# THE MOTHER'S A·L·M·A·N·A·C

REVISED

## MARGUERITE KELLY
AND
## ELIA PARSONS

Revised by Marguerite Kelly

*Illustrated by Rebecca Hirsh*

DOUBLEDAY

New York London Toronto Sydney Auckland

PUBLISHED BY DOUBLEDAY, a division of
Bantam Doubleday Dell Publishing Group, Inc.
666 Fifth Avenue, New York, New York 10103

DOUBLEDAY and the portrayal of an anchor with a
dolphin are trademarks of Doubleday, a division
of Bantam Doubleday Dell Publishing Group, Inc.

Library of Congress Cataloging-in-Publication Data

Kelly, Marguerite.
  The mother's almanac, revised / by Marguerite Kelly and Elia Parsons :
illustrated by Rebecca Hirsh.
     p.   cm.   Includes bibliographical references and index.
   1. Child rearing—United States—Handbooks, manuals, etc.
2. Mothers—United States—Handbooks, manuals, etc. I. Parsons,
Elia. II. Title
HQ769.K367   1992
649′.1—dc20                              91-28592
                                              CIP

ISBN 0-385-42624-0

*To Tom
and Kate and Mike and
Meg and Nell*

*To Dick
and Ramon and Nadia
and Amalia*

This revision is indebted to Karen Van Westering, the same remarkable editor who nurtured the original edition of *The Mother's Almanac* as well as *The Mother's Almanac II*; to John Duff, for guiding the manuscript through production; to Rebecca Hirsh, for more of her whimsical art; to Heidi Almy, Claudette Best, Maria J. Burrington, Beverly Lemmon and Martha Mechelis—the five splendid mothers whose thoughtful comments helped to update this edition; to Tom Kelly, who is as fine an editor as he is a father to our children (and he is a very fine father), and to Kate, Mike, Meg and Nell, for keeping so closely in touch with their parents, and for bringing Steve Bottorff, Madelyn Greenberg and Tony Rizzoli into our family. Finally, a special thanks to Emily and Marguerite Bottorff and to Sally Rizzoli, who let us relive our yesterdays even as they enliven and delight our todays. It's nice to know that life can get even better.

—Marguerite Kelly, 1992

# CONTENTS

# PREFACE

The updating of this book was a long time coming, and brought some real surprises. So much had happened in seventeen years, and so much had stayed the same.

We must have mentioned the record player a hundred times in the first edition—for tapes were fairly rare when it was published and CDs were nonexistent—and we talked more about the car harness and the car bed than the car seat. In those days, that was just a lightweight contraption that hung over the front seat, so a little child could see better.

Even the grammar was different then. In the first edition we used the standard "he," "his" and him" as our generic pronouns; in this one the gender alternates from chapter to chapter. As we said then and repeat again, however, our advice applies to both boys and girls in almost every case. Any boy should be able to play with dolls or cook or take modern dance without anyone's doubting his masculinity, just as any girl should feel comfortable with hammers and worms and trees to climb. As new studies are finding, sexual choices depend on genetics and body chemistry, not on the way children play or even the way their parents treat them.

Although children haven't changed, they've come under much tighter scrutiny. Hyperactivity—which seems to get a new name every Tuesday—had just been "invented" in 1975, and allergies, though long recognized, were seldom considered the cause of it or any behavioral problem.

There have been other changes. Natural childbirth is more popular with mothers than it used to be, C-sections are much more popular with doctors and breastfeeding is increasingly popular with both. Although mother's milk was once the choice of only the very educated and the very poor, today most mothers at least try to nurse their babies, and this deserves a big hurrah.

Lifestyles have changed most of all. By the end of the seventies it was clear that motherhood was still a full-time job, but appliances and processed food had turned housekeeping into a part-time responsibility, and not a very satisfying one at that. Women still had a need to accomplish, but they didn't have the chance to be fulfilled. It was hard, they found, to get that excited about dust.

Their dissatisfaction, as well as the high cost of living—and the urge to live better—sent mothers out to work, but nothing sent them faster than divorce. The divorce rate in 1975—already too high—soared in the next fifteen years, and the experts are only just reporting what the children of divorce have always known: the pain is terrible. Today we're on the cusp again, as more and more couples—and more and more therapists—are trying harder to make marriage work and now the divorce rate is finally beginning to subside. This deserves another hurrah.

Working mothers brought many changes to the workplace and the home too. Although many women worked in 1975, the number was much smaller and their husbands usually didn't help much around the house or with the children either—a situation that is blessedly beginning to change. Hurrah No. 3.

Working mothers, whether single or married, have also made day care commonplace and preschool almost a necessity, but now day care often starts in infancy and preschool begins before their babes are out of diapers. Today we have play school for the one-year-old, rather than the two-year-old, and nursery school for Twos and Threes, instead of Threes and Fours. This leaves the Fours in Pre-K—a year of schooling which sprang up out of nowhere. It's all part of the rush to get children ready for today's more academic kindergarten, a class that seems more and more like first grade every day. Oddly, the more children are pushed ahead, the more old-fashioned their clothes have become—which probably doesn't have anything to do with anything—and the more their test scores have dropped in later years. This must have something to do with something, but nobody quite knows what, or how long the problem will last.

Most things are much the same, however, in life and in this book, with only a tuck here and a new paragraph there. Some mothers still see television as the great babysitter, and others see it as the great threat, but today they can be much more discerning—and so they are. Parents now choose fine, commercial-free videos in place of bad television, and teaching shows like "Sesame Street," rather than mindless cartoons. The payoff is great. Good tapes encourage good books and Big Bird's emphasis on the ABCs makes reading seem easier, which has brought a boon to the publishing trade: the children's book market is growing lickety-split.

Parents, however, are the ones who encourage books most and *The Mother's Almanac* still urges them to read to their children more than anything else. You'll find an expanded list of wonderful books, as well as a brand new list of videotapes, in this edition. We also include our many techniques and recipes to help children use words and art and music—and ladders and stilts and a balancing board—so they can express themselves in many ways. And of course, we still offer the cooking, gardening and refinishing recipes that young children can do with their parents, both to strengthen their self-esteem and to weave them into the fabric of the family.

The core of our advice, however, concerns the heart and soul of a child, just as it always has. We still believe that values must be taught, laughter encouraged and children must get—and give—respect. Even our discipline, which is perhaps a little gentler today, still follows an authoritative, middle-of-the-road path, which was rather new when it was published but is now commonplace. The popularity of both permissiveness and autocracy has dwindled as parents found that these extremes not only backfire in adolescence but they fail to teach a child the most important lesson of all: self-discipline.

Since the development of the child is still the same as it's always been, so is our reporting of it. Infants really do see and smile and respond when they're born, which has been amply proven by the experts—a relief, since that was only mothers' wisdom back in 1975—and children really do grow up at the same pace, and in the same order—mentally, physically, emotionally and morally—as they always have.

Children are also just as much fun, and as rascally as ever, and their parents still love them just as much. This is far more than you can ever believe, unless, of course, these children are your own.

MARGUERITE LELONG KELLY, 1992

Today we can plan our families so well that babies are a sign of love, a sign that parents are ready to swaddle them in all the affection and respect they need.

Now we can wait for the right job, the right home, the right income, and then we find—no matter how ideal the conditions—that it's as hard to rear the first child as it always was.

Motherhood brings as much joy as ever, but it still brings boredom, exhaustion and sorrow too. Nothing else ever will make you as happy or as sad, as proud or as tired, for nothing is quite as hard as helping a person develop his own individuality—especially while you struggle to keep your own. In motherhood, there's so much to learn, so much to give, and although the learning gets less with each succeeding child, the giving never does.

If only to make ourselves feel better, we assume that new mothers today, like new mothers yesterday, have a lot to learn about child care (and cooking and gardening and making love too). Enthusiasm is not enough. Somehow techniques must be found, but today you can't look for much help from grandmothers—since they've got their jobs downtown—and you can't learn about babies from the big family next door, since there isn't any big family next door. Still, you don't want to muddle along. The quicker you solve the problems of motherhood, the more satisfied you'll be and the less you'll sound like the young and old biddies who go about wishing they had had "the second child first."

As immodest as it sounds, we think we've found ways to help you nurture your child in the critical years before first grade. These answers, gathered from our errors and our successes, our friends and our research, all ripened in the years of intro-spection and deliberation that it took us to write this book.

We have divided it into three parts, but the first is perhaps the most important because it covers the realities of family life—not just the routine, the problems and the crises, but the way you teach your child to become independent and self-disciplined. This will be his strength for life and this is your strength too, for a child who can take care of himself will be a happy child, hungry for all the enrichment and creativity you can offer.

In the second section we consider the influences that give this enrichment. The memory of picking apples on a country ramble or taking part in a family celebration can never be erased. We talk about these adventures here, as well as the values you instill and how you can do it (through pets and gifts and chores) and the enrichment of books and schools and theater and records. The influences you give your child in the early years will be as much a part of his structure as the bones in his body.

Finally, there are the avenues of expression you offer your child, which we cover in our last section. Here we tell you about the traditional arts and drama and crafts; the experiments your child can make in science and reading and the proficiencies he can learn. The skills of the kitchen and the workshop and the garden will give your child a lifetime of self-confidence. We hope you will find the recipes fine enough to use them yourself, long after he has grown.

There is no way you can expose your child to every enrichment, nor do we think you should. You're not creating a genius in the arts and sciences, nor a Renaissance child who excels in every discipline, but instead you're rearing a quality child who is eager to draw the best out of life and glad to return just as much.

Since everything you do—or don't do—affects your child, we wrote not just a how-to, when-to book, but a why-to book. We speak to the mother, since she usually has much of the day-to-day responsibility, but most of our advice applies, of course, to fathers and grandparents and sitters too.

The ages we give for particular achievements or games or recipes are arbitrary and based on our children and their friends. They certainly aren't precise or scientific (for neither are children) and will vary from child to child by many months. You also may think these ages are too optimistic. Perhaps they are, but we've found a child learns much quicker if you teach him the ground rules and have faith in his ability (and we have a lot of faith). Certainly we've come a long way since Dorothy Canfield Fisher, an avant-garde thinker for 1915, said, "The actions of a human being, even of 15 months of age, may not be without significance to a sympathetic eye."

Motherhood, we find, is more than a craft; it is an art. Like any other, the more inventive you are and the harder you work at it, the better the pay, for nothing is as rewarding as the love of a happy child.

MARGUERITE LELONG KELLY
ELIA ESTHER SANCHEZ PARSONS, 1975

# REALITIES

There are many times in parenthood when happiness thrusts your spirits higher than the stars and the pleasure of loving makes living a throbbing delight. This is normal, but like sex, much too brief.

There are other, fortunately fewer times in parenthood when tension leaves no room for joy and self-pity can rend your soul. This is normal too.

As probably typical mothers we have known much more happiness than sorrow, but also, typically, we muddled through a dreary routine of confusion with our first children, through days and weeks that should have been better and disasters that need never have happened.

Somehow with our good husbands we have helped seven children finish their first six years during which we discovered, through the same painfully original research all mothers gather and forget, a number of ideas that worked and a great many others that did not. There were times past—we can admit it now—when we despaired of our children and particularly of ourselves. Motherhood was not for us.

One night one of us walked in tears and in the rain to the neighborhood bookshop, looking for some guide to cope with a two-and-a-half-year-old terror. Only Gesell was there to say that this too shall pass, but it wasn't clear how it happened and why or what we could do to make it pass any faster.

Once one of us knew the lonely agony of waiting out the weeks for a stillborn son and learned to treasure the fullness of life in the midst of its emptiness.

Parenthood, we found, was much harder and less predictable than we thought it would be, and even now, as our children require less physical care each year, we find they need continually more emotional attention from us. This is typical too and another surprise.

We made mistakes more often than we expected, of every sort, but with love they were corrected more easily than we expected too.

We found there were many options in child care, each reflecting a parent's attitude toward her child and herself. This made it clear to us that parents must evaluate their own viewpoints together, honestly and often, so that their child may grow up with clear and consistent direction.

By the time we thought we had some of the answers, we found that Lydia Maria Child, a forgotten pioneer of women's lib, had found them before us—childless though she was. In 1831, she published *The Mother's Book*, which remains unique in the field of child care. She not only loved children, she enjoyed them. In later books, American children have been ignored, denied, idolized, pampered and despaired of, but seldom enjoyed.

Today, we have a grand number of books to teach the techniques of a happy sex life, but there are still very few books to teach us how to grow happy children. Both accomplishments are fun to learn, but since it takes such a little while to start a baby and so long to nurture a child, we pass on to you what we wish we had learned in the beginning, without a family trial for every error. This is a book that sees children through the eyes of a parent, not a teacher or a doctor or a psychologist, and sees them in the context of a family, and not as the center of the world.

Like Ms. Child, we think we have found techniques to make child care much happier and much less trouble. We feel we have learned, through research and through experience, which toys and games and crafts are necessary, not for play, but for work. These are the tools of childhood, as much as skillets and typewriters and hammers are ours.

We believe every activity in which a child invests his time will teach him something in return—either positive or negative—and, therefore, parents must consider what they want their children to learn, both in skills and in values. This is a learning time for parents too.

When Freud taught the world that children had psyches, it disturbed the balance of family relationships—as it should have, for the balance, if not unworkable, was unjust. The heavy autocracy of Calvin and Victoria had stifled generations of children. No total credo has replaced it, however, and parents have been groping for new rules ever since. Children often drift uneasily in search of a niche while parents, in fear of mashing an id or an ego, pass the scepter of authority back and forth like a baton in a relay race.

We feel there is another position.

Although we consider parents the king and queen of a family, we think they must respect their subjects now, if only to avoid the guillotine later.

Respect is inherent in the fairness with which a child must be treated, and respect is the one commodity every parent has the duty to demand. We hope this compilation will help parents give this respect and receive it, so that a child may inherit the legacy of stability he deserves.

We believe a child's respect for himself is increased in ratio to his competence. This is his key to self-love, the basis of a confident, complete adult. It will give him the bedrock to enjoy and withstand the pressures of our society.

Mothers, as well as children, feel these pressures, but perhaps they feel them less in other, single-ethnic countries. Women in America, where all the qualities are stirred in one big melting pot of mores, don't have one national standard, they have them all. In addition, the pride of a new mother forces her to compete with her own mother (and *his* mother), not as they were once, young and inept, but as she knows them now—older and very ept indeed.

American women, urged by the women's magazines, spend the first ten years of their marriage trying to keep their sanity—or if they are college graduates, trying to find their "identity"—while pushing to be first the ideal employee, then the ideal wife and finally that most mythical creature of all, the ideal mother.

There is, of course, no such perfection, but it will take years before you find out.

Fortunately, the glory of birth transcends such anxieties, for you are overcome by its blessing. Time and effort have made the most extraordinary things in the world—like canyons and temples and concertos—but the most remarkable of all creations must be: new people.

To you and your husband, the first baby is a miracle. For forty weeks you have known he would have everything you loved best about each other in a perfect marriage of the genes. By the time he arrives, with his father's big ears and a pointed head, you are much too pleased to care.

With each pregnancy you will expect that magically right combination of genes again. It starts love going for the new baby before there is anything to see or even feel.

The firstborn, however, will continue to grasp your emotions in an unexpected way. No pregnancy and no baby are as exciting as the first. Only he can make you feel so foolish, so confused, so frightened—or so exhilarated. Every action, every day are novel to you and to him. Every reaction, every emotion, every expectation, yours and his, are more intense, all of your lives.

You won't love this miracle child best, but you always will love him differently. It works out well enough. You also will have special feelings for the baby of the family or the only girl or the retarded child or the family clown (every family with more than two children has a clown). Each child has one extra line to your heart, which no other child can replace. You can tell your children about this when they are older, and you should, because a child should know his own special place in the family.

With your later children you will be less experimental and more relaxed. You will enjoy them much more, be bored a little more and find them much less miraculous. But no matter how many children you've had, you will be overwhelmed each time by your power to make life and to shape it.

When you are pregnant for the first time you feel superior to every frazzled mother chasing children in the supermarket and you know you'll never be that way. Savor that confidence. This faith in your own maternal wisdom won't reach that peak again until you are a grandmother.

Despite the current mythology, life with babies does not mean an occasional bad day when your Four spills his paints on the top-grade kitchen tile and the dishwasher breaks down. This is a normal day, even a good one. When motherhood is in full flower and you have two or three babies under Six, you not only won't have money for a dishwasher, you're overdrawn at the bank.

As a new mother, it's more normal to be tired for weeks at a time, to be quick to cry, to be sure your husband is a devil with the girls at the office. You will look back wistfully to the job you left with the same distorted vision with which you once had looked forward to marriage. In those days you believed what you read in the magazines—that every good wife "whipped up" silky skirts (long, for evening), refinished furniture (with a French polish), and if she dieted, it was gourmet-style. You thought you'd have drinks before dinner every night (with homemade pâté on the side), make love to the beat of blue grass and keep the house clean without help—and easily with it—even if you went back to work.

After three or even two babies, you realize that wives don't live this way any more than men—and women—lead glamorous, proposition-filled lives at the office. In fact, if you're an at-home mom, you might even spare your husband a little sympathy. You may have more calamities and longer hours than he does, but at least you're the boss, even if your child doesn't know it. In shaking down the realities of marriage you will find, as one wise young wife said, "Happiness is getting there."

The honest reason for having children is your own fulfillment, and to rear them well can raise your marriage to glorious heights.

These years, when your children are under Six and underfoot, are your years of apprenticeship. Now you will learn simplified routines, safety precautions, an acceptance of the inevitable miseries most of the time and a plan of escape for the rest.

You will give more time to others—and have less time to give—and you will learn more about organization than a management trainee at General Motors. You will learn to give sit-down dinners for twelve—the height of logistics—to paint walls, mend sheets and collect for charity, and you will do these things even if you have a job, although you won't do them so often. The extent of your investment now will determine the richness of your growth. You will have more years without children than with them and they will be your years of harvest.

Every child is born with trust and then spends the rest of his life hanging onto it.

Your child instinctively knows he can count on you now, because he always has, and he'll keep his trusting nature if you go to him when he cries, giving food when he is hungry, warmth when he is cold, entertainment when he is bored.

The child whose needs are attended with reasonable speed in the first year will learn, as he should, that the world is a dependable place. This trust in others gives him the base he needs to develop trust in the most important person in the world—not you, but himself.

We believe if parents love their child and respect him, he will love the whole world and be kind to it; if his curiosity is nourished as a child, he will become an imaginative, creative adult; if he is self-sufficient when he is small, he will learn the tough joys of independence, and if he has wide, firm boundaries when he's young, he will reach for freedom when he's grown.

We could pretend your child will be a joy if you just give him paints, books, action, adventure and attention. This is not so, for your child must be civilized too.

No matter how deep your love, you won't enjoy his company much if he depends on you for everything—and then doesn't bother to say thanks. A child is precious little fun unless both of you operate within a framework—loose as it may be—of discipline, of safety and of decent manners. These boundaries, which you lay before first grade, will channel his bold spirit. This lets you trust him enough to loosen your reins, helping him conquer his world even as you fence it.

A skill, like talking, is worth helping a child achieve early for the happiness it brings, but other skills bring great satisfaction too. This is why we think a One should start to feed himself, a Two should begin to dress himself and a Three should make his bed. Each small job a child masters gives him new psychic strength.

In this way he will become independent, for a child builds his self-confidence not on what you can do for him, but what he can do for himself.

This independence is the prelude to the sense of responsibility he needs to care for pets, to do his chores—even to make simple gifts, for charity is not indigenous to children and indeed it must begin at home.

Although a child's makeup is set genetically, his values, his stability and, to an unknown extent, his intellect are determined by you. Malnutrition of the mind or the body will suppress both mental and physical growth. If you accept the premise that you can help your child raise his intelligence—and what mother doesn't?—you must realize that you can limit it too.

We think parents have no right to withhold knowledge on the highly questionable theory that intelligence is fixed. No one has ever reached his full mental capacity, nor has anyone ever fulfilled his potential for goodness or love or happiness either, but it does not mean that we should stop trying. It is difficult enough to be a mother; let us forgo the role of God.

According to nutritional studies, a proper diet can raise an I.Q. as much as twenty-two points and, conversely, an improper one can drop it and even cause retardation. Other studies show sweeping differences between babies whose environment has been either creative or sterile. If findings on rats are applicable to people, the more stimulation a baby receives, and the earlier he receives it, the more his brain grows in size and in weight, and therefore in intelligence.

The brain has been compared with a giant computer, more sophisticated than any ever manufactured. The cortex, where knowledge is banked, can store millions of facts in its circuits in a lifetime, but only if the circuits have been programmed for use. The methods of measuring intelligence are still inexact, but authorities believe the brain reaches half capacity by the time a child is four, three fourths of capacity by the time he is eight and total growth around the age of seventeen. If a child has enough of the right stimuli, you can stretch his horizons for life.

We believe a child is quick to learn instinctively, but with help he learns quicker and likes it better. His furious chase for knowledge is basic—a joyful, endless quest. A child, of course, should not be pushed into learning, but parents have the obligation to offer it. Any activity, however, that makes either of you nervous, tired or cross should be dropped, for as we all remember from our childhood, a bored or boring teacher is the quickest way to curb curiosity.

Whatever you teach your child should be in an easy, comfortable atmosphere where he may dare to reach any of a number of goals—or even dare not to try. A happy child certainly will not feel he must excel in all areas, but he should be able to investigate them, through enrichment, through work and through creativity. Education comes in many packages.

Your children will be at home for eighteen years at least, but you will be bound to them, for better or worse, for the rest of your life. Your children and, heaven help you, their children will be home for holiday dinners and for occasional loans. Since you only can stand such intimacy from your best friends, you may as well rear children who will be your best friends as well as suitable companions for all mankind.

It takes hard work and hard thinking to rear good people. The job is interesting, although the hours are bad, starting from the first day.

# FUNDAMENTALS

The planning you put into any project will decide how well it goes, and this is especially true when you're having a baby.

Your psyche and your body have nine months, a dozen books and a trusty obstetrician to help you prepare, but after seven babies we can tell you: you need more than that.

## BEFORE

Your baby will nest best if you eat right, take your vitamins, nap when you're tired and walk briskly to keep your body in tone, starting, if possible, about three months before you conceive. Your good health will get your baby off to a stronger start.

Everything may go just as well if you didn't follow these rules, but you shouldn't trifle with the thou-shalt-nots of pregnancy. The list gets longer every year, as researchers find so many things can affect your unborn baby.

You mustn't go twenty-four hours without food or take prescriptions or over-the-counter medicines without your doctor's permission or use a sauna or a hot tub or even dye your hair (but you can color it with a rinse). You shouldn't smoke either, because it can slow the baby's growth and increase the chance of asthma in the first year, or have caffeine and, of course, you can't drink alcohol. It may be safe for some women to drink at certain times in their pregnancy, but no one knows precisely who they are or when it's safe, and the risk of retardation and other birth defects is too great.

You may have to give up many things, but sex, thank heavens, is still safe—unless there's been some bleeding—and it's safe right up until the membranes break.

For every *shouldn't* in pregnancy, there seems to be a couple of *shoulds*, and most of them concern the foods you eat. Three meals a day are a must, for every nutrient you eat is washed into your blood, and a fourth of that blood goes to the placenta, which governs the growth of the baby. If you don't get enough good nourishment—and get it regularly—the baby won't get enough either. You even have to chew your food well, to help your body break down the food better and get the most nutrition from it.

Altogether you'll need about 2,400–2,600 calories a day—300–500 more than you had before you were pregnant—and you'll need even more if you're underweight, or under emotional stress or have had a baby, a stillbirth or a miscarriage within the past year. Since your diet calls for so much high-calcium, iron-rich food, you won't have many calories left for chips and chocolate bars.

Even without any junk food, you'll gain twenty-four to fifty pounds, with about five in the first trimester and a pound or so a week thereafter, for an ideal weight gain of maybe thirty-five pounds. While this may seem too much, you'll get a baby who weighs in at around eight pounds, which means a baby who is easier to deliver than a bigger one, more alert than a smaller one and less likely to have colic, too.

Plan on having four servings of milk or milk products—whole or skim, lactose-free or not—every day and whole milk with any fat-free meal; three servings of grains; two well-washed fruits or vegetables including one that's rich in vitamin C, like tomatoes or potatoes, and two leafy green vegetables. They can be served raw or steamed but they should be as fresh as possible and the darker the better. A variety of colors gives you a variety of vitamins.

Above all, you'll need seventy-five to one hundred grams of protein a day divided between four to six servings with turkey, steak, fish, cottage cheese, soy-anything, eggs and beans giving you the most, and in that order.

You can add a little zest with herbs and with spices too—if you don't get heartburn—and you can even have salt. Doctors now think it can prevent toxemia, rather than cause it, but use iodized salt, which can help prevent thyroid problems, and avoid the hidden sources of salt, or you may take in too much. Bicarbonate of soda is full of it and so are canned soups, lunch meat and snack foods. You don't want to eat many sweets either, since refined sugar spikes—and then drops—the blood sugar, while fruit and honey do not. Also you don't want to eat or drink anything that's been doctored with artificial sweeteners, additives or preservatives, since they affect some people poorly. Finally, you need to drink two quarts of water a day to metabolize the protein, circulate the blood and prevent urinary tract infections.

No matter how well you follow the rules, you still will go through the doldrums of pregnancy, for it's a long time between your conception in June and your delivery in March.

You may have known that doubts would crowd your mind, but you will be surprised by the tedium and listlessness, the queer aches and fancies. You were prepared for the queasiness, which is common in the first trimester, and the craving for odd foods, like pickles, in the second, which is not, but you didn't know how much you would still want to make love in the third trimester, and how silly you would look when you did.

Nor did you have any idea how the knowledge of this pregnancy would consume you, intruding itself into every thought you had and popping awkwardly into your conversation, unbidden and it almost seems, unappreciated, even by your dearest friends. Somehow they forget your due date, again and again, while strangers look you up and down and tell you exactly when the baby will arrive, which is usually a month before it's due.

You may be annoyed when other people think your belly is their business, but you have more important things to worry about.

## CHOOSING THE O.B./MIDWIFE

Either an obstetrician or a midwife can deliver your baby, depending on your health and their qualifications.

The o.b. should be board-certified, the nurse-midwife should be certified and both should have at least five years of experience and a comforting personality.

You want someone who won't rush you through your appointments or your labor, who won't scare you with a thousand scenarios, who won't make you think your worries are silly—even when they turn out to be—and who will involve your husband every step of the way.

Each specialty has its pluses and minuses.

An obstetrician is essential if you have any signs of diabetes or high blood pressure—which can last for the duration of the pregnancy—or if you're having a multiple birth or have had a certain type of Cesarean and need a Cesarean again or if the baby just won't get out of a breech position.

Even if you have no problem, a medical degree can bring you great peace of mind during your pregnancy. Friends, and particularly strangers, are shockingly free with horror stories they've heard from someone, somewhere, and you'll be especially vulnerable to such folks if you decide to have a midwife.

A nurse-midwife, however, is often ideal since she only takes women in the low-risk category—and most women are—and has a back-up doctor on call and an operating room just ten minutes from the birth center or the home birth, which means thirty minutes, portal to portal. This has produced a success rate that's very high, a cost that's quite low and an appeal that's getting stronger all the time. Mothers report that this practitioner usually gives longer appointments than obstetricians; teaches more about pregnancy, childbirth, nutrition and breastfeeding; stays with the mother throughout active labor as well as delivery; and doesn't resort to painkillers, C-sections and episiotomies as often as doctors.

Before you decide, interview a couple of candidates from each specialty to find which practitioner suits you best and whether you want to follow the traditions you've known or the ones you're trying to build. Any choice you make is fine, as long as it's informed.

## FIRST TRIMESTER

You won't look pregnant in the first three months, but you sure will feel different. Never has your body had to work so hard or been filled with so many inglorious little complaints.

You'll often be sleepy and tired, tired, tired. And no wonder.

You're dealing with more hormones than ever before, and this, plus the iron you take, and maybe a sudden drop in your blood sugar, can make you queasy, especially in the morning. The doctor won't be alarmed—nausea is supposed to be a sign of good health—but he may have you skip your vitamins for a while, or take a little $B_6$ or drink some milk at night, eat more proteins or more pasta and rice, drink peppermint or ginger tea, or keep soda crackers or a banana by your bed to nibble on when you wake up. He'll also tell you to rest more, get up slowly in the morning, avoid smelly or fatty foods—or any food that makes you feel sick—and to eat a little something every waking hour. What works for one person doesn't work for the next, so you'll probably try many tricks before you find one that works (or you'll reach the second trimester and the nausea will go away on its own).

Queasy or not, you won't be very hungry in these first few months, but you'll still collect a little fat on your hips—which will spread a bit—and your thighs. Nature—always sure that a famine is just around the corner—is setting up her reserves.

Your breasts may get more tender and larger too, so you'll need a good bra, since it's the lack of support (and heredity and poor nutrition) that may make them sag later, not breastfeeding.

The support you really want will come from a small library of pregnancy books, and from your doctor, who will seem almost saintlike to you before the pregnancy is done. Never will you give one person so much power. He'll first verify the drugstore test, and then take your history, do a blood work-up and give you a thorough internal exam. After that you'll see him once a month for an external check-up, and a urinalysis to make sure you don't have a bladder infection. You'll also get a glucose test at some time in your pregnancy, to check for diabetes; an AIDS test, if you want to put your mind at rest, and an AFP test, which helps to rule out spina bifida.

If you're over thirty-five, the doctor also may order a chorionic villi sampling (CVS) in this trimester, or an amniocentesis in the next. Even though there is a slight chance of a miscarriage in both, they can screen for many disorders. The CVS may be the better test, however, if there is a skilled technician in your area, since it's given around the ninth week, rather than the sixteenth, and the results are usually quicker too. But the technology is evolving so quickly that these dates may get earlier and earlier.

The doctor may also order a sonogram, which usually isn't necessary, but it is a hoot. This ultrasound test, which turns sound waves into a picture on the screen, will check the amniotic fluid, the baby's due date and position and tell you if you're having twins or if the baby has any major physical problems. If you're going to get the test, however, you may as well go to a

## BEDREST

Sometimes pregnancy doesn't always go as we hope and expect, and then the doctor may prescribe bedrest—the most common treatment, one of the oldest and one of the best. The doctor may put you to bed until the twenty-fourth week, to prevent a miscarriage, or in the second trimester, to stabilize your blood pressure, or in the last trimester, to prevent early labor—or in some cases, you may have to go to bed for most of your pregnancy.

To lie on your side—but not your back—day after day, will be the most important job you've ever had, and the most difficult. Guilt and inadequacy and fear—and boredom—can make it much worse, but like most duties, bedrest gets easier if you stop fighting it.

You'll feel better if you put on your makeup and a clean nightgown when you wake up every morning, and your household will function better if you hire a high school or college student to be a part-time housekeeper or at least hire a preteen to run errands for you after school. If she's having trouble in school, she may let you tutor her as part of her pay.

You can give a lot of orders from your bed, but it will be your own achievements that make these days pass faster and more happily. Set a small goal for yourself each morning, to be accomplished by the end of the day. It's time to figure out all the things you *can* do, not all the things you *can't* do. You won't have this much time again for years.

You can organize the family finances and pay the bills; write a master grocery list—including brands—to be copied, so you and your husband can check off the items you need each week; get your cookbook and the family pictures in order; write the family history for the baby, with all the interesting sagas (and the scandals, too, as long as the people are dead); learn how to knit or crochet; do volunteer work for a charity and clip grocery coupons for your husband or to thank your friends and neighbors for all their help.

You can even teach yourself new computer skills if you can buy, rent or borrow a laptop computer and you can study a foreign language and take natural childbirth lessons if you have a VCR.

No matter how much you accomplish, and how much help you have, you'll still need a great deal of emotional support. Ask the doctor or the hospital to give you the number for the telephone confinement line in your area, which will put you in touch with other bedresting mothers-to-be, or those who have been through it. There's nothing like talking with your own kind.

center that specializes in giving it. It's bound to have better equipment than your doctor and a very experienced sonogram reader.

### SECOND TRIMESTER

By the start of the fourth month, pregnancy begins to be awfully real. Now you go into maternity clothes—so thrilling in the fourth month; so tiresome in the ninth. Look for those with easy comfort and lighter weight—since pregnancy makes you hotter—and get one smashing party outfit, to make you feel glamorous, even in the thirty-ninth week. Consignment shops often have great maternity buys, especially party clothes.

Everything about this baby is growing lickety-split. The twentieth week, and the thirty-sixth week, are the two greatest times of his growth, and this will be reflected by both your appetite and your weight. You can expect to be much hungrier in the fourth month and to gain the most in the fifth and sixth months.

Your breasts get still bigger—to accommodate your growing milk glands—and they may get lumpy too and even secrete a little colostrum—that vital fluid your baby will suck until your milk comes in. Even your nipples will darken, but that—and the almost invisible line around your belly—will be your only permanent changes.

Your new shape—or your doctor—may send you to a pregnancy exercise class, to keep your body toned and your weight in check, and to give you and your baby more oxygen. You'll also need to hold in your belly—so the muscles stay taut—and to rub it with cocoa butter, just as old wives tell you to do. This may not prevent stretch marks, but at least you'll feel like you're doing something about them.

Other changes may turn into problems in this trimester.

Pregnancy may make you feel faint and dizzy, which your doctor will probably blame on your changing hormones or a drop in your blood pressure if the baby is pressing on some of the bigger blood vessels. If you get up and move slowly, it won't happen so often.

Leg cramps may bother you too but they'll usually go away if you take 300 mg of calcium gluconate; swollen ankles will improve if you keep off your feet for at least a little while every day, and your dry hair and dry skin will get better if you shampoo less and use aloe vera on your skin at night.

If heartburn keeps you awake, avoid big meals and greasy, spicy foods, and if constipation troubles you, exercise more and eat apples, raisins, figs, dates and prunes (especially at night), whole grain cereals, salads, six to eight glasses of water a day, and—if your doctor agrees—a couple of grams of vitamin C. Hemorrhoids can be another problem, which will call for you to walk often, drink lots of water, eat grains and raw vegetables and use a topical cream.

Cravings can be annoying too. You can indulge them a little, but if the calories are empty, they'll give you nothing except perhaps a pound or two.

It's the changes in your baby that will interest you more than your own complaints however. By the sixteenth week your baby already has a sense of taste, an aversion to light and what seems like an ability to do cartwheels. Although he has been wiggling and wriggling right along, you now can feel the sensations when he moves around and they are, quite simply, sensational.

You'll find that he's lulled to sleep when you're moving around and active when you sit down to rest, but he'll calm down when you stroke or even lay a hand on your abdomen or play soft music, for your baby lives in a little bathtub and fluid is a great conductor of sound. Even though the loud, rumbling rhythm of your body is keeping time with your heartbeat, he can still hear outside noises, for the wall between you is really quite thin and his hearing is very acute.

Gentle sounds can put him to sleep but favorite voices can also startle him into action. Little Sally, in fact, would move about every time she heard her father, the actor, on stage—and she was only four months along. Your baby will know your voices, but talk to him, read aloud and sing songs directly to him too: you're reaching into his soul. Bonding begins very, very early.

Near the end of this trimester you may feel some Braxton-Hicks contractions, which really began in the eighth week, even though you didn't notice them. These rhythmic tightenings start at the top of the uterus, flow down until the womb hardens into a ball and then they relax—a routine that can be slightly scary, but it's really good for you. These contractions not only strengthen the uterine muscles, but they circulate your blood in and near the placenta and may make labor easier too, for they will help to thin the cervix before delivery.

These new physical signs will impress you with the reality of this baby and make you want to learn how to care for him better than any baby has ever been cared for before. Red Cross courses can teach you infant C.P.R. and other measures you'll probably never need, but other mothers will teach you how to bathe and diaper a baby best.

Your husband needs to get some experience, too. In child care, as in sex, practice may not always make it perfect, but it sure makes it better—for both parents. With encouragement, your husband can learn to be as capable as you in every phase of child care except breastfeeding.

You can both learn what to do if you babysit for your neighbors, nieces and nephews or join the neighborhood baby-sitting co-op, and accumulate credit in advance. It takes practical experience to learn how to feed a baby best and what to do when he cries.

Other expectant parents volunteer in the children's ward of a hospital, changing babies, rocking them, singing to them. Basically, you are giving love, a commodity that expands with use. It also will help you show affection to your own baby, for most of us are very shy with our first-borns.

So much begins with your own moods. Motherhood can be as bleak as the worst pregnancy or as joyous as no pregnancy ever was. You need to develop a serene, relaxed attitude, even if you have to learn some relaxation or meditation exercises, so your baby will be more serene and relaxed after he's born.

### THIRD TRIMESTER

By now, you'll be too tired to look for more experience and more advice and too busy making arrangements, even though you're still determined to do whatever must be done, at home and at work, and then to do just a little bit more.

Don't feel guilty when you slow down. Your extra weight demands new concessions. You'll also find it easier if you wear lower heels; cock one foot up on a stool when you stand; tuck in your fanny like a Vogue model; sit much more than you stand; take warm baths and use a heating pad on your back.

No matter how cumbersome you feel, however, this is no time to cut back on your doctor-ordered diet, even if you think you're gaining too much weight. Your child is adding an ounce a day in the last eight weeks—about a pound every nine days—and needs more nutrients than ever, for his brain is developing faster in the last four weeks of pregnancy—and the first four months after his birth—than at any time in his life. You need even more protein in this trimester for the lack of it now can slow down the development of his brain, and cause problems with his learning and coordination. You do want to eat five to six small meals a day near the end of pregnancy, however, rather than three to four bigger ones, so you'll feel more comfortable. There's not much space left for food.

The baby has taken over your life as well as your body.

You and your husband will probably start natural childbirth classes in the seventh month. It's usually safer for the baby to be born without drugs, but even if you plan on anesthesia, these exercises may help you handle the pain so well you won't need as much of it. And yes, you do want your husband in the delivery room with you. This sets the tone of unity and equality in your new family and it's only fair. He helped start this production; he surely should be there for opening night.

It doesn't matter whether you choose the Lamaze method, which is based on breathing techniques, or the Bradley method, which stresses relaxation, but the teacher matters a great deal. You need someone who is warm and friendly and inspires self-confidence; limits the class to five or six couples and explains the whole birth process clearly; shows the famous film about three kinds of birth; teaches the exercises well and tells you how to avoid anesthesia or a C-section if you can, but doesn't make you feel guilty if you can't. She knows that the health and safety of the baby and the mother matter most.

Above all, you need a teacher who will tell you how to cope when you get home from the hospital. Having a baby is hard work—they don't call it labor for nothing—and you'll be quite tired and shaky for the first two weeks and fairly tired for the next four. And that's if you have help. If you don't, you may be very, very tired for the next six to eight months, and much more susceptible to postpartum depression.

You'll need someone to take care of the laundry, the housework and the cooking for the first two critical weeks after the birth—someone who will diaper the baby, bring him to you to nurse and put him down again, and even bring you a roast beef sandwich at midnight. The better

### DIAPERS

Disposable diapers are mighty tempting—and almost essential on a trip or for an emergency—but give cloth diapers a try if you have a washer and dryer. They're much cheaper, they're environmentally better and they have fewer chemicals next to the baby's skin. If you're using cloth diapers, buy

4 dozen prefolded cloth diapers
4–6 diaper wraps OR
6 pairs waterproof pants
6 diaper pins

If you use a diaper service instead of washing your own, choose a service that will give you the same diapers every week, and will adjust the Ph factor to suit your baby's skin, so he won't get a rash if he sits around in wet diapers. You'll also want to order an extra batch of diapers at first, so you'll never run out.

Whether you primarily use cloth or disposables, keep both types on hand.

you're cared for, the quicker you can get on your feet, so plan now to hire this helper if your husband or a relative can't be home with you.

You'll also have to find a pediatrician now, maybe a diaper service, and, of course, to decide where you'll have the baby.

An obstetrician will usually deliver only in a hospital, and will give you a couple of choices. The nurse-midwife, however—who takes only low-risk women—may deliver in a hospital, if she has privileges there, or at home, but more likely she will use a birth center, approved by the National Association of Childbearing Centers and near a back-up hospital. Whether you deliver at a birth center or at home, you'll have to be within ten minutes of the hospital, so you can get a C-section within thirty minutes, if necessary.

Each of these options—the home, the

birth center and the hospital—has certain advantages, depending on your point of view and your health.

The planned home birth is the cheapest delivery of all and often more comfortable than a hospital birth, and it's generally quite safe, since you can have a baby at home only if you have no known problems. Even the baby is less likely to get an infection, since a hospital is full of sick people and germs abound even under the most sterile conditions.

You can expect the home birth to be both less of a production and more. You'll be expected to have a copy of your prenatal chart, some disposable pads and paper towels and a bed made up with an extra set of sheets over plastic, to be removed when you've delivered the placenta, to leave the bed dressed in clean sheets. You will also need someone to take care of any older children at home, as well as a packed bag and a car in the driveway, in case you need to go to the hospital after all.

The nurse-midwife, assisted by a labor and delivery nurse, brings sterile gloves, a cord clamp, eye drops and vitamin K, if it's required; a bulb to suction the baby's nose and mouth, a baby scale, a birth certificate and in case there are problems, an oxygen tank and drugs to stop the mother's bleeding.

The birth center is a compromise between home and a hospital. It's much easier for the midwives to deliver in the same place, but it has the amenities of home. Here you drink sweet raspberry tea during labor, for energy, and perhaps bathe with your husband in a Jacuzzi, to speed your labor along. You'll then deliver—maybe in a four-poster bed—with friends and family around if you'd like, go home four to twenty-four hours later and pay considerably less than you would at a hospital.

Most couples, however, prefer a hospital, if only to satisfy their anxious parents.

Your o.b. probably has privileges at two hospitals and will encourage you and your husband to tour them both, make your choice and fill out preadmission forms, which will simplify registration when you check in. You want to see which hospital has the friendliest, most attentive, most professional nurses—since the nurses, not the doctors, do most of the tending—and whether you want to use a delivery room or a birthing room. You'll probably choose the one where you think you'll feel most comfortable, and most secure.

The delivery room is full of tools, tubes and dials everywhere—like something out of science fiction—with a huge mirror overhead, so you can watch the production; oxygen at the ready if you feel queasy; glucose if you feel faint; and those wretched stirrups on the table, which make it easier for the doctor to deliver but much harder for you (and which you'll ask him to lower, please).

The birthing room, which looks about as homey as a motel room, has oxygen and an IV too, as well as a birthing chair and a bed which can be adjusted to let you deliver lying down, squatting, or more likely, at a forty-five degree angle, so your husband can sit behind you and massage your back. Just make sure the room is often used—a sign that the hospital encourages deliveries here—and that it's close to the operating room, in case there are complications.

Whether you plan to have natural childbirth or not, choose a hospital that has an anesthesiologist on duty around the clock and a sonogram machine that's always available.

The hospital should fill other requirements too. It's best to deliver in a place that will let you have a private labor room with its own bathroom; a labor nurse you'll share only with one other patient; a delivery room that is warm enough for a newborn, and a lactation expert on staff to help you when you start to breastfeed. You also want a hospital that doesn't insist on continuous monitoring and will let you walk the halls in labor, drink juice instead of having an IV, and keep the baby with you for at least an hour after the birth and then either stay in your room or in a nursery right next to it.

Above all, you want a hospital that has a Cesarean rate of 11 percent or lower if it's in a city, and about 5 percent if it's in a middle-class, low-risk suburban neighborhood. The higher the percentage, the more likely it is that you'll have a Cesarean.

You also need to choose the kind of room you want after you give birth.

Rooming-in is generally the best arrangement for a nursing mother, so the baby can stay with you unless you have company. This will give you and your baby the chance to know each other well before you go home, but it also means that you'll be getting up with the baby day and night, and this can be quite tiring.

If you sleep very lightly and don't have a lot of stamina you might consider a modified rooming-in instead if it's available. In this case, the baby stays with you during the day but spends the night in a nursery next door, just on the other side of a window where you can see, but hardly hear him. The nurses will give him bottles through the night, if he's on a formula, or bring him to you to nurse every two to three hours if you breastfeed, so you can sleep better between feedings.

The pediatrician you choose is another major decision, and it should also be made now.

### CHOOSING THE PEDIATRICIAN

The pediatrician you choose, like the house you buy, will affect your life for years. Both are long-term contracts and hard to leave, so both should suit your style. It's a decision you'll want to make by the seventh or eighth month of your pregnancy, particularly if the pediatricians have waiting lists in your area.

You'll be seeing this doctor about nineteen times for well-child checks in the next six years—and more for illnesses—and you'll be calling her many, many times for

guidance on even the most trivial issues of child care. You can see that it's not a choice to make lightly.

Look for a doctor who is board-certified, has at least five years of experience, is affiliated with a teaching hospital and, if possible, has offices near you.

Although your obstetrician will recommend several possibilities—if you ask—your friends may have the best suggestions, for you probably like the same kind of people.

Make appointments to interview these doctors—even though you'll probably pay for their time—to find out their views on breastfeeding and their methods for seeing a sick child, as well as the office hours, the call-in hours and the cost for visits and immunizations. You're not just meeting the doctor, but studying the atmosphere of the office, for it will reflect the respect she feels for her small patients and their parents.

It should be a friendly, orderly place, with a short waiting time, some toys and a special area for sick children to sit, if possible.

There are also more direct signs that mark a good doctor.

You want a pediatrician who treats parents as equals, not underlings; who takes the time to talk to each mother and who gives you the advice, diagnosis and instructions herself, rather than leaving these jobs to her nurse.

This kind of doctor is hard to find. Most pediatricians seem to come in two varieties. One is so casual she not only will forget your name and your child's name too, but she'll tell you blithely and consistently to "trust your own instincts," until you won't dare admit how desperate you feel in the baby's bleating hours between midnight and dawn.

The other type of pediatrician is concerned about your instincts too. She wonders if you have any. To this doctor, your child is her property, which she lets you watch because she is too busy.

It's hard to foresee the power that the

pediatrician will have over you. The obstetrician, who is so important in pregnancy, will mean little more to you than a friendly plumber once the baby is born, while the good opinion of the baby doctor will matter very much. If the doctor thinks you're a dunce, you soon will fit the role. This will make you so unsure of yourself you may have to change doctors to feel comfortable.

There is an art to dealing with a pediatrician, which you can master early by acting reasonably self-sufficient, without hand-wringing, but with enough curiosity to ask the reasons for her directions. Even the most curt doctor will give you the smattering of basic medicine you need to make the many intelligent little decisions that motherhood requires.

The pediatrician will know you're serious about learning more if you take notes every time you meet with her, particularly at the hospital, for this impression sticks. Even if you never look at these notes again (which you will), she will see you as a capable person.

### THE LAYETTE

You will want to buy a basic wardrobe for your baby before he's born, but this is all you'll need for the first three months, if you are willing to wash every other day.

6 terry-cloth jumpsuits
4 kimonos
6 undershirts
2 bibs
1 large box disposable diapers
1–4 dozen prefolded cloth diapers
1 diaper wrap
2–4 diaper pins
1 bunting
2 sweaters
1 hat
4–6 receiving blankets
1 carriage blanket
6 bassinet sheets or pillowcases
4 crib sheets

You'll underscore this image if you keep a rough chart of the first couple of weeks, or during a bad patch. By recording everything your baby does, and when he does it—when he cries and eats and sleeps and has a bowel movement—you can order your thoughts before you call the doctor. And if she says there is no problem but you're still concerned, stand your ground and be heard, even if you have to call back the next day.

The chart will also help you see patterns as they develop so you can plan your own time around your child. Without it, your hurry, your concern and your fatigue may make you forget and you'll never know what to expect and when. This can turn motherhood into a maze.

Even without a chart, it won't be long before you can decipher your baby's moods and fussy ways better than anyone—even an M.D. You really do have a maternal instinct and you really can trust it.

Even after you've settled these details, there are still a thousand things to do in the eighth month. Now the need for a layette and a nursery not only seems urgent, but you might think it should be as perfect as your baby. That's not the case, of course. The easiest equipment is often the cheapest, and it's often secondhand. The baby won't care and you shouldn't either, as long as it meets the safety requirements.

The baby won't be the only person who will need attention. Since the laundry routine dissolves with a newborn, your husband will need extra shirts, shorts and socks and you'll need more underwear, socks, stockings, some new sweats and maybe some blouses that button down the front, so you can nurse discreetly.

Between now and delivery you will also pack The Suitcase and build a grocery bank—by buying extra staples and convenience dinners every week, since you can't count on a helper to cook for you too. You can even freeze big batches of spaghetti and chili in small bags to take care of the

## THE SUITCASE

The packing of your suitcase is recommended by the end of the seventh month, for babies are notoriously poor in arithmetic. This is what you need for a two- or three-day stay:

- 2–3 nightgowns
- 1–2 nursing bras
- robe/bed jacket/ slippers
- 4 pairs underpants
- toothpaste/toothbrush
- talcum/deodorant
- makeup
- shampoo/hair dryer/curlers/hairbrush
- list of key phone numbers
- a novel
- loaded camera
- split of champagne and 2 glasses
- cookies/crackers for guests
- wraparound skirt/ blouse
- baby's outfit/2 diapers

You'll wear the bra under your nightgown, for nursing mothers need extra support and protection from leakage too, and though the hospital provides the sanitary napkins, you'll also need to wear underpants, for your flow will be heavy at first.

The phone numbers will make you feel efficient and thrifty too. Few hospitals keep phone books in the rooms and you'll be charged if you call information. The makeup is at least as important, for it will make you feel glamorous, but leave the perfume at home. You want your child to bond with your smell, not Chanel No. 5.

The camera is another necessity. With one-hour development service so common, you can send snapshots to new grandparents or home to an older child before you even get there (and no, the flash won't hurt the baby's eyes).

And the champagne? It's essential too, even though you will do little or no drinking after that if you're a nursing mother. Chill it in an extra pitcher of ice and count your blessings with a toast. You and your husband can't be too sentimental when you've just had a baby.

first two or even three weeks after the baby is born. Today's chores will be tomorrow's salvation.

It's the ninth month that seems downright endless. There are still loose ends to tie, o.b. visits to make every week and maybe another sonogram to check on your due date and the baby's good health, but mostly you just fret to yourself. It's hard to feel pretty and energetic now, and there are so many aches and twinges to worry about—especially in the middle of the night—and so many dreams to come true.

Even if you don't wake up to pee every few hours, that ripe belly of yours makes it hard to sleep, and you feel so very tired. Welcome to that sweet state of suspension, when you only have two to three weeks to go. (Or maybe just a day.)

This is the time to consider, to reflect, to respect the privacy of your mind: you have a wonderful, enormous adjustment ahead. While you focus on yourself more and more, everyone else focuses on you too. Well-meaning friends and relatives will inundate you with calls until "Still here?" becomes the most dreaded phrase of all. Now you may stay inside and even stop answering the phone: the true meaning of confinement.

Just as it seems like pregnancy is forever, some little old lady will stop you to say that you've "dropped" and she'll be right. This is the lightening as the baby slides down into the pelvis. Although this puts more pressure on the bladder, and makes it a little harder to walk around, it's much easier to breathe and to be a little more comfortable, but not all the time. Your baby is making at least twenty small moves in an hour in the last seven days, which is a welcome, but distracting sign of his good health.

Now that you're in the homestretch, you'll notice that your vaginal mucus gets thicker and your o.b. may tell you that your cervix is softening or you've started to dilate, which can be quick or take many days.

You pass the time by taking slow walks with your husband, renting movies, talking, wondering, retreating into yourself even more, but the occasional contractions may unnerve you. They get stronger, more frequent and more painful as you near term, which can be the onset of labor if you're expecting a second or third child, but it's probably just those Braxton-Hicks again. Although they thin the cervix, it's hard to count your blessings. False labor can hurt more than the real thing at first, but unlike real labor, it will go away if you change your activities or walk around.

And then whammo, you feel compelled to scrub the kitchen floor and unpack those bags from your grocery bank. Some of this is fine but save as much of your energy as you can: there's more important work ahead. Finally, about a day before labor starts, you notice that your vaginal mucus is tinged with pink—the bloody show and another sign that labor is about to begin.

## DURING

No two women follow the same pattern of labor and no woman has the same sort of delivery each time, but most of them have an early warning system and most first labors usually take about twelve hours—twice as long as later ones.

When contractions start in your lower back and lock your body like a chastity belt, you'd better record their time and length. You'll know the labor is real if the pains are regular, if they last a full minute, if they're so intense you can't laugh and talk when you're having them and if you can't make them go away. If they're more than ten minutes apart, however, go back to bed, and get as much rest as you can. No one ever had a baby in her sleep.

This two- to six-hour delay is a good idea. You'll be much cozier, you'll progress much better at home and you can eat enough carbohydrates to keep your energy high even through a long labor. The hospital, with its surreal atmosphere and its many intrusions, makes most mothers-to-be more tense, which slows down labor a little and may lead to problems. The longer you labor at the hospital, the more likely it is that someone will install a fetal monitor. This will slow your labor down further, since you can't walk around very much with an external monitor and not at all with an internal one.

A long wait in the hospital also encourages the doctor to order oxytocin. Even though this hormone can be very helpful, the cervix must be dilated, soft and paper-thin before it is given, since it can stimulate contractions but not dilation. The tight cervix, as well as the fetal monitor it requires, can cause distress in the baby—two factors that can lead to a Cesarean.

Your doctor will probably want you to stay home until the contractions are just five minutes apart or until the membranes break, spilling amniotic fluid as clear and warm as spit. It's a sign that you've gone from early labor to active labor and you've dilated about halfway.

When you are ready to go to the hospital, grab a thick towel to sit on in the car. Labor makes you self-conscious enough without sitting in a big, warm puddle if your waters break on the way.

You'll want to take a sweater too—the labor room can be chilly—and remind your husband to wear sneakers, since he'll be on his feet for hours. You'll also need to take some snack food and fruit juices, for labor will make you both hungry and thirsty. Just don't tell the anesthesiologist. He won't like you to eat in labor, in case you throw up while under a general anesthetic, but a full knockout is unusual, even with a Cesarean, and it's nothing the doctors can't handle.

You'll be surprised that your arrival hardly ripples the businesslike air of the hospital, just as if you weren't carrying the once and future king. After a few quick questions, a nurse will put you in a wheelchair—as insurance usually requires—and whip you straight to the labor room. There the doctor or the midwife will check you and cheer you and the labor nurse will listen to your belly every fifteen to twenty minutes with a Doppler—an ultrasound stethoscope which gives you the same results as a monitor. For the rest of the time, you and your husband will be left alone in one of the most suspenseful times you'll ever have together: you arrive as two but you'll leave as three, and everything in between is a mystery.

As the labor gets stronger you may even feel shivery and have a few moments of panic as you go from work to hurt. Now the contractions come every three to four minutes, last sixty to ninety seconds and you try to remember your Lamaze: which positions will make you more comfortable? when should you start your breathing? how can you focus your concentration? what can you do to move labor along? The books say active labor lasts one to two hours, but it seems like eons to you.

You might try nipple stimulation to make it go faster or your doctor might order an enema or insert prostaglandin gel into your vagina but mostly you'll walk the halls. You may even hear a woman moan, "Oh, my God," again and again, and you'll be so afraid you'll sound like that when you get further along. Since no mother ever admits that she did, we like to think it's a tape that hospitals play to keep their ladies in line.

Any fear you have of delivery is based almost entirely on a fear of the unknown, and particularly a fear of making a damn fool of yourself, for there is pain in labor and you don't know how you will react to

it until it happens. Fortunately, the pains are so instinctive and constructive (and interesting) that you will behave quite properly, and they're so intense you won't remember it if you don't.

By the time you enter transition, the dilation is almost complete, and you can probably expect one to two tough hours, with contractions every two to three minutes, and, if you're lucky, a nurse who lays warm compresses on your perineum—between the vagina and the rectum—to ease the painful pressure. Just when you think you can't take any more, you'll have an undeniable urge to push, which calls for

## GRIEF

Most pregnancies and most births are quite marvelous, but none are perfect. There are sure to be some small problems, some anxieties, and very occasionally, a tragedy.

A miscarriage, a stillbirth, or the death of a child is devastating, and a birth defect can be a heartbreak, but these crises are much worse, and much more prolonged, for couples who go through them alone.

If you suffer one of these terrible losses, look for the self-help group that deals with your situation. The consolation of those who have walked in your shoes can help you get rid of your guilt and anger a little sooner and accept and even find comfort and kindness in the clumsy words of friends and strangers. This is especially important if you've lost a baby through Sudden Infant Death Syndrome, which probably takes the heaviest emotional toll of all.

Support groups, and perhaps some counseling, will protect your marriage too. Husbands and wives go through the same stages of grief, but they express them differently, and at different times, which puts them out of sync with each other for a long time. Your differences will be easier to accept and you'll even quit blaming yourselves and each other if you have the right support.

Grief can either weaken or strengthen a marriage, but it never lets it be.

an internal exam to make sure you're dilated all the way. If not, you may have to pant or blow until you're ready.

When you are, you'll be whisked to the birthing room or the delivery room for the second stage, which lasts one to three hours and doesn't hurt as much, but does require intense concentration to push the baby down through the birth canal. Imagery helps, and so does eye contact with your partner, low lights, soft voices, an open mouth and a relaxed jaw when you push. Now you learn to go with the flow: if you push, the pain goes away.

At this point the doctor is very attentive to your bottom—even massaging your perineum to try to avoid an episiotomy—but he may have few words for you, especially if you deliver in a teaching hospital. This is the best kind—because it usually has the finest doctors and the latest equipment—but if you have an interesting delivery, you may also have a group of students who stand just below your navel to get a lecture in obstetrics. And you won't even care.

Finally, you'll see the top of the head come out, go back, come out, crowning three to five times, and then suddenly the baby emerges. You haven't had a baby. You've had a miracle.

Within seconds he turns from a limp, purplish gray little body to a bright red, squally baby and a beauty, even though he's covered with a waxy-white substance, his head perhaps misshapen from the birth canal, and genitals that are huge compared to the body itself. When we first saw our son we pointed in disbelief and said, "What's that sticking out?"

The baffled nurse said, "You mean his nose?" and we only could say, "If that's his nose, send him back."

## CESAREAN

A Cesarean birth is just as fulfilling as a vaginal birth, if you've been prepared for the possibility. It helps to know that a Cesarean is very safe, taking only ten min-

utes or so to lift the baby out of the womb and about an hour to repair the mother.

It also gives you one beautiful baby. He may be bloody from the incision and have extra mucus to be suctioned out—since it isn't squeezed out in a vaginal delivery—but his head won't be squeezed like a cucumber either.

A Cesarean is major surgery, however, and it shouldn't be done unless it's truly necessary. And yet one pregnancy out of four now ends in a Cesarean rather than a vaginal delivery—not one in twenty as it was in your mom's day. Some blame this high rate on the fetal monitor, which can be tricky to interpret and can slow down labor. Others blame it on doctors who are impatient with a lengthy labor, or who want the convenience that comes with a planned operation or the extra money that a C-section brings or who are afraid they'll be sued if they don't operate and something goes wrong.

You're less likely to have a Cesarean if you have a conservative doctor—one who delivers only about 5 percent of his babies abdominally.

Twins, a breech birth, diabetes, heavy bleeding or blood pressure problems may make a C-section necessary. A C-section may also be done if the placenta is blocking the birth canal or if the woman has a vertical internal scar on her womb from an earlier Cesarean, even if the scar on her belly is horizontal. Only her medical records can give the doctor this information, since the internal and external scars may not go in the same direction.

In most cases, however, a Cesarean becomes necessary because the baby is too big for the pelvis—and the contractions less effective—or the labor just isn't getting anywhere.

Fortunately, only 10 percent of these operations are true emergencies and there's almost always time for a second opinion and some key tests to see if a problem actually exists.

A sonogram can tell if the baby is actually overdue or if you conceived later than you thought, and it can check the position of the baby and the placenta too. A pH reading of the baby's blood—called a fetal scalp blood exam—isn't done in many hospitals but it is another fine test. It reveals the baby's oxygen level, which tells if he's really in distress or if the monitor is just overreacting—something that often happens.

Whether you expect to have a C-section or not, talk with your o.b. about it beforehand. Tell him you want a low, horizontal incision of the womb—a bikini cut—if he does have to operate, so you can have a vaginal delivery next time. Ask for an epidural too, which would kill the pain below your waist, but still let you see and touch the baby as soon as he's been cleaned up. You'd miss that experience with a general anesthetic, because it would put you to sleep.

Also ask the doctor to let your husband join you in the operating room—a sterile sheet keeps both of you from seeing the operation itself—and to let him stay with you for a while in the recovery room, so he can help you hold the baby while you nurse. This is especially nice to do in that first half-hour, before the anesthesia wears off, and it's important for both you and the baby to have this contact. It's also usually quite safe. Most C-section babies are perfectly healthy and need no special newborn care, aside from the love that a mother gives best.

If you do have a Cesarean, you can expect to stay in the recovery room for two to three hours with a nurse monitoring you carefully and reminding you to wiggle your toes, take deep breaths and cough gently every few minutes. After that you'll be trundled to the maternity ward for three to five days. The first few days may be pretty tough, especially if this is your first Cesarean, and you may need a prescription painkiller every three to four hours. If you have gas pains—which may hit about three days after any abdominal surgery—your grandmother will order chamomile tea and your doctor will order aspirin. They're both good bets for this discomfort. Aspirin also can handle the afterpains—those uterine contractions that occur for four to five days after either a vaginal or an abdominal birth.

Despite the aches and discomforts, the baby can go to your room as soon as you'd like, and for feedings every two to three hours as long as someone is with you. By getting the doctor's permission in advance, you can have the orders written on your chart, to make sure the staff follows them.

The doctor will also have the nurses sit you up about eight hours after the delivery and even have you do some exercises in bed. They'll also ask you to take deep breaths to fill your lungs completely, which prevents pneumonia and gets rid of the anesthesia in your body and the gas in your gut, and they'll have you out of bed within twenty-four hours of the birth to prevent complications. You also need to walk so you can go to the bathroom often, for the pressure of a full bladder makes the pains worse.

Any exercise will make you feel better and so will solid food, which you can have about two days after the birth. Only then can you get rid of that IV you've been dragging around, but in the meantime drink a lot of water, juice and broth, which will make your body work better.

Once you get home, you'll have to rest most of the time for the first week with someone handing the baby to you for feedings, even though the bassinet is next to your bed. You'll still need to take it easy the second week with your husband or a helper doing all the chores, for heavy lifting and stair-climbing are forbidden for two weeks, even if you have other children to tend.

Since you are also recovering from major surgery, you probably won't mind this inactivity too much. Unless it was planned, however, the C-section may make you sad. It's tempting to bemoan what might have been, instead of reveling in the moment, especially when other mothers tell you about the glorious experience of Natural Childbirth. You can only ignore the sorority of the pious and know that it's better to have a healthy baby by C-section than to put the baby at risk. A Cesarean is a medical victory, not a maternal failure.

You've been bonding for nine months; you have a lifetime of bonding ahead. So what if you miss some moments in the delivery room? There are times to regret, but the birth of a baby—by any means at all—is the time to rejoice.

## AFTER

The doctor will suction the baby's mouth and nose, so he can breathe better, and then cut the umbilical cord—a symbolic job he may give to your husband. He'll also check the baby's heart rate, breathing, muscle tone, reflexes and color a minute after the birth, and then five minutes after—which gives him the Apgar score to see how well the baby's doing—and the nurse will wipe off the baby lightly, and lay him on your chest. Every one of your senses will respond to his, and his to yours. Your baby already knows your voice—he's heard it for months—but if you're allowed to hold him, he bonds to your smell in the first ten minutes.

It's like holding a piece of heaven. With great satisfaction, wooziness and perhaps some nausea you will only have eyes and ears and heart for the baby, with a little left over for your husband. The pain of a few stitches—if any are needed—or the

few contractions it takes to get rid of the placenta, will be ignored as you wallow in the greatest contentment you have ever known. The baby is in a state of quiet alert for about an hour—if you haven't had many drugs—and you are in your glory.

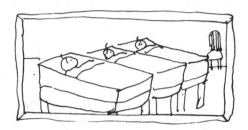

If you have the baby in a birthing room, the doctor will let you stay there but the delivery room usually calls for a transfer to the recovery room, until the effects of any anesthesia are gone and you don't feel sick anymore. Here women groan and you have nothing to watch but the clock and the other ladies, who still look pregnant too.

The better hospital will let you nurse your baby there—if you haven't already—then the baby will be taken to the nursery to get a heel-stick blood test to rule out PKU, and a shot of vitamin K, some antibiotic for his eyes, a hospital wristband and oohs and aahs from the nurses. After another visit with your husband, too poignant ever to forget, you are rolled to your room and into bed, cleaned up and amazingly ready to make a few celebratory calls to your family before you fall asleep.

If your baby doesn't wake you up soon, your body will. Everything about it is a little out of whack—and so different from what you expected.

By the ninth month of pregnancy, you thought about only two things: making babies and making love. The idea of sex, in good old missionary style, became almost an obsession. Now you only think about your baby and your bottom.

Almost as soon as you are comfortable, a nurse slides a cold bedpan under you, runs the water and tells you, honey, to perform. Then there are the miserable afterpains, which hurt as much as early labor, except no one holds your hand and says, "You're marvelous!" The stitches start to heal, which hurts too, because they shrink as they absorb, and you realize you are constipated and confer regularly with the nurses about it. Sometimes it's mighty hard to feel maternal and impossible to feel sexy. Your breasts swell painfully, even if you are a bottle mother and have had a shot to stop the milk. Finally, you weigh yourself—and you've lost only ten pounds. You take a good look at yourself, see a few stretch marks and a bulging belly and realize that the wraparound skirt you packed to wear home is not going to be wrapping very much.

And doctors wonder why mothers have postpartum blues. It's like two days after Christmas when the presents fall apart. None of these small problems will knock you out of your newfound bliss, however, but it's still hard to think of yourself as a mother, or ever being as adept as the nurses.

As nice as they generally are on the maternity floor, their deftness in handling your baby makes you feel as awkward as you did on the first day of your first job. Even your husband looks like an intruder when he visits, for if some jewel of a nurse should treat you like an Earth Mother, no one ever treated a man like an Earth Father, more's the pity. Champagne was invented for days like this.

You can prevent some of the blues if you put yourself together as quickly as possible after the delivery. Shower soon (for giving birth is a sweaty process) and wear a ribbon in your hair, put on makeup and put on your own nightgown instead of the hospital special.

The rest is a matter of recognizing that the slings and arrows of maternal fortune are normal, and soon and simply cured.

It's true that your tush aches after the birth, but it will feel better if you put ice on the perineum for the first twenty-four hours. If you had stitches, you'll also want to take sitz baths every day, do vaginal exercises (see page 34), squeeze a bottle of warm water on this area when you go to the bathroom, and expose the stitches to the air occasionally for the next two weeks, when they'll dissolve.

---

### MEMORIES

When you aren't calling your friends, admiring your baby or catching a snooze, try to write down your memories of the past two days, and what it feels like to be a parent. One loving mother takes out these notes and reads them to her children on their birthdays, to remind them again of the joy they brought, right from the start.

---

The afterpains hurt for the first one to two days, usually when you nurse, but the nursing helps the uterus contract. The contractions will hurt less if you empty your bladder before you breastfeed, take nonaspirin and be patient. You'll also sweat a lot and need to drink a great deal of water for days after the birth, which is fine and a good way to lose weight.

Fatigue is a problem too. It will seem like you're nursing the baby every two minutes at first, and it will be fine if you do, because the colostrum is awash with antibodies and because it will flush out his gut. This may lower his chances for jaundice, since meconium—the black, tarry waste in a newborn's bowel—is full of the bilirubins that cause it. He still may get jaundice anyway—30 percent of all newborns do—but it's almost always a mild case, easily fixed by putting the bassinet in a sunny window—for sunlight helps all babies—and by placing him under special lights if necessary. You'll know the baby may have jaundice if he's hot, sleepy and lethargic or if the whites of his eyes look slightly yellow or the skin has a yellow cast after you press his nose, arm, leg and belly, but the pediatrician will tell you what to do.

You can expect the pediatrician to visit

you the day after delivery and return at least once before you go home, to tell you, in fifteen minutes or less, about the care and feeding of your baby. It all seems so simple.

### CIRCUMCISION

Victorian doctors used to circumcise males to discourage masturbation later—which obviously didn't work—and turn-of-the-century doctors did it to prevent asthma, madness, syphillis, cancer, tuberculosis and other popular problems, which didn't work either. Still the custom has stayed with us. Today the United States is the only industrialized country that still circumcises most of its sons for medical reasons, and usually without a local anesthetic.

The number is dropping very fast, however, because studies show that babies can indeed feel pain, that circumcision can cause unnecessary problems and that more and more insurance companies are refusing to pay for it.

There's seldom any reason for parents to okay this operation unless they want their son circumcised for religious reasons, or think the boy will feel different from his friends or his dad or they're afraid he'll need a circumcision years later. This happens sometimes, but it's quite rare.

If your son isn't circumcised, keep his penis as clean as you'd keep his ears, without pulling the foreskin to clean beneath it (any more than you'd pull his ears). You can pull it back gently in about a year, and easily in about three years, the way nature intended.

If you do want your son to be circumcised, however, have the pediatrician examine him first to make sure he's healthy, that his blood clots quickly and that there is no penile deformity—since that can't be corrected as easily if the foreskin is re-moved—and ask the obstetrician to use a local anesthetic.

### BREASTFEEDING

Formula is fine, but mother's milk is better, both for you and your baby. Breastfeeding will not only fulfill you as a mother, but it's free, convenient, nutritious, and can prevent many childhood illnesses and allergies, and possibly obesity too. It even has special proteins to promote brain development. In fact, today most pediatricians think breast milk should be a baby's only food for the first four to six months, and almost the only milk he gets in the first year.

Although it seems hard at first, any healthy mother can produce good milk, no matter what size her breasts, and sometimes even an adoptive mother can be successful. The more you feed your baby, the more milk you'll make, as long as you give the baby little or no water or supplements at first, which would make the baby nurse less and would slow down your milk supply.

You still have to relax, however, have faith in yourself, rest enough, drink at least two quarts of water and eat five hundred more calories a day than you did before you got pregnant. You have to skip caffeine too, so you won't keep the baby awake, and alcohol, and avoid any food or drink that gives him a rash, constipation or gas, as well as junk food, which gives you nothing but calories and gives him nothing at all. If you'll follow this regime, you'll get your energy back in about six weeks and you'll lose your extra weight in about six months, at the rate of about a pound a week.

You'll need two to four cotton nursing bras, with a flap that unsnaps for easier feeding, pads to catch any leakage and blouses that button up the front. Also keep

a receiving blanket handy to drape over your baby and your breast if you nurse in public, so you won't embarrass anyone—or yourself.

You also need some good instruction on nursing before you have the baby, again before you leave the hospital, and any time you run into a problem. Your old Lamaze teacher, or someone from La Leche League—the support organization for nursing mothers—can help you, or the lactation expert at the hospital. This advice is particularly important if your family or friends think nursing is silly or out-of-date, for new mothers need plenty of encouragement.

Breastfeeding is natural, but it isn't instinctive. You will be clumsy at first, and your baby will be too: furious at his hunger one moment, losing the nipple the next, then dropping to sleep in the middle of his meal. You both have a lot to learn.

You have to learn how to brush your baby's cheek with your nipple when he loses it—so he'll root around toward it—and to keep him awake or make him eat faster by tapping his cheeks, massaging his back, his belly and his legs, or by rubbing the bottom of his feet or changing his diaper when you switch from one breast to the other. These tricks usually wake a fellow up.

Much of your success will depend on how well you position the breast and the

baby. Although in time it will probably go better if you sit up rather straight, well propped by a pillow or a rocker, you'll want to start off lying down on your side, tummy to tummy, and preferably in the first hour or two after his birth, for one of the great bonding moments of motherhood.

To nurse, suppress the breast away from his nose—so he can breathe—and slip the nipple straight to the back of his mouth, to stimulate the sucking reflex and keep your nipple from getting sore. This also lets his gums cover the areola, so his chin presses on the sinuses below the nipple, which empties your milk ducts and lets him get his fill.

The colostrum—which is all your baby gets in the first few days—gives him the fluid he needs and a great many benefits too. Colostrum may be thin and watery-looking, but doctors call it liquid gold. It's much richer than breast milk; it's high in protein and low in sugar and fat—so it's easy to digest—and it's full of antibodies to fight all the new germs he will meet.

You'll know he wants to eat if he cries, opens his mouth and turns his head from one side to the other, rooting around to find the nipple. Both you and your newborn will need frequent nursing sessions at first—about ten to twenty minutes on each side—every one to three hours to get your milk supply going, which quickly turns into about eight feedings every twenty-four hours. This will get your womb back to its normal size in about six weeks, for the uterus contracts with every nursing. These nursings may hurt a little at first, but the pain is sweet.

You'll start producing milk instead of colostrum between the second and the fifth day and you'll know it by the look and feel of your breasts. There is often a lightening or a sort of sexy, tingling sensation—the "let-down reflex"—and then you see your baby swallow. That, and your soft, empty breasts afterward, and maybe some leakage of milk in between nursings, are sure signs that your milk has come in.

Your breasts will also get hard, warm, swollen and maybe tender and lumpy when you start making milk, and you'll have to offer the baby both breasts every two to three hours, even if you have to wake him up. If you don't feed him this often, they may get red and shiny and so engorged that you'll need to lean them into a pan of warm water before you breastfeed, or squirt out some milk first, to soften them a little, and you may even need to put ice packs on your breasts between feedings if they really hurt.

Sore nipples can become a problem too, if you don't position the teat well. Pump a little milk to soften the areola before nursing, massage your breast while he sucks, apply cold packs to your breasts after you nurse, and smear thick, pure vitamin E on the nipples after they air-dry. The problem should go away in a few days and certainly by the tenth day.

Altogether it will take six to eight weeks for you and your baby to feed with ease, but there are sure to be some setbacks along the way. Just when you think you've adjusted to breastfeeding, the help leaves, the confusion overwhelms you and your milk may diminish quickly. It's time to go back to the basics. Drink much more water—especially when you nurse—get two to three short naps a day, eat a better, more varied diet and nurse more often to increase your milk.

You also want to relax before you nurse and to massage your breasts lightly. This will stimulate the let-down reflex, so the baby gets the milk from the back of the breast. Two thirds of it is stored there and this "hind" milk is twice as fat as the "fore" milk he gets first.

You may also be dismayed when your baby is at about two to three weeks old and again at about six weeks, when he can't seem to get enough to eat. It's not that you're making less milk, but that he's hit a growth spurt and suddenly needs much

more. It's nothing to worry about. The supply will catch up with the demand in a few days.

You may also be bothered around six to eight weeks, when your breasts no longer seem so full. That will simply tell you that your milk production has adjusted to his needs. As long as he gains five to seven ounces a week, and wets eight or more diapers a day—without drinking any water—you know he's getting the twenty to thirty-four ounces of milk he needs each day. Although you don't want to give any bottles in the first month, he should have occasional bottles of breast milk after that so he'll get used to a rubber nipple, and he can have formula sometimes after about two months. Once your production has stabilized, this won't affect your supply.

Your milk won't even be affected much if you get sick and have to take medicine, since only 1 percent of the dose—or less—enters the breast milk, and many medicines can't get into the supply at all. Some drugs can be dangerous to a baby, however, and you should check with your pediatrician before you take any prescription or over-the-counter medicine. She'll probably have you take the dose right after a feeding, for the medicine only stays in the breast milk for two to four hours.

### Expressing Breast Milk

Breast-feeding and technology have finally joined forces. If you can't master the artful technique of expressing your milk by hand—and most mothers say they can't—there are some good manual and electric pumps to do it for you. The results are invaluable. Not only will your husband be able to give some of the feedings but you can get out of the house much sooner and more often than you expected and life will seem more normal.

An electric pump, which is too expensive to buy, is best and can be rented from the hospital, but a good manual pump is affordable. There is, however, a great difference between these pumps, and you'll want to ask the pediatrician to recommend the best one. Before you do that, however, see if you can't express milk by hand, because it's so much simpler.

Start by massaging the breast lightly to let down the milk, then press on the sinuses, which are in a circle about one-and-a-half inches from the nipple. To do this, put your thumb above the nipple and your index and middle fingers below it, and then push straight in, rolling the thumb and fingers forward to express milk directly into a plastic bottle liner. Move the hand around the breast to press all the sinuses, then switch to the other breast.

Whatever method you use to express your milk, plastic bottle liners are ideal for storage. Close them with rubber bands and refrigerate them—where they're good for forty-eight hours—or date then and toss them in the freezer, where they'll keep for three months.

### Working Mothers

Working mothers can use this method too, if they can find a quiet place at work to express their milk two to three times a day and then store the bags in an insulated container with a reusable freezer gel pack. Even if there is a refrigerator at the office, you need the container to keep the milk cold on your way home.

Although the mechanics of breastfeeding are fairly easy to solve if you work, the fatigue is not, for a nursing mother needs plenty of rest. You'll have to go to bed early at night and have your husband or a hired helper do most of the housework. Even so, you'd be wise to wait until the baby is about four months old and eating a few solids before you go back to work, so he won't need as many feedings.

If your baby is younger, you can still feed him four times a day if you nurse him early in the morning, when you're still in bed; again before you leave him; as soon as you get back in the evening; and then just before you go to sleep at night. It's tiring, but if your baby gets up a burp or

two, all will be right with his world and yours.

### Weaning

Eventually you'll want to wean the baby, of course—or the baby will want to wean himself, which is ideal and often happens at the end of the first year. Some babies take to the cup right away, but a bottle is preferred by most.

If you initiate the change, you'll find it easier to wait until your child is eating some solids, and then drop one feeding a week, cutting out his favorite feeds last.

But beware. Breastfeeding has become almost a cult to many women and someone is sure to lecture you whenever you quit, even if your baby is a toddling Two. This is silly, of course. Breastfeeding is the completion of a natural cycle, not a test of your maternal ability. Love and nestling matter more than milk, and you can give it with a bottle as well as a breast, as long as you're willing to cuddle and talk to your baby while he feeds.

This weaning will make you sad, but it will be a relief too, although you may be nonplussed to find that your breasts are smaller than they were before you got pregnant. Don't worry. They'll be back to their normal size in about six months.

### BOTTLEFEEDING

Bottlefeeding may be best for you and your baby if you're going right back to work, or you're ill, or you've adopted, or you're uncomfortable about nursing or tired of it, or afraid of being tied down or simply if bottlefeeding has always been the custom in your family. The choice is completely yours and like everything else in the wonderful world of grown-ups, there are pluses and minuses.

On the positive side, it frees you up a little, and gives your husband and the baby some special time together—including, we hope, that 2 A.M. feeding. A good stretch

## TEMPERAMENTS

Take a hard look at the newborns in the hospital nursery. They may have black hair, red hair or no hair, and small lumps and bruises and strangely squashed heads—the sign of their four-centimeter trip from inner to outer space—but somehow they all look alike.

And then you look again. Children, it turns out, come in at least fifty-seven varieties. They not only look different but their temperaments are different too. Although their health, their families and their nurturing will affect their behavior, they are already set in their ways. You can expect the baby who kicked and carried on in the womb to be an active child, and the one who made gentle moves to be more placid.

The experts say you can even detect their temperament by the way they're built. In the purest cases, the sturdy, square little mesomorph, with his big bones, strong heart, and heavy muscles, is noisy, on the go, and if possible, in charge, while the long, skinny ectomorph has feelings as thin and sensitive as his skin. You'll know him by his round shoulders, slight muscles, small appetite, and a disposition that is often quiet, shy and introverted.

The endomorph, however, is soft and round, with little hands and feet; a digestive system big enough to handle all the food he likes to eat, and a spirit big enough to love the whole world.

The sooner you can recognize these differences, the more you can appreciate your child.

digest and more allergenic than formula. The pediatrician will therefore choose a formula that comes in three varieties, all of which are fine, as long as you buy them before the expiration date and none of the cans are dented. The easiest will be those ready-mixed little bottles that need no refrigeration and are great for traveling, but they're wickedly expensive. This leaves you to make the formula with a liquid, which is much cheaper, or with a powder, which is cheapest of all.

Whether you bottlefeed your baby right from the start or after a few weeks, you will discover a well-kept secret: a bottle baby needs a fairly well-organized mother. You have to keep formula and bottles, or plastic bottle liners, in the house at all times, and make up a bottle of water, which you probably won't use, and about eight bottles of formula a day. This will give you a twenty-four hour supply, which is as long as you should keep formula anyway.

And now comes trouble with a capital T. The pediatrician may want you to sterilize all the bottle-making equipment for the baby's first six months even if you have a dishwasher with extremely hot water.

This exacting little job can seem monumental to a new mother, but a new father handles it just fine. It won't seem so hard when you get your strength back, but even then you'll need a positive attitude. Bottles should always look half full, not half empty.

To sterilize, put a rack in a pot, fill the pot with about two inches of water and add the glass or plastic bottles—if you use them instead of liners—as well as the caps and discs, the measuring cup and spoons, the tongs and a knife and then boil, covered, for at least ten minutes. The water you'll need to make the formula should be

of sleep at night will give you back your energy quicker than anything else.

On the negative side, there is the cost and the trouble. Cow's milk would be the easiest to give, of course, but it has the wrong kind of fat, too many minerals and too little sugar, and it's much harder to

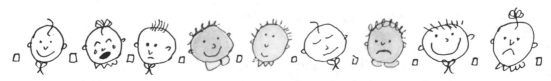

boiled in another pot for at least ten minutes and the nipples in a third pot for about three minutes, but not longer or they'll soon get gummy.

To make formula, use the tongs to lift out everything to air dry on a paper towel, and then make up the bottles when they're cool enough to handle. Pour the water into the measuring cup and add either the liquid or the spoonfuls of powder, leveled with the knife, so you don't add too much. This would give your baby too much fat, protein and minerals, including salt, which would make him thirsty (and make him cry). You also don't want to open the can of liquid formula until you first rinse the top with hot water in case the lid should fall in. They use a lot of bug spray in supermarkets.

Put the nipples upside down in the bottles and cover them with the discs—a nicety you'll forgo in a few months—and then screw on the tops and refrigerate immediately so bacteria can't breed. Once they're cold you can transfer them into an insulated container if you're going out, but wherever you feed your baby, try to warm the bottle first. An infant will take it cold, but he really doesn't need that shock to his young system. Since a microwave may get the formula too hot, heat the bottle in a saucepan half-filled with water—a bain-marie, we call it in Louisiana—until the formula feels no hotter than sweat when you shake it on your wrist.

When you feed the baby, put a bib on him—formula stains are tough to remove—and hold the baby in the crook of your arm, with the bottle at a forty-five degree angle, so the whole nipple is full of milk. If it isn't he'll get air bubbles in his belly, and bubbles hurt.

You also want to hold him as closely and as gently as you would if you were nursing, rather than prop the bottle, since this can lead to an ear infection. Propping is seldom necessary anyway, and even twins can be held at alternate feedings. This will give a sense of tranquility to your baby and give you the chance to gather your thoughts, read a book, visit with an older child—or admire the one in your arms.

### BURPING THE BABY

Whether you feed your baby with a breast or a bottle, be sure to burp him at least once during the feeding as well as afterward. No two babies burp alike, but until you know his style, bring up the bubbles by rubbing up and down along his spine, especially between the shoulder blades, while he falls over your hand or your shoulder. This pressure forces more gas from the solar plexus area where it often collects. If you lay your baby on his stomach afterward, the last bubbles usually come up in about fifteen minutes.

## GOING HOME

By the time you have been in the hospital for two or three days, you know you can conquer the world. Then you go home. It takes such energy to dress yourself and the baby, to gather the flowers and say goodbye to your roommate and the nurses (who are now your best friends) that you are tottering by the time you climb the few steps to your front door. That's why you should ask your husband to tidy the place before you get home. It isn't that you wouldn't want to do it yourself, but it's overwhelming to realize that you can't.

During pregnancy you prepared yourself well for the problems of fitting three people together in one household—and now there are four. The presence of a mother's helper, as essential as she is, can shatter this fragile situation.

Your helper, whether a relative, a neighbor, or, if you should be so lucky, a baby nurse, won't do everything the way you think it should be done—and it doesn't matter at all. It won't hurt you to let your mother-in-law have her way; you will have your way for years. Your helper is there to worry about the baby. You worry about yourself.

It is much harder on you to have company at home than it is in the hospital, so your husband should ask friends to stay away for your first few days at home and to keep their visits short for the first week after that. Have a note put on the door when you want to sleep (just blame it on the helper) and unplug the phone. We knew one dear lady who traveled across town by bus to see us, feathered hat, white gloves and silver baby spoon, and then only stayed ten minutes.

"It's not proper to stay longer with the sick, my dear," she informed us, for which we blessed her seventy-five-year-old sense of etiquette.

You will loll about the first week, avoiding stairs to prevent strain on the uterus. The flow probably will stop about three or even four weeks after you deliver. To prevent infection, change pads frequently, take showers often (but not baths or douches), and when you start to make love, use condoms, both for contraception and hygiene.

### THE BABY BLUES

If you're like so many new mothers, you may start to feel low about two to three days after the baby is born, and be restless, teary, wakeful, confused and agitated for a few hours or days. Some of this reaction is caused by fatigue and excitement, but not all.

Your body has been on a hormonal roller coaster for nine months. Your estrogen and progesterone levels shot up fifty times higher in pregnancy, and then—within hours of the baby's birth—they dropped even lower than they were before. Your thyroid level went up in pregnancy too, and it will drop slowly about two to four weeks after the birth and stay low for

about a year, which can make you feel depressed.

Worry, lack of sleep or money (or both) and too much—or not enough—help from friends and relations can make your moods worse and send hormones into a greater tizzy. Occasionally the baby blues even turn into postpartum depression—a miserable joy-robber that comes in two varieties.

Some new mothers have wild mood swings between the fourth and the fifteenth day after delivery, and then slip into depression, and others find that PPD creeps up on them between the twentieth and fortieth day, when they turn sad, listless and tired, with swollen ankles, delayed menstruation, a low libido, a disturbing new weight gain and maybe insomnia.

The more tired, fearful and anxious the mother becomes, the worse the PPD, but you won't reach the desperation point if you tell the o.b. as soon as the first signs of PPD appear.

Your doctor may order an antidepressant unless you're nursing, (but not a tranquilizer, which masks the symptoms, or the pill, which can cause depression). He'll probably prescribe natural progesterone too (but not artificial progesterone, which can make PPD worse), and 10 mg of $B_6$, since the body often needs more of this vitamin for the first thirty days after delivery.

The doctor will also tell you to eat bananas and oranges for their potassium; to have a small meal every few hours to keep the blood sugar steady and to get more sleep, especially at night. Your husband can give the baby a bottle as well as you can, or at least bring the baby to you to breastfeed, then change and burp him and put him down again when he's finished. He may not think it's necessary and you may not think it's worth arguing about, but this is one request that should be nonnegotiable. If you don't get your strength back in about six weeks, you'll be exhausted for many months.

It doesn't matter whether other mothers can lick the world with a baby on each hip. If you have PPD, you have more hormone activity than they do, or you're more sensitive to it, and either way, you need help, especially if you are afraid you'll hurt yourself or the baby. This requires a quick call to Parents Anonymous (see Resources), another call to the doctor and an understanding husband. PPD is a problem, but it's nothing to be ashamed of.

With or without intervention, the miasma of gloom will slowly lift after eight to nine months, as your body chemistry gets back to normal, but if you're still abnormally tired or depressed after a year, get the TRSH test to see if you need extra thyroid. It's expensive, but much more accurate than the regular thyroid test. Sometimes PPD is just that simple.

## ON YOUR OWN

When your child is born you need to undergo a rebirth yourself to meet the many emotional and physical demands of motherhood.

You may cope well with the anticipated, positive pains of labor, and then be dismayed by the unexpected, negative aches of afterbirth, stitches and the brief, if prominent, postpartum blues when you discover you are nearly as fat as you were a month before and a sexpot you clearly are not. Now you realize that you can't handle every situation, and your resolutions are about as flabbly as your figure.

You've begun the most creative phase of your life, but you often feel overcome by its problems. The vibrancy of your new job will sustain you, however, if you count your blessings at least as often as your burdens.

Rest is another essential. Stay in your nightgown for the first week—the quicker you get dressed, the less help you'll get— and steal every bit of sleep you can for the first six weeks. It takes most mothers at least that long to recover from the impact of birth, but if you are too energetic it may take months longer. Exhaustion creates a real postpartum depression, and you will be too tired even to recognize it. If you're nursing, fatigue will diminish your milk supply too, and that will just make you feel worse. It will also increase your bleeding and could make it last longer than three to four weeks, which will just tire you more.

Your adjustment to motherhood will also be quicker if you and your husband occasionally escape for an hour or so, starting when your baby is about ten days old. Choose a place where you can sit when your knees start to quake and stand when your bottom starts to hurt.

Companionship is important—and so is sex. Most o.b's ban intercourse until the six weeks' check, but most new mothers do not. Three weeks is much more like it. They just don't tell, figuring it's better to have loved and hurt than to wait another month. And so will you. Sex is a lovely tranquilizer and the quicker you return to the good life, the quicker your new family gets settled. Just make sure your husband uses a condom to prevent infection—and pregnancy.

You also need to include your husband in all the new routines of family living. The more you encourage him to take care of his child—and the more you let him do it in his own way—the sooner the three of you will turn into a real family.

It's true that some drudge said, "Women's work is never done," but you don't have to drag around from 6 A.M. to mid-

night to prove it. If you do, you will be a very tired bedfellow and have no fun at all.

You have to change your way of thinking too. From now on life must be lived in fifteen-minute snatches, and even then it will seldom go smoothly, particularly if you have more than one child. If by some fluke one day is serene, you can bet the next one will be a pip. New problems teach you new solutions, but they have to be changed almost as often as diapers.

For your own ego, you need to feel successful at the end of each day. If you make lists of your intentions at breakfast, you only will have a record of your failures at dinner. Instead, keep your time fluid and your goals general. Caring for a baby all day is as demanding as the toughest job you ever had, and you must organize your time at home as wisely as you did at work: the hard jobs are tackled in the morning. As long as you're at home, the afternoon is for taking walks, cooking dinner—the simplest routine. Eventually this will seem so respectable you can follow this pattern for the rest of your life.

You also need to do some things for yourself. There are at least two times a day when you should look and smell good: at night when you go to bed and first thing in the morning. This fresh-up will make the transition easier if you go back to work, and even more important, it will be good for your own self-esteem. When you have a baby you leave the mainstream of society, and it's very easy to look as pitiful as you sometimes feel. This doesn't score points with anyone.

Get dressed as soon as you get up— unless you're ill—and wear perfume, lipstick, jewelry and even stockings in winter.

Motherhood, like any other job, should be respected by everyone, and most of all, by you.

Part of this respect is expressed in the speed with which you get a good figure again. There are those of us who have babies and then spend the rest of our lives waiting hopelessly for the Rubens woman to come back in style. Or we wait for the weight to disappear—as if wishing could make it so—but that's not likely either.

It's true that you'll probably drop ten to thirteen pounds when the baby is born, three-and-a-half more pounds in the next twelve days and still more in the next four weeks, but you'll still have to wrestle with the last five to ten pounds. And no one can do it for you. This is annoying, but a small price to pay for a baby.

In Greece, new mothers have traditionally bound their hips tightly and immediately with a length of linen, six feet long by a foot wide, to push the organs back into place, but it takes more than that to put a figure back in shape. Your body won't return to normal unless you exercise, and neither, in fact, will your vagina, for which we give exercises too. You'll like these more.

### ABDOMINAL EXERCISES

You might be able to bring your weight to normal within six weeks, but your muscles won't be the same as they were before unless you do postnatal exercises. Start them after the bright red bleeding stops— and quit for a few days if it should start again.

Begin each exercise by lying flat on your back on the floor, but preferably on a rug, adding new exercises on the specified days.

On the first day of this regimen, with your hands at your sides, take five deep, slow breaths, right from the abdomen. That's all.

On the second day, spread your arms horizontal to your body, with elbows straight. Raise them, bringing them directly over your chest until the hands touch, doing this five times. And that's all to that too, but even this gentle exercise is tiring when you have just had a baby.

On the third and fourth days, raise your head slowly until your chin touches your chest, expelling your breath as you lift your head and leaving the space of an orange between your chin and your chest, so you won't get a bulging tummy muscle. Do this ten times.

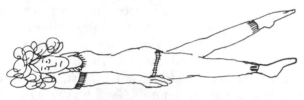

On the fifth day, raise one leg as high as possible, toes pointed, keeping the knee straight and your hands at your sides. Keep the other leg flat on the floor. Alternate legs, raising each one five times, a little higher on the sixth and seventh days.

On the eighth day, raise your right knee to your belly, so your foot is pulled back to touch your bottom. Straighten the leg and lower it, alternating each leg five times.

On the tenth day, spread your legs slightly and pull your feet toward you enough so that your knees almost bend at a right angle. Lift your bottom so your weight rests only on your shoulders and your feet. Contract your anus at the same time.

On the twelfth day, cross your arms on your chest and raise your head and shoulders slightly five times. When you're stronger, clasp your hands behind your head, cross your ankles (or tuck them under a chair to hold your feet down) and

raise yourself slowly until you're sitting, keeping your knees straight while still pressing your back to the floor. By then you're exercising ten to fifteen minutes a day, and will be fit for a more strenuous workout when the baby is about six weeks old.

### KNEE-CHEST EXERCISE

Your doctor probably will recommend this exercise, which helps the organs fall back into place, but it generally is not started until several weeks after delivery.

Do it twice a day after urinating. Begin with two minutes each time and gradually increase to five.

Lying on the floor, face down, raise your bottom up in the air with your head resting on your crossed arms and the rest of your weight on your knees. They should be about eighteen inches apart, the thighs should be perpendicular to the floor and the back should be straight.

### VAGINAL EXERCISE

Birthing naturally enlarges the vagina, even with stitches to tidy it again. Tighten it by repeatedly firming the muscles between your thighs, as if you were restraining your bladder—a little exercise called the Kegel. At first these muscles will seem so flabby you can't believe you're constricting at all, but if you do this every day for about three minutes you can rebuild them easily. It's a pleasant pastime and can be done anywhere, except maybe standing on your head, and if done often enough it will add an extra dimension to love-making. The dedicated do up to one hundred Kegels a day.

# THE CHILD

◇　　　　　　　　　　　　　　　◇

A child goes through many stages and the most dramatic occur between birth and first grade. Each brings pleasure, each brings pain and every one of them will make you react. If you know what to expect, we think your reactions will be wiser and the joy of these years will be multiplied, for both of you.

## INFANCY

During infancy your baby learns at a faster rate than he ever will again in his life. In the first four weeks he will learn to breathe regularly, lift his head and return a smile and sometimes a laugh.

He is born knowing a great deal more, however. He can recognize your smell in the first ten minutes (just as you can soon tell his smell from all other babies), and he knows your face within the first day and can tell your voice too, and where it's coming from. Tests show that a newborn's senses are so acute he gets upset if his mother's voice seems to come from another woman's mouth.

A baby sees best when he's eight to ten inches away from you—just about the distance from your face to your breast when he nurses—and he can recognize colors. He likes contrasts, circles and stripes and complicated patterns better than plain colors and simple patterns. Best of all, he likes a friendly face, as we found when little Marguerite would be soothed by the picture of her dad taped to the inside of her bassinet, or even the "smiley" picture her mom would draw for her.

The sense of touch is just as strong, particularly on a baby's lips and hands—nature's way to encourage him to nurse—but his whole body responds to your touch, for the skin is his largest organ. After months of being bathed, jostled and bounced around, your baby wants to cuddle, to mold himself to you just as he did in the womb, and to be petted and massaged, rocked and walked.

Even his sense of taste—so often ignored—is exquisite and your newborn can discriminate between salty, acidic, sweet and bitter. A baby may not know what they are, but he knows what he likes.

These abilities are stronger at some times than at others, but they shouldn't be pushed any more than they should be ignored. Just be attuned to your newborn. You'll automatically respond to the things he likes best.

He needs to hear your voice in everything you do—singing, humming, talking. He should be exposed to as much variety of sights, sounds and smells as possible, which will make him happier and brighter too. A baby who is treated to different environments will meet more germs, but gradual exposure will help him tolerate them better. The more he's kept in a sterile situation, whether restricted in activities, noise or people, the less stimulated he'll be.

Your child needs mobiles or stabiles in every area where he is stationary for a long time, such as a crib or an infant seat. They

can be quite inexpensive or homemade, so you can change the pictures every few days if you have the time. A baby thrives on bright colors, geometric shapes in black and white, patterns, glittering foil, tassels. Leave the pallid colors and static designs for the pale in spirit. A picture on the television set is no substitute for growing plants, a music box, bells, a fish tank and mirrors.

A walk is excellent too. A leaf shaking in the breeze or a moving skyline will enliven your baby's mind the way a Picasso feeds your soul.

A playpen is best now, not as a cage, as it is sometimes used later—and shouldn't be—but as a cozy place where he can watch the world go by and with greater protection from drafts than he would get lying on a blanket on the floor.

Most of an infant's waking hours should not, of course, be spent in a play-pen, a bassinet or even an infant swing. He won't last for more than a half-hour in any

## THE NEWBORN

You and your baby will settle down in about six weeks, but his first two weeks, when he's a newborn, will worry you most, if only because you watch him so much. A newborn is likely to have a dozen unexpected little conditions, and none of them means a thing.

You may be anxious about his lumpy head—the aftermath of a vaginal delivery—but don't worry. It will soon get round and smooth again, whether you massage it or not, but since he'll like you to do it, that's reason enough.

The genitals look strange too, because they're large for his small body, but they may be even larger for a few weeks. The high hormones you had when you delivered can make them swell and the baby's breasts may get puffy too, whether you have a boy or a girl.

You may be concerned if his eyes are swollen or red for a few days, which happens to many newborns, or because he can't always keep both eyes on the same object for months, which is natural too. Or you may think something is wrong because he doesn't make tears when he cries, even though his head and neck can get quite sweaty. You'll get tears enough in four to six weeks.

Your baby's skin may also peel from his palms and the soles of his feet, which is very common and goes away after the first few days, while a baby—especially a preemie—may be born with a light fuzz on his back which rubs itself away in a week or two.

Another baby may have a rash on his body because his sweat glands are plugged, but you can get rid of it by washing his skin with mild soap and rinsing him well.

Cradle cap—a scaliness that covers a baby's scalp and maybe his eyebrows—is another nonproblem, but it makes many mothers fret. Rub his head and brows lightly with baby oil if it bothers you, then brush his hair gently and shampoo his head every day for about a week.

If your child is breast-fed, you also may be concerned about his little white tongue and the blister he may get after he nurses, but they are of no concern either. If you're still worried about these or any conditions, call your doctor. She'll decide what you should do, if anything.

You do want to pay attention to your newborn's tender reactions to the weather, however. Since a baby thinks eighty-five degrees is just the right temperature until he's about twelve pounds, you have to keep him much warmer than you might think. Dress your infant in an undershirt, diapers, a stretchy jumpsuit and a receiving blanket, and keep him in heavier clothes at night if your heat goes below sixty-eight degrees. You don't want to take him out in chilly weather either, until he's three to four weeks' old and has been gaining weight at a steady clip. Even then, lay a blanket or a sheepskin under him—to block the drafts—and put a hat on his head. Babies lose a great deal of heat without it.

one position if he is awake and neither would you.

## THREE MONTHS

Everyone, even a small baby, tries to express himself, and he can if you don't anticipate his wants. Let him give the first yell before you feed him and let him try to turn over by himself. He likes to scoot around his crib, grunting and puffing, to reach a rattle, for he learns by doing. Your help should be given at the end of that increasingly wide period between his first attempt at achievement and his first scream of frustration.

If necessity is the mother of invention, frustration is the grandmother. Every child needs a little of this frustration, but the smaller the child, the smaller the dose. This is not only to establish his place in the pecking order, which it does, but to force him to figure out other ways to accomplish a job. In this way you show respect for his ability. You will manifest this respect in a thousand ways and the only way you can do better is to find a thousand more.

He coos by four months and will talk early if you encourage him. Compared with other animals, however, a baby is a very slow learner, for he has choice as well as instinct, and many more jobs to learn. His concentration is intense and he may forget his last skill temporarily while he learns the next one.

## SIX MONTHS

When your baby is six months old, you may be tempted to get pregnant again. Obviously, you are a Perfect Mother. Your baby is a babbling delight. Your household practically runs itself, even if you have gone back to work. Regretfully, we must tell you that your schedule is as light and your child as undemanding as either will be until he leaves for college.

This is an idyllic stage now. All he needs for happiness is good health and a revolving set of small activities to sparkle the day. If you supplement this with about five minutes of playtime out of every half-hour he is awake—unless he's being fed or bathed—he will love you. And if you don't do this, he will love you just as much, but he may not be as jolly or as quick. Besides, if you play with your child you will have a fine time yourself.

Soon your baby will start to sleep less and move about more. When he can crawl, you will give him enough freedom to feel important and enough protection to keep him safe. He will pull himself to his feet, but he needs your help to sit down and then learn to push a chair around a room, like an old lady with a walker.

## ONE

The changes in a child's behavior come not around the first birthday but when he learns to walk. Your whole attitude must adjust to this new skill. Although your baby is harder to handle now—awake more, demanding more—he will compensate for it by becoming an independent person, more striking every day. Each new angle of his personality will tighten the bindings of love. When you share his achievements with your husband you draw your family closer together and even the weariest day ends positively.

## FIFTEEN MONTHS

Now your child is "into everything," but you can say it with pride, for he is happy and tractable (a glowing reflection on you).

You even may be self-confident enough to give wise, park-bench advice to the mothers of those rowdy mid-Twos, just alas as we did, for you have reached the age of the Expert Mom. Your baby is seldom dirty, his nose never runs green, and if he talks, he actually says "yes" as often as "no." More to the point, he sleeps two hours each afternoon.

You are, we're sorry to say, as unfeeling as the svelte young bride who tells her middle-aged neighbor how easy it is to diet. You just haven't gotten there yet.

## MID-ONE

Now you will keep more of your opinions to yourself and you certainly should. Not only is your child no genius, he can't even remember simple obedience. In another year, new mothers will be telling you where he went wrong. Your only comfort will be the rightness of these "wrongs."

When your child becomes rambunctious, congratulations. This is your compliment for helping him grow into a curious, climbing, inventive child, with a new command of his own body and mind. Don't take it away now.

A child makes his major moves toward independence between mid-One and Three. He must reach out of his limited environment of cleanliness and acceptable behavior. Now he will sink to what may seem a disastrous ebb, with stitches, bruises, and perhaps a minor concussion in the next eighteen months, before turning into an angelic Three.

Eighteen months is a pivotal time, when many mothers simply give up, for now the novelty of child care wears thin. Earaches and high fevers complicate life even more, and every day you are more tired than the day before. Your child follows you everywhere and when he doesn't you know he's getting into trouble. Your temper frays as your fatigue increases, just trying to keep up with your toddling child. It's your job to draw his physical boundaries very carefully, childproofing every part of your house.

It may seem easier to keep him dependent on you through your restrictions and your coddling, but this curbs both self-confidence and curiosity. It is curiosity that makes a mid-One seem so defiant,

until by the end of the day, you can only pity yourself and ask, "If I'm such a good mother, how come Susie's such a brat?"

Your child's behavior makes more sense when you realize that he can understand a process only if he undoes it first and repeats it often.

When he does flood the floor—by flushing the john and the diaper too—you will look angry or sad and he will be less likely to do it again (even though he knows you are wrong), because he loves you. He doesn't want to make you unhappy. A child who knows the warmth of love, its frequent hugs and kisses and the sweet silence of affection, will return love with full generosity. Everything he does is geared to love and acceptance, first by himself and then by his parents. He'll be surprised to find that the capers that amused you as a One are considered naughty now and will be even worse later. He must understand that you sometimes dislike his actions, but you never dislike him. You just learn to say over and over to yourself, "What will it matter in a hundred years?"

Now your pattern of living will change almost every day, generally about a day too late. All of your intentions—of toilet training and table training and even (although you didn't tell anyone) of teaching him to read—will be postponed one to five years. Although there will be difficulties in the next eighteen months, they are more than offset by the joy of watching your child's individuality unfold. The overwhelming, awed love you felt when your child was born is nothing compared with the love you feel now. Your involvement with this child makes him more precious every day.

The extent of your husband's inclusion or exclusion in the routine of family living is just as important to the father as the child. It will decide whether he will be a valid husband and father or merely a weekend warrior. It is absolutely essential to keep sharing the child care as well as the good experiences (and a few of the bad) with your husband every day. These exchanges are the cement of marriage.

Probably the smoothest way for three or more people to live together is to merge some interests, and this is done most naturally through work. By now your child has eaten some of your burned dinners and seen you break a few dishes. He knows you need help too. He just isn't sure you know it.

When you or your husband do a job, your child should be asked, when possible, to help. Let him hold the wood to be sawed and load the washer or scrub the windowsills with you. He will enjoy most those chores that you prefer, since pleasure is contagious.

For play, spend about ten minutes an hour diverting him with some new activity. These interludes should be given at your convenience and when you're both content. If you wait until your child is cross before you play with him, you will have to play twice as long to make him happy again.

Probably no more than half of the playtimes are spent with toys, for there are so many and often better things to use. He enjoys planting seeds, wearing odd hats, having a tea party with you and feeding the goldfish—often too much.

### TWENTY-ONE MONTHS

If your child didn't hear the starting gun of rebellion at mid-One he certainly will now. While this highly necessary period of achievement will give him the security no blanket ever can, it's quite likely to put a temporary crimp in your own self-confidence.

You probably are experiencing the first throes of desperation since your child had colic:

*Motherhood is real.*
*It is forever.*
*It is not a game.*
*You cannot divorce your child.*
*There is no way out.*

These reactions are normal. They call for balm, never shame. There isn't a mother alive who hasn't felt this despair, this resentment and guilt, and it is particularly strong with the first one or two children, because their behavior seems so inexplicable to you. You have put your child's environment in order, rearranged his schedule, bought him new toys and still he gets bolder every day.

Now it's time to take care of you. You will need more time alone and whatever special treats you can afford so you won't feel so sorry for yourself. This need cannot be overestimated, and it will last for another eighteen months.

### TWO

We know a doctor who said, in a back-of-the-hand consolation to a weeping mother, "Well, if there's anything worse than Terrible Two, it's Terrible Two-and-a-Half."

Actually, we think Two is a dandy age, all year long, but it's almost as exhausting as it is exciting. This is the age to consider before you plan another child. You may be healthy enough for another pregnancy and efficient enough to handle an infant on demand, but whether you have the stamina to cope with another Two again is the question.

He is as much fun as a present: you never know what to expect but usually you like what you get. No matter how bad he is (and he will be quite bad), he is a delight. The moods of a Two swing like a pendulum. Your child will be funny, kind, destructive, ebullient, flirty, furious, curious, but always imperious, for a Two knows what he wants, at least until he gets it.

At this age, he won't give you much chance to do anything but keep track of him. Accept it. This is his year.

You need your husband's strength to keep in perspective the rebellion of your Two and you also need your husband's companionship to share the silly things he says. The joy that is shared is twice as great, but there is only one other person in the world who will be as amused and pleased by your child as you are, and that is his father.

These may be depressing words if you're a single mother, but it doesn't lessen your need to share the latest news about your child with another appreciative grown-up. Find one other special person with whom you can share these stories—your sister, your desk mate at work or another parkbench mother—someone who will listen and beam when she should. There's always a lot to report now.

You will watch your child take apart block towers, and when you're not watching him, he takes apart the sewing machine and the radio and anything else he can find. He bites the dog and bathes the cat; smashes ants and chases pigeons. He mixes salt with sugar, milk with juice and then shrieks if his peas touch the meat on his plate. He climbs out of his crib and, given half a chance, will climb right up to the roof, and every time he knows he shouldn't. Even so, he doesn't want to make a damn fool of himself, or of you.

His curiosity runs in every direction. By now every little girl knows that her tush is more fun than her toes and little boys are practically born with an erection. However, we're a long way from Tahiti and a Two already knows enough to masturbate under the covers, no matter how enlightened the parents and that's fine. Even a Two has a life of his own.

His personality develops rapidly and his control over his body and his speech makes his growth rate seem phenomenal, but don't expect him to work on more than one skill at a time, or to do equally well in talking and in doing. He may only be Two, but he's smart enough to know that he should build on his strengths.

He will get angry when he works, often furiously so, and sometimes when he plays his exhilaration almost smothers him. These are times when he is out of control—his control and yours. This is a trademark of Two.

Rachel summed it up, in one glorious tantrum, when she shrieked "I am an *Angry Woman!*" While a Two's inabilities infuriate him, his accomplishments make him so proud his vanity is huge and he abuses his power as blatantly as a young teenager. The treatment is the same. You are sensitive and understanding, but you don't take him as seriously as he takes himself or as seriously as you took him last year or as you will take him again next year. If you do, each problem of the moment will become more important than either of you want it to be, for with your cooperation, he will dramatize every trifle to its ultimate crisis.

Instead, use strong safety precautions and watch carefully to prevent trouble, but unless it's major, you should look the other way when it comes. This is the time to use a low voice, a kiss and even more praise for his goodness. If you never learned tolerance, you will now.

To control a Two, remember he has feelings. To control yourself, remember these feelings in the morning and maybe ten more times a day. Although you will get angry, consider the damage before you scream. Some things may not merit as much fuss as you think at first. When you overreact you will be embarrassed afterward, even though only one other person will know how silly you were. Unfortunately, that other person will be your child.

We think you will find child care easier

if you analyze your anger. Your bad temper today really may be caused by fatigue or low blood sugar or maybe the milkman reminds you of your creepy cousin or maybe you haven't made love in four days.

If you help your Two begin to be self-sufficient, you will give him the present of a lifetime: independence. He needs to achieve this attitude now, and if he does he will look like a winner to everyone, particularly to the person most important to him—himself. He can learn to dress himself if his clothes are simple, if you're not too particular and, like anything else, if he gets the practice.

A child also needs to make some simple choices for himself as a part of his independence. If he has no choices he will be rebellious, but if he has too many he will be indecisive. It is difficult to begin to hold a Four accountable for his actions if he has had little chance to exercise his will at Two. Offer an either/or choice at this age—between apple juice and orange, for instance—whenever his decision is only of consequence to himself.

With the help of his parents, a Two talks in sentences, but speech is just one way to communicate. Give a child clay and he will sculpt as loud as he can shout. He needs to try every avenue of self-expression you can think of—in art, in the kitchen, in simple crafts, in the workshop, in the garden. He can do a little bit of everything but never very well. He needs more and more books and tapes to encourage quiet times and will find a morning spent with friends in a play group is better than in a department store with you.

With your good example a Two learns to give, not just through making presents but by helping others. He is able now to hold an electric hand mixer for you, to vacuum and to hang his pajamas on a low peg. He even can strip shellac with you when you refinish, as long as you watch him carefully. Compliment him often and give him no job that takes longer than his ten-minute attention span or he will associate boredom with work. Don't expect

perfection and, in fact, feel lucky if you don't have to do the work again. When you must, do it when he's not looking, so he won't feel ridiculed. This undercuts his self-confidence badly.

Although the pediatrician may say mid-Two is the most difficult age, all the children we know reached it at about twenty-six months. For all the solutions and techniques you use, living with a Two is like living with dynamite. Just when you think everything will blow apart like a plot from an old Hardy Boys story, the fuse begins to sputter.

He gets saucier every day until, by twenty-six months, you are drained. Nothing surprises you anymore. You may even be too numb to notice that his self-control, and therefore yours, increases steadily every day between twenty-six and thirty months, with just enough backsliding to keep you in your place. It's amazing you love him as much as you do.

As our favorite Irishman used to tell us, "If you hang long enough, they say you get used to hanging."

### MID-TWO

When your child settles into mid-Two, he is less mischievous but so rigid you're sure that if you fall down the steps at noon on Wednesday he would have you repeat it every noon, or at least every Wednesday.

Your demanding mid-Two needs to be reminded that parents run the show. Do this by changing the routine a little each day—a different plate for breakfast, a different story at bedtime—so he won't get so set in his ways.

He enjoys order in others and regularly returns the cat to his bed, but seldom his toys to their shelf. Nevertheless, a child needs a place for everything and the responsibility of putting away a few of his own treasures. He develops a sense of order through his own efforts, not yours.

This need for order is a paradox, for a Two dismantles everything he touches. Don't think of it as destructive, but "unbuilding." It is the taking apart, over and over, that teaches construction.

For your own peace, expect much less of your child, laugh a lot and insist that he nap or at least rest an hour or two a day. It doesn't matter whether he needs it or not. You need it. If you keep the custom your Three will nap again, if only to oblige.

### THREE

A Three is almost too good. Even when he's bad he has the wit to understand reason, for now he begins to see what fairness is all about. He can share better and take turns, for he revels in people, whether they are the realistic friends from storybooks, or from the games he invents or from the neighborhood. He likes to visit and enjoys overnighting with a friend, partly to pack a suitcase, and even may want to visit relatives for a few days.

He cooks, gardens, paints, makes his bed and spends a lot of time feeling proud. If he isn't in day care, he yearns to start school now and we think he should, although he catches many more colds and you find the "hurry, hurry" syndrome inevitable. You also find that it isn't possible to rush a Three.

He has much energy and uses it fairly well, which makes him more settled, especially if he gets daily exercise outdoors, like tricycling and walking, and some work on indoor play equipment. Early talkers are curious about words and letters and "Sesame Street" may have taught him to recognize at least some of them, but the more active child will talk less and may need your help to speak in complicated sentences. Your child also may need help with puzzles, for the longer he takes to coordinate the small muscles, the more restless he'll be. This makes concentration difficult.

At Three, there still will be a few accidents with the pot, unless he's reminded to use it, and a few tantrums too. He will give up his bottle in public, suck his thumb when tired and want to be cuddled any time.

Although you or your husband may have demanding jobs and may often be away from home, you should each arrange for time alone with the child at least once a week. Sons and daughters must develop deep individual relationships with their parents now. There are some lessons that are almost too hard to learn twenty years later, and this is one of them.

### MID-THREE

A child usually changes now, as he does about every six months. Behavior improves about the middle of an even year, but gets worse, as now, in the middle of an odd one. At least the turf is familiar.

This is the age for exploring new worlds. Our Mali did it by running away from home (around the corner to the neighbor lady), but Ramon did it by announcing that he wished to lunch by himself. As we watched, he marched to the corner stop sign, sat down, ate his sandwich and marched home again. That's how babies grow up.

A mid-Three not only begins to flex his independence, he also wonders about your omnipotence, testing it more each day. He doesn't need to be near you when he plays and can restrict certain toys to certain areas. For the first time, your house isn't one big playroom anymore.

Schedules may need changes with a later bedtime so a child can see his parents for more than a few stories and some good-night kisses. Plan a long rest for your child so he won't fall apart every evening when you walk in.

## FOUR

A Four is to childhood what a circus is to show business—a lot of laughs, but enough uncomfortable moments to keep you off-balance. A Four tries everything, as he should, but his initiative is often your despair. Alone in a room he will nail your rickety antique chair together and if you still haven't missed him he will paint it for you too.

A Four is suddenly much bigger and more energetic, but inevitably clumsy. We found that classes in modern dance or tumbling are a dandy way to help a child control his body, and have even seen them give him enough basic coordination to bypass the awkwardness in puberty.

You will find your Four needs your respect even more now, for he feels on top of the world one time and surrounded by giants the next. We remember our generally amiable Nell, who put every child's anger into words when she stamped her foot and cried, "Even though I'm only three feet tall, I still have my rights!"

Every measure of respect you give a child, from knocking on his door before you enter to keeping the secret he shares, will be returned tenfold as he grows up.

Self-dramatization is another way for your Four to figure out his place in the world. He regrets that babyhood is over, but he's too interested in the rest of the world to dwell on it much. Some grown-ups, other than his parents, assume great importance and he has long talks with friends about God, whether you go to services or not.

You will want to write down everything he says now for a Four is so free, poetry springs spontaneously from his lips.

Your child will be very serious one moment, ridiculously silly the next. Boys and girls kiss each other, show bottoms

and use scatological language, all of which they think is hilarious. To some children, dirty words become so commonplace that adults only can blink in disbelief, as we did when our Meg, in a sudden hush at a family reunion, said, "Pardon me, please. I farted." Or another day, when she spilled her milk at dinner and said, "Oh, shit!"

When chided, she cunningly lied (for Fours do lie).

"I was speaking Spanish," she said, and added that she had learned it from a neighbor of great Latin propriety.

"She said to me, 'Meg, don't put your foot in the shit.' "

May you follow that old Spanish proverb—especially if you have a Four.

## FIVE

A Five is a giver, passing peanuts to company and making presents as if every day were Christmas. Like many of us, he is at his best in the morning and his teacher may appreciate him more than you do. He is unself-conscious: singing, performing, playing roles and chatting with all the garrulity of a Fifteen. At this age, he is in harmony with himself.

Your Five, as nice as he is, does wish everyone else were as fine as himself. This sanctimony often leads him into situations he can't handle. He becomes quick to tease now, but whines just as quickly if teased in return. He also is likely to be cross or even have tantrums again, for your Five is so sociable and so adult you may forget he is still a young child. He needs twelve hours of sleep at night, an hour of afternoon quiet and much more fruit and fresh vegetables and milk than potato chips, cookies and sodas.

He wants to read his own books now, to make sense out of the numbers on the yardstick and to find the answers to concrete and even abstract phenomena, like rain and gravity.

By Five, your child's personality and talents become sharper every day. Already you can see the general field he probably will enter as an adult (although you won't try to guide him at all). The child who likes to collect and sort rocks and seashells now is apt to be scientifically curious all his life and the child who wants to paint every day will keep a strong interest in art. His weaknesses are balanced by his strengths. He won't excel in everything, but it won't bother him for another year.

## SIX

The behavior of your Six runs the gamut, but basically he is a comformist, needing to do whatever other Sixes can do, but not too differently. Even his pictures are increasingly rigid.

He can dress himself completely, but can't tie his shoes, and will wash his hair every week, sort of, but seldom comb it. He still won't wash his face or pick up most of his toys unless told and often helped.

Now he makes his own breakfast when necessary, cares well for special toys, can play soccer, but not baseball, and carries a lunch box on any possible occasion. He needs many adventures and much hard exercise, but he shouldn't start any new lessons, like music or dancing. First grade

is quite enough, even for the most self-confident Six.

When he does begin school, he will adore his teacher, whether he loves reading, writing and arithmetic or not. A Six cares what his classmates think of him, but is quick to sock someone who disagrees with him—and quick to cry if he's punched back. Now your child expects more of himself but so does everyone else. Once he turns Six, the teachers, the neighbors and even the other Sixes will treat him with more justice than mercy, for accountability begins in earnest now. This is one of the harshest realities a child must face, but each bit of respect and kindness, of toughness and competence you've given your child will form the backbone he needs to stand tall for the next few years. This is the time, like the young teenage years, when it will be hard for your child to feel he's master of his own fate. With your continuing encouragement to be independent, however, the transition will be easier.

Every mother has real goals for her child, as well as fantastic ones.

"My daughter will be President one day *or* find a cure for cancer." (You know she'll actually do both.) It is the real qualities—of kindness and integrity, curiosity and imagination—that count, for you are no longer rearing just a lovable child but shaping a likable adult. Now you begin to accept your child for what he is and realize that followship is just as important as leadership.

By Six, he has been given enough trust by you to go through life expecting candy and just enough doubt to keep him from taking it from strangers.

## ADOPTION

Adoption may be the ultimate sign of love—by the birthmother, who gives her child away so he can have a better life; by the adoptive parents, who take him into their hearts; and by the baby, who gives love back, measure for measure.

Adopting a child is never a decision to take lightly, and never without talking to others who have been through the experience. An adoption workshop or support group can help you deal with your questions and concerns, and what may be your terrible sense of inadequacy. As you'll discover, the ability to have a child has nothing to do with the ability to be a good parent.

The group will also give you the latest information on agency placements and on private and overseas adoptions, as well as the costs, which vary greatly and aren't always related to the results.

The counselor and the other parents can help you make some tough choices too. You'll have to decide whether to adopt a baby or an older child, and if you can handle the extra pressures that come with one who is handicapped or from another race. You might even decide to take a foster child or perhaps to take a series of foster children on a short-term basis. Some of the most demanding options can also be the most rewarding.

You'll find out about the home study— that scary visit that must be done by a social worker before you can adopt or foster any child, from anywhere—and how you can—and should—get as much information about the child as possible if you do adopt. You—or your child—may need to know his medical history or his family background one day, and it is much easier to get this information when the placement is made than to look for it years later.

You'll also learn about the extra pleasures and problems if you adopt a child from another country or another culture. There are ways to weave this heritage into your family traditions and—when the racial difference is obvious—to deal with the awkward questions of strangers, or the hurtful comments from relatives.

Your child may not look like anyone in your family, but he will think and act as they do, because you and your husband will rear him in much the way that you were reared and the way your parents and their parents were reared. The actions and reactions of each generation have been passed down and your ways will be a distillation of their ways. This will make your child a part of them as well as of you.

You'll also learn how to handle the whole adoption issue as your child grows up. His adoption is central to his past, and there should never be a time that he didn't know about it. It's a matter of working it into your conversation naturally—a little here, a little there—the way you talk about nutrition or sex. Many small talks teach a child best.

Your child will want to hear the whole delightful scenario of his adoption once or twice a year, or maybe every night for a while, if he's going through an insecure patch. Tell him about that magic moment when you picked him up for the first time and how you brought him home. Show him the pictures of his welcome home party and tell him who came to see him. Let him know that it was the best thing that ever happened to you; that he was a chosen child; and that you will never, ever give him up. Every child is instinctively afraid of being abandoned by his parents, but the adopted child has been rejected once and is even more fearful about it as he gets older. The more he's reassured now, the better he can handle it later.

Generally, a child under Seven is interested in the details of his adoption, but not for very long. As far as he's concerned, you're his mom; his dad is his dad; and what's the big deal anyway? Abstractions are confusing when you can think only in concrete terms.

Time enough, in the years ahead, to

tell your child why his birthmother couldn't take care of him. A lifelong openness about his adoption—without either the glamorous or the sordid details—is healthy and should keep him from thinking he was a prince in disguise—a favorite fantasy for any child—or that he was so wretched he had to be given away.

You'll also want your child to know that you will help him find his birthmother when he's grown—and if she wants to be found. Many adopted children need this information, if not to put their pain to rest, then to figure out this missing piece of their past. It makes them feel whole. This search will put your love to its ultimate test, but it won't destroy your bond, and in fact, it will strengthen it. Honesty fortifies a relationship better than anything else.

By talking easily about the adoption, a child feels free to bring up the subject when it troubles him and to realize that adoption is just another way of being born. One set of parents bears the baby; the other bears with the child. The first takes nine months; the second takes a lifetime.

## TWINS OR MORE

Multiples are magic. They multiply the fun and the joy they bring, and they also multiply the help and the money you'll need. You'll never have enough of either, of course, but you and your husband can bridge most of the gap with shortcuts and clever tricks, heartfelt prayers and laughter. Twins will teach you more about thrift than a New England banker, and more about priorities and efficiency as well. Studies show that mothers of twins are more flexible than most mothers and solve problems better too.

You can jolly one baby in your arms while you rock the other in a cradle, but family dinners often turn into quick-start suppers and sometimes sandwiches on the run.

The transition from pregnancy to motherhood can be rocky if the multiples

are a surprise or premature, or if they caused a sudden Cesarean—or if you try to get along without any help, particularly if you have older children. That's silly, of course. You need someone to help you with the twins for the first two weeks, and then someone part-time for a few weeks more to clean house, put the evening meal together or care for the twins while you nap or bathe. Most of all, you need someone to play grandma and to give you encouragement, especially for breastfeeding, which can seem pretty overwhelming with twins.

If you have triplets or more, you need more help of course, on a regular and preferably a volunteer basis. A relative or friend might organize it for you for the first few months—the greatest present you could get.

While you probably can't nurse triplets—at least not every feeding—many mothers find that it's feasible with twins and it's certainly worth trying. You may even be able to feed both of your babies at once, just as you can with a bottle, but the sleepy one may not want to eat when the other one is hungry. Twins don't always follow the same schedule if they are fraternal or if their weight is quite different.

Your husband can help you with this—as he'll help with so much else—by giving each twin a supplemental bottle every few days for the first six weeks, using either a formula or the breast milk you've expressed. After two to three months, your milk supply will be well established and you can gradually decrease the number of breastfeedings—even down to one to two times a day—without losing your milk supply—and then your husband can take over more feedings. It's a choice many working mothers make and it's fine for the babies, but do have your husband hold them close, so they can see his face and have that skin-to-skin contact babies need so much.

All of this will make you both so tired for about a year that you forgo many of the pleasures of life. Even sex takes too much energy, most of the time, but you can still cuddle together and count your blessings. Twins are hard work but they also seem to pull a family together, even when there are older children, because everyone learns to count on each other. No father of twins ever said he felt left out, and no older child did either.

The diapers, the feeds and the wash seem almost continuous, especially for the first three to four months, which makes it hard to do something spontaneously with the twins, or to do anything for yourself unless you plan it. And so you should. Daily trips to the park or walks with another mother every day are almost essential, even if it's cold. There's nothing like the wonder of nature to make you appreciate your own small wonders.

While the mother of a singleton will be good company, you'll get your best ideas from parents who are just a few steps ahead of you. You'll find them in your local chapter of Mothers of Twins, which is a great source of firsthand advice and secondhand twin strollers, car seats and high chairs, as well as the latest information.

You'll learn that twins don't match the idealized picture of two little people who look alike, act alike, dress alike, think alike. Instead they act like siblings who are less than two years apart, with a friendship that will change and grow, just as all friendships change and grow. Identical twins tend to be closer than fraternal—who are, after all, simply siblings who have

the same birthdate—while identical twin girls are usually closer than identical twin boys and boy-girl twins are the least close of all. All girl twins—especially fraternals—tend to be more outgoing and gregarious than boys, but all twins seem to have their share of friends.

In most activities they follow the same behavior patterns as single children. They may look like they're playing together and they may share with each other a little earlier because they have so many chances to do it, but they're really playing side by side until they're Two or Three, just as other children do. They do tend to be more empathic with each other, however, to negotiate and collaborate well, to make friends easily and to be more self-confident, as if they can count on two people instead of one.

You'll also learn that the intelligence of twins varies, as it does for all children. Twin boys, however, may have more language delays and some reading problems

## TWINS

Twins turn up in about one birth out of a hundred and a third of these pairs are identical. Other multiples are much rarer, with triplets born once in 10,000; quads once in a million, and quints just once in 20–40 million, and almost all of these groups are a mix of fraternal and identical babies.

Nobody knows just why an egg splits into an identical pair of boys or girls, but researchers do know that fraternal twins, which come from two separate eggs, are increasingly common, and they follow certain patterns. Your chances are higher if you've used a particular type of fertility drug or have just quit taking the Pill, and if you're black; have had up to four babies; are between thirty-five and thirty-nine—since older women often release more than one egg in a month; or if you have fraternal twins on your side of the family. When it comes to twinning, your husband's genes don't count.

until the early teens, and all twins may take a little longer to talk than other children. They then tend to speak in a kind of shorthand with shorter words and sentences but will get on track with their buddies when they're about Five. They won't develop a secret language, however, unless they have few playmates, or parents who don't chat with them much. It will help if you talk to your twins often—individually and together—putting your faces close to theirs and enunciating clearly.

These babies need and enjoy one another, but they need and enjoy you and their dad much more. Try to give each of them a little time alone with each of you every day. Feed them separately when you can, once or twice a week, and walk one of the children, while your husband stays home with the other, and then switch twins and do it again.

The children also need you to notice their differences and their strengths and to get others to notice them too. Even a low mirror hung on the wall will invite identi-cal twins to look for—and find—their own distinct characteristics. Give them different toys and clothes, encourage different interests and different friends. The better your twins define themselves, the more self-confident they'll be.

You need to encourage their independence by Two, by helping them make their own individual choices, even if you have to call one of them aside, so they don't echo each other.

When it's time for school, most parents find their twins do best if they're in pre-K and kindergarten together, but let each of the twins go alone sometimes, so they can get used to the idea if they are separated in first grade.

The push to help them keep their individuality must be renewed when they start school, for teachers often look for similarities instead of differences. Insist on talking about one child at the start of a teacher conference, and one at the end, or even arrange for two separate conferences. It's a strategy you'll follow for years, and your twins will bless you for it.

# ◇ MECHANICS ◇

Child care can get so complicated that you can spend most of your prime time on the mechanics of motherhood instead of the pleasures.

Whether you have a job or not, you need to learn the tricks of this trade too, so you can take a half-hour to bathe and dress your baby if you want—or do the job in seven minutes flat if you must.

## DIAPERING

Sixty thousand diapers later, we find that the mother who can change her baby quickly has one less job to resent. We think it should be a production only the first time.

Change even the tiniest baby at a waist-high table, so you won't get a backache. Lay the diaper over him for an infant often wets during a change and a boy is liable to catch you foursquare. Slip the diaper he'll wear under his fanny and if it's a cloth one, twist it at the crotch, in a figure eight, for double thickness and a tighter fit. If you pin the back over the front, it stays on better.

Wash the baby's bottom each time you change him, either at the table or over the bathroom sink. Use a soapy cloth to wash, a wet one to rinse and a towel to pat the skin dry. Washing the skin removes bacteria—the main cause of a rash—which is one of the baby's most common and least necessary problems. It is also cyclical, since the saltiness of the urine burns any

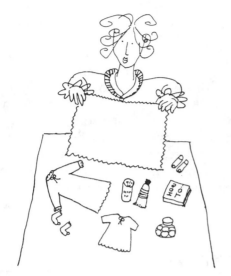

chafed skin, making the rash worse and the fussing more.

You can also prevent a rash if you smear the clean area with petroleum jelly (the cheapest, best but least attractive coating you can use), or use cornstarch, but not talcum powder, which can be bad for a baby's lungs. It's also a bad idea to use waterproof pants when your child has a rash, since they hold heat and help bacteria breed faster.

Although many mothers don't rinse dirty disposable diapers—if they have a diaper can with a tight lid—you have no choice with cloth, even if it's from a diaper service. Rinse it immediately, for no one likes to find one soaking in the toilet, and then wring it and put it with the wet ones. If you wash your own, and do it every day or two, they'll need no soaking and neither the job nor the smell will overwhelm you. For a young baby, diapers should go through the washer twice—the second time without soap—as the residue can be too caustic for his skin. Both the rays of the sun and the high heat of the dryer will kill any remaining bacteria.

To prevent most of the squirming while you change a young baby, fix a mobile above the changing table, strap him into place and give him two special toys, one for each hand, for balance. At nine months you can change him standing on a straight chair in the middle of the room. His newly

developed depth perception won't let him fall (at least not more than once), and it keeps him in place without force.

Expect to diaper your baby for nearly three years, although a Two should be encouraged to get his own diaper when he needs it and to put the wet one in the hamper for you. This is an early step in toilet training.

## BATHING

A baby is sponged only until he loses his umbilical cord—about ten days—and then he has the treat of a real bath. This is such a nice job, it's almost always a father's favorite part of child care. The bath needn't be daily, but it probably will be because it's such a pleasure to see your baby have a good time.

Wash an infant in a sink, a basin or a little inflatable tub, but never a bath table, for it's unstable and a nuisance. Cushion the bottom of the sink with a towel, the way you would wash crystal, and add several inches of water, no warmer than spit. Soap him all over, even his head, and hold him like a football, for he's slippery. Because a bath is at first a stressful situation, talk and sing to him all the while, the way you always should when you think he might become fearful. Rinse, dry and rub him with lotion, for water removes skin oils. Some babies have such dry skin they should be bathed only a few times a week.

His bath is his joy for the next few months and soon he'll sit up and splash so much you'll graduate him to the tub. Before putting him in it, make sure the spigot

isn't too hot or that it's covered with a faucet protector, because he'll be sure to touch it. A bathtub seat is good too, so he can sit up in safety, but you still can't look away for a minute.

It's easier to make the baby comfortable than you. The tub bath probably will give you a backache, since you'll be leaning over, and a few other aches, as you'll discover when you've been goosed by a plastic duck the next time you bathe. You can avoid the backache if you sit on a low stool, or if you bathe together, which is the easiest way for both of you to get clean and to play too, and you can avoid the ducks if you keep them somewhere else when you're in the tub. We put them in a bag made by sewing one end of a face towel on a hanger, doubling it and sewing the side seams together.

A One will adore his bath, because he thinks it's such a happy, sexy thing to do, and will hate his shampoo, because the soap may sting, but he needs both. The more he feeds himself, the more food he rubs everywhere, including his head.

Shampoo his hair by rubbing a soapy washcloth on his head, but when he's older he may forget his fears if he can watch in a hand mirror as you sculpt fancy hairdos out of suds. A little conditioner, mixed in with the shampoo, makes the hair much easier to manage, if you let it set for a few minutes.

Soon he may be afraid of the bath itself and you may be like an harassed mother we met, whose pediatrician told her to ignore the fear; it would pass in three weeks. Actually, it lasted much longer, she said, but by the time three weeks had passed, she couldn't remember when the baby hadn't been afraid of his bath so it wasn't a worry anymore.

For practical solutions to this fear, your child will get almost as clean if you let him play naked outdoors with the hose or with a bucket of water, or let him bathe in a small, plastic tub that sits in the bathtub. A child can also be enticed into the tub with an addition of bluing or bubble bath with mineral oil, or for that matter, of you. Always remove him before you pull the plug, for he has no concept of size and may be afraid of going down the drain. If he's still scared, take comfort. By the time you have another child, a bath won't seem so important. We think our Mali may still have some of her original belly button lint.

## DRESSING

We found dressing our first babies a complicated job, for which we went up and down stairs like yo-yos, and though we never ironed very much, the laundry seemed ominous. Babies later, we learned to carry a day's supply of clothes and diapers downstairs in one arm in the morning and a child in the other, like a football. We even found it took only four minutes to iron four little batiste dresses (a day's supply). Like us, you also may find the joy of looking at a fancy-dancy baby is worth the effort.

A baby is dressed in the same way he is diapered: strapped on the changing table in the early months or standing on a straight chair later.

It is the buying of the clothes that makes dressing either easy or hard. To simplify your life, choose simple clothes, with few buttons and easy neckholes. Since bootees are kicked away so quickly, buy pajamas with feet and dress babies by day in tights or white socks (so they'll always have mates).

A child needs no shoes until he walks, except to placate clucking grandmas in the park, but when you do get them they should be pliable and have enough space at the toe to fit the width of your thumb. Put a strip of adhesive tape across the bottom of a leather sole, to prevent a slip, and another inside the back of the heel, to stop sock eating.

Study the labels of all clothes you buy. Miracle materials and fluffy packing can mean almost anything. A snowsuit should never be made of slippery nylon, for a baby wiggles so much he can slide through your arms. The hat should be connected to the collar of the suit, to avoid drafts on the neck. To prevent the loss of mittens, pin them to the cuffs of the snowsuit or run a length of yarn through the sleeves and pin a mitten on each end.

Carry a sweater for your child in the summer, for most supermarkets are over-cooled, and protect his tender skin at the beach by dressing him in a shirt and hat and using sunscreen.

For safety, buy bright colors for any outerwear or bathing suit, which helps you find your child quickly, and for your budget, buy only in two colors—like navy and scarlet, yellow and orange or green and brown, so coordination is easy. You not only will need fewer clothes, but you'll feel organized. It also helps your child put himself together, which we talk about in La Toilette (see page 113). You can expect

**FIREPROOFING**

For safety you may want to fireproof your child's much-washed pajamas and bedding, for its original protection lasts only through about twenty launderings. The boric acid is sold at the drugstore. To make this recipe:

**Combine:**
9 oz. borax
4 oz. boric acid solution
1 gal. warm water

Soak the clean clothes in the solution until it impregnates them completely, then dry as usual.

a Two to begin to dress himself, a Four to put on his shoes, a Five to lace them and somewhere, somehow he'll learn to tie them between kindergarten and college.

## EATING

The same nutrition chart your fifth-grade teacher pointed to in Health and Safety still applies today: two to three servings of milk or cheese, four of fruit and vegetables, four of bread and cereals and two servings of meat or fish a day. A good diet not only keeps a family healthy, but it helps to keep everyone content from one meal to the next, for food affects dispositions so much. You'll fortify your child best with a varied diet of proteins and complex carbohydrates, but go easy on eggs, lard and butter, particularly if there is a record of heart disease in the family.

The need for protein remains very strong, however, even if the sources change. In fact, protein is so important that a major long-term shortage of it in the first year of life can cause retardation. Cells are made, repaired and destroyed every day and it is protein that builds and repairs them, no matter what your age.

Although all foods contain some protein, the quality is much higher in some foods than in others. Eggs, fish, dairy products, nuts and chicken have the most, but you can multiply the quality by combining the right foods, like red beans and rice or macaroni and cheese—to get a protein almost as complete as an egg. Serve beans and lentils more often than chicken and fish; chicken and fish more often than beef, lamb or veal—and when you do serve red meat, make it rare.

The best meat and poultry are raised without hormones and antibiotics and the best fruits and vegetables are organically grown, but all of this is expensive and hard to find—and this isn't a perfect world. Just do what you can.

Other preferred foods are a little more affordable. Since heat destroys so many nutrients, it's best to use cold-pressed oils and unheated honey, which may be sold with health foods in your grocery store. For more vitamins and minerals, use natural rather than processed cheeses, brown rice, iodized salt, dark flours, raw fruits, steamed and raw vegetables (the more colorful the better) and pure semolina pasta.

The fresher the fruits and vegetables you serve, the more natural sugar they contain. Older ones convert the sugar to carbohydrates, which don't satisfy the body's basic need for sugar. Neither, unfortunately, do brown and white sugars, honey, corn syrup, fructose and dextrose—all synonyms for sugar—and they're often added to processed or prepared foods, from corn-bread mix to canned peas. Nutritionists blame these sweeteners for half the ills of the world and they may be right about some of them. They don't have any food value, they kill some B vitamins and they really can cause hyperactivity and irritability in children. Add sugar of any kind sparingly and instead serve fresh fruits whenever you can. Certainly you'll let your child splurge with sweets sometimes, but a well-nourished child will crave candy less.

You also want to use as few processed foods as possible because they have extenders and flavor enhancers, which are costly and have no nutritional value, as well as dyes, additives and preservatives, which can upset and even wreck the behavior of some children.

If your child eats a fifth of his food when he snacks, then it must provide a fifth of his daily nutrition. Aside from fruit and vegetables, the best snacks are nuts and cheese, with bread or cookies enriched with soy flour or wheat germ.

All snacks should be served with milk, water or pure fruit juice perhaps diluted with water, but please, no sugared fruit drinks or sodas if your child is thirsty. Frequent glasses of water are much better for him, especially during hot weather—the start of a good lifetime habit—but use fluoridated water, not bottled water, to prevent cavities.

## INFANCY

No matter whether you breastfeed or bottlefeed, you need to feed your baby when he's hungry and burp him when he's full. It's quite a lot for both of you to learn. Your little baby has been fed continuously for nine months and now he's got a stomach that goes from full to empty in three to four hours. It takes time to get used to so many big swings every day.

While a breast-fed baby is nursed when he cries, a bottle baby is a little harder to read. If he has finished a full bottle within the last hour, he may still be hungry, but he probably has a little gas instead. First burp him, hold him, give him warm water and then hold him and burp him some more. If he's still fussing in about a half-hour, give him a bottle of formula, put up your feet and forget your other jobs.

It's the night and day rules of self-demand that need a little guidance from you. Some babies can't tell time worth a hoot.

Since you want your baby to learn that daytime is playtime, don't let him sleep for more than four hours at a stretch between 10 A.M. and 8 P.M. Wake him gently, offer to feed him, give him a bath and a massage, or just talk to him. If he wasn't hungry before, he'll be hungry now. At night you need to keep the lights low when you feed and diaper him and don't talk much or play. Whether he sleeps a lot or a little, he'll soon be more wakeful when you want him to be. When he's about twelve pounds, he'll sleep through his 2 A.M. feeding, which is much better than sleeping through his 2 P.M. feeding. You can then tell people—and yourself—that the baby is sleeping through the night, even though the night starts at 11 P.M. and ends at dawn.

However, if some night you're very tired and ready for bed and the baby hasn't had anything to eat for two to three hours, wake him up for his feeding. Sometimes it's your turn to demand.

## FOUR TO SIX MONTHS

Pediatricians usually want parents to start solids between four and six months—whenever the baby drinks more than a quart of formula a day or wants to breast-feed more than once every three hours. Begin with rice cereal, and then add bananas, pears and applesauce, either from the store or blended at home. In time you can even blend your supper into a baby dinner (see page 57), as long as it's not too strongly seasoned, and it's a mixture of foods you've already tested.

A careful pediatrician will have you serve each new juice or food, including each type of cereal, every day for five days and without any other new food, since you can't isolate a problem food if you serve several new foods at once. If your baby is allergic he may get a diaper rash or the heaves or the miseries or he may dislike it intensely, which may signify an allergy too. An allergy generally disappears if the food is stopped and then introduced again at One, but if you keep giving it to your child, the reaction will probably get worse.

### PROBLEM FOODS

Children are most sensitive to milk, grains, eggs, citrus, spinach, starches and seafood, which is why doctors have you test them so carefully and one at a time. Honey can also cause trouble, since a baby can't digest the spores it may contain, and that can cause food poisoning. Don't let your child have any honey at all in the first year.

A pre-Two never is given raisins either, or nuts, melon, corn, cherries, berries or chocolate, for they're too hard on the digestive system and some of them can choke a young child.

## NINE MONTHS

A child sucks much less now, and begins to surrender his thumb or his pacifier. Now he wants to chew instead, and likes to gum a bagel—better for him than a teething biscuit, which is sweet—or a steak bone, and is ready for a few finger foods, like small slices of banana. Everything will taste better to the child who can feed himself, but he'll make a horrendous mess. Just lay paper or plastic under his high chair and have a sponge ready to wash his face and hands when he's finished, or you'll have to wipe everything that he touches.

You don't of course, give him books or any toy when you're feeding him, because this is telling a child to play while he eats. It's time for him to learn that eating should be an efficient job, completed in about twenty minutes in a calm, pleasant atmosphere and without being coaxed to eat one more bite for Mom. When a child is cajoled to eat he discovers an unholy power. We think food is neither a plaything nor a weapon. Instead use positive discipline, congratulating him with cheers of "All gone!" When he starts to fiddle with his meal, it's time to take it away.

He enjoys a yogurt and fruit dessert now, which you can make yourself. You're lucky if he likes it, for yogurt helps the body make its own chain of B vitamins. However, it works so hard in the small intestine it can keep a baby wide-eyed, but not fretful, the first night he eats it.

Your child's plate should have suction cups on the bottom so he can't throw it on the floor too easily—or no plate at all. A high-chair tray does nicely. He can sip from a cup you hold, but he can't manage a spoon for another six months. Since he puts not only food but everything else into his mouth now you can expect frequent bouts of diarrhea.

## ONE

Now he can hold his own cup if you wrap a rubber band around it so it won't slip through his hands. The cup also should be too heavy to tip easily—one more way to help your baby feel adept. A cup with a spout is also a great help and he can drink from a juice box as soon as he can pull through a straw. Just keep the box in its plastic container, so he won't squeeze the juice everywhere.

Sugar has been a favorite since birth, when he had his first belt of sweetened water, but his appetite drops so fast now, you can't afford to give cookies to satisfy what little hunger he has. Although a child triples his birth weight in his first year, he gains only three to five pounds in his second.

Even so, he still continues to need five small meals a day: a full breakfast; a mid-morning snack; lunch; an after-nap snack; and dinner. This same schedule lasts until first grade.

For snacks, give your child juice, fruit or raw vegetables and any protein, like cheese. No fruit should be given less than an hour before the next meal; it would be like a dessert before soup. In any case, avoid snacks without vitamins, such as dry cereal or potato chips, for simple carbohydrates only guarantee fussy behavior.

### MID-ONE

As mothers, we must have made most of the mistakes you can make in child care, especially in eating and we've been astonished to find that the bad patterns were so much easier to set than the good ones.

In no time our toddlers learned they could skip lunch and get sweeter, bigger, earlier snacks from their anxious mothers, just because they were hungry. This was folly, of course, for a heavy snack in mid-afternoon simply makes a child too full for dinner and then too hungry to wait patiently for breakfast the next morning.

We watched other mothers offer simple snacks, yet hardly notice themselves allowing a steady flow of dry cereal, cookies, fruit and milk until the next meal was barely touched. Either way will encourage a finicky eater and a whiny one too. He'll be a terrible pain until you decide that a meal isn't a nonstop production.

### TWO

Although you won't demand that your child clean his plate, you won't give second helpings or desserts until he has. Obviously, if he has some food left on his plate he isn't hungry and your refusals should be explained like that.

Considering that his taste buds are so much more intense than yours, you shouldn't expect him to like everything you like, and he particularly may not like the texture of some foods. They may be too gritty, like roe, or spongy, like liver, or slimy, like oysters. Other dishes, like stew, have their flavors combined, which bothers some children. Still, you should put a bit of everything you cook on his plate and expect him to taste it, on the grounds that this may be the day he is old enough to like it, even though he hated it when he was younger (such as a week before). Unless your child has an allergy, an illness or a birthday, you should never cook a special meal for him in exchange for peace at the dinner table. If you do your child will restrict his diet more and more until you're ready to divorce him if you ever smell hot dogs, tuna fish or peanut butter again. Having worked ourselves into that box, we found only one sure, if painful, exit. This method is a lot of trouble, but if you're desperate enough it's worth trying.

Begin when you're willing to stay indoors for several miserable days, without company, without any treats in the house and, to be kind, when your husband is on a trip. First, tell your child he no longer can have snacks or desserts until he will eat what he is served at meals. Then cook every outlandish dish you can think of until, after a certain amount of fasting, he'll find that even lamb curry or crab imperial tastes good. You can expect some backsliding afterward and when that happens, you simply quit desserts and snacks again until he comes around again.

### MID-TWO

When your child outgrows the high chair, his company at the dinner table is less and less charming. Somehow he's expected to act as grown-up as everyone else and instead he'll talk while you're talking (the way he plays next to his friends but not with them). He will feed the cat, spit out his meat, hide his peas in his bib and spill his cup at least once. (We remember one ghastly night when two children spilled a total of eight glasses of milk.) These are the same things your child does when he eats lunch with you in the kitchen, but it's much more annoying at dinner, when you've tried so much harder. Regrettably, a pre-Five can't be much better than this and you'll spend the next few years finding ways to escape, none of which will be too satisfactory or permanent. Realistically, you should know that in eating, as in everything else, the solutions that work one week will collapse the next, for your child isn't static, thank goodness.

If you think your child would profit by having family meals—and we do—you need to decide how frequently you can stand it. It should be no less than once a week, however, and probably couldn't be more than four, although we know one organized mother who had her three pre-Fives eat with their parents nightly—but only for ten minutes. First she gave them an early dinner alone, without dessert, followed by a communal bath, and then invited them downstairs in their sleepers for

salad, which one of the children usually made. It was served as a splendid first course for the parents and a last course for the children and worked very well, although the youngest child, at Nine, still thinks a good dessert is green and oily.

The rest of us endure, but less grandly. If you can tolerate four family meals a week, you might plan on a pickup supper of sandwiches another night, an adult meal at a restaurant or with friends at your house or theirs on still another night and a late and fancy dinner for you and your husband at home—a corny routine but it improves your cooking and helps you feel civilized.

The other basic solution: have your child eat with you once a week, and feed him early on the other six nights. For this you can 1) cook your own meal in advance to give him some of it; 2) save a plate from the night before; 3) freeze TV dinners from your leftovers; or 4) feed him dinner at noon and a sandwich for supper.

A child's separate dinner shouldn't be a production and it doesn't deserve all the resentment it generates, but, somehow, cooking two balanced meals every night can make you feel like Milly the Martyr. That's one reason we settled for family meals. They should be served with style: food should pique a child's sense of sight as much as his sense of taste. You'll find candlelight makes everyone's behavior better, for a child is awed into near goodness and you can't see enough of the badness to correct him too often. A little wine will also make you feel better and we recommend that too.

You can help your child act his best by using a booster seat or a seat that clamps to the table, or just sit him on pillows or phone books high enough to let him handle silverware well. Strap him to the chair so he can't leave when he feels like it, but don't expect him to last longer than twenty minutes. This means that even soup must be served alongside the dinner plate, for to a Two, dessert is the only course worth waiting for.

### THREE

Your Three almost seems grown-up to you now—and to himself. An early Three eats pretty neatly and pretty well, and prefers meat, pasta, fruit—and sweets—but even some vegetables are tolerated now.

And then that dear child hits mid-Three, and he balks at food as he balks at everything else. Just look the other way and keep very little junk food around, or he'll demand that instead.

By now he has sampled a few soda pops in some Garden of Delight with Grandpa and wants some more, any time. You may succumb, giving soda to your child as often as water, which starts a bad pattern.

Besides their high sugar content, many sodas contain about half as much caffeine in a twelve-ounce can as you'd get in a cup of coffee. Since your child weighs so much less than you, 40 to 70 mg of caffeine will affect him much more, causing him to be jumpy, wakeful and cross. Your Three will do much better with water, milk or juice, none of which are addictive.

### FOUR

"You take what you want and you eat what you take" is the motto of the Amish smorgasbord restaurants in Pennsylvania and their way suits our independent Four very well. A picky eater can serve himself from your own simple buffet, taking as much as he wants (but including a vegetable) and finishing it all.

A Four usually has a fair appetite, however, which gets better as he nears Five, and may adore some foods, and despise others, especially if the texture is gritty. A Four will drink all of his cup if he pours for himself. For this he still needs a small unbreakable cup (but not a paper cup, for it tips too easily), and a small unbreakable pitcher.

A Four also is big enough to have a proper lunch with you at a department store and little enough to enjoy it.

### FIVE

Fives like to eat—in part because they like to please—but these convivial children often dawdle, seldom eat as much at one meal as another and almost always like simple, bland, smooth foods best.

Snacks are heartier now and a Five likes nuts or raw or dried fruits as well as cookies and milk. Your child usually will eat a whole sandwich for lunch and enjoys pared carrots, celery and seeded cucumbers from a jar of water in the refrigerator.

### SIX

If your Six doesn't have extra sweets every day, his eating habits will be normal in first grade and he won't be so tempted to join the lunch box contest, where each child jockeys for more sweets and treats than all the other children. A lunch box needs milk or juice, a sandwich, some fruit or raw vegetable, two cookies and perhaps some nuts. Sodas and candy bars give a child nothing.

He'll be welcome to have dinner with you at night now because he eats nearly everything that is cooked for the adults and with manners that aren't too offensive, even to visitors. However, you may have another child by now and you and your husband will want to eat alone at least once a week. Let your Six join you for one more quiet evening, and live with a one-ring circus the rest of the time. Once more you lower your standards and enjoy the show.

These are some of the best, easiest and healthiest foods you can make.

## YOGURT

YIELD: 4½ CUPS

The best yogurt has no preservatives and since it should be a part of the daily diet, you may enjoy making it yourself. It's cheap and easy and an older child will like to help you, if only to watch it bubble. The milk must be scalded first to kill the bacteria, and containers and utensils must be very clean. Use either fresh or reconstituted milk—whole, low-fat or skim—with extra milk crystals for more thickness.

**SCALD**          **1 qt. milk**

**ADD**            **½ c. milk crystals**

Cool for 10 minutes. Meanwhile place 5 wide-mouthed 8-oz. glass jars in a pan with warm water up to their necks. When the milk feels warm on your wrist (about 110°)

**ADD**            **3 tbsp. plain yogurt OR**
                   **1-oz. pkg. yogurt culture**

Stir with a metal spoon. Pour into the jars, cap them and cover the pan. The cover and the bath help distribute the heat evenly. Keep the pan on a heating tray, over a pilot light or in any place warm enough to stay about 110° for 3–10 hours. For a mild flavor, heat 3–4 hours, refrigerating just when the yogurt stops bubbling and has turned to custard. For a sharper taste and thicker consistency, heat overnight, or for 10 hours, before refrigerating.

Serve yogurt with a spoon of honey if your child is more than a year, or with fresh fruit, and if the taste of the yogurt is too sharp, add a little cream. Never add sugar or chocolate, however, since either may kill B vitamins. Save 3 tablespoons to start a new batch within 5 days.

## BABY DINNER

In a covered pot, and using no salt or spices

**COMBINE**        **1 c. water**
                   **1 chicken breast**
                   **¼ c. rice**

Simmer 20 minutes

**ADD**            **3 whole carrots**
                   **¼ lb. green beans**

Simmer 10 minutes longer

Blend or process the meat with enough of the cooking broth to make it moist. Mash the carrots and then the beans. Store separately in individual servings in the freezer sealed in plastic sandwich bags, or in a plastic ice-cube tray, which must be bagged and tied. Defrost a meal at breakfast, so it's ready to heat for lunch. As your child gets a few months older and can chew better, you can grate these ingredients instead of blending them and you can use your leftovers too.

## SPROUTS

A Two likes to eat sprouts and especially to grow them. Serve raw, either by the handful or in salads, or combine with cooked vegetables. Their chemistry undergoes an almost magical change from seeds to sprouts, creating a very high value in protein and vitamin C. Any seeds you grow need constant dampness and, of course, no soil. They mature in 3–5 days, according to their size. Buy them from supermarkets or health food stores, but don't buy gardening packets, for these seeds may be chemically treated. In a bowl overnight

**SOAK**           **½ c. wheat berries OR**
                   **mung beans OR alfalfa seeds**

Line a big tea strainer or colander with cheesecloth or a paper towel to contain moisture. Pour the seeds into it and run cold water over them twice a day. Don't cover them (or they may mildew) and keep them out of sunshine.

## SLEEPING

A newborn sleeps best on his tummy, for the pressure brings up bubbles better. He likes to nestle his head in the corner of the crib, cushioned as it probably was in the womb. He'll probably sleep fourteen–eighteen hours a day, heaven and colic willing, and can sleep for six to eight hours at a stretch when he's about twelve pounds.

### THREE MONTHS

Now he plays in his crib for as long as an hour before breakfast, if he has a mobile, a crib gym, a board book and a soft tinkling toy to amuse him. He'll nap every afternoon, but his morning naps grow shorter. In the next few months you may find he can tell you which of his many blankets has the magic to put him right to sleep—and it's never the one you knitted.

### SIX MONTHS

There are many ways to handle bedtime now, but don't nurse your baby until he falls asleep, or he won't learn to go to sleep on his own—the first step toward independence. This is the time when you begin to adjust the baby's sleeping schedule to fit yours. We put our Kate to bed at 10 P.M. to fit her father's late shift, for there's no rule that says a baby must sleep from 6 to 6. Besides, 10 A.M. is a civilized time for a baby and a mother to wake up.

If your baby is still one of those determinedly early risers, however, treat his wake-up call as a nighttime feeding. Go to him quietly, change and feed him and put him down with new toys, or hang a basket outside his crib and fill it with different toys every night after he's gone to sleep. This ritual—and dark shades to hide the dawn—may buy you an extra hour or two of sleep.

### NINE MONTHS

When Ramon was this age, a nursemaid would have been heaven—not for the days, but for bedtime. Fortunately, his father enjoyed the ritual of putting him to bed and it was their special time for years.

### ONE

Gradually the morning naps disappear until your baby settles into a two to three hour sleep after lunch. Finally, you can have more order to your day.

### MID-ONE

The vivid dreams start now, and with them, some fears. We recommend a night light or a hall light before these fears ever start and certainly a soft doll or a stuffed animal in the bed. All of us need the reassurance of an old friend, and bed is certainly the best place for an old friend.

One day, if he's a climber, he'll surprise you by crawling out of the crib. Since it's safer for a child to climb out of a low bed than to scramble over a high one, it's best to lower the rails and admit that he no longer can be contained.

### TWO

You'll find your Two needs positive discipline for he'll have invented a dozen ways to postpone bedtime. Set bedtime four hours after he wakes from his nap, so he'll be sleepy, and precede it by restful activities—a bath, a soft song, warm milk or a story read in a sleepy voice. Give him lots of kisses, lay him down firmly and don't be in a hurry to answer his calls or you'll start a new tradition. The more rituals you have, the harder it is to enforce the bedtime and the more rewards you offer—water, a cracker or a toy—the more reasons he has to call you again.

### MID-TWO

This child is ready to quit his nap now, just when you need the respite the most. We've found that every mother of a mid-Two is adamant about her child doing one of three things: he must eat everything on his plate, be toilet trained or take a nap. To us there's no choice. A child's nap is the glue that holds a mother together. He'll fight against it, stay awake and probably scream at you, but keep the practice just the same and call it a rest.

### THREE TO SIX

A Three, with more pedal toys, more playmates and maybe a nursery school, will be tired enough to sleep, but he won't return to the nap unless you and he have continued the pretense. We think a child is much easier to live with if he has enough sleep at night—about twelve hours—and you'll be much easier to live with if he sleeps or at least rests one more hour in the afternoon. Some children can adjust to less sleep, but others scarcely cope.

A Four will go to his room for quiet play or to look at books, and to please you, he may pretend to nap. Sometimes he will. If he does, he must get extra exercise afterward unless you don't mind a very late bedtime.

If your child still has trouble going to sleep, the bedtime you set may be unrealistically early. We think the hour can be flexible until nursery school begins, but be more relaxed about it on weekends. A little whoopee time is good for the soul.

One of the nicest habits a child can begin, from his viewpoint, is a visit with you in the night, a pattern that sets nicely in less than a week.

The family bed gets pretty tiresome for most of us, however. Instead, you might invite your child in for a cuddle every morning, or on Sundays, while you read the paper, and let him sleep with you all night if he's very sick, so you can care for him and catnap too.

It's the night-to-night routine that can be so disturbing.

If he needs you, go to him, stay in his room, even get in his bed if it's big enough. If you think that's a poor solution ask the tired, resentful parents who share their bed with a wiggly, leaky child from 3 to 5 A.M.—every 3 to 5 A.M.

When our Kate had that miserable habit, we introduced

## JAKE

One day when we were feeling in charge, we said we saw Jake galumphing around the neighborhood the night before and wasn't he a sight. Just that, nothing more.

Kate, without trying to resist, asked about Jake and immediately she was greeted with great surprise.

"You mean you don't know? You mean I never told you?"

Incredulous, we told her about Jake, who had made himself at the city dump out of bits and dabs that were there. He used drainpipes for arms and legs (we went to look at our drain pipe) and ice trays for shoes and applesauce cans for his kneecaps and elbows. He made the middle of himself out of venetian blind slats, vertical, so he could be cooler in summertime. His head was a gallon paint can, the same color that was in her bedroom in fact, and he had light bulbs for eyes. Jake wore a saucepan for a hat, but mainly so he could bow to the ladies and show off his fine curls of 0000 steel wool, his only vanity.

Jake was nine feet tall and carried a plumber's friend.

When he walked he went ka-plink, ka-plunk, ka-plinkety, plinkety-plunk, but only the grown-ups could hear him, and not even all of them. Every night he made his rounds, visiting little children to make sure they were sound asleep and tucked in their own little beds, where else. If they were, the front door opened magically and he came in, very pleased with himself, and went up the steps, ka-plink, ka-plunk and with many, many squeaks, he bent himself enough to go through the bedroom doorway. He straightened up his nine feet in time to bend down again to kiss the nose good night. It is the nose, Jake said, that was responsible for good and happy dreams and it certainly seemed to work for Kate.

The first time she slept the whole night in her own bed, she found a little gift from Jake. This wasn't a bribe, because it wasn't promised, but a thank-you present, for letting him come in out of the dew. If there's one thing Jake hated it was wet weather (the rust, you know). The other thing he couldn't abide was sand, because it got in his joints, but since Kate was so special, Jake always trudged to the seashore every summer to make sure she had good dreams on her vacation.

Jake never promised gifts, but very occasionally left one or a funny note or a picture if the child had stayed where she belonged.

There must be 1,024 variations of the sandman routine and you probably will be more comfortable making up a Jake of your own. It's fun for you, it stretches your child's imagination—and it works.

## TO SLEEP—OR NOT TO SLEEP

It's harder for some children to put themselves to sleep than it is for others, but it's a basic skill all of them need to know. A child must trust others, but first of all, he must trust himself.

You'll do your child a favor if you put him down after his story, with a kiss and a hug and the clear impression that you know he can go to sleep on his own, so there's no need for you to hang around. It will take him five to ten minutes, and a little fussing and some scrunching around, to make the transition from wakefulness to sleep and then one night he bleats for you, again and again, maybe in the middle of the night, and begs to get in your bed. Some parents think the family bed is a great idea, others give in so they can get back to sleep. Unless you want to take him into your bed, night after night, however—for that's how quickly this habit starts—its better just to go to him, pat him, say, "I love you," lay him down—and let him be. You may have to do this again and again, every five to ten minutes, for an hour or so—not angrily but a little more businesslike every time—and then do it again the next night and the next. By the end of the week, the problem is almost always over, no matter how old the child, or whether he's been sleeping in your bed for months.

## TOILET TRAINING

A child has little control over his bowels until Two, the bladder until mid-Two. A Three can stay dry through the night. If you start toilet training too early you'll have to wait months before your child can

control himself, and you both will feel like failures. The older your child, the less you need to explain, for with his natural curiosity he has followed you to the pot, flushed it for you and asked many, many questions. Eventually he tries to mimic you and will tell you about every bowel movement he makes—after he makes it.

When your child has stopped rebelling—between mid-Two and Three—you can have your turn. This is the end of pamperdom.

We found ourselves angry when we realized our daughter was old enough and smart enough to pull down her wet diaper and hand us a dry one. Clearly it was time she trained herself. We told her so emphatically and were businesslike about it. She was expected to be trained like the rest of us. We gave her one week to do it—a deadline she met.

There may be other ways to train a child but let us tell you. We've never met a mother whose exasperation didn't trigger the training.

You'll find it calls for single-mindedness on your part. Plan a full week to train your child, and this means you won't go out at all, unless he's asleep for the night, and you'll invite no special company to distract you. It's your job to make training easier for your child and each success he has will make success more likely the next time. Basically, toilet training is just one more step toward his independence.

If possible, train your child in summertime; you'll have less laundry. We recommend buying twenty pairs of dime store underpants, better and cheaper than half as many training pants, which have to be changed when they're wet anyway, and dressing your child in pants or dresses that have no straps or other complications. Handicaps aren't needed during the training week.

Your child also needs a potty on every

floor, because his feet can't run quite fast enough. It either should be a chair or a special seat on the toilet with a step to reach it, since a toilet is gigantically high to a Two. Everyone wants his feet to touch the floor when sitting in a chair, especially if the chair has a hole in the middle. Children are as afraid of falling into a porcelain pot today as our foremothers were of falling through the privy a hundred years ago. It's the curse of the age.

One enterprising mother of a competitive little boy found a child's urinal with a target painted on it. In his striving for a high score he trained himself to hit the bull's-eye in just two days.

When training begins, explain to your child that he should sit on the pot when you ask him, until he learns to sit without being told at all. Don't let him stay longer than ten minutes or not at all if he objects. You won't, of course, play games or read stories, for this teaches a child that pot time is playtime, but do stay with him if he likes.

With your reminders, he'll go to his potty about eight times a day. Let him sit there as soon as he wakes up—not when you wake up—leaving a bell in his crib or bed if you usually don't hear him. He'll ring it, you can bet. He sits on the pot again right after breakfast and after lunch—the two times he's most likely to have a bowel movement—as well as after juice in midmorning and after a nap, after supper and before bed. And any other time he mentions it.

Your child will be very proud of his successes, which you'll praise. Let him empty the potty in the toilet, even though he spills a little, and let him flush it himself. You may flush too quickly and hurt his pride.

It is important not to overreact to a bowel movement—or the lack of one—or to thank him for doing one for you. It's really not the most important thing in the world and a great deal of emphasis is a distortion.

Ask him to tell you when he makes a mistake—and he will if you don't fuss—and to help you clean it. Have him put his wet underpants in the diaper hamper, get fresh ones and put them on without any help, for you want him to learn how good it feels to stay dry. You'll not even use diapers at night and, yes, you will do a lot of wash, but there's a good chance you can put the diapers away after a week.

If your child hasn't trained himself in a week, one of you isn't ready. Go back to diapers with as much good grace as you can pretend. Who ever wore them to college?

## POSTLUDE

Once a child is trained, he should learn to pee in an assortment of places—in other people's bathrooms, in a meadow, in the ocean, from a boat (always downwind), never in a pool. By Four, he'll insist on using every facility he can find. We know one little girl who, in the midst of the model rooms at Sears Roebuck, insisted to her distracted mother that she had to go potty. She insisted and insisted and then she disappeared, returning in a few minutes and reporting that she had indeed found the pot.

"I picked the pretty blue one," she said loudly, pointing to the floor display nearby.

## BEDWETTING

All children occasionally wet the bed until they're Eight. A cold night, too much water before bedtime, a case of nerves or plain laziness may be the cause.

A Five who consistently wets the bed will be embarrassed about it and may feel unhappy about himself. For this reason, we feel a mother can't treat bedwetting lightly and must help the child overcome the problem, but never with threats or bribes. It's time to look to the latest research instead.

More and more doctors agree that bedwetting is often related to something a child eats or drinks, and occasionally to something in the air. An allergy can make a child sleep as though he's drugged—because he is—and it can make the muscle in the bladder swell too. If it does, the bladder will hold only one-fifth as much urine as it should and it will spasm too, but the child will be too sleepy to go to the bathroom.

If that's the problem, the bedwetting will go away when his hips have spread a little—usually between Ten and Fourteen—or in about five days, if he avoids his allergy (see Allergies, page 128). It may mean taking milk or apple juice or pork chops or whatever out of his diet until he's a little older, but a pre-K would rather do that than wet the bed.

# THE FAMILY

Sometimes we think a *ménage à trois* would be easier than an old marriage and a new baby. Many parents feel resentment, most feel ineptness and all undergo unexpected changes. The carefree husband may become the overprotective papa; the shy man suddenly blooms; the complete woman falls apart; and girlish wives grow up.

No matter how young or old your marriage, your first baby greatly affects the essence of it. The style of your life is interrupted. Nothing is impromptu but little can be planned. You can't even make love without worrying about the next feeding. Because of so many nursemaid jobs, the baby becomes the catalyst for friction.

Like most new mothers, we succumbed to that awful joy of giving our husbands small commands—and many—just to prove there was someone in this world we could manage. Fortunately, we couldn't get away with this petty tyranny for long, for they knew they were as capable as we were, if not as practiced. If you never ordered your husband around before, this is no time to start. Instead, he should have the same primary jobs that you have—diapering, feeding and bathing the baby, and with little advice from you. If you let him follow his instincts, no matter how much they differ from yours, you are showing respect. This is the keystone of good parenthood but it goes against the mores of a millennium.

It has been natural for a woman, kept in her place for so long, to make motherhood appear full of inscrutable nuances that no man could master. This was nonsense, of course, but she had to gather her laurels where they grew: Only women were gentle, sensitive and soft enough to attend to a little baby; only mothers were patient enough and natural enough and interested enough to keep up with a Two. This strange mystique developed until sooner or later only the mother could communicate with a teenager except it turned out that she couldn't, and neither could the father. He never had.

Even though fathers do much, much more around the house than they used to do, and much more for their children, your husband may have a hard time meeting these commitments. Today's father, between his work and his commuting, often is away from home twelve vital hours a day, five days a week. Not only does he have little energy left for his baby, but if his dad was a commuter too, he's had a slim model of fatherhood to follow.

The problem is compounded if you also work outside your home. Somehow you both must find time to be with your child, individually and together. Schedules may need changes, perhaps with a later bedtime so a child can see his parent for more than a few stories and some goodnight kisses. Plan a longer afternoon rest for your child, so he won't fall apart every evening when you walk in. In this way you'll encourage intimacy between both parents and child, an intimacy that comes only with frequent, direct involvement. To care and be cared for bind two people as tightly as a newborn's grasp.

You also have to show respect for yourself as well as your husband. For all the initial joy and sense of importance your baby brings, you're entering a time that will test your sense of self-worth and decide the shape of the rest of your life. And what an unsettling experience it is.

The Hamleting you felt as a teenager will be nothing compared with the irresolution that can hit you now for your personality can be submerged under the deluge of work as wife and mother, especially if you stay at home. You've tried so hard to get to the "happily ever after" and now you're wondering—after what? Although you can accomplish many things, none are done as well as you'd like and it's been a long time since anyone asked what you thought about foreign policy or much else either.

The less money you have, the more impossible your situation will look, for a lack of money can gnaw at your happiness and the simplest solutions are overshadowed by the problems they create. It's particularly galling to see other couples your age, who seem to have the same income as you, do so much with it (even though they complain twice as much about all the things they can't afford). Take heart. As we always discovered, they have Parent$. Somehow that knowledge helps.

To make the pressure-cooker atmosphere worse, you probably are lonelier now than you ever have been. Old friends move away but others don't fit as well into your new life, any more than you fit into theirs. Now you'll have to start a serious search for new friends.

Once when our constant companions were a One and a Two, we marched through a stranger's gate, uninvited, and introduced ourselves to a young mother and daughter—the start of a long friend-

ship. We continued this brazen pattern for years, for that day we learned a truism: all young mothers are lonely.

As the months go by, however, no number of good friends will solve your problems. The complaints of early motherhood, listed singly, may seem silly, but taken cumulatively they can become monumental, rotting the whole fabric of marriage.

First decide exactly what bothers you most about motherhood. Is it its inherent disorder? its debts? its loneliness? its lack of privacy? its sameness? its hard work?

The important part of any problem is its admission, for only then can you reach a solution. You may need time alone every day, to play the guitar or read. You may need a maid a few hours a week—who doesn't?—or someone to help with the heavy work once a month. Some mothers feel reincarnated by a visit to the hairdresser and others are happy with a few hours a week to window shop or go to church without a crying baby. Others like to rent a sexy movie or have a late dinner at home with wine and candlelight. You need to find two or even three solutions to get reasonable serenity. Since the problems often change, so should the cures.

Even if you can't afford the beauty shop, you still need the luxury of at least one perfumed bath a week and time to set your hair and manicure your nails. Send your child to a neighbor (a favor you'll return), turn on the answering machine, and enjoy. It won't be the best, but it beats nothing.

This attention to your *toillette*, as the French say, is necessary and is equal to the shaves you ask of your husband on the weekends. The way you let yourself look is almost as important as the way you spend your time. One is generally reflective of the other.

It becomes strangely easy to get out of the habit of bathing regularly unless you keep to a fixed time, no matter how brief it is or how busy you are. Otherwise you'll find yourself putting it off in the morning

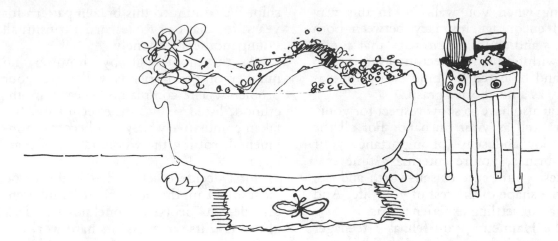

because you've used all the hot water to wash baby clothes, or until naptime, except the baby is hungry again, or finally until night, but by then you're just too tired.

Of course, a bath without interruption will be rare for years. By the time your child is Three you'll bathe with an audience of not only your child, but a few neighborhood ringers and every animal you have but the goldfish.

Your main problem may be the enormous amount of housework. If you feel overwhelmed by it, ask a friend to help you once a week and you, of course, will help her just as often while your children play together. Even mending with a friend will make you feel less like a druge. Unless you have a job, too, you can't expect your husband to do half of the housework, since you don't help him at the office, but you certainly can expect him to do some of it, and to help with dinner and the baby and to handle some weekend projects.

Basically, all solutions must come from your own attitude. You'll decide whether to watch soap operas or read a book; fill crossword puzzles or learn to be a better cook. Unless you're prepared to work at it, motherhood can become very depressing. You need to accomplish a little bit everyday—something that can't be undone by another wash, another meal, another day of dust. A day in which nothing new is learned or nothing permanent is done is a day wasted as far as your psyche is concerned, for none of us ever stops growing.

The solutions you develop will help you deal with motherhood, and your marriage, which needs regular reinforcement too.

We think every couple should get away together maybe once a season. Even a camping trip for a day (and especially a night) will do, leaving your child with a neighbor (and promising to do the same for her). But be prepared. Your pre-Three will scarcely speak to you when you return.

As you and your husband and your baby work out an easy relationship, you'll decide again whether, or when, to have another child.

Whether you're adopting babies or having them by the bagful, you should remember that each parent should give ten to fifteen and preferably twenty minutes of undivided attention to each pre-Six each day. The size of your family should depend on the time you think you can give, not only now but during those vital Middle Years, between Six and Twelve. This is the time when parents and children seal their bond tightly enough to carry them through the adolescent years.

It's an effort for two to live happily, but it requires much more effort for three (or four or five or six).

## SITTERS

An evening a week with your husband—and without your child—is an investment in marriage. New parents need to reinstate themselves often as a couple, whether they go to a fancy restaurant, or just nuzzle again in the back seat of the car. The best mothers aren't mothers all the time.

You can usually find the cheapest, most responsible child care if you join a baby-sitting co-op of parents, who pay each other in time rather than money. There are many other possibilities, however, and your preference will vary as your child gets older. An infant, we feel, receives the best care from someone who has been a mother, but an active boy of fourteen is dandy for a rambunctious Four. A responsible preteen girl is ideal to watch the baby during your nap or while you spend time with an older child for it's her last chance to play with dolls and her first chance to play grown-up. When all else fails, bonded agency sitters are reliable, but exorbitant.

A good sitter, like a good mother, pays primary attention to the child—not the telephone or the television. Even a teenager will accept this rule if you emphasize it enough. You need a sitter who sleeps lightly or not at all, who can diaper and burp a baby, who can cook simple meals, and above all, you need a sitter who is

### EMERGENCY NUMBERS

Always keep a list of emergency numbers next to each telephone extension—stress makes you forget the most familiar numbers—and leave a signed, undated authorization to give your child emergency medical treatment, which hospitals usually require, as well as your insurance number.

| | |
|---|---|
| Fire | Pediatrician |
| Ambulance | Drugstore |
| Poison Control | All-Night Drugstore |
| Father's Office | Neighbor |
| Mother's Office | Neighbor |

kind. You also need a sitter who is quick-witted. If you have doubts, ask yourself how she would handle a burglary, a fire, a convulsion. Obviously a scatterbrain won't do.

We remember how blessed we felt, returning home to check on an address, when we saw our three pajamed pre-Fives lined in a row on the sofa. They were spellbound by their dumpling of a gray-haired sitter who smiled benignly as she explained a book of cartoons to them. We were blocks away when the soft, sweet words finally registered: "And in this picture the little children are boiling their parents in the big pot."

Charles Addams, the cartoonist who brought vampires to Main Street, remained a favorite with the children for years, and so did the sitter. She was a very kind lady.

### SITTER RULES

Maggie and Susan, two pretty girls who have sat with more children than any mother ever will, believe these rules will guarantee you good sitters. We agree.

◇ Ask for references—and check them.
◇ Establish your rates when you hire the sitter, not when the job is finished.
◇ Allow no company; babysitting is work, not play.
◇ Tell your child in advance if you're going out, who will sit and when you'll be back, since it's your return, not your leaving, that worries him.
◇ Ask the sitter to come fifteen minutes before you leave, so she and your child can adjust to each other—a time for which you'll pay.
◇ Provide your sitter with sober transportation after dark, coming and going.
◇ Show the sitter where you keep your list of emergency numbers for police, fire and poison control, the doctor and a nearby friend, and a signed undated permission slip in case she has to take your child to the hospital. Add the number where you can be reached each

time you go out and call if there is any change.

◇ Show the location of lights, thermostat, flashlight, thermometer, television and phone.

◇ Leave a key for any double lock and explain all locks and alarm systems.

◇ Explain the care a pet might need, but put it in another room if the sitter objects to it.

◇ Ask your sitter to take phone messages.

◇ Supply all sitters with coffee, tea or sodas, something to eat, a lamp to read by and if you'll be late, a pillow and blanket.

◇ Tell your sitter if any part of the house or any food is off-limits.

◇ Leave a fairly specific menu if you can't feed your child before leaving.

◇ Tell the sitter if your child has any allergies.

◇ Give precise, written instructions if your child needs medicine.

◇ Leave at least one book to be shown or read to a child of six months or older.

◇ Specify which television program or video your child may watch.

◇ Show the sitter which clothes your child should wear and where to find the diapers and lotion.

◇ Leave a pacifier, magic blanket or another consolation.

◇ Tell her your child's bedtime or naptime if you can't tuck him in before you leave and tell her the rituals he likes.

◇ Tell the sitter the discipline you allow— but it should never be as stringent as your own, for it's not given with your love.

◇ Expect a sitter to tidy up after herself and your child, but never after you.

◇ Get home when you've promised, or call if you'll be late, but never stay more than an hour extra.

◇ Have cash or a check ready to pay your sitter when you get home—not next week—and pay for a half-hour if you're fifteen minutes after the hour; a full

hour if you're thirty-five minutes past and a tip if she's done a good job.

## BABYSITTING COOPERATIVE

Unfortunately, sitters are hardest to get when you need them most—when there's so little money between paydays and not much then.

We overcame these problems best through a babysitting cooperative of parents who sat for each others' children—the ultimate in credit economy and good times. The co-op brought new friends to us and to our children, it had only two meetings a year and it was free: we paid each other with the preprinted tickets we had earned and we even used them for extra baby gifts.

The large, diverse co-op we joined, in transient Washington, D.C., had only the necessary ten families when it started, but it has thrived. Now, many years later, and with many more working mothers, it has 250 families split into four sections and is more viable than ever.

If your neighborhood has no co-op, it's simple to start one. It only takes a steady flow of play money between buyers and sellers and a lot of mutual respect. For viability, a co-op seems to work best with a president, a treasurer and a monthly secretary; a minimum of ten families and a maximum of eighty (although we've seen it work with more); and an initial printing of scrip—about 3,000 half-hour tickets the size of those "Get Out of Jail Free" cards.

It is also much simpler than it sounds. In the co-op, you or your husband will sit at your own house in the daytime—which will give your child a playmate—and sit at the gadders' house at night, so their child can sleep in his own bed. The tickets you earn will pay for your sitters when you go out.

Even a single parent can use the co-op, if she takes daytime sits on Saturday or Sunday—or takes care of a child for the weekend—and then uses co-op sitters when she goes out at night.

We found that this is the way a co-op runs best:

### Duties of a Member

◇ Sit at your home by day, the child's home by night.
◇ Arrange all daytime sits yourself.
◇ Ask the monthly secretary for nighttime sitters twenty-four hours in advance, but find your own sitter on shorter notice.
◇ Give twenty-four hour notice to the sitter and the secretary if you cancel your plans to go out at night—so the sitter can make other plans—or pay a one-hour penalty for a last-minute cancellation and two hours for Saturday night.
◇ Arrange a co-op replacement or pay for a sitter if you cancel your promise to sit without twenty-four-hour notice.
◇ Make calls to the secretary before 10 P.M. and almost never on Sunday.
◇ Tell the sitter beforehand if your child is sick.

### Payment

◇ Pay only in scrip.
◇ Figure time to the nearest half-hour, giving two hours of scrip for two hours and twelve minutes and two and a half hours of scrip for two hours and sixteen minutes, but don't pay the sitter for her time if she comes earlier than you asked.
◇ Pay immediately after a sit to avoid controversy later.
◇ Pay a minimum of two hours for any evening sit.
◇ Pay an extra hour for Saturday night.
◇ Pay double after 1 A.M. and for Arsenic Hour—between 5–7 P.M.

◇ Pay double for children from two families, triple for children from three families, whether the families are in or out of the co-op.
◇ Pay only one extra hour for children in a group house and for long-term house guests, since they are members of the extended family.
◇ Pay a flat eight hours for your child to spend the night at the sitter's home, beginning no earlier than 7 P.M. and ending no later than 9 A.M.
◇ Negotiate your own pay scale for a full weekend.

### The Operation of a Co-op

◇ Full-time members sit and use sitters day or night, while part-time members use them only in the day.
◇ A new member receives a loan from the administration of thirty hours of scrip, in sixty half-hour tickets, when she joins, which she must repay when she leaves.

| name | date | time | sitter |
|------|------|------|--------|
|  |  |  |  |
|  |  |  |  |
|  |  |  |  |

◇ Every new member must be sponsored by another member and every old member must get a replacement if her sponsor leaves, so someone is responsible for her thirty-hour loan if she leaves without paying it back.
◇ Each member can sponsor only three members at the same time.
◇ A member should give a small coffee to introduce anyone she sponsors.
◇ Every member pays a small fee—to cover mailing costs—and fourteen hours of scrip a year for full-time membership and seven hours for part time to pay the officers—a debt that's due twice a year and prorated for new members.
◇ A member, if out of town for three months or more, may become inactive and pay no dues.

◇ Members may buy scrip from others at a rate set by the administration.

◇ A member may repay two thirds of her loan of scrip at any time.

◇ Members must either sell scrip or give it away if they accumulate more than twenty hours above their loan—even if the loan has been partially repaid—to keep the economy viable.

◇ A member will not be reimbursed for lost scrip.

### Duties of the Administration

◇ The co-op is run by a president and a treasurer, and, if more than eighty families belong, a vice president, with a change of leadership every six months, and each month they choose a different secretary from a pool of volunteers.

◇ The president shepherds the flock, processes new members and distributes new membership lists every six months with the name of the husband and wife, the addresses and telephone numbers of home and office and the name and birthdate of each child.

◇ The treasurer keeps a separate reserve of scrip in the co-op bank to loan to new members, prints scrip as needed and balances the intake and outgo of tickets and money each month.

◇ The secretary fills every sitting request as soon as possible, calling every member—starting with those who are lowest in scrip—until the sit is filled.

◇ The president, the vice president and the treasurer each receive three hours compensatory time every month.

◇ The secretary receives a half-hour for each part-time member, one hour for each full-time member and an extra half-hour from all members in December, since it's such a busy month.

◇ The administration adds another monthly secretary when the membership exceeds forty families, and the two secretaries divide the membership and the pay.

◇ The administration meets in executive session each month with new and old secretaries.

◇ The members meet twice a year and whenever 20 percent of the membership may request it.

◇ The cooperative may make by-law changes if 30 percent of the membership attends a meeting.

◇ The administration may drop the name of any member from the list who doesn't use the co-op for six months.

◇ The administration may ask a member to withdraw, but only after receiving a written complaint and conducting a closed hearing with both members involved.

### Secretarial Help

Two mimeographed forms make a secretary's job much easier. The first is a record of sitting requests for the month, with columns for the name, date and the time of the sit so she can enter the sitter's name as she fills the sits. This quickly lets her see if there are any outstanding requests.

The second form is filled in with the

| name | phone | scrip | 1 | 2 | 3 | 4 | 5 | 6 | 7 | 8 | 9 | 10 | 11 | 12 | 13 | 14 | 15 | 16 | 17 | 18 | 19 | 20 | 21 | 22 | 23 | 24 | 25 | 26 | 27 | 28 | 29 | 30 | 31 |
|---|---|---|---|---|---|---|---|---|---|---|---|---|---|---|---|---|---|---|---|---|---|---|---|---|---|---|---|---|---|---|---|---|---|
| | | | | | | | | | | | | | | | | | | | | | | | | | | | | | | | | | |
| | | | | | | | | | | | | | | | | | | | | | | | | | | | | | | | | | |
| | | | | | | | | | | | | | | | | | | | | | | | | | | | | | | | | | |
| | | | | | | | | | | | | | | | | | | | | | | | | | | | | | | | | | |
| | | | | | | | | | | | | | | | | | | | | | | | | | | | | | | | | | |

names of active members and their scrip balance—to show who needs to earn more tickets—and a calendar of thirty-one spaces. This lets the secretary mark the busy evenings as the members mention them—from sitting dates to night school classes—so she only needs to call those members who might be free.

## WORKING MOTHER

Every mother agonizes over the most basic choice in motherhood: to go back to work or not. And she agonizes not once, but a thousand times. It's a tough decision and a fairly new one. Women once worked until they got pregnant; now they work until they get Social Security.

Our foremothers stayed home to care for the children—and the house, the garden, the meals, the sewing, the wash. Today the children still need to be cared for, but appliances, convenience foods and ready-made clothes have turned housekeeping into a half-time job. Since mothers, like nature, abhor vacuums almost as much as vacuum cleaners, life has taken on a new twist. More than half of all mothers of preschool children now work at least part-time.

Even the woman who hadn't really wanted to juggle her job and her family felt the pressure of the times. It was lonely and embarrassing to be the only stay-at-home mom on the block—the one who couldn't find company when she wanted a cup of coffee, and couldn't afford little luxuries either.

Just when it seemed that an outside job was the only option, there's been another turn-around. Today more and more mothers feel secure enough to turn their backs on Supermom and to follow their own dreams. Now the question is not whether to work, but when, and how much. The choice is completely personal and never simple—a reflection of your style and your needs. Your husband can help you weigh the pros and cons, but you must make the final decision. Money plays a big role, of course, but it shouldn't be the main one unless the need is critical.

First you have to define yourself, as if money weren't an issue at all. The best mother is a happy mother, and you have to know who you are to know what you really want. Some women are born to work; some are born to stay home; most of us are settled in between. Just as no two babies are alike, so are no two mothers.

You'll almost surely need to work if you're a single parent, but you also need to work if you have a career so interesting that you can't bear to stay away from it; a profession so demanding you have to work to keep up with it; a job offer so fine you can't resist it.

A job is also the best answer if you thrive in the competitive atmosphere of an office, or if you would feel isolated and angry without the challenges you enjoyed at work or if you're a highly focused person who likes to concentrate on one job until it's done. This intensity wins gold stars at the office but it can overwhelm you at home, since life is lived in twenty-minute segments with a baby and few things ever really get finished.

You may also want to work because you're just plain bored at home. You may not be as interested in babies as you'll be in school-age children and there's no need to wait around until you are. We all have our favorite ages.

A job can be very hard on other mothers, however. If you've longed for this time with your child, or feel surprisingly wrenched at the idea of a daily parting—or even if you just feel much more content at home—you should try to stay with your child for a few years.

You'll also have a hard time working at a job if you're a perfectionist. If you think it would be difficult to choose between a family walk at night and folded laundry, you're probably not ready to go back to work. Perfectionists can't do both—unless they have live-in help or a very helpful husband—and a baby comes first. Or you may simply be too anxious to have a job. If you're sure that no one can care for your child as well as you can, you're probably right, for your standards may be impossibly high for someone else.

If you don't have strong motivations, one way or the other—and most women don't—you'll make a healthier decision if you consider your baby and your own peace of mind. Some babies seem to need more attention from their parents than others, but all of them probably do best if one parent is home a good deal of the time for the first three critical years.

You also need to weigh the stress that comes with work, and how well you would handle it. Most of the time everything will go quite well—unless the child gets sick, or wakes many times in the night—but it still takes a big effort to meet a split-second schedule day after day. The relentless, cyclical effort required to care for a job, a child and a home can consume your strength until there's none left to play with your child.

Now consider your marriage, and the stresses a job will place on it. The more you work, the less time you and your husband will have for each other, unless you consciously plan for it—and so you should. You'll also have to share the chores and the child care, and that's not so easy, since it means sharing your authority too. You can bet that your husband is going to do any work his way or not at all—and he has that right, just as you have the right to do chores your way. Just lighten up and be glad he's willing to help. You may even have something to learn.

Finally, you want to take a fresh look at your money situation, and figure out whether you'd be working for the basics or the extras, and which is which. You do have to pay the rent and save for a down payment, but ask yourself if your first

house has to be as fine as the ones your friends have bought. If they're that grand, they probably had some family help anyway. Remember: you don't have to live like anyone else and neither do your children, nor do they need a big collection of clothes and toys. It's attention they want from you, not things.

If you would be working for the extras, ask yourself: how important are those fancy toys? the restaurant meals? the second car? the processed foods and frozen dinners? the magician at the birthday party? If you don't watch it, the luxuries of one year become the necessities of the next.

Then think of the money you'll save if you stay home. You'll not only save on child care, transportation, lunches and clothes, but you can save even more if you go to the sales and the thrift shops, stay in an apartment a little longer than you'd like and use a babysitting co-op instead of a paid sitter.

If you do stay home, however, some part-time outside work—temporary or regular, paid or volunteer—is still essential for even the most dedicated mother of a pre-One. You can't shut the world out of your life just because you've had a baby. If you do, you'll feel your mind shrink to the size of a prune and the restrictions of motherhood will make you feel claustrophobic. It takes so little to lift you, but without some reassurance from the outside world, you can sink so low. Realistically, motherhood lasts forever, but its duties have a comparatively short term. You must maintain your independence so you can allow your child to be independent too.

The longer you wait to get out of the house regularly, the harder it will be to believe you can ever leave such a dear baby. Every day he pulls the lines to your heart a little tighter. If these lines are too tight, however, the effect will be as stifling for your child as it is for you, for he also needs some outside influences every day or so. The more people he sees, the less rigid he'll be.

Whatever your choice, however, it won't be fixed or final, and it will probably change with the age of your child and the size of your family. Only one thing is certain: you have every right to start a job, or stop it, without feeling guilty.

### VOLUNTEER WORK

If you can get along without the money, volunteer work can bring enormous rewards, for nothing else can be so demanding and so satisfying, and nothing else can teach you so much either. When you work for a cause, you learn how to organize, to run meetings, to hire and fire, to unwrap red tape and to tie loose ends.

Although you may only go to this office one morning a week, you can multiply your time by doing some of the work at home—a good way to keep your mind stimulated while you bake cookies with your Two.

There are more tangible rewards too. The diversity of volunteer work can define your strengths and your weaknesses, sharpening old skills and teaching you new ones. A volunteer job also lets you assume as much responsibility as you want, for your job description, like your hours, can be very loose when an employer pays with a smile and a thank-you and time off when the baby is sick.

Such work can often lead to a paying job later. The federal government, for instance, may count volunteer experience if the job calls for the same skill, since it takes as much expertise to supervise forty workers for a mailing for eight hours as it does to supervise one worker for eight weeks in an office. If you take the civil service exam, you can parlay your experience into a higher rating, either to get a better government job or to ask for a comparable salary in the private sector.

### PART-TIME

A part-time job can be ideal, particularly if you're a professional. If you work in your field just one day a week, you'll probably be able to keep in touch with it.

A part-time job can also be more lucrative than you might think, since you won't have to buy lunch if you work half-days and you won't have to pay so much for child care either. Many mothers find that they can work for three or even four days a week—or from nine to one, day or night—and net almost as much as they would get for a forty-hour week. Employers like it too, since a part-timer usually gives the boss her prime-time energy and without as much cost to the company.

You may even be able to get a part-time job from your old boss, if you can get along without medical benefits. As long as your husband is covered, you probably don't need it, and it will save your employer a bundle.

In another approach, you can ask for different hours or locale, but be ready to defend your proposal. First think of all the problems that might be involved—and then think of the solutions—before you make your pitch. If you want to do at least some of your work at home, a computer and a facsimile system can save expensive office space downtown, but your boss may not think of the savings unless you remind him. As long as you go to the office every week or so, he'll keep you in mind for raises and promotions and you'll still feel like part of the team.

You might also consider job-sharing,

where your employer lets you share your work with someone else. It will be up to you to find the right person, however, and for you and your co-worker to pass on all the instructions to each other. No boss wants to give the same orders twice.

There are other and sometimes better jobs that will let you stay home with your child, which may have nothing to do with your work in the Other Life. You might keep the books for a small business, type manuscripts, do survey work, make curtains or slipcovers for a fabric store, take care of children after school, or sell toys or cosmetics through a home distribution business. As long as you stick to your interests, you'll probably like the work, and the IRS may let you deduct the cost of your home office.

A part-time job in a home office has another advantage. Once you find out how nice it is to be your own boss, you can possibly turn your services into a full-time job when you're ready for it, and still work at home if you want.

## FULL-TIME

A full-time job is essential—and practical—for millions of women, but it will be much less stressful if you can wait until the baby is at least three months old and preferably six or more, for it can be very wrenching to leave your child too soon. You'll know when you're ready.

Your anxiety will be hard to handle no matter when you start. If you don't want to leave the baby with a stranger—although the sitter won't be a stranger very long—you and your husband might consider alternating your schedules—so he works nights and you work days—or you can ask your boss to let you do at least some of your work at home, or to let you work four ten-hour days, or perhaps you can become a day care provider at home, so you can take care of your own baby while you care for other children.

Whatever you do, and whatever your schedule, the results will be better if you set your priorities before you start and lower your expectations. You simply can't expect to clean the house as well or as often if you have a full-time job, or to do much civic or church work either.

Ideally, you need enough sleep and enough good food to keep up your energy and a job either so interesting it keeps you lively or so simple you can forget it the minute you leave. If you're married, you also need a husband who's willing to spend as much time on the housework, the yard, the car and the repairs as you do, with each of you doing what you like to do best, and splitting the baby care, for a child needs to connect with both parents as much as he can. Traditions die hard, however. Although fathers are much more involved with their children than they used to be, nine out of ten of them don't do many day-to-day chores or bathe the baby either. If your husband is one of these nine, this will leave you with a job and a half, and a baby who gets shortchanged, unless you hire someone to do what you cannot.

Your husband will be more likely to do his part if you work out a share-and-share alike list of duties before you go back to work, so the list can tell him what to do, instead of you. You don't want to squabble about chores at the end of a workday, when you're both tired and hungry.

Since it's much harder to go from work to home than from home to work, you want to arrange other ways to make the transition a little easier at night. Ask the caregiver to see that your child has a high protein snack an hour before you get there, so he won't be so cranky, and give yourself ten to fifteen minutes to relax. A short wait in the car, before you see your child, or a shower when you get home or a lie-down in your room with the lights out will seem like heaven. You can even invite your child in for a snuggle, for the dark will calm him down, especially if you talk low or turn on very soft music.

## CHILD CARE

Once you do go back to work, regardless of the age of your child, or whether you work full time or part time, at home or outside, you mustn't feel guilty about it. You and the baby will do just fine if you have a relaxed attitude; if you look at the job as one more adventure to be enjoyed, and if you have the best, most reliable sitting arrangements you can find.

No matter which kind you choose, however, your child must be prepared for it. Any child will need some special comfort, like one of your perfumed scarves and—for the child who can talk—full, matter-of-fact information: you're going out, just like Mommy; you'll be home every night, just like me. Since the unknown is so scary and the abstract so unreal, it would help if you actually took your Four to work, then turned right around and went to the day care operation, so he could see where you would be all day and how quickly you could get to him. Once a child knows what to expect, he won't be so anxious.

Begin the sitting arrangement a week before you actually start work, because your child will need you around for at least part of the time the first few days, no matter who takes care of him. If he's in unfamiliar surroundings, bring him home after lunch, since a nap in a strange place can be the last straw for a child.

When you do leave him full-time, he should know just what he'll be doing all day and what he'll be doing when you get back, since he tells time by his activities, not by the clock. Finally, you should never, or almost never, be late. A child can always adjust to a working mother if the arrangements are good, and his mom is on time.

Your true importance will, perhaps, be your big shock if you're a first-time mother. In your heart you'll be afraid that your dear little child might like the sitter best, and then you slowly realize the truth. It would be as impossible for your child to prefer someone else as it would be for you to prefer another child. Once you cross that emotional hurdle, child care won't be nearly so threatening.

There are many choices you can make, and the right child care for you is the one that suits your family best.

### AT HOME

There are three types of caregivers who might care for your child at home—a mother's helper, who would come by the day, and an au pair or a nanny, who would live with you. An at-home arrangement can be the best for the pre-One, but it's the most expensive and requires the most careful kind of checking, for this sitter will be alone with your child all day.

In any case, you want a sitter who's healthy and active; who speaks English well enough to understand your orders and handle emergencies; whose references check out completely, and who is affectionate, easygoing and responsive—just like you. This is the sitter who'll play with your child on the floor, eyeball to eyeball; take him on outings every day, and encourage playmates—even if they only stare at each other at the park. Most of all, you want a sitter who is kind and talkative, whatever her language. If she treats your child's sobs with silence, or warns of bogeymen or spankings, she can create serious fears.

You can get the best if you pay a little more than the customary salary, or give a "reliability bonus" for prompt and regular attendance, since the sitter's dependability is essential for a working mother. Your peace of mind is worth a few extra dollars.

You also should establish the two-week vacation, the holidays and the sick days you'll give—in writing—before she starts, as well as the Social Security and unemployment you'll pay and the chores you'll expect her to do. This may even include driving, if she has a valid license and a clean record.

Of the three at-home sitters, the mother's helper is often the best, since she'll do the heaps of laundry and the many time-consuming chores that come with a young baby. When the choice must be made, however, she knows that loving a fussy baby all morning is more important than cleaning the house.

Although you will lose a chunk of your privacy, you may want to hire a live-in—either an au pair or, in the words of the rich, a nanny—if you often work late or on weekends.

According to mothers who have had them, an au pair—who is usually between eighteen and twenty-five and from a small town or another country—can be great or ghastly. This will depend on her maturity, and whether she has a boyfriend back home. If she's unattached, if you make her feel like part of the family, and if you work through an agency that specializes in au pairs and screens them well, you should have a good experience.

You can expect your au pair to take care of your child and do light housekeeping for about nine-and-a-half hours a day, five-and-a-half days a week, with one full weekend off every month and a two-week vacation, and to stay about a year. For this you'll pay her slightly over a hundred dollars a week—based on the 1990 dollar—and give her meals, a private room and her own television—if only so she will keep out of your space when she's off-duty.

The nanny, however, who has usually taken a two-year training course in child care, is a cross between a sitter and a governess, and she doesn't do windows or houses either. Instead she devotes herself to the child, and though she'll cook and clean and maybe do laundry, she'll do it only for the two of them. In exchange, she gets her own room and TV, usually stays for four to five years, gets a paid vacation and benefits, and is paid much, much more than any other help. She is usually worth it too, as long as you get along and you give her enough psychological space, for a good nanny usually keeps a little distance from the family.

## DAY CARE

Sometimes a relative will watch your baby at her house, which is cheap and often very good, but this arrangement can be fraught with friction, especially if she's unpaid. A member of the family often thinks she can interfere with your methods, the way no sitter would dare to do.

Child care methods in family day care, however, or in a day care center—particularly a center connected with your work—tend to be more predictable, since you have a chance to observe them beforehand.

You're looking for a safe, happy atmosphere, where your child will be treated with affection and respect and where parents are expected to treat the providers with respect too. Anyone who is good enough and dedicated enough to take care of your child deserves consideration, as well as smiles and compliments, and as much notice before you take a vacation—or leave your provider—as you would expect to get in return.

This equality should be woven throughout your relationship, so you feel free to exchange information about your child, to make sure he is getting the best.

There are some negative aspects to any day care operation, of course, and extra illnesses lead the list. Since children from One to Three share their germs better than they share anything else, you'll have to keep your child out of day care when he is sick, and keep him home until the fever has been gone for a day. You can send him to a day care center designed for sick children, but it's better to let him stay home, in familiar surroundings, which means that you have to have the names of reliable backup sitters or an agency handy or plan to stay home yourself.

### Family Day Care

If you want your child to be with other children, and yet still be in a home, try family day care instead. Here the provider is licensed—after a police check, a medical checkup and a home visit by the social worker—and is usually allowed to care for up to six children at a time at her home, with not more than two of them under Two.

Even with all this official approval, you'll want to have a thoughtful interview with the provider yourself, to see that cleaning supplies, medicines, liquor, vitamins and knives are out of reach; empty electrical sockets are covered; gates—but not accordion gates—are at the top and bottom of the stairs; windows are screened; toys are sturdy, and the provider has a car seat for each child of forty pounds or less and a seat belt for each older child.

Each child also needs a place to hang his coat and take his nap, and there should be a quiet nook to let him get away from the action too. A card table draped with a sheet makes a terrific hideaway, but it may not look like much to you, especially if the children have left some canned goods on the floor, after playing a game of store. As long as the house is clean, however, a little mess is perfectly all right. In fact, a tidy,

tidy place should give you pause, for it may mean the provider would rather tend the house than the children.

You'll want to make sure the provider serves very little junk food and processed food, of course, not just because fresh fruit and homemade foods are better for your child's health, but because they're better for his behavior too.

Ask what activities the provider has given the children in the past month, both at home and in the neighborhood. An imaginative provider will take the children to a museum or a petting zoo about once a month; go to the library every week for a story time; and give them daily walks and outdoor play. You're looking for someone who usually sets up paints or clay for a while every day, reads them a story every two to three hours, limits them to maybe a half-hour of television twice a day, and gives them lots of snuggles, fitting the children into her own schedule, like any mom.

Above all, you want a provider who has about the same values, the same philosophy and the same humor that you do, and who seems to like her little charges almost as much as her own.

You can tell a great deal by the way the children respond to her, but you'll have to ask about the discipline. You want her to give about the same kind that you do, but more gently. A child can take the very occasional spanking from his parents, because he always knows that they love him, but he won't feel so safe with his provider.

Even if everything seems perfect at this family day care, you want your child to spend a half-day with the provider before you sign the contract. This agreement should not only give you both a two-week trial, but it should spell out the rules and the costs. You'll be expected to pay a set amount each week (and on time), even if your child doesn't go; to pay extra if you're more than fifteen minutes late to pick up your child, and to pay for one week of vacation and six holidays, as you would to a day care center.

*Day Care Centers*

A day care center should meet the social, intellectual, emotional and physical needs of your child as completely as you do, and most directors will insist that it does. You can't tell how a center is run by the way it looks in the brochure, but you can tell a great deal by an interview, a morning of observation and by the way the children act. In a well-run center, the children look happy to get there, and happy to be there, most of the time.

This center will have a director who is organized enough to run her job well and relaxed enough to enjoy it, in part because she has a teacher and one or two aides—men and women—for every eighteen children in each age group. Since the staff members take care of the total child, they will not only be articulate, smart, patient and creative, but they will offer a lot of hugging, lap-sitting and cuddling so a child can dare to show his sadness and his anger, as well as his joy. This helps a child keep his individuality, which is tarnished easily when he spends most of this waking hours as part of a group.

The center should meet other criteria too. The room should be clean and well organized, the playground should have several pieces of climbing equipment and there should be room to run outdoors, and, if possible, inside.

No center should be so perfect that it is self-contained, however. The children need short walks, other playgrounds and small field trips to make each day different from the next, as well as interesting activities on their own turf. These are often woven into creativity, as they are at one well-run center, where the children market for yellow foods on "Y" day and then, with great importance, cook their yellow lunch.

Food and sleep are most important to day care children, for the constant company and continuing activity often make them hungrier and sleepier than they would be at home. Each child should have a nutritious hot lunch, and morning and afternoon snacks—all processed as little as possible—as well as breakfast for those who come early and an extra snack for those who stay late. Each child also needs his own cot and blanket for the regular daily nap (and for an irregular morning one if he'd like).

You also want to ask how much the teachers and aides are paid—since the centers that pay a little extra usually attract the best staff—and how long they have to work each day. Because teachers and aides must give so much of themselves, none should work longer than seven hours—and this includes an hour for lunch. Although the teaching staff works on staggered shifts, aides often substitute at lunch or when a teacher is sick, so they must be well qualified, either through schooling or experience. Warmth is not enough.

The staff should involve the parents with a few hours of volunteer work a month too so they will be on a more collegial basis, and should hold regular meetings with them as a group. The teacher also should give a progress report to each set of parents regularly, to let everybody exchange information about the child. This makes child care smoother at school and at home.

Even if your child is in the best of all day care centers, he'll need an extra amount of privacy at home to make up for the lack of it at school, and he'll need an extra amount of undivided attention from you and your husband at night. Day care is a supplement to parents, never a replacement.

## SINGLE PARENT

In the beginning the single parent has more troubles, more fears, more loneliness and less money than most other parents—but she often has more joy. There is something supremely satisfying about tackling—and doing—a very tough job, even if it means eating beans and rice every day for a while and crying yourself to sleep.

Once you've reached the turning point, when you know you can handle a separation, divorce or widowhood with dignity and dispatch, you develop an authority no one can ever take away from you. There's nothing like experience to give you a graduate degree in motherhood. It's getting from here to there that's hard.

This can be a little easier on you, if you get some help. Look for free support groups that deal with death or divorce—or the problem that caused it. Or go to a single-parent workshop, where you will meet others in your situation and learn how to handle your child and your anger, as well as find legal and financial aid from both government and private sources.

Even a six-year-old will profit by being in a group with other children facing the same uncertainties. It also helps if some of them are older and a pace or two ahead, so he'll know that he will soon feel better too. This is especially true if you and his dad have divorced. According to some studies, it takes five years for a child to get over divorce—and that's with therapy.

If there isn't a group for him—and they're hard to find unless you live in a city—you could put your child into art or play therapy for a few months. It's hard enough to be a single parent; don't try to be a full-time therapist too.

You're bound to be a part-time therapist for your child, however, and possibly the best one, for a single parent usually deals with her children in a way that is quite satisfying and one all parents should copy. The pressures of your new life make it much more likely that you will admit your mistakes to your child, if only because you're too tired to keep them to yourself, and this is sure to please him. There's nothing a child likes better than knowing that his mom can be wrong too.

You'll also find that you're much more candid with him than you once were, not to weigh him down with worry, but to let him know that you depend on him, just as he depends on you—that you guys are on the same team.

This will make him seem a little more grown-up than most young children, but he still will have the one fear that haunts all children in a single-parent home. No matter what the age, they have the same unspoken question: if you go away too, what will happen to me? Don't wait for your child to ask you, since he almost surely won't. You need to make the arrangements and then tell him about them too, in a casual, matter-of-fact way. Even a four-year-old has the right to know who will care for him if you get sick or have to go away.

While you're making plans for your child, make a few for yourself. You occasionally need to get out in the evening with other women and on dates. It will remind him that you have other friends, and it will remind you to make an effort to keep them. Every mother is a person first.

## REMARRIAGE

Divorce—with all its sound and fury—is very upsetting to a child, but a second marriage can be almost as disturbing. Here is this child, surrounded by love and joy and plans and excitement, and suddenly no one has much time for him. Even if your child is barely old enough to talk, he will be aware of the signs of change all around him, and change is scary.

A Four may talk about the remarriage, ask a few questions—maybe even ask if you'll still love him—but he won't let you know that he's truly worried, or wondering where he'll fit in.

If you or your ex-husband are going to marry again, your child needs constant reassurance. He should know all about your plans and the role he'll play in the wedding and, if possible, the vows.

In one lovely remarriage ceremony, the parent and the stepparent promise to love and honor each other and then they promise to love, honor and care for the child. At that point they give him a small medallion on a chain (see Resources, page 390), so the child knows he is truly part of the new family. This kind of inclusion can make all the difference.

## STEPPARENTS

A stepchild can bring you many joys and many stresses too.

These stresses are inevitable, because there is a strong, primitive link between a child and his natural parents. You don't want to undercut these links, but you do want to forge a strong new one of your own. This will be the kindest thing you can ever do for this child, and it will be the smartest thing you ever did for yourself. A good relationship with your stepchild won't ensure a happy marriage, but a bad relationship can endanger it.

The child—whatever his age—needs you to treat him as fairly, lovingly and respectfully as you would treat your own child. All children in the family—stepchildren or not—deserve even-handed attention and even-handed discipline. If you don't give it, they will play one parent against the other and the relationship with your stepchild will turn into one long competition.

You can't compete with the first wife either, no matter how much she may annoy you or how much you may resent the child support your husband must pay. If you get ensnared in those traps, you will be tense with your stepchild, who will think he's causing the tension, for young children are terribly egocentric. Even if he could understand what was going on, it would tear his loyalties apart and at a time when he's trying so hard to be true to them.

If you find it tough to be gracious, imagine a walk in the child's small shoes, shuffling from one house to the other and from one set of rules to another. The younger the child, the less he can understand this revolution in his life. It's your job to be so steady the stepchild knows he can always depend on you, and so loving he will want to depend on you.

The stresses will still be there, but you'll handle them best if you know what to expect, so you can sidestep some of them, laugh at others and rise above the rest, most of the time.

## GRANDPARENTS

Grandparents can be one of your child's great strengths, but you'll have to set the tone. You need to act so competent they won't try to take over and so considerate they won't feel put upon and you'll have to keep them so well informed they'll want to stay in touch with your child, as well as with you, even if they don't live in your area.

The links you forge will depend on you. You're the one who sees those first smiles, hears those first words and takes all of those snapshots. If you share the information freely, the grandparents will want to share themselves. This may not be easy for them to do, particularly if they're busy and working, or if they're naturally reticent people, but if you keep reaching out, your child can bring you together, even if you've never gotten along that well with your parents or your in-laws.

It's particularly important to encourage the connection with your in-laws, even if your marriage has been broken by death

or divorce. Grandparents have the right to know their grandchildren and grandchildren have the right to know them and their heritage. You'll do this best if you accept the grandparents as they are—if only so they'll accept you—and let them know that their grandchild needs them. And he does. Children need people who are happy just to ooh and aah over them, to watch them and snuggle them, without being in a big hurry to do something else. They need someone to show them pictures of their mothers and fathers when they were little—an unbelievable sight—and to tell them how they behaved, and misbehaved. This can be very reassuring to a Four.

If the grandparents are reluctant to sit, listen to the nuances in their conversation. It may not be the request that bothers them but the details. They may not like to sit as long or as late as you want, or to be asked at the last minute, or they may rather sit in their own home, where they feel cozy, or in yours, so their place won't be turned upside down.

Even if the grandparents live far away, you can stay in touch with regular low-rate weekend phone calls and particularly if you give them a tape recorder and some blank tapes. Ask them to sing and talk to your baby, so you can play their voices to him, and when he's a little older ask them to read his favorite stories on a tape, for him to turn the pages while he listens. And by all means, send them tapes of the baby's first words, and later his silly songs and jokes. Grandparents and grandchildren will never really be strangers, as long as their voices are friends.

The video camera is another great way to patch the distance, even if you only live across town. You can rent one when you get together, and then your Three can play the tape as often as he likes. It will enchant him as much as the ones he plays of your wedding and his first birthday party.

There will be time when a close connection with the grandparents may make you feel a bit competitive, but never forget: your child still listens to you most and loves you best, by a very wide margin. The grandparents may give him a little extra candy and a little extra attention and he may demand too much of you for a day or two after they have visited, but we all need to be spoiled sometimes. Just brush his teeth well, put the rest of the candy in the freezer and give him a kiss when he weeps. Parents know best, and your child knows it.

# BEHAVIOR

Discipline—the most misunderstood word in the language of motherhood—is just another way to show your love.

A child's behavior varies from age to age, from good to bad and then when you think you can't stand it anymore, to good again. To help you anticipate this behavior we've written a chronological account of what you can expect and what you can do about it. Basically, all solutions revolve around the boundaries you set. They are the essence of discipline, and every child at every age needs them to feel comfortable in her society and to feel the security that comes from knowing that someone cares enough to bother.

There are, we found, two sides to discipline—the positive, which makes a child want to be in these boundaries, and the negative, which keeps him there. However,

it will be the physical limits, like the rim of a coin, that hold these sides together and the good manners you'll insist upon that will add the luster.

The ratio of positive to negative discipline determines her behavior. Your attitudes are fed into your child's makeup as surely as chromosomes at conception and can be almost as hard to change. Her character is like a fallow field. Something is going to grow there and whether it will bloom with dandelions or daisies depends on the seeds you sow.

Having tried more methods of discipline than we care to remember, and a few we'd rather forget, one secret became clear. The more positive we were, the less rebellious the child. Each successive child was easier to handle, not because the child was more disciplined, but because we were. We finally learned that since a young child's capabilities couldn't be raised, our standards had to be lowered.

You can be as relaxed with your first child as your last if you remember that the best discipline, like the best medicine, is preventive. It begins at birth, when you help your child get good food and enough sleep and exercise and activities—and especially praise—that make all of us happy.

Because respect is the heart of any relationship, all discipline must include it. When a child's rights are accepted, she'll begin to accept the rights of others. This is why you knock on your baby's door before you enter; correct your naughty Two in private; ask permission of your Three to see her latest drawings; and tell your child to hurry only when you must.

A child learns well from a person who respects her, who lets her enjoy some time alone and who takes a few minutes a day to explain concepts or to listen single-mindedly to her ideas. The respect you give now—or don't give—is returned in kind ten years from now.

Part of this respect hinges on the amount of safety and freedom you're willing to give your child, especially during her first years. Personally, we found it much less fatiguing for ourselves and less provocative for our children if we let physical boundaries say no, instead of us. This extra freedom buoys a child's ego, keeps you calm and, most importantly, prevents at least some of the accidents that beset families. The more active and inquisitive your child, the more precautions you'll have to take.

If you let your child stand up in the grocery cart, you'll pick some groceries, and possibly your child, off the floor and if you keep your ornaments on low tables, you'll sweep away a lot of memories. When you remove a temptation, you remove a rule and the fewer rules there are, the easier your child can live in dignity with the important ones that are left.

Even if you follow the philosophy of preventive discipline your child will need some corrections. For this we have the techniques of positive discipline (The Light Side) and negative discipline (The Dark Side).

The positive side of discipline is your anchor and the basis for the discipine you give in puberty, when the whole cycle is repeated and reinforced. You'd be wise to learn it now and learn it well.

Parents and policemen share a similar technique. Both operate best when one of their team is the "good detective." Although you and your husband need to be fairly consistent in your discipline, your approach will be different. If both of you are tough at the same time, your child will feel abandoned, and if both of you are soft, she'll have trouble handling criticisms later from other people.

The kind of discipline you give will

depend on her behavior and on her age, but your child will be Three before she can begin to be held accountable for her actions. Until then, she needs you to praise the good (even as there is less and less to praise), ignore most of the bad and try to postpone the spankings until she reaches that magic age. After Three, she'll need very few, if any, for reason usually works better than force.

Even if your child stays within every boundary you set—which she won't—we still must urge good manners too, from the table to the telephone, for manners and kindness are really the same.

We hope you won't think us as old-fashioned as our mentor, Lydia Maria Child, but we think every member in a family must have enough self-discipline to be kind to each other. This is the trick of a contented household.

# AGES AND STAGES

The behavior of boys and girls can vary by weeks at first, then by months and occasionally by as much as a year, with boys often running about six months behind girls by first grade. After the first year, their behavior follows the same path, however, winding its way through hills and valleys. You'll find your child acts better around her birthday, then sinks to new lows around the middle of the year—a breaking apart so she can put the pieces together in a new and better way.

## INFANCY

There are few flat statements we would dare make about motherhood except this: love never spoiled anyone, especially an infant. The cries of a helpless baby must be answered, even if neither of you knows what's the matter. If a child learns she can depend on you in her first year she'll obey you in later ones, for she listens best to people who listen to her.

In the early months you give milk, kisses and a steady change of diapers and scenery to keep her comfortable and interested, assuaging most tears before they fall. The baby should learn early that a crib is for sleeping, a playpen is for playing and a high chair is for eating, or you'll pluck toys from the applesauce and scrub dried bagels from the crib rails. When you simplify life your baby learns to do her jobs, like eating and sleeping, with dispatch. This is the way she begins to discipline herself.

## SIX MONTHS

This is the easiest age of all, but you still will need to second-guess her more every day. She will squirm when you dress her, which is why you strap her in place on the changing table, and she will throw toys from the walker for you to return. In this game, according to some experts, a child is sorting out the relationship between the movement of her fingers and the bang on the floor, but we suspect she's simply sorting out the relationship between baby in her walker and Mama going off her rocker. If you hang a few toys from the tray on lengths of elastic, she can reel them in for herself and the game will pall. For every problem there is at least a partial solution, if you think about it long enough: a comforting idea two years from now.

## NINE MONTHS

When she crawls, you'll have to forget how she was going to respect property. It's too much to ask of a pre-Three and certainly of her friends. She needs an increasingly childproofed environment to protect her from herself and make life easier for you.

### ONE

Now you become a master of diversion, swapping the hammer she found for the pull toy that rattles, and when that doesn't work, using a cross, no-nonsense look to carry your message. Since you mean so much to her, this often is discipline enough.

### FIFTEEN MONTHS

Suddenly, your child will get bolder every day—and she should. She needs to learn enough daring at this stage to last the rest of her life.

Although she doesn't want to damage anything, not all of her experiments will be successful. That's the way it is with scientists. One thing is certain: she'll be much sadder when she breaks one of her toys than when she breaks one of yours— just the way you are. It's as hard for her to understand the value you place on a teacup as it is for you to see the importance of her little plastic plane.

Your reaction to her experiments should be measured. A certain amount of cat catching is all right; too much is cruelty and must be stopped. Every child must feel her food a little bit, and at every meal, but you must decide, at every meal, when she has gone from eating to playing. Now you'll correct her with body English— physically removing her from the scene of mischief—but don't fuss or even mention the transgression or she'll have to cry about it to keep her dignity.

Fifteen months is the first watershed in motherhood, when you're likely to let your child's bewildering quest for independence sink child care to a service level. Though you still confer with the pediatrician, there is that universal inclination to exaggerate, depending on how the last week went. Frankly, we found it very hard

to be objective in those brief sessions and think a husband probably gives the best day-to-day advice now. He not only has a greater stake, he makes home visits.

To keep a light heart, you also will need to evaluate your child together regularly, as unemotionally as if you were talking about someone who didn't belong to you. A child lucky enough to have two parents should have the guidance of both.

### MID-ONE

You will be giving some rules, but not too many, for motherhood is an easy power to abuse. Without any rules at all a child would be the tyrant of the first grade, or at least, a most unpopular person.

When you make a rule, your child will need at least a week to absorb it, and still it must be repeated. Speak clearly, directly, eyeball to eyeball, holding her hands and using the same words each time. She'll concentrate on the new rule so hard you can expect her to forget most of the old ones for a while.

Your child will have a much better chance to be good if you give a direction she can obey and if you're willing to see that she does. When you don't care enough to follow through, she certainly won't.

Everyone likes praise—the more we get, the more we want—which is mighty helpful to remember when dealing with children. You can always find something good in a child's behavior, which guarantees more of the same. However, you mustn't praise everything with the same intensity, or she'll value none of it, nor must you praise everything good that she does, or she'll become addicted to praise and yet feel oppressed by such constant attention.

The indirect compliment often is best, beginning with a mid-One. No matter how preoccupied your child may appear, she hears every word you say about her to others. We found there was no finer way to say "I love you" to a child than for her to eavesdrop on a compliment, particularly if you're talking to her father. Conversely, an overheard criticism is so powerful that it's almost an intolerable method of rebuke and shouldn't be used.

When your child disobeys, which will be often, your criticism must ring with kindness. If your standards are too exacting, your pre-Three will become either very anxious or very naughty. She knows she can't win.

You surely have gone through the agony of a correction from a favorite boss—who wasn't even twice your size—so you can appreciate the power you carry. Just multiply it by ten. Your love and acceptance are more important to your child than anything else in the world.

She can understand being put in a corner for scrubbing the toilet bowl with your toothbrush, but the enormity of a spanking horrifies her. This should be the extreme punishment reserved for extreme behavior, such as running in the street or playing with fire.

### TWENTY-ONE MONTHS

Sometimes you can see what's making your child behave so poorly—and then there are times when even the best pediatrician can't figure it out. That's what is called a stage. If we remember that we all need more love in the bratty periods of our lives, it's a little more acceptable. Guide her with matter-of-fact praise for her goodness—for sharing a toy or coming when called—as if you expected this behavior all along and give more and more physical exercise to work off tensions. When she doesn't obey, there are many

reasonable methods of correction, most of which center around her isolation to a corner, or for a tantrum, to her room. The respite will be even better for you.

### TWO

A Two, like a young teenager, is building a lifetime of self-confidence, and like a young teenager, she needs her boundaries as loose as you dare to make them. This lets her think she is making her own decisions.

To do this, give few commands, always prefaced with an advance notice, and then give enough time for a child to obey. Also be sure to say your pleases and thank-yous, as you would to anyone else.

Although you may phrase an order politely, your child should know she has limited options. You don't ask, "Shall we go walking now?" but give her a specific option instead: "What will you take on your walk? Your magnet or your magnifying glass?" (Please remember she may take the plumber's friend instead or anything else to show you that she's master of her own destiny.) By giving her lesser choices, her independence is preserved and so is yours.

A change in a basic rule should be an event and if it's less than that you're breaking too many rules.

Your child should be like a special free-wheeling Twelve we know who explained happily to her mother that her good friend Babs was reared with great strictness.

"Just like me," she said, to her liberal mother's astonishment, explaining, "She can do anything she wants—only she better not try."

You'll set slightly different boundaries from any other mother, for each of us has a different threshold of tolerance, which no one can know but you—not your sister, not your neighbor, not even your doctor. You may draw the boundary very tightly in one area, very broadly in another, but to be comfortable, you must draw it yourself.

Any correction for breaking these boundaries must be quick, private, without humiliation or roughness and always followed by a kiss within about ten minutes. It also must be directed to the action and not the child. There's a great difference between telling a child that it's bad to throw a ball indoors and telling a child she is bad for throwing a ball in the house.

The closer your child gets to twenty-six months the lower your spirits will sink, for this is the nadir. You may rant hysterically and have tantrums too bizarre even to tell your husband, like the mother who sprayed the instant whipped cream all over her little child's head—after the child had done the same thing to her sofa. This behavior is normal for both of you, for to be charitable, a Two is as trying as she is funny—and she is very, very funny.

She is also a rather uncivilized person. Now she slowly learns that her family won't condone fighting, sauciness or physical or verbal attacks. It's not only uncivilized behavior, it's a pain to be around. In fact, we even think it's a poor idea for a child to name a doll or a punching bag after her baby sister and hit it when she's mad, for you're trying to teach her to live by her wits and not her fists. A child can learn to work off most of her aggressions with a good dig in the garden, a workout with some bread dough or a hammer and nails.

## MID-TWO

You can teach a mid-Two a little about giving but it isn't easy, for getting is more her style. Now she's beginning to learn right from wrong and like one of our favorites may say, "No, no, no" while emptying a bottle of Chanel No. 5 on her overalls.

There may be stages now, yours and hers, when you're just getting through the days as best you can, like a reformed alcoholic, one hour at a time, one day at a time. This is when you need a sitter for an hour every afternoon, or a job on the lunchtime shift of the neighborhood restaurant or some volunteer work, so you won't take your child so seriously. You need to have a rest every day, a Mother's Pickup in the afternoon (see page 118) and to see how many times you can say "yes" instead of "no."

As always when you have a problem, you need to keep a daily chart too. Record what time your child fell apart and when you did, what you both ate and how many no's you gave in a day (and how many you needn't have given). Sometimes you can see patterns and, therefore, solutions, but since it takes so long to chart and figure you may see her behavior improve anyway. That's because she's nearly Three.

## THREE

No one wants to be as good as a Three. This child becomes an accessory before the fact, instead of after it, and, therefore, so angelic you can see what a fine mother you are. She'll be even better if you tell her exactly what you expect of her and why before she asks.

A Three is not unlike one of our teenagers who was outraged at a certain job required of her, until we explained the need to do it.

"You know, Mother," she flounced, "even a teenager will do something if she has a reason."

At Three, a child can connect kindness with courtliness and likes to practice good manners. Help your child get along well with company by letting her have frequent visitors and telling them your house rules before they start a game. Above all, teach your Three how to share. It's a hard lesson to learn, but it's the basis of generosity and fundamental to love.

There are some pitfalls in discipline now, for your child may act so adult you forget she's just a baby. This is when you can overreact to her misbehavior and catch

yourself using the same angry words your
parents used with you when you were
young. The methods you use to discipline
your Three will affect her values for years.

If, for instance, dessert is a reward for
a clean plate then she'll think she should
be bribed to eat.

If you say a shot won't hurt when it
will or you'll be home soon when you
won't, she'll begin to doubt your word.

If you promise money for a job, she'll
put a price tag on family cooperation.

If you put property rights ahead of
personal rights, you'll rear a materialistic
child.

If you take the blame for her mistakes
she'll never learn to be accountable, and

If you don't make a big fuss over her
sometime, she won't feel she's worth the
trouble.

### FOUR

The Four (known as the out-of-bounds
Four) is as funny as the Two, but she's
more rational, because she talks so well
and because she often lets her conscience
be her guide. Now she needs to be the big
shot: faking bravado, telling outrageous
lies and playing grown-up. When Ramon
asked, "May I call you by your first
name?" we answered, "If you want to, but
you're the only boy in the world who can
call me Mother." So Mother it was.

Your child needs more special duties
now, more independence and wider
boundaries every few months to reward
her reliability.

She changes so quickly that clever handling one month, or even one week, will
be a witless bore the next. Never continue
any job or reward or routine to the point
of boredom, either hers or yours. Today
you might draw a fine Goodness Chart
(see page 89) on which to paste gold stars;
next week you might start a Job Jar (see
page 226); and days later you may change
her nap and bath schedule to make her
behave.

She'll be stubborn quite often now and

insist on doing things her way. It helps to
remember that you are bigger than she is
and if not smarter, at least you know
more. You're still Big Mama and what you
say goes.

### FIVE

A Five can meet her own high standards as
long as you let her get enough sleep, good
food, plenty of praise for good behavior
and plenty of love all the time. Serious
arguments start now and you must remember: it takes two to make a stubborn child,
and the other one is you. Try not to make
a big issue of something that doesn't matter.

We can remember once shrieking at our
Five, "Dammit! Quit That or I Will Hang
You by Your Thumbs in the Doorway
Until Tuesday!" Whereupon her blond-
haired visitor rolled her big blue eyes and
said thoughtfully, "My mother always
boils us in oil."

### SIX

A Six is an interested, interesting, reasonably obedient child and, like the Texas
politician, she knows you go along to get
along. This is the age of conformity and
she needs to please her buddies, her
teacher and the neighbor lady, most of
whom seem to have your standards, thank
goodness. This is the time to appeal to
your child's courtliness by having her open
the door for you. To do this, always stand
in front of it without saying anything until
she opens it out of impatience and then
you slip through first, fast as a flash, and

thank her for her good manners. She'll even think it was her idea.

When school begins, you'll forget most of her poor behavior and feel a certain amount of confusion and shame over the discipline you gave at one time or another.

At least mothers have improved since our pal Lydia Maria Child said, "Call me modern if you will," for her opposition to spanking and advised other punishment.

"Do not shut the child in the closet, but simply tie him in an armchair when he has been naughty."

Now we use whipped cream.

<hr>

## ◇               BOUNDARIES               ◇

Motherhood can be fairly easy or it can be quite anxious, depending on the limits you set. We set quite a few.

### CHILDPROOFING THE CHILD

A newborn can be very strong and can flip over without a warning, as we remember to our amazement when our hungry Mali rolled over to her back in a rage at only five days old. Always strap your child in place on the changing table, in the car seat or in the infant seat, and later in the high chair and the stroller.

While a disabled mother may find it essential to harness her toddler, even a spiral cord, attached from the child's wrist to the mother's, is a fairly unnecessary safety measure for a healthy parent.

We would oppose it totally (perhaps because it looks so demeaning) if it weren't for that horrendous trip alone with two pre-Twos, when one disappeared at the airport. Ordinarily, a mother should set aside more time for her errands and carry fewer packages. A child's hand is much nicer to hold.

Just as you teach your child that "hot" can be dangerous long before she tries to cook, you also should teach her that streets are not playgrounds—especially if you live in the city. You'll watch your child carefully, but by mid-Two, she can understand the concept of danger. Let her help you fill a paper bag with some impersonal ob-jects—twigs, a plastic teacup, an inflated balloon—and help you leave it in the street for a few minutes at rush hour. A bag of breakage for her to examine is a graphic lesson in caution.

When your child is Three, you can trust her on the sidewalk if you draw boundaries in chalk on the cement or on the ground with a stick. These barriers will be as difficult for her to cross as a chasm. Expand these boundaries every few months, according to her own expanding sense of responsibility.

We don't think any pre-Six should cross streets alone. Any streets. If traffic is very light she'll forget to watch for cars, and if it's heavy she'll have trouble noticing everything at once. A young child, no matter how bright, has trouble gauging distance in relation to speed.

### THE HOUSE

Most accidents, like most tantrums, can be prevented.

Block the top and the bottom of any stairs or you'll be running up and down all day to keep track of your child.

Use a gate in any doorway you don't want her to cross. You also can slip a sock on the knob, fastened with a rubber band, which a child can't open (and possibly you can't either).

At the start of each day, put your wastebaskets out of reach—it's much easier than picking up the trash again and again—

and check the floor for small items that could choke a child.

Have no matches, cigarette lighters or space heaters within reach, plug empty electric sockets with blanks and band the head-splitting edges of low tables with foam tape, especially if they have marble or glass tops. Lay rugs over skidproof pads, jam books into their shelves so tightly a child can't remove them, close bureau drawers so your little climber won't turn them into a ladder and cleat any window cords so your child won't wrap them around her neck.

Realistically a child can respect no more than one treasure in a room. The rest of your breakables can be handled two ways. Either put your treasures out of reach or stay in the room with your child and say "No" to her and her friends every time they touch an ornament. In either case a child will learn not to touch them when she's Three—and not before. Naturally, for us the easy way won every time, but occasionally we think you should take an ornament from its shelf, talk to your child about it, let her look at it, smell it and caress it to see why in the world you like it so much. Then put it on a higher shelf so she won't investigate it on her own. In this way your pre-Three can be trusted as long as twenty minutes awake and alone in one room.

### THE KITCHEN

The kitchen is a pre-Two's favorite playroom. To keep it safe, turn the pot handles inward on the stove and boil and fry foods on the back burners and simmer on the front ones. Sweep up broken glass and then pick up the small shards with a wet paper towel. It works like glue, if not like magic.

Don't use a tablecloth if you have a toddler—she'll just pull it down and everything with it—and use safety catches if you need to keep drawers shut.

Use and immediately discard those household cleaners you don't need regularly. Store the rest in a high cupboard,

locked if your child is a climber. Babies taste new foods regularly and drink juice from odd-shaped bottles, so sampling a little lemon-flavored furniture polish isn't as peculiar to a child as it would be to you. Three tablespoons of it can kill a One and a fingerful of dishwasher compound is nearly fatal at that age. There are a quarter-million lethal household products available, most of which aren't labeled poison (see Poison, page 133).

A young child may be especially intrigued by whiskey and cigarettes, which can be toxic and they should also be kept out of reach.

### THE BATHROOM

A bathroom requires special precautions for no one place has so many lures in so small an area. Since your child will turn on the shower (and frighten herself witless), you need to reduce the hot-water thermostat to medium if possible, and keep a faucet protector over your tub spigot, so she can't get burned.

Use only plastic glasses in the bathroom, to avoid breakage; keep any razor out of reach, put all medicines and vitamins in a locked cupboard in childproof safety bottles and throw away obsolete drugs. Your child, as smart as she is, can't understand why sweet cough syrup is all right one day and verboten the next.

Even the toilet is unsafe for a mid-One, who can topple into the bowl and drown, and a late Two should never play alone in the bathroom either. Sooner or later she'll lock herself in, or flush a diaper down the toilet or squiggle pictures from the toothpaste tube. When you have time to join her, let her flush and brush as long as she wants. This curbs a little of her curiosity. In the meantime, fix the door so she can't lock it.

### THE CAR

The most careful, sensible parents often ignore the laws of safety and good sense when they step into an automobile. We can't think of any place you need them more. A baby held in a passenger's arms is much less safe than a baby in a carrier. The less a person weighs, the farther she'll be thrown forward in a sudden stop. Even with air bags, restraints are still essential. With nearly two thousand young children killed in automobile accidents every year,

you just don't have the right to relax these boundaries. All states now require restraints and so does your own common sense. Your child is irreplaceable.

Your baby needs an infant carrier from the time she leaves the hospital until she can sit up by herself and weighs about 20 pounds; then she graduates to a car seat. Look for government-certified, highly rated car seats and learn exactly how to install and use them, or they won't really be safe.

You'll also want a car seat that lets you lift your child in and out of it with some ease. It will still be fairly awkward, but it would be worth it even if safety weren't a factor. When a child is buckled in place, she can't block the rearview mirror or yell in your ear.

You can switch your child to a seat belt when she weighs about forty pounds and you'll need as many belts as you have passengers, including the car-pool children. If a child won't wear her belt, however, don't bother to start the motor. Tell her why, but only once, and don't say another word until she surrenders. A few of these silent scenes—which never last more than ten minutes—make a child cooperate, if only out of boredom. If she unbuckles when you're driving, the treatment is the same. Pull over to the side of the road and wait, even if it means getting out of the car and standing outside. That's how we learned to wear seat belts ourselves.

# THE LIGHT SIDE

Every child tries to rule the house, but you'll never meet the child who really wants to, and you'll pity the one who does, for she is never happy. Although parents are in charge, we do think you should respect your child enough to listen to her ideas, especially on family projects. Even if her suggestions are bad, she'll like to examine the options too and learn that she's the very important, very junior member and not the focus of the group.

Some families hold structured weekly meetings, but for us informality works best, in a setting where everyone has a full chance to speak. We never put a question to a vote, however, unless we don't care what happens (or like a Chicago alderman, we know what the outcome is going to be).

We think you'll find this positive approach to discipline will let your child make a few decisions, so it will be easier for her to accept the many you make. Still, every mother should shrink herself in half and imagine what it feels like to be ordered around all day. The more a person is told what to do, the more recalcitrant she grows. Dignity becomes so precious that your child will stall every request and say no to every order, even as she complies.

Your orders will range from the simple request to the urgent command and not one should be given unless you're willing to enforce it immediately. A child learns quickly how many times you're willing to repeat the order before you mean what you say. It may be once or it may be seven times. If you shorten your fuse she'll believe you the first time and if you have her tell you when she's done, you won't have to tell her again. Otherwise, you'll be a nag.

### GOODNESS CHART

Goodness deserves recognition. A chart full of gold stars on the bulletin board guarantees compliments. Use any accomplishments you want, but not too many.

| bed | ☆ | | | ☆ | | | | |
|-----|---|---|---|---|---|---|---|---|
| teeth | | ☆ | ☆ | | ☆ | | | |
| dishes | | ☆ | | | | | | |

### QUIET RESPONSES

A child is often blamed for a noisy household but it's the mother who decides how noisy it will be. A lively family is a joy, but senseless clamor eventually shatters everyone's nerves. There are ways to avoid it, all hinging on respect. If you whisper

when she shouts, the loudest child will lower her voice the way you do when your boss has laryngitis. If she doesn't, tell her you can't hear for all the noise. Eventually, you may shout less yourself.

### EASY OBEDIENCE

Discipline is easiest if you take a positive point of view. It's never "Time for you bath," but "It's time for your duck to have a swim," and it isn't "Bedtime," but "Let's hurry to bed so we can read a long story instead of a short one."

Although your maneuvers get more sophisticated, the positive technique still works—even, we were surprised to find, for a Seventeen.

**MEET MR. BUZZER**

Children between Two and Five often obey best if someone else gives them their orders, rather than you. Paint a face on your kitchen timer and let Mr. Buzzer decide when a turn is up, or when it's time to wash hands or go to sleep. He even lets you give stickers and hugs to a child who can pick up his toys before he buzzes.

### ADVANCE NOTICE

A Two especially needs a ten-minute warning before bed or a bath, a meal or a walk, so that she can adjust to the idea. After that, you should have a "Let's go/no-nonsense" attitude she can respect, although she may try you out with a game of procrastination. At this point, resort to body English. Pick her up, give her a smile and get on your way.

### WARNING

Every child finds obedience hard sometimes, but there are a couple of techniques to make it easier.

We found it best to give our children a stern "To the count of six" or whatever, but the punishment was never specified, which made it more dicey.

Choose whatever number you think will give your child time to finish the job, counting slower or faster so she can obey. Or try the same threat our Creole aunt would use, "I'm going to *claquer* you!"

We quickly did as we were told, since we didn't know what that meant and now our children do the same. And we still don't know what it means.

### GIVING CORRECTIONS

It's hard to discipline a child when you're angry. If you're furious—no matter how justified—give yourself a time out, by going in another room, taking a dozen deep breaths, splashing cold water on your face, having a cry—anything rather than lashing out too strongly, verbally or physically.

When you do chastise your child, put your hand on her arm. You'll know you have to be more gentle if you start to feel her skin crawl away from your touch, even though your tough little guy looks so stoic and unrepentant.

If you fuss too much, apologize afterward, and then apologize again at night, even if you have to wake her up. Parents have too much power to let themselves abuse it.

### INDOOR SUMMONS

Unless you think your child is in danger, don't go to her when she yells. If you hear, "Come see how many doodlebugs I caught for you," just call to say where you are and say absolutely nothing more. She'll come to you.

If you want to talk with your child and it's not an emergency, call her name and say where you are and if she answers, "What?" or "Why?" don't answer back. Sooner or later she'll learn to call, "Coming, Mom" (in ten to twelve years), especially if you tell her later that you were calling her to get an ice cream cone. In the meantime you will have a little more peace

than most mothers, and probably more doodlebugs.

### OUTDOOR SUMMONS

No mother can call loud enough to be heard by her child a half block away. You either will sound like a shrew, or the other children will mimic you and embarrass your child. Use a whistle or a bell instead.

### INSTANT OBEDIENCE

Every mother has a special tone to warn her child of danger, which requires instant obedience. This is the sharp, serious voice that keeps her on the curb or away from the hot spigot and if it doesn't, you might give a single swat on the backside to emphasize what you say. If you use the same tone—or the same swat—to tell your child to put down a vase or pick up her toys you'll dilute your control when you need it.

### ALLOWANCE

We include this subject in discipline, not because we think it should be there, but because so many other people do.

To us, an allowance is just another way to give a little love—not essential for a pre-Six but nice for her to have. We think you and your husband should remember that the gift of an allowance, like any gift, has no strings attached and should never be given as a reward nor withheld as a punishment.

A child shouldn't be paid for communal work any more than you should be paid for driving the car pool or for cutting the grass. This is the difference between a family and a business.

The allowance your child receives is her own, to be used as she likes. Whether she wants to spend it on candy or sock it away in a sock or throw it in the gutter is her business. Although you will encourage some thrift, she needs to experiment for herself. However, since a preschool child is so likely to lose her money and because we don't believe in giving children much in the first place, we keep our stipends very low.

A Five will enjoy perhaps a quarter a week, graduating to fifty cents by Six, when she finally can begin to appreciate money. After that, we follow the advice of a pediatrician who gives her nine children annual increments of fifty cents a week at every birthday, so that a Seven receives $1.00, and an Eight gets $1.50. This regulated schedule, of whatever sum you set, eliminates any whining about who deserves raises and when.

*MAKING UP*

Most quarrels with your child are over in minutes, but some arguments are so angry they can fester for hours.

Whether you're right—or wrong, as mothers often are—you surely said more than you meant, for which you should apologize quickly and, since you're the

adult, you should apologize first. After that comes the big make-up.

A Three will welcome a quiet visit at bedtime and a chance to mend the ties. We found darkness sheds a special light on lovers and small children, unlocking words too tender to say by day and softening any tough ones. Now she can understand why you got so mad and forgive you for getting as mad as you did. Somehow what was inexplicable to her by day becomes quite sensible by night and a problem that was hopeless to you in the morning has a fresh solution.

# THE DARK SIDE

No matter how well you handle your child, neither of you will be perfect, even some of the time. There will always be enough weeping and punishments to make you appreciate the good days.

If you think there isn't enough sunshine you may be saying no too many times. To give you less to fuss about, simplify the rules of the house and remember: your child's sense of injustice is more acute now than it ever will be again in her life. It takes great wisdom to fit the punishment to the crime.

*FUSSINESS*

If an infant is fussy, she may be bored, for not even a baby likes to stay in one place for more than a half-hour. Move her often, from tummy to back/to the bathtub/the carriage/the *very* gently sloped infant seat/the sling/the blanket on the floor or a rest in your arms, with or without a feeding.

A brand-new talker is especially apt to fuss: she can't find the words to tell you what's wrong. You can tell your child instead. Our friend Carol quickly calms her son down by saying, "I know you're hungry. We'll have lunch as soon as we finish this errand."

When a Two won't eat, won't take a bottle, won't play—and won't stop fussing—take her temperature, for she may be sick. If she's simply out of sorts, put her quickly to bed so she can glue herself together in privacy and without any special treats. If a child is given a lollipop when she's cross, she'll think poor behavior is supposed to be rewarded.

A Four to Six gets sent outdoors to run back and forth a dozen times, then is retired to her room to rest with books or tapes.

### THE CORNER

By mid-One the bloom of rosy motherhood gets paler every day, and it's time for some negative discipline. Corners must have been invented for this.

When your child disobeys, escort her to The Corner "to think about it" or simply put her on a special out-of-the-way chair for this time-out. In either case, you'll have to hold her shoulders in place the first few times until she'll go there when she's told. Expect a mid-One to last no more than two minutes, a Six no more than ten. Set Mr. Buzzer, your friendly kitchen timer, to tell her when she can come back.

### WHINING, FOUL LANGUAGE, BACK CHAT

Some of us can stand a child who whines or who talks back and some of us can stand one who uses nasty language, but you shouldn't put up with much of either. If you tolerate this sort of thing at Four, it's bound to escalate.

We no longer wash out young mouths in the manner of our foremothers, but disinterest can be just as effective, as long as you show it every time. Tell your child you can't hear her when she whines, won't listen to her when she's fresh and don't want to be around her when she uses bad language. And then go about your business, without giving her any attention at all. She may test you more at first, but since she wants to be heard, she'll soon come around. Give her a big kiss and a welcome back.

### BICKERING AND WRANGLING

Every household has its fractiousness, but you can make some of it less likely most of the time and refuse to put up with the rest.

We finally have learned it's easier to prevent a fight than to settle one. That's why it's best for Fours—visitors or brothers and sisters—to be interrupted every half-hour with a small adventure, a story or something to eat before they start to fuss. Sixes can last almost an hour without wrangling.

### FIST FIGHTS

Children must learn to resolve their differences for themselves—up to a point. A fist fight is that point, we think, particularly if one child is bigger than the other. Separate your fighters, putting them in different rooms, for it's hard to fight an absent enemy.

A Three begins to understand that words start fights—and stop them. When all of you are calm (in about ten minutes), talk over the quarrel to show each child the other's point of view—but never talk so long that you have a rematch.

The discussion can be such a bore a Six may find a fist fight rarely worth the bother.

### NEIGHBORHOOD SQUABBLES

If your child is in a neighborhood quarrel, listen to both sides as the arbiter, not the champion. The mother who automatically believes her child is right is as unfair as the one who always takes the word of an outsider. Each situation is different. If you must punish do it with dispatch, discretion and, of course, in private.

## BITING

Even at six months, a child discovers she can bite you, pull your hair and kick while you change her. It won't be funny at all at eighteen months and then she must be corrected. We remember a sweet and simpering Two who would admonish her squalling baby brother with "Temper, temper," even as her teeth marks flared red on his arm. She never did it again after we put her own arm in her own mouth and gently pushed her own chin up until she bit it. This same technique works for hair pullers and pinchers too, but kickers go to the corner.

## TANTRUMS

A child has a tantrum when she's tired and frustrated, and the power of her own temper may frighten one child while it may embarrass and anger another. Hugs and reassurance calm the first child best, but the second one needs a little solitude, to save her dignity and yours. In either case, you don't give the child what she's crying for or she'll learn to have a tantrum wherever she can get the most attention: on the escalator at the department store or crossing the street while you're holding two packages and an infant. As awkward as it is, haul this screaming meemie to the quietest area you can find and let her be. Even if she holds her breath until she turns blue, she'll stop if you stop looking. Strangers aren't worth such dramatics. When she has contained herself, give your affection freely and plan your day a little better. There will be many fewer scenes if you run your errands in the morning when your child isn't tired, and if you give her fifteen to twenty minutes of single-minded attention every day—before she cries for it.

## LYING

A child who lies is either afraid of you—or she's Four. For a Four, just roll your eyes, listen to the brags and tell her she'll write great stories one day. Honesty comes easier at other ages if you ask the right questions. After the curtain is pulled to the floor (again), ask, "How did that happen?" not "Who did it?" or "Why?," since you know who did it and who cares why. When a child is given a yes/no choice she is more likely to lie her way out, which can become habitual with the crafty Five.

If your child lies, try to cure it with magic first. Send her to the next room, tell her to spin herself around three times and when she comes back she'll be able to tell you the truth. It's a trick that works for many infractions, for it give the child an excuse to change her behavior without losing face.

If magic doesn't work, send her to The Corner for ten minutes, and if she keeps on lying, just ignore her until she's back to her old honest self again. When your child does tell the truth, however—whether she does it immediately or later—give her your praise and a big kiss. This is the way she learns that honesty is more important than a broken rule—or a broken vase.

## JEALOUSY

We remember holding three bottles every afternoon—one for the new baby, another for the two-year-old sister and with a stretch of our fingers, a tiny bottle for the doll, who, her mistress said, was very, very jealous.

If your child is mad because there's a baby in the house, help her talk about it and keep her busy with more diversion and exercise. Show lots of love and show it before she falls apart. If your children nap at different times—though tough on you—you can give them each individual attention. You should know though that no matter how much attention you give your firstborn, she'll never quite forgive you for having another baby, no matter how close the children become. The emotional demands of your first child are much greater, so you must learn to give more, and give most of it when the younger one isn't around to get jealous too. On the days when jealousy almost consumes your child, she may be tired or coming down with another cold.

### GRIEVOUS BEHAVIOR

A child can accept a spanking if you don't do it often, don't do it hard and don't do it frivolously. It's better, however, if you don't do it at all. A spanking makes a parent feel awful afterward and it teaches a child very little about self-discipline.

Since it often takes one or two children to learn that spankings don't work very well, you'll probably spank your first child, sooner or later. One firm swat on a well-padded bottom isn't the end of the world, but don't give more than one swat; don't hit her anywhere but her bottom; don't spank her if she's younger than Two or older than Six; don't let anyone but you or her dad spank her—not even grandparents or sitters—and don't ever shake your child. This can cause brain damage.

If you must spank, be sure the crime is serious enough to fit the punishment. A Two might be spanked if she runs in the street or plays with the stove or matches or touches the power tools and a child between Three and Six might get one for being way out of hand, or she might even get a "pantsdowner" for hurting a person or an animal or other extremely naughty behavior. When you give this spanking, however, use your bare hand—not a hairbrush or a wooden spoon—so you can

gauge your force, and don't spank at all if you're at the point of absolute rage. It's so easy to hurt a youngster and the guilt you'll feel certainly will hurt you. When you're that angry, your punishment should be later, tough and verbal.

If you insist on giving a spanking, wait long enough for your child to remember why you were so angry, but don't wait until you're completely calm or until your husband does the job for you when he gets home. A spanking given in cold deliberation will frighten and confuse a child for she sees no love in it.

It's time to reconsider your discipline if you're spanking your Two more than three or four times in the whole year or giving more than one or two spankings a year for a child between Three and Six. This tells you that she needs more supervision to keep her out of trouble, and better discipline when she gets into it.

If you find that you're spanking your child every day, however, or spanking very hard and repeatedly, look for other causes for your anger, and other cures. A little talk by phone to Parents Anonymous (see Resources, page 389), or a few of their free support meetings, will help you get back on the track.

### STEALING

There is a little larceny in everyone's heart, but you can expect a Four, Five or Six to put it into practice at least once. Whether she does it again depends on the way you treat it the first time. If you act as if it were a joke she'll steal again, and if you cover up for her she won't learn to be responsible for herself.

We think any child who steals from someone's home must apologize to the owner privately, but in person, and return the loot. If she steals from a store, however, we think she should pay for it with her own money—and by mail, since only the most hardhearted manager can resist a weepy little child and that would undo the lesson before it was learned.

It was our Kate who, at Five, coveted a fifteen-cent art gum eraser from the stationers the way we might yearn for French perfume. When begging didn't get her the eraser, she simply carried it home in her underpants and surprisingly forgot all about it until it bounced out of her dirty clothes that night.

Through tears she had to dictate a letter of apology for us to write, copy the words on her ruled paper, tape fifteen of her nineteen pennies onto the paper and mail the letter herself. The store manager was so pleased at her display of "honesty" that he gave the story to a newspaper and wanted to give Kate a dozen erasers too.

We hid the newspaper, declined the reward and witnessed the overnight reformation of a little girl who learned that a shoplifter's life is not a happy one.

This may sound like tough treatment, but honesty is a tough lesson to learn.

### PLAYING WITH FIRE

Fire stirs such primitive emotions you can expect your child to be fascinated by it and the more it's forbidden, the more fascinated she'll be.

When our first Five played with matches one Sunday morning (to the delight of his little sister), each was spanked by both parents and marched to the closest fire station for a tour and a stern lecture by the fireman. Afterward we let Ramon help build fires in the barbecue and said he could strike matches in our presence if the itch ever got too bad. It never did again.

With trepidation we let our later girls light fires at Five, under supervision, and for them the fascination bordered on disinterest.

### DANGER

The most dangerous thing about danger may be all the warnings about it. Parents tell their children to watch out, but so do sitters, pre-K teachers, grandparents and their little buddies who watch the evening news.

With all these warnings it's easy for a child to feel totally responsible for herself and that's the scariest idea of all. All children should know the rudiments of self-protection, but mostly they should know that they are never alone. There is always someone to help them.

It's a fine line to walk. Boys and girls need to think that most people—including strangers—are good and true, but not all.

Even your Three must learn that no one—not even someone her own age—should touch her anywhere that is usually covered by clothes, which stops those doctor games before they start. Teach her to keep away from anyone who gives her a funny feeling in her tummy, or makes her scared or nervous when he touches her or who does it only when no one is around. You want her to know that she mustn't go somewhere with him—and without you—or do anything if it has to be done behind a closed door or kept as a secret, even if she's asked to do it by someone she loves. Your child must also be taught that she can say no to a grown-up, even Aunt Tillie who's begging for a kiss good-bye. If she's not allowed to practice her no's, she'll never learn that her body is her own—the most important lesson of all.

Tell her that those were your rules when you were a child, and those were her dad's rules too. By putting yourselves on her level, she will feel safer and by listening to her opinions about grown-ups—without rebuke—she'll know she can always tell you if someone makes her feel edgy.

Your advice must be almost casual, however, and given without showing any sign of fear. You don't want your child to think that there are bogeymen—and bogeywomen—everywhere.

Mothers must give so much to their children, but they have to take some things away—like a layer of innocence.

# MANNERS

There are days and weeks, as we all have learned, when only sex and good manners hold a marriage together. With a child there is only good manners.

The *Babees' Book*, a collection of medieval etiquette for children, advises them to stand until told to sit and "Do not claw your flesh or lean against a post."

"Keep from picking your nose, your teeth or your nails at meal time," it said, and advised them not to eat their food with a knife.

Mothers are still giving the same rules today, with about the same effect.

A Three likes to learn the reason for every rule of etiquette, although some seem pretty silly. When a child sets the table, for instance, tell her the knife blade faces inward so it won't hurt the person at the next place. And that's the essence of good manners. Nothing should be done or said that could possibly hurt someone else, especially someone's feelings. This is why a child shares her toys, tiptoes when someone is sleeping and stands to show a visitor how welcome she is.

Don't let us mislead you. Your child won't have truly good manners by first grade, but if she's been exposed to them early they will be natural to her later.

## SHARING

If you want your child to have friends, she must have good manners, which is the reason she must learn to take turns and share toys.

Some possessions are so new or so beloved that a child just can't bear to share them, and that's all right. Ask your child to tell you which ones they are and then put them away before company comes.

To a child, a toy is an extension of herself, the way money is to some adults. Unlike an adult, however, she has no fi-

nesse at all when she grabs her playmate's wagon and this brings grief every time.

A child finds it equally hard to share power or status, which makes her resent a new baby or a sitter or a visitor. Chickens and children know you can shift up or down in the pecking order but never sideways.

Teach your child to share just as you teach her anything else—slowly, by example and with a few tricks. Start as early as mid-One, just for practice, but expect little success for at least another year. If a rocking horse is in dispute between mid-Ones, only distraction will work, but mid-Twos will regulate their turns with a timer. Children find it easier for Mr. Buzzer to tell them what to do (see page 89).

By Three, you'll find a cupcake teaches sharing quicker than anything else. Give one child the knife to divide it—and the other child first choice. It will be cut exactly in half, without complaints from either party.

## CONVERSATION

Good conversation is like city traffic. Words are slipped in when the path is clear, but each interruption is like a little crash.

Drive safely.

Since your child will start interrupting as soon as she starts talking, she needs to be taught the stop-and-go of conversation, learning when to speak and when to listen. It's easier for her to take turns when she's having a conversation with just one person, especially someone her own age, but it will be years (would you believe, a decade?) before she can talk easily with two or three adults at the same time. She should start learning this fine art early, since it doesn't come naturally.

You begin to teach it when the two of you are visiting alone, by using clear diction and a pleasant voice, looking her in the eye when you speak and letting her talk as much as you. Slowly, she'll understand that you pause when you finish a thought and that's when she has her say.

When you have company you'll want to include your child in some of the conversation before you send her out to play, but treat her as a participant, not a performer. This is basic courtesy. If you were in a room with two other people who wouldn't talk to you, you'd feel excluded and if they talked to no one but you (or talked only about you), you'd be embarrassed. A child is no different.

Whether you're talking to your child alone or when you have company, you can't permit her to interrupt constantly. If you do you'll catch that most common disease of motherhood: prattle. It creeps up on you slowly until sometime after 6,413 interruptions you realize that you can't finish a sentence, let alone a thought, even when there's no child around to interrupt. Having had virulent cases of prattle ourselves, we think you'll find it easier to stop interruptions before they become a habit. To do it, touch your finger to her lips when she interrupts and keep talking until you've finished your thought. She has to learn that anything short of a disaster will keep a few minutes.

Telephone conversations are a special problem. The phone is every mother's salvation, but your child will find it hard to believe you're having a conversation when you're not opening your mouth. If you have a running conversation with her while you're on the phone she'll think that phone calls are meant to be interrupted and this will irritate your friends. Avoid some of the problem by using the telephone when your child is asleep or outside; by using a portable phone when she's awake, so you can go to her when she needs something, and by having special activities for her when you're on the phone. The morning comics make a good coloring book.

### TEA-PARTY MANNERS

A mid-One learns her table manners best at tea parties. We used a tiny, cheap and very proper china tea set, the kind that pleases a mother as much as her child, and greeted our first daughter after her nap with a proper "How do you do, Mrs. Jones." She shook the paws of Mr. Bear and Mrs. Giraffe and sat down at the low table, which had a napkin, a plate and a cup and saucer at each place.

The cookies were in the middle, the sponge was out of sight, the juice was in the cups and Kate poured from the teapot as needed. She also graciously ate the cookies for Mr. Bear and Mrs. Giraffe to spare them the embarrassment of leaving their food untouched.

### MEALTIME MANNERS

We once heard a father of four ask a Chinese restaurateur how his children ever learned to feed themselves with chopsticks, to which Dr. Chang replied, "You've seen the way American children eat spaghetti with a fork? It's the same way. Not very well."

A Three is ready to have some meals with her parents. Conversation and good table manners are hard to choreograph and harder to perform. Whenever your child joins you for a Sunday dinner, or any special occasion, she'll behave better if she uses the same kind of plate and silverware you do. If you use candlelight and ask her questions (as you would of any company), she'll behave with some gentility. One mother and father ask each of their children to tell them something that made them very happy that day, and something that made them very sad. This shows children much more interest than asking, "How was day care?" and it teaches them the mannerly art of telling a story.

A Five should eat with parents as often as possible, for manners, like tennis, can only improve with practice. She certainly won't learn them magically on the day the grand duchess of the family arrives for dinner.

### COMPANY MANNERS

Your Three learns to make her manners quicker if you let her spend the first half-hour in the living room when you have company, because example always teaches best.

Here she'll learn to shake hands, take lightweight coats and pass the cheese and crackers. Eventually your child begins to see that party manners are so natural and nice, they're good enough for every day.

By Six she should be able to talk with your guests almost as comfortably as she does with her own, but one hopes, with more decorum.

### CAR MANNERS

Just as your child needs to learn the art of conversation, so must she learn the art of silence. It can become essential when you or your husband are driving on a freeway. For us, hand signals worked best.

When you bring your thumb and forefinger almost together: quiet.

When you squeeze them or clap your hands: absolute quiet.

And when your child claps her hands for you, it's time to do a little listening yourself. With your good example, she probably won't overuse this privilege.

These same signals work when you're on the telephone.

### TELEPHONE MANNERS

It takes a Four to talk well on the telephone, but she should answer it only when she knows how. Your friends deserve that courtesy.

Begin teaching her at mid-Three by ringing her toy telephone for her to say something such as, "Hello, the Johnson residence, Betty speaking."

She can answer your phone when she is adept enough to chat a minute and careful enough to remember most messages, and by then she'll be Five or even Six. Until then she may respond, as Kate did when she said, "Yes, 584-4854. Wait! How do you make a 5?"

### TOO MANY WHYS

A child asks "Why" for two reasons. Either she asks once because she wants an answer, or she asks over and over again because she wants attention. To break the cycle, give an answer as detailed as you think she can understand, then have your child explain it back to you. This turns a whiny why into a conversation.

# INDEPENDENCE

There is nothing instant about learning.

Your baby masters a skill by repeating it over and over, the same way he one day will learn to add and subtract or drive a car. Learning is layered and each new skill is built upon the last. The more you teach a child, the easier he is to handle, the less he whines and the less he says "no." You can't force your child to learn, but if you put him in a situation where it's easy, where he is regarded as a capable person, his abilities will soar.

He learns not by watching, but by doing. He does need encouragement but more than that, he needs simple step-by-step, eye-level demonstrations, slow of movement and of speech.

Even after he learns a skill, he'll need at least twice as much time as you to do the job. Try not to hurry him, for the child who is rushed regularly, like the child who is often corrected or ridiculed, will perform only under stress—never very well and with little joy.

Any adult has learned a skill, like cooking, and then has burned the pot. A child needs the right to err too, without your making a production out of every mistake. Regressions are common in all areas and ages, but they are more obvious in children. Praise the new skills and ignore the lapses. A positive parent seldom produces a negative child.

Remember—the time you spend shaping an independent child will result in a teenager self-reliant and self-confident enough to be a giver, not a taker.

# ◇ COORDINATION ◇

No child under Six is as proud of his mental skills as he is of his physical ones. He measures himself by the way he handles his body.

Your baby's play is work to him, from the day he is born. He builds every move on his gradual understanding of distance, size, shape and quantity.

It takes an accumulation of knowledge for your child to turn over or stand, but when he finally triumphs he will look more exultant than an Olympic winner. Nothing is as exciting to a child as success, especially when it's hard to achieve.

One of our best friends, short and slight at Ten, is completely in tune with his body. This isn't, we're sure, because his parents are athletic, which they're not, but because they refused to let his delicate build hamper him. Instead they gave him an environment that let him have a thousand small victories a day.

Even at Two he was encouraged to throw pebbles at a brick wall, hammer nails into soft wood and climb up and down a stepladder, not as a show-off, but as a worker. He operated alone, although a parent was near to keep him in bounds and they praised some of his efforts, but never all, so he could believe their sincerity. Today his coordination is so sure that he plays goalie on the neighborhood teen-age soccer team, and his self-confidence is so solid he thinks it only fitting.

Since every person has a different ability to run, swim, climb, aim and catch, your child may need more practice and more help than another, but don't work with him if his ineptitude makes you cross. His skills are a measure of his ability, not yours.

Finally, a child should be encouraged to work and play in his own fashion, as baffling as his approach may be to you, for he seldom tries anything by himself that he can't accomplish fairly soon. He does need you to show him a new skill, like jumping, as soon as he has learned an old one, like walking.

Physical dexterity gives a child the self-confidence he needs to depend on himself.

### INFANCY

The more a baby squirms, the easier it will be for him to inch about, but he needs help with his coordination. Give him a daily workout and place him on a hard, safe surface, like a playpen floor, so he can roll over more easily. A slightly sloped infant seat, while making no physical demands, stimulates his curiosity, which propels a child to move more than anything else.

Grasping is a baby's first skill. He instinctively will clutch your finger at birth but he'll do it on purpose at about two months. Give toys that are easy to hold. A small doughnut shape is precisely what he needs to hook his finger and thumb, rather than a large, stuffed animal.

### THREE MONTHS

You can develop his arms and legs better by increasingly strenuous daily exercises. Hold out your forefingers and let him pull himself to a standing position on your lap—an easier place than his crib—for as long as he likes. This exercise strengthens his body, but he's the only one who knows when his back is ready to feel the strain of sitting and standing and you shouldn't hurry him or make him stand when he wants to sit.

He'll also learn to use his body better if you put some toys just slightly out of his reach. If they're colorful he'll try harder to grab them. By four months, he clasps his arms like pincers to clutch the bigger toys. As he develops better coordination between the things he sees and the way he handles them, he is learning the same hand-to-eye skill he'll one day need to read and write.

### SIX MONTHS

At this age you should offer anything to your child squarely to his middle, so he can decide for himself whether he's right-handed, or left-handed or ambidextrous.

When your baby learns to sit, he'll topple over often, since he doesn't know how to lie down again. Once he feels comfortable sitting, he's ready to play So Big. "How big is Jamie? Soooo big," you say, stretching your arms until pretty soon he'll hold up his arms too.

In the next few months your baby will start crawling, and now the fun begins. Dress either a son or a daughter in long pants to protect the knees—dresses are impossible for little girls to crawl in anyway—and give your child plenty of room to roam. He'll use the furniture to pull himself upright, but watch him carefully. We've never seen a baby who could sit back down the first few times without help. If you gently clip the back of his knees with one hand while you catch his back with the other, he'll learn to fall squarely on his bottom.

You have to watch your crawler closely, however, because a baby thinks every surface is on the same level until he's about nine months, which causes him to crawl from sofa to floor as if they were side by side.

If your child is a climber before he has learned depth perception—our sympathy. You'll be his constant companion. A swing, a walker, a jumper and a playpen help contain the vertical child.

### NINE MONTHS

If you don't believe your baby uses a lot of fuel now, follow him around the house for a half-hour, doing whatever he does: sitting up, falling down, crawling, lifting. Even discounting the size of the objects he deals with in relation to his size, you will be exhausted by the work—and he won't be fazed.

We think that teaching a nine-month-old to climb up and down stairs is a smart use of time. It's helpful to you and safer for him and makes him feel proud and brave. You will, of course, lock the gate when you can't go with him, for you have to be ready for anything with this age.

You also have to be careful with his boundaries even if you live in an apartment, as one wacky caper taught us. Ramon, who practically lived in his walker, got a good-bye kiss from his father and then noticed that the apartment door was left slightly ajar. In a flash he scooted down the hall, straight to his friend's door, where he pounded, was admitted and was eating his friend's breakfast bacon before his mom could put on some clothes. Time: two minutes. A lesser-known reason for mothers to dress before breakfast.

### ONE

If a One isn't walking, he'll be a most adept crawler and the more adept he is, the less reason he has to walk. When he does start, you'll be rightfully wary, for his propensity for trouble will skyrocket, and you'll be weary too, from listing to starboard on those shuffling walks, stretching your forefinger low enough for him to reach.

### FIFTEEN MONTHS

Once a baby can walk, he wants to do more and more with his upright body: run, walk backward, jump. Between his first and second year he'll master these after a thousand falls, a few goose eggs and maybe some stitches.

When his legs are steady, take him in a stroller to different terrains—grass, cement or sand—for short walks there. A child has so much to discover.

Now he loves the push-and-pull toys, because they give a sense of mastery. When our Meg was this age she found a small, twenty-five-cent wheelbarrow in a junk store, which she wheeled everywhere, precariously, carrying all her goods with her. It was a pastime that lasted for at least a year and taught coordination better than any toy we ever saw.

### MID-ONE

This child is ready for a wheel toy he can sit on and push with his feet, for he is peripatetic now. He likes to splash in calm water—a lake or a pool—but often won't lift his face if he falls in it. For this reason, you must watch him very, very carefully when he's near water (even a big bucket or a toilet bowl) and empty the wading pool immediately after use—a practice to continue for at least two years or whenever a younger child visits.

### TWO

Whether your Two is a swashbuckler or a dreamer, he needs every chance to climb, both in and out of the house. Climbing equipment develops such coordination of the arms and legs and such self-confidence that it's even worth a long walk to a playground. In any case, your child needs to walk every day, as much for the exercise as the enrichment.

### MID-TWO

A mid-Two is a whiz with his wheel toy but he probably isn't ready for a real tricycle for another six months, unless he can alternate feet when he climbs stairs. This is the skill he needs to pedal a trike.

Nothing makes a mid-Two feel more like a daredevil than a chance to balance along a low brick wall—a compulsion to play Harold Lloyd that some of us have to this day.

He loves a rocking horse too, for it's so sexy to bounce on it, and the bigger the bounce the sexier the horse.

### THREE

By Three, your child should be able to go on 20–30-minute round-trip walks, and will like to play outdoors: climbing, running, triking and wrestling. He can toss, bounce and kick a ball (but not catch it).

In the bathtub he may try to blow bubbles with his face barely in the water.

## FOUR

A Four has mastered the tricycle and can move on to a scooter—a short-lived love. He likes a rope ladder and tries to slide down the biggest slide in the playground— the one with the three bumps. Despite the equality of the sexes, boys are more likely to wrestle like puppies and an old mattress on the basement floor is ideal for them. So is a punching bag, but boxing gloves are silly for a pre-Six. As for walking, a Four can go as fast as you but only in short spurts.

A Four needs to feel capable for he compares himself constantly with his friends and needs to be as adept as they.

## FIVE

A Five finally is able to pump a swing, if you teach him. It takes an amazing combination of physical skills. He likes to show how far he can jump, how high he can climb a tree (not very), how fast he can run, how long he can skip. No matter how big and confident he feels, however, he doesn't like to compete in any sports but soccer and T-ball, and then only if the coach is very relaxed.

A Five may be ready for a small sixteen-inch bicycle if he wears a safety helmet—a practice you want to start early. Training wheels aren't necessary, however. Having put them on the first bikes—and removed them almost immediately—we're sure of this: a Five is too old for a four-wheel bike. He'll have a few more spills without the trainers, but he'll learn quicker and feel much braver. Make sure he rides on a sidewalk, in a park or any place completely free of people or cars, however. He can't be responsible for balance and safety at the same time.

### BAT AND BALL

We found our son could hit a ball by the end of his fifth summer, after his father had made a target for him by tying a plastic ball—the kind with holes—to a string and hanging it from a line strung between two trees. It dangled just above Ramon's waist, so he could swing at it again and again, aiming either for a moving ball or a still one. Though it flipped around and all over the clothesline, it always returned to the same level—a splendid game to play all alone and every hit brought immediate pleasure.

## SIX

The Six who liked soccer and T-ball last year is apt to love them this year. He also can take part in a game as complicated as softball, if he plays with kind folks, like his parents. He's ready now for a game of pitch and catch and likes to bat a ball, roll an automobile tire and float and swim under water and perhaps can pass a beginner's swim test.

## EXERCISES AND GAMES

### INFANT'S DAILY WORKOUT

Changing time is the best time to exercise your baby. Hold his feet as you pedal his legs gently, and eventually he'll return the pressure against your hands.

### CATCH FINGER

Your baby—from three months to three years—will like this game. Hold your forefinger so he can try to catch it before you snap it down. He'll laugh greatly when you let him win, which should be at least half the time.

### CRAWLING

When a child lies on his tummy and uses his arms to push his shoulders from the floor, you know he's ready to crawl. Get alongside him on the floor and show him how, first by crawling yourself. Next lift his left hand and right foot together, then switch to the other hand and foot, loco-motive-style.

You probably would have learned to dance by yourself, but it was quicker and easier when you had a partner.

### CLIMBING STAIRS

At nine months, a mountain is for climb-ing.

When your firstborn begins to crawl and has decent depth perception, teach him to climb up and down stairs, even if you have to go to someone else's house to do it. He'll be one less package for you to carry and he'll feel very important too.

This skill is taught best by crawling upstairs yourself, which your child will imitate, even as he laughs. Any child loves this scramble, with never a thought to getting back. At the top he may cry (or fall backward), until he learns to slither down on his tummy. This is taught gradually, a few steps at a time, by literally moving his arms and legs backward, then carrying him the rest of the way, for he'll just want to go upstairs again. With some practice, your child will climb to the top and come slithering down at a terrific speed, con-trolled by catching onto the balustrades.

Even when he starts toddling, he still may scramble up and down the stairs on his belly for months before he dares to walk up a step at a time. When your child is a little bolder—usually by Two—you'll see him teeter at the top, then cautiously walk down—a great sign of derring-do. We almost negated the adventure by saying each time, as our child swayed from tread to tread, "Don't fall down the steps, Katy!"

This was silly, since she didn't want to fall and a warning couldn't have stopped her. As we learned, if you're going to broaden your boundaries you'll have to broaden your faith.

### WALKING

When a baby starts to walk, he gets a wonderful new view of the world. He can get it sooner if you don't carry him every-where and if you bicycle his legs daily. Some say a baby also walks quicker if he has a walker, for he feels protected enough to be daring, but be very careful. Many a walker has tumbled down the stairs, baby and all.

Generally it's better to teach your child to walk behind a chair as he pushes it, or to walk in front of you, hanging onto your forefinger. Finally, he takes a few ecstatic steps alone, usually clutching a toy in each hand. As he gains stability he'll depend on the walls for balance instead. This quaint native custom, with its trail of fingerprints, continues until he's about Twelve (yes, years, dear).

As for shoes—they're not necessary in the first year or so, but they will keep his feet warm and safe and they'll keep little old ladies from fussing at you. Put him in soft shoes, like sneakers, when you go out and let him run around barefoot at home.

### BALANCE

The earth is a wobbly place to a child. He needs practice to feel steady.

For a Two, drag thick yarn on the floor in a simple pattern, so he can walk on the twisty string. An older child will make his own complicated patterns.

You also can place a wide plank, 4'–6' long, on bricks or blocks of wood, 6" above the floor for a young child, higher for an older one. A child automatically walks this plank a dozen times a day, without even wondering why it's there. If you want to make a permanent balancing board, see page 163.

### SWIMMING

The sooner you give your child the chance to swim, the quicker he'll take to the water. If you're lucky enough to have a pool in your area that offers swimming lessons for babies, take advantage of it. A baby can learn to paddle above water in his first year and loves every minute of it.

Whether you can give him lessons early or not, you can prepare him for swimming by letting him feel the buoyancy of the water, bouncing up and down in it with him. Later pull him along, but with his face out of water or he'll be scared. A Two may jump into your arms from the side of the pool and a Three may hold tight to your hands while you stand sideways to buck the ocean. Once a child learns to bubble, he may be ready for more advanced lessons, but be careful to find an instructor who can teach the rudiments of swimming and particularly of breathing, in an easygoing way.

We think life jackets are usually necessary in any water and essential in the ocean, for a small swimmer needs all the protection he can get in the surf. The one exception: a swimming pool, for a life jacket in this still water can take away the healthy fear of water every child should have. If you do get one for the pool, however, be sure it's certified for safety and can support his weight, because a child in any kind of support—even the simplest plastic tube—will depend on it to stay afloat.

Even when your pre-Six can swim, you must watch him very carefully. Lifeguard or not, the buck stops with you. And if you have a pool in your yard, be sure that it's protected by a locked gate and, if possible, a cover, and that you know mouth-to-mouth resuscitation (see page 133). Neighborhood children are sure to visit, whether they're invited or not.

### Bubbling

Most children are afraid to go completely under water, even at Four, because they don't know how to bubble. We helped Mali, first by demonstrating this silly game, then by doing it with her.

We shouted, "One, two, three," dropped to the floor of the pool and bounced straight up again. After a few times and enough laughter, we grabbed Mali's hands, counted again and went down together, over and over, until she learned to blow bubbles as she came up. It worked, but we don't recommend it until your child is comfortable in water to his waist.

### POSTURE

Good posture is essential for physical dexterity. But you won't teach it by saying, "Sit up straight."

Your ribald Four likes to know that flesh is laid on bones, which he can understand better if he dangles a cardboard Halloween skeleton, bending his arms and legs and finding the same bones in himself.

Once he's familiar with his skeleton, sit on the floor together and reach back and touch your own spines with your fingers. Bend over, wiggle your backbones and feel the vertebrae move. Twist your bodies into all kinds of shapes, freeze and breathe deeply so he can teach himself that he breathes more easily when the vertebrae sit one on top of the other. Now ask him to stand sideways in front of a mirror, with his ears in line with his shoulders, not in front or behind them. Any child will accept occasional, simple corrections of posture later if he first learns why.

### PITCH AND CATCH

Nothing teaches coordination better than a ball.

An infant should have several balls which he can follow with his eyes and later can throw and chase. One ball

should be large and colorful, one should be bumpy enough for a good grip and one should be made of foam rubber, because it's so light and it's good for years and years of indoor play.

When your child learns to sit, spread his legs apart and roll a ball between them, the first game of catch. The child who walks steadily will lift the ball, throw it—and be amazed to see it land behind him. A Two can kick the large ball, throw the indoor one into a laundry basket and can hold his arms tightly together to catch a ball if his father throws it with great care. A Three will love a wide bat and a large ball and a Four is ready for a rubber ball bigger than a tennis ball but small enough to fit in his hands. He'll throw it overhead and underhand on his own, but he'll do it better if you show him how and let him shoot into a low basketball hoop. A Five can play T-ball and kick a soccer ball and even learn the basics of these games, and a Six will try to bat a softball with his friends, none of whom will succeed either.

We don't think a child can kick and throw and chase a ball too much, for nothing will make him more nimble.

### BEANBAGGERY

A Two likes a beanbag better than a ball because it stops right where it lands. On a dawdly day, suggest that your child throw the bag high and catch it on the move or hold it between his feet and hop with it.

Let him pitch the bag into a chalk circle, a game made harder if he shuts his eyes first, flings it over his shoulder or tosses it first with his left hand, then with his right.

A handful of dried beans sewn in an odd glove makes a fine bag—an easy job for a Four (see page 317).

### SPORTS

If you or your husband like sports, you're bound to encourage your child to try them, and if you don't like sports, you ought to encourage him anyway. The more agile and adept he is, the better he will feel about himself.

Some particularly physical pre-Threes—or particularly klutzy ones—will profit by a low-key gymnastics program, but most of them just need a chance to run around on the playground or climb all over the equipment every day.

### LEFT-HANDEDNESS

One boy in ten—and fewer girls—are left-handed (and probably left-footed, left-eyed and left-eared too).

You won't know if your child is left-handed until he's Two, or even older, and until then you hand him each toy, each cookie, squarely to the center, so he can choose with either hand. He may eat with one hand, throw a ball with the other and then switch around from age to age, before you suddenly realize: you've got a little leftie. There's nothing you could or should do about it and you certainly don't want to make an issue out of it or make him self-conscious. He'll be fine. Just set his milk to the left, so he won't spill it as easily; give him left-handed scissors (and one day a left-handed baseball glove or lacrosse stick) so he has as much chance to succeed as anyone else. Ask his kindergarten teacher to give him left-handed scissors too, as well as a left-handed desk and some special help to learn how to print without smearing the letters. If you are not left-handed yourself, you'll also need to get some leftie friend of yours to teach him how to tie knots and sew. Your child won't be able to translate your right-handed instructions into left-handed instructions any better than you can.

Fours, Fives and Sixes want more of the same and they like team sports too. Most of the players will barely figure out the goal of the game and all of them will be very hazy about the rules, but they will like the chance to make new friends, chase each other and wear a uniform. A few of them may actually learn how to work together—the whole point of a team sport—but that's asking a lot, even of a Six.

Still, your child will feel like a winner, if he tries the right sport, at the right time. A swim team is usually too much pressure for a Five or even a Six—unless he's a true water baby—and ice hockey is too expensive for most parents. You would not only have to pay for the coach and the ice time, but for new skates and probably a new stick every year and usually for new protective gear too, since it must fit the size of the child to keep him safe.

This leaves T-ball and soccer, if you can find a team that's small enough for every child to play at least half of every game. Even then you'll want to observe a practice before signing him up. So much depends on the coach. He not only should know the game well, but he should know how to teach it to little children.

You're looking for someone who encourages all the children to play their best, not just a few stars; who finds something good to say about each of them at every practice and every game; and who never, ever, embarrasses a player, even if he

thinks it would make the child try harder.

Just as the coach and the players have rules, so do the parents.

You have to get your child to every practice, because his team depends on him, but only watch every second or third game unless he really wants you to be there, or you might make him feel pressured. When you do go, cheer all the children—not just yours—and give your own lots of praise afterward, but please—no criticisms and no instructive replays. If you tell your child how to play the game, he'll think you're pushing him—and he'll be right.

You'll know you're expecting too much if you get a knot in your tum when he misses the ball. Winning usually doesn't mean very much to him and it shouldn't mean that much to you.

If you don't act as though winning is so important, your child will begin to learn that the only person worth competing against is himself. It's one of life's great lessons but don't expect him to learn it very soon. Eventually your child will try to do better today than he did yesterday, but this concept is too much for him to understand now. A Six still plays for the moment, and if he's allowed to go his own way, the moment is very sweet.

### T-Ball

This ingenious game follows the same rules as softball, but it has no pitcher or catcher, making it much safer and easier and one of the funniest games you'll ever watch. Here a weighted T sits on the ground, with a lightweight plastic ball balanced on top, about bat high, and the child takes a swing. The bat—and the spring of the T—sends the ball flying. The right fielder will probably run to left field to catch it (and probably miss it); then someone will throw it to one of the three basemen, who will miss it because he wasn't there anyway. Players never stay quite where they belong in T-ball, and nobody cares. A sports-minded Three can bat this ball alone or with you, and a child from Four to Six can join a coed T-ball league. It's as much a hoot for the players as the parents, although probably for different reasons.

### Soccer

Teenagers have used our quiet city side street for their impromptu ball games for years, but our favorite game was a soccer match after Thanksgiving dinner, played by a mix of children from Four to Forty. To the joy of the young, the Fours—and the Fourteens—clearly played better than the Forties. Soccer is either the great equalizer or a lesson in humility, depending on your point of view.

Soccer—football to the rest of the world—calls for great skill and speed, but even pre-K's can play this game with some success. Children find it much easier to kick a ball than to hit it or throw it, and girls find it as much fun as boys, which isn't always the case on other coed teams.

In soccer the faster children play the line positions, trying to kick the ball into the other goal; the sturdier one plays in back, trying to keep the ball out of their goal. These little players look like a swarm of bumbling bees, chasing the ball up and down the field and loving it. Soccer brings success as sweet as honey and a very fine time.

If you need a better reason to buy your child a uniform and shuttle him to practice and a game every week, consider these: soccer builds a child's oxygen intake and his stamina; it teaches him to run faster; it steadies his balance—the child has to kick with one foot while he stands on the other—and it strengthens his self-esteem. And he has a very fine time.

If you don't want your child to sit in front of the television all afternoon, you have to give him something better. Like soccer.

---

# TALKING

The articulate child is blessed for life. We believe in early talking, not because your child (and thereby you) will seem brilliant, but because the sooner he talks the happier you both will be. Language is one of the best ways a child can feel in control of himself. It lets him tell you his stomach hurts or he's lonely or he's afraid of things that go squish on his plate. When a person can't express himself, he's frustrated and angry.

At birth a baby gasps his first breath and cries out at the tickling of his feet. His furious screams will never be so welcome again, but for weeks this is the only way he knows how to talk to you. Within his first year he'll babble every sound in every tongue on earth—most of which he'll forget when he learns your language. The average child is said to know perhaps three

words when he is One and sixteen more when he is fifteen months old. We think a mother can extend this vocabulary considerably.

It's not how much you talk to your child but how well you talk to him that counts, for a child understands many words before he can use them. You'll want to speak slowly, precisely, to tell him whatever you're doing, using the same words every time. You should tell him the name of everything he eats, wears and what you're shopping for and you should explain why you're going someplace or doing some particular thing, the way you would to any friend. And above all you should read to him starting with the simplest board books at three months, for books give words a special importance.

### INFANCY TO SIX MONTHS

By six weeks your baby will communicate with you through cries and smiles, but when he's about three months he will coo—the single most enchanting sound a child will make. It's important to follow your instincts, answering him coo for coo, your faces close together. This is his first conversation. He'll make new sounds every week—some because he's so happy; some because he's so tired and some because he's so mad. Frustration has its place. Although some of his sounds aren't as pretty as a coo, you'll want to repeat many of them. The more a child exercises his vocal chords, the faster his voice box develops. This lets him control the sounds he makes: the key to talking.

Talking is a game that's more fun to teach than any other and it delights a baby, if only because of the single-minded attention he gets. We learned our technique from a marvelous, toothless, eighty-year-old Irishman who stood over the carriage of his marvelous, toothless, four-month-old granddaughter for a half-hour saying, "Hell—ooooooo," over and over. Finally, like a trumpet player watching a fellow suck a lemon at the bandstand, Kate was compelled to imitate him until she could sing it back—not very well, but enough to satisfy them both.

Only grandfathers have this much patience, but your child will still profit by a three-minute exercise.

### NINE MONTHS

His attempts at talking will be almost impossible to understand, but give him the respect of listening to his language as well as he listens to yours. Otherwise, he'll grow discouraged and instead of speaking in two-word sentences by eighteen months, he might take an extra year to talk that well.

Keep repeating his sounds with delight when he says anything that might be a word. He'll be so pleased it will become a word, whether intended or not. As long as you each know what a particular sound means and he uses it consistently to describe the same thing—it's a word. If your neighbor doesn't know that "boom-boom" means vacuum cleaner or "putat" means pussycat, that's her problem. As long as you respond to your child's words with standard language, you aren't teaching baby talk.

Whenever you dress him, you'll put *socks* on *feet* and *hats* on *heads*, pointing to each as you do it. You'll touch his eyes and his knees and his forehead and elbows and say each word as you go. One day he'll surprise you and touch his eyes when you say the word and you'll know it's time to teach him about eyebrows and eyelashes too.

### FIFTEEN MONTHS

By fifteen months he can fetch familiar things for you, if you ask him in short, one-thought sentences—and if he isn't ornery that day.

### MID-ONE

Your child may stop talking while he masters a new skill, like walking. The more active he is, the less patience he'll have for talking, for children are as single-minded as anyone else. They can't learn how to walk and talk at the same time any more than they can grow taller and fatter at the same time.

Even the most nonverbal mid-One can understand everything that concerns him, whether you're talking to him or not.

As soon as he is familiar with one word, use a synonym to increase his precision and his scope. In this way, big comes large, huge or tall. Be specific when you talk, pointing out not a "baby dog" but a "puppy," adding the color in another year and eventually the breed.

## TWO

By Two you should require your child to say "please" and "thank you"—just as you do—and help him enunciate clearly, without baby talk. Speak in complete sentences and expect the same of him, which helps him think more clearly.

Soon you can use more complex language games to teach adjectives and adverbs and reinforce his vocabulary even more by using books and tapes, and singing nursery rhymes and by watching some television too. Shows like "Sesame Street" teach new words very well. Your child may talk even quicker if you put your own silly words to music, like "Here comes the plumber/Looking like a drummer."

The plumber may think you're a little daft to introduce him that way, but he'll have something to tell his wife that night.

## STUTTERING

Of all the small problems that can unsettle parents, stuttering often unsettles them most. Somehow all the important things that come out of the child's mouth are not as important as the way they come out.

Generally it's nothing to worry about. Most children between mid-Two and Five tend to stutter once or twice a day, or more often if it's near their birthdays or Christmas; if there is a good deal of excitement or tension around the house, and if they simply have more to say than they can manage. The true stutterer, however—usually a boy—has regular difficulty with a particular word or part of a word, and has a certain stuttering pattern. There are many patterns—all of them complex—and probably many causes too.

If you're not sure whether your child has a problem, or if it worries you, take him to a certified speech-language pathologist for an evaluation. This takes several sessions but it's worth it, since a true stutterer needs speech therapy before school starts if possible. You'll learn that stuttering may have a neurological, psychological or even an allergic basis, or it may be caused by a learning fault or poor rhythmic control. The therapist will teach your child various techniques to change his speech patterns, slow his speech and relax his throat muscles, and she'll teach you to make eye-to-eye contact with your child when you talk; to be patient with him, and to pay more attention to his words than his stutters.

## THREE

Until a child can be understood clearly, he'll whine more, fuss more and have more temper tantrums to exorcise his frustration.

Some children are late talkers because no one talks to them or because the conversation is too fast to follow or because the full-time sitter doesn't speak their language.

If a child screeches, "Ee, ee, ee," and points to something he wants and his parents automatically give it to him, that child will have no reason to build a vocabulary. That's how our Nadia, the charmer of the preschool set, got along almost entirely in pantomime until she was Three.

Still other children are slow to talk when they're told "no" too often, for it takes nerve to make words.

Occasionally, a child may have a physical problem. We remember a family with more children than money whose Four never talked until he had a tonsillectomy. A few days later he knocked hard at a neighbor's door and sang the full lyrics of "The Isle of Capri."

You can use our techniques to help a child of any age to talk, but the older the child, the swifter his progress.

## FOUR

Every day, as your child needs less and less concentration to develop physical skills, he'll astonish you with his huge collection of words and the queer ways he puts them together.

Help him learn a few new words each day—not fancy, "look-at-me" words (or you'll have an aggravating little show-off) but words with enough variety for him to choose exactly the right word for the right moment. In fact, synonyms can be your social salvation. The experts would never agree with us, but we think sex organs should have nicknames unless you're talking to your child about sex. We remember too well when our Kate and Mike, Four and Three, plagued their crusty bachelor uncle at a party, asking if he had a ding-ding. He may have been annoyed (no doubt about it), but at least he could ignore it more easily than if they had chanted, "Uncle Tom, do you have a penis?"

### FIVE

By now your child should know his full name and address, but he should know home and office telephone numbers too—a matter of simple rote. Since a Five is so sure of himself, he will never get lost, although he'll be distressed how often you do.

Teach him to ask help from policemen, mailmen and mothers, no others, for he must learn not to talk to strangers. This is a lesson we completely skipped with our outgoing Meg, who, at Seven, classically insisted she had never met a stranger. When we explained that a stranger was someone her parents had never met, she brought home a very large and inebriated fellow she found on the sidewalk.

"Jack," she said, "I want you to meet my mother. Mom, this is Jack. Now he's not a stranger any more. Can he have some coffee and then can I go to his house to watch television?"

He did and she didn't—and we got a television.

## TALKING GAMES

We found talking games were the best way to make a child feel comfortable with words—their shadings and their tempo—and make him crystallize his ideas. Most of the games, which lasted for years, centered around the parts of speech.

Start with the Grandfather's Drill at four months and well before the first birthday graduate to Nouns, then Verbs, then Prepositions. Adjectives and Adverbs, which are not as necessary, come in his second year. Your games will sound like Dick-and-Jane readers, which may explain why a Two likes these books so much and a Six does not.

### THE GRANDFATHER'S DRILL

All sounds and words are taught the same way—starting as early as four months.

It may seem silly to try to teach words so soon, but it doesn't hurt if it's a way to show love and not a demand for performance. Babies, like all of us, revel in attention. This technique works for the next three years.

Practice first before a mirror, speaking slowly and enunciating each syllable, so you can see your mouth and lips and tongue synchronize to make a particular sound. Do the same with your child, talking at eye level and inches from his face, so he can see "bye-bye" and "Dad-dy," as well as hear it. Say a word over and over, slowly and distinctly, the way you would teach a foreign language. To a baby, it is a foreign language. Do this as many as twelve times at a stretch, and your child will soon try to imitate you.

Continue teaching each new word slowly and close to his face, even when he begins to speak fairly well.

In another year your child will wrestle with difficult sounds better if you use props—a candle flame or a feather to emphasize the breathy "wh" sound of "what," rather than the flat "w" sound of "water."

### NOUNS

Most of the first words you teach will be nouns, which you'll do by naming everything you touch and then by teaching Guessing Game I before he talks and the second game when you think it's about time that he did.

### Guessing Game I

At nine months our amusing friend Suzannah enjoyed this ancient dialogue, with her mother asking—and answering—every question.

"Where is Suzannah's shoe? In the refrigerator?

"No!

"Under the table?

"Nooo.

"On the dog?

"No, no.

"On Suzannah's foot?

"Yes!"

Suzannah didn't learn how to say shoe that day, but she did learn what the word meant and her mother referred often to her daddy's shoes and the newsboy's shoes and the fact that the dog had no shoes. Everything on a foot was a shoe; there were no slippers, socks, or sandals for another nine months.

### Guessing Game II

Almost every child will point to what he wants, instead of trying to name it, which will annoy you more and more.

When he points to his juice next time, pick up the salt cellar, the pot holder, the tea strainer, saying, "Is this it?," "You mean this?"

And finally, when he is almost furious, "Oh, the bottle. Say BOT-TULL," and say the word face to face, several times, after you give it to him. He may be too annoyed to say it then, but he'll try the next time or the next.

### VERBS

Action verbs are taught more easily than any words, as you hop, skip, walk and run, saying the words as you go. He'll think it's very funny. When your child says, "See," "Go," "Look," he's speaking in complete one-word sentences—a comfort.

### PREPOSITIONS

The abstract concepts of prepositions are the hardest words for a child to understand and about the most important, for it's hard for a conversation to make sense without them.

Play a game of hide-and-seek with a small toy, placing it *on* the table or *behind* it, *before* it, *under* it or *over* it. You'll do most of the hiding and most of the looking and all of the guessing, calling out each preposition until you find the toy.

A child can understand the simplest prepositions in a few weeks, even before he learns to talk.

### ADJECTIVES

When your child has mastered a word like "ball," roll one to him gently. Rub his fingers on it, saying, "Round ball." Go about the room, pointing out everything that is round. Try to roll a block so he can see the difference. Tell him it's square, then show other things that are square. This is the prelude to these abstract concepts.

Your little girl's dress and her dolly and especially herself are pretty, an adjective to be used often and in front of the mirror.

Your child will learn "hot" and "cold," because you touch his fingertips to the spigots; "loud" and "quiet," because you yell and then whisper; "dirty" and "clean," because he looks at himself before his bath and after; and "sweet" and "sour," because you touch lemon juice and sugar to his tongue when you cook.

A Two begins to learn colors, and as soon as he does, you should define them more accurately—not blue, but navy; not red, but scarlet.

Every time a child learns a new adjective, he can describe his world more precisely than before. In this way a child can tell you, often with novel insight, how fog tastes or a kitten leaps or a sunbeam rests on his shoulder. These descriptions don't just spring from his mind, for the use of words, like skills, is built a layer at a time.

### ADVERBS

A Three can understand such adverbial concepts as here and there, if you physically put yourselves—here and there.

He'll like the adverb game best though, for it's the beginning of charades and funny enough for the whole family.

To play it, each person walks/sits/looks: slowly, sadly, loudly, softly, gaily, proudly, fearfully, bravely, happily, sillily, and whatever otherly you and your child can invent.

# LA TOILETTE

"Ah, *chérie*, make your toilette, if you please," our old *tante* would implore each morning, for to her, an unkempt child at breakfast was a sacrilege. Today we agree and insist our children wash, dress, brush their teeth and comb their hair before coming to the breakfast table, a routine they began learning by Two, mastered by Six and sometimes practiced on their own by Twelve.

Just as you had to learn how to take care of your child, so must your child learn how to take care of himself. This is the essence of independence.

## CLEANLINESS

### BATHING

When your child is Two, your bathroom will be your cleanest room, because you have nothing to do for twenty minutes a day except scrub the tiles and wipe the medicine chest. This is how long it takes him to bathe himself—a soaking sort of job—which is one more sign of his independence.

A Three scrubs too, washing handkerchiefs, underpants and the ring in the tub—not too well but with vigor—and by the middle of this year can be trusted alone in the bath and even with his two-year-old sister. By the time he's Five, any fear of the bath is gone and he can wash his hair, if you're not too particular.

### WASHING UP

A child, starting at Three, should wash his hands and face before and after meals, and by Four he can sit on the edge of the tub and rub his feet back and forth in the running water to get them clean—a great help if he often goes barefoot.

He'll find the hand washing is fun, but you'll have to keep his nails short so they won't show dirt, for it takes an Eight to scrub them clean. The face won't fare much better. Just have him splash it and rub it reasonably clean on the towel. Which is why we buy black towels.

### BRUSHING TEETH

Your mid-Three likes to watch his favorite person—himself—when he brushes his teeth. Hang a magnifying mirror from the bathroom towel rack, to dangle about two feet above the floor. He'll do a better job for such a splendid fellow. He won't brush his teeth well, but he'll learn the right technique and initiate the habit.

Let your child pick his own toothbrush—so he'll want to use it more—but see that it's a soft one.

Bacteria from food forms a plaque on the teeth when it's twenty-four hours old, and this can cause decay. Your child needs to brush the teeth on all three sides. He should brush vertically, flicking the bristles outward and scrubbing the molars any way he can. If the gums bleed, don't worry. It's part of the gum-toughening process and will stop in a few days.

An older child may like to use dental floss, which you'll cut. Teach him to slide it between his teeth to remove bits of food.

### COMBING HAIR

Conditioner makes hair easier to comb but our Nadia, like most young children, had such a sensitive scalp that she still preferred to brush her own hair, counting the strokes as a distraction—a job she could do by Six.

When her hair was a little smoother, she used a comb with widely spaced teeth and we taught her to hold it at an angle, making quick little strokes downward, un-tangling first the ends and working slowly up to the scalp.

We combed—and occasionally cut—the snarls for her.

## DRESSING

Before a child learns how to do a job, he must learn how to undo it, the same technique you use when you carefully take apart a chair to learn how to upholster it.

In this way, a Two can put on his socks, but he would rather take them off. He'll spend a lot of time removing his shoelaces but he won't be able to replace them for at least a year, or tell his left shoe from his right for another. He'll put on his pants and shoes and shirts many times, over many months, before he always does it right. In the meantime, he'll be furious every time he puts both feet in the same pants leg.

He'll button some things, but seldom correctly, for he almost never starts at the bottom, and he'll pull on his shirt backward. Still he considers this dressing himself, and so do we. If you keep your standards low, your praise high and his clothes simple, he'll be dressing himself completely, quickly, and competently by Three. Until then you'll help only before he reaches despair, and as casually as possible. This lets him pretend that he could do it himself if he weren't in a hurry to do other, more important work.

A child not only needs help sometimes to dress himself, but he needs help to keep his clothes. Since he'll remove at least some of them when he visits, if just to be convivial, it will pay to order labels that give your last name and your phone number. Iron them on the inside of his collar and his waistband and paste them inside belts, boots, shoes—and your umbrella. You'll be surprised at the rate of return.

To keep mittens, hammer grommets through the ribbing and the jacket cuffs, snapping the mittens to the cuffs—or just use safety pins. You also can attach one mitten at each end of a length of yarn and run it through the sleeves.

## PUTTING ON A COAT

There are two laborious but self-sufficient ways a child can put on his coat. They almost always are used in good nursery schools and almost never used at home. They should be. The happiest children attend to themselves.

The first way is a test of your housekeeping. A Two can put on his coat by throwing it on the floor, spreading it to show the lining. Have him kneel just behind the hood and, looking like a pint-sized Houdini putting on a strait jacket, slip each hand into an armhole, flip the jacket over his head and shove his arms through the sleeves: Even the hood will flop on his head.

Dust him and send him out to play.

An older child can lean his coat against the back of a low chair, sidle his back to it and slide his arms into the sleeves.

## BUTTONING

Your child will feel like a chowderhead when he struggles to button his clothes. Help him, not by doing it, but by teaching him to button from the bottom up. This way, the buttons and buttonholes have a better chance to come out even. A right-handed child should push the button halfway through with his right thumb and forefinger and grab it fast on the other side with the left thumb and forefinger, before that button gets away. Particularly inept children will use their teeth, which is fine too.

The success of the job is more important than the technique.

## ZIPPING

There will be zippers in your child's life, so teach him how to outwit them, most of the time, and buy coats with toggles or Velcro closures for the rest.

Like all dressing skills, your child first will learn to unzip his clothes before he can zip them. A Three can zip a placket, but it takes another year before he can zip a jacket.

When he learns that the tab has to be pulled all the way down to the bottom of the track to undo a zipper, he's ready to learn to zip. It requires such manual dexterity you have to explain each step graphically and congratulate him freely. Teach him to pull the tab to the bottom of the track until it touches the metal catch. He must keep it steady while he fits the other side of the zipper into it.

Be sure to tell him to hold the bottom of the zipper with one hand while he pulls the tab with the other, or the teeth won't mesh. Your child should learn to lock the zipper by pressing the tab flat after he zips—especially important for a little boy.

## BOOTING

The fine art of booting is seldom taught at home and hardly learned until first grade. Here is a method we devised to make life less complicated for a mid-Three.

Keep an 8-inch square of wax paper inside the back of the boot so the heel of the shoe can slide into it easily. This method works even if his new shoes have almost outgrown his old boots. He can use the same paper repeatedly.

## RIGHTS AND LEFTS

Most pre-Sixes don't know their lefts from their rights generally because they haven't been taught in a comprehensible way. Paint your child's right toenails with a permanent felt-tipped pen and match it with a big dot of the same color pasted to the inner sole of his right shoe. He'll know his lefts from his rights in a few days, but he may never be able to look at his right foot without thinking the nails should be green.

### LACING AND TYING

You never should bother to show a child a skill unless he's interested, whether it's toilet training or tying shoes.

Even with Velcro, all children go through a period of unlacing any shoes they can find. When your child has passed this stage, teach him how to lace a shoe. This concept is tricky to master, unless you're willing to demonstrate the same techniques a half-dozen days in a row. Don't use a cardboard toy shoe. It's the shoe on the foot that interests him.

Dip exactly half of a white lace in vegetable coloring so your child will see the colors crisscross. If he starts lacing at the top of the tongue, instead of at the bottom,

it will be easier. This trick can be learned by a mid-Three, but it takes a dextrous Four or an average Six to tie his shoes.

Frankly, we were never able to teach any of our children this skill. Instead, they learned to tie from a fellow Five. After tying the half-knot, Claire had them make the standard loop with one end, another loop with the other and tie the two loops together in a second half-knot.

If you want your child to tie in the standard fashion, perhaps he can learn from a neighbor.

# PROBABILITIES AND POSSIBILITIES

With parenthood comes a crowd of obligations, often unexpected, but most of them as inevitable as rain. Your child will get sick—and so will you—and sometimes she'll get bored and scared, but it's the day-in, day-out crankiness that can wear you down. You can expect your child to get at least a little cross between 5 and 7 P.M.—every 5 and 7 P.M.

While the bother of routine living will nibble your soul, the bigger problems can swamp it. When you have a second child,

you'll have to shepherd your first through the pain of having a rival and when you move across country you'll have to deal with her adjustment while you're dealing with everything else.

You may have to struggle with a disability, either in your child or yourself, and find the pity of strangers almost as hard to take as the problem itself.

And then there will be those big questions—of sex, of death, of divorce and many others too—and they always come when you least expect them. Not surprisingly, most important questions are hard to answer, but if you know what to expect, you can handle them more wisely.

Although there are few simple solutions in child care, there isn't a situation you'll meet that others haven't met before.

For this, be grateful. Every mother who has ever lived has found some ways to make things better. You just have to discover which ones will work for you. The search is worth it, for the easier you find motherhood, the happier you'll be.

# MISERIES

Some miseries are inevitable. No matter how creative, enriched and self-sufficient your child, motherhood can be the most dismaying job in the world at times. For us, it was the third child who brought calm to our house, but it could have happened sooner if we had figured out the right solutions to deal with the extraordinary bits of life, like fears and illnesses, or the very ordinary chaos of car pools and the daily Arsenic Hour. It turned out to be a matter of good preparation, lower standards and the knowledge that this too shall pass.

### ARSENIC HOUR

*Between the nap and the twilight
When blood sugar is starting to lower,
Comes a pause in the day's occupation
That is known as the Arsenic Hour.*

When you were pregnant there never was a moment you could forget it, even when you wanted to. Although you may not have asked the doctor, you worried about the wine you drank before you knew you had conceived and if it was safe to make love so often. You walked every day, slept eight hours at night and every nap you took was wrapped in virtue, but most of your attention went to the food you ate— the milk, the liver, the fruits.

This regimen gets harder and harder to follow by the end of the baby's first year and yet you both still need the three essentials every day—enough sleep, enough

physical and mental exercise and enough of the right foods—the same things, in fact, that you once took so seriously.

Without them there is bound to be a daily collapse, first of the child and then of the mother, which almost always strikes between five and seven. Experienced mothers jokingly call it Arsenic Hour and an astonishingly high number of other mothers begin to look forward to it as Sherry Hour, which is no joke at all.

The full quota of sleep at night is necessary and so is an afternoon nap for your child, even if you have to pretend that you think she is resting while she climbs in and out of her bed.

You need a half-hour of exercise, not to make you tired but to make your body alive. Vacuuming, cooking, dusting and driving do not constitute exercise. Walking, biking, playing hopscotch and touching toes do. Your child, like you, needs at least one special interlude a day to renew the soul, which seldom happens unless you make it happen.

However, it is the third essential—the quality of the food you both eat—that decides why 5–7 is so much worse than any other time of day. This is the time when you pay for any imbalance accumu-

lated from the day's diet. An overdose of carbohydrates and sugar—of cookies or alcohol or the caffeine in sodas, tea and chocolate, as well as coffee—drop the blood sugar level. This causes fatigue and bad temper. We think safety comes in many guises and good nutrition, as dreary as it sounds, is as sensible as a gate on the stairs or a lock on the poison cupboard.

Even these preventive measures aren't quite enough, however. Try to take your child for a short walk before dinner, or simply surrender him to television. This is a perfect time for a video or for "Sesame Street," if you only let him watch for a half-hour or so.

## MOTHER'S PICKUP

We've never known a mother of a Two who couldn't use a boost. This one has enough potassium to spark your metabolism in the morning or steady your nerves for Arsenic Hour. In a blender

| COMBINE | 6 oz. orange juice |
| | ½ banana |
| | 1–2 ice cubes |
| BLEND | 2 minutes |

## ERRANDS AND CAR POOLS

Trips to the pediatrician and the supermarket can be simply dreadful and at least some of them will be, no matter how efficient you are.

Buckle your child in a safety-tested car seat or a seat belt for even the shortest errand, to contain her as well as keep her safe. Take along a small special toy, keep a package of crackers in the glove compart-

ment, and play sing-along tapes as you drive. They're a godsend in a traffic jam. Keep paper and pencil and playing cards in your purse to fill time in a waiting room.

### TO THE PEDIATRICIAN

For the first four years, trips to the doctor can't be avoided and are bound to involve a twenty-minute wait and some confusion. Minimize it, dressing your child in simple, everyday clothes (no pediatrician wants a fashion show) and bringing a few toys and something for him to eat or a bottle if you don't breastfeed.

Still, a doctor can't jab a baby with a needle, poke a stick down her throat and a thermometer up her bottom without initiating an anxiety she'll remember next time. You can help a baby with sympathy but never tell a One that a shot won't hurt. The best thing you can do for a young child is to keep her entertained in the waiting room. For a mid-One draw a face on your palm, with one eye in the life line so it winks when you bend your hand.

A mid-Two will like to fish into an envelope of geometric shapes cut out of cardboard. Your child can close her eyes and tell the shape by feeling it. And a bag of colored zippers—to zip and unzip— appeals to a Three.

At mid-Three, the anxiety is over and your child should feel comfortable with the pediatrician—or you have the wrong pediatrician. A child is usually in awe of her doctor; but yours may be like the fresh little girl in our old *tante*'s joke, whose doctor, knowing the child's aversion to skivvies, looked down her throat and said, "Aha, Sarah! You're wearing no underpants!"

To which she replied, "Why don't you turn me upside down and see if my hat's on straight?"

### TO THE SUPERMARKET

If you must market with your child, buckle her in the seat of the cart, even if you have to bring a belt with you. You need early and very firm rules for her safety—and your sanity.

A Two can face you, standing on the axle between the front wheels, as if the cart were a fireman's truck. We called our Mike a fireman and brought his fireman's hat to wear—the only thing that kept a child like that from plucking a can of peas from the bottom of the pyramid.

Let your child decide on one family treat before she gets to the store, but tell her you won't buy anything else she asks for when she gets there. If she starts begging for more, return the treat you've put in the cart—a tangible way to show a child you mean business. Some people call this bribery and some people are right. It's all in the way you phrase it. Not, "If you'll be good, I'll buy you some treat," but, "If you won't be good, I won't buy you any."

We still wince when we see the corn chips. We never bought any because we never knew the children liked them, and we never knew they liked them because they never remembered to ask until they got to the store. Poor little tykes.

### CAR POOLS

Before your child is Five you and your husband will probably participate in car pools, which will mean hilarity, noise and camaraderie for your child, and a little more free time and, possibly, much chaos, for you.

After a combined nineteen years of car pooling, we know that there can be benefits only if the car pools are limited to five or six children, if you have that many restraints, and if the adult adheres to a few rules. On this we are ruthless.

You must have your child ready to go out the door when the driver beeps, and if your child is sick you must cancel in time for the driver to avoid the trip.

If you drive, be punctual. Buckle children in place and allow no nonsense. If they get rowdy, pull to the side of the road and wait, in silence, which calms them much quicker than commands. When you deliver, stay until each child has entered her house.

If you're going to be out of town on your duty day or if your child is sick or you are sick or your car is sick, you still must drive or get a replacement—or send a taxi.

### TO THE BARBERSHOP

Trim your husband's hair, then your child's, each sitting on a high stool. Once you've played barbershop at home, the real adventure is less frightening.

### TO THE GIFT SHOP

This is one time you should tell your child, "Hold your hands behind your back." You can expect almost absolute obedience, for a child doesn't want to break anything either, but she can last only about fifteen minutes.

## FEARS AND FANCIES

Fears may start in the first year and all children will have some by Six. They stem from dreams, shadows, stories, television and even overheard conversations, for a child is a literal creature who believes exactly what she hears. In fact, when you read "Amelia Bedelia" stories to your child, you'll find she also thinks it reasonable to "dress the chicken" in a sunsuit rather than fill it with corn bread. When you also look at life from the underside, your child's behavior will make more sense to you.

A baby as young as seven months may be afraid her parents won't return, even when they leave the room, for out of sight is out of life then. This fear of desertion peaks at mid-One, although later she deliberately uses her tears to pull on your heartstrings.

By Two a child has found some reason to fear loud noises, strange dogs, sharp needles and hot stoves. A little of this is good, for a child without fear is like a child without antibodies. She has no protection. She needs to know that fears are normal, to be discussed as matter-of-factly as anything else. If you show too much concern she may think you're scared too, but if you can help your child turn the fear into a fancy it usually disappears.

The vividness of a fevered dream may last for life, but the fears need not. Our Meg, at  mid-One, was terrified to cross any bridge by car until, at Three, she mentioned how scared she was the time the car went over the bridge. When we explained that she must have dreamed it, the problem dissolved instantly—a surprise, for most fears are more tenacious.

Some dreams are so real, a child wants to climb in your bed for comfort—a poor idea—but you can give her some hugs and then let her stay in a sleeping bag on the floor in your room for part of the night. If you're too rigid in dealing with her fears, they'll just get worse.

Your child may become afraid of daydreams too, of sliding down the drain, like a sliver of soap, for she can't judge sizes yet, or she may develop a galloping fear of elevators or of the ubiquitous Stranger. Give your child plenty of hugs and listens and tell her that you're the one who takes care of her and you do it pretty well. Many young children have been warned so much, about so many things, that they think they have to protect themselves, which can be an overwhelming idea.

If your child withdraws from most play or regularly acts out her fears, she needs professional help. Don't hesitate to seek it.

### THE GREAT PENIS SCARE

The penis is an extraordinary creation, but as strange as it looks to a child, the lack of it looks a lot stranger. When a little boy first sees a little girl completely, he is appalled. Obviously, she lost it. And when a little girl sees a little boy for the first time, she's sure she did.

That anyone could be so careless or so forgetful can frighten a child, though temporarily. The fear will be much less, or not at all, we think, if boys and girls see their friends and their parents naked sometimes. Trust your Four to carry on further investigations—fearlessly.

### DESERTION

The most self-confident child may feel abandoned sometimes, as parents shuttle to work, to shop, to parties. Although you won't stay home if your child sobs when the sitter comes—that would reward the tears—you will need sitters who give comfort more than cookies.

No matter how hard you try, however, not all sitters will be good and none of them will be able to comfort your child as well as you or find the teddy bear as quickly. The fear of desertion should be under control by Three, however, if you handle it positively.

For a baby of six months, play peekaboo first by hiding your eyes behind your hand, and then by hiding yourself behind the door. Your quick reappearances help a child have faith that you will always come back.

You also need to be very candid with your child. Tell her, even before she can talk, when you're going out and where, who will sit and when you'll be back and tell her in the same conversational way you would talk with a Six. A child can accept the fantasy of the tooth fairy or Santa Claus as games of love, but never the pretense that you'll "be back in a few minutes" when you know you won't. Honesty is not a plaything.

## THE DARK

This particular fear is the most common and we think the most preventable, since there's no rule that says a child must spend ten of every twenty-four hours in the dark. Either use a night light before the fear ever begins or open her door into a softly lit hall. A Three will like her very own flashlight too. It turns a midnight trip to the bathroom into an adventure, but tape both ends shut or she'll take it apart by noon.

A light sleeper is more likely to develop a fear of the dark if she isn't tired enough, either mentally or physically. See that your child has much more to do in the day, and more playmates—and, as a last resort, cut out her afternoon nap. All of this will make her sleepier at night.

When little Emily suddenly became fearful, her mother filled a clean spray bottle with water and a dab of French perfume, then shot a little of this "dream spray" on her pillow to make the fears go away. It was a lot cheaper than the drops of cologne her own mom once dabbed on her pillow, when she was a little girl.

## NIGHTMARES

A fear is scary and a fancy is fun, but both can spring from the same source. When that same imaginative Meg had a nightmare about a bear in her bed, her father immediately chased him out of the house, loudly and with a broom, and said he went to live down the street with Uncle Tom. For years we would drop over to visit Harry the Bear (for that was his name), who wore electric socks and slept in an empty bathtub. Unfortunately, he always was asleep or in a snit or out for a soda when we called, but by turning a nightmare into a charade, the fear had turned into fancy.

# HEALTH HAZARDS

Motherhood is one long internship in paramedics. When your baby is born, the doctor will insist that she's as close as the telephone, ready to answer every question, day or night—and then she goes on a trip or you go on a trip or the questions just seem too silly to ask.

In the first year you'll vacillate between being too casual and too anxious, perhaps as extreme as one careful mother we know who panicked when she picked up her baby and found the impossible—a dry diaper. Obviously something was wrong with her plumbing.

First she kept a careful record of everything that dear child did for the next twenty-four hours (for she didn't want to sound frivolous), left a message with the doctor's office and waited, frozen, by the telephone. The minute it rang she gave a full, nonstop account of the cries, the naps, the amount of formula left in each bottle and a description of each bowel movement until—inevitably—the man on the phone interrupted to say that it sure was interesting, ma'am but he was the piano tuner.

It's foolishness like this that will make

you slow to call the doctor until—inevitably—you treat the baby's cold yourself for days before seeing the pediatrician—and then you find out that your child nearly has pneumonia.

It's important to take the baby's temperature if you think she might be sick and—fever or not—to call the doctor if you're worried or just have a question. It may be embarrassing, but this is the way you learn to distinguish between a cry of hunger and a cry of fatigue, which takes a few months, and between fussiness and an earache, which takes at least a year. The healthiest child may have a fall or a fever and the most attentive doctor will go out of town. It will be your day-to-day experiences that teach you to handle the small crises alone.

By the time your baby is grown, you'll think you know enough to write your own prescriptions—which you won't—or enough to write a book—which you will.

## HOME MEDICINE

We don't dare pretend to prescribe medicine, but we can't pretend that you can get along without home remedies. You need popsicles and lollipops quite as much as you need a thermometer and a hot water bottle, and you need to know how to handle a fever in a hurry when the doctor can't be reached. Common sense is the common denominator of motherhood, and a few rounds of sickness help you learn it in a hurry.

### INFANT CRIES

The pediatrician, if she is the casual type, will tell you that you will recognize your baby's needs by the different sounds of her cry. This is seldom true. By the time you learn to interpret a baby's complaints you

probably have stopped having babies. However, there are only a certain number of things that can be wrong and it doesn't take long to check them.

A baby cries for a reason, and sometimes you can find out why and correct it and sometimes you can't. Nevertheless, it's your job to comfort her and sympathize. You want sympathy when you have a hangover or a crick in the neck or a bad case of the blues. Babies get miserable too and there are times when they need to be rocked and loved and crooned over whether it registers on the thermometer or not. This attention takes precedence over almost anything else, except possibly cooking dinner. Now you learn to cook with a baby in a sling, or on your hip, tribal-style. It can be done, and it really is much less distracting than hearing your child sob in her crib.

A baby likes to be rocked and to be held close, on your left side—the instinctive position for mothers—so she can be near the heartbeat she knew in the womb. This probably is the first imprinted stimulus a baby receives and it should be reemphasized after birth. A muffled clock—although its beat is different from yours—can soothe a child in her crib the same way it soothes a newly weaned puppy, but your baby will like a tape of your heartbeat better. Other children are soothed by a tape of white noise, or the whirr of a vacuum or a ride in the car or the stroller, even at night. Most of all, you will find—like many mothers and many studies before you—that the more a baby is cuddled, the less she cries.

### COLIC

There is a difference between a stomachache, which is occasional and erratic, and colic, which may be caused by an immature digestive system, or by a sensitivity to a food that's passed through your breast milk or to something in the baby's formula. When your child draws up her knees, tenses her belly and cries at a regular time every day, that's colic. And when you put a warm hot water bottle on her stomach and give her a warm water bottle to drink and rock her for hours and you both cry, that's colic.

Mothers in some European countries will soothe an unhappy baby by swaddling her tightly below the waist but without diapers, leaving the rest of her body unfettered by clothes. Any solution you try will make you feel better, and perhaps the baby too.

In other generations parents walked their colicky infants back and forth, and again doctors find it a good idea. Today they say that babies are consoled by the objects they pass as they go up and down the room, as well as the comforting heartbeat of a parent.

### HEAD COLD

A head cold is dreary for anyone, but it's miserable for a nursing baby, since she can't have antihistamines until she's six months old.

If your baby can't suck and breathe at the same time

**MIX**  1 t. salt
1 c. tepid water

Drop this solution in each nostril and lay the baby on her back. The saline nose drops will liquefy the mucus in about ten minutes and the baby will swallow it. If she's still gurgling, use the nasal aspirator to draw out the liquid mucus before you nurse.

### PACIFICATION

Most first-time mothers don't want their baby to have a crutch, but second-time mothers will take any crutch they can get. We're with them.

Some babies need to suck more than others, and for them a sugar tit was invented. This is the old Southern device of a clean rag dipped into sugar and water (and some say, occasionally bourbon) for a substitute nipple. Today we wouldn't try that without (1) checking with the pediatrician, (2) triple-rinsing the cloth to remove all traces of detergent and (3) sterilizing the water. With this amount of trouble, you may as well skip the sugar tit, and of course, the bourbon, and either give the baby a pacifier or put up with some fussing in the early months until she finds her thumb. A thumb is preferable to many parents because it will never fall out of the crib at midnight for you to find on the floor while she screams. In any case, a baby will probably suck as long as her nature intended, whether she has a sugar tit, a pacifier or a thumb, and she'll probably stop between Two or Three.

If your baby has trouble settling down one night and snuggles in her crib the next, it probably has nothing to do with her day. Instead, notice which bunny or blanket is in bed with her on the happy nights and make sure it's always there. If she has chosen a magic blanket you may have to scramble to get it washed and dried between breakfast and naptime, but it's still better than a fussy baby.

### SPITTING UP

If your baby spits up to be sociable after every meal, sponge it from her clothes with a rag dipped in baking soda and water. This absorbs the odor. If you're going out, take a soda-soaked wet sponge in the diaper bag, so your baby will smell sweeter. Spit-up, which is so routine to you, can upset those who have no young children.

You'll also want to spray a prewash onto the spot until you can wash the clothes—especially borrowed clothes. This is particularly important if your baby is on a formula, since it usually stains much more than breast milk.

## TEETHING

Your baby will probably cut her first front teeth between four and nine months and her first molars at Two (and if there aren't any accidents, she'll start losing her front teeth around Six, growing her second set in exactly the same order as the first teeth appeared).

A baby chews a great deal to cut a new tooth, drooling steadily, but she doesn't need you to rub the gums. It's one job she can do herself, and she should, for she'll know when to stop. Too much rubbing may cause a bone infection. Instead, help her teethe by giving her a stale bagel to gnaw or a small hard rubber toy. You also need to protect her from the dozens of small things she'll try to put in her mouth. Besides the risk of choking, they often carry germs, which is one reason why teething babies often catch colds. Unless your child gets sick, teething generally causes little pain except for the few hours it takes for a tooth to cut through the gums. Or so the doctors say.

When there is more pain, give a lot more love and kisses and help her sleep better by bicycling her legs and taking her on longer walks. Because sucking makes tender gums hurt more, let your child drink milk from a cup or enlarge the holes in her bottle, and give her fruit juice popsicles to numb the pain.

When her molars come in, she will drool twice as much, have a runny nose, look pale and be a little cranky.

## CRANKINESS

After a child is Two, you'd think she could explain her crankiness, but this is often hard even for a Six. She has no idea she's cross because she didn't sleep enough or eat a healthy snack. A child's frame of reference is so small, she doesn't know what she should complain about, as we found when the doctor took wheat from the diet of our brilliant, if fussy, young friend. Her disposition did improve and her headaches went away—a problem she never had mentioned. At Five, she thought her head was supposed to hurt. It always had.

Another child may be cranky because her jacket isn't warm enough or her shoes pinch her toes but it usually takes an Eight to explain even these problems.

Suspect pinworms if your child has a bad temper, the fidgets and an occasional tummy ache. You can see tiny white worms in the stools or by shining a flashlight on a bare bottom at midnight, when they come out to play. A prescription and some extra care get rid of them quickly, but these parasites spread easily, especially in urban areas, and a great many children get them every year.

## DIARRHEA AND CONSTIPATION

The most proper mother talks about her child's bowel movements at parties the way she used to talk about politics. After your baby has had diarrhea or constipation a few times you'll understand her concern. It's miserable for the whole family. Diarrhea is almost inevitable between six months and two years, for it can be a sign of many things, including an allergy, parasites or an infection. In fact, the same germs that cause a cold, tonsillitis and a stomachache often travel to the intestine, unless you curb your child's diet. Her normal caloric intake is too much when she's sick. The doctor will probably veto fats and carbohydrates to prevent or control diarrhea, ordering a simple, bland diet of apple juice, grated raw apple, gelatin, banana, low-fat cottage cheese, skim milk and dry toast, or the more stringent BRAT diet—bananas, rice, applesauce and toast. Give an occasional lollipop before she rebels, since it's only eighteen calories, and have her drink a great deal of water or the electrolyte supplement your doctor will order. Diarrhea often causes dehydration, which happens quickly and is one of the most serious problems that can befall a child.

Constipation, which can be caused by

an allergy, antibiotics, a yeast infection and heaven knows what else, is helped by changing your child's diet to include whole wheat or dark bread and by adding two tablespoons of prune juice to her orange juice if she won't take the prune juice straight. A drop of corn syrup added to her water or formula is also helpful and so is extra vitamin C, if your doctor says its okay.

Both constipation and diarrhea are improved by plain, unsweetened yogurt, that ancient, extraordinary food that makes centenarians commonplace in Bulgaria. Experienced travelers take it before and during an overseas trip, for it has a special strain of bacteria that, taken regularly for a few weeks, is said to prevent dysentery.

## CROUP

If you hear a seal barking in your baby's room, run to her quickly. You've got a case of croup on your hands and you have to move fast.

This illness, which can strike pre-Sixes quickly and usually at night, can develop if the larynx gets inflamed and swollen. This makes it so hard for a child to breathe that she barks and coughs and scares herself—and her mom—witless. Hug her tight, call the doctor and then aim the cold-air vaporizer right on her face with a sheet draped over the crib to make a tent and trap the steam.

If you don't have a vaporizer, turn on all the hot water taps in the bathroom and get your child's face as close to the steam as you can without burning either of you. These treatments may be all you need but the doctor may still want you to take her to his office or the hospital if your child has never had croup before. If you can wait until morning, however, put some stuffed animals or books under one end of her mattress to keep her head raised and open her windows wide, keep the vaporizer going and stay with her until morning. Another attack that night definitely calls for a trip to the hospital, but you can

probably handle future attacks on your own. A tendency to croup usually goes away by the time your child is Five.

## SORE THROAT

Almost any sore throat can be helped by gargling three times a day with this tepid solution, which a Four can do.

### The Gargle

| COMBINE | 3 oz. boiled water |
| | 1 tbsp. hydrogen peroxide |
| | ¼ tsp. salt |

The results are worth it, despite the taste, which lasts three to four hours, unless you give her a mint and a kiss. If her throat still hurts after the first day, or if fever develops, call the doctor.

## STOMACHACHE

Any stomachache that lasts more than a few hours can be serious and you should call the doctor. However, with us it always seemed to happen when we were traveling far from home, and every time we were sure it was appendicitis.

As a friendly nurse once taught us, appendicitis generally starts from the left side of the stomach, wanders to the middle and then settles on the right, usually causes a slight fever and reacts to poking differently from gas pains.

A child who can talk fairly well will cooperate when you examine her, so long as she doesn't know which symptoms are which, for then she may be too cooperative.

Have her lie on the bed, arms relaxed at her side, and poke all around her abdomen with stiff fingers, slowly and firmly. If it hurts more when you push them in it's probably gas, but if it hurts more when you pull them out it may be appendicitis, and you need a doctor and a blood count to test for an infection.

### FEVER

All children run fevers sometimes. It's the body's way of fighting an illness.

Each pediatrician has her own procedure for dealing with this symptom. Learn beforehand how she wants you to bring down a fever, because somehow children seldom get very sick during office hours. This way you can spare yourself the agony of standing by helplessly while your child's fever soars.

The doctor will probably want you to use a digital thermometer to take your child's temperature whenever she feels warm to the touch, and to call her if a baby under two months is running a fever of 100, rectally, or under 102 degrees for a pre-Two. There is less urgency for an older child, but 103 degrees, or a five-day fever of any degree, is cause for a call, and probably a visit to the pediatrician to look at your child's ears and throat, listen to her chest and take a culture.

Any child under Five with a fever of 103 degrees or more is a sick child. High fever is nature's way to burn up an infection, but it is a danger, especially to a pre-Two. Intense, prolonged body heat can cause delirium and convulsions, and on extremely rare occasions, it can even cause brain damage. Not all high fevers can be prevented, but their effects can be minimized.

### Thermometers

A rectal thermometer, which registers a half-degree higher than an oral thermometer, is the more accurate and it only takes one to two minutes to get a reading, but even a One feels the indignity of being spread-eagled on her tummy with a thermometer up her bottom. Sit next to the telephone to take her temperature, and let her listen to Weather or Dial-a-Prayer or anything else that will talk to her nonstop. By Three, you can usually trust her to keep her mouth shut when you take her temperature orally.

If your child objects too much to both methods, slip either a rectal or an oral thermometer under her armpit and keep her still for four to five minutes.

### The Chart

Keep a list of each temperature reading and the time, and record all symptoms. Pediatricians rightfully get very irritated at a mother's vagueness, for a record of the ups and downs of an illness can help them make the right diagnosis.

### Treatment

As soon as your child runs a fever, pump her with liquids. Give her anything she will drink or suck, including crushed ice, gelatin, lollipops and popsicles, but avoid milk, which is hard to digest. The higher the fever, the more liquid the body needs to keep from drying out.

If your child has a high fever, put her in a room away from hot or cold air vents and near the telephone, so you can make additional calls to the doctor. Turn off any lights that may shine directly in her eyes, remove any extra clothing and cover her only with a double sheet. Some doctors recommend wrapping a naked child in a wet towel covered by a dry one and holding her for a half-hour to bring a high fever down. Others think a parent should sit in a full tepid bathtub with her child for thirty to sixty minutes—a strange middle-of-the-night adventure. And, of course, there is nonaspirin in liquid, tablet and suppository form, which takes at least twenty minutes to take effect, to be given as the doctor prescribes.

Your child will begin to sweat as her temperature goes down. Change her, give her more water and check her every hour. These are only temporary measures until the virus has run its course or an antibiotic has cured the infection. If the doctor does prescribe an antibiotic, however, have her order live acidophilus too, to prevent a possible yeast infection, for an antibiotic kills the good bacteria in her intestine as well as the bad, and then yeast grows rapidly, which can cause other problems. The body has to stay in balance to stay healthy.

### Vomiting

If a child runs a fever and vomits too, call the doctor again and sit right by your child for she can dehydrate quickly in this condition. Give her gum if she's old enough to chew it, water by the spoonful every few minutes or bits of ice to suck on. Too much liquid drunk at once will cause more vomiting.

### Convulsions

A convulsion is brought on by a temporary dehydration of the brain, caused by high fever. It's the body's defense against the high fever of an infection or a virus and nothing is as dramatic. We have watched several and they have never lost their chilling effect.

In a convulsion the child's body goes rigid and shakes hard. The eyes roll back, the jaw snaps, the neck arches, the tongue flips back, and thick saliva forms around the mouth. Although panicked, you have to lay your child on the bed or a rug, clear any vomit out of her mouth with your finger so she won't choke, turn her on her side to let the saliva run out and then dip her in tepid water in the bathtub to bring the fever down fast. It will seem like hours, but a convulsion lasts only a minute or two. The child then goes limp as if in a faint, and falls into a calm sleep. Put her in a safe place, call the doctor immediately and prepare for a rapid trip to her office or the hospital.

And now you know why mothers tell their children to wear their galoshes when they go out—and why they keep telling them for the next eighteen years.

### Dehydration

Vomiting, diarrhea and fever can cause dehydration quickly in young babies, and the younger the baby, the more serious it is. It is also completely preventable. You'll know your baby is getting dehydrated if the skin on her tummy won't spring back when you gently pinch an inch—for dehydration makes skin lose its elasticity—and when her urine is dark; her eyes look glassy or sunken; and she doesn't shed many tears or pee very much.

Your doctor will probably have you give her an electrolyte solution and also recommend crushed ice in tiny, frequent amounts, weak tea, popsicles and milk or formula, cut in half with water.

### FAMILY ILLNESS

Life is grim if you succumb to an illness, but it's even grimmer if you don't. Just lying on the sofa—dressed and looking green—won't get any sympathy from your family. Instead they will spill more things than ordinarily, make more noise and look as pathetic as possible each time you remind them, "Mommy's sick." You still will be expected to cook and diaper. And at this point you may as well hang a scarlet "M" around your neck for Martyr.

It's time to give up, call your husband, put on a nightgown and go to bed. Only then will your family take you as seriously as you take yourself. In fact, your child will be so surprised she may tiptoe and whisper, off and on, for as long as two days. Your husband will be respectful, and

he may not give you breakfast until noon, but he will take charge.

When the whole family gets sick, however, you will probably have to run the show, dispensing medicine, diapering babies, serving meals and, resentfully, mud-

## WELL-BABY CARE

This is the first century in the history of the world when parents can confidently expect their babies to grow up. There are very few little tombstones anymore. We can thank antibiotics—as overused as they are—surgery, car seats and especially immunizations and well-baby check-ups for this spectacular change. It all amounts to prevention, and if necessary, early intervention, to keep your child healthy and safe.

Even if she never gets sick, the pediatrician will see her at least a dozen times in the first year; four times in the second year; twice in the third year and then every birthday thereafter. The check-ups will include the PKU test at birth, annual blood and urine work-ups; vision, hearing and tuberculosis tests, and the critical round of vaccines.

It's a wise and loving parent who gets her child innoculated on time against the greatest threats of childhood—polio, diphtheria, whooping cough, tetanus, rubella, measles and mumps as well as bacterial meningitis and three other serious infections, which are prevented by the new HIB vaccine. Only the vaccine for whooping cough—the pertussis part of the DPT shot—is controversial, but no charge against it has ever been proven, and it's protected countless children from brain damage and death.

This is the schedule to follow:

| 2 months | 4 months | 6 months |
|---|---|---|
| polio | polio | |
| DPT | DPT | DPT |
| HIB | HIB | HIB |

| 15 months | 18 months | pre-K booster |
|---|---|---|
| measles | | |
| mumps | polio | polio |
| rubella | DPT | DPT |
| HIB | | |

dling through, but lie on the sofa as much as you can. Soft-boiled eggs, dry toast, gelatin, low-fat cottage cheese and tea with lemon will seem like a banquet to everyone. Give plenty of liquids to prevent dehydration. Pass out lollipops to assuage tears and use television, videos and cassettes to get you through and lie down as often as you can.

This dismal togetherness may be eased somewhat if you have made friends with your neighbors. Tell them everyone is sick and ask for their help unashamedly. As our Atlanta friend says, "We can all get through if we 'hep' each other."

## *ALLERGIES*

Allergies may be the hidden handicap of childhood. Once they're tracked, they can be cured or contained fairly easily, but the symptoms are so diverse that they're seldom suspected.

You probably know that they can cause a runny nose, a sore throat or asthma. But they also can cause an earache, a headache, a stomachache or even achy joints as well as rough or scratchy skin, colitis or cystitis, constipation or diarrhea, bedwetting or soiling. They can even cause personality changes, for allergies can affect any part of the body, including the brain. Crankiness, hyperactivity, sluggishness, poor concentration, confusion, depression, anger, fatigue, deep sleep and night terrors can be triggered by an allergy, and some allergists even think it can cause symptoms that look like Tourette's syndrome—that rare condition which can cause tics or even make the child speak in obscenities or sound like an animal.

The effect of allergies on behavior is particularly hard to track. If you and your husband have been pretty good parents, and yet your child doesn't act like other children—especially your other sons or daughters—you have to ask yourself: Does this behavior make sense? If it doesn't, you're probably looking at some minor, chronic problem, like allergies.

Many allergies—both physical and behavioral—are reflected in a child's face. A reaction to milk, for instance, may make her get puffy or wrinked around the eyes or get dark circles under them—allergic shiners, they're called—or they may make her earlobes turn red, while the same allergy may make another child rub her eyes or swipe her hand across the tip of her itchy nose a dozen times a day—the allergic salute.

Surprisingly, most pediatricians know very little about allergies, and even pediatric allergists often disagree about them. Some don't believe that a child can be as allergic to foods as to inhalants, because it is hard to read any allergic reactions in young children, particularly to foods. Other allergists dismiss the possibility because they think only a small number of children react to food at all. Or they think that children are merely sensitive to foods, rather than allergic to them. Parents don't care about percentages or semantics of course; they just want their child to feel well.

Fortunately, parents are usually the best people to test for allergies, and they can do it if they use care and keep a careful diary. It will taken a written record over a week or so to show if your child is worse at night—a sign that she may be bothered by the kapok stuffed into her teddy bear or the padding under her rug. Another child may react after she's been around cleaning supplies or a fabric softener, paint or gasoline, mold in the basement or the freshly cut grass outside.

An allergenic food is much harder to track, however, since children eat such a variety of foods, with so many ingredients. Also it can take several days for the body to process the food and trigger the sensitized cells.

Milk—in some form—is the biggest offender, followed closely by corn, eggs, orange, apple or grape juice, pork and peanut butter. Other children—particularly hyperactive children—react to dyes and preservatives as if they were poison and sometimes to salycilates in aspirin, almonds and many fruits.

If you think a food bothers your child, you should allot two to three weeks to the testing, prepare all her meals and snacks yourself and keep very good notes to monitor her reactions. Otherwise you'll get quite confused.

This can put a lot of pressure on your child unless you and your husband go on the diet with her, which is a good idea. You may find that your own nagging little health problems go away, since allergies are often inherited. You may even be bothered by the same foods, although you may not react to them the same way.

To manage the elimination diet you first must clear the most allergenic foods out of her system for five days. Do this by cutting out all milk, beef, pork, wheat or corn products, as well as processed foods, citrus fruits, tomatoes, chocolate, eggs, peanuts, yeast, sugar, additives, preservatives and dyes and anything else she eats or drinks more than once a week. This will probably leave you with chicken, lamb, rice, oats, pears—usually the last allergenic foods—and a few other fruits and vegetables.

If your child is worse than ever after a couple of days, that's a promising sign. She may be allergic to one of the most common foods in her regular diet, for a child often loves the thing that makes her sick, and they bother her most as these allergens leave her body. This child will want another fix as badly as a smoker wants a cigarette.

These cravings should fade on the fourth day and she should be much better by the fifth day. You can then start adding one food every twenty-four hours and always in pure form—a glass of milk, an egg, a tomato, unbuttered popcorn, a handful of peanuts—until you've tried all her regular foods. If she reacts to any of them, keep those foods out of her diet for six months and then give them to her again, trying one every day or two. Once she's built up her defenses, she may be able to eat the problem food every four to five days without any bad effects.

This is a tiresome test, but a Four will usually cooperate if you explain it carefully, give her a shiny badge and tell her it says Allergy Detective, Junior Grade. Children want to feel good and be good, even if it means trying this diet.

## CALAMITIES

Living in the city, we soon learned to appreciate the solitude of country life and were lucky enough to have spent a few vacations on a secluded farm and some on a quiet beach. This happy isolation fed our souls but forced us to grapple with emergencies we never had handled before. Every vacation had its sunburns, bee stings, infected bites, cuts, bruises, even bad scratches from an attacking peacock, fishhooks in the head and one near drowning.

We learned to pack salt, soda, vinegar, peroxide and cornstarch and in fact to use these first-aid treatments successfully before the doctor could be reached.

### BURNS AND SUNBURNS

Apply cool water immediately to a burn, both to keep the layers of skin from separating into blisters and to lessen the pain. It takes at least ten minutes to cool a minor, first-degree burn. Even a package of frozen food on the burn will help.

A sunburn almost vanishes if you first wash it with vinegar, then cover it with a cold wet towel until the skin feels cool.

For faster overall treatment in case of any large burn—no matter what its cause—wrap a wet towel around the child before going to the hospital. A child under Three can get dehydrated quickly from a large yet minor burn.

### POISON IVY

Poison ivy and poison oak are still making children miserable, but nature also gives parents six hours to prevent it: the poison ivy oil has to be on the skin that long before it can cause a rash. If you think there's a chance that your child was exposed, use pre-packaged alcohol wipes to get rid of it, or scrub her well with a brown soap, or at least a deodorant soap. You also need to wash all her clothes well and wash or wipe her shoes, for the oil can last for months. If she gets a rash anyway, it will start in twelve to forty-eight hours and may last for two weeks. Treat it with love and kisses, calamine lotion—which works pretty well in the beginning—and plenty of hot baths, to ease the itching for a few hours at a time.

### BUMPS AND CUTS

Ice will keep a bump from turning into a goose egg if you put the ice in a plastic bag and flop it on the bump like a pillow. Crush the ice first, because the bits won't feel as heavy on your child's head, and watch her carefully. The doctor should be called if she vomits or gets pale, sweaty or sleepy—all signs of a possible concussion.

Ice is often the treatment for cuts too. Although steady pressure on a cut will make the blood clot more quickly, try an ice pop for one of those small frightening cuts on the inside of the mouth or on the lip. It usually stanches both the blood and the tears rather quickly.

Ice does the job for other minor cuts too, but it will intensify the pain for a few minutes until the skin is numb. Just rub the cut with an ice cube, and to keep your child quiet, give her another cube to suck.

Some mothers, more daring than we, use ice, a kiss and a butterfly bandage on small cuts, but frankly we never hesitate to let the doctor or the hospital staff decide when stitches are necessary.

Although we are no food faddists, we have had spectacular luck using vitamin E on small cuts and even stitches, as well as minor scrapes and burns. We simply smeared on the contents of one 100 I.U. capsule three times a day for three days.

The results were always good, if curious, with the top layer of skin toughening and peeling, leaving a fresh pink skin beneath, to be coated one more day. This helped prevent scars, and though it may be our imagination, we think it made stitches less noticeable too.

### SPLINTERS

A splinter can cause an infection and the blood will need stimulation to flush it away. Soak the area with this solution.

#### All-Purpose Solution

The water should be as hot as the child can stand for ten minutes.

**COMBINE**     **1 pt. boiled water**
                   **1 tsp. salt**

If part of the splinter is exposed, you can use tweezers to pull it out. If it's completely under the skin, heat a needle over a flame to sterilize it, then freeze the spot with ice to numb it and gently poke the needle under the skin to fish the splinter out. If you can't remove a very deep splinter, your child may need to see a doctor and even get a tetanus shot.

### SCRAPES AND SCRATCHES

The skinned knee is to childhood what the Purple Heart is to war: a badge of courage. Every fall is a sign of derring-do.

Give it a kiss, wash it well with hydrogen peroxide, get out all debris, dry it with a tissue, and put a bandage on it, if it makes your heroic little child feel better. The scrape can heal just as well without it.

### BITES AND BEE STINGS

Some mothers report that lemon juice rubbed on a child's skin will actually keep mosquitoes from biting, but most of us only think of that when we have to treat the bites.

The itching caused by bites from mosquitoes, gnats, flies and spiders can make a child miserable. Vinegar, if used immediately, will lessen the itching and a hot poultice of the All-Purpose Solution will ease the swelling. It it's near the eyes, use half as much salt in the solution, applying first a hot compress for ten minutes, then a cold one in two hours and a hot one again two hours later.

For a bee sting, pull out the stinger if you can see it or suck the poison and spit it out, then shake meat tenderizer over it. The enzyme breaks down the venom because it's a protein. There may still be a little swelling, which ice should help, but take your child to the hospital quickly if she gets pale, sweaty and has trouble breathing—all signs of an anaphylactic reaction.

### TICKS

Ticks can carry Lyme disease, Rocky Mountain spotted fever and other illnesses, but you can avoid them if you can avoid the ticks themselves. Some ticks are so small they are impossible to find on the skin, so have your child wear long-sleeved shirts and tuck her pants in her socks if you go for a hike in any tick-infested area with high grasses and shrubs. You also need to check well for larger ticks when you get home, especially in her scalp.

If you find one, soak a wad of cotton with alcohol, nail polish remover or salad oil, and press it over the tick so it will let go, then twist it and pull it out. Call the doctor if your child gets a rash, a headache, a fever or swollen joints within three weeks of the bite, to see if blood tests and perhaps antibiotics are necessary.

### SPRAINS AND STRAINS

Apply ice for the first twenty-four hours, then soak the sprain in a hot All-Purpose Solution or in epsom salts. A child can keep her foot or hand in a bucket more happily if you add marbles or pennies for her to handle (or footle, or that matter).

If she has any problem walking or picking up a toy, however, have her checked by the doctor, for a broken bone isn't always painful enough to make a young child complain.

### BROKEN BONES AND CRACKED HEADS

Sooner or later, your child will break a bone and if she doesn't, she will roughhouse so much you may think she has.

Sometimes the most minor fall can injure a child, so you must watch her closely after she takes a tumble. Sharp, localized pain, blacking out, double vision, paleness, cold sweat, chills or vomiting are signs that your child should be rushed to the hospital.

If it's a broken leg she probably won't be able to stand on it, and if it's an arm, she might not be able to make a fist, or indeed bear to lift it to any position other than the one in which it was broken. It's

much harder to tell about the skull, the ribs or the bones in the hands and feet. An X-ray is the only way to be certain and the quicker the better. The doctor must either set a broken arm or leg before there's any swelling, or wait until it subsides—a painful twenty-four hours—and she must treat a concussion immediately.

If you suspect a fracture, keep your child warm to offset the shock to her system and call your doctor. She'll either send an ambulance or have you take her to the hospital yourself. If you drive, lay your child next to you, buckled in place and covered with a blanket, and with an ice bag on the tender area to minimize swelling. The doctor also may have you give her sips of cola on the way to settle her stomach, and if he suspects a concussion, will have you talk to her constantly to keep her awake.

Vomiting and drowsiness are the two main signs of a concussion. It requires bedrest and usually hospitalization.

### CHOKING

A child who is choking—who can't talk, cough or breathe—needs help fast. The younger the child, the gentler you'll be, but it may take some force to clear the way.

A baby should be draped face down on your forearm, with the head lower than the trunk, and hit forcefully four times between the shoulder blades. If that doesn't work, drape her over your hand, press your fingers between her belly button and her rib cage and give sharp upward thrusts.

An older child needs you to stand behind her, wrap your arms around her waist and make a fist with one of your hands, using the other hand to thrust the fist in and up, rapidly, just below the breastbone—the Heimlich maneuver.

If that doesn't work, look into the child's mouth. If you can see the food or the toy, put you finger into her mouth and try to sweep it out of the mouth.

## POISON

If you think your child has had cigarettes, whiskey, vitamins or even a teaspoon of any nonfood, like liquid wax or a dishwasher compound, call the Poison Control Center—a number you should keep next to each telephone. They'll check the ingredients before you try to get her to throw up, since a caustic, like lye, would do as much damage coming up as it did going down. If they want her to vomit, they'll have you put your finger down her throat and tickle her tonsils or give her syrup of Ipecac—an emetic that belongs in every medicine chest. They may even have you take her to the hospital. Unless you go by ambulance, have a friend drive you so you can give your child fluids and if she falls unconscious, you can give mouth-to-mouth resuscitation—a technique to learn before you ever need it.

---

### MOUTH-TO-MOUTH RESUSCITATION

This technique has saved thousands, but you have to know it—and practice it—before you can give it. This is what you'll learn in class:

Have someone call the rescue squad, while you lay the child on the ground, then wipe anything out of the mouth with your thumb and tip the head backward, so the tongue can't clog the throat. Hold the jaw steady, and pinch the nose with your fingers, so the air can't escape—both necessities during the entire procedure. Cover her mouth with yours. To the mental count of 1, 2, 3, breathe out in a gentle puff, then turn your head aside to let the old air expel from her lungs while you draw a new breath for yourself. Keep an even rhythm, twenty small breaths to the minute for a baby under one year, and fifteen bigger breaths a minute—1, 2, 3, 4—for an older child, and do this for at least fifteen minutes or until breathing is regular. Anyone who has had to have resuscitation should be seen by a doctor and hospitalized for 48 hours for general observation—an essential in the case of a near drowning.

---

## HOSPITALS: EMERGENCY AND OTHERWISE

There's little to calm the frenzy of an emergency, but you can handle it better if you know what to do in advance—and you should. There's bound to be at least one disaster in the first six years.

Learn the location of the nearest hospital, the hospital your doctor uses and any special procedures she recommends.

She surely will want you to call her even if you feel too frantic to spare the time. She can advise first aid, and decide whether your child needs hospital or office treatment. Home visits are almost impossible, since few doctors will leave a roomful of patients, and if it's that urgent, the child should be in a hospital to get the necessary tests and medical or surgical help.

If your child does need hospital treatment, the doctor will alert the emergency room and, if necessary, call an ambulance. If you call yourself, the driver may take your child to the nearest hospital, no matter what you want. If you can't reach your doctor and you don't know whether you have an emergency or not, go to the hospital—the safe-not-sorry principle.

You'll be dashing out of the house, but do grab a special toy, your insurance identification and a blank check too (whether you have money in the bank or not). Officious nurses sometimes delay help until they are sure the hospital can be paid. The toy is to placate your child because the wait may be long—emergency rooms take the most serious cases first—and because she'll be cross, since she can't eat or drink anything until she has been treated.

If your child will be hospitalized for more than a day you'll want to return with a few special toys from home and some snapshots of the family and maybe of the pussycat. Even if you're with your child she'll be lonely, for the friendliest hospital in the world is still remote. If your child needs surgery, a good hospital will try to minimize her anxiety by letting you wait

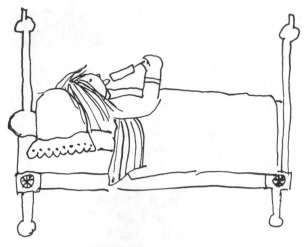

with her outside the operating room until she's sedated and will probably let you spend the night in her room.

When you know in advance that your child will be hospitalized, she should be told what will happen to her there. A pre-Three can't understand much besides tea and sympathy, but an older child will profit by a book about hospitals and a visit there beforehand.

She also needs to know about anesthesia and why doctors wear those silly-looking pajamas and caps. She'll want to know that the bed in her room will be stiff and narrow with crib rails, but if she's there for an operation she'll travel to and from surgery strapped onto an even taller, skinnier cot on wheels—an interesting trip.

Of all the routine hospitalizations, we found a tonsillectomy was the scariest, not because of its slight danger, but because it was preceded by so many illnesses we wondered, "If this doesn't work—then what?" A child has these same qualms too, we think, and needs special cheer. Our Kate, still groggy from a tonsillectomy, was enchanted by the beautiful Spanish doll on her pillow but Nadia enjoyed her send-off most. On the night before the operation we turned a favorite family dinner into a party with a special dessert and with friends—at the doctor's suggestion. The food kept her adrenalin high and since she couldn't eat much for several days, she needed a full stomach.

If your child is having this operation she should know that it will hurt to swallow or even to talk at first, improving rapidly until, on the fifth day, she will have a brief few hours of real pain as the stitches draw tighter. On the other hand, she will have more ice cream, ginger ale, popsicles, gelatin—and soup—than she's ever had in her life: the silver-lining principle.

## CONVALESCENCE

A convalescent child needs sympathy and many simple things to do. She also needs socks on her feet, since she spends only as much time in bed as her body needs and she'll seldom put on her slippers.

When health is low, impressions are deepest. Our girls still remember an occasional rose on a sick tray, with food served on doll dishes and a lollipop to stir their tea (the only spoon we could find, we said). It's nice to feel treasured when you're sick.

A convalescent child is frustrated easily. She can't even decide what to do without feeling weepy. To keep her a little happier, you can provide her with more tapes, more stories aloud, more loving and a few simple toys she can use to invent her own games, such as a flashlight, a magnifying glass, playing cards and some paper clips as "fish" for a magnet.

An older child finds a jelly roll pan is a good base for a puzzle or a coloring book, for its rim catches anything loose, but a bed table made from a cardboard box is good for the child who will be laid up for a long time.

To make one, turn the box upside down, so the bottom becomes the table-top. Remove the flaps and cut two semicircles on opposite sides of the box, to fit over the patient's legs. It will look like a two-way covered bridge.

◇ EXCEPTIONS ◇

Whenever your life gets complicated, you will have to spend extra time with your child to compensate for it, since any change, for better or worse, strains a family. No matter how much you welcome another baby, a cross-country trip or a little renovation in the house, you can expect more tension. You may face a temporary situation, like moving across town, or it may be the grinding long-term problem of dealing with a disability. Both sorrows and joys will exhaust you but the grit you develop will enrich you too.

The solutions you find must be peculiarly your own, for no circumstances are ever the same. However, since nothing in this world is unique, the answers that other parents have found can be the most helpful of all.

## HYPERACTIVITY

Hyperactivity is one of those scary buzz-words of parenthood—an umbrella term for the impulsive, fidgety child who can't concentrate, can't sit still and can't be counted on to do what she should. It can undercut the strongest little ego and unsettle the most stable family, unless parents know how to help their child handle it.

But first you have to identify it. Children are normally bouncy, frisky people and it's hard to know where the bounce ends and the hyperactivity begins, particularly if this is your first, or if you're a quiet sort of person with a rowdy sort of child.

Although the severity of their problem varies widely, hyperactive children generally have many of the same characteristics. They are easily distracted children who sleep poorly at night and are restless by day, and whose attention spans are so short they find it hard to finish what they start. They have sudden tempers and major mood changes and are quick to act, quick to cry and want what they want right away. Their motors run in overdrive.

Hyperactive children are more allergic, and they have more colds, more illnesses, more asthma, and more middle ear infections, particularly as babies. And when they get older, they have more learning disabilities too.

You might suspect your child is hyperactive if she was extremely active in the womb and was often fretful and frequently awake in infancy and if she hated to be cuddled. A hyperactive toddler may have fierce and frequent tantrums, bang her head or bite her hand or rock herself until the whole crib shakes, but mostly she's busy getting into the medicine chest, going out on the roof or taking off on a walk—alone. This child needs much more supervision than most, for she finds it as hard to discipline herself as she would to read *War and Peace*.

A hyperactive Four is not as bold as she was at Two, but she's probably still clumsy, has trouble handling crayons and small toys and has taken a long time to be toilet trained. The real problem will show up when she starts pre-K. The hyperactive child is so self-centered she has a terrible time following orders and tends to bother other children, no matter how much or how well she is disciplined.

If you think your child is hyperactive, the pediatrician will first rule out low blood sugar, high lead levels, sleep apnea and other possible causes, and then probably tell you that the cause is still unknown. Some experts think hyperactivity is born of a slight abnormality in the brain, or a shortage of blood to one part of the brain, while others blame it on an allergy or a sensitivity, or perhaps an imbalance of trace metals. You probably want to test for food allergies first—which you can do yourself—since many parents say they can get rid of the hyperactivity by getting rid of a food or an inhalant (see Allergies, page 128). This is not only the least expensive and most conservative approach, but it's the easiest.

If that doesn't work, or you don't want to pursue the allergy theory (and it is controversial), the doctor may want a psychologist to evaluate your child and then prescribe a stimulant. Oddly enough, this often calms a hyperactive child, but it has to be monitored carefully, for there can be side effects—including a slower growth rate in some children—and there is increasing concern about this treatment.

Whether you look for the cause or treat the symptoms, your hyperactive child needs a fully childproofed home; wider, clearer boundaries than most children; and more supervision. She also needs an order and structure to her day, and to all the events within her day. This child gets rattled enough; she doesn't need many choices.

Most of all, a hyperactive child needs parents who know how hard she tries to be good (and she does) and who make it clear that they love her, no matter what.

## THE SECOND BABY

Tell your child about your pregnancy when you tell your other friends. Some mothers can wait until the sixth month; we lasted six weeks.

After the initial queries, your child will scarcely mention the subject. She hasn't forgotten. You need to explain how life begins, develops and is brought forth, even if she doesn't ask. Let her listen to the heartbeat and feel the baby move.

Instinctively, you will push your first child from the nest, encouraging independence much faster than you would have done. Don't be alarmed. This is good and healthy. Mothers don't have the stamina to handle more than one litter at a time, whether they are cat mothers or people mothers. Even a One will react well to your expectations if you compensate with a special camaraderie—a relaxed trip to the pet store, a breakfast picnic in the park.

There are other specific ways to prepare your child for the new baby. She'll resent the baby using her crib, but she won't resent it so much if you put away the crib and provide a new bed and new bureau for her at least six weeks before you expect to deliver. Only then will you set up a bassinet for the baby. Right now, the first child comes first.

In the last months of pregnancy you'll want to take her to a party or a tour for siblings at the hospital, or at least tell her what the maternity ward looks like, who will take care of her when you're away and how the new baby will eat. We should warn you: your child will be more curious—and more jealous—when you feed the baby than at any other time, especially if you nurse. We think you'd be wise to ask a friend to show her how her own baby eats. It will help her get used to the idea, but not very much.

As luck will have it, you'll go to the hospital in the middle of the night, but be sure to wake your child and tell her you're leaving. You'll also want to telephone her after you deliver. She'll accept your news—probably in silence—but she may be distraught unless the baby is a carbon copy of herself.

Our Mike sat in self-exile on the front steps all day, after hearing the news of a third sister. Only his father could lure him in again, but the next day he was consoled enough to announce it with lollipops to his friends.

You may be able to let your firstborn visit you at the hospital and see the new baby for herself, but if not, a camera will help your firstborn adjust to the tininess of the infant.

Take pictures immediately of the baby alone, with Father, with Mother, and all three together. She may as well get used to the idea. A one-hour developing service— or, if possible, a camera that develops its own film—will let your husband hurry the pictures home.

Your child can absorb the impact alone, then show the pictures to her friends and probably scribble on them and flush them down the toilet. That's all right. They're her pictures, and you probably will never see them again.

When you have a new baby, you may be ashamed of your love—not the rather prosaic love you feel for your newborn, but the overwhelming love you feel for your first child. This difference is completely natural. Each day you care for a child brings a new degree of love, no matter how bad either the day or the child. It will take months for your newborn to find her niche, and until she does, she won't know what she's missing.

On the day you come home, let your husband carry the baby into the house so you can hug the firstborn and make a great fuss over her. Give a wrapped present from the baby, perhaps a rubber doll and bottle, so she may feed her baby while you feed yours, and maybe one superpresent, like a toy piano. She'll like these gifts and she may like the salt and pepper packets and flexible straws you bring from the hospital but the real present you bring will be you.

Let your child show the new baby to any guests, and hope that they have the grace to bring a present to her as well as for the baby.

Your firstborn will want to touch him, smell him, tickle his toes, sing to him, hold him and later help you bathe and dress him. Everything you allow her to do shows your trust, but do stand by. She may never hurt the baby—at least not much—but there are bound to be times when she'd like to throw the baby out with the bathwater. It won't be a patch on the jealousy she'll feel in three months when everyone koochy-coos the cooing baby and nobody notices her or brings her presents.

The first few times your older child sees you breastfeed, she may ask for a taste or pretend not to notice, or, as ours did, she may astonish you by yanking down your bra before company and commanding, "Feed her." The more distracted you are when feeding the new baby, the worse your firstborn will react. She'll realize almost immediately that you can't control her while you nurse the baby. That's why you should try to have morning and afternoon feedings wherever you think your older child will be most content.

One well-prepared Four we know, the paragon of his set, accepted the idea of a baby completely until his mother came home with a new sister and a colossal cold too. She didn't have quite enough energy to nurse both the cold and the baby and none at all to visit with Robbie. On that first day, when his father thought he was napping, he wrote on his toys with crayons

## THREE SONS

There must be a special place in heaven for mothers of three sons. You certainly can tell them on earth. They're those ladies with amused, bemused faces and an amazing tolerance for disaster—for they have learned that shouting doesn't help.

No other combination of children, not even twins, can create so much chaos or camaraderie. Even the most introspective child will join the team—them against you—and like all good players, they encourage each other to bigger feats of daring.

We recommend the advice of so many successful mothers of three boys. Give them as much outdoor playtime as possible, and indoors, set up two rooms: one for sleeping, with nothing but beds and bureaus, and the other for playing, with much climbing equipment. With three children, one is bound to be quieter than the others and he probably will need a corner somewhere else.

You will be frazzled in the early years but when your boys grow up, we think you'll find yourself perhaps more treasured than most other mothers.

---

and on his walls with felt-tipped pens, spread glue on the floor and ran his mother's clothes through the dishwasher. His mother could only stagger out of bed and say, "Why, Robbie, why?" Fortunately, his behavior was as temporary as it was disastrous.

Another favorite Four, picture-book pretty with brown eyes and yellow curls, climbed on a stool at our house one day and pronounced, ex cathedra, his own rules to care for the new Suzannah:

"You *Don't* Drop the Baby When You're Holding Her in the Air!

"You *Don't* Push Down on the Baby's Soft Spot!

"And You *Don't* Press on the Baby So Hard You See the Whites Under Your Fingernails!"

Aside from these essentials, there probably aren't any other rules your firstborn needs to know.

## DISABLED CHILD

We agree with a noted anthropologist—and a grandmother—who said that children "trash a marriage," even as they enrich it. Indeed they do, and the more problems a child has, the more a marriage can be hurt—and the more it can be enriched. Stress brings out the best and the worst in everyone.

If you have a child who is disabled, either mentally or physically, she'll need much extra care and therapy too. So will you. Some exceptional people can endure alone, but you won't know if you're one of them until it's too late.

You and your husband will need more respect for each other than other couples and more respites together. You also will need support and guidance from others, either through group counseling—which costs money—or through parent meetings of the local organization that deals with your problem, which are free and usually better.

The problems of these parents will mirror your own concerns and their solutions will guide you. You'll find out what tests and treatments might help your child, where to get good consults, who's doing the best and latest research, how to handle the medical bills and how you and your husband can still get along, even though you don't always see the problem the same way or at the same time.

You'll even find out how to help your other children adjust better, which is critical. Siblings often feel their needs couldn't possibly be as important as the needs of a handicapped child.

There's no reason to invent the wheel—especially when the roads are so rocky.

## DISABLED PARENT

In one more marvel of nature, the disabled mother learns to cope in a hundred ingenious ways, as if the challenge of her role were a sport in itself. One dear friend, battling braces and crutches—and still a more dedicated mother than most of us—found it was a matter of adjusting the equipment and resolving the small, terrible tasks of motherhood so thoughtfully that she didn't feel overly tired or silly because of her solutions.

If you have a back problem, you'll be more self-sufficient, as our friend was, if you have the playpen raised by extending the legs or by mounting it on a platform.

The feeding table was better than a high chair, she felt, because lifting was less of a strain and the table was safer, because tipping was almost impossible.

Changing was done at waist level until the baby was old enough to stand on a chair and a harness was used outside since the straps were easier to catch in an emergency than her child's hand—and since her child loved it so much, her dolly wore one too.

Stooping is the biggest problem any mother has, but it's especially hard if you have a bone or muscle problem. We recommend the large plywood pincers to pick up the clothes and toys from the floor, but you can have fewer toys to fetch if you tie them to the playpen with elastic so your child can reel them in for herself.

If she still makes trouble for herself and then cries about it, she's been in the same place too long, like any child.

◇ # TRANSITIONS ◇

We all go through normal, stressful passages in life—some long, some short—and they can be quite unsettling for children. They instinctively resent it—even a crosstown trip in the car—if they don't know why they're doing what they're doing, or when it will be over (and so would you). If children know the reason for all the steps involved in a move, a trip or an afternoon of errands, and if you make it simple enough for them to understand—they will behave much better.

Try to look at these transitions through the eyes of a child—and with the patience of a saint.

## TRAVEL

It can be maddening to travel with a child, but there really are ways to make it easier.

### AIR TRAVEL

An airplane ride of even two hours alone with a small child can cause anguish. We've seen the young mother in tears, struggling to walk those endless corridors to get from one gate to another to change planes. She

carries her baby in one arm and her house in the other.

If you travel with a child you must plan the trip to the last minute. When making your reservation, ask the airline to have a stroller, a cart or even a wheelchair waiting at the airport, at your connecting flight, and at your destination. You can load it with everything, which is especially helpful at the end of the flight for that long trek between the gate and the baggage claims, when you can finally get a skycap.

You also need to ask the airlines for a seat on the plane with the most leg room—generally the bulkhead seat on the front row of the coach section. You'll have space to change her on the floor or to let the baby play there on a blanket when you're in flight. This will give you more freedom, for a pre-Two is a nonpaying passenger who has no seat of her own, although you may want to take her car seat along in case there is an extra space she can use. You can always check the car seat if the plane is full.

Pack everything else you need for the flight in a lightweight shoulder bag—petroleum jelly, disposable diapers, packaged premoistened towels, a large bib, a sweater, a few teething biscuits, two small toys, her magic blanket, some food and maybe some bottles. Remember: a pre-Two gets no meals at all; an older child may not like what she's served—and the plane may be delayed.

Since you may have to carry this pack, the baby, your purse, and perhaps the car seat and a coat, you may want to hold all of it beforehand to see if you can do it. Nothing will force you to jettison the non-essentials quicker than this little test.

Until your baby is about six months old, you will find it easier to carry her in either a front or a back sling, but a skittish toddler may need a spiral cord with one end attached to your wrist and one end attached to hers. This is one of the few times to use this piece of baby equipment, but it can be very helpful, if your child has had a chance to use it once or twice before your trip so she can get used to it.

A Two to Six can walk—although the airport stroller can be helpful even for a Four—and at this age your child can wear a backpack with her own precious possessions—books, crayons, paper, stickers, coloring books.

To prevent your child's brief but painful earaches on take-offs and landings, give her a bottle to suck or gum to chew.

No matter what your child eats, she'll get properly dirty, which may surprise the people who meet you. They always seem to expect an immaculate mother and child. To give the appearance of cleanliness, have your child wear a large bib or *tablier*, the sleeveless apron with pockets worn by French schoolchildren. Remove it just before you get there.

If you weren't able to reserve a bulkhead seat, ask the clerk at the airport to move you next to an empty seat or to the kindest, most tolerant-looking grandmother on the plane. And our best regards to you both.

## CAR TRAVEL

Regardless of the tempo of your car trips, you'll need some basic tricks to keep your sanity, and keep your child reasonably happy and safe. (See Car Pools, page 119, and Car Manners, page 98.) You also should observe her regular eating and sleeping schedule, and take some old toys and some new ones, to be disbursed as

needed. You'll need to sit with your child in the back seat occasionally, to pet her and play with her before she starts to fuss. It's most important for her to run, stretch and pot every two hours—a schedule we found can be synchronized even in a large family if you limit the intake of fluid for the toilet-trained to four ounces of water or juice between stops.

We found a large breakfast in a restaurant was the one meal we could afford to order, because you get so much more for your money, but lunch and dinner were picnics, literally if not vernacularly. Fruit, crackers and cheese are good on-the-road snacks, but avoid candy and chips, for they make a child thirsty.

### Infancy

This is the simplest age to travel.

Although you can carry more equipment in a car than you can in a plane, the list of supplies is just more of the same. Expect to change your baby in the car and wash her bottom at least once during the day, as well as morning and night, to avoid diaper rash or she'll be very fussy.

### Six to Eighteen Months

From now on, a tape deck or a little portable tape player will be your salvation in the car. Raffi tapes, as well as crackers and small surprises, make car travel pleasant now and so does your own attitude. If you act as if you're having a good time, your child will enjoy it more, and if you change her into pajamas at night, her life won't seem so disrupted.

### Mid-One to Three

We find this is the most difficult time to travel with a child, as it is to do anything, for she isn't flexible enough to enjoy an adventure. Her concentration time varies between five and fifteen minutes, at the

most, and she's tremendously active. She needs to use her energy, so longer, more frequent stops are vital.

This child is old enough to accept strange beds but not strange foods. You'll need to stop in time to order your meals or prepare them so she can eat at her regular time. At this age continuity is essential.

### COUNTING CARS

Keep score on the number of station wagons vs. trucks, convertibles vs. sports cars, or red cars vs. blue ones. You'll soon be bored with this game—but not your Four.

### Three to Six

Any child needs extra cuddling and coddling when she travels, but now she revels in a trip if it's treated as a Great Adventure, with much anticipation and map reading, sing-alongs and tapes, which can be more peaceful for you if she uses a headset sometimes. Car games, however, are still a favorite pastime. For some reason, children like to make the highway one big contest.

### ALPHABET GAME

A Five can find all the letters of the alphabet on signs (but not on license plates, which go by too fast for him to read). Start with the letter A, go on to B and follow the alphabet. The letter you're looking for doesn't need to start a word. The first to get to Z wins a big hurrah.

### Car Sickness

We thought car sickness went out of style with the pompadour until we had our Nell, who got carsick from the time she was a baby.

If you have a child like that, avoid all rich foods while traveling and take a non-prescription drug for motion sickness with you. It will cause drowsiness too—a welcome side effect.

For mild queasiness, rely on chewing gum, pretzels, crackers and hard lemon candies, but for the pea-green stage, give sodas. A caffeine-free cola drink will settle the stomach best.

Since car sickness embarrasses a child so much, you should treat it very matter-of-factly. Carry a few throw-away plastic bags, a damp cloth to wipe her face and sit her next to an open window and, preferably in the front seat, which can help. As our other children would tell Nell when we couldn't slow down on a freeway, "Aim for the Cadillacs, sweetie."

## MOVING

In the next few years you'll choose a pattern of living that probably will last for years, and this pattern is directed by the place you live—a small town, a farm, a suburb, a city. It's a much more serious decision than it may seem at first, not just because the influence of a neighborhood is indelible, but also because, to some children, a move can be drastic. However, you can soften the impact if you give your child a role to play. The emphasis should rest, not on the travails of moving or some awful reason for it, but on the joy of the adventure.

Before you begin to look for a house or an apartment, talk with your child about the important things it should have. Will there be a tree big enough to hold a tree house? a shady spot near a faucet for a sandbox? a little room just fit for a child her size?

Even a Two should be included in a little of the house hunting, if only to feel her opinion counts (although you won't, of course, ever let her think it counts above the opinion of her parents).

Before you move you'll go through a nearly endless litany with your child, as early as mid-One: yes, we'll take the sofa and the rug and your lamp, and no, we'll throw away the carrots and the broken vacuum cleaner and the trash can with the hole in it. By the time you've discussed everything in the house, from teaspoons to toilet paper, you're ready to pack.

If you can afford the luxury, buy boxes from a truck rental company. They'll be new and flat, so they won't take up much space until they're packed, and they won't have the bugs you might get with the grocery store boxes. An older child can open them up for you as needed, but a Two can throw the spices in a paper bag, take the toys from the bathtub and carry the potty chair to the moving van.

When we moved seven doors up the street, our Nell and Claire, a neighboring Six, amazed us first by tying three thousand books into bundles of four, and then by hauling them to the new house by doll carriage, by wagon and by dolly, by golly. It took a week, but it's hard to say who was more pleased—Nell or us.

Although you are busier than ever now, you must expect to give your child more attention during moving days, or they will be a nightmare. You'll need neighbors to watch your child when you do the bulk of the moving, but the child who leaves her pleasant house to visit Grandma for two weeks, then returns to a new, albeit pleasant house, will be jarred by the impermanence of her life. A child

adjusts, of course, but the adjustment will be easier if she also is part of the move.

Once you are in your place, organize your child's room first, for as disorderly as she may be, she needs order around her to feel at peace. The living room can wait.

## RENOVATION

To live in a house during its renovation, as so many families do, is a test of fortitude for everybody. Its confusion is tough on a marriage and tougher still on children, unless you make some basic decisions.

Your meals must be the simplest, your housekeeping almost nonexistent and you must have some small area of calm—if only a tidy, well-painted nook in a room, with comfortable chairs to sit in, lights to read by and a floor clean enough for crawling.

Your child needs to keep her regular routine somehow and some extra toys. Buy whatever seems special but cheap, for toys are damaged easily during a renovation and good ones may be a waste. Your child also will need extra loving, just as you do, for the restoration of a house can be depressing and always takes longer and costs more than you thought.

Your child will need to play outdoors or visit friends more often than usual, since she can't have company or run around the house so well, and she has many "no's" there anyway. You also will need sitters to take her out too so you can work in peace.

You must be careful to protect your child from an overdose of plaster dust—often the start of allergies—and to have your water checked in case some old pipes are made of lead. Be careful about the sanding of old paint too, for it can carry

lead particles into her system. Your pediatrician can keep a running test on the lead levels in her blood, if you see signs of listlessness. From the many children we know who have thrived in this crazy milieu, however, these problems can be controlled.

You can expect other, more obvious physical dangers, but be surprised how your toddler will skitter to the edge of the big hole in the floor, as our intrepid Michael did every day for fifteen days until the new stairs finally were in place. Despite all the tools, wires and lumber that abounded, the only blood drawn was by his unhinged mother, who nicked his ear while cutting his hair.

You should tell your child what the workmen are doing during each stage of the renovation, both for her own information and because she'll ask your workmen if you don't and their time is expensive. Explain also the work you do yourself and the principles involved, showing her how the holes you punch in the lip of the paint can will drain the extra paint back into the can and how a wet sponge makes a plaster patch smooth.

If renovation does nothing else it imposes a remarkable sense of self-sufficiency on a child, for even a One realizes when you have tolerated as much chaos as you can and that she'd better try to muddle through alone.

We found a Two makes a good apprentice or, as Michael called himself so seriously, a "workin-ing man" (his only ambition in life for three more years). At this age a child will fetch tools for you, if she's taught their names, but you won't ask for the screwdriver for that's unsafe in a fall. A Three can tell brick nails from brads and what a tenpenny nail looks like too. This child lays the level on every horizontal she can find, but a Four is much more sensible.

She measures instead, flipping out the six-foot rule like a master carpenter. While a Four will be helpful one minute, and gone the next, a Five is a whiz and curious about everything. She'll be intrigued when her father shows her an old disconnected switchbox and with it can understand the principles of electricity, even if you can't.

A Five is also a pretty fine worker. Under a tough time pressure, we organized a crew of Fives to give radiators a first coat of paint and the work was surprisingly good. We found our Six, that diligent child, was eager to scrape paint from the windowpanes and in fact was considerably better than her sister (a blasé Twelve) and could haul a prodigious amount of trash outdoors, too.

A renovation, we found, brings out the best—and the worst—in all of us. You'll be amazed how fast the money goes, and how hard you work together. You'll be shocked at how cross everyone becomes when the work drags along and how proud everyone feels at each bit of progress.

A child will never forget which balustrade she refinished, which tile she laid, which prisms she washed. For that sense of accomplishment alone, a renovation is worth it.

◇ # QUESTIONS ◇

Some of the toughest moments you'll ever have—and the most memorable—will be the ones you spend explaining life well enough for your child to understand a little of it. She's deeply curious about the world and who made it and wars and how they kill—all questions that deserve your thoughtful analyses, as simplified as they might be, for you'll find that any idea that intrigues you will intrigue your child too.

This is why a Two, as flummoxed by newscasts of the latest crimes as you are, needs explanations. Each year you can talk about the news a little more cogently, until your Five will be ready, as our Kate was, to grasp the sarcasm of most Herblock cartoons when we explained them and to realize, when she was Six, that if she could read her primer, she could read the big headlines too. When a child tries to understand the whole world, she has a slightly better idea of her place in it.

Although she may ask you about the nightly newscasts, the questions that could affect her own life fascinate her so much she may not be able to ask them at all. That's why she needs to know that parents

might divorce each other, but they never can divorce their child, and she needs to know this even if you and your husband have never considered divorce. Since your child will know parents who do separate, you need to have these conversations or she may go through a fearful stage when every argument she overhears is one more sign of doom.

We also think you have to talk with your child about the bugs (and the bunnies and the people) that die and return to enrich the land and about the bugs (and bunnies and people) that procreate and why and how. The abstract is confusing to a child but the more you translate it into simple terms, the less confusing it will be.

## SEX

Once a precocious Five climbed on her grandmother's lap and said, "Tell me, *Grandmère*, tell me about sex."

The old lady—French, worldly and delighted—settled happily into a full, if delicate account.

"Now, *ma chère*, is there anything else you wish to know?"

"I just want to know how to spell it, *Grandmère*."

A child's questions about sex are generally like that.

Beyond a daughter's, "How come I'm so plain and he's so fancy?" most children let the subject slide unless they're in a crowded elevator or in church. Bring up the discussion yourself, so you can explain it at your convenience. A child needs to know a little about everything, including sex, even if she hasn't asked.

She should know you think bodies are beautiful, and she will if she sees you and your husband walk around naked occasionally—which won't embarrass a pre-Five—and if she can touch your bodies, which shouldn't embarrass you, but probably will. If you accept your child's natural curiosity about sex now she won't feel the shame it so often brings later.

When she is toilet trained, she (and, of course, he) begins to touch the genitals, obviously and regularly. You won't, of course, tell her that masturbation is bad, because it isn't, but you will tell her not to do it in public, because it bothers other people. It also can reflect boredom or a need to urinate, as well as a pleasant interlude, so you want to keep your child busy and well pottied.

We may be old-fashioned, but we think there's more to sex than human reproduction. The sex act is improbable enough without plucking people out of the regular pattern of nature. If you want your child to believe that intercourse and birth are normal, or even believe it at all, she needs to know that there are a lot of ways to make a baby.

A Two will be pleased to find that an insect is the yenta of the flower garden, matching pollen to seeds and collecting nectar as its reward. Although many insects pollinate the flowers, the bee, with its nectar-to-honey cycle, explains it best.

Show your child the flowers, colored to attract the bugs, and let her smell their different perfumes. This helps her understand that while brilliant flowers may need little scent, the white flowers often compensate with a much stronger smell.

Have your Two help you undress a flower, like an iris, big enough to hide no secrets. Let her jiggle the stamen and see the yellow pollen fall from its stalks to her finger, just the way it falls on the wings of a bee. She can track her finger down the bright yellow stripe of the petal—like a runway for a bee—right to the pistil, where the ovule of seeds swims in nectar. The pollen is bound to fall from her fingertip, just as it falls from the bee, fertilizing the seeds and giving us flowers next year.

And after you've explained all that, go inside and have a honey sandwich.

A Three can find the stamen, pistils and pollen in any flower without help. She likes to examine the blossom on an apple tree now and check the ovule as it swells to become the fruit itself, with its nest of seeds protected in the center.

If it's at all possible, a child should watch the birth of kittens or puppies—without touching them of course—and see an animal nurse its young.

Our two daughters, as foster parents to nearly one hundred gerbils over the years, were distressed one morning when Exter, the father of them all, cringed in a corner of his cage. Though he'd been up all night helping to deliver the tenth litter, the children were sure he was ill, but by afternoon Nadia ran in shouting, "Don't worry any more about Exter! He and Zester are mating again!"

By using so many natural examples, your child will understand cross-pollination of people more easily.

Since you'll probably be using biological names for the sex organs, don't be surprised when your child sidles up to a

stranger—the stranger the better—and asks loudly and publicly if he has a penis? or better yet, if she has a penis? This is not altogether accidental. Your child may look innocent, but she knows that something about babies, beds and bottoms is very exciting and that people wear clothes for more reasons than to keep away the chill.

Gradually between Three and Six you'll explain the hows, whys and wheres of human reproduction enhanced by a month-by-month picture book of fetal development—usually when you or a friend expect a second baby—and of course you'll tell her that sex is an expression of love.

You can expect boys and girls of Four to kiss often and possibly play feelie more than a couple of teenagers. Truth to tell, we found an advanced Six with his fly unzipped on top of a dainty Five with her panties to her knees. They may have learned by looking through the keyhole, but we prefer to think they were simply inventive. Keep a close eye now, but don't be too alarmed if your child experiments, for by Seven she'll be too modest to try and even too embarrassed to recall her wayward youth.

No matter how much a child enjoys her experiments, she'll never believe the same of you. After perhaps dozens and dozens of small talks about sex with our curious little girls, one suddenly asked, "But you only do it when you want to make a baby, right?"

The question astonished us, but our answer astonished them more.

## DEATH

Death is shocking and the acceptance of it comes almost as slowly for a child as for you. Be frank if you anticipate the death of someone dear to your child, so she can have the chance to say good-bye too.

There are times when death is so sudden or inexplicable you can attribute it only to plain bad luck. Whether you're religious or not, don't pass the buck with phrases like "God needed her more," which can anger a child and undercut her faith, or euphemisms like "Aunt Harriet was called away," which will baffle her. What seems like harsh reality to you will be logical to her, if you treat it as a natural part of the life cycle. We think a child can make better sense of the ashes-to-ashes concept if she commemorates death with life, by planting a tree in the yard or even a daffodil bulb in a window box.

A Four, we think, is old enough to attend a funeral, but no child should have to see a beautified corpse. That can be eerie enough to make a child believe in ghosts.

In a way we felt blessed, toward the end of a difficult fourth pregnancy, to have had the chance to tell our children that the baby couldn't live after birth. When they had absorbed this idea we explained the medical problems specifically to remove the mystery and any fear that they could die the same way. Naturally there was grief when the infant died and we all wept and comforted each other. It was an event that enriched our lives even as it saddened us, and, in fact, was a catharsis for all the children in the neighborhood.

Today our children still talk about their dead brother as if they had known him, occasionally assigning him the role of angel when they play pretend. This isn't because we told them he was an angel, but because

this death added a new dimension to their games—and a certain status too. Children, like old Latin ladies, enjoy pathos. We remember our Tía Tata, at eighty-eight, weeping all day on the anniversary of her mother's death and our Tante Nini, who wore full mourning for various relations for eighty-four of her hundred and two years.

Many young children will never be faced with the death of someone they know, but the idea shouldn't be foreign. We found a casual procession of snakes, gerbils and goldfish explains life and death better than we ever could.

The first funeral was an event when all the children in the car pool gathered at seven-thirty one morning to pledge allegiance, sing "God Bless America" and plant that first Peruvian guinea pig to die of the dread "wet bottom" disease. It took our animal lovers, Nadia and Meg, about seven funerals before the ritual was perfunctory. Death had become a way of life.

## DIVORCE

Today divorce is epidemic, striking almost one out of every two couples. Now you'll find yourself explaining it to your child frequently, either because you or your neighbors are taking this step.

If you and your husband are considering divorce, you first want to do everything you can to save your marriage, including counseling together for at least a year. If marriage is hard, divorce is much harder, particularly on a child, and the older she gets, the harder it is.

Unfortunately, the death of a marriage is almost inexplicable to a child, for it seems so sudden to her. She's dumb-founded that two adults can't get along with each other well enough to live together—especially her parents. The thought that love can start—and stop—will haunt your child, for if her parents can stop loving each other, they just might stop loving her.

No matter how bad your marriage or how smooth your separation, the first year will be very hard on your child. She may behave as usual at home, although perhaps more quietly, then have sudden tantrums or periods of confusion or inattention at someone's house or at her day care center.

If she is in school, have a conference with her teacher as soon as you and your husband have decided to separate, so she can give your child the extra support she needs. Above all, you'll need to have many little talks with your child about the divorce, for one big talk is never enough to assimilate such news. Even a nonverbal mid-One should be told—in twenty-five words or less—although she can't comprehend the idea.

Of course you won't give a pre-Six any tangible reasons for separation—they're none of her business—but she's such an egocentric, she inevitably assumes some of the blame herself. Both you and your husband must cushion her with as much love and time as possible, even though you're under so much stress yourselves.

A pre-Six, that ultimate loyalist, can be fractured by a split, but it won't be so bad if you and your husband don't snipe about each other—the same rule you follow in marriage. This lets her keep pretending that her parents, if not Superman and Supermom, are at least sort of super. This is a need all children have.

They also have a terrible need to keep in close, and if possible, daily touch with both parents, and for this, joint custody is best, although it isn't always possible. If two people can't agree in marriage, they seldom find it easy to agree when they're divorced.

If you don't share custody, you should encourage frequent visits with her father (and he should encourage visits with you, if he has custody). Otherwise it's easy for a child to glamorize (or condemn) the parent she never sees. Even if your ex-husband should have a serious problem, like drinking, we think your child should spend some time around him. Slowly she'll learn to accept her dad as he is—or not. The decision eventually belongs to your child.

Since young children have an oversupply of female company, a child in your custody—boy or girl—needs to be around older men, whether she has a weekly visit with her father or not. If you pay a teenaged boy to take your child out for an ice cream or a bike ride a few times a week, it will help a good deal. To a young child, a teen-aged boy is man enough.

Even with a job and the double duties of a single parent, you'll also need some outside activity so you won't focus on your child too intensely, and she won't think you belong only to her. A support

group will help you keep your life in balance.

From a child's point of view, there's very little good you can say for divorce. Since you're doing what you think is best, you must ignore the guilt you feel (for some of it is part of every marriage, every death and every divorce) and treat your child with as much sensitivity as you would like to be treated yourself.

# INFLUENCES

If you want your child to become an interesting, bright adult, you have to give him an interesting childhood. Of course, your baby can develop into a complete person—competent, respectful, honest and independent—but without enrichment, his life will be like a room without windows. There won't be any sunshine or the chance for him to see the dazzling world outside.

From the moment your child is born, you and your husband will make a series of decisions, often unconsciously, which either will limit or stretch his world, depending on the influences you offer. They determine how far he can see and, ultimately, how much of the world he'll want to see. His values, his friendships, his adventures and his environment will shape him into a three-dimensional person—and you're the lady who'll do most of the shaping.

In 1831, our favorite arbiter of maternal behavior, Lydia Maria Child, quoted an educator who concluded that "the heaviness of the Dutch" and "the vivacity of the French" began in the nursery. She said, in those pre-Freud days, "The Dutch keep their children in a state of repose, always rocking or jogging them; the French are perpetually tossing them and showing them lively tricks."

Naturally a Dutch mother shouldn't try to act like a French one nor should a French mother pretend that she's Dutch. Some of us are quiet, some are loud; some shy, some not and this temperament is innate. Any way you treat your child is fine, as long as it's natural to you. If you rear him in your own style, he'll grow up to share many of your interests and your own brand of humor too.

You may be contained or you may be effusive, but you must be loving, for love and learning go together. Each is dependent on the other. Studies show such a strong relationship between the two that institutionalized babies can be markedly slower to learn and even can become irredeemably retarded when they lack not care, but caring. Your praise, freely given in words and kisses, invites your child's love in return, because love is a response, not an instinct. This mutual love will be his greatest preparation for life, particularly in his first year, when he needs you the most.

A well-loved baby is like a sponge, ready to absorb all the information in the world, if he has the surroundings, the excitement and the values that make it easy. Your baby, who at first seems to need nothing but diapers, milk, diapers, sleep and diapers, actually needs a great deal more. He has been coddled and nestled those weeks in the womb and has prospered by it; now he wants challenges and chances.

A child needs daily outings—from carriage rides to backpacking—and the stimulation of seeing people of all ages and in many situations. This is how he becomes a little more sensitized each day. Any equipment he uses—in his room, the backyard, the playground—will influence him. It needn't be expensive but it should both prod his imagination and improve his coordination.

Much that he learns will be drawn from books and from television programs, so both should be chosen with care. The marvel—and the violence—of a TV show seen only once may live just as long in a child's mind as a much-read storybook, since film has the extra impact of movement and sound.

Toys are invaluable too, if they're the right ones, and worse than useless if they're not. Select them judiciously, buying only half as many as you think he'll need—and then he will have only twice as much as he should. There are aids that will open his mind—a magnet, a padlock, a magnifying glass, playing cards and, especially, a library card—for every one of these makes a child ask questions. When he learns to wonder about small things, he will learn to wonder about everything.

No matter how much you enrich your child, you still can't supply all the influences he needs (nor should you). His family background, his friends, his play group and his nursery school or day care all will color his image of the world. The effect of these outside influences on your child will depend on the emphasis you give them.

Tempting as it may be, however, don't agonize over everything he does and everyone he sees or your child will think he's more important than he is, and he'll feel stifled too, because he'll have so few decisions left to make for himself. The child who is allowed to make his own choices (and his own mistakes) can find his own affinities, which is as it should be. He isn't cloned in your image.

Just as he develops his own interests, so must he develop an awareness of the intangibles, for they will govern his values. This awareness follows, we think, when you help a child be a responsible person, letting him care for pets and expecting him to do some chores too, as a contributor to the family. We also believe he should make presents as often as possible—the first of his many lessons in sweet charity. The strongest influences he'll ever know are the ones that will come from within.

It will be the total enrichment of the mind, the body and the spirit that turns him into an individual, as unique as his footprint.

# SURROUNDINGS

The surroundings you give your child will never be perfect, but if they're chosen with care they'll help him progress naturally from hours of action to moments of solitude. When a child can mesh his activities with his environment he'll feel a little more confident at the end of the day than he did at the beginning.

---

◇       **CHILD'S ROOM**       ◇

You don't want your child's room to be like anyone else's room, because you don't want your child to be like anyone else—not even you. Still, like every mother, you're bound to superimpose yourself on your child in many ways, including the surroundings you give him, but gradually you should grow so attuned to him that his room will mirror his own personality. You'll need to make few changes in his first six years except in the bed, the toys, the paint and the pictures.

### INFANCY

Years ago, when cleanliness nearly won the race with godliness, a sanitary, superwhite nursery would have been a storybook setting for a baby. Today it would look like a scene in Kafka, for so much of a baby's growth depends on the stimulation he receives. A study of two groups of institutionalized babies, each given the same amount of cuddling and physical attention, showed that the babies with mobiles, patterned sheets and posters were much more attentive than those kept in a white, picture-free room. Once you've seen a small baby ogle the drawings on his crib sheet and try to trace their outlines with his fingers, you won't need a study to tell you that color and design give a child extra richness. This is why the walls in his room should have pictures and from the ceiling you should hang a kite or a piñata, a bird cage or a balloon.

A lighted lamp is another important stimulus in the nursery: the shadows it casts will mesmerize a baby for minutes at a time. Also include a goldfish in a bowl and a green plant, for beauty is as necessary to a baby as it is to you, and as every mother knows, nothing is as beautiful as something that grows. If the light is too scant in the room for photosynthesis, put the plant under the lamp and replace the bulb with one made especially for indoor gardening.

The basic necessities of his room should be assembled before you deliver. They won't be many but they should be colorful, functional and safe (see Equipment, page 155). Besides a crib, you'll need a rocking chair, a soft light for night feedings and a shelf for his toys. You also must have a bureau to hold his clothes and a sturdy changing table to dress him. The best one we ever saw was a combination of

153

the two—a converted Salvation Army dresser, circa 1920, without its spindly legs and mirror. It was big enough to hold all the baby's clothes, its drawers were soaped for smooth sliding (for a mother needs no added aggravations when she's changing the baby), and it was painted brightly, with wooden alphabet blocks for pulls. The bureau top had a tie nailed to its center to strap the baby in place and was covered by a long quilted pad, to keep him comfortable.

Unless you live in a one-room apartment, you'll find it convenient to have at least one other changing area and some extra clothes in each part of the house to save steps, and another bassinet, to give your child a change of environment. You also may want to tack the ribbons from baby presents on the back of a door, with clothespins tied to the ends of them, to clip bootees, caps and mittens. If it's easy to take walks you'll take more of them.

### THREE MONTHS

When you buy the crib, get one that's sturdy enough to last through several babies (if not yours, your friends').

At this age, your child should have a crib gym with rings to pull as well as a toy bolted to the slats. A mirror is another good visual aid and a spellbinding one too, for it catches and refracts light in as many patterns as snowflakes under a microscope. Since your child will have neither the force nor the tools to break the glass, hang the mirror from the old bureau onto one end of the crib for the next few months. He'll be glad for such handsome company.

### ONE

You can't believe how lively your child has become. He needs strong screens or guards on his or any low window or a screw in the sash to control the height it can be raised. Some babies now are able to rock a crib right across the room and for them you must set the wheels of the crib on hard rubber casters.

### MID-ONE

By eighteen months a crib may be a cage to your child and escape is his only solution. For this climber, keep one side lowered so he can scamper out in safety or put him in a regular bed. Choose a sturdy one, low to the floor, with a firm mattress and a portable guard rail. He still may fall out of bed, but the falls are closer to the floor.

Whenever your child switches to a bed (unless it's the day before the baby takes his crib), his pride will be huge. We remember our Kate asking the postman, the druggist, the carpenter and every other fellow she met if they too slept "in a big girl's bed." She got many happy, if ribald replies, but she certainly could understand their pleasure.

### TWO

By Two, a child's room should encourage independence. There should be a tidy place for toys, low hooks for coats in the closet, more shelves for his growing library, a pajama bag to feed every morning, a laundry hamper to feed at night and a gadget that screws into the switch plate, so he can pull a string and turn his light on (and off and on and . . .).

Your child can begin to learn where to find his clothes if you label the top edge of each drawer with a felt pen: "socks," "pants," "shirts," which he sees as he opens the drawer. A child quickly memorizes what the words look like (although he won't recognize them anywhere else) and can put away his own clothes in a couple of years.

Since a Two generally has more toys than at any other age, you'll need to make space. Dolls and stuffed animals are decorative but out of the way if you sew a curtain ring on the back of each one and hang them on cup hooks you've screwed to the back of the door.

### THREE

When your child has stopped dressing and undressing himself every day as a game, hang a rod in his closet low enough for him to reach. Let this rod—a broomstick will do nicely—rest in a pair of rope slings that hang from the pole above. The upper one will be for good clothes that he shouldn't wear without permission; the lower one for his everyday clothes. It's an important distinction for a clothes-happy child.

### FOUR

This child has a new project every day, each more involved than the next. Let him work with these projects on a folding card table so they won't be stepped on.

### FIVE

A Five and a desk are meant for each other, perhaps now more than ever again. He wants to draw, to print, to play school quite as much as he wants to climb.

### SIX

When your child is Six you'll analyze his room and himself. Suddenly the low shelves are too low, the toys are outgrown, the pictures look silly. His personality must dominate, if it hasn't before. A precise little girl will want a place for her dollhouse and her collection of small boxes, as well as one high shelf to hold the tiny glass animals, whereas another little girl, like our Nadia, may turn her room into a zoo of gerbils, snakes and fish. A Six doesn't want his room redecorated suddenly; he has enough changes at this age. When you interpret his interests as they evolve—even if this is stretched over a year or so—the room will suit him better. At least that's our excuse for taking so long.

◇ # EQUIPMENT ◇

Your baby needs more equipment than you may have thought at first, because he'll be happier if he's moved from place to place.

The quality of his equipment depends on your income or your ingenuity in shopping at secondhand stores. You may have a better idea of how to spend your money when you realize that your infant will sleep at least fifteen hours a day—three of them during naptime—and take probably two more hours to eat. On this basis, the crib and the infant seat, and later the high chair, are the most important expenditures. In addition, your baby probably will spend two hours a day in a sling, another hour in a carriage or stroller (which may be used indoors in place of a bassinet), an hour in a playpen or on a blanket on the floor, another hour in the swing, perhaps some time in a car seat and less than a half-hour in his bathtub.

## BEDDING

A farmer's daughter once told us about the joys of the annual threshing season in Indiana, when she got her new straw tick. She would dive into it night after night until the mattress was hard and she had burrowed a niche all her own. This need for enclosure is primitive and shouldn't be denied to an infant. That's why we think for the first six weeks a baby should be kept in a cradle, a bassinet—which is easier to find—or a bureau drawer, for there he can nestle and feel secure. The mattress of this or any bed must be firm, for the sake of his back, and should fit tightly, to prevent suffocation.

### BASSINET

Every woman has grown up with fantasies about motherhood and how she would care for her children. We saw one mother satisfy one of her whims by transforming the bassinet—sturdy and wide-based, of course—into a bed fit for her princess. You can do it too, if you had a fancy wedding, by gathering one end of your veil into a large embroidery hoop and suspending it from the ceiling, so it falls like a canopy over the bassinet: a proper way to honor royalty.

### CRIB

This piece of equipment should be the best of all, to be safe. The slats must not be more than 2⅜″ apart, the cornerposts no more than ⅝″ high, and the crib should be built as solidly as a piece of gym equipment—for that's what it becomes. Use a firm mattress, as big as the crib, so he won't get stuck between the mattress and the sides, and snug-fitting bumpers all around to protect the baby's fontanel from hitting the slats.

### BED

When the crib becomes more of a gym set than a place to sleep, it's time to buy a bed. Then he'll have a trampoline. The simplest bed will do, as long as it has a firm mattress and good springs, but forget about a youth bed, which has to be replaced in a few years, and forget about a bunk bed too. It needs an acrobat to change the sheets. If you want more sleeping space for overnight guests, we find a trundle bed works well.

## CARRIAGE

Strollers are so fancy that carriages are almost a thing of the past, but they still are quite lovely, they give the baby a nice rocking motion and they can be used as a bassinet for a nap, either indoors or out. Unless you can leave your carriage outside, however, get one that is so lightweight you won't mind pulling it up and down the steps and curbs. You also want one with as few plastic parts as possible for a summer baby, because plastic holds the heat. In winter, lay a couple of receiving blankets over the sheet, to protect him from drafts.

## INFANT SEAT

This will give your baby a whole new slant on the world and give you a place to put him wherever you work in the house or while you shovel in the applesauce. Begin

using it after the first month, propping it only a few inches at first, to protect his back. At any age be sure to strap him in place for safety.

You can expect a three-month-old baby to be happy in an infant seat for a total of an hour a day, at least, exclusive of feedings, but by four months, he probably will be too busy or too lively to sit in it without tipping.

## SLING

People babies have something in common with marsupial babies; they like to be close to their mothers. There are many types of totes on the market that let you carry your baby on your chest or on your back or on your hip while you shop or bike and especially when you must console him and cook dinner at the same time. Since the designs vary probably more than in any other piece of equipment, you have to look hard for the one that suits your needs best. The finest carryalls are made of strong fabric with enough support to cradle a very young infant and with tucks that can be removed during the first years as the baby grows—but these are never cheap. An older child needs a carrier reinforced with an aluminum frame, but not before four or five months. Try out the many varieties before you buy or borrow, since you'll probably be using it every day and you'll want it to be comfortable for you and the baby.

And since you want your baby to be safe, always use the restraining straps and bend from the knees if you have to lean over, so the baby doesn't fall out of the sling.

## CAR SEAT

A government-certified seat for infants is the only safe way to drive your baby home from the hospital, or anywhere else—even if you're only going five blocks away. It's a fairly new idea.

For years a car seat simply kept a child

in place while raising him high enough to see. Fortunately, all states now require all children to be buckled at all times, which precludes any ride in the back of a pickup truck. You'll need a padded, molded infant carrier until he's about twenty pounds, and then you'll switch to a regular car seat. Both of these must be government-certified for safety and held in place with a seat belt. Even so, you'll have to follow the manufacturer's installation and buckling directions to the letter, or even the best car seat may not protect your baby properly.

Your child will be forty pounds, or about Four, before he can use a seat belt safely, because the pelvic structure of a smaller body can't stand the pressure of the belt in a sudden impact.

And yes, it is a certain amount of trouble to buckle a child in place, but it's impossible to replace him.

## SWING

The portable swing isn't essential, but it may be the family's favorite piece of equipment. Its steady rocking motion soothes the fussy baby and his fussy parents too.

Look for a swing with sturdy, widespread legs, and—if you can afford it—one that's powered by a battery, rather than mechanically. The baby either swings in its bassinette or lolls in a seat at no more than a 25-degree angle. Even so, you shouldn't keep your baby in the swing for more than a half-hour at a time, and no more than a total of an hour a day until he is old enough to sit well on his own— about seven months. But by then he'll be ready to conquer new worlds anyway.

## PLAYPEN

To some mothers, a playpen can be mighty handy for the first few months, because an infant can see out of it much better than he can see out of a crib, and this is what he likes. Look for a pen with slats no more than 2⅜ inches apart, but don't get a mesh

one if it lets you lower one side, for an infant can fall into the pocket and suffocate. And don't use the pen at all after he starts to crawl. By then he'll consider the playpen a jail, for nature wants a crawling baby to explore. When this happens, you'll have to depend on gates, locked doors and your own sharp eye to keep your child within safe limits.

You can use the pen much longer as outdoor equipment, sitting him in it for at least a quarter hour at a time after a snowfall, if he's well bundled, or for as long as an hour in summer with blocks, a few plastic pots, a trickling hose and no clothes at all. Keep the pen out of the glare on a hot day and bind each of its legs with two-faced sticky tape to stop the ants from joining him and his teething biscuits.

The pen also may be used for an extra bed for a pre-One and a place to keep the Christmas tree when you have a Two.

## HIGH CHAIR

Because your child will spend more than an hour a day in a high chair, it should be both safe and convenient. Having tried every sort from the secondhand store—from a cane-bottomed antique to a five-way combination of bleached wood and plastic—we find the best is one that has very few places for a child to stuff spinach. It also should be sturdy enough to be hosed down every month or two, have a strap to keep him seated and be steady enough to contain him even when you forget to tie him into it. A Two needs a tray big enough to use as a desk when he draws or sculpts, as well as when he eats. A feeding table may be easier at this age instead of a high chair, but we don't recommend it unless you have a big kitchen. A child's equipment shouldn't take up a disproportionate amount of family space.

When he gets too frisky for a high chair—or thinks he's too grown-up for it—switch him to the little seat that clamps to the edge of the kitchen table or sit him in a booster seat.

## STROLLER

You need to get the best stroller you can find, because you'll use it more than any piece of equipment except a crib. Don't go by their cost however. Very expensive strollers are often so heavy and bulky you'll either stay home rather than wrestle it outside, or you'll rush to the mall and grab the cheapest one you can find. As usual, the middle course is best.

Ask a friend to go stroller shopping with you—and to bring her baby to test-drive him around the store, since all strollers handle fine when they're empty. You'll find that a stroller is too hard to handle if it's heavy—since it's the baby's weight that centers the stroller—and the lightweight, umbrella stroller can't support an infant's back well, although it will be great when he can sit up on his own.

You want a stroller of a middling size and weight that changes from a well-padded bed to a little chair easily—a sturdy, wide-based number that's easy to handle, with axles between the wheels so they go in the same direction. There should also be a tray in front to hold the things he brings, and a low—and therefore safe—basket in back to hold whatever you buy.

You'll want to check the height of the handle too—if it's short and you're tall, you won't like to push it—and see how quickly and easily it folds, and how much space it takes. Or as one young mother said: Get a stroller that comes from the same country as your car, so it can fit in the trunk.

## WALKER

A walker has been the joy of many babies and the despair of most doctors, for this piece of equipment is safe if it has a wide wheel base and if it's used right, but it tips easily when a child scoots over a threshhold or a rug, or goes near the top of the stairs. Let your child use it only on the first floor, and only on wood or tile, and don't let him use it more than an hour a day, because it puts too much strain on his young frame and it may take him longer to walk.

## GATES

Gates are a necessity once your baby starts to crawl, for you don't want to be the sort of mother who always says, "No." A gate across a doorway and at the top and bottom of stairs will give both of you a feeling of freedom, but don't get an accordion gate, or your baby may wedge his head in it. Look instead for a gate with an expandable bar so the child will stand on one side of the gate, and the bar will be on the other, and out of his reach.

# ◇ BACKYARD ◇

A preschool child needs a place to play outdoors if possible, but unless you have only a small patio it needn't consume your whole yard. A child isn't meant to dominate the outside any more than the inside. Rather, establish one or two pockets of space—one with climbing equipment and one for a Sandbox (see page 163) and a wading pool (in which you'll never leave any water). With this layout, a pre-Three is happy in a 10′ × 10′ area and 15′ × 15′ will suit a Three to Six. A first-grader, however, usually feels a backyard is too babyish, no matter how big it is, unless it is so enchanting everyone will want to play at his house.

The pocket you devote to climbing equipment should be covered with small wood chips or four inches of smooth pea gravel, since grass won't grow there anyway. Also, some of the backyard should be shaded, because no one likes to play for hours in the hot sun. If you don't have a shady spot, plant a quick-growing tree, like a fig, to make it that way.

Any play equipment must be bought with great care, for the standard, relatively inexpensive gym sets often will rust, bolts will loosen and children will hurt themselves. We think it's better to buy one good piece of equipment—like a slide with a rustproof bedway—and make the rest.

Because your child likes to get in and out of places, over and over again, your lawn furniture will be his fort. That's part of motherhood. One parent we know succumbed enough to let the family's aluminum canoe rest on the grass for the children to play in, and another father built a tree house without a tree, putting a small, A-frame house on stilts, with a knotted rope to reach it.

# ◇ CO-OP PLAYGROUND ◇

In many cities, particularly in older neighborhoods, an empty lot can stand vacant for years. This is a silly waste of land, for inevitably there are young families in nearby apartments whose children have little outdoor space to play. A cooperative playground can be the answer. We suggest only that if you do want one, don't wait for others to make it, for that might take a long time.

We found it took the proceeds of a neighborhood carnival, three weeks and a lot of hard labor for a dozen families to convert a big lot into a safe, scythed, fenced playground with equipment made of telephone poles, railroad ties and cement conduits, and dressed up with benches for parents, a load of dirt and some sod, all donated by businesses. By renting the land with a token $1-a-year lease and by buying a $100,000 accident insurance policy for $40 a year, the owners of the lot and the parents who built the playground had legal protection, even though it was never needed. It did take some regular community upkeep, but because dogs were banned and trash cans were supplied, the work was minimal.

Every playground has two main needs: a shady area for hot weather and a little hill, no more than 8' high. You may not be lucky enough to have a tree on the property, but you can have the hill, so Ones can scramble over it and the bigger children can play King of the Mountain. A hill in the middle of a playground also keeps grade school children from using it as a ball field, which, aside from the dogs, is the single biggest problem of a public park.

To build the hill, first have clean fill dirt dumped in one spot and then ask parents and children to run up and down it, again and again, to pack the earth. Water and cover with sod, then scatter grass seed occasionally before an expected rainfall so new grass replaces the dead grass.

The equipment in any park must be very sturdy, which either means that you build it yourself or buy it from a school catalogue—a most expensive method. To make equipment, call the public relations department of major city offices, and especially of businesses, which can deduct their donations from their taxes. We were able to get 3' cement conduits to set on their sides in cement (so they couldn't roll). Once installed there was always a child or two inside, just sitting and thinking. Old telephone poles became fanciful horses, with goofy faces and rope tails. They also did nothing at all, but were so popular their backs were worn to satin in a few weeks. Other poles were cut into logs, notched at the ends and fitted together to make square forts, like huge Lincoln logs. Railroad ties edged the sandbox and others were erected, by the Herculean efforts of the mothers and fathers, to form a stanchion for swings. These were hung with ropes using leather seats for slings. One cautionary note: we recommend swings *only* if you can build a low barrier—perhaps out of something as simple as 2″ × 2″s and chicken wire—far enough in front of the path of the arc to deflect a toddling child.

Climbing equipment can be made from lead pipes cut to any length and threaded to fit the joints. The rungs should be no more than 16″ apart and the structure itself no taller than 5', with the uprights sunk into holes filled with concrete. An old tree trunk, either rooted in place where it grew or imbedded in cement, is a less complicated piece of climbing equipment for a pre-Three. Bind a heavy chain around it tightly several times and nail it into place, so the chain makes grips for a child's feet.

If you don't expect theft to be a problem, you can make a Basic Board, with a stanchion (see page 163) to provide a combination balancing board/seesaw/slide.

You will need to build a few benches too, so mothers have something better to do than hover over their children. A Saturday morning spent in a park of your own making can be quite as nice a social outing for you as it is for your child.

---

## ◇  HOMEMADE EQUIPMENT  ◇

Some of the best equipment your child can have will be the pieces you make. Since carpentry is hard for us, we recommend some shortcuts, such as the hot glue—a thermoplastic material—which shoots from an electric gun, bonds in sixty seconds under heavy hand pressure and withstands a two-thousand-pound stress without any screws to reinforce it. Of course, the surfaces must be cleaned free of any old glue, roughed lightly with sandpaper and dusted before new glue can bind.

Any equipment will be stronger, however, if it's held together with nails or screws in addition to the glue. For this type of construction, paneling adhesive is easier than hot glue since it doesn't set as fast. To apply, squirt the adhesive from a caulking gun onto the clean, dry wood, pressing the pieces together for ten minutes until the parts are joined. This step leaves both hands free to screw the pieces together.

Soap any screw for easier threading and pre-drill all holes except those that go into the studs, where you want the tightest fit possible. Roundhead wood screws are supposed to be best, because they leave no rough edges to scratch a child; lag screws, which must be tightened with a wrench, have, as one adept father told us, "great authority."

### TOY BIN

You wouldn't like to sew if you had to root through a big box to find the needle, the thread and the pieces of each pattern. A toy box has the same effect on a child. Instead, we suggest an open, wooden bin,

6' long, with slots about 6–10" apart to separate the beads and blocks, noisemakers and toy trucks, construction games and plastic letters. It will hang flush to the wall, as high as your child's waist, and look like a long, skinny version of an old-fashioned washtub.

You can make it if you have patience—and a patient helper. Although you can cut the pieces and drill the holes, you need four hands to put it together.

**ASSEMBLE** one 4' × 8' sheet of ¾" interior plywood
  ten 3" No. 12 roundhead wood screws with washers
  hot melt glue
  8- or 10-penny finishing nails

Draw guidelines on the plywood before sawing the pieces.

**CUT** one 6' length, 15" wide
  one 6' length, 12" wide
  one 6' length, 4" wide
  two truncated right triangles (15" × 12" × 12" × 4")

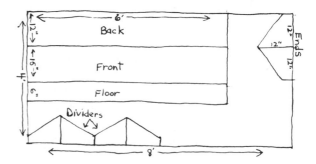

The piece with the 15″ width will be the sloping front of the bin; the one with the 12″ width will be the back; the piece of wood that's only 4″ wide will be the floor of the bin. The truncated triangles become the ends of the bin, with the 4″ edge meeting the floor and the 15″ edge aligned to the front of the bin. One 12″ edge rests against the back of the bin and the other 12″ edge forms the top. The four dividers, to be cut from the leftover plywood, will be the same shape as the ends, but slightly smaller. Don't cut them until the bin is glued together, however, so you can make the pattern fit better.

There are two preparatory steps to take before you assemble the bin. First, use a wood rasp, or a plane, to file down one long edge of the floor piece so there will be a broader surface for gluing—or better yet, borrow a circular saw so you can cut this edge at an angle. Next, measure the distance between the studs in the wall—usually about 13–15″—and mark where the bin will be hung. You then drill five holes across the top of the back piece and five across the bottom of it so they will align with these studs. Drilling the holes now makes it easier to hang the bin later.

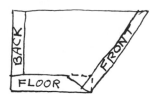

To assemble, fit the back piece perpendicular to the floor of the bin, to look like an L. The rasped side of the bin's floor should be forward, and face the ceiling. Now glue the floor to the back.

If you haven't had help before, you'll need it now. Gluing is tricky, for this hot thermoplastic sets within sixty seconds. To make the hot glue bond, shoot only two feet of it at a time and quickly press the boards together for about two minutes. When tight, spring out the floor piece just enough to feed another two feet of glue

into the joint and then repeat this step again. And again. And again.

Now you're ready to glue the two ends in place. Outline the L on the end of the back and floor with a quick drizzle of glue and press the truncated triangle over it. Glue the other end in place the same way.

The front piece should be put in place now, resting on the rasped edge at the 45-degree angle and fitting between the two ends. Shoot the glue from both top and bottom—any way you can—to hold the front in place. Now you'll probably want to hammer some 8- or 10-penny finishing nails into the front and back pieces to hold the ends in place. It's not necessary, but it will give the bin extra strength.

For dividers, first make a pattern by fitting a piece of cardboard into the bin. With the help of a short prayer, it should be about 14¼″ × 3½″ × 11½″ × 11¼″. Draw the measurements on the plywood and cut out the four dividers. Shoot glue on the bottom, back and front edges of a divider and quickly ease it into place. Do this to the other dividers, gluing each one into place before starting on the next. File any rough edges and fill all crevices with the glue, so small toys don't get caught.

You're now ready to prop the bin on blocks and level it in place. To hang the bin, slide a washer on each screw and drill through the hole in the bin and into the studs.

Even though you'll sand and paint this wonder, it won't be very beautiful (plywood seldom is) but it is sturdy—and it works.

## WORK TABLE

When your child is mid-One, he'll like to paint and sculpt on the breakfast table or, ideally, on a low table and chair in the kitchen where he can have your company—and your supervision.

By Three, he needs a bigger work space with room enough for friends too. The kitchen is still the best place, but the size of the table is more important than its location. We recommend a long, smooth table made from an old or unfinished door and mounted on legs.

## SANDBOX

Our favorite kind of sandbox is filled with gravel—the smooth, small pea gravel that comes from a riverbed. The stones are too small to hurt when swallowed, don't stick to clothes, don't attract cats and are cleaner than sand.

To make a sandbox, use a rigid plastic pool, about 4' in diameter. Dig a hole in the ground, almost as deep as the pool itself, and lay short lengths of 2" × 4"s around the edge. Drop the pool into the hole and adjust the wood so the rim of the pool is supported. Punch holes in the bottom of the pool for drainage and fill with pea gravel.

If you do use sand, we recommend the sterilized white sand packaged for sandboxes—not because we're fanatics about cleanliness, God knows, but because this kind is a little less sticky. Cover any sand with a screen when not in use, to keep the neighborhood cats away.

## BASIC BOARD

This equipment, which can be used either indoors or out, is simply a board with four strips of wood across its underside, letting it convert quickly from a Balancing Board to a Seesaw to a Slide.

ASSEMBLE     one 8' plank, 8" wide
four 7" lengths of 2" × 2"s
hot melt glue OR
eight 2" No. 12 roundhead wood
    screws with washers
sandpaper
polyurethane

Place the lengths of 2" × 2" across one side of the plank with one strip at either end and the other two strips each 1" from the center. Glue the strips in place or slip a pair of screws through the washers and drill them from the top side of the plank into each strip of wood. Sand the rough

edges of the wood and paint it with polyurethane.

### BALANCING BOARD

A narrow board, raised slightly above the ground, teaches coordination better than any other piece of equipment. For a teetering Two, lay the Basic Board over two bricks—one at each end, abutting the strips of wood. Graduate to cinderblocks at Three.

### SEESAW

To use the Basic Board as a seesaw, you'll need to make a stanchion, with plumbing pipes cut to size and threaded at the hardware store. Once in the ground, it will look like a big, square croquet hoop.

ASSEMBLE     two 1½" pipes, 2' long
one 1½" pipe, 1' long
two 1½" elbows
premixed concrete

The longer pieces are the uprights, the shorter one the crosspiece. Use the elbows to join them together. Dig two holes, 6" wide, 14" deep and about a foot apart. Fill with concrete and imbed the uprights to a depth of 12". Once set, a Four and a friend can drag the Basic Board to the stanchion and center the board across the crosspiece: a seesaw. The strips on either side of the crosspiece will hold the seesaw in place.

### BEGINNER'S SLIDE

To a true climber, everything vertical is his turf and he almost never misjudges his space. Unfortunately, he has a lot of poor imitators, which is why a child in the beginning needs instruction and a small slide.

We once watched Mike at mid-One, a Buster Keaton in rompers, when he saw his first slide—a tall playground wonder. He watched, eyes wide and feet apart, as three experienced children ran up and slipped down. In a moment, he went up the steps and down the slide, whirled around in exhilarated confusion and then ran up the slide and slid down the steps—amazingly without injury.

To create a Beginner's Slide, simply hook one end of the Basic Board over the foot rail of the bed, if you use it indoors, or lock it over a low wall or the seesaw stanchion. The strip on the end will hold it in place.

## INDOOR LADDERS

There was a time when we left a 7' wooden stepladder set up in the middle of the dining room, so Mike, at Two, could go up and down, up and down, all day, but by the time he was Four, we found a much better solution. Straight wooden ladders—the kind with round rungs—can be hung horizontally from the ceiling or bolted to the wall. The ladders can be any length; the children, however, should be older than Two.

### HORIZONTAL LADDER

A horizontal ladder hung from the ceiling makes a spectacular apparatus for swinging hand over hand, as long as it clears 40" on either end, so a child won't bang into the wall.

ASSEMBLE        1 wooden ladder
                4 No. 0 hooks
                4 lengths 2/0 twist chain
                4 padlocks

Since the ladder should hang about a foot above your child's head, the length of the chains depends on the height of both your child and your ceiling.

Screw the hooks—the kind that hold the porch swing—into ceiling beams with one chain dropped from each hook. Loop a chain around each corner of the ladder, wrapping it under the side of the ladder, over the rung and then under the side

again, to prevent slippage. Padlock the loops into place. Your child soon will realize that he must take a flying leap from a chair to catch the first rung, which is why you might want to keep an extra mattress on the floor. Raise the ladder as he grows taller.

### VERTICAL LADDER

This climber takes little space because it's bolted flat against the wall although far enough from it for a child to fit his feet on the rungs.

ASSEMBLE        one ladder
                three 40" lengths of 2" × 4"s
                six 2½" No. 10 flathead wood screws
                    with washers
                nine 4¼" No. 16 roundhead wood
                    screws with washers

Because the ladder will receive heavy use, it must be attached to 2" × 4"s—the crosspieces—which then are attached to three studs in the wall. The studs usually are

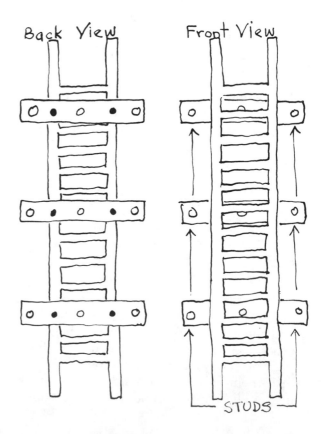

about 13–15″ apart, but measure first to make sure. Drill three holes through each crosspiece—to align with the studs—but don't attach them to the wall until they're screwed to the back of the ladder.

It's easier to attach the crosspieces to the ladder if you first drill the holes you need. Drill a pair of them through each crosspiece—the same distance apart as the uprights of the ladder. Then drill three more sets of holes, ½″ deep, into the back of these uprights—one near the top, one near the bottom and one in the middle.

To attach the crosspieces to the ladder, use the flathead screws (with their washers), threading them through the holes of the crosspieces and into the holes in the uprights.

To hang this Vertical Ladder—a heavy, two-people job—thread the roundhead screws, each cushioned by a washer, through each of the nine holes in the crosspieces and screw them into their corresponding studs.

## SWINGS

Nothing is quite as sexy as a swing (except, of course, sex). So let your child enjoy. Start with a portable swing in infancy—battery-powered, if possible—and work up to an old-fashioned four-seater lawn swing at Two, a rubber tire at Four, a traditional swing at Five and, finally, a heavy manila rope, knotted at intervals, which is rugged and tricky enough for a Six to climb and daring enough to sail through the air like Tarzan.

## BASKETBALL

Small boys like to imitate big boys, but it isn't possible in basketball unless you adjust the hoop. This gives a Four the same break as a Fourteen.

The hoop should be hung about 16″ higher than your child's head and attached to a high fence, the side of your house or within the carport—anywhere that he can retrieve the ball over and over, without

losing his dignity. Raise the hoop as he grows.

Because you'll be using the same hoop for years, we think the standardized, heavy-duty one is best. Let him use a soft, light ball at first, graduating to a real basketball at Six.

## STILTS

By the time your child is Six, he'll yearn to stand as tall as you. God bless stilts. These are sturdy, easy to make and safer than they look.

| ASSEMBLE | two 5–6′ lengths of 2″ × 2″s |
| | two 6″ lengths of 2″ × 4″s |
| | two 4″ lag screws, ¼″ in diameter |
| | two 3½″ lag screws, ¼″ in diameter |
| | 4 washers |
| | paneling adhesive |
| | sandpaper |
| | paste wax |
| | polyurethane OR paint |

When a child stands on stilts they should be no higher than his head and no lower than his shoulders, with the steps 1′ above the ground for a new stilter and as much as 2′ for an advanced one.

The two 2″ × 4″s form the steps of the stilts. To make them, cut off a triangle, 2″ × 3″ × 6″, from each one, which removes a sharp corner that could scratch your child's leg. Smear the 6″ side of a step with the adhesive and press it against one side of the 2″ × 2″ pole, at the height you want. The 4″ side of the step should be on top to support the foot. Now glue the other support in place.

When the glue is dry, drill a hole, 4″ deep, through the pole and into the step, 1½″ below the top of the footrest, and drill another hole, 3½″ deep and 2″ lower. Wax each screw before inserting it—so it will be easier to turn—and slide it through a washer, so the pole won't split under pressure. Tighten with a wrench and screw the other step in place. Sand the rough edges of the steps and coat the stilts either with the polyurethane or the paint to avoid splintering, but neither sand nor paint the foothold itself, for this would make it too slippery.

To teach your child to stilt, have him stand on the porch step that's even with the footrests, and tuck the poles behind his shoulders, wrapping his hands around them from the back of the poles to the front. Then have him mount the stilts and march away, and, yes, it will take several days, and many spills, for him to learn.

# RICHES

There are a few necessities a child must have—like love and food and shelter—and then there are the riches, which are almost as important.

A child can get along, no doubt, without books and theater and music and television too. If she has no friends, she'll invent some, and if she has no sense of her heritage she won't even know what's missed. Deprived of toys, she'll play with anything from a soap bubble to a firefly and if she isn't sent to preschool that's all right too. She'll still learn her lessons in first grade.

Just the same, childhood isn't the time to strip her world, but rather to embellish it. It's the trappings that give us the good life, that add the civilizing touch. The riches you bring your child, and the quality of them, will be treasures she draws on for the rest of her life.

---

◇                    **HERITAGE**                    ◇

---

You help your child's individuality grow in many ways, but an emphasis on her heritage is one of the best. When she can understand where she comes from, she will have a much better idea where she wants to go. Each time you continue a family custom or resurrect an ethnic recipe or use the language from generations past, you're giving her a stronger sense of herself. To keep this heritage alive, you and your husband will want to blend the customs of your families, even as you add a few of your own,

such as the way you let your Four use your great-aunt's favorite teaspoon for Sunday dinner.

If you live near your relatives, your child will be that much richer, for each visit with them—even when you have little in common—introduces her to her culture. She's part of a family and the family should include her bizarre cousins as well as her stern old grandfather. There are such affairs as a family reunion—so much trouble for everyone and so tempting to postpone—but these memories fill the attic of her mind with such riches she'll still rummage through them fifty years from now.

Like the rest of us, however, you and your husband probably live so far from your hometowns that your child must rely on you to weave these memories for her, and the best way to do it is to tell her about her people—alive or dead. Your child wants to hear all the stories, whether they're silly or sad, but she especially wants to hear about her parents when they were small. The simplest account will charm her, as it does Nadia each time she hears about her daddy playing hooky in first grade, but like all children, she admittedly likes the odd stories best, and so did we.

We remember our Tía Tata's vivid apparitions of the devils and the lesser-known virgins as if we'd seen them ourselves and we believed completely (as she did) her story of the Mexican revolution that made her cross-eyed and how she was cured by her nana, who pasted orange peels on her temples. We also recall, in color and sound and smell, that glorious day our wild Tío Pepe brought a drunken turkey home for dinner—because drunken turkeys, he said with a flourish, were easier

to pluck. To be sure, the turkey didn't agree and, made bold by tequila, zigzagged around the patio, gobbling wild turkey songs until the womenfolk finally cut off his antics. And then the plucking was just as hard as ever. In another age, a scene like that would have been the basis of a whole new feast day.

Every family has its wackiness, its excitement, its embarrassments and its gaiety. Your child should be a part of it all.

## THE BULLETIN BOARD

This sense of heritage your child needs is fed early when she sees family pictures around the house. Our friend Sarah, at six months, had her own picture gallery, where snapshots of grandparents, uncles and cousins were pinned to a bulletin board in her room. Her parents pointed to the faces (whether she had ever known the people or not) and called them by name until she was as familiar with them as the pictures in her book. By One, Sarah could hold these pictures herself (in her more peaceful moments) and never destroyed any at all. We wish we had used bulletin boards too.

---

◇                    **FRIENDSHIPS**                    ◇

We remember our old Tante Margot, the *grande dame* of her village, who would mutter at family reunions, "God gave me my relatives, thank God I can choose my friends."

A child is never too young to start trying, as we realized when we saw a snapshot of Meg and her two buddies on their bellies in a playpen— happy as pigs in clover and all only three months old. People are social

animals, whatever their age. Although babies won't play cooperatively with each other until Three, they all answer each other's babble, touch each other's hair (and occasionally pull it too).

For the first two years, the size of a playmate is more important than the age. When a larger child plays with a smaller one, he almost always bumps her over, because the bigger child has more ballast.

You can expect a pair of Ones to play together for as long as a half-hour before one of them cries. By fifteen months, your child will need to visit with friends and preferably with only one friend at a time. Because she may do very well with one playmate but be at her worst with another, she needs to know many children to select the ones she plays with best. This is true at every age.

Ideally, you'll seek a few children you like and she likes and whose mothers you like too, even if it means introducing yourself to likely women in the grocery store. Every young mother is in the market for more friends. This may seem like the last straw if you work, but your child needs to grow up knowing that friends are at least as important as errands, chores, parties and even work.

When you have little children, a park often is the best place for them to play together, since they can share playground equipment much better than they can share their toys at home. Besides, in a park a child can make friends with those eccentrics she might never meet otherwise, like the dizzy old lady who feeds squirrels and the crusty fellow with his racing form. It's variety that makes life interesting to a child. Any cross section of perspectives gives texture to a child's personality for it helps her think about the world from many angles.

By mid-One your child wants the companionship of other children more and more, and a play group becomes important if she isn't in day care (see page 74). It may be easier and cheaper to keep your child at home—no doubt about it—but she won't benefit as much. Although a play group is almost no different to a mother from a morning of small visitors, to a child it's quite special. The undivided attention from the duty mother and the regularity of the schedule give it some status and the rest comes from the formality of its name. Although this child barely can talk, she knows enough to call it "school."

A Two wants company all the time, more's the pity, and this means a constant eye. Every time you invite a young guest, you probably will invite her mother too.

With both of you watching, you may be able to keep up with them.

When your child starts nursery school—usually at Three—you may think you can taper off her social life, but soon she discovers that a peanut butter sandwich tastes much better when she eats it with a classmate.

A Four, you'll find, is a great plan maker and a friend is included in any plan. This child may learn her numbers and letters just to telephone invitations to a friend and loves to have you take pictures of her with her friends so she can hang them about her room. By Five, she becomes so selective you won't make or accept any invitation without her approval, but you should continue to ask a variety of children to visit so she won't lose the daring she needs to make new friends when she begins first grade.

Friends are so important to a Six that she spends a lot of time wondering how much she means to them, then cavalierly drops them into slots—"best friends," "second-best friends," "sort-of friends" and "yuks"—their rank somewhat depending on their sex. At this age a boy begins to prefer boys for friends, while a girl wants to be with girls no matter how hard you've tried to rear your child without any bias.

Any Six wants to roam more than a sailor on liberty. If she had her way, she'd travel up and down the block with a flock of other children all day, going from house to house for a snack here, a television hour there. You'll want to allow this only occasionally, for on a regular basis the group becomes more important than any other influence. No matter how nifty these children are, they can't offer her as much as her parents. Besides, the child who can visit with two or three children at a time, instead of many, will have a chance to make close friends. It's as important for a child to have quality friendships as it is for her to have quality care.

# SCHOOLS ◇

◇

We once knew a lady with six children in school, grades one to six, and she said if she had it to do again, God forbid, she would say to each child the moment she awoke, from the very first day: "You're beautiful! You're marvelous! You're fantastic!"

"I would say that every day, a hundred times a day, for six years," she said, "and then maybe that child would be ready for first grade."

Although school seems unimaginable when you're holding your baby, this is the time you're preparing her for the great big world, first by giving her independence and later by sending her to a preschool where she can put it into practice. If your child is in day care, that's school enough, but if you stay home, or if you have a sitter come to your house, she'll need more.

A play group is great for toddlers (or a "play school" as every Two insists on calling it) followed by preschool. This will mean a nursery school for your child at Three and Four or nursery school the first year and pre-K—for prekindergarten—the next. Each step in this gradual program has a different goal to help your child get ready for one of the watersheds of life: kindergarten.

If you keep your child at home until then a miasma will settle over her, which makes even a good little child whine, pinch the baby and ask, "Why?" about everything when she plainly knows most of the answers. This good little child needs a lot more action, more friends and more ideas than you're able to give. She will profit as much by a few mornings away from you as you do by a few evenings away from her.

A father ironically often tends to be more protective than a mother and may think preschool is silly, expensive and, although it may be all right for other children, it isn't necessary for any child of his.

True, it almost always costs too much money and takes up too much time, but personally, we've never met a child who didn't profit from a good preschool—nor a father who wasn't pleased with the results.

Once your child starts school she discovers new toys, new friends, new accomplishments and revels in field trips even though she's been there before with you. Although you might offer ideal surroundings at home—terraria and toys, canaries in cages and pizza every Tuesday—it will be the challenge of being a member of this first democracy that multiplies all of her enrichments. When your child meets the same dozen children regularly she learns the pains and the pleasures of belonging to a group, where everyone else has just as many rights as she does. She also finds that while some children do some things better than she does, she excels in others.

In nursery school the shyest child learns to fend for herself, without a mother's intervention, and she learns that the bigger her vocabulary, the easier the fending. While she learns new independence, she also meets a fresh measure of authority. A child in preschool truly believes that she can't cross streets, not because you've told her so often but because her teacher told her once.

## MOTHER'S DAY OUT

The Mother's Day Out programs are great for pre-Threes and give beleaguered mothers the chance to go off on their own one to three mornings a week. They are also a dandy way to meet other mothers, and they cost very little since they usually operate in suburban churches, using Sunday school rooms that would otherwise be empty during the week.

Of all the schools our children attended—and they were as varied as snowflakes—there wasn't one that didn't benefit them in some way. However, if you think you must choose between a bad school and no school at all, then your child should stay at home—or you should start your own school. It is a lot of trouble, but we think the more familiar she is with the idea of school, and the earlier it begins, the more comfortable she'll be in first grade. This is how you teach your fledgling to fly.

## PLAY GROUP

A play group seems to work best if it involves four congenial mid-Ones of relatively congenial mothers, who live near each other. Ideally, the children are about the same size, so they don't topple each other over, and no more than four months apart, and they meet twice a week on a regular schedule, for no more than two hours. Rotate the sessions among the four houses, with each mother taking a turn. You'll need a push or pull toy for each child, two wheel toys for the group—for children now begin to learn about sharing—some big cardboard boxes, a few three-piece puzzles and toys, some clay and, of course, books and tapes.

A play group has no structure at all, but it does require organization. As we learned when we found a mid-One hanging out of a third-floor window, you can't take even five minutes away from the children while you prepare juice. Do this before the group arrives and also tidy the play space, wash the breakfast dishes and lock any room you don't want a child to enter. Some days your presence hardly will be needed and other times you may have to do a song and dance in a funny hat to keep some jollies in the day.

The play group can graduate to a public facility—a church, a school or a settlement house—by Two, with mothers providing the toys and juice. You can double the number of children, use two duty mothers and split the cost of juice, cookies and secondhand toys.

## PRESCHOOL

Admission to preschool, on any level, depends on the child's readiness, which varies with each child. Certainly all children shouldn't start at the same age. However, since it often takes a year to find the right school and get to the top of its waiting list, you should start looking far in advance.

Nursery schools are usually run in the morning only, from three to five times a week, accepting children no younger than mid-Two but generally between Three and Four.

Pre-K, however, is a five-day program for four-year-olds, and though it isn't found everywhere, it is increasingly available in public schools, where it is free or nearly so, and in many private schools, but there the tuition is nearly as high as it is for first grade.

Some of these schools even let the more mature children stay until 3:00 for a low-key program several days a week, although it's almost never free, even in public school.

Most kindergartens, public or private, are run for three to six hours, five days a week, in the same protective atmosphere found in a nursery school and pre-K but with more emphasis placed on numbers and letters. Also, because the class size is often twice as big as a nursery school, the waiting list is much shorter in a private school and seldom encountered in a public school, where there is a place for every child.

## FINDING THE RIGHT PRESCHOOL

There are aptitude tests to tell students whether to go to a school for engineers or one for architects, but there are, alas, no tests that tell parents what kind of nursery school their child needs. Where one child may need a place to expend tremendous physical energy, another needs an orderly, almost serene setting and a third may thrive in a highly creative school. Certain schools are better for some children than they are for others. Generally, the younger the child, the smaller the school should be, no matter what the ratio of children to teacher.

You and your husband need to analyze your child candidly, assessing the strong points and the weak ones and deciding which atmosphere makes her happiest so you can find the school that will provide it best. These evaluations should be made together, for this is another, albeit small, watershed in your marriage.

Most preschools are private and these generally have an arts-and-crafts direction. The rest are usually cooperatives (since they're cheaper), and in these the parents develop the philosophy of the school and hire the teacher to carry it out. Because of this, there are many differences among the schools, and you must observe them carefully for they can be very good or rather awful. Whether your child goes to a public or private preschool, it will draw so much of your energy and your time that you'll want to study various established philosophies before you commit yourself. This will help you choose among Montessori schools, which are work-oriented; Waldorfs, where art, reading and science are woven together; or the creative, freer Country Days. The religious schools, which consciously stress values, can be another good option, but they come in many, many styles. Look for one that meets the same criteria and uses the same discipline that you'd look for in any good school.

No method is perfect, but the more you know, the better you can judge all of them. Ideally, a school should be strong in all areas, but be realistic when you look. Perfection is hard to come by. The best schools of any sort are elastic enough to handle children with a variety of personalities, backgrounds and abilities, enhancing their good days and helping them through the bad ones.

If you're the methodical sort, you might find the schools in your area through the licensing department of your city government, but frankly we've never known anyone that methodical and think you can get the same help from friends, neighbors, local churches, parents in the park and the people in your car pool. You'll have to observe the schools, however, to see how good they are, for this information is too important to take secondhand. Do this without your child and stay a full morning at each school to see the complete picture.

Even a mediocre preschool may be better than none, but if you're not going to switch her to pre-K, it has to be good enough to keep her interested until Five. If the songs, the games and the activities are just a repeat of the first year, you may be tempted to put her in kindergarten too soon.

When you think you have found the right school, ask if your child can explore it, but only after the children have gone for the day. Since you may be looking for a school as much as a year ahead of time, your child will be too young to mesh with these older children. She's not ready to do this until the teacher thinks she's practically ready to start school, and then she needs to visit, so she'll feel comfortable when she does begin. Her admission date should depend on her maturity, which seldom follows a calendar.

Since she'll need about six weeks to adjust to school, don't plan to enroll her less than two months before—or after—you plan to move, take a job or have a baby. One shake-up at a time is enough for a child.

There will be some adjustment problems in the most stable situation, for it's a wrench to go into the big world. A good school expects it, however, and a good teacher can handle it.

### JUDGING A PRESCHOOL

A well-run preschool, like a well-run any kind of school, is a happy place, where the children are happy to go in the morning, dawdle in their leaving and openly like their teacher and each other.

From a physical point of view, the room should be light and airy with running water, a tape player, a pet and shelves low enough for children to reach all toys and supplies for themselves. There also should be an easel for every four children, a wheel toy for every two and at least one plant and one rhythmic instrument for each child.

The class needs a corner for housekeeping, one for block-building and another for dress-ups, with a suitcase of costumes as well as a heap of shoes, canes and even a crutch or two although probably no hats. The threat of lice has made them a thing of the past in many schools.

A preschool particularly should have an area for quiet play with books, puzzles and small interlocking blocks, which help the fingers become more dexterous. Children also need a place indoors to jump, dance, tumble on a mat and climb gym equipment, all of which help them coordinate their arms and legs better (and give them a jolly time too). If there's no room for gym equipment outdoors there should at least be space for trikes and trucks.

Although the most beautiful setting can't compensate for a bad teacher, a good one can make a dowdy place come alive when the program is exciting enough. This is easier if the school limits a class to fifteen children and gives the teacher an aide.

A good preschool chooses a teacher who recognizes that children are working when they play and respects each child for it. This respect should be the strongest underpinning in any school, flowing not only between the teacher and the children but among the children too. When there is this respect, children can be themselves, working at their own pace and in their own style, keeping their small eccentricities as long as they don't disrupt the class or offend anyone too much.

Each child should be able to go to the

bathroom without waiting for the bell to ring (because heaven knows, that's her business), but there must be some rules in a school. A school will be a happy place as long as these rules are sensible and the children know the reasons for them—such as returning a toy to its shelf so others may use it, but not so the room will look tidy. In fact, unless a school has signs of pleasant disarray, we'd have to question its priorities.

Although there will be small personality clashes in any school, the children should be so absorbed in their work and play that there will be little time for quarrels and none for boredom.

### JUDGING THE TEACHER

Sometimes a school can have an excellent facility, a strong philosophy—and a teacher who doesn't quite live up to either. To us, the quality of the school is more important than the quality of the teacher, because one is more permanent than the other, but if the school itself is weak, the teacher must be much more competent.

To run a classroom well, a teacher should have the day blocked into chunks of time, so children can complete their work and slip easily from passive to active play, without having to be herded.

When you observe, you should be able to see that the teacher obviously cares about each child and makes each one feel better about herself, but still stays in the background. This lets children develop easy friendships, so they will seek help from each other as well as the teacher.

We've found the best teachers have had several years of practical experience. They are imaginative and enthusiastic, have good speech patterns, clear ideas of discipline and are open with parents about the way they handle general problems, but discreet about the specific children involved.

We've also found that a man teacher may offer more to young children—especially boys—than a woman, since many children spend so much time with women. Something as simple as hammers and nails aren't used in most nursery schools, not because of safety but because many women teachers don't handle them adeptly and so they don't encourage their use.

A good teacher is a good disciplinarian but, like you, sets boundaries as wide as possible and uses praise and positive techniques to guide the children. This sort of person diverts the demon of the day before mischief is made, comforts a downcast child before she cries and uses carpentry, climbing and clay modeling to channel energy constructively. Above all, this teacher corrects a child only when it's possible to follow through, and then only in private and never, of course, with a spanking.

In these ways a teacher treats all the children with equality and with respect—the only way they can learn to treat others the same.

## THE COOPERATIVE

A cooperative, as the sociologists say, is a learning experience. You may have to hire teachers—and fire them—schedule mothers and keep them to it, interview applicants and agonizingly reject a few, which doesn't seem to faze the child and always hurts her mother very much.

You may have to supply the cookies and juice for a month or paint the bookcases, but the better the co-op, the less a parent will be expected to monitor the classroom. However, all cooperatives use parents to help on field trips and the best ones take advantage of the special talents of parents, having them teach carpentry, modern dance or cooking. To help with the children is the most tiring—and stimulating—job you can have in a co-op, for children draw as much out of you as you're

## SUNDAY SCHOOL

For most of us, religion is part of our culture and our heritage, and a child has the right to this legacy too. It not only will help her figure out where she stands, but it can give her the strength to stand tall.

Your child's week-in, week-out experience at church or temple will also make it easier for you to explain bedtime prayers to her and help her understand what religion is all about. You'll even benefit yourself, for Sunday school will make your pre-K act a little better at weddings, christenings and bar mitzvahs.

Even then her behavior won't be great when she goes to a regular service with you, but you can expect her to behave pretty well if you don't let two children sit next to each other; if you don't make eye contact with her when she misbehaves—since this only encourages more of the same—and if you don't expect too much. A pre-Three usually needs to go outside for a little walk at half-time, and sooner if she starts to cry, talk loudly or throw pennies in the air, and an older child will need a book or a doll to keep her busy. Don't bring more, however, since she will distract others and she won't learn much about religion, which is, after all, why she's there.

It's hard to give up a precious Sunday morning, but religion will be another anchor in her life. If she ever needs special help, she'll always know where to find it.

---

willing to give. We think it's the most rewarding job too—even if you or your husband have to take time off from work—to take some co-op turns. It will give you the chance to see how your child gets along on her own turf. Little children particularly need fathers around them and the school often takes on a livelier air when they're there, since they usually haven't been preconditioned by those dreadful monthly co-op meetings. To us they are the most difficult and dizziest part of a cooperative. Here, for some metaphysical reason, the most charming, intelligent women turn into somber ninnies when they talk about the health, safety and education of their children.

At least some of this is inevitable and we predict you'll natter like the rest of us over milk vs. orange juice and why cookies should be baked with honey instead of sugar (and, of course, they'll be home-made). You even may endure, as we did in one of the drearier cooperatives, an hour-long discussion of the daily projects. There we remember the imposing teacher from Britain, much given to Freudian slips, who announced that the children would make styrofoam ornaments for the Christmas tree "which little boys particularly will like," she trilled, "and when they're done we'll let them roll their little balls in glittah."

It's silliness like this that puts the nursery school business in perspective.

## PRE-K

Despite many stops and starts, preschool has been going on ever since the Puritans started it, in the 1600s. Only the pre-K is new.

This fine invention recognizes that Fours really are a breed apart. These little eccentrics, hedged between the good and golden years of Three and Five, are wilder than they'll be for years. They definitely listen to their own drummers and the beat is purely ragtime.

This often makes them tired of their gentle little nursery school and yet they're still too young for kindergarten. Although they have the same needs as Fives, their attention span is shorter—10 minutes is long enough to sit and listen, thank you—and though they can also get along fine in a class of 20, they get along much better if there are three teachers instead of two.

On paper, the pre-K plan of the day may seem much like the plan for kindergarten, but the pace of pre-K suits the pace of the Four much better. It is faster, the noise level is louder, the centers are free-flowing. The Four might build with blocks, but it will be a garage one minute, a boat the next, while a Five happily builds blocks around the single theme of the day or the week.

This is the year that Fours work on their skills: to take care of themselves with ease, to dress themselves and go to the bathroom alone, to share toys, to wait their turn (within reason), and to express themselves better, verbally and creatively. Most of all, they learn to feel good about learning.

## KINDERGARTEN

A good teacher—particularly a good kindergarten teacher—looks at the whole child and the whole world, weaving the art of language with the science of math and nature, and then adds social studies to the mix.

The class may look like three hours of fun and games, but everything is channeled to help Fives think a little better, a little more clearly. They are expected to "read" with understanding—even though the teacher does the actual reading—and to write with creativity, even though the writing is just scribble at first.

When the teacher reads a story, she asks the children how they think it will turn out—and then invites them to figure out the main character and the plot and to change their predictions as the story unfolds. These aren't easy tasks at Five, but if your child understands the sense of what she reads, she'll want to read more.

When these Fives write, they keep journals, guessing at sounds as they go, and then telling the teacher the story so she can decipher it at the bottom of the page. To your surprise—but not to the surprise of the teacher or the children—you can more or less read and understand these very short essays without any help by the end of the school year. These exercises in reading and writing will make your

child comfortable with letters, teach her the basic sounds and help her get ready for first grade. They will even make her a better speller than the children who learn to read before they ever try to write.

In kindergarten the children are encouraged to use real objects to make math make sense, for these children are too young to understand numbers unless they can touch them. By moving Cuisenaire rods, bottle caps and pennies around—adding here, subtracting there—the rote learning in grade school will be necessary only to help them remember what they already know.

Kindergarten will teach your child many things, but the greatest of them are these: to be self-confident, to work independently, to solve problems without running to the teacher. This is the foundation she needs most—and she'll depend on it for the next sixteen years.

## FIRST GRADE

The first-grade teacher is often dandy, whether the school is public or private, but from then on, there will be that one excellent teacher, whose name your child will never forget; one penny dreadful, whose name she'll try to forget; and two mediocre ones, whose names she'll forget soon and their faces too.

There seems to be no way you can put a child in a building with at least a dozen classrooms and thirty children to a class, without scaring her a little bit. It takes a strong, strong child to be ready for this.

It is self-confidence—not "reading readiness" or even reading—that makes a successful first-grader. This child must be tough enough to be teased by older chil-

dren, to say "I don't know" in front of a roomful of other children, to throw up in the hall without crying too much. A first-grader must want to learn what everyone else is learning and at roughly the same time, and she usually can if she's a Six, for this child conforms to her surroundings as fast as a lizard to a lily pad.

A Five has a much harder time in the first grade, as we've learned through poignant experience, for she measures herself not against other Fives, but against other Sixes. This child may not be overwhelmed at first, but then be swamped as she advances until, in the pivotal sixth grade, the younger child is likely either to surrender or rebel with sloppy work, poor behavior or a shyness that will twist your heart.

Most states set a cutoff date for kindergarten and first grade and the school won't accept a child if her birthday comes after that date. This helps to group children of the same emotional age, but if you think your child is still too young, talk out your concerns with the teacher before she starts. Sometimes it's wiser to let a child go to kindergarten for another year (especially a boy, since boys usually develop about six months later than girls). This delay, and extra enrichment programs to whet her yearning to learn, will give your child the dignity of going to school, without the responsibility of keeping up with older children. It's nice to be that big frog in a little pond. Next year she can be the big lizard.

---

◇                     # TOYS                     ◇

While many of the best toys and game come out of your head and out of the supplies and equipment in your house, a child still needs her toys and play equipment the way you need your VCR, your tennis racquet and your morning paper. You can expect any toy or game that has lasted for generations—like blocks or a ball or a wheel toy—to be fun for all children, for a good toy, like a good teacher, makes learning a delight.

A mechanical bear does bring the laughs—which are important—but a toy also can be a tool. It may challenge the mind, like dominoes; build coordination, like a gym set; encourage creativity, like blocks, or it may quicken the imagination the way a rag doll permits more fantasy than a perfectly costumed bride doll. The more a toy invites a child to participate, the better it is.

The best toys are geared to a child's size and age and require little instruction and supervision. If you don't have to hover over your child like a hen she can learn how much she can do for herself.

Not all children like the same kinds of toys and their preferences show up early. One child may be attracted primarily by wheel toys, another child by balls she can kick and throw, a third child by paints and other art supplies and the fourth child will want anything—from a doll to a cradle—that fulfills an innate need to nurture. Plastic nuts and bolts, which require a mechanical ability, can enthrall one child and frustrate another, regardless of sex. Although you'll begin to recognize some of your child's preferences at the end of the first year, others will take more time to surface.

When you see your child get bored or angry with a toy, it's either too old for her or she finds it pointless, and in either case it should be put away. Other toys simply aren't good enough for your child to use. These are the ones that are made to be bought, broken and replaced within weeks. We find they make a child feel clumsy, guilty and eventually irresponsible, until she may learn to mistreat all toys.

A toy should be well made, safe and sturdy, so it will last as long as the child's interest, and it should be so much fun it will stretch her attention span because she can't stop playing with it. Some toys in particular are put to such heavy use that they should be the best, like push and pull toys, a rocking horse, building sets and a wagon. It is always better to have a few fine timeless quality toys than a shelf full of licensed fads.

If you can afford it, your child should have a few faddish toys, of course—so she won't feel left out—and some battery toys too, but use the rechargeable cadmium batteries. They are actually cheaper because they last much longer, although you'll have to cover the battery door with duct tape. Otherwise little fingers will open it and roll the batteries to that mysterious place where toy parts hide until the child is too old to play with the toy.

### CARE OF TOYS

All children mistreat some toys sometimes, but occasionally one energetic child will be hard on all of them, the same way she may be hard on her clothes. If your child uses a metal truck as a battering ram, a push toy to bang on the floor and a block to throw like a ball, she needs clearer boundaries. You still can have peace and she still can play with gusto if you let her ride her truck outdoors, use a real hammer to pound on wood scraps—under your watchful eye—and only throw a foam ball in a particular part of the house.

You also can help your child take reasonably good care of her toys if they're not crowded; if she can reach them easily, and if she can keep all the pieces together.

When a toy does break, either put it aside until you can repair it or throw it away. If you let broken toys accumulate, they'll depress you so much you'll start to notice the cracks in the plaster instead of the daisies on the table.

When you buy new toys—not many more than are needed—you'll be wise to store some of the old ones, if only so your child won't look so pampered. This is a good instinct to follow. Too many toys can overwhelm a child. In self-defense she'll limit her choices anyway, playing with only a few of them. It will be easier if you rotate all but the favorites, putting away a third of the toys every few weeks. When you take them out of storage they'll look to her like long-lost friends—a great deal better than they did when she saw them last.

### BUYING TOYS

Buying toys takes some expertise, a sharp eye and much restraint, like shopping the sales. It's a trial-and-error process. Count yourself blessed if you succeed 75 percent of the time.

A child needs some new toys when many of the old ones are outgrown, lost, broken or boring, which usually happens about twice a year. The dilemma of selecting the right toy for the right child at the right age is one that's never completely solved. It's tempting to give the toys you once coveted—which is all right if you had the same tastes then as your child has now—or to buy them too soon, as if she were a prodigy—and that's never all right.

Most manufacturers suggest such a wide range of ages that a mother is encouraged to offer a toy early and the child is sick of the sight of it by the time she's old enough to use it. In this area, at least, we feel it much better to go too slow than too fast. Besides, the waste of a good toy will make you feel as irritated as you do when

you buy shoes that are too small or food that no one eats.

For safety, a toy should be nontoxic and nonflammable and it shouldn't be too noisy either. A toy also should be washable, have smooth edges, no pins or buttons that can be removed and no springs that can catch the fingers, toes or hair. No toy should be made of glass, of course, nor of brittle plastic either, for this also breaks easily and can scratch a child.

If your child is under One her toys should be too large to be swallowed, should have no cord over 12" long—since it could wrap around her neck—and it certainly shouldn't have any small, detachable parts that could lodge in the windpipe, ears or nose. A parent has to take special care in selecting toys for an older child when there's an inquisitive baby crawling around. Some toys, like marbles, are clearly dangerous for a baby and others, like a metal truck, depend on the driver. If you have any doubts about the safety of a toy for your household, don't buy it.

Although all good toys are educational, some require more guidance than others. If you buy a toy that needs a teacher, remember: you'll be the teacher. You may have to give frequent lessons with your child to make these toys come alive.

A first-time mother may assume, as we did, that her child will learn to count magically with an abacus. How foolish we were to think that a child in her innocence could decipher this inscrutable tool. Certainly we couldn't. Of course, the children obligingly pushed the colored beads from side to side and whirred them around the rods, but they never could learn to add and subtract with it—or learn Chinese either. If you want your child to enjoy an abacus or any other toy that requires specialized knowledge, you'll have to learn to use it yourself.

Even if you know how to choose a safe,

sturdy, interesting toy, you might not know if it will be any fun, and that's the most important part of all. A few select toy stores may have clerks informed enough to advise you or they may let your child play with the samples. However, be wary of her impulsive judgment, for a pre-Six is dazzled easily by the biggest and the brightest and anything that's advertised on TV. The way to find out which toys she likes is to watch the ones she chooses time after time, when she visits friends or goes to play school. The type of toys that enchant or challenge her the most will be the ones she'll treasure at home, but keep one caveat in mind: no toy will mean as much to your child as the time she spends with you.

## INFANCY

The toys for a baby in her first six months are designed to awaken and then sharpen her sense of sight, sound and touch. A baby needs exciting surroundings everywhere—especially the ceilings—and she is fascinated by sophisticated black and white designs. She'll look at them more in the next few months than she ever will again in her life. Kites are great, but mobiles are better. To make them, dangle anything that's vivid, shiny or amusing on ribbons, thread or nylon fishline, tying them to clothes hangers, embroidery hoops or simply to straight sticks. The hoops can be hung from cup hooks in the ceiling, and the sticks or the hangers can be poked between books in a tall bookcase.

No matter how many gifts she has received, you'll want to add a few simple stimuli for her each week, like magazine pictures hung on the kitchen wall. A ball of aluminum foil may not be beautiful to you, but she'll be so pleased. She also will like a silver rattle, because it's shiny and has such a clear, tinkly sound, and she needs a music box, soft toys, a hard rubber ring that looks like a doughnut and at least one activity toy fastened onto the playpen and the crib. Above all, you will want her to have some warm, cuddly stuffed animals—especially a monkey. The face enchants most babies.

### SIX MONTHS

In quiet moments, a stuffed animal, like Peter Rabbit, may be this child's delight—the beginning of a long and loving relationship. It's the other moments that keep parents so busy.

Once a baby can sit up and crawl, she becomes interested in undoing everything she can. During the next three months she'll learn to toss toys from her crib, pull yarn out of a basket and empty your purse. As her crawling improves she empties shelves, boxes, drawers and anything she can open and reach. She should never think that this undoing is bad—because it isn't—but neither should you let her undo everything she sees, for you'll soon resent it. She'll be content if you give her a plastic jar with a top to unscrew, a box of spoons to spill, an aluminum drip coffeepot to take apart—none of which she can put back together, of course, but that's all right. A child has to learn to "undo" so she eventually can learn to "do": to nest blocks, to fill shelves, to put a puzzle together.

She has more and more waking hours now and small toys aren't enough. This is the time to give her a few board books, small enough for her to hold—if you haven't already—and buy or borrow a walker or a doorway swing.

### NINE MONTHS

The best toys for this age are the artifacts of everyday life: hats, eggbeaters, pipes, keys, new paintbrushes, pots and pans.

Parents demonstrate their use over and over—much more often than they show their child how to stack blocks.

### ONE

When your baby starts prowling around the house, you may decide she needs a playroom. She doesn't. She has one already and it's always the room you're in. In another year, when her curiosity sends her off on her own adventures, you'll worry every time she leaves your side and you should. This year feel blessed that she follows you instead.

Since you want your child to explore life when she's an adult, now is the time to start. Provide a special basket or shelf, cupboard or drawer in every room to hold her toys and some of your discards too, choosing them according to the room. This is the way you continue to define her boundaries, for your home, like yourself, shouldn't be dominated by a child.

She needs scarves, a pocketbook without a catch, a tie and a big hat in your room, where you want more quiet. Hang a net sack in the bathroom for her rubber toys and provide some low, open shelves in her room for books and stuffed animals. She'll like to play with water in the kitchen, pouring from one container to another and will love pots and pans, for if you use them daily, she has to figure they're fun. Encourage her to bang one with a wooden spoon, to fit the lid in place and eventually to nest a pot into a bigger one.

Her own store-bought toys probably will be kept in the living room, where you at least can read the paper in comfort while she plays. Either a small rocking horse or the considerably more exciting horse on wheels or a ride-on truck are excellent toys and so are the simplest peg-pounding toys of beginning carpentry. Sometimes the old toys are the best ones.

What looks like play to you is work to a child and she thrives on it. Everything she does has a purpose to her. As soon as a child walks she should have a push toy and a pull toy, the brighter the better, especially if they have their own special sounds as they move. These toys are her tests of skill as she maneuvers them through doorways, down the stairs, around corners.

A One needs a couple of dozen books, a sponge ball to toss inside and a large colorful ball to chase outside, a doll to cuddle, a few new bath toys and things that open and shut like a jack-in-the-box. Now she likes musical toys, like a bell, a harmonica, a maraca and, if she doesn't run with it, a wooden horn.

### MID-ONE

Your child's quest for independence takes on new dimensions at mid-One, and the tools she works with are more important than ever. She doesn't need a great many toys, and many of the best ones will be homemade, like Flour Clay for sculpting (see page 303) or beanbags (or snowballs) for pitch and catch and for target tossing with you outside. Crayons, if she uses them in the high chair, are good now, and so is a small broom, a bubble pipe, a noisemaker and peg puzzles.

Her energy seems enormous now and it appears to increase every day as she is able to give less attention to the mechanics of moving and more attention to getting herself there. One child will run almost constantly and when she's not running she's pushing herself around on a little wheel toy. Another will become a climber of extraordinary skill. At this age you're likely to find her shimmying up the bookcase or sitting on top of the refrigerator with neither of you having any real idea of how she got there. No matter how much natural climbing instinct you think she might have, she still needs to be taught how to climb and slide and balance and you need to teach these skills before a calamity makes you sorry you didn't.

A mid-One uses a kitchen chair as the first two rungs of a ladder and pushes it before her everywhere she goes. This may be why she appreciates having her own sturdy stool so much. She'll use it with marvelous importance, backing her fanny onto it as if it were a throne, carrying it like a silver tray and climbing on it to reach even the lowest chair.

An indoor slide and, if you can stand it, an indoor sandbox on legs are used for the next few years, but your child also needs to play outside every day. Although you may have a well-equipped, well-protected backyard, you can expect her to go in and out of the house almost as if she were caught in a revolving door. Personally, we've never seen a mid-One happy to stay alone for more than fifteen minutes—if that long. Whether she plays outdoors or in, it's the plumber's friend, above all other toys, that most young children like best if they're given the chance. It's a horse, a hat and a hundred other things. You don't have to show your child how to use it; she knows instinctively. And if she leaves it outside, someone else will gallop away with it immediately. So far we've lost seven.

### TWO

A child's life is either chaotic or organized, depending on instruction. Learning the use of toys, step by step, makes them more interesting and makes her feel more competent.

A puzzle teaches concentration, trains the eye to isolate shapes and helps coordination—if it's easy enough. If not, put it away for weeks or even months, for nothing is more frustrating than a puzzle that's too difficult. We speak from experience, for to us, nothing's harder than those three-piece wooden puzzles cut on the color lines: no hints at all. Whenever your child gets a new puzzle, scribble across the backs of all the pieces with a crayon, using a different color for each puzzle. When you have to separate a half-dozen puzzles, you'll find it a bit easier to sort them by the color of the scribbles on the back than by the color of the pictures on the front. Be careful, too, about the kind of puzzles you buy. Even though they're hard for grown-ups, wooden puzzles are the most durable, the most expensive and the best, and cardboard puzzles in a frame are the worst, for the thin pieces are hard for a child to handle.

A Two also needs toys to pull and push, but now they should have a function: a doll carriage, a wagon, a wheelbarrow. Of the three, we think a wheelbarrow is best, for it's big enough to transport many treasures and it develops a child's sense of equilibrium because it's tricky to handle. Your child can also master a tricycle—and you can master your child—if you get the small, lightweight European trike with a long removable handle that's inserted in the back. You'll use it to guide her safely across streets and over curbs, and to push her along when she's tired, and this "I do it meself" Two will never even know it.

Blocks teach coordination too. Now your child needs a dozen of those lovely big cardboard bricks that she can both stack and climb on and she also needs a peck of small wooden blocks in geometric shapes. They needn't be expensive—secondhand ones run through the cycle of soap and hot water in the washer will do fine—but they have to be smooth. Avoid the painted ones if you have a young baby or a puppy in the house who may chew them, since they're cut from soft wood. However, you should know that any child left in a room with the cheaper, brightly painted blocks and the unpainted varnished ones used by the best nursery

schools will choose the brighter ones every time. So much for the experts.

Your Two won't be exuberantly building, jumping or climbing every moment of the day. It only seems that way. Some of the time she's relatively still—making music.

There are two types of musicmakers—those that make noise and those that make musical sounds. For noise, get a toy piano, a large whistle, a cheap, twangy guitar. For music, get a marimba, a tambourine and a durable bongo drum of wood and hide. A beautiful, marching drum from the toy store is a waste, because the skin is usually made of paper and when it breaks—almost immediately—it makes a child feel both incompetent and destructive. However, she'll enjoy a cylinder drum she's made from a grits box, because it's tougher and she expects much less from it.

Your child will like your old magazines, which you might mark with big, red X's to identify them—and to protect your new ones. A stack of this X-rated literature will keep a toddler busy for a full ten minutes, so we recommend several stacks around the house.

### MID-TWO

A child's play space at home, indoors and out, should be geared to much more demanding exercise now. Since she climbs constantly, she'll use your furniture less if you hang a Vertical Ladder bolted to the wall (see page 164).

Toys should be more complicated for a mid-Two and some should be toys she can order around. She needs sturdy trucks she can ride and guide, snap-together blocks she can build so they don't fall apart every time she moves and a sexy rocking horse that will gallop when she bounces. Now she can toss her beanbag toward a basket and pound her hammer, again and again, at the head of a nail.

Many of the props she needs are compact and some are homemade. They're necessary to help her enact the dozens of

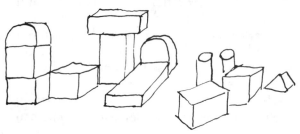

different roles she fantasizes every day. Every time a child pretends she's a supermarket checker, a carpenter or a bus driver, she's trying to answer her own curiosity and forcing her imagination to stretch itself. It will stretch more if she has a basket with a handle to carry her possessions, a tunnel to crawl through, a cloth to hang over a card table for a house of her own and a variety of hats.

Wooden boxes are good to hold special

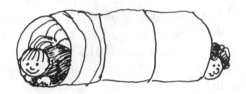

sets of toys, but cardboard boxes—any shape, any size—are the joy of any child. A mid-Two will be as content with four or five of them as she would be with as many new toys (and your house will look tidy too).

The boxes should be big enough to sit in, to push, to pull, to stack. A child enjoys them even more when you refer to them by the proper names she gives them: a boat or a wagon, an island or a tower. Each time you encourage her imagination, it grows that much bigger.

### THREE

As a child approaches Three, her behavior becomes more predictable. Now she has a stronger preference for certain types of activities—boisterous or quiet—but any child should have some of both. This opens her world much more. If your child is quiet, she still needs toys that make her run, chase, swing, swoop or jump, just as a rambunctious child needs books and soothing tapes to enjoy her solitude more.

By Three she'll profit by having her own sturdy little tape player and a rack to hold her tapes. You'll find she knows which ones she wants to hear, because she can read the odd marks and scratches as quickly as you read the labels.

Real games begin to be favorites now too. Threes may be ready to play Uncle Wiggly and Crackers in My Bed—a dandy matching game—and will like to look at books and watch videotapes when they're quiet, but don't let us mislead you: the only time they're really quiet is when they are asleep.

Dolls—and stuffed animals—are very important to the nurturing sort of child, while the little storyteller uses them for props. This makes many Threes beg for Barbies or G.I. Joes, although little boys may want the fashion dolls and little girls may want the soldiers, to the dismay of their parents. It's nothing to worry about. In either case, the dolls are quickly stripped, and then the child has a terrible time dressing them again.

This is a great age for running around and you may be shocked that your Three wants a gun. Children have pretend shoot-ups, whether they use their fingers or a stick or a plastic pistol, but the children who have homemade props seem to have less interest in war games and quit them much earlier. One gun we don't mind is the water pistol, especially the kind that doesn't look like a gun. It's a good outside toy and you'll want to replace it as soon as it's lost or broken for it releases a great deal of exuberance and brings a lot of laughs. Bubbles are another pleasure, in the bathtub or outside, but the bubble-making wand is definitely an outside choice, since its homemade mix leaves a slightly sticky residue. It's worth it though, for it makes such marvelous, parabolic shapes, and the recipe is always on the package.

Your Three does love her large, bulky toys, such as a tricycle or a Big Wheel, a rocking horse, or her big plastic car, and she needs a sheltered place for them. Let her park them in the carport, the basement or her bedroom, but they should definitely be put away or it will seem like they're taking over the house.

She'll still need a shelf or a drawer in each room for her smaller toys, so she can be near you, but most of the toys should be kept in her own room.

Never expect to store toys in the boxes they came in, for they're not sturdy enough. Instead, keep them on shelves or in strong cartons, baskets or cloth bags. Some toys, such as her interlocking plastic blocks, small cars or magnetized wooden trains, can be grouped together but don't throw them into a toy chest. Even if it has a safety hinge, it's still a poor way to store toys and it breeds disorder.

Since disorder confuses your child as much as it confuses you, help her sort her toys, but do this only once or twice a week. If a child gets too concerned about keeping her toys in order, she won't like her friends to play with them either.

### FOUR

If she hasn't already, your child soon will have very sure opinions about what toys she wants for her birthday, Christmas or Saturday night. They are inspired by the toys her playmates have, the ones used in nursery school, and, of course, by those she sees advertised on TV. Fortunately, she likes so many things it's easy to choose the ones that fit you both.

Children like to dress like cowboys, nurses, sailors, farmers—any costume that creates a role. Your Four will like to play house with a stove you've made out of cardboard (see page 321), go outside to throw a small rubber ball with one hand like a ball player and play "road safety" with her tricycle, toy car or scooter. This makes her feel grown-up, and makes her aware of traffic long before she crosses streets.

She also wants to use scissors on every piece of paper she can find and to put a jigsaw puzzle together. She can work her puzzle best on a tray, so you can put it away when she's bored with it without disturbing the picture. Until she learns how, help her turn over all the pieces, face-up, and then separate the borders so she

can make the frame. She can assemble it faster that way, which makes her proud.

Games become increasingly important now. If your child is anything like Alison, expect to play Candyland 1,042 times this year, as well as Dominoes—a Four can match the pictures on the tiles or the patterns of dots—and will probably be ready for Memory and Clue, Jr., before the year is done.

The child who enjoys small toys will love a farm with animals or some miniature cars. For more robust play, consider a tumbling mat or a mattress on the basement floor, a rope ladder to hang from a strong limb of a tree in the backyard—and an old tire to hang from another, if you don't mind pushing—and T-ball, a game to play alone or with friends. She'll also adore the chance to play on a slide every day, either in the park or her own yard and needs a large sturdy but lightweight ball. It's good to throw and chase too, and to use in games of dodge ball, kick ball and foursquare when other children come over.

### FIVE

A Five, that great collector, has defined interests and saves rocks or toy cars or dolls. The most ardent doll collector also wants a bigger carriage and a dollhouse with all the paraphernalia although she's not ready for fancy dollhouse furniture yet.

A Five should have a small assortment of brushes for artwork, a deck of cards to

play the standard favorites—Old Maid and Fish—as well as many stories on tapes and in books. For favorite board games, look for Sorry, Chutes and Ladders, Guess Who, Pictionary, Jr., and Uno and if you have a computer, you might give your child a game that demands hand-to-eye coordination and a lot of eye-tracking. This is one way to help a child get ready for reading.

Now you can introduce a needle and embroidery thread, a small potholder loom or a game like pickup sticks, so your child can practice the same pincer movement she will use every time she holds a pencil at school. While these pastimes appeal to some children, others still can't get enough physical exercise and will like a soccer ball to kick and a knotted rope to climb, and can pump a lightweight swing now if you teach her. Don't give your child a bike, however—even though the wheels are only sixteen inches—unless you think she will wear her helmet, for you want her to start this lifetime habit as soon as she starts to ride. She should also be able to go fast enough to keep the bike steady, without training wheels. They only turn a two-wheeler into a four-wheeler and make a child more fearful.

A great amount of a child's playtime may be spent in elaborate "pretend" games, where her old Big Wheel becomes the family car and the gym set is her house. Other games require no props at all and you may hear yourself saying that your child never plays with her toys anymore. Neighborhood games like Statue, Mother,

May-I and Red Light/Green Light are as popular now as they ever were, and their appeal will only grow over the next few years.

## SIX

We've found girls beg for the biggest, most complicated dolls at Six, and then prefer the plain old baby doll that does nothing but drink from a bottle (for your Six to share secretly) and wet her diapers. Although dolls are beloved by many little girls, woe to the boy who likes them too. Despite the women's movement, children still feel somewhat pressured by society, if not by their parents, to accept the stereotype roles of boy and girl, until all boys think they must be rough and tough and all girls must be scared of worms. This is silly, of course, but it won't happen to your child if you encourage her to choose the toys and books that let her follow her own interests. Just as a One may pick a puzzle over a beanbag, so should your son be able to cook and your daughter be able to play games with the guys.

Boy or girl, almost any Six wants to fly a kite (especially if she's helped to make it) and to push a tire like a hoop and she thinks there's nothing finer than having a clubhouse—in a tree, a cave or a garage. This obsession reaches its peak in two to three years.

A pair of stilts will delight this child too (see page 165), although she must practice every day for many days before she can take more than a few steps on them and she will love to play Twister with her friends. She's still too young for roller skates, however, because she can't coordinate her legs that well, and she still may be too young for a bike, unless you can take her to a nearby park or a cul-de-sac. A Six just isn't mature enough—or steady enough—to ride in the street alone or on the sidewalk if there are neighborhood toddlers around, even if their mothers are watching them.

When Sixes play inside, the card table

is often the center of their activity. This is the age for rowdy card games, like Pig and Spit, but it takes a couple of rather serious, logical children to play checkers. Most Sixes are ready for Junior Monopoly, Junior Scrabble (the picture side), Chinese checkers and Double Trouble, however, but expect some double trouble of your own in any of these games. Sixes just aren't great about losing and if your child really can't handle it, it's best to put competitive games away for a while.

The rest of a Six's indoor time is almost always spent playing with the possessions that now define her life. School, and all its trappings, makes a Six want more pencils (colored, please), sharper scissors, lots of well-lined paper, and containers for the things contained, like a pencil case and a backpack. These aren't exactly toys, but they serve the same purpose: they help a child learn and they make her feel good about herself. The newly minted status of a schoolchild needs to be polished.

# ENRICHMENT

## BOOKS

You have more control over the books you offer your child than you have over almost any other influence in his young life. To our way of thinking, the only books that can harm a child are the ones so static and so boring that they destroy every child's natural love affair with literature.

You'll watch this sweet romance flower with each child and each time it will be as poignant as before, and perhaps you'll be lucky enough to see your Six, as we saw Nell, when she clutched her new library book and said, "I can't wait to get to the exciting part! Did you know, it always comes after the middle?"

Storytime, we've found, is one of the best ways to deepen a parent-child relationship and also to increase a child's attention span. To hold her interest, your voice should be light and expressive and your child should be able to comprehend

most books so well she can save many of her questions until the story is finished.

We find a child thrives on thirty minutes of storytelling a day, although it naturally will be broken into several short sessions for a mid-One and in one or two concentrated periods for a Six.

To a child, a story must be either real or preposterous, funny or informative. While Ramon, a serious Two, insisted on books full of content, the rest of the children wanted as much wackiness or, at the least, as much whimsy as we could find. It's for you to stretch a literal child to fantasy and a fanciful child to realism by offering some books that pull her natural inclinations in other directions.

The younger the child, the more familiar the setting should be (although this is a rule made for breaking), but any story must have a happy ending. Above all, it must be well written—no matter what style—so it pleases both of you every time you read it. If your child's books bore you, you've chosen the wrong ones. You'll know it when you catch yourself saying, "In a minute," whenever she asks for a story, and when you're finally cornered, you read the book, a yawn for every page. If you do this too often your child won't like books—any books—when she learns to read for herself.

Phoniness, in either text or illustration, also will be sensed immediately, for you can't trifle with the honesty of children. We believe the worst books are those abridged, assembly-line specials at the supermarket, and we found it much cheaper and wiser to buy high-quality books, either paperback or secondhand. Look for winners of Caldecott awards (for art) and Newbery awards, for their stories, as well as those books that have been honored by Parents Choice or been named a notable book by the American Library Association.

Today most bookstores have a wide selection of children's books, and many cities have stores that just sell children's books, and their quality is superb.

Even so, you'll want to have weekly trips to the library for most of the titles, and for the story times.

Just as all children's books shouldn't be read by children (nor by anyone else), neither should children read only children's books. Every young child should be exposed to poetry—good adult poetry—not only to learn to appreciate the rhythm of its sophisticated beat (as opposed to the amusing, political doggerel of *Mother Goose*) but because poetry has the scope and precision to conjure pictures that prose can seldom paint. The very brevity of poetry will give you time to read it again and again, so your child can draw a richer meaning every time.

We once baby-sat for a Three named Cassandra, who met us at the door with a book of poetry from her father's shelf, flipping straight to the page she wanted to

hear. She could and did match every thumping line of William Blake's

> *Tiger, tiger burning bright*
> *In the forests of the night*

and not as a rote performer, but as an involved participant, grasping heaven knows what marvelous images from it. She died a few years later, in one of those fluky accidents of illness that haunt every parent, but we can't help thinking that she had drawn more joy from one part of life, at least, than most people ever do.

### SIX MONTHS

A baby should have her own small, sturdy board books like *All Fall Down* and *Garden Animals* in her crib by now, because she learns to feel comfortable with books and to study the pictures, taste them, caress each page. And because you get a little extra sleep in the morning. An adept mother masters the art of staying abed, and a well-practiced art it should be.

### NINE MONTHS

Now she wants you to point out the pictures, naming the boy, the girl, the mama and papa, saying each word distinctly. She may try to say "moo" if you point to the cow, and have often said it yourself. *Pat the Bunny*, with its wonderful textured pages, is a big favorite now—just as it was for you—and so is *The Petting Zoo*, which is another fine touchie-feelie book. These curious babies love books of photographs too—they know they have so much to learn—and the multiethnic *Baby's World* is a real eye-opener while *Goodnight Moon* puts her to sleep. This is still the book your child will take to heart at night, every night.

### ONE

A One begins to turn the pages and will be content with a mail-order catalogue for a long time, pointing to all the toys, shoes and clocks she sees with "oohs" and "aahs" as she goes along.

Now her books can have more intricate drawings and she likes to find the ladybug or the butterfly in the background, which not only increases her vocabulary but makes her concentrate longer.

This is a good age to invest in some classics, like *The Real Mother Goose*, with its famous checkerboard jacket, or the charming alphabet book by Kate Greena-

way. She is sure to like the illustrations by Ezra Jack Keats, a master of picture books, and those by that blessed fellow Maurice Sendak, for almost all his work is a joy, starting now with *Chicken Soup with Rice*.

There are children who are restless before you've turned the third page and for them you need to be the most careful in choosing books, finding those with almost no text but with dazzling colors, or those that involve some action. Also, when you can run like a deer or jump over a candle-stick together, your child realizes that she is a part of a story or a rhyme, and will like story time much more.

## TWO

A Two needs books that are so good you'll enjoy reading them almost as many times as she will enjoy hearing them. She should have fresh library books each week and at least ten books of her own, new or used, paperback or hard cover, poetry or prose, and another ten every year thereafter.

Your Two will take reasonably good care of books now and should be chastised if she doesn't. Generally, a child won't destroy books if she likes the stories.

A Two will recite nursery rhymes with you, for the cadence has much appeal and she likes to see their pictures decorate her room. She is happy with the artwork of

both Jose Aruego, whose flowers fairly spring from a page, and Pat Hutchins, whose animals teach prepositions as they move through the books. It may surprise you but the work of Tana Hoban and Donald Crews, which may seem so static to a grown-up, is as fascinating to your child as Georgia O'Keeffe would be to you.

## MID-TWO

A mid-Two is so rigid that the book that makes her happy one night is the book she'll want to hear every night, which we wish we'd known before we had impulsively bought Kate that book about a wretched child named Eukalalie. Although any Two gets caught on one particular book, you still will need a variety from the library to make reading more pleasant—especially for yourself.

Your mid-Two will want to hear about true situations, for she is the greatest fan of realism since Daguerre gave us the photograph. She wants to know about letter carriers and firefighters and her parents at the office—which tend to be quite dreary books—but she will be just as charmed, and so will you, with the realistic, if zany, *Let's Be Enemies*, or *A Little Night Music* and any book about that amusing dog Spot.

Small books with small, detailed drawings are lovely but your child will be enchanted (and who isn't?) by Brian Wildsmith's orgy of color in any books he illustrates.

At this age she will weep for "one more story"—especially from the sitter—for she has learned to manipulate an adult's love of books into a later bedtime. For this your only defense is to offer two stories and stick to that, or offer one story and ritualistically read "one more"—almost never exceeding your limit.

## THREE

Since a Three is good enough to know when she's naughty, she enjoys books with mischievous children, like *The Temper Tantrum Book*. Some books now should be informative, like *When I'm Sleepy*—the book that helps children imagine what it's like to sleep like any of many animals—which is a fine introduction to the differences in nature, adjunct to the many zoo trips now. Other books you offer may be a combination of reality and fantasy, as in *Mr. Little's Noisy Car*, one of a nice series.

Books in a series may be your salvation—or they may not. Personally, we found the ones about that Little Engine That Could, Dirty Harry and George, the obstreperous monkey, were dreadful, but the children did not—perhaps because the little engine tells children they really can achieve, and the little monkey says it's okay to be curious.

If it truly bothers you to get stuck with a group of books you don't like, spend some time going through many series with the children's librarian, skimming one of each set yourself before introducing it to your child. When you find one you like, you know you can introduce the whole set to your child with confidence. We would recommend the books of Dr. Seuss and Rosemary Wells now and any books about Frances, that nice, nice bear. She teaches children to handle the dark, the new baby sister and just about anything else. Pop-up books, so good for a gentle child, are a delight too. Look for *A Is for Animals* and *How Many Bugs in a Box?*

### FOUR

At this age there are books for every interest and excellent ones in almost every category. If your child is impatient, you can choose pop-up books or those with scant text but with sophisticated drawings or story line. For most children, however, the art shouldn't overpower the story anymore.

A Four needs to have the world explained to him and enjoys the See How It Works series now and the marvelous Magic School Bus series too.

Besides learning the usual facts about a farm, a city, a small town and some of the skills and professions of the people who live there, she needs to begin to know why there are wars, why there are jails, why we have traffic laws, governments and manners—and what happens if we don't. Books that take up these subjects force you to exchange ideas with your child and this is the grist for so much of the talking that lies ahead.

Your child is ripe to appreciate wit and likes *Stone Soup*. There is also *Fanny Mc-Fancy—A Passion for Fashion* (the title alone makes it worth reading), *A Day With Wilbur Robinson*, which is so great for boys, and the Judith Viorst books, which show that some storybook families act real. With all these new books, don't forget the classic *Winnie-the-Pooh*, but first tell her that it's about a little boy and his nursery full of stuffed animals. Without this explanation, she may be confused; we certainly were.

Four is the time when a child likes to hear her language turned upside down too, as it is in the Amelia Bedelia series. She enjoys daffy, contemporary poetry, as well as the old-fashioned *A Child's Garden of Verses*.

We also recommend the stories you make up yourself, for although the plot may be scrambled, it will be different from any story any child has ever heard.

### FIVE

Now her appetite for reading is bigger every day. Your child wants to hear that leaves turn red when the sap is drawn from the branch; that melanin makes animals—and people—black; that rain is just warm snow and that a baby grows in the womb. She wants Greek myths and legends now and stories and folk tales that tell about the culture and customs of other people, like *Mufaro's Daughter*, *Uncle Nacho's Hat*, *Berchick*—about a Jewish homesteading family—and *The Wednesday Surprise*, about a grandma who learns to read.

There is the sophistication of the Madeleine series, about elegant living in Paris, or for that matter, the charming Babar books, about elegant living among the elephants in Africa, or the hilarious poetry in *Meet My Folks!* Since this is the age when your little girl is quite likely to think herself a princess who got swapped in the crib, the stories about kings and castles will make her feel right at home.

### SIX

You may want to introduce resource books now, like the simplest supermarket set of encyclopedias, or a children's book on gardening or one on cooking, such as *Kids Cooking*, which comes with its own measuring spoons. There are more and more good history books for children, but we do recommend Leonard Weisgard's *The Plymouth Thanksgiving*.

When you read to your child from these books, they become such familiar friends she will turn to them naturally for information when she begins to read well.

There are many good, easy readers on the market, but some of them are imitative and often not that easy to read. Give care-

ful consideration to these books, because a poor choice will bore a child after the first few readings and she may decide that it's boring to read to herself. Or skip the consideration entirely, and give your child the *Bob Books* with each little book slightly

### STORY TAPES

Story tapes are terrific for a child between Three and Six (and Thirty and Sixty too), if they're narrated by good actors with imaginative voices—and they usually are. Give your child the right to play them on her own little tape recorder during rest time, and to take along when you'll be in the car for several hours or stuck in rush hour traffic. It's a good way to share some of the longer stories, like *Stuart Little*, but don't, of course, use tapes as a substitute for reading aloud.

Not all tapes should be store-bought, as we used to say down South. You and your husband can send blank tapes to your parents, and to your own brothers and sisters, so they can record stories and songs to send back to your child, but cover the holes on top of the tapes when they're returned, so your child can't record over them. The quality won't be professional, but your child will love them just the same, because they are sent to her. It's a particularly nice, inexpensive way to strengthen long-distance connections.

While stories and songs are lovely, forget about the tapes that teach colors, numbers and letters, which are no fun to be heard alone. If they're used at all, they should be used at pre-K and kindergarten, or when brand-new first-graders play school.

Foreign language tapes fall in this category too. They're boring if a child listens all alone, but folk songs in another language are fun and so are well-done language tapes for children, if the sitter—or someone in the family—is foreign and will play them to your child and talk to her in the language too. The child who learns a second language early is blessed, for it can make all foreign languages easier to learn later, but the main teacher should be a real live person, not a reel of tape.

harder than the last. They are very, very simple and truly wonderful.

You'll want to continue to read to your child long after she has learned to read, because it will be years before her ability can catch up with her interests and because it's such a warm, friendly thing to do. Books about animals are lovely, and fairy tales become so enchanting now and your child's span of interest so long that you can expect absolute, knee-hugging silence when you read the Tasha Tudor stories.

There are also the splendid *Macmillan Book of Greek Gods and Heroes*, the non-sensical poetry by Edward Lear, and the many fine classical English stories by Milne and by Kenneth Grahame.

Your child will also be enchanted by the Waldo books, tracking that busy fellow through dozens of complicated pictures and learning a lot in the process.

Perhaps it's our own proclivities, but we find any books that make us laugh are very good books. That's why we read to our Sixes from James Thurber's splendid book *The Wonderful O*, about the fellow who had hated the letter *O* ever since his mother got stuck in a porthole and they couldn't pull her in so they had to push her out. He left that letter out of his king-dom later—your child will be happy to know—and Ophelia Oliver became Phelia Liver.

That's very ribald to a Six.

## STORY-TELLING

Not all stories have to be written before they can be told.

When Mike was young, his father started the wacky Michael J. Smithfield stories, which proved that any story is good if (1) it is improbable; (2) specific numbers are used, like 17 or 1,224; (3) treasure is discovered; (4) there are bad guys, who are adults, and good guys, who are children; and (5) the hero and his family and his friends look just like the listener and his family and his friends and even have the same first names.

Naturally these stories end well and reflect great glory on the children in them, who use their quick wits and many tricks to catch the pirates and the burglars.

Now Mike makes up his own stories for the children he babysits and the for-mula is the same, although the victories are more vulgar and possibly more beloved: his small heroes always catch the villains the same way—they pee on them.

## BOOK LIST

Many of the books we list are our personal choices—beloved by our children, by their friends and by us. Some of the books are prizewinners, many are in paperback, most are in the public library, and all are waiting to be read.

### BOARD BOOKS

*ABC*—Jan Pieńkowski
*All Fall Down*—Helen Oxenbury
*Baby's World*—Stephen Shott
*The Book of Babies*—Jo Foord
*Cat*—Juan Wijngaard
*Garden Animals*—Lucy Cousins
*The Going to Bed Book*—Sandra Boynton
*My Toys*—Sian Tucker
*The Petting Zoo*—Jack Hanna

### GOOD READS

*Alfie Gets in First*—Shirley Hughes
*The Bare Naked Book*—Kathy Stinson
*A Bear Called Paddington* (series)—Michael Bond
*Boxcar Children*—Gertrude Warner
*The Caboose Who Got Loose*—Bill Peet
*Caps for Sale*—Esphyr Slobodkina
*The Cat in the Hat*—Dr. Seuss
*Cherries and Cherry Pits*—Vera B. Williams
*Chicken Soup with Rice*—Maurice Sendak
*Curious George*—H. A. Rey
*A Day with Wilbur Robinson*—William Joyce
*Elizabeth and Larry*—Marilyn Sadler
*The Gnats of Knotty Pine*—Bill Peet
*Good Dog Carl*—Alexandra Day
*Gorilla*—Anthony Browne
*Home Place*—Crescent Dragonwagon
*I Love You, Mouse*—John Graham
*In Christina's Toolbox*—Dianne Homan
*The Jolly Postman*—Janet and Allan Ahlberg

*King Bidgood's in the Bathtub*—Audrey Wood
*The Last Time I Saw Harris*—Frank Remkiewicz
*The Little Engine That Could*—Watty Piper
*A Little Night Music*—Charles Micucci
*Lonely Doll*—Dare Wright
*Madeline*—Ludwig Bemelmans
*Make Way for Ducklings*—Robert McCloskey
*Millions of Cats*—Wanda Gág
*Miss Rumphius*—Barbara Cooney
*Mr. Little's Noisy Car* (series)—Richard Fowler
*Napping House*—Audrey Wood
*Noisy Nora*—Rosemary Wells
*No Kiss for Mother*—Tomi Ungerer
*The Paper Crane*—Molly Bang
*Phoebe's Revolt*—Natalie Babbitt
*Picnic*—Emily A. McCully
*Pretend You're a Cat*—Jean Marzollo
*Sam Who Never Forgets*—Eve Rice
*The Shopping Trip*—Helen Oxenbury
*Shrek!*—William Steig
*Stone Soup*—Marcia Brown
*The Story of Babar* (series)—Laurent de Brunhoff
*The Story of Z*—Jeanne Modesitt
*The Tale of Peter Rabbit*—Beatrix Potter
*Tar Beach*—Faith Ringgold
*Teddy Bear* books—Susanna Gretz
*Thomas' Snowsuit*—Robert Munsch
*Tiki Tiki Tembo*—Arlene Mosel
*Tom and Pippo's Day*—Helen Oxenbury
*Uncle Wizzmo's New Used Car*—Rodney A. Greenblat
*The Velveteen Rabbit*—Margery Williams
*The Very Hungry Caterpillar*—Eric Carle
*Wempires*—Daniel Pinkwater
*The Wheels on the Bus*—Paul Zelinsky
*When I'm Sleepy*—Jane R. Howard
*Where's Waldo?*—Martin Handford
*Why the Chicken Crossed the Road*—David Macaulay
*Wild Baby*—Barbro Lindgren
*Winnie the Pooh*—A. A. Milne

## GREAT READ-ALOUDS

*Charlie and the Great Glass Elevator*—
   Roald Dahl
*Charlotte's Web*—E. B. White
*Eloise*—Kay Thompson
*James and the Giant Peach*—Roald Dahl
*Land of Oz* (series)—Frank Baum
*Little House in the Big Woods* (series)—
   Laura Ingalls Wilder
*Many Moons*—James Thurber
*Stuart Little*—E. B. White
*The Thirteen Clocks*—James Thurber
*Trumpet of the Swan*—E. B. White
*The Wonderful O*—James Thurber

## FOLKTALES AND FAIRY TALES

*Berchick*—Esther Silverstein Blanc
   (Jewish)
*Dream Wolf*—Paul Goble (native
   American)
*Fairy Tale Treasury*—compiled by Virginia
   Haviland
*The Flute Player*—Michael Lacapa (native
   American)
*Girl from the Snow Country*—Masako
   Hidaka (Japan)
*The Keeping Quilt*—Patricia Polacco
   (Jewish)
*Macmillan Book of Greek Gods and
   Heroes*—Alice Low
*Mufaro's Beautiful Daughter*—John
   Steptoe (Africa)
*Tale of the Mandarin Duck*—Katherine
   Paterson (China)
*The Talking Eggs*—Robert D. San Souci
   (Creole)
*Uncle Nacho's Hat*—Harriet Rohmer
   (Mexico)
*Victorian Fairy Tale Book*—Michael P.
   Hearn

## POETRY

*Animals, Animals*—Laura Whipple
*Beneath a Blue Umbrella*—Jack Prelutsky
*A Child's Garden of Verses*—Robert Louis
   Stevenson
*Chinese Mother Goose Rhymes*—Robert
   Wyndham

*Growltiger's Last Stand and Other
   Poems*—T. S. Eliot
*Mother Goose*—Michael Hague
*Mother Goose Treasury*—Raymond Briggs
*The Orchard Book of Nursery Rhymes*—
   Zena Sutherland
*Poems of A. Nonny Mouse*—Jack
   Prelutsky
*The Real Mother Goose*—Blanche F.
   Wright
*Ride a Purple Pelican*—Jack Prelutsky
*Sing a Song of Popcorn*—Beatrice De
   Regniers
*Small Poems*—Valerie Worth
*Tomie dePaola's Book of Poems*—Tomie
   dePaola

## SCIENCE AND NATURE

*Autumn Harvest*—Alvin Tresselt
*Eyewitness Jr. Books*
*From Seed to Plant*—Gail Gibbons
*Gorilla Builds* (series)—Derek Hall
*How to Hide a Chameleon*—Ruth Heller
*Tigress*—Helen Cowcher
*My Visit to the Dinosaurs*—Aliki
*The Very Busy Spider*—Eric Carle
*When We Went to the Zoo*—Jan Ormerod

## TEACHING BOOKS

*A to Zoo*—Carolyn W. Lima
*Animalia*—Graeme Base
*Anno's Counting Book*—Mitsumasa Anno
*Ashanti to Zulu*—Margaret Musgrove
   (Africa)
*Bob Books*—Bobby Lynn Maslen
*Fish Eyes*—Lois Ehlert
*Holes and Peeks*—Ann Jonas
*How Many*—Fiona Pragoff
*How Many Bugs in a Box?*—David A.
   Carter
*Is Your Mama a Llama?*—Deborah
   Guarino
*Kids Cooking*—editors, Klutz Press
*Machines*—Anne Rockwell and Harlow
   Rockwell
*The Magic School Bus* (series)—Joanna
   Cole
*See How It Works* (series)—Tony Potter

*Toolbox*—Anne Rockwell
*Truck*—Donald Crews
*The Village of Round and Square Houses*—Ann Grifalconi (Africa)
*William the Vehicle King*—Laura Newton

## HOLIDAYS

*Christmas* (the King James version)—Jan Pieńkowski
*A Christmas Story*—Brian Wildsmith
*Halloween*—Gail Gibbons
*Hanukkah*—Jenny Koralek and Wanda Gág
*My First Passover*—Tomie dePaola
*The Plymouth Thanksgiving*—Leonard Weisgard
*Thanksgiving*—Gail Gibbons

## FAMILY

*Are Those Kids Yours?*—Cheri Register (overseas adoption)
*Arthur's Baby*—Marc Brown (new baby)
*Born Two-gether*—Jan Brennan (twins)
*Charlie Anderson*—Barbara Abercrombie (joint custody)
*The Day We Met You*—Phoebe Koehler (adoption)
*Do I Have a Daddy?*—Jeanne Warren Lindsay (single parent)
*Everett Anderson's Nine Month Long*—Lucille Clifton (remarriage)
*A Family Is a Circle of People Who Love You*—Doris Jasinek and Pamela B. Ryan (family differences)
*Hard to Be Six*—Arnold Adoff (siblings)
*Horace*—Holly Keller (interracial adoption)
*Nobody Asked Me If I Wanted a Baby Sister*—Martha Alexander (new baby)
*No Kiss for Mother*—Tomi Ungerer
*Peace at Last*—Jill Murphy (working mother)
*Peter's Chair*—Ezra Jack Keats (new baby)
*Piggybook*—Anthony Browne (working mother)
*Through Moon and Stars and Night Skies*—Ann Turner (overseas adoption)

*We Are Having a Baby*—Viki Holland (new baby)

## QUESTIONS

*The Accident*—Carol Carrick (death)
*Badger's Parting Gifts*—Susan Varley (death)
*Becoming*—Eleanora Faison (death)
*Beyond the Ridge*—Paul Goble (death)
*Dinosaurs Divorce*—Laurene Krasny Brown and Marc Brown (divorce)
*The Divorce Workbook*—Sally Blakeslee Ives, Ph.D.; David Fassler, M.D.; Michele Lash, Med A.T.R. (divorce)
*Moving Gives Me a Stomach Ache*—Heather McKend (moving)
*Our Brother Has Down's Syndrome*—Shelley Cairo (retardation)
*Sam's Story*—Fiona Chin-Yee (SIDS)
*To a Different Drummer*—Mary Ann Dockstader, M.A. and Laurene Payne, B.A. (learning disabilities)
*When Someone Very Special Dies*—Marge E. Helegaard (death)

## GROWING UP

*David Decides About Thumbsucking*—Susan M. Heitler, Ph.D. (habits)
*Dinner at Auntie Rose's*—Jane Munsil (manners)
*Going to the Potty*—Fred (Mr.) Rogers (toilet training)
*Hospital Journal*—Ann Banks (health)
*How You Were Born*—Joanna Cole (sex)
*A Kid's Guide to First Aid*—Lory Freeman (health)
*Sam's Potty*—Barbro Lindgren (toilet training)
*Toilet Tales*—Andrea von Konigslow (toilet training)
*A Very Noisy Girl*—Elizabeth Winthrop (manners)
*What Do You Say, Dear?*—Seslye Joslin (manners)
*What's a Virus, Anyway?*—David Fassler, M.D. and Kelly McQueen (health)
*Your New Potty*—Joanna Cole (toilet training)

FEELINGS AND FOIBLES

*Alexander and the Terrible, Horrible, No Good, Very Bad Day*—Judith Viorst (the miseries)

*Bedtime for Frances*—Russell Hoban (bedtime fears)

*Big Al*—Andrew Clements (popularity)

*C Is for Curious*—Woodleigh Hubbard (feelings)

*A Chair for My Mother*—Vera B. Williams (money)

*A Cool Kid—Like Me*—Hans Wilhelm (fear)

*Elbert's Bad Word*—Audrey Wood and Don Wood (foul language)

## AUTHORS AND ILLUSTRATORS

These are the names of authors and illustrators—classic and contemporary—that we've found are almost always associated with good books:

| | | | |
|---|---|---|---|
| Verna Aardema | Janina Domanska | Ezra Jack Keats | Jack Prelutsky |
| Janet and Allan Ahlberg | Roger Duvoisin | Steven Kellogg | Edna M. Preston |
| Aliki | Barbara Emberly and Ed Emberly | Phyllis Krasilovsky | Ellen A. Raskin |
| Mitsumasa Anno | Marie Hall Ets | Robert Kraus | Anne Rockwell |
| Edward Ardizzone | Louise Fatio | Albert Lamorisse | Anne Rose |
| Jose Aruego | Aileen Fisher | Munro Leaf | Richard Scarry |
| Frank Asch | Marjorie Flack | Edward Lear | Maurice Sendak |
| Natalie Babbitt | James Flora | Lois Lenski | Dr. Seuss |
| Byron Barton | Michael Foreman | Leo Leonni | Peter Spier |
| Ludwig Bemelmans | Mem Fox | Barbro Lindgren | William Steig |
| Michael Bond | Don Freeman | Anita Lobel | John Steptoe |
| Sandra Boynton | Wanda Gág | Arnold Lobel | Robert Louis Stevenson |
| Gail Brandenburg | Paul Galdone | David Macaulay | Ianthe Thomas |
| Jan Brett | May Garelick | Robert G. McCloskey | James Thurber |
| Leslie Brooke | Gail Gibbons | Emily McCully | Tasha Tudor |
| Marc Brown | Mirra Ginsburg | Margaret Maher | Janice M. Udry |
| Margaret W. Brown | John Goodall | Kenneth Mahood | Chris Van Allsburg |
| Anthony Browne | Kenneth Grahame | James Marshall | Judith Viorst |
| John Burningham | Kate Greenaway | A. A. Milne | Rosemary Wells |
| Virginia L. Burton | Eloise Greenfield | Else H. Minarik | E. B. White |
| Randolph Caldecott | Deborah Guarino | Martha Moffett | Laura Ingalls Wilder |
| Eric Carle | Martin Handford | Evaline Ness | Brian Wildsmith |
| Carol Carrick | Virginia Haviland | Joanne Oppenheim | Garth Williams |
| Donald Carrick | Lilo Hess | Jan Ormerod | Margery Williams |
| Rebecca Caudill | Eric Hill | Helen Oxenbury | Vera B. Williams |
| Lucille Clifton | Lillian Hoban | Jan Pieńkowski | Marie Winn |
| Miriam Cohen | Russell Hoban | Peggy Parish | Audrey Wood |
| Barbara Cooney | Tana Hoban | Katherine Paterson | Don Wood |
| Donald Crews | Shirley Hughes | Bill Peet | Dare Wright |
| Edgar P. and Ingri d'Aulaire | Ted Hughes | Susan Perl | Paul Zelinsky |
| Alexandra Day | Pat Hutchins | Jerry Pinkney | Charlotte Zolotow |
| Laurent de Brunhoff | Janosch | Daniel Pinkwater | |
| Tomie dePaola | Susan Jeffers | Watty Piper | |
| | Ann Jonas | Beatrix Potter | |
| | | Fiona Pragoff | |

*Fanny McFancy—A Passion for Fashion—*
    Patricia Thackray (possessions)
*The Gorilla Did It—*Barbara Shook
    Hazen (accountability)
*Joyful Child—*Peggy Jenkins, Ph.D. (joy)
*Let's Be Enemies—*Janice M. Udry (anger)
*Max's Choice—*Debra L. Wert (drugs)
*Not a Worry in the World—*Marcia
    Williams (fears)
*The Squeaky Door—*Laura Simms
    (bedtime fears)
*Tales of the Perfect Child—*Florence Parry
    Heide (self-consciousness)
*Tight Times—*Barbara Hazen (money)
*The Wednesday Surprise—*Eve Bunting
    (empathy)
*Weird Parents—*Audrey Wood (shame)
*Where the Wild Things Are—*Maurice
    Sendak (fears)

## MAGAZINES

*Ladybug,* for prereaders and new readers
*Your Big Backyard,* on nature for the
    young (National Wildlife Federation)

## MUSIC AND TAPES

From the day she is born—and long before—a child absorbs every sound she
hears, which is why we feel at least some
of them should be beautiful. That's what
music was made for. Her introduction to
it will be the lullabies you sing, the music
box that tinkles, a soft piano passage.
She'll be startled by any loud or sudden
sounds and will be soothed best, we found,
by tapes of chamber music or Gregorian
chants—good reason for good background
music.

The smallest infant is entranced by just
a few notes on the guitar or the bassoon,
so if either you or your husband play an
instrument we think you should try to
entertain your baby with it for a few minutes a day. By three months she may smile
to show you her preference for E minor
rather than C major when you strum a
chord, which will make you want to play
more and more for her for the next few
years. This will be the best audience you'll

ever have. The charm of these little interludes will linger long after your child has
grown.

Whether you can play an instrument or
not, you still should whistle while you
work and sing to your child too, even if
you can't carry a tune. She'll like sad
songs, happy songs, any songs and sometimes she'll like to feel your throat while
you sing.

This won't be enough for a One. She
wants simple melodies and clear rhythms
so she can try to clap her hands and bounce
to the beat. It's hard to believe, but this
bumping and grinding focuses her interest,
another way to stretch her attention span.

Just as you want your child to respect
musical instruments, so must she learn to
respect people when they play them, but
this, we tell you sadly, takes years longer—
especially if you're the player. For some
inexplicable reason, your child surely will
feel she must hug your knees when you
play the violin the same way she babbles
when you read the paper. All your anger
won't change it, but it will hurt your performance, so if playing is what keeps your
soul in balance, you'd better do most of it
when she's asleep or out visiting.

A Two doesn't sit still for music either
(nor a Three, nor a Four)—nor should she.
Music is to be enjoyed. Perhaps this is why
outdoor concerts seem designed for a Two,
for they give her plenty of room to move
and she'll intoxicate all those around her
with her enthusiasm for the music.

This child is ready for baroque music,
hearty marches by Sousa and some folk
songs and sea chanteys sung by Raffi, Burl

Ives, Woody Guthrie and Pete Seeger. The words in every folk song should be so easy to hear she can learn them if she wants. At Three your child will like Saint-Saën's *Carnival of the Animals*, Brahms' Hungarian dances, Prokofiev's *The Ugly Duckling* and Carl Orff's *Music for Children*. You should also play the best of jazz, of soul, of country and rock—any kind of music at all as long as it's first class. If you have tapes, rather than CDs, you can even let her play them on her own portable player, since they're practically indestructible now. This will give her the chance to play the songs again and again or to hop around to the rhythms with her friends, without having to wait for your help. Just don't let her play the music too loud or you won't let her play it so often.

Back in the old record player days, we had a rugged, tree-climbing friend named Tom whose love of music was so great at Three that he was trusted to play the family's finest records on the family's fine turntable. Soon he was dividing his time between climbing trees and listening to music, until at Four, we watched him approach a young stranger—the oldest and therefore most important child at a birthday party—with, "You know what I like best? Beethoven's *Ninth*." To which the Seven astonished us all by replying, "Me, too." It turned out he also had played his first records at Three.

Your Four may not be ready for Beethoven's *Ninth*, but he surely can enjoy Tchaikovsky's *1812 Overture* or Dvořák's *New World Symphony* or Bruch's *Scottish Fantasy*. Certainly you'll want to get Prokofiev's *Peter and the Wolf* too. (We're partial to the Milton Cross narrative.)

Sometime before Five, a child will be ready to go to an indoor children's concert, at least on an infrequent basis.

A Five enjoys songs in a foreign language, which she will imitate in an enchanting way. She also will like Mussorgsky's *Pictures at an Exhibition*, Holst's *The Planets*, Stravinsky's *Firebird* and Grieg's *Peer Gynt Suite*.

Before first grade we hope your child will have attended not only that proper concert but also a ballet or two where she can watch the dance meld with the music, and a musical, like *Oklahoma!* or an operetta, like *H.M.S. Pinafore*, or for a total fusion of the arts, a light opera such as Menotti's *Amahl and the Night Visitors*, even at a high school performance. Most children, to be sure, won't grow up to be musical giants, but all children should be exposed to so much music when they're young that they will love it for life.

### Cassette Tape List ©

Good music is like magic. It can make a sad child smile, a bored child sparkle and a cranky child forget to crank.

### GRAND MUSIC

*Appalachian Spring*—Copland
*Carnival of the Animals*—Saint-Saëns
*Children's Corner*—Debussy
*A Children's Overture*—Roger Quilter
*Cinderella*—Prokofiev
*Daphnis and Chloe*—Ravel
*Dolly Suite*—Fauré
*Eine kleine Nachtmusik*—Mozart
*Grand Canyon Suite*—Grofé
*The Magic Flute*—Mozart
*Mr. Bach Comes to Call*—Classical Kids Series

*Mother Goose Suite*—Ravel
*The Nutcracker*—Tchaikovsky, read by
    Christopher Plummer
*Peter and the Wolf*—Prokofiev, read by
    Sir John Gielgud
*Romeo and Juliet*—Tchaikovsky, read by
    Claire Bloom
*Scenes from Childhood*—Schumann
*The Skater's Waltz*—Strauss
*Sleeping Princess*—Tchaikovsky
*The Snow Queen*—Tchaikovsky, read by
    Natalia Makarova
*Swan Lake*—Tchaikovsky
*Typewriter Song*—Leroy Anderson
*The Young Person's Guide to the
    Orchestra*—Benjamin Britten

## GREAT MUSICALS

*Annie*
*Annie Get Your Gun*
*Babes in Toyland*
*Chitty Chitty Bang Bang*
*Fiddler on the Roof*
*Gigi*
*Hans Christian Andersen*
*Mary Poppins*
*The Music Man*
*My Fair Lady*
*Oklahoma!*
*Snow White and the Seven Dwarfs*
*The Sound of Music*
*South Pacific*
*West Side Story*

## FUN MUSIC AND FOLK MUSIC

*Abiyoyo (and Other Story Songs for
    Children)*—Pete Seeger
*Adventures in Rhythm*—Ella Jenkins
*African Folk Tales*—Ossie Davis and Ruby
    Dee
*All for Freedom*—Sweet Honey in the
    Rock
*American Folk Songs for Children*—Pete
    Seeger
*Baby Beluga*—Raffi
*The Best for Boys and Girls*—Burl Ives
*Birds, Beasts, Bugs and Little Fishes*—Pete
    Seeger

*Dinosaur Rock*—Michele Valeri and
    Michael Stein
*Doc Watson Sings Songs for Little
    Pickers*—Doc Watson
*Howjadoo*—John McCutcheon
*Jump Children*—Marcy Marxer
*Lamb Chop in the Land of No Manners*—
    Shari Lewis
*Let's Make Music*—John Langstaff
*Lullabye Classics*—Terrence Farrell
*Mother Goose Nursery Rhymes*—Hershey
    Kay
*My Street Begins at My House*—Ella
    Jenkins
*Music for Little People*—Sweet Honey in
    the Rock
*Music for Ones and Twos*—Tom Glazer
*Nursery Days*—Woody Guthrie
*Rhythms of Childhood*—Ella Jenkins
*Tickles You*—Rosenshontz
*Singable Songs for the Very Young*—Raffi
*Sing A to Z*—Sharon, Lois and Bram
*Song for Singing Children*—John
    Langstaff
*Songs to Grow On*—Woody Guthrie
*Travellin' with Ella Jenkins: A Bilingual
    Journal*—Ella Jenkins
*We Are American Children*—Ella Jenkins

## THE ARTS

### *THEATER*

Any legitimate theater—no matter how
bad—has advantages over the best television, for the electricity of live drama is
unforgettable. Also, when the cast takes
its curtain call, a child can see that everyone is all right, whatever happened on-
stage.

At Two or Three we like to introduce
theater with a puppet show (but not a
Punch and Judy, which is grim at any age)
and then at least one play a year for a Four,
a Five and a Six.

While your child won't draw the same
meaning from a play as you do (for she
looks at everything from the underside),

she still will feel its richness. You'll find she gets even more pleasure if you occasionally play a tape of the production, which may be easy to find in the library if it is an old standard.

A child can discover Shakespeare in happy style with the musical *Kiss Me, Kate,* and go on to such comedies as *A Midsummer Night's Dream* or *As You Like It.* Again, this isn't hard to do if you live near a city, since there are often Shakespearean productions outdoors during the summer.

A child, as early as Four, will be delighted with a comedy like *You Can't Take It with You,* by Kaufman and Hart, or one by that master, Molière, and by Six she'll be quite as thrilled by a mystery like Tom Stoppard's *The Real Inspector Hound* as she is with a children's classic like *Pinocchio.* The tickets are affordable if you go to a high school or even a college production.

Of course, not all theater should be confined to plays and musicals. Besides modern dance troupes, there are classical ballets, which are often more appealing since they have story lines. We think your child is almost sure to like *The Dance Lesson*—that funny ballet—or one of the grand ones, like *Sleeping Beauty,* and Bal-

anchine's *Stars and Stripes* will make her march for days.

Sometimes you can find a good student production, but for ballet we'd rather scrimp for a professional company. This may be cheaper than you think since you'll buy balcony tickets, where your child can see better from above than she can from the orchestra, and you'll go to a matinée.

Even if the cost of the tickets bites into your grocery budget, your child will remember an afternoon at the theater a lot longer than she'll remember a week of spaghetti.

## MOVIES

Of all the outings we've ever taken with the children, one of the nicest of them was a six-hour, air-conditioned orgy of the Marx Brothers in the middle of a heat wave. Generally, we're not so greedy.

Even if you have VCR movies and air conditioning at home, an occasional movie at a real theater is a treat, if the quality is high—and a dismal experience if it's not. There's no reason to endure a simplistic Walt Disney when both parents and child would be happier with a zinger like *Superman.* Adventures with a child are meant to be enjoyed by adults too.

Movies even give you the chance to teach your child movie manners, which are becoming a lost art. It's up to you to train your child to be quiet in the theater, even if she can talk during the movie at home. The best lessons are learned early.

## VIDEOS

Your child will see some movies at the theater or on television, but it's cheaper and often more fun to see them on a VCR. You don't have to put up with commercials, you can stop the tape as often as you want, and you know what you're getting.

You also get quite a bit. A good video—short or long—generally enriches little children more than a good program on TV, since films are usually better made, and therefore more powerful.

They also often lead to more reading, rather than less. Parents regularly report that their children want them to read *The Wind in the Willows, The Lion, the Witch and the Wardrobe* or *The Little Mermaid* after they've seen the tapes.

Videos must be chosen with caution, however, and played with restraint.

Although they are seldom as memorable as books—because a book makes a child's imagination work much harder—they can be much scarier. If a child can't handle the words or the scenes she hears or reads, she will instinctively screen them out, but she can't avoid them if they're backed up by pictures.

Watching too many videos can be a problem too, no matter how fine they are. They are not only as mesmerizing as TV, but they can make a child physically antsy and mentally passive, and can create a dependency too. A couple of hours of video a week, in addition to five to ten hours of television, is plenty for a preschooler.

Even then a child should see only short videos until she's about Five, or a long movie broken into segments—the younger the child, the shorter the segment. She'll look forward to the next installment the way she looks forward to chapters in a book, and so will you.

Short stories and segments are particularly good for that hectic half-hour before you leave for work, or when you first get home. This will give you the chance to organize yourself, and give your child the chance for some quality entertainment.

It isn't as hard to find good videos as it is to choose them. After almost a hundred years of moviemaking, there are some dillies out there—more than your child can ever see.

Although most video stores don't stock many titles for children, you should be able to find a large selection to borrow from your public library or to buy at certain bookstores and through catalogs. Look for the splendid children's videos from Rabbit Ears Productions and especially from Weston Woods, which has many films in Spanish too.

You want films that will entertain and enlighten your child, spark her imagination, stretch her knowledge and make her laugh and sing, or even make her cry, if she's going through a rough patch and needs to get rid of some tears. Above all, look for films that are so well made, and so free of violence and bigotry, that they

will subtly teach her to pursue the best in life, as well as in film.

For short films, begin with the joyous computer-generated animation of *Tin Toy*, *Luxo, Jr.*, and *Red Stream*, which are all on one tape. They will enthrall a Two, who may even be ready for *The Red Balloon*—one videotape that's even better than the book. Some of the Disney shorts with their sing-along songs or clips from their movies are good at this age too, as well as *Raffi in Concert*, then graduate to *Tales of Beatrix Potter* and *Golden Fish* at Four; *Star Child* and *How the Rhinoceros Got His Skin*—just one of an animated series—at Five and working up to *Mufaro's Beautiful Daughter* and some of the National Geographic specials by Six.

Even though a pre-K has trouble watching a whole movie, a musical like *Mary Poppins* or *The Adventures of Milo and Otis*—that gem about a cat and a dog—are terrific for the fanciful Four—and all Fours are fanciful. Go next to *Alice in Wonderland*, *The Lady and the Tramp*, *Peter Pan* and *The Secret of NIMH* at Five and finally *An American Tail* and *The Princess Bride* at Six. Even the Shirley Temple version of *The Little Princess*—despite all the liberties taken with the plot—is good at Six, and so is *The Wizard of Oz*, if you're there to hug your little prince or princess tight during the tornado scene. Don't, however, forget the grown-up movies like *Singin' in the Rain* and *The Yellow Submarine*, which will delight you too, and give the family some good times together.

As fine as these commercial films are, your child will have some special and perhaps unexpected video favorites, such as the videotape of your wedding, and the tape of her birthday parties (but not, thank you, the birthday of a younger brother or sister). Try to make a birthday tape for each child, adding to it every year, even if you have to rent or borrow a video recorder. It's well worth doing.

Don't wait for special occasions to make home videos, however. Your child will be delighted with vignettes of her life as she goes to nursery school, plays under the hose and takes her doll—or her dad— for a walk. A few minutes here or there will add up to a fine tape.

### VIDEO LIST

These are some of the best videos available, long and short, and the earliest age a child will probably like them. In some cases the publisher is noted, if there is more than one version. A few films are made up of pages from the book and listed as iconographic and others are drawn for the video and marked "animated." The rest are live.

### SHORT FEATURES

These are short films or a group of short stories which can be watched individually.
*Cloudy with a Chance of Meatballs*— animated (2)
*Katherine Hepburn's World of Stories* (2)
*The Adventures of Curious George*— animated (3)
*Children of Wax* (African folktales)— animated (3)
*Corduroy and Other Bear Stories*— animated/live (3)
*Foolish Frog and Other Stories*—animated (3)
*Frog and Toad Together*—animated (3)
*Happy Birthday, Moon and Other Stories for Young Children*—animated (3)
*Mike Mulligan and His Steam Shovel*— animated (3)

*The Mysterious Tadpole and Other Stories*—animated (3)
*The Red Balloon* (3)
*Smile for Auntie*—animated (3)
*The Tale of Jeremy Fisher and The Tale of Peter Rabbit*—animated (3)
*The Tin Toy/Luxo, Jr./Red Stream*— animated (3)
*Abel's Island*—animated (4)
*The Cat in the Hat* and *Dr. Seuss on the Loose*—animated (4)
*The Elephant's Child*—animated (4)
*Golden Fish* (4)
*Koko's Kitten* (4)
*Jay O'Callahan: Herman and Marguerite* (4)
*Pecos Bill*—animated (4)
*Rainbow War*—animated (4)
*The Reluctant Dragon*—animated (4)
*The Snowman*—animated (4)
*Tales of Beatrix Potter* (Children's Video Library)—animated (4)
*Tell Me a Story* (African folk tales) (4)
*The Three Robbers and Other Stories*— animated (4)
*The Ugly Duckling* (Random House)— animated (4)
*The Velveteen Rabbit*—animated (4)
*Where the Wild Things Are*— iconographic (4)
*Winnie the Pooh and the Blustery Day*— animated (4)
*Winnie the Pooh and a Day for Eeyore*— animated (4)
*Babar the Elephant Comes to America*— animated (5)
*Christmas Stories*—animated (5)
*The Dr. Seuss Video Festival*—animated (5)
*The Fabulous Adventures of Baron Munchhausen*—animated (5)
*Family Circle Storyland Theater*, vols. 1–4 (5)
*Five Lionni Classics: The Animal Fables of Leo Lionni*—animated (5)
*The Fool of the World/The Flying Ship*— animated (5)
*How the Rhinoceros Got His Skin* (series)—animated (5)

*The Mouse and the Motorcycle*—animated/
live (5)
*Mwe Bana Bande* (African tale)—(5)
*Pinocchio* (Disney)—animated (5)
*Star Child*—animated (5)
*The Story of Babar the Little Elephant*—
animated (5)
*The Three Little Pigs* (Faerie Tale Theatre)
(5)
*The Wind in the Willows*, vols. 1–3—
animated (5)
*Bim, the Little Donkey/White Mane*—(6)
*A Cricket in Times Square*—animated (6)
*The Emperor and the Nightingale*—
animated (6)
*The Legend of Sleepy Hollow* (6)
*Mufaro's Beautiful Daughter*—
iconographic (6)
*Pickwick Papers*—animated (6)
*Really Rosie*—animated (6)
*A Stowaway in the Sky* (6)
*The Village of Round and Square
Houses*—iconographic (6)
*Mister Rogers: When Parents Are Away*
(day care) (2–6)

## LONG FEATURES

These films last fifty minutes or more, but
you can break them into installments.
*The Little Mermaid* (Disney)—animated
(3)
*The Wind in the Willows*, vols. 1–3
(HBO)—animated (3)
*The Adventures of Milo and Otis* (4)
*Cinderella* (Disney)—animated (4)
*Mary Poppins* (4)
*Peter Pan* (Disney)—animated (4)
*Pinocchio* (Faerie Tale Theatre) (4)
*Robin Hood* (Disney)—animated (4)
*Swiss Family Robinson* (4)
*Alice in Wonderland*—animated (5)
*Charlotte's Web*—animated (5)
*Lady and the Tramp*—animated (5)
*Peter Pan* (Disney)—animated (5)
*The Secret of NIMH*—animated (5)
*An American Tail*—animated (6)
*Annie* (6)
*Bedknobs and Broomsticks* (6)
*Cinderella* (Faerie Tale Theatre) (6)

*The Court Jester* (6)
*The Frog Prince* (Cannon's Family Movie
Tales) (6)
*Hansel and Gretel* (Cannon's Family
Movie Tales) (6)
*Hansel and Gretel* (Faerie Tale Theatre)
(6)
*The Jungle Book* (Korda) (6)
*The Lion, the Witch and the Wardrobe*
(series)—animated (6)
*The Never Ending Story* (6)
*Oliver!* (6)
*Princess Bride* (6)
*Singin' in the Rain* (6)
*Sleeping Beauty* (Disney)—animated (6)
*The Sound of Music* (6)
*Superman*—(6)
*Tom Thumb* (MGM) (6)
*Yellow Submarine*—animated (6)

## LEARNING

*The Animal Alphabet*—animated/live (2)
*Baby Animals Just Want to Have Fun* (2)
*Bill Cosby's Picture Pages*, vols. 1–6 (2–6)
*Learning About Numbers* (Random
House/Sesame Street) (2)
*Richard Scarry's Best ABC Video Ever*—
animated (2)
*Don't Eat the Pictures*—art (3)
*Banana, Banana, Banana Slugs!*—(4)
*Bears!*—(4)
*Dinosaurs!* (Golden Book)—animated/live
(4)
*Earth Creatures*—(4)
*Here We Go* (series)—transportation (4)
*Dinosaur!* (Children's Video Library)—
animated/live (5)
*The Greatest Adventure Stories from the
Bible* (series)—animated (5)
*Reading Rainbow: Digging Up Dinosaurs*
(5)
National Geographic: *Among the Wild
Chimpanzees* (6)
*Show Off!*—special tricks (6)

## MUSIC/DANCE

*Baby Songs* (series)—animated/live (1)
*Carnival of Animals*—animated/live (2)

*Raffi in Concert with the Rise and Shine
    Band* (2)
*A Young Children's Concert with Raffi* (3)
*Mister Rogers: Musical Stories* (4)
*Peter and the Wolf and Other Tales* (5)
*Uncle Elephant* (5)
*Who's Afraid of Opera?* Vol. 3: *The
    Barber of Seville/Lucia di
    Lammermoor* (5)
*The Nutcracker* (6)
*Petronella* (6)

### TELEVISION

It's hard to imagine any influence that can
be both so good and so bad for a child,
but television is it. Nothing else is so easy
to supply, so hard to deny, so intelligent
when it's good, so dreadful when it's not.

Too loud, it can damage the eardrums,
too near, it can hurt the eyes, and too
often, it can dull the senses. And after all
that, we still approve of television. With its
cable competition, it gets better every year,
not because the shows are better, but because it gives you so many choices. It is an
art form, an entertainer and a teacher, and
it is an inescapable part of our society.
Sooner or later, every child sees television
somewhere, so she may as well begin to
learn how to watch it in moderation and
how to judge its quality.

Sometime between Six and Twelve
you'll be shocked to find your child—your
bicycling, book-reading, games-loving,
moderate child—wants to do nothing but
watch the set all day long and the trashier
the show the better she seems to like it.
This too shall pass, but it will pass easier,
we think, if you have thoughtful and consistent rules in the early years.

You shouldn't let your child sit any
closer than six feet in front of the set, raise
the volume above a normal level, keep it
on during meals or let bedtime slide "to
the next commercial."

Although you may enjoy the freedom
of an electronic babysitter, you have to
limit the time, allotting, we feel, no more
than five hours a week, starting at Two,

and seven to ten hours by Six. It also isn't
wise to let your child watch for longer
than an hour at a time, for it can make her
cranky to be inactive any longer. To be
realistic, a sick child will watch more television, but she can't tolerate it for more
than two hours at a time.

Sick or well, don't let your
child look at any program
without permission. Gen-
erally all children get a
great deal out of "Mr.
Rogers' Neighborhood"
and "Sesame Street"—
and "Reading Rainbow"
for kindergartners and first-graders—but
you should see one show of any series
yourself before okaying it for your child.
You're the arbiter, for it's your child who
will be affected if the show is too silly or
too adult or if the pace is too fast. Gentle
Mr. Rogers may bore you, but his frequent
pauses give younger children the chance to
answer him. Even if they don't talk out
loud, the learning is imprinted and the
attention span is stretched, while "Sesame
Street," which is excellent for many children, goes very fast. This can make the
pre-Four—and the hyperactive child—
quite nervous.

You particularly want to avoid violence, especially if your child is under
stress. While every child will see some
violence on TV, remember that the senseless fighting in a cat-and-mouse cartoon
has as much impact on a pre-Six as a scary
movie. A nature show, with the ritualistic
bluffing of the animals, and the occasional
spilling of blood, is about all she can handle, but she'll handle it better if she has
company. As little Lucia discovered, nature shows give her some great cuddling
time with her dad.

Just as a child may be mesmerized by
violence, so might she be transfixed by one
bit of vacuous nonsense after another.
Such blather is an assault on the mind and
can hold a mother spellbound too—as we
should know. It's so easy to use old movies
and quiz shows to counter the lonely,

rainy afternoons, but this expediency has its price. The more you watch television, the more your child will too, even while she's playing with her toys. This can make her passive as well as inarticulate, for it's hard for either of you to talk and watch television at the same time.

Television shouldn't be a constant factor but a small event—a supplement to the day's adventures.

When you and your child work together with letters, she begins to learn them but when she also sees the letters on an educational children's show, this lesson is enhanced. In the same way, the child who is taken downtown to see the parade in the afternoon and then sees it again on the evening news will have a slightly broader concept of the world and especially her important place in it. She'll be sure she's in the picture at least a dozen times.

### MUSEUMS AND ART GALLERIES

The best museums for children are children's museums—usually only found in

big cities—but many museums have special exhibits for young children. You can add a lot to the adventure wherever you go, by the way you handle it however. Plan to cover a small amount of territory, but let your child choose which display to visit and, with gentle guidance, which sculptures and paintings.

Point out how artists once used fruits and vegetables and egg whites to make and bind their colors, how they learned to paint pictures in perspective and paint portraits with such remarkable eyes they'll follow your child wherever she walks in the room.

Finally, although the day is a treat for you too, do go home before her interest flags. Like any other outing, you want her to want to come back for more.

# VALUES

It's hard to cradle a newborn in your arms and realize that perfection isn't automatic. You're sure that anyone who can achieve such beauty in only nine months should have no trouble with his faith, hope and charity in twenty years.

This isn't so. You have to teach your child the virtues the way you teach him to dress himself or make his bed—by example, by insistence and by giving him the chance to make choices, and make mistakes. As long as he knows you love him, even when he's jealous and greedy and full

of the faults that beleaguer us all, he'll be a better person for trying. It's maturity he's learning, not perfection.

If the values you try to live by are honest ones, they'll be your child's solace and his strength later, and if they're materialistic, hypocritical, rigid or simply never discussed, there will be repercussions too, for without this shield, his legacy is weak. As distressing as it sounds, we can never forget that the drunks in the park were all children once.

Although your child is born with

hope—the expectation that he'll be fed and cared for—it's the love with which you swaddle him that will make him trust you and therefore trust himself. This faith in himself generates the self-confidence he needs to be daring at Two and also at Fourteen, when it takes a lot of chutzpah to be an individual, no matter how much teasing he gets from his friends.

A child learns to respect others if he is respected—not as a prince but as a person, albeit small. This teaches him to accept others as they are, which is the essence of charity. The presents he makes, the kittens he cuddles and the work he performs are all tangible expressions of charity, which help a child learn to give that most important present: himself.

You will find your pre-Six is so egocentric he'll be able to recognize injustice instinctively, especially when it's applied to himself, and in this way he begins to understand about justice. The child who is treated fairly will be able to treat others the same way.

You do want your child to become a prudent adult who can handle money cautiously and weigh consequences before he acts. This lesson begins early and is learned not by your preaching but by his errors.

When he starts to handle toys with some care and wear mittens in the snow, you'll know he realizes that a little trouble is better than broken toys and icy fingers.

The Carry Nations of the world have given temperance a bad name, but a child must learn moderation. He has to curb his love of candy and television the way he curbs his temper—the first steps toward self-restraint.

Your child must understand that it's not enough to be good and kind and prudent and true, since he still needs fortitude when the rest of the world is not. While a child must build the courage to finish the fights that he starts—even when he knows he's going to lose—he also needs the courage to face the tough realities of life and endure its small succession of sorry problems. As every mother knows, there are weeks and, heaven help us, even years when love is stretched quite thin. That's what fortitude is for.

Although your child must realize that he's responsible for every decision he makes, he can't make sensible ones unless he's supported by the old-fashioned virtues. Character is built, like a wall, brick by brick.

---

◇                              **GENEROSITY**                              ◇

---

You may not believe it of a Two, but the younger your child, the easier it is to live with him. As he gets older, however, each member of the family pulls stronger in slightly different directions, which adds stress to any family. The understanding that each of you has for the other will depend on the generosity in your house, for giving in and giving are often the same.

Your child can be a giving person if you cultivate his empathy—that sixth and most delicate sense—so he can learn how to express all the love he feels. This is why we think a child, as early as mid-Two, should make a housewarming gift for a new neighbor, a bouquet of dandelions for the sick and have pets on which to squander affection. Later perhaps he can help you wash and mend the outgrown clothes to fill a huge Daisy Box, as we used to do for our Aunt Kay. There all the clothes were collected for her friend Daisy, who had even less than we did. As nineteenth century as this now seems, a child who is able to give hand-me-downs, as well as get them, can understand the essence of generosity. The more you give, the richer you are.

Although your child may be unknowingly direct, his kindness can match his candor, as it did when we heard a Four ask solicitously of the neighborhood arthritic, his torso bent horizontal as he walked, "How are you today, Mr. Find-a-Penny?"

Your child needs some friends who are disabled, not as a favor to them, but as a favor to himself, for he's the one who's enriched. It was Mali who said about one of our closest friends, "I know Charlie is retarded, but I really like him just the way he is." This acceptance of people is the essence of generosity.

The ability to accept others isn't limited to the poor or the sick. Your child needs to realize that eccentricities are as reasonable as red hair and, in effect, are not his business. Tolerance is expanded, for instance, when he chats with the old ladies on the bus—strangers though they are—for everybody has a story and the more stories your child hears, the more he understands about people. He begins to see that good health is not automatic, that poverty is not preferred by the poor, that some people are smarter than others (or kinder or prettier) and that, Pollyanna though we sound, there is good in everyone. Sometimes, in fact, it's a sport in itself just to find it, and a child rather enjoys that too.

## GIFTS

A giving child doesn't simply sprout like a mushroom on Midsummer Eve. As much

as he wants to share his love, he needs you to show him how.

You'll watch him instinctively experiment with the game of give and take (especially take) at nine months, when he hands you his teddy bear again and again, but always for you to return right away. The game gets more sophisticated by mid-One, when your child offers you one of his two precious cookies, but still he would weep if you ate it. Your effusive "thanks, but no thanks" may seem overdone until you realize that it's as hard for him to give away that cookie as it would be for you to give away your paycheck.

This appreciation you show helps him understand the joy of giving a little better. Soon your Two, if encouraged, will make some Curried Peanuts to give to the neighbor lady and find pleasure in her compliments. By Three he'll make a few presents for his favorite people, on his own initiative. A Four begins to see that a gift needn't be shiny and store-bought to be enjoyed, and in another year he can carry the custom of giving a little further. Now he recognizes that the work he does for others—in the kitchen, in the workshop, in the garden—is another way to give. By Six, a child is learning to give of himself, without expecting any immediate return. This is a sign of maturity.

Some of his gifts, like the Winter Blossoms (see page 208), are so pretty you'll hate to part with them and others, like the Coat Rack (see page 206), are so homely they require as much charity from the getter as the giver. Although the presents he makes may not be beautiful, each one he gives will help him give more freely the next time.

## CURRIED PEANUTS

There are those of us who are addicted both to curry and to peanuts and find these make a dandy combination. A Two can make this present but a Six still won't have the palate for it—which means you'll have as many gifts as you expected. Into a paper bag

ADD         **4 c. cocktail peanuts (not dry-roasted)**
        **1½ tsp. curry powder**

Let your child shake the bag as much as he wishes. Lay newspaper on the counter, then dump the peanuts into a colander, rattling the pan to remove the extra spice. If the peanuts taste too strong to you, rub a paper towel among them to remove the excess, and if too bland, add a little more powder. Divide into four 8 oz. bottles for giving. No seal is required.

## KITTY WHEEL

Just as you provide toys for your child, so should your child provide toys for his pets. This one is especially good for the Three who still loves pull toys.

ASSEMBLE       **6′ string**
      **1 empty thread spool**

Have him poke the string through the hole of the spool for you to tie it, leaving a long tail for him to pull, like a wheel, to the giddiness of both your child and the chasing kitten.

## COAT RACK

There once was that awful moment at his father's birthday dinner when we watched Mike instinctively realize that the bug collections he had heard about weren't quite like the one he had made for his dad: one water bug, four dead roaches, three flies (one squashed) and a doodle bug, all pinned to a piece of cardboard he had painted a scurvy green. Actually, this present was a milestone, for he had made it days ahead of time. Usually Mike—never one to plan in advance—made a coat rack every Christmas Eve and once on the very day itself, when he postponed his present making just a whit too long. This coat rack is quick for a Two to make, and it works.

SAW       **1′ length of 1″ × 2″ wood**

Do this for him. Into it, have him

HAMMER       **four 8-penny nails**

You'll have to hold the nails in place while he hammers—a true act of faith. He can paint the wood with felt-tip pens himself or color it with crayons or paint it with watercolors. Hang immediately and with love.

## POTPOURRI

This is one of the easiest presents a Three can make, since it requires so many brief steps over a long period. It's also one of the nicest. The potpourri will last about a year in sachets or for a few months in an open dish as a room freshener. The newest blooms smell strongest.

In a measuring cup, and without packing them

COLLECT       **5–6 c. rose petals**

Have your child spread the petals on a window screen and dry them under his bed for a few days until they're crisp and dry. They will shrivel to about 2 cups. Put them in a quart jar and cover.

ADD       **½ c. non-iodized salt**

Cap tightly, shake and leave for a week.

ADD       **1 tbsp. crushed cloves**
      **1 tbsp. mace**

Cap again, shake and let steep for six weeks.

## CATNIP TOY

Children like frisky cats and this present makes a cat quite frisky indeed.

CUT       **6″ square of felt**

In the middle of the square

LAY       **3 tbsp. catnip**

Fold the felt over the catnip. A Three can staple it shut, a Four can cut the material too, and a Five can pin the edges and then sew the felt together with embroidery thread. Any age, however, will like to decorate it with squiggles of a fabric pen, or let him paste bits of felt or braid on it with white glue.

DRY       **1 hour**

## SCOUR FLOWERS

This fluff of net will scour dirty pots, pans and bathtubs and makes good gifts for aunties and grandmas. A half yard of net, 48″ wide, will yield 12 flowers for your Four to give. Out of newspaper

**CUT**             **4″ × 18″ pattern**

You'll find it easiest to have your child do the cutting on the floor. Lay the pattern on top of the net, starting at one corner. Have your Four kneel on the pattern to hold it in place and cut around it, repeating until all the net is used.

**CUT**             **twelve 10″ lengths of string OR yarn**

He can gather the net lengthwise for you to tie in the center, leaving a loop at one end so it can be hung from a towel rack.

## DRIED WATERMELON SEEDS

Preheat oven 225°

Watermelon seeds dried in July make squirrel food in January. Let your Four wash them first in a strainer, then spread on a cookie sheet.

**BAKE**             **30 minutes**

Stir every 10 minutes. Cool and package in plastic sandwich bags for winter.

## MEDITERRANEAN POLISH

YIELD: six 4 oz. bottles

Any Four who can make salad dressing can make this furniture polish. Use cider vinegar for dark woods; white vinegar for light ones. This is used instead of paste wax, to be applied lightly and buffed.

**MIX**             **1 c. vinegar**
                    **2 c. olive oil**
Bottle and give.

## TRANSPARENCIES

Preheat iron: Warm

A Four can make this, but under supervision, for it must be sealed with a warm iron. Between two sheets of wax paper

**LAY**             **autumn leaves OR**
                    **fern fronds OR**
                    **pressed flowers**

Iron both sides of the paper, trim the edges, and poke

a ribbon through a hole at the top, so it may be hung from a window for the sun to shine through.

## PLAY CLAY

Since all neighborhood children seem to have two or three birthdays a year, you need a small supply of presents at the ready. We find this clay just right for a Five to help his mother make. You will need two boxes of salt. In a 6-quart bowl

**COMBINE**         **3 c. salt**
                    **6 c. flour**
                    **3 tbsp. powdered alum**

When well-mixed

**ADD**             **6 c. boiling water**

Pour all at once and stir until well blended—a job for you. Lay newspapers on a table and over them lay 2 large sheets of wax paper. Dump the dough onto them and have your child spread it with a wooden spoon.

**COOL**            **10 minutes**
**ADD**             **1 tbsp. salad oil**

Be careful to sprinkle the oil evenly over the dough. Help your child divide the dough into 6 portions.

**KNEAD**           **7 minutes**

Do this to each batch—a 20-minute job if you both work at it. As you work it the warm dough will absorb any loose salt and flour, be smooth to the touch and make your hands tingle. To each batch,

**ADD**             **few drops food coloring**

When the color is well mixed, store in a plastic sandwich bag, tie with a ribbon and refrigerate until the next party.

## DRIFTWOOD PICTURES

A Five can make this gift alone. On a small weathered plank

**STAPLE**          **3–5 spring flowers**

Daffodils look nice, but whatever the flowers, the arrangement should look like a bouquet. At its base

**STAPLE**          **a bow ribbon**

At first this picture looks great, and then it looks dead, but after a few weeks it dries with a primitive charm—

or maybe you just get used to it. Another present for Aunt Rosie, but give after it's past its middling stage—which means it has to be made a month in advance.

## ALUMINUM FOIL

Aluminum foil comes in many weights and widths, but for the following recipes you'll need foil that is 35-gauge, 12″ wide and found in arts and crafts stores. It can be cut with a child's scissors, bends easily, holds its shape—and scratches, so your child should wear gloves when he works with it.

French Bread Pan
This pan—a nice present for the auntie who went to gourmet school—will bake two loaves of French bread and looks like a rounded W, because it's been shaped with a rolling pin. (She'll never guess what it's supposed to be.)

**CUT**              **17″ length of foil**

Fold the 12″ width in half and have your Five first press a firm crease in the foil and then pull it apart, so it looks like a tent. The rolling pin is laid down one side of the crease and rolled to the edge, forming a trough for the dough. Do this on the other side—now it looks like a couple of "U's"—and fold down the tips of each corner so they won't scratch anyone. The pan will squash easily but can be reshaped easily too.

Hurricane Lamps
Your Six can cut, curl and staple this lamp together in ten minutes, if you do the measuring first. It will look like an upside-down crown.

**CUT**              **15″ length of foil**

Mark one long edge of the foil every 1½″ and draw a line from each mark 9″ toward the other side. Have your child cut along the lines to make foil strips and then curl them around a rolling pin to make a fringe of the strips. Staple the short sides of the foil together, turning it into a tube, and rest it on its fringe. If the candle is low, curl the fringe tighter to shorten the height of the lamp.

## WINTER BLOSSOMS

A lovely Virginia lady taught us how to bring cheer to a neighbor on a January day—a gift for no reason at all. Have your Six cut forsythia or fruit branches in November, when the tiniest buds have formed. With a hammer, let him

**MASH**              **3″ base of stem**

Put the stems in warm water, with no leaves or buds under the surface, and keep the vase in a dark closet for about six weeks. Replace the evaporated water with cool water as needed. When the buds are fat, transfer the branches to a well-lighted room, or for faster blooming, to a window sill. Start only a few at a time so you can have blossoms for many weeks and always let one branch bloom in your child's room.

## BOOKENDS

Two covered bricks make good bookends, as elegant or as casual as the material itself. Burlap or brocade are both handsome. Have your Six

**CUT**              **11¼″ × 13″ of material**

The fabric is glued to the brick—a messy step—so your child should cover the work table first with newspaper. Over it, have him stand a clean, dry brick on its end and drip white glue down its four sides. Wait 5 minutes for the glue to get tacky. Have him cover the sticky newspaper with a fresh sheet, then lay the brick across the short end of the fabric. Roll it slowly toward the other end, pressing it down hard against the material to make it stick. Smooth any wrinkles and have him seal the seam, but you should close each end with more glue, so that it looks as tidy as the back of an envelope.

## HAIR RIBBON TREE

This gift takes some forethought and is good enough for a Six to give to his little sister, for her to festoon with ribbons.

When you're on a walk, look for a small branch on the ground, no bigger than ½″ in diameter, with enough twigs on it to look like a miniature tree. Have your child put the branch in a large cardboard box or over newspapers.
Over it he should

**SPRAY**              **white latex paint**

Aim downwind (so the fine mist doesn't get in his lungs), and have him turn the branch gradually to get an even coating. In a bowl

**MIX**        ¾ c. plaster of Paris
                 ½ c. water

Pour into a 2–3″ container, the kind that holds cottage cheese. You also can use Patch Plaster (see page 332) but it takes longer to set.

**REST**        10 minutes

Have your child imbed the branch, helping him hold it in place for the first 5 minutes or until it can stand alone.

**DRY**        30 minutes

Tear away the carton and let your child cover the sides of the plaster base with felt-tipped markers or a fabric skirt. To make it, use pinking shears to cut a strip and sew the ends to make a tube. Turn the fabric inside out, pull it over the base, and hold it in place around the top while your child anchors it with a rubber band. Flip the material over the band so it falls like a gathered skirt.

## HERB GARDEN

This makes such a great gift, you should plant an extra garden for yourself. Your Six can plant the seeds in peat pots—one variety for each pot—but the present will look fancier if he plants them in eggshells, broken in half, and then puts the shells back into their carton. Identify the seeds on the inside flap, like a candy sampler—your job.

**MIX**        1 c. vermiculite
                 1 c. scalded sphagnum moss
                 1½ c. water

Your child can make drainage holes in the base of each eggshell cup with a pencil point, then fill them with the moss mixture. Into each cup

**PRESS**        4–6 seeds of parsley OR basil OR
                   thyme OR rosemary OR sage OR
                   oregano

**GERMINATION**      10–30 days

The garden will need little or no watering if your child slips the carton into a plastic bag, ties it shut and keeps it in a warm place—an instant hothouse. He can give this present when the sprouts have 4–6 leaves and are about 1½″ high, so they can be transplanted either to a bed outdoors with full sun or to pots where the herbs can get 4–5 hours of indoor sunlight.

## SWEDISH RYE BREAD

YIELD: 2 loaves

There must be a patch of heaven that smells like anise and orange. Since this bread keeps at least a week without refrigeration, it makes a grand gift for a Six to make. Read the general directions for making bread (see page 354) and then, in a large bowl

**DISSOLVE**      2 pkgs. yeast
                     1½ c. warm water

When the yeast bubbles—in about 10 minutes—

**ADD**        ¼ c. molasses
                 ⅓ c. sugar
                 2 tbsp. softened butter
                 1 tbsp. salt
                 1 tbsp. fennel
                 1 tbsp. anise

**GRATE**        2 tbsp. orange zest

Stir it into the bowl

**ADD**        2½ c. rye flour

Stir the flour into the bowl, one cup at a time.

**ADD**        2–3 c. white flour

You've added enough flour when the dough stops sticking to the sides of the bowl. Rest the dough, covered, for 10 minutes, then knead, adding more flour if necessary. Stop when the dough is golden in color, its texture smooth and it springs with a life of its own. Roll dough in a greased bowl, cover with a towel and let rise in a warm place.

**FIRST RISING**      2 hours

Poke for readiness, punch down dough, divide it, cover it and let it rest for 10 minutes. Butter two 8″ × 4″ loaf pans and shape dough into loaves. Cover.

Preheat oven 375°

**SECOND RISING**      1 hour

**BAKE**        30 minutes

Lower heat to 350° and cook 10 minutes longer. Remove from oven, butter tops and place on racks. When slightly cool, remove the bread from the pans. Wrap in foil.

# RESPONSIBILITY

◇                                                                    ◇

A child must learn to be responsible for four things: his toys, his clothes, his pets and himself. Frankly, it's much, much easier to forget about the pets and take care of the rest yourself, but it's quite unfair to your child. The longer he waits to learn the rudiments of responsibility, the more difficult it will be to assume them until one day he'll be looking around for his old mum to make his excuses, pay his bills and babysit his children.

It's your job—the hardest one of all, perhaps—to teach your child to be accountable for his actions.

When your Four spills the milk he must realize, as Harry Truman once said, "The buck stops here." It's his job to wipe up the milk and no, he won't do it well, but when he's a few years older, he'll do it better and much more willingly than he would have if it had never been expected of him before.

Day-to-day duties, as well as the unusual ones, are simply part of the giving that must be expected of each member of a family. The more responsibility you encourage in your child, the more freedom he can carry. This is a connection to be stressed all his life, for no job seems too onerous when it has its reward.

The Five who can clean his hamster cage alone or the Six who can pick up most of his toys will be a self-confident child and proud to have earned the respect that comes with his accomplishments.

## PETS

Just as there should be a boy in the world for every girl—a pretty notion—so should there be a pet for every child. It's easier to find the right one if you eliminate the wrong ones first.

Canaries and parakeets, we've found, aren't good pets for a child (although they're lovely for a mother), for the cage is too complicated for small hands to open without eventually letting the bird escape.

Most animals shouldn't be kept in captivity at all, no matter what they tell you at the pet store. There is the small dime store turtle that lives in water and often carries salmonella, the exotic iguana that thinks the temperature in a hothouse is just warm enough and then there is the monkey, which has all the faults of a baby and few of the virtues. It doesn't coo, it has a fur full of allergens and it's sure to be, as the book says, "either shy or vicious" (ours was both). A monkey also must have a year-round heat of 80°, a huge cage cleaned at least four times a week and if you need one more argument, most likely a dead mother. According to our veterinarian, a baby monkey usually can't be captured unless his mother is killed first.

Your child can—and should—enjoy wildlife, but unless a species has been domesticated, it isn't ready to be owned. A fox, a raccoon and even a deodorized skunk can charm you, but they have powerful smells and revert to offensive habits easily when kept as pets. Instead, let your child fill the birdbath with water for the cardinals, toss grain to the chipmunks and, God forbid, the pigeons, and plant morning glories for the squirrels. Our favorite squirrel, a reprobate named Floyd, would nuzzle these flowers and hallucinate drunkenly every morning.

While we've ruled out many pets, there still is a long list left—the fish, the box turtle, the iguana (if you'll give him a heater—or if you happen to live in a hot-house), as well as snakes, gerbils, rabbits, guinea pigs, dogs and cats—every one an animal that offers a child a special bit of joy. You almost can see the electricity that flows between your child and his kitten, and his fascination when he watches the gerbils mate and his wonder when they birth. The life—and the death—of a pet is high drama to a child.

Even with the best of care, a pet usually has a rather short life expectancy, but his death, although tragic, is still a child's most gentle introduction to the natural cycle. The sorrow of death can never be greater than the gift of life.

A pet is easiest to care for if he's lively, happy and healthy, and for this he must have shots if necessary, a good diet, a clean home and enough room to move about. The bigger the animal the more often you'll have to clean after him and the warmer his blood, the more gentle the handling must be. In truth, you're looking not for an animal that suits your child, but one that suits you, for although he'll be in charge of the tender loving, you'll be left with most of the care.

Every child, as early as One, should learn as much about his pet as possible—how much food and sleep and exercise he needs and how he can help you feed him and clean his living quarters. The more your child helps, the better he'll learn the likes and dislikes of his pet, until by Four, he'll be sure he can care for him better than anyone in the world. By Six, he'll think he's doing all the work and if you're lucky, he'll be able to by Eight, but not without regular reminders—a custom to follow for years.

Like so many mothers, you'll find that pets instill a sense of responsibility and kindness and generosity in a child, teach-ing him that although love may be a lot of trouble, the trouble is quite worth it.

## FISH

Fish make interesting pets, for you can start with a simple goldfish when your baby is only a few weeks old and graduate to schools of tropical fish before he's Six. If you treat fish with a certain reverence, your child will try to do the same, but a Two, no matter how accustomed he is to a fish bowl, will try to grab his fish with his fist, will feed it too much—and will be very sorry to see it floating on its side. He'll be better by Three, if he helps you care for the aquarium and feed the fish.

Any fish should be fed only twice a day and never more than the fish can eat in a few minutes, so the bacteria count in the water stays low. If you have a tank with a pump, you need to add more water only when it has evaporated noticeably. Gravel isn't necessary, except it makes an aquarium prettier, hides any droppings and anchors plants.

### Goldfish

This flashy fish needs little oxygen, is happy with flake food and content to live in a small bowl of water at room temperature. Change the water every two to three days. Have your child draw the water from the tap twenty-four hours before you add it to the aquarium, so the lethal chlorine can evaporate. For a more exotic and equally easy pet, get a Siamese fighting fish, which can survive with just enough water to keep it wet.

### Mollys, Swordtails, Guppies, Platies

Most fish lay eggs to reproduce, but these fish give live birth, which all Threes like to see. A large female will reproduce every four to five weeks.

Food—Give twice-a-day feedings, alternating between flake and freeze-dried fish food.

*Lodging*—Use a five-gallon tank with a pump but have a smaller one ready for the babies, for these parents are so forgetful they may swallow their young as if they were bait. Transfer their children with a fish net and use an air stone in this small tank to provide oxygen, but no pump, for it can suck in such small fish.

### Tropical Fish

These splendid fish are very expensive and all beautiful, with the red barbs and silver angelfish the cheapest and the heartiest. You'll want to buy a few of each because this looks more natural, and if they travel in schools, like the zebra, you'll need even more so your child can see the formations. However, the tiger barbs, the oscars and other aggressors should live in a separate tank, for they nip the fins of the more peaceful passersby.

*Food*—A tropical fish likes variety in his food, as he had back home. Alternate the flake food with freeze-dried foods or frozen brine shrimp, giving only two meals a day.

*Lodging*—A ten-gallon tank will house twenty to thirty fish, depending on their size. The water should be as it is in their native habitat: warm, running rapidly and acidic, with a pH factor between 6.6 and 6.8. For this, you need a heater to keep the temperature between 78°–80°; a pump to feed oxygen into the water and a pH kit to test the water regularly, so you can add the right chemicals to make it acidic enough. All these supplies are available from the pet store and are never cheap. Some fish look better in a dark tank, while others are seen best with more light. You can control this by the color of the gravel, the natural light near the tank or the electric light attachment on the top of it.

Plants aren't necessary; except as a place for the fish to play hide and seek, but they add beauty, so your child probably will want them. To grow, use the light attachment, but only in the evening and

for no more than four to six hours, or they will photosynthesize too much and destroy the pH balance of the tank. Anchor rooting plants, like the amazon sword or the corkscrew valve, in gravel, but anacharis, cabomba and the hornwort simply float about.

For simpler decorations, your child can add the rocks, slate and even driftwood he collects, but scrub them first and check the pH content of the water afterward, for these additions can change it.

### CATS

Mid-One is a good age for a kitten. A toddler seldom is nimble enough to catch him, and if he does, the kitten has twenty sharp ways to defend himself. There's nothing like a cat to teach a child what cause and effect are all about. By mid-Two, when a child is as quick as a cat, neither will want to tangle with the other.

Your cat is more likely to be healthy if you get him from a healthy, well-fed mother cat, rather than a pet store. Even so, he still will need vaccinations for feline distemper and for leukemia at nine weeks, with boosters four weeks later and annual boosters after that, and he may need to be inoculated against Lyme disease too. Most vets also give a rabies vaccine, since every cat usually gets out sooner or later.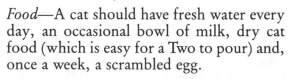

*Food*—A cat should have fresh water every day, an occasional bowl of milk, dry cat food (which is easy for a Two to pour) and, once a week, a scrambled egg.

*Lodging*—A cat, that independent creature, will sleep where he wants and go in and out of the house three times while you're still struggling to get the baby and the groceries inside. A cat does need a litter box and will train himself to use it immediately if you give him a swat when he misbehaves and then scratch his paws in the litter a couple of times. However, accidents can happen when he's mad at you or when his box is too dirty. You also want to keep the litter box in a place that's convenient for the cat but away from a toddling child. Cat feces can carry a disease that can make a child seriously sick.

*Sex*—Because of the explosion of the cat population, most veterinarians think cats should be altered. If you have a male, we definitely think he should be castrated, for he'll spray the same place again and again when he's sexually aroused and if he chooses an overstuffed chair instead of a screen door, you can only throw it away: the smell is that noxious. With a female, however, it would be nice to let her sample the good life once, as long as you're absolutely sure that you can place the litter (or keep the cats). It's also great to let your child know the wonder of a boxful of mewing kittens, looking like tiny lions with their eyes sealed shut and legs too limp to hold them. A female cat goes into heat at six months and if you don't get her spayed, she will go into heat every three to four months thereafter, if she's an outdoor cat, for with cats, as they say, "copulation controls the ovulation cycle." As far as we can see, this is another way of saying a female cat is either pregnant, mothering or in heat most of the time. Gestation takes fifty-nine to sixty-six days, and then the kittens will be born in some dark place, like a bureau drawer, and usually moved by the mother to a dry, clean, dark place, where she'll want them to stay until the kittens can see and walk. They will nurse about six weeks, and the mother can be spayed immediately after they stop.

### BOX TURTLES

A mid-Two enjoys a pet box turtle because he can pick it up without hurting himself or the turtle. This animal doesn't bite, is quiet and unobtrusive and doesn't need to be fed regularly. At least, no one's ever seen a skinny turtle—or a fat one either. A turtle can live for weeks indoors without any obvious means of support, seems to last forever in the garden and is supposed to get a diamond in his carapace each year he's with you.

*Food*—A turtle will eat greens, strawberries, hamburger and an occasional banana.

*Lodging*—If your turtle gets sluggish indoors in winter, it means that the temperature in your house is probably too cold for him to be hungry but not cold enough for him to hibernate. Either put a light in his box to make it warmer or take him outside where he can hide.

*Sex*—It seems impossible to contemplate, but it must be true. Our Hilda proved it when she went to the beach with us, laid her egg in a blanket and left it—unnatural mother. Alas, we didn't know enough to wrap it in damp sand in the hopes that it would hatch.

### ANTS AND OTHER INSECTS

All children are bug collectors at heart and none too selective about it. Roaches are quite as interesting to a Two as their cousins, the butterflies, and the ants that sneak into the kitchen are so fascinating they leave them sugar cubes.

You can buy an ant farm—a clear plastic box full of sand—from the toy store, so your child can see how they live, but then you have to order the ants from a supplier or gather them from your backyard. This works, if they come from the same colony, but our luck with homegrown ants has been very poor and we tried other insects instead. A silk moth in a jar with mulberry leaves or a caterpillar with whatever leaves he likes to sit on will also entrance a Four for a few days, but do keep the lid on tight, with a few holes punched in it.

By Six, books about insects usually interest a child more than the insects themselves, thank goodness. Books are so much more manageable.

### GERBILS

A Four is ready for that bright, alert little rodent, the gerbil. Generally, gerbils are so friendly they want company, but unless you think they want lots of company, choose a pair of the same sex. They will play mostly by day, for unlike hamsters, they're diurnal animals.

With gentle treatment, a gerbil will eat out of your child's hand, but will also try to slip out of his cage if he thinks no one is watching. Our Nadia and Mali have learned that curiosity is the downfall of the runaway, so one child taps her fingertips on the floor and the other grabs his tail when the gerbil comes forth to investigate. It takes some petting to settle him enough to go back into the cage again, for too much noise or rough play frightens a gerbil and then he may bite, which can develop into a habit. This doesn't hurt the child, but it does hurt their friendship.

*Food*—Gerbils like dry seeds, shelled nuts, grain, cereals, crackers and bread crusts, as well as grass, fruit and vegetables—especially lettuce, carrots and apples. Either hang a bottle in the cage for water or add a cut potato, which supplies water too.

*Lodging*—An aquarium with a heavy lid is good, for gerbils, like other rodents, can chew through plastic, wood or cardboard. Use fresh newspaper, which they will tear to pieces for bedding, but only clean the cage monthly since gerbils seldom urinate and they need the same nest as long as possible. The oil they exude on the paper is a protection. Add a tin can and an old shoe for them to climb into and a mirror to admire themselves.

*Sex*—Gerbils are better at making more gerbils than they are at anything else, happily giving your child a litter a month after the first year. There usually are six to eight in a litter—tiny, pink, hairless and with their eyes shut tight, although Nadia has found there's only one in a litter if she's fed the mother dry dog food. The babies burrow into little nests of paper their parents have shredded and after three weeks of suckling, have wonderful brown eyes and brown fur.

A gerbil mother is such an elitist she'll eat any ill-formed child—a Darwinian example that is too graphic, we found, for a young child. If one of the litter is either lame or overly quiet, put him in another cage.

The babies also may be attacked if the cage is too crowded, if noise makes the mother nervous, if she doesn't have plenty to eat and drink and something to chew every day, and if you touch them, for she may not recognize their smell any more. Otherwise, Nadia assures us, gerbils make excellent parents. Because they do need some peace before the next litter, put the babies in their own quarters after the third week, with dry seeds and water and some paper from their parents' cage—a touch of home. Now your little girl has enough presents for the next six to eight birthday parties.

### GUINEA PIGS

A guinea pig can soak up as much affection as your Five cares to give. There is little else this dear animal can be except a terrific cuddle figure. If pampered he can live for seven years, although four months was our record.

A native of South America, a guinea pig (or a cavy, as it's also called) has either short or long hair, straight or tousled, and generally comes in white, black, orange, or mixes thereof. The Peruvian is the prince—the most expensive, the shaggiest and the funniest, for it wiggles along the floor like a big, fuzzy caterpillar.

His squeals and his grunts are his only protection and when he feels at home, he uses them to chatter to anyone who comes in the room and seems to think all conversation is directed to him. In fact, we found our cavy, who lived under the sideboard, talked straight through every dinner party.

He's a better talker than he is an athlete, for he can't jump or climb. However, he needs to run constantly, although not necessarily on a tabletop, for while he can scamper around and around it for quite a while he will, contrary to popular notion, fall off after a while.

*Food*—The guinea pig is a vegetarian. Balance his diet with commercial guinea pig pellets, apples, lettuce, celery tops, dandelions, grass and clover, but avoid onions, peppers and potatoes. Give him a salt spool from the pet shop, a bowl of water and, twice a week, a half-teaspoon of edible linseed or cod-liver oil.

*Lodging*—A guinea pig is sensitive to temperature changes and must live in an airy, draft-free, well-lighted house. Make a wooden hutch—which he can't gnaw—and cut a hole at each end and cover with screening, so he can watch the world. Inside put a skinny ramp of plywood to multiply his running space and cover securely if you have other pets.

Use a thin layer of sawdust, straw, cat litter or wood shavings to absorb the moisture and add a toy, like a treadmill, for him to spin. Clean the hutch weekly and occasionally wash it with a mild disinfectant.

*Sex*—If you have a pair of guinea pigs, the boar and the sow must be separated when they are a month old, for they can begin mating this early. This may be fun, but it isn't good for the sow until she's six months old. For this reason, each sex will need its own hutch except for the month when you mate them and the new male babies will need a hutch of their own, since males will fight unless they've been living together continuously.

You can assume that a sow that's been in the mating pen for a month is pregnant, so put her in her own hutch to avoid premature delivery. It takes sixty-five to seventy days to produce a litter of one to six babies, but the wait is worth it. These children are born with hair, teeth and eyes wide open. They begin to run when they're only an hour old and can eat solid food in two to three days, but they'll continue to nurse for three to four weeks, when they must be separated from their parents, with the males going to one hutch, the females to another.

## RABBITS

Your Five or Six is old enough to care for a rabbit, and it's a pleasant pet to care for. It's gentle, clean, quiet and big enough to romp in a fenced-in yard. A rabbit likes to be petted by its owner but he doesn't like noise, confusion or being picked up by his ears (who does?). Teach your child to lift him by the nape of the neck with one hand while supporting his rump with the other.

*Food*—A rabbit is a vegetarian who eats twice a day, preferring a deep bowl for his food, another for his water and a salt spool to lick. He does well on commercial rabbit food balanced with stale bread, lettuce, spinach, clover, pea pods, dandelions, carrots, potatoes and apples. It's tempting to give him other treats, but if a rabbit doesn't eat properly he'll get "pot belly"—a sign either of worms or a lack of protein or both in any animal.

*Lodging*—The hardest part of rabbit keeping is the building of the hutch—and then the cleaning of it. It should be made of wood and hardware cloth, but if you keep a big rabbit indoors, the hutch shouldn't be made of chicken wire or be too near an electric cord, for big rabbits have big teeth—and together that meant the untimely end of poor Heather Lapin. Outdoors is better, no doubt about it. Build the hutch flush against the house and on stilts, 2 feet above the ground. It should measure 4′ long, 2′ wide, 3′ high and have a sloped roof that extends over the sides to keep out the rain. One side should be hinged for easier cleaning and there should be a small room of plywood partitions for privacy. Rabbits like a clean cage, with a bed of cat litter, hay, straw or peat moss (but not sawdust, which sticks to the fur). This should be changed twice a week and disinfected occasionally, although a proper hutchkeeper tells us that a rabbit deserves clean bedding every day if he only dirties a corner of his cage. In fact, many vets say that rabbits are so civilized they can be trained to use litter and live inside.

*Sex*—A doe is ready to breed at eight months, but not earlier. Leave the doe and the buck alone for a few days until the doe begins to growl at her company. That's when she's had enough of the buck. Give her a hutch of her own for the pregnancy, which lasts 30–32 days, and expect her to want less affection, less noise, more food and a little milk. She'll start making a nest of her bedding about a week before she's due and must be left alone then and for the two weeks after she births, without being touched. When the babies are born—generally in a litter of eight or more—they are hairless, with their eyes closed. They mustn't be touched either—not until they have fur and their eyes are open—for the mother either may kill them or stop caring for them. Give the babies solid food at three weeks and add milk to their diet for the next three to nine weeks.

### SNAKES

A nonpoisonous snake makes a nice and curious pet, although you shouldn't get it unless your child has handled one and asks for it, for even a Four has strong feelings

about snakes. We've found a garter snake is best, and even the female, while bigger than the male, is still small and gentle. No snake, however, is slimy and none seem to mind writhing in a small child's hands.

Teach your child to hold the snake midway along his body and use his thumb and index finger to hold his head, just under the ears (if he had ears). Like any nonpoisonous snake, it will stick out its forked tongue, not to bite but to feel about a bit. Don't be alarmed.

*Food*—Keep your snake on the same diet he had at the pet shop, which varies not from species to species but from store to store. Our snake liked to dive into a bowl of water every week to catch a live goldfish, chasing it with great cunning and tossing it in the air until he could swallow it head first, so the fins couldn't scratch his throat. We found we could switch fairly soon to a much cheaper diet—a small piece of frozen fish or some freshly dug earthworms placed in the water bowl every other week.

*Lodging*—Because a snake is almost solid muscle, he can push the top from any cage if it isn't heavy enough and because he's so squirmy, he can slide through the smallest opening—as we found after the big black snake slipped from his second-floor home and turned up in the backyard across the street, which was not considered funny by the lady in the backyard. That's why you need to have the cage ready before you buy your snake. An old aquarium is good, with a sturdy screen top and a hole cut in it to fit a 60-watt light bulb. This must be lighted all day to keep him warm enough. Have a hardy plant and a stick in the cage for him to curl around and a rough rock, so he can rub against it to scrub away his skin when he sheds—two to three times a year. Keep a 3″ layer of aquarium gravel in the bottom, which must be washed before using to get rid of the fine dust since it can hurt his eyes. Dry the gravel for several hours in a 200° oven and cool it before putting it into the cage. Change the gravel every two months when you clean the cage.

*Sex*—We had hoped a pair of garter snakes would produce babies, since they are among the few reptiles that have live births, rather than lay eggs, but captivity chilled that romance.

### THE IGUANA

Sometimes nature plays bad tricks on children, giving them a great love of animals, and a batch of allergies too. The green iguana—clean, calm, quiet and odorless—is a good option for this child, or for one who is disabled or chronically ill, and needs things to watch as well as do.

Only get an iguana for a gentle child, however. Although this animal won't bite or claw your child, he may drop off the end of his tail if it's pulled, or at least get so upset he'll stand on his hind legs, puff his dewlap and look fierce, which can be scary.

Generally, he'll watch his owner with beady black eyes when he plays the harmonica—as if he really knows him—but he probably doesn't, since an iguana isn't very bright. He can climb and run fast, however, and according to one delighted owner, "is pretty pleasing to look at." Think of the iguana as a snake with character, or a modern-day, pint-sized dinosaur, which probably has more appeal.

Go to a clean, reputable pet store—maybe one that specializes in reptiles—and get an animal that was hatched three to six months ago. He'll probably be a foot long, grow to five to six feet and live for maybe ten (or twenty or thirty) years.

*Food*—Keep moistened dog kibble in the refrigerator to feed the iguana, as well as a daily ration of greens and of yellow vege-tables—the darker the better. Dust the food with vitamin bits designed for reptiles—so he'll stay beautiful—and always keep fresh water in his dish.

*Lodging*—The colder it is, the less active the iguana will be, for he's a tropical beast and needs the room to be at least 79°, or to have a heated rock from the pet store and maybe a heat lamp in his aquarium too. Get a fifty-five-gallon container, add a perch to play on, a shoebox to hide in and shred newspaper in the bottom with four to six inches of hardwood mulch for bedding, but never add corn cob pieces, which can make him sick. Empty the cage every two weeks, clean it well and then disinfect it before adding new paper and mulch.

Once the iguana is less skittish, you can take the top off the aquarium, run a plank from it toward a platform near the ceiling, and connect the two with a towel, so he can scamper about and hide in the folds, as if it were a cave. Like Vladimir, our handsome iguana friend, he may even live in this contraption and just use his aquarium to pot and to keep his food and water dish.

*Sex*—The iguana doesn't have much of a sex life outside of the jungle or the zoo, unless he runs into a lady iguana down the street. It's one less thing to worry about.

### DOGS

If you or your husband want a puppy, fine—but don't pretend you're getting it for your child, any more than you'd get him a six-week-old baby. They need an equal amount of attention.

Even a smart puppy (the sort we've heard of but never owned) requires a lot of time and a certain amount of money. Beginning at eight weeks, your dog will need to be inoculated against distemper and four other viruses, with two boosters in the next eight weeks and every year thereafter. He'll also need a rabies shot at sixteen weeks, with boosters as often as the law requires, and daily or monthly tablets to prevent the lethal heartworm, and a little operation too. Unless you want your dog to be a parent, either sex should be neutered.

He also will need a course at obedience school with you, for he has to learn some acceptable behavior—and you have to learn to accept the rest.

Even the best-trained dog will bark (usually during the baby's naptime) protecting you from all those people who come to your door, but never enter, like the postman and the newsboy. Your dog will be doubly suspicious if they're of a different race from you, for although a dog is color blind, his other senses are keen and you can expect him to be prejudiced whether you are or not.

The younger the dog the more trouble he'll cause, since a puppy goes through stages just like a child. He'll teethe, not on rattles but on old shoes, new shoes, pillows, rugs and sometimes plumbers. This happens between three and six months and must be helped by much exercise, many toys and a lot of your time, or it will become a habit. Dogs, like children, get into mischief when they're left alone.

House-training will be your biggest problem, and it usually isn't possible to solve it until your puppy is about eight months old—the equivalent of a four-year-old child. To teach your dog, take him on six walks a day, about five minutes after he's eaten, and give him a biscuit when he performs. In the house, keep the dog and his bed in a small area at first, with five to six layers of newspapers nearby, until he's old enough to last to the next walk. He'll use this same place every time if congratulated and given a biscuit, but if you act angry, he'll choose another place, perhaps hiding his mistake so well you won't find it before the rug or the floor has spotted badly. During the night, put your puppy on a small porch or in the bathroom, with a rug of newspapers, both to train him and to protect his paws. They're made to walk on grass and dirt, not on a cold, hard floor.

For a similar but much quicker method, many mothers suggest crate-training instead, which takes a month or less, even if the animal is just a few months old.

Here the puppy is kept in a small crate without letting the children bother him. The crate becomes his home, and since a dog won't soil his own living quarters, he will only pot when he goes on walks.

*Food*—A dog should have 100 nutritious calories a day for each pound he weighs, divided into four meals a day at first until, by eight months, he eats one big meal in the morning and a little one at night. Give him canned, dry or moist dog food with some additions, but not table scraps. These are so rich and tasty they make standard food seem boring. Canned food is good if it's a mix of cereal and meat but it's expensive since it can be 76 percent moisture. Soft, moist dog food is fine for trips, because it needs no refrigeration, but the cheapest is dry food, which can be mixed with a little warm water. Supplement it with cooked meat (but not pork), an egg or cottage cheese, but these shouldn't make up more than a fourth of his food. An all-meat diet is especially bad for a dog and even can kill him.

A puppy can eat as much dog food as he wants, but don't give vitamin supplements for they can damage bone growth.

*Lodging*—A puppy needs a ticking clock wrapped in a towel for consolation, to sound like his mother's heartbeat, and any dog should have a bed of his own. Most prefer it to be in the house, and often in the child's room, no matter who feeds him. To a dog, it's the playing that counts.

*Sex*—If you decide to breed your dog, the female is mature enough to whelp after she's been in heat twice. Look for a gentle, prospective father in advance, so the offspring will be gentle too, and take her to his house twelve days after the start of the menstrual discharge. Leave her there three days to be sure of consummation (and to give her a good time) and check afterward with the veterinarian, for some like to give another round of inoculations then.

Gestation will last nine weeks. The puppies open their eyes at two weeks and can be weaned at five.

## WORK

For centuries people have blessed and blamed Calvin for his philosophy that all work is good as long as it makes you tired and gets you rich. Calvin and the pre-Three have a little bit in common.

Every young child glories in work, not as some puritanical penance, but for the sweet reward of doing a job and eventually of doing it well. You never heard a child say he wants to lie in a hammock all day when he grows up. Your child may want to be a trashman or a farmer or a bus driver, but he would never want to be a dilettante, even if he knew the word.

It's important and productive—and initially quite troublesome—to teach your child how to be helpful, but work draws your child closer and closer into the family structure. Although it may seem easier, don't put off chores until he naps. For one thing, he doesn't sleep that many hours a day, and for another, he wants to help you.

If you welcome his help, his efforts will be positive, if bumbling, but the next time he'll do the work a little better. It may be some years before he does a good job but,

fortunately, with his short attention span, he won't attempt anything for very long either. This won't detract from his pride, and his healthy attitude toward work will give him the stamina to endure those dreary classes and dull jobs that plague us through the years. As one determined mother told us, faith, hope and charity are all very well, but over the years, it's fortitude that counts.

After mothering for what amounts to a ridiculous number of years between us, we've found our children have grown to like the work we like, as long as we've taught them to help with it when they were very young.

Many first-time mothers consider the only true learning to be academic and we couldn't disagree more. It's work that builds a child's coordination and sense of order and it is the success of this work that builds self-confidence—all necessary for arithmetic, reading and writing.

When Kate and Mike and Meg were Six, Four and Two—often demons by day but almost angels by night—we sought our solace in many ways, including prayer. It was hard to believe that we would pass this way but once.

On their knees in nitey-nites, they earnestly said this prayer together, which made the next day seem possible to us and the last one not so bad:

*Help me to work,*
*Help me to play,*
*Help me to learn a bit each day.*
*Teach me to wash,*
*Teach me to scrub,*
*To hang my clothes and clean my tub;*
*To put my toys upon the shelf,*
*Help me, dear Lord, to help myself.*

If nothing else, this prayer will help your child realize that you weren't put on this earth to be a nursemaid, and it may help you see that your child is as eager to care for himself as you are for him to do it. He just needs a mother to guide him.

A child can understand the instructions best if you speak to him slowly, at eye level, and show him how to deal with his work safely and neatly, dividing the job into segments so he can see each step clearly. The chores you have him do should be requested in a matter-of-fact, let's-go manner, and when the work is done you must inspect it and praise it promptly before he undoes it again (as he almost surely will). However, we think you should never give money for a job, even as an allowance, for then you're putting a price tag on cooperation. Within a family, a father, mother or child needs only the satisfaction of completing a job and not a cash bonus, since the feeling of accomplishment should be its own reward. This is the difference between a business and a family.

### MID-ONE

For a child to be self-sufficient, we believe in starting chores by mid-One, when he gets the morning paper for you and helps unpack a few groceries, working up to bigger and bigger jobs before first grade.

Except for child-sized mops and brooms, we even think your child should use your equipment, like your vacuum, and by Five, your iron, set very low. Good tools make success that much likelier.

### TWO

The real jobs begin about Two, all of them small enough to be finished without pressure from you. It's better, we find, to have the closet floor cleaned well than to tell a

Three to tidy his room, for one can get done and the other is impossible. By breaking a job into stages of time, the improbable, at least, is in sight. If he balks, you're demanding bigger jobs than he can handle or thinks he can handle.

A Two, as scattered as he is, will empty wastebaskets with you and tidy a little too. He also should help you undo many of those things he has done. He'll like some of the jobs, like washing fingerprints from woodwork, but don't remind him where they come from; he knows. It's obvious you don't want them there or he wouldn't be asked to remove them.

### THREE

By Three, your child wants to run errands and offers to help with chores—not picking up toys, of course, but real chores— like sweeping and dusting and polishing silver and shoes. If you've encouraged his help in the past his work will begin to be quite satisfactory, for his competence comes with practice.

### FOUR TO SIX

A Four will step and fetch for adults and he'll rake the yard for you now and dig, both where you want him to dig and where he wants to dig, so you must work nearby.

Your child may learn some things far earlier than most children, depending on your own abilities. We once knew a chef who claimed his Four could separate a dozen eggs without breaking one and a seamstress whose Five taught herself to use a sewing machine one day while her mother napped.

A child will learn everything much faster if you let him learn by trying, and he'll fail sometimes too—just like you. When you let your child dare to try—and fail—you're showing respect, for a child has the right to make mistakes too. Bear with his errors in judgment, whether it's making his bed or pouring his milk. If there are too many failures, quit for a while, and you'll know the meaning of the old proverb: There's no use crying over spilled milk.

Your child gains self-confidence with each new chore he masters. He wants to learn more, do more, see more—because he knows he can. You'll find his capabilities increasing in direct ratio to the praise he earns, until one day you'll be astonished at the efficiency of your masterful Six. And you, dear heart, will face a revelation: your Six is more help than not.

### ORDINARY

No matter how you live, you have to do some routine housework every day and so should your child. It's nothing to feel apologetic about. The job may get boring after he thinks he's mastered it, but still he must be expected to do his share of what we call "the common good." It sounds more noble than housework and if you offer a variety of jobs, and don't expect too much, he'll do them fairly well.

A little child leaves you with little time or energy to clean house, especially if you also have a job, but a tidied house will help you keep your psyche in order.

Go from room to room, wearing a big, pocketed apron to hold all the little things that are out of place, picking up and putting down items as you go. You can expect

### ERRAND RUNNING

Someone once said that if whales had thumbs they'd rule the world, for that's how smart they are. Teach your child, starting at mid-One, that it's smart for him to use his thumbs for something more than putting in his mouth. He should clasp them over anything he carries, for he'll be much less likely to drop it. You also will teach him to carry anything with both hands, telling him approximately 117 times a year for the next ten years. He'll remember for himself most of the other times.

a mid-One to help you if you encourage him to follow you about and hand him each toy or box to return when you reach the place where it belongs.

### The Blitz

In the late afternoon, when the world seems so fragmented, set Mr. Buzzer, your friendly timer, for fifteen minutes and shout, "The Blitz!"

For this you and your child—a Three or better is best—should scout the room as fast as you can, picking up and putting down until, like a parody of Mary Poppins, the living room is tidy and the bell has rung. When your life is stripped of clutter a couple of times a day, you can appreciate it more and no one will mind the effort much, since the time is limited.

With any kind of warning from company, we still can shout, "The Blitz," and as a family, put the house together in fifteen minutes flat. If it's still a little chaotic when the bell has rung, we still stop just the same. Enough is enough.

### Vacuuming

A One often is terrified that your noisy vacuum will swallow him as if he were an old paper clip, for sizes make no sense at this age. This fear both overwhelms and fascinates a child and he may follow you, rushing forth to touch the machine,

shrieking, running away and then following you again. The reaction may get so bad you'll have to vacuum when he sleeps, but by mid-One, fascination should prevail. Now he'll imitate you, eventually with the vacuum but first with make-believe props, perhaps as our Kate did the day the priest came to call. She came down the stairs, ever so politely, saying nothing but "buzz-buzz-buzz" as she pushed the nozzle around each balustrade. Unfortunately, she was using an old douche bag.

Since a small child often is scared when he sees small items sucked into the vacuum, collect them first by hand, the way a professional cleaner does to prevent a blocked hose. Let your Two fit the attachment to the wand, push the plug into the socket and start the motor. He can vacuum for you, actively if not well, and by Four be expected to do a good job on the baseboards of one room a week. We think the living room is best so that company, once prompted, can praise his work.

Don't expect perfection, however. The vacuum is such an awkward contraption, you can hardly expect a Two—or even a Ten—to handle it well. Heaven knows we can't.

### Dust Mopping

A dust mop must have been invented by a genius with a degree in childhood education. You need only teach your Two to run it around the floor without lifting the head (so the dust doesn't scatter) and to contain his cleaning to small areas or a hallway, so he doesn't skip too much of the floor. Carry the mop to the window for him,

almost closing it on the handle, then let him twist and pump it up and down to shake the dust free.

### Sweeping

This is an irritating job for a child, because he can see just as many mistakes when he's done as you can. Sweeping is easier, however, if give your Three his own child-sized broom and dustpan and considerable instruction too. Teach him to pick one spot in the center of the room and sweep toward it, starting from the corners, so he doesn't have to sweep the same spot twice—a technique he'll follow automatically in five or six years. It will take that long to get reasonably good results.

A child needs to see that the efficient way is the easiest way every time.

### Mopping

A preschool child isn't old enough to mop a floor, or even part of one, by himself, but a Four should be expected to mop up his spills with a small mop of his own, even though you'll do it again afterward. He has to realize he's responsible for his own actions—and his mistakes.

### THE CHILD'S ROOM

You'd never tell your child to "paint the house" or "go to the moon" but when you say, "Clean your room," it overwhelms him just as much. Truth to tell, it probably overwhelms you too, for it's hard to know where to start.

When just a few toys are out of place you put them back automatically and feel quite satisfied with your lot: that's what motherhood should be about. Unfortunately, that's your child's idea of tidying too, no matter how messy the room.

You can expect your One to pick up his teddy bear sometimes without being told, and a Two may take care of his bear and a good truck. A Three may put away the tea set too, and a Four may have about four toys that he treasures enough to stow away. To expect more of a child is to expect the impossible. Instead, you'll have to pick up the toys with him, doing almost everything when he's Two and almost nothing by the time he's Six, if you chat with him while he works, giving only occasional aid.

As in any other complicated job, you must break it into segments—"Now, let's put away everything that's under the bed" and then, "on the bed," then in it. Next it's the bureau top, then the night table, the chair, the desk. Finally, you get a broom, sweep the rest into the middle of the floor, and sort the mess together.

You can make your child enjoy order by helping him tidy his room twice a week, so it never gets totally in shambles, and then seldom mentioning it in between. When you help your child keep his possessions reasonably in place, the cleanup will seem possible. If you can't, he has too many possessions.

### Bedmaking

Along with the presents of a third birthday come the first real responsibilities, and bedmaking is one of them. If you handle it right your child will think it a prize for growing up—for a while.

For years his bed will be not just a place to sleep but a comfort in trouble, a trampoline, a tent, a zoo for stuffed animals. With this kind of wear he needs to learn how to put his bed together almost as easily as he takes it apart.

### Three

Begin teaching him to make his bed several weeks before his third birthday, not because it will take that long to learn, but because it takes that long to fit the job into his routine. He should do it when he makes his toilette—before he's ever entitled to breakfast—and he should straighten it after his nap.

To give your child a chance to do the work well, the bed itself should be away from the walls on three sides, so he can get around it easily.

For any bed, use a fitted bottom sheet and square-corner the top sheet and the blanket when you change the linens, for in his hilarity they are kicked away easily. On top of it all, use a quilt. It shows wrinkles much less than a bedspread.

To make the bed, help him pull the top sheet back to remove the toys, the pajamas, the apple cores and cookie crumbs. Next, have him pull the sheet forward again and then the blanket, folding back the sheet's wide hem so it will be on the right side. Help him tuck in the sides of the sheet and blanket but he can drag the quilt across the bed himself. By Four the job becomes automatic—more or less.

### Five

Bedmaking becomes more precise for a Five and now he can learn to square-corner his own top sheet, like nurses do in a hospital. Little girls, we found, are particularly adept at this, not because they like housekeeping but because they usually like to play hospital better than boys.

Have your child tuck in the sides of the top sheet, as before, and fold the end of the sheet onto the bed. Each corner is then turned onto itself, to make a right angle, and the sheet is tucked under the mattress. This secures it and looks like the side of a triangle, as crisp as the flaps of a display package at the post office.

When your Five graduates to a spread, he can make a neat job of the pillows if you teach him to fold back the spread and lay the pillow slightly over the fold. This makes a tidy tuck when he pulls the spread into place. When you tell your child the reason for each step he will understand the job and do it better.

To be realistic, we find a child makes his bed perhaps four days out of seven, and for us, that's a lot better than no days out of seven. When you find he forgets, have him make it right then, even if he's just getting ready for bed. You should make it for him only when you change the sheets and a Nine, we discovered, can do that too.

## THE PLEDGE

Growing up in the Deep South may have inspired Tennessee Williams to write remarkable plays but all we did was make remarkable promises in the style of Scarlett O'Hara.

There was that pledge to our Tante Margot to wear perfume, "always, *ma chère*, always," and to our dear Aunt Kay who said, in her moonlight-and-magnolia drawl, "Honey, if you're ever in a situation (and mind you, I don't know *what* that situation would be) when you can wear only mascara *or* underpants— always wear mascara."

These still seem like perfectly sensible promises to pass on to our girls, and we've also had our children take the Carton, Can and Bottle pledge, just as we did. Under no circumstances can these be on any table—not for breakfast, not for lunch, not for dinner. The manners your child shows when he eats are mirrored very much by the niceties of his surroundings. This small trouble is quite worth it—especially after you teach your child to set the table.

### THE TABLE

Bread is the staff of life, and the table is the heart of the family.

### Setting

Once at a bazaar we bought a checked oilcloth place mat—pink and pinked to look like a pig—which taught Kate, at Four, to set a table much quicker than we could.

The mat had a brass ring sewed to its snout on the left, and with a waterproof marker, a fork was drawn to the left, a circle in the center for a plate and to the right a knife, a spoon and a circle for the glass.

We made more mats for the rest of the family, for it was hard for Kate to reverse the order when she set the other side of the table. We drew a kitchen picture of the other extras needed at the table—the trivets, the salt and pepper and the serving spoons—so she wouldn't be embarrassed by repeated reminders.

By Six, a child can learn about salad forks and soup spoons and how you set silverware from the outside toward the plate, according to the order they'll be used. A Six also can learn to serve on the left and clear from the right, and he should, for if a child is going to learn a job, he may as well learn correctly.

### Clearing

A Three can clear a table, if you don't mind picking up the bones and silverware he drops. Personally, we do, which is why we wait until Four.

He should clear from the right, one dish at a time. You mustn't let him stack dishes, of course, both because it isn't pretty and it isn't safe. Your child will be Eight before he can carry a plate in each hand, but in the meantime, he should carry one plate in both hands, with one thumb on the rim and the other straddling the silver that is balanced across the middle. This prevents many accidents.

A Six will also take away the unused knives, the trivets and the salt and pepper before dessert, but you'll have to remind him every time.

### Washing Dishes

The most recalcitrant, into-everything Two will be pleased to wear a big plastic bib and stand on a kitchen chair for a half-hour at a time for the privilege of washing dishes. Whether you have a dishwasher or not, take advantage. It's the best way we ever found to have a second cup of coffee in peace.

There will be reasonably little trouble if you prepare the scene, first by washing and drying all the breakable dishes and sharp knives—for a pre-Six should never wash these—then by covering the floor by the sink with newspapers, for much water will spill. Finally, set up one pan in which to wash dishes and another to rinse them.

Put the silverware, tin mugs and plastic dishes in one empty pan in the sink and teach your child to run warm water (which he'll run almost cold) and to measure soap (which he either won't use or won't measure). You'll have to show him how to rub the dishcloth on all sides of each cup and spoon and fork and to put them into the other pan on the counter when he's finished. When he's tired of washing, dump out the soapy water for him and put the pan of dishes into the sink for him to rinse under running water. And rinse. And rinse.

He can put the dishes in the drainer himself but don't expect your child to dry them or even to put them away when they're air-dried, for there's little fun there. That's just as well, since you'll probably do them again when he's not looking. It takes a Ten to do dishes well—if you're lucky.

### THE LAUNDRY

Clothes inevitably mean trouble, but they don't have to mean so much.

### The Hamper

Mother's liberation begins at the laundry hamper. By Three, a child should put his own dirty clothes in the hamper—automatically. Insist upon it.

### Washing

A little girl at Three thinks hair ribbons and handkerchiefs are charming, but by now she should wash her own. Let her do it in the tub, when she bathes, and smooth them over the mirror. This irons them dry. A little boy will settle for washing his underpants.

### Ironing

Ironing isn't dull to a child, and if it's taught right we don't think it's dangerous either.

A Two likes to use a little ironing board with a nonheating dime store iron, but a Three quickly graduates to one that heats a little. We had our Fours use this iron too, since they were so rambunctious, but a Five is ready to use your sturdy board, lowered to scale, and your regular iron, learning exactly where to keep the dial. He won't want to hurt himself and, in fact, will be even more cautious than you. The weight of this iron and today's synthetic clothes let him smooth any wrinkles, whether imaginary or not. Teach him to iron the sleeves and facings and the pocket and collar before he irons the rest of his shirt.

### EXTRA-ORDINARY

While every child should do some routine work every day, the unusual accomplishments are the ones that count. His pride in any job will last as long as the work looks good—which is why anyone would rather shine a window than make a bed.

## Cleaning

Ten minutes of scrubbing anything will let your child release a whole morning's worth of angries. As in all work, don't expect much, be thankful for what you get and work alongside for less mess.

## Walls and Woodwork

Use a sponge to clean walls and woodwork because a Two can squeeze it easily. This solution also cleans bathroom tiles, but your child will need a nailbrush to clean the grout, and even at Five he will need you to wipe the spatters.

BASIC CLEANER—In a nonaluminum pan

| COMBINE | 4 c. warm water |
| | 4 tsp. washing soda |
| | ¼ tsp. ammonia |

Stir to dissolve the soda. The ammonia is included both for its cleaning power and its smell, which discourages a child from tasting it. The soda is the magic, erasing dirt but not color from both latex and enamel and leaving no trace to be rinsed. Make a fresh solution each time you use it, so the soda doesn't settle.

## Furniture

A party needn't give your furniture a hangover. The white rings usually disappear with this recipe, but if the cleaned patches make the rest of the furniture look dull, you may have to revive it all.

RING REMOVER—Your Three will think this job is a lark—briefly. In an ashtray, have him

| COMBINE | cigarette ashes |
| | lemon juice |

Do this yourself, squeezing just enough juice to make a paste, then have your Two rub it on the ring, around and around with

### JOB JAR

We've found a simple, impersonal job jar appeals to the gambling side of every child as early as Four.

Taking an idea straight from the comics, we cut twenty to thirty strips of paper, printed on each one a little job that needed doing and dropped them all into a jar. The normal reluctance to work not only disappeared, but the children would rush to shake the job jar, even before breakfast. They would fish out the daily orders for us to read, like "polish Daddy's shoes" or "wash the fingermarks from the kitchen switch plate" and then act as though we gave them a present. We don't know why, but the printed word causes fewer moans, much laughter and a zest for work. At least for a while.

his finger, as hard as he can. The very light grit should remove the ring, but if you don't know any smokers, silver polish works too, for its base is rottenstone.

## Windows

A Four can learn to shine a few windows so hard you'll scarcely know there is any glass there.

Have him crush newspaper into balls, a sheet at a time, to rub on the glass, but avoid the Sunday funnies, for the colors will smear it. Give him a plastic mister filled with Basic Cleaner and a cloth to wipe the sash and the window frame before he sprays the glass, so the dust won't smear it.

He needs you to show him how to wrap his finger in paper and poke the paper in the corners and along the edges first, since these are the hardest parts to clean, and to do it before he shines the whole glass. Explain that even a grown-up must spray and shine a window at least three times on each side to get it clean or he'll be disappointed in his speed.

If possible wash one side of the windowpane while he washes the other, so you can admire each other's work and point out any dull spots as you shine. If he leaves smudges, polish them yourself when he's not looking, for you want your child to think that he did a great job, no matter how the sunlight hits the glass. That's how standards are set.

When your child has washed enough windows he may even stop making monster faces against the pane when it gets steamy, although we do know an otherwise charming Fifty who can't resist it yet.

### Pictures

This cleaner would interest any child, even if it didn't work. But it does. Let your Three use it on a gold-leaf frame or an old oil canvas. Any paintings you get from the junk store can find a new life.

**HALVE**       **1 onion**

Rub the canvas or the frame with the wet side of the onion, cutting a fresh surface as the juice evaporates. Wipe with a dry rag.

### POLISHING

A Four, we discovered, is a polishing fool. Perhaps it's because children like mirrors so much, but no job pleases a young child more than shining wood, metal or leather so it's glossy enough to see his face in it.

### Shoes

Twos, like Sixes, can polish shoes and belts—and tables and chairs and the ends of their noses. That's why we avoid colored waxes, either liquid or paste, and instead recommend saddle soap—a safe, colorless protection.

Have your child dip a damp cloth into the soap and rub the leather with it until the foam disappears. Let the leather dry for a few minutes, then shine it with a dry cloth. A Six will like to shine all the shoes in the house every week—for about three weeks.

### Silver

The silver presents that may have seemed silly when you married seem mighty sensible when you have a Two. They're the only things in the house he probably can't break. Your child can even polish them for you, but only give him one piece at a time, so he won't go to the next before the first one is fairly clean. Silver polishing is one job that can be perfect and by the time he's Six it will be, but only if he is limited to one or two pieces.

Cover the table with newspaper and give him some polish, an old diaper or a rag and a small, solid piece of silver, but not the more fragile hollowware, for we've had sugar bowls bend and crack like paper straws. Let him rub the silver as hard as he can, all over, then wash it in soapy water, rinse it and rub it dry for luster. Satisfaction is seeing yourself smile back in silver.

### Copper

A Four wants immediate, obvious success when he works and this polish gives it. In a bowl

**MIX**       **1 c. salt**
                         **¼ c. vinegar**

Have him rub the copper with a cloth dipped in this mixture and then rinse it. You may have to rinse it once again, since any residue turns to verdigris. When working with several children, let them add an extra ¼ cup of salt, so the polish makes a stiff paste, and pat it on the copper like a crust on a ham—an amusing task. This coating dissolves the tarnish in about ten minutes, although they still will have to rub the metal to get a sheen, concentrating on any dark spots. Rinse well.

### Marble

Marble cleans well, if your Four is willing to put a little oompah into his work. The powdered pumice can be bought at a well-stocked hardware store and the chalk dust (or calcium carbonate, as it's called) can sometimes be bought at a drugstore. Your child also can make his own chalk dust by putting a few pieces of his white chalk in a paper bag and pulverizing them with a rock or by putting the chalk in the blender. In a pint jar

**COMBINE**
½ c. chalk dust
⅓ c. powdered pumice
⅓ c. baking soda

Stir until all the shades of white are blended into one. To use, shake several tablespoons of the mixture into a bowl and have your child dip a well-squeezed sponge into it so the dust doesn't fly as much as it would if you shook the powder directly onto the stone. Have him scrub the marble hard and in any direction. Rinse with a clean sponge.

### WAXING

Paste wax gives furniture much more protection than commercial liquid wax and is much safer, for the liquid waxes on the market are highly toxic yet often smell so nice that a young child may be tempted to drink them. Paste wax is also much tougher. It can be buffed to a shine many times without using more wax (and thereby hiding the wood itself) and it holds its shine much longer. Wipe the wood first with a wet sponge—dried milk will make white spots under the wax—and then wax. The petroleum solvent in the wax will clean away any other dirt as it covers the wood. We like bowling alley wax best because it's so impervious that a drink won't leave a white ring on furniture and the floor won't spot in toilet-training season.

### Floors

A child will be delighted to help you buff the floors if you skate up and down the waxed boards together wearing thick socks or pillows tied to your feet. Nothing is funnier to a Four than his mother taking a pratfall.

### Furniture

Have your Five drop a plug of wax, the size of a quarter, into cheesecloth, an old cloth diaper or a rag. The wax oozes through the cloth as your child rubs the wood, giving it a thinner coat and therefore a better shine. Have your child rub with the grain of the wood, let the wax dry for twenty minutes and then have him buff it with a dry cloth—again with the grain—until he can press the wood with his thumb without leaving a print. Buff often and wax only when finger marks can't be erased with a soft dry cloth.

### American Polish

If you want a matte finish, use a safe, homemade liquid wax. We recommend the Mediterranean Polish (see page 207), which is simply olive oil and vinegar, or this one, which has no tempting color or odor. It's a classic furniture polish found in "ye olde shoppes" at about five times the price it costs to make it. A Three with a funnel can mix it, if you give him the right amounts, but it takes a Four to apply it. Into a measuring cup

**COMBINE**
¼ c. turpentine
¼ c. vinegar
¼ c. boiled linseed oil

Pour the mixture into a jar, shake it well and rub the wax on the furniture with a soft cloth. Polish dry in twenty minutes.

# ADVENTURES

Every day you and your husband add a little more to your child's legacy, and money is the least of it.

It's the time you spend with her and the way you spend it that determine the richness of her heritage. The summer walks may seem a bother, the fishing trip too much, but they set the mood for talking—a habit once set that can never be lost.

The adventures you offer should be frequent and varied, with good planning for the special ones and spontaneity for the rest. Just as you prepare for her outings, so must she help you prepare for the family celebrations. When you let your child make a pecan pie for Thanksgiving or arrange the flowers for company dinner, you're giving her memories for a lifetime. Which is as it should be. They'll be your memories too.

---

## OUTINGS

Each day should have a focus of its own; no one wants to drift like flotsam. For you, the focus may be the digging of a garden bed or the teaching of a class—for the child, it's more likely to be an outing. Any size will do. The smallest baby will sleep better for having had a half-hour airing in the stroller.

As your child gets older, these excursions—from a ride on your bike to a camping trip—become essential and their quality will depend on you. We've found a happy outing with a child is no more accidental than a happy childhood. It takes good planning and good timing. If a mother appears casual on an outing it's because she's organized enough to feel free. Some organization is achieved through practice, but a great deal is the result of thinking a problem through before it becomes one, taking enough food and equipment to let you decide to stay where you are a little longer but not taking so much that you'll feel too burdened to leave home.

The best excursions, at any age, have a goal but the goal needn't be designed for children. If it makes you happy to go to a garage sale to look for a table, your child will be happy to see if there are any puzzles there. As long as you're willing to visit with her on an outing, rather than treat her as a tagalong, she'll have a good time.

Children also need outings with people other than mothers. Grandpas, aunties, neighbor ladies and the teenage boy down the block are good companions, but fathers are even better. Each one of our children likes to ankle around the neighborhood with her father for a chance to talk alone. The children take turns in no particular order; the child who seems to need the visit the most gets the priority.

Just as outings shouldn't be only a

mother's job, neither should they be limited to a certain time of day. Looking for the stars is as enthralling to a child as looking for morning glories.

### INFANCY TO ONE

Once the first few weeks are past, a walk is good for the soul, in almost any weather. Use a lightweight carriage or stroller so the walk won't become a chore and on cold, windy days, lay a blanket over your baby and under her too, for better insulation.

Wherever you go, you'll need to bring enough diapers, a bottle of water or formula, something for your baby to eat, a blanket on which she can nap and a damp rag for her sticky fingers.

### ONE

Although you'll use the stroller until your child is Four, she should do some of the walking herself, as soon as she can. The more she walks, the longer the outing will take and the shorter the distance will be. Two blocks is a long, long trip for a One. If you want to get somewhere with this child, the happiest way to go is by bike as long as you both wear helmets, and the best carrier for her is a plastic seat, molded so her legs will be protected from the spokes.

### TWO

Now you'll do anything to divert your Two, and if you're a full-time mother, your house will reflect it. It either will be rather tidy, because you've gone visiting friends, or quite messy, because your friends—and their small children—have been visiting you. It all depends on which mother is organized enough to get out first. You and your friends can compromise once in a while and go somewhere else together. At this age your child will want to visit a firehouse, go to a band concert or begin the first of her many trips to the library.

Along the way she'll stop to hunt and gather, picking up fist-sized pebbles which she can scrub and oil for her windowsill or bits of bark and moss for a terrarium. She'll dig for worms in the park and will like to keep a few in soil in a glass jar with a punched top, so she can see them aerate the earth. Tell your child what they're doing, for there is so much she wants to learn and she can't imagine all the questions herself unless she knows some of the answers.

### MID-TWO

A long walk works very well now, leaving her as satisfyingly tired as an hour on the jungle gym. If you take several children—and you will, for a mid-Two is a sociable creature—you can safely hustle them more across streets by stretching your fingers and having each child grasp one of them, then curling your fingers shut into a fist. You'll feel like a cow at feeding time, but safety comes first.

A mid-Two is energetic enough for an occasional, nap-free day, which permits a big adventure. You can drive to a hilly park for a short, backpacking trip, with fruit and cookies in her knapsack or tied in a bandanna on a hobo stick. If you live near brackish water we suggest crabbing—an amusing family project—or a dig for mussels, using a table knife to cut the shells loose from the reeds along the banks at low tide (and far from sewers), and if you live near the Mississippi, you can catch crawfish in the ditches in spring.

### THREE

A Three is so full of curiosity and goodness, she'll like a parade (any kind of parade), can sit through a puppet show and is eager for the weekly story hour at the library, although it may be another year before she's ready for its movies.

This child will ask you about everything—and wait for the answers. A Three wants to know the names of the stars and the streets and with your help she'll notice the architecture and the fusty housetops of the city. We've found that walks help a child observe her world better than almost anything else. She can drive through the neighborhood twenty times with you and not notice as much as she will when she walks a single block.

When you go out with your Three, take a lunch bag to hold things she wants to bring home. She's such a collector, in fact, that she needs her own museum: any shelf or cabinet that is strictly her own and too sacred to be touched by lesser people—like you. When you respect her precious bibelots, she can respect yours a little better.

### FOUR

Your Four is a powerhouse of energy. She'll splash in the water until her lips turn blue and hike until she should be too tired to crawl. When she's not using her own energy she likes to see others using theirs: the monkeys swinging at the zoo, the cyclist on the high wire, the players at the high school baseball game. She's still delighted with the freedom of the countryside and she'll find a run in the fields just right.

### FIVE

At Five, the countryside takes on a new appeal. She'll find the fields are full of a hundred wondrous kinds of weeds, good for gilding, for bleaching (see page 234) or just for investigating. We've found it isn't the collection that sharpens her wits but

the collecting. A metal detector will make a day at the beach even better, but nature usually provides enough props. Your child never will forget how many kinds of daisies she once saw on a single day, particularly if you dry them. Snapshots aren't the only way to reminisce.

A Five likes to imitate grown-ups so much, she'll be delighted to go out to dinner or shop and will think it's a lark to spend part of a workday with you or your husband at the office. In fact, she's so contained now she'll hardly bother the other people who work there. This outing has another advantage. It helps your child see how you spend your time when she's not around and she gets to see her picture and her art on display.

The best outings she takes, however, will be the ones she takes alone, running errands for you next door to the neighbor lady, and farther away too, even if you have to walk her across the street and wait discreetly within eyeshot to guide her back again. We've found a Five enjoys these adventures even more if you send her on her tricycle or her scooter. This isn't for the joy of the ride as much as the sense of importance it gives her. As everyone knows, a person of affairs must have a set of wheels.

### SIX

All children should have a purpose in whatever they do, but a Six demands one. She's a bit of a pain this way. She doesn't want to take a walk; she wants to take a walk to see the tulips in the park and she doesn't want to shop for a pair of jeans; she wants to shop for a pair of green jeans. This child will whittle her life until it fits into a neat, narrow slot, unless a good friend like you keeps her free.

She needs a variety of outings—from a fireman's carnival to the ballet—shared with a variety of people. This flexibility at home will make first grade that much easier for her.

## NEIGHBORHOODING

You might think your child deserves an adventure every day—and she does—but some of the best ones are simply the walks you take in your own neighborhood. What seems boring to you is a subtle parade of changes to a child. The rhythms of nature aren't learned so much as they're absorbed.

### COLD-WEATHER PLANS

If you're lucky enough to live in a snowy climate, take advantage of it. A One will like to sit strapped onto a sled and be pulled to the store, but a Two is ready to slide down small hills on a tray or a little sled, if the snow is well packed and it isn't too deep.

Although it takes a coordinated Eight to roller skate well, a Three can stand on ice skates and shuffle around the pond with only a few more falls than she'd have anyway (which is a lot of falls), but since it's a great adventure, there won't be many tears.

Warmth is the secret of a happy time in the snow and layers of clothes are the secret of warmth, for they trap the air. The layers must be thin, for bulky clothes will make a small wearer top heavy and clumsy and that is embarrassing. Dress her in a couple of shirts and a sweater under her jacket, two pairs of tights or thermal long johns under her overalls, boots and a pair of thick socks. She needs two pairs of mittens—the second to be given when the first pair gets wet—and a hat that covers the back of her neck.

Whenever you go on a cold-weather adventure, take warm soup and hot chocolate with you, for the air gets mighty chilly when the sun is hidden. A disposable hand warmer—available from a ski shop—helps too and take many tissues, for a runny nose on a snowy day is as inevitable as a pratfall.

### FOUL-WEATHER PLANS

A child has such a great amount of energy she needs outdoor play every day and in almost any weather. She can romp in the rain just as she does in snow, if she's well bundled and booted and doesn't have a cold. For a child, there's hardly anything that beats a parade: stamping in mud puddles, marching underneath an umbrella or beating a pot with a spoon. For you, there's hardly anything more depressing than a week of rain. Endurance becomes a game, so you might as well play it. This is the time to widen your boundaries, invite more of her friends to visit and resign yourself to big, messy projects.

When the rain is light, you can walk to the library together or try to follow the arc to the end of the rainbow. By the third bleak day a bowl of hot soup at the mall, and a good run down those wide tile aisles, will be more enticing than any pot of gold.

### NIGHT WALKS

It took our Nell to teach us that the dark is as magical to babies and first-graders as it is to other romantics, for she was the one who said she hardly could wait to trick-or-treat on Halloween.

"Daddy takes me," she said, "and a walk in the dark with my daddy is the best sort of walk there is."

Which is what won her a walk with her daddy every night since.

### OVERNIGHTING

Most parents leave their baby with friends or relatives for a weekend, to take a little vacation or to paint a room in peace, but they seldom think of it as a holiday for their child. While you won't insist on it unless it's an emergency, by Two your child may think an overnight with a good friend is one of the most exciting adventures she can have—even though she may back out at the last minute.

To be able to pack her own suitcase (diapers and all), will give your child a fine feeling of independence. It also teaches her that all mothers are not alike—or that, in some ways, they're exactly alike.

We remember one of our Fives who came home from an overnight and reported with relish, "You know Mrs. Walker? She calls her son a chowderhead too!"

There's nothing like motherhood to make a woman explode and there's nothing like an overnight to help a child accept it.

### FINDING

When you were pregnant, it seemed as though every woman you saw was pregnant too. And then when you had your baby, something mystical happened. You never saw pregnant women anymore, just other mothers with little babies. It depends on what you're looking for.

Children have their natural attractants too. With some it's feathers and some it's worms and one little boy we knew found beer can openers everywhere he went. In fact, we suspect that the Victorian custom of string saving wasn't started by its scarcity at all but by a harassed housewife who had little time, a lot of children and too much imagination ever to say, "Go out and play." When you say, "Go out and find," you help a child keep busy and curious too. String is a good place to start.

It's remarkable how much string there is in this world, just waiting to be saved: in parks, in alleys and especially near mailboxes. Help your child tie the ends together to make a growing ball of it. It will seem like money in the bank to her.

### COUNTRY RAMBLES

You may have to take a subway to get there, but every child deserves at least one tramp through the woods in the spring and in the fall—and a lot more often if you can. A country walk takes on new interest when your child is old enough to help you find moss, birds' nests and rabbit warrens in the woods and dragonflies and tadpoles in the pond or the bayou. Since you'll be doing the planning, you'll probably look for the things you like best and your child is sure to get interested in them too. You need to take a bag for whatever you collect and maybe one of the dandy Peterson field guides to help you identify trees or rocks but probably not birds, because they fly away before you can get a good look at

them. We preferred weeds and wildflowers and for this you'll need to take scissors and maybe a cake tin in case you decide to cut some. If you pick many, ask for permission first (some owners are very touchy about this), and avoid endangered species. Collect only from a field of many, cutting no more than one bloom to a stalk to assure reproduction, or take flowers from an excavation site, where they would be destroyed anyway.

Since poison ivy often is found in the

woods, bathe your child with a deodorant soap when she gets home and wash her clothes too, or the irritant will infect her skin the next time she wears them. (See Poison Ivy, page 130.)

### WEEDING

This is a beautiful adventure in late fall and easy enough for a Two and you. By this time nature has dried the reeds and grasses, pods and burrs on their stems. Break or cut them near their base, choosing as great a variety of color and shape as possible and include many of the fluffy weeds for filler to make a winter bouquet—the sort popular in colonial America.

A Three can arrange them for you, if she uses three times more weeds than you think she should, for that's the secret of this dried arrangement. Let her add city flowers too, like hydrangea that's dried on the bush. These will last for years and the memory of the walks will be so vivid your child can tell you where she picked each one.

### Bleaching Weeds

A Three can bleach some weeds for you, which gives more variety in color and still keeps to a monochromatic scheme.

**COMBINE**      1 qt. water
                 2 tbsp. bleach

Dip the heads into the solution for several minutes—until their colors change. Dry on newspaper.

### Gilding Grasses

When you get home from weeding, have your Four spray some dry reeds and grasses with gilt—a few at a time, outdoors and in a box to contain the mist. This should be done lightly, since a complete gilding looks gaudy, and arranged with only a few in a vase for a Japanese effect. Large branches, like dried brown magnolia, look elegant with this dusting of gold, although your child might not think so unless you tell her.

### WILDFLOWERING

The wonder of the woods will stay with you longer if you keep some of the flowers in a bouquet (see pages 312–16). Most wildflowers wilt within an hour of picking, but some hardy ones like Queen Anne's lace, black-eyed Susans, ox-eyed daisies and the beautiful blue chicory are sturdy enough for handling and plentiful enough to pick.

If you're planning to pick flowers on a walk, take a cake tin with a tight lid or a self-sealing plastic bag, either of which will keep the flowers alive for several days. However, if you're just going to pick flowers in a field near your car, take a bucket of wet sand and have your Five stick the stems in it to keep the flowers fresh until you get home. Once there, put the flowers in a glass.

**ADD**          2″ very warm water

Let them revive in a dark, damp place (under the sink is fine) and then either show your child how to press them in a book (see page 313), dry them in the delicate silica gel method (see page 314) or arrange them in a vase (see page 261). In a vase

**ADD**          water
                 1 quick squirt detergent

You can use soap, too, including bar soap. Stir until the water clouds, then add the flowers. Change the solution every three days.

### Transplanting Wildflowers

You can move wildflowers to your own garden if you have permission from the owner; if you're sure they're not endangered; if you leave many of the same species; if you take a jar of water along and some small self-sealing plastic bags, and if you use considerable care.

Very small plants will suffer less shock than large ones, for transplanting plants is as difficult as transplanting people. Still, a Five can do all the steps.

Have her draw a circle in the dirt with her finger about 2″ around each plant she wants and then dig straight down with a spoon to catch all the roots. Pack each plant in its own bag, with as much of the soil as possible. Add a little water and seal it shut.

Choose a place in your yard where the plants will have about the same amount of sun that they had back home. Have your child dig a hole for each plant—the size that she dug in the woods—and fill it twice with water. A plant goes in each hole with its own dirt around the roots. She should press the soil firmly to hold the plant upright and eliminate air bubbles and then water again. Probably only 50 percent of these plants will live, which isn't a bad lesson for a child to learn.

### ROCK HUNTING

Maybe it's because a Two is so close to the ground, but she always wants to pick up anything she sees—especially rocks. She'll find that some are sharp like coral and slate, some are round and smooth like pebbles and others are crumbly like sandstone, and once in a long time she may find one with a fossilized print of leaves or bugs or tiny creatures from the sea. With your help, it won't be long before she can sort the metamorphic rocks, like marble, which were formed by pressure, from the igneous rocks, made by a spewing volcano, and the sedimentary rocks that come, of course, from sediment. If your child is going to have a rock collection (and they all do), she may as well know what she's talking about.

### BERRY PICKING

"Doubtless God could have made a better berry, but doubtless God never did," said William Butler, the sixteenth-century poet.

We think every child should pick fruit (or vegetables) at least one time in her young life and, though you may have an affinity for raspberries, Mr. Butler's strawberries are much easier to pick, for they are ground level, very obvious, and have no thorns.

We've found berry picking is hot, dusty and unforgettable. Every summer for the rest of her life your child will conjure the smell of berries ripening in their beds of straw.

To offer this adventure, find a farmer who shares his crop on a pick-and-pay basis and go early in the day, when it's not so hot, and early in the season, when the fruit is best. Don't, however, go the day after a rain, for rain diminishes the flavor and texture of berries, if you make strawberry preserves.

A pre-Three should wear a shirt and hat and use sun screen, since the sun is strong in an open field, and she should at least arrive in a stroller, to mollify the farmer. Take shallow, lightweight pans, lunch, juice and a picture book. The flat pans—one for you and one for her—should have handles and be no deeper than 4″ or the weight of the berries on the top layers will mash the lower layers. Line them with paper towels before leaving home, to protect the fruit from bruises. Your child will enjoy the book and the treats in the shade when she's tired.

Before starting, teach your child how to pick the berries. They are ripe when the color is deep red and the stems break easily from the hulls. The smaller ones are generally more flavorful, although you can expect her to pick the biggest, fattest berries she can find. Pick the less vivid ones yourself, for underripe fruit contains more pectin and this is what you need for jam.

We've seen a One sit quietly for a half-hour between the rows, picking berries with great care—and eating most of them. A Two and especially a Three will put most of the berries in the pan but she won't last longer than a half-hour either. A Six can pick for twice that long and any child is content to amble through the rows for perhaps two hours if she has stopped for lunch. This is long enough for you to pick about ten pounds—as much as you can preserve without wishing you'd never gone at all.

Once home (and these farms always seem to be at least an hour from home, no matter where you live), both you and your child will need a fat nap before making the preserves.

### Strawberry Preserves

This experience will be as fresh to your child as the berries themselves. Your Two can help you hull the berries and your Six can cut out most of the soft spots, although you must remind any child to touch this fruit very gently. Don't expect her to have the patience to help you make more than one batch, however. Four cups of berries are best, although we like to work on such a grand scale that we double it.

## FREEZER JAM

YIELD: 4 8–oz. jars

This puddly jam is perfect for a rambunctious Four to make, because it needs some active chopping but no cooking at all, and it's the perfect gift to give in winter, because it tastes so much like summer. In a large bowl

**CHOP**     4 c. strawberries, hulled and
                  cleaned

Your child can crunch them with a potato masher so the berries are in small pieces—but not crushed—or she can process them, very quickly, with you standing by. Pour the berries and juice into a bowl. In a measuring cup

**COMBINE**   ¼ c. sugar
                  1 (1¾ oz.) pkg. pectin

Mix well and add to the berries.

**WAIT**     30 minutes

Into the bowl

**ADD**      2 c. sugar

Have your child stir this in slowly, and then stir and stir, until the sugar dissolves—about 5 minutes. Fill clean

jars almost to the top—a job for you—clean the rims and tighten the lids. Let the jars stay on the counter for a day and a night, then transfer them to the freezer, but refrigerate them once they're opened.

## OLD-FASHIONED PRESERVES

To cook these preserves, you'll need a pot three times higher than its contents, to prevent any hot syrup from splashing over the brim, and to bottle it, you'll either need jars with caps and rings or glasses with paraffin. In a colander have your child

**WASH AND HULL**   8 c. berries

Drain. Pick them over yourself, cut out any bruises and put the berries in a big bowl. In a large pot

**BOIL**          6 c. water

Pour enough boiling water to cover the berries (your job) and let them sit in this bath for two minutes, to cook them slightly. Drain—again your job—and put the berries in the cooking pot. Into it

**STIR**          4 c. sugar
                  1 tsp. lemon juice

**BOIL**          15 minutes

Stir occasionally.

**ADD**           4 c. sugar

Stir again. Although the syrup is hot now, a child can do this, if the pot is tall enough to be safe, she uses a long wooden spoon and she stands next to you on a kitchen chair.

**BOIL**          5 minutes

You needn't skim the fluffy scum, since it will stick to the high sides. To test for readiness, dip the spoon into the pot, cool it momentarily and let the syrup drip back into the pot from the side of the spoon, a step too dangerous for a child, we think. Show him how the syrup falls from the spoon into points like a *W*. If you stop now, the berries will float in a soft jelly, but if you cook it a few minutes longer the jelly will reach the thicker sheeting stage of 220° and the two drops will marry into one, like a *V*. This gives a firmer base—a decision your child will want to make for herself.

Now you're ready for Open Kettle Canning.

## OPEN KETTLE CANNING

If you let your child can a few jars of preserves, her pride will be great, but it will be even greater if you use 4-ounce jars or large baby food jars instead of the standard half pints. There will be twice as many.

Canning isn't as complicated as the cookbooks describe, particularly if you preserve jams or pickles or chutneys, which have a high acid content. Mold will be your big enemy and this is controlled if the jars are sealed well.

This is what you need:

flat rack
roaster with cover
jars OR jelly glasses
metal rings
lids OR paraffin
tongs
dull knife
ladle
large wooden spoon
many potholders

Lay the flat rack in the roaster and add the jars, upside down, with the metal rings and the lids (if you are using them), the tongs, the knife and the ladle tossed between them.

**ADD**            5″ water

Cover. Bring to a boil.

**BOIL**           20 minutes

Leave the top on the pan until you're ready to ladle the preserves into the jars, which your child can do with you if the preserves and the jars are cool—and you don't mind the mess. If you're using the old-fashioned rubber rings or the lids with rubber rings pasted in them (the prettiest kind), put them in a saucepan and pour boiling water over them 20 minutes before filling the jars.

Spoon the preserves into the jars almost to the top and have your child jockey the knife up and down to eliminate air pockets. Wipe any drippings from the threads of the jars and either cap them tightly or pour melted paraffin into them to form a seal—a job for you.

Scrub the outside of the jars—the glass usually clouds when boiled—so the fruit inside will look beautiful. Refrigerate the jars sealed with wax, but you're supposed to put any others on a dark shelf to save the flavor. Personally, we'd rather keep them in the middle of the kitchen table where everyone can see them. So would a child.

## SUPER OUTINGS

No matter where you live, you mustn't let your neighborhood dictate the way you live; in fact, it should do just the opposite. A child needs one zingy adventure a week in a completely different environment, whether it's walking the busy city streets or sitting on a riverbank.

Although a child has short staying power, she'll want to visit the places that interest you—for just a little while. Let her investigate the monuments and fountains, the courthouse and city hall, the art galleries and the theater (see pages 197, 203).

She also needs to see the wild animals at the zoo, the silly chickens in a barnyard and the galloping horses at the circus, just as she needs to see the rabbits and the birds in the woods, the frogs in the ponds and the seashells on the beach. It may take a thousand questions, but this is the way a child learns how animals eat and where they sleep and why they look the way they do. It isn't that your child will learn so much but every exposure will make her curious to learn more.

### THE BEACH

It's the planning that determines the success or failure of an outing with a child, especially a trip to the beach. You don't want to burden yourselves with extra baggage, yet your day can be spoiled if you forget vital clothes or the right food or drink. The wind and water, the glare and sunshine, encourage extra hunger and thirst, and always, we're sure, more bowel movements for the child in diapers. It must be something about the air.

You'll need more diapers than usual, more towels, and more to eat and drink too, but not caffeinated sodas and sugary snacks, which can make a child cranky. Your child will need:

    beach blanket
    towels
    disposable diapers
    tennis shoes
    bathing suit
    child's hat/shirt
    extra outfit
    sweater OR
        sweatshirt
    life jacket
    Wind Screen OR
        umbrella
    ball/pail/shovel
    suncreen/zinc oxide
    food/drink

Your child will need to drink much more water and juice to prevent dehydration, but she won't need as many toys as you think. The bucket and shovel are usually enough, and if your child is at the ocean, she'll soon use a seashell instead of a shovel.

While toys aren't so important, a life jacket can be critical. Having gone through a desperate hour when an Eight and a Nine were swept away in a riptide (good swimmers though they were), we strongly recommend that your child wear a life jacket in the ocean and indeed in any water except perhaps a swimming pool. It's such an easy precaution to take and it's a good way to remind your child that she must respect the water.

Although you can see the vivid jacket at a distance, she may not be wearing it when she plays on the beach. Since all patches of sand look the same to a child, it's mighty easy for her to wander away, but you can find her quickly if her bathing suit is brightly colored too. The tennis

shoes protect her feet against hot sand or a rocky shore; the sweater or sweatshirt against sudden winds, and a hat and a shirt protect her skin when she's playing on the beach and maybe even in the water if she's already had enough sun. This is easy to remember when the sun is dazzlingly reflected by white sand or water, but an overcast sky and soft breezes are just as dangerous.

A baby under six months can be in a playpen shaded by an umbrella or the Wind Screen (see below), but she can't have any direct sun at all. After six months, she can be in the sun more and more, particularly if her skin is dark or olive, but even then she should stay out of the intense sun between 10 A.M. and 2 P.M., and periodically sit in the shade the rest of the time. Above all, she should be covered with a broad-spectrum hypoallergenic, waterproof sunscreen with a rating of at least 15. Give her this rubdown several times a day and after she's been in the water for a while, even if she has a tan or if the day is cloudy. Neither tan nor clouds can block cancer-causing ultraviolet rays.

A very tanned and tough-skinned Four—the sort who spends weeks at a time at the beach—can usually skip the extra clothes, but she'll still need sunscreen and maybe even some zinc oxide on her nose if it looks pink. Tell her she looks like the lifeguard.

If your child does get a sunburn, put her in the shade and rub her quickly with cool water from the picnic chest—the best treatment for all burns—or cover her with a towel dipped in cool fresh water. One of the best treatments—a towel dipped in a 50-50 solution of vinegar and water—may have to wait until you get home, unless you pessimistically packed the vinegar. If you're going to the ocean, that's not a bad idea.

### Wind Screen

This piece of equipment is sometimes better than an umbrella, easy for an adult to make and considered a necessity on the Riviera—so it's said.

| **ASSEMBLE** | 3 yds. 45″ sturdy cloth |
|---|---|
| | four 4′ dowels, 1½″ thick |

Any heavy, closely woven fabric, like canvas or vinyl, is fine, but the dowels must be at least a foot longer than the width of the material and sharpened with a hatchet at one end to stick into the sand.

| **SEW** | four ¾″ tucks |
|---|---|

Do this across the width of the fabric, making one tuck at each end and the other two at one-yard intervals to form equidistant pockets for the dowels. Midway on one side of the screen

| **SEW** | 36″ grosgrain ribbon |
|---|---|

This should be done in the center of the ribbon only, but go back and forth several times with a small machine stitch, so it will be strong. Roll your supplies in the blanket and lay this bundle in the Wind Screen. To carry the screen, roll it like a sausage, securing it with the ribbon. It will easily fit under one arm.

When you get to the beach, jam the pointed ends of the dowels into the sand to form a wall to break the wind. Unless it's high noon, the screen will cast enough shade to protect your child and you too.

### Marine Lab

Show-and-tell, the thrill of any preschool, becomes more marvelous to the Five who has something notable to show. This lab is one of the best—or the worst—ideas, depending on the squeamishness of your child, since to make it she must drop live insects or small sea creatures into denatured alcohol. Although death is instantaneous and painless, you'll want to offer this experiment with discretion. To carry the alcohol, use a wide-mouthed jar with a tight lid. Into it

| **ADD** | fly/grasshopper/beetle |
|---|---|
| | sand crab/jellyfish |

Your child—and all her classmates—can observe the specimens through the jar, with a magnifying glass to examine them from all angles.

### Wall Hanging

One of the loveliest wall hangings we've seen was made by a Four at the seaside, because her mother had been organized enough to take the patch plaster for a vacation. If you do take it, have your child

| **GATHER** | rocks/shells/crab claws |
|---|---|
| | leaves/grasses/reeds |

Into her bucket she should

| **STIR** | 3 cupped handfuls patch plaster |
|---|---|
| | 1 cupped handful sand |
| | 3 cupped handfuls sea water |

She should add more water if it isn't soupy enough and more plaster if it's too wet. Have her pour it into three paper plates and then arrange the shells and grasses into a collage, after waiting a few minutes so they don't sink through the plaster. Over each plate

| **SPRINKLE** | 1 handful sand |
|---|---|

Peel the plate from the plaster when it's dry, shake the extra sand loose and paste a picture hook on the back to hang it on the wall or simply prop it in the back of the bookcase.

### CRABBING

This is a sport that suits our small talents better than fishing and it seems to suit our

children too, perhaps because it gets so raucous. There's just one drawback: you can crab only in brackish water.

The investment required is quite small—but then so is the catch. Keep only those crabs that are five inches across the shell—the legal limit—and expect more silliness than supper.

You can also expect your child to be bitten at least once (for crabs are craftier than children), for which you only can give sympathy. She probably will fall in the water too, a good reason to wear the life jacket. This is what you need:

crab net or box trap
line
sinkers
bait
knife
life jacket
tall basket

Plan to crab from a pier or a riverbank, in brackish water, preferably around a channel and when the tides are changing. A Two can operate a trap, a Three can manipulate a line, a Four thinks she can net a crab, a Five sometimes can and a Six can do both jobs at once. When using a crab net, cut several lines for each person, long enough for the string to reach bottom when weighted with a sinker or a rock. Tie the bait—such as a chicken neck or some fatback—just above the sinker and tie the lines at intervals to the pilings or to small sticks that you jam in the sand. Reel in the lines often, using both hands. Do this gently and quickly, with the net held just below the water to swoop beneath any crab that might be hanging on. We think it's best if a parent holds the net and a child

pulls in the line. It's a wacky way to teach cooperation and you'll catch more crabs too.

If you use a box trap, tie the sinker and the bait in the middle of it and drop the trap until the line is slack, the sign that the four sides of this box have fallen flat on the sand for the crabs to walk inside (for crabs are more greedy than crafty). Once the line is jerked taut, the sides flip back into place and capture the crab—all principles of crabbing that a child must understand if you want her to do it well.

Keep any crabs in the basket, without water and lightly covered from the sun. They take about ten minutes to cook in a covered pot of boiling water. A Four can season as you would for Boiled Shrimp (see page 350), but transfer the crabs yourself, using long-handled tongs to grab each one from the rear. Still, you can expect at least one crab to escape for an unforgettable chase in the kitchen. Your child will like that very much. You can tell by the way she screams.

### FISHING

As soon as your Four finds that someone has invented fishing, she'll want to try it. No matter how little she knows about it, in her mind fishing is the sport of kings.

It took a handsome grandfather to teach us how to make it the sport of small children too, instead of the disappointment it so often is. Our gentleman friend, a perfectionist like all good fishermen, feels you need to do some fishing yourself before you try to teach its techniques, while we belong to the "let's bumble along together" school. Whether you practice first or not, this outing needs some preparation with your child, even if you're an expert.

She will want to know the names of the fish she might catch, and she also should know about the innate courtesy anglers have for each other—speaking quietly so the fish aren't frightened from your hook (and from theirs) and even showing courtesy to the fish, tossing back any that are too small to eat.

In fairness to your child you'll want to tell her that fishing at times will be uncomfortable and boring and tiring and, truth to tell, it may be unsuccessful too. This not only won't daunt her, she'll still plan a fish fry for the whole preschool.

In fairness to yourself, you should know that when a parent and a child go fishing, the child fishes—and the parent explains, untangles and pours juice, with little time to drop a line. Some outings, like adult fishing, are simply not made for children, which is why you leave your Four at home when you really want to fish. Apartness has its place.

The equipment you use when you fish together should be simple and the same for both of you. If you bring a fly rod, your child will want to cast it and since it's too complicated for her to handle, it becomes a weapon. This is what you need:

| | |
|---|---|
| metal tackle box | knife |
| 2 bamboo poles | nail clipper |
| line | screwdriver |
| several sinkers | first-aid kit |
| several bobbers | life jacket |
| several leaders | juice and snack |
| assortment of hooks | bait |
| 5′ stringer | |

The night before you go, spread your equipment about the living room and show her how it works, rather than waiting until you reach the water, for it will be hard for her to learn in the midst of such excitement. With your child's help, thread the poles with the bobber midway on the line, to be adjusted as you fish to suit the depth of the water. Tie the hook on the end to the leader—the wire that makes it easier to change hooks and keeps the line less snarled. The sinker is just above it, to hold the bait deep in the water. Your child should be told the reasons for everything, although they seem obvious to you. When you're finished, wrap the line around the pole, stick the hook into the bobber for safety and let her stow the extra supplies in the tackle box.

## FISH FARMING

Not all fishermen follow the classic rules nor do all fish eat the same food. Ben, a mid-Two, caught a bucketful of fish at a well-stocked fish farm in Georgia, and he did it with just the bamboo pole his auntie had rented and the bait she bought at the farm—marshmallows dipped in sugar. Who would have guessed that trout have sweet teeth?

You need the stringer to keep all the fish you catch and the knife, the screwdriver and the nail clipper to remove them from the hook and to cut new line—a regular duty when you fish with a child, for she tangles it often. We find it's better to throw away a few pennies' worth of string than have a child dance around while we spend a half-hour untangling her line.

In this modern age, worms are still the best bait, for a child can slide them onto the hook easily and they stay in place better than meat or dead insects. If possible, help your child dig the worms before you leave, for she'll think it's a lark, but you may need to buy some too, for you should have at least two dozen.

Fish seem to bite best on a clear day and since it probably will be sunny, have your child wear a hat and sun screen. She needs a life jacket too, whether you fish from land or from a boat. It's one less thing to worry about.

We prefer the dock or the shoreline for a novice fisherman, choosing a place with few reeds or logs to tangle the line. An older, more experienced child can fish from a boat, but only if you know the currents, the channels and the day's weather report.

To bait the hook, thread it through the worm, hiding the point within it. Drop the line over the edge, keep quite still and talk, if you can, in whispers. When fish begin to nibble, the bobber starts jiggling. Wait until the fish takes a few big bites (which you can see by the way the cork plunges), then pull the pole sharply and quickly upward, so the hook becomes imbedded in the fish's mouth. This single, sudden action, successful or not, is so exciting to a child it will make the waiting worthwhile.

Take the fish off the hook for her, for she may scratch herself trying, but let her run one end of the stringer through its gills. You can tie the other end to the oar lock and then let her throw the fish into the water to keep it alive, because the freshest fish always taste best.

To be realistic, you probably won't catch enough fish for the preschool—or for dinner—but you'll know the pleasure of a quiet, lazy day when whispers bring secrets to life.

### THE CIRCUS

If you take your own flock and their friends to see the clowns every year, you learn a lot about children and circuses.

Children find the circus is a great adventure but a scary one. This is one time when food is a good diversion. We brought enough to give a treat before every high-wire act, when they might be frightened. You'll need a wet washcloth to wipe sticky hands, and for each child take:

    roasted peanuts
    popcorn
    candied apple
    peanut butter and jelly
        sandwich
    soda

Although some of this is available at a circus, the cost is prohibitive and the hawkers are never there when you need them. Save the soda as long as possible, and if you must take your child to the bathroom, go in the middle of an act. At intermission the bathroom is like the fourth ring of a three-ring circus.

When you take five children or more, you can expect at least one to wander. For this we recommend a helium balloon—their only treat—tied to the wrist, or have them wear vivid hats or sweaters so you can follow them more easily.

### CAMPING

Camping gives you time to hike and fish, find rocks and wildflowers and generally fall in love with nature again, for all you have to do is simply eat and sleep.

There are as many styles of camping as there are styles of living, and it can be as encumbered or as free as you wish. Some campgrounds are for tenting; some have close-packed spaces for RVs only, and with all the amenities of home; some have cabins and even prepare the meals for you and some have a little of each.

We tend to go tenting, relying on our old station wagon, a top carrier to hold the gear on the roof and few fancies. You can find much of the equipment you'll need in your kitchen, and you may be able to borrow a good deal of the rest in the beginning. Avoid extensive purchases until you know if you like camping and, if you do, what camp style you like best.

A camping trip, we found, is a pleasure if everyone helps, but a bore to anyone, including a young child, if she must watch others work and has nothing to do herself. Since we find it hard to assign jobs when we're busy setting up camp, we plan the work before leaving home, by sorting and organizing the paraphernalia on the living room floor. You'll find this is a good time to teach your Five the square knot—an invaluable lesson—and to show your Two how to zip and unzip the screen door of the tent. Otherwise, you'll have a tentful of mosquitoes. This is what you need:

tent, with floor
plastic tarp OR ground sheet
nylon rope
sleeping bags/firm rubber pads
campfire blanket
towels/washcloths/dish towels
packaged premoistened towels
changes of clothing
toothbrushes/toothpaste
liquid/laundry/bar soap
insect repellent/sunscreen
first-aid kit
life jackets/compass
hatchet
large flashlight/lantern/candles
cold chest
propane gas stove/matches
skillet/saucepan with lid
oven rack
long-handled fork/spatula
sharp knife
can opener/corkscrew
canteens
large water jug
paper plates/plastic flatware
large plastic bowl
self-sealing plastic bags
plastic trash bags
aluminum foil
food/wine/marshmallows
salt/pepper/condiments/herbs
collapsible fishing pole
cards/Frisbee/ harmonica
magnifying glass/binoculars

If camping with an infant, you also will need a portable crib or playpen, a collapsible stroller or sling and the same necessities outlined in Travel (see page 139).

An older child will need sturdy shoes, rubber boots for wet ground, a sweatshirt with a hood (for the nights and early mornings can be chilly), enough clothes to last through the stay, a friendly toy and the canteen, both for hikes and for that midnight drink of water.

She also should have the fishing pole and the life jacket if you think you may camp near a stream.

The tarp is to lay over the tent floor to keep rain or dew from creeping up from the ground. We bought the waterproof, torso-length foam-rubber pads only for the adults since a child accepts the hard ground as her lot in life.

The insect repellent should be the one sold at camping stores—a cream that doesn't burn the skin or the eyes.

You can mix food in the plastic bags and wash dishes in the bowl. By taking the oven rack, you can cook more food over the wood fire—a sensational taste. Since it's harder to prepare meals when you camp, you should serve the most satisfying foods—the best breads and natural cheeses, the freshest of roadside fruits and vegetables and eggs. Because of the space shortage, you'll need to buy perishables every few days but you can carry the dried foods, like soup and pancake mix.

We also recommend taking Banana Cookies, Homemade Biscuit Mix and Spanish Granola, all from our Cooking section, for camping seems to call for the heartiness of natural foods. It also calls for a sense of festivity—hence, the wine.

### At the Camp Site

After making an initial one-night trip—to see if we actually could do it—we made many trips, lasting from two days to two weeks.

This experience taught us that it's easiest to stay two nights in the same place and to choose a secluded campsite, so our children didn't disturb other campers—nor they disturb us. We found most campsites sell dry wood, many have laundry facilities, all have trees to hang the clothesline and many are close enough to town for you to find a supermarket and a laundromat.

### Pitching the Tent

To give you an idea of your child's capabilities, a Two can be in charge of the tent stakes, unpacking them and handing them over one at a time. A Three can lay out the tent poles, a Four can fit them together, a Five can help to pitch the tent and a Six can bang a few stakes in place, if the ground isn't too hard.

Once the tent is pitched and the tarp is laid, decide where each person will sleep, lay the bedrolls in place and hang the flashlight. This gives a child great comfort for as soon as this is done, the tent becomes her home.

### Cooking and Fire Building

Whatever you do during the day, return to base at least three hours before dark. This will give you time to prepare dinner (for everyone is much hungrier, much earlier than usual) and it will give you time to wash dishes, brush teeth and build the campfire before dark.

When you camp, almost all the work involves cooking the meals or cleaning up after them. With more than one child, we find we must alternate the jobs for everyone wants to pour water from the big, squeezable jug and no one wants to gather the sticks. The cooking is done on the propane stove, which your Five will like to pump, although she can do only a few strokes.

Everything you cook at camp has its own touch of glamour and dinner is the focus of the day. If it's too simple or if your child has nothing to do, she'll be bored. We find there's bound to be some dish a child can prepare, whether it's Grilled Corn or Bean Salad, so long as you use the same safety precautions that you

do at home. As for yourself, you can cook almost anything at camp that you can at home, depending on your spirit.

Before dinner, your child can begin to lay the fire. A proper fire has the most inflammable material at the bottom with drafts to fan the wind. A Four is ready to assemble the paper in the center, with a pyramid of small sticks over this heap and a bigger one of larger kindling over it all. After you've lighted the fire and it's caught well, lay the logs—an adult's job. Before dark, have your child find green sticks on which to roast the marshmallows.

The prize of our day comes when we lie on the blanket with our children to

watch the falling stars and point out the constellations with a flashlight.

### Problems

For us, getting to sleep is no trouble in the brisk, outdoor air, but getting up in the morning is difficult. The ground is wet with dew, the bed is warm and it may be a long walk to the bathroom or, if you're a more primitive camper, the slit trench. If you think your child would be embarrassed to walk around in pajamas, let her sleep in her clothes. It may be that—or a wet sleeping bag.

Water, in one way or another, is the menace of every camper. Children splash in ponds, sleeping bags get damp, rain drips in the stew and the best of tents will leak a little in a downpour. That's all part of the Great Adventure.

If you find you must cook in a slight rain, you can cover the area by throwing the tarp over the clothesline and tying each corner to a tree. When water comes in the tent in a storm, we recommend towels bunched to absorb it and a meal in town while the clothes and the sleeping bags are in the laundromat dryer. The treat is almost worth it.

### Pulling Up Stakes

When you leave your campsite, take one last patrol to make sure the fire is out and to pick up any litter so the area will be ready for the next lucky family.

## SHISHKABOB

SERVES 6

This recipe is one of the most adventurous ones a Four can cook, for it gives her a dozen important jobs. Have her make the marinade at home, but she'll soak and cook the meat at the campsite. You also may want to buy the meat before you leave home if you're cooking it the first day. In a plastic bag

| PACK | 1½ lbs. lamb or beef cubes |
| --- | --- |
| | 2 green peppers |
| | 4 yellow onions |

Use a jar to make the marinade. In it

| COMBINE | ⅓ c. salad oil |
| --- | --- |
| | 3 tbsp. soy sauce |
| | 3 tbsp. vinegar |
| | 3 garlic cloves, minced |
| | 1½ tsp. sugar |
| | ¼ tsp. pepper |
| | ¼ tsp. steak sauce |

At the campsite, remove the green peppers and onions and add the marinade to the bag of beef. If you do this after lunch, the meat will be tenderized by dinner but do hang the bag from a branch so the animals can't reach it. In the meantime, have your child

| COLLECT | four 2' sticks, ¼" in diameter |
| --- | --- |

Whittle one end of each stick (your job) for your child to thread the ingredients more easily. Soak the sticks briefly in water (her job), so they won't burn. On these skewers

| ALTERNATE | meat cubes |
| --- | --- |
| | green peppers, seeded and cut in eighths |
| | onions, peeled and quartered |
| ROAST | 20 minutes |

Turn to brown on all sides. The onions can also be cooked separately, sealed in a package of foil with 3

tablespoons of butter and laid over the coals. Shishkabob is served with rice, cooked on the propane stove.

## BANNOCK

SERVES 6

If you take Homemade Biscuit Mix (see page 356) with you, your Six can make this bread on a stick for dinner. Have her find 6 straight green sticks 1" thick and 2' long. Sharpen one end of each stick yourself as a stake to drive into the ground. In a plastic bag

| MIX | 2 c. Homemade Biscuit Mix |
| --- | --- |
| | ½ c. water |

Have your child knead the dough in the bag 20 times, adding a little more mix if it's too sticky. Divide the dough into 6 pieces and snake one around each stick, near the top. When the coals glow, poke the pointed ends deep in the ground at an angle over the fire. Slowly turn the sticks twice so the dough will brown evenly on all sides in about 15 minutes.

## CAMPFIRE BEANS

SERVES 8

Sometimes campfire dinners need all the help they can get. In a saucepan have your Four

| MIX | two 30-oz. cans pork and beans |
| --- | --- |
| | one 10½-oz. can tomato soup |
| | 1½ tbsp. dried minced onion |
| | 1 tsp. instant coffee |
| SIMMER | 10 minutes |

Do the small amount of stirring yourself, since a camp stove is not so steady.

## POTATOES IN MUD

This is a great project if you have time, a fire, a shovel and a Three. Dig thick mud or have your child make it with dirt and water—enough to cover medium-sized potatoes with a ½" layer of it. Into a fire of hot coals

| DROP | mud-covered potatoes |
| --- | --- |
| BAKE | 1 hour |

Turn them with a stick midway. The mud will get darker in some spots as it bakes as hard as a clay pot and you'll be amazed to find it leaves only a trace of dust on the skin when your child breaks them open.

## GRILLED CORN

Try this recipe only with fresh-cut ears of corn, still in their husks. Drop the ears in a bucket of water.

| SOAK | 15 minutes |
|---|---|

The rest of the jobs are yours, although a Two will feel she's completely responsible. Lay the corn over gray coals.

| GRILL | 20–30 minutes |
|---|---|

The bigger the ears and the wetter the husks, the longer they'll take to cook. Turn the ears every 10 minutes and, when tender, peel back the hot silk and husks.

| ADD | salt |
|---|---|
| | butter |

The taste is terrific.

## BROWN BEAN SALAD

SERVES 6

You may think this recipe has odd ingredients to take on a camping trip, but living in the woods is no reason to eat dull food. Let your Five

| STIR | one 21-oz. can kidney beans, drained |
|---|---|
| | 1 green onion, chopped |
| | 2 tsp. oil |
| | 1 tsp. vinegar |
| | 1 tsp. cumin |
| | ¼ tsp. salt |
| | ¼ tsp. garlic salt |
| | dash pepper |
| ADD | 2 tbsp. chopped parsley |

## GRILLED CINNAMON APPLES

SERVES 4

It takes a Six to count as high as this recipe requires and it will take her a satisfyingly long time to do it. You can use ripe pears instead of apples and in either case,

the dessert will be fresh, pink and bubbly. Have your child

| CORE, QUARTER | 4 apples |
|---|---|

On 24″ heavy-duty foil

| LAY | apple quarters |
|---|---|

Over them

| SPRINKLE | 150 cinnamon candies |
|---|---|
| | 2 tbsp. butter |

Fold shut and seal by folding the edges together. Lay the foil package on the grill over a smoldering fire.

| ROAST | 30 minutes |
|---|---|

### BACKPACKING

Backpacking, far more adventuresome than camping, is a long, long hike, with at least one night spent outdoors and every person carrying her share. That's why a child who backpacks either must be a steady walker—generally no younger than Four—or an infant you carry in a sling.

Even so, it's only practical to backpack with an infant if your baby is breast-fed and if you can distribute your load of food and equipment between at least two other adults, for only the most experienced backpacker can handle more than a forty-pound load and you have the baby to carry.

To prepare an older child for backpacking, you must help her get into condition, preferably starting as early as mid-One when you put away the stroller and have her walk whenever you have the time and she has the energy. This helps a child develop the muscles and stamina she will need. A good walker is ready for a one-mile hike at Two, but she should wear rugged boots and carry her lunch in a small knapsack on her back.

When you can hike so long you have to stop and cook a simple meal, your child should have small jobs to do, as she would in camping. By Four she also must be responsible for more equipment, carrying her own fork, spoon, plate, cup and canteen in her gear.

By the time your child can walk five miles without any bellyaching, your family is ready to start backpacking together.

It seems to take as much precise planning and preparation as the coronation of a king. You can backpack in national forests, national parks and some state parks, all of which have maps of their trails showing the terrain, the sources of water and where you can build a fire and pitch a tent. These maps are found at the information centers in the national and state parks, but to backpack in the wilder, less-crowded national forests, write the United States Geological Survey, Map Distribution Office, 507 National Center, Reston, VA 22092. They'll send you an index of the state where you want to hike so you can send money for the right map. You can also contact the state park service—or the National Park Service—to reserve cabin space at a state or national park if you don't want to camp outdoors.

It's best to choose a trail that brings you back to your starting point, so you can return easily to your car, and one where you can camp near a spring or lake, so you won't have to carry water too far. (Water from a spring is always drinkable, but chlorine tablets will make any water safe.) You'll want to avoid areas with steep climbing—not because your child can't climb up, but because it's hard for her to climb down—and you definitely want to leave the trail at least as clean as you found it.

### ADULT'S BACKPACK

This is what you need for backpacking. You can borrow many of these items until you set your own priorities, but get the lightest things you can find.

| | |
|---|---|
| backpack | large plastic trash bag |
| 2-person tent | pliers |
| plastic sheet OR tarp | flashlight |
| sleeping bags | map/compass |
| canteen | first aid kit |
| stove | toothpaste/brushes |
| wineskin OR | soap |
|   collapsible plastic | insect repellent |
|   jug | sunscreen |
| aluminum pot | chlorine tablets |
| aluminum skillet/lid | raincoats |
| paper plates/cups | bandannas |
| flatware/sharp knife | matches |
| small plastic jars | toilet paper |
| nylon rope | dried foods |

Since the gas is in your feet when you backpack, you must have shoes that fit well and either cotton or wool socks, thick enough to be absorbent. A two-person tent is big enough for parents and a pre-Six, if all the gear is stored outdoors. True backpackers tell us that the pliers have many uses, especially for picking up live coals when you make an oven to bake

### CHILD'S BACKPACK

Backpacking, like nothing else we know, forces your child to decide what is essential in life—the big, old teddy bear or the scraggly old blanket. After she's carried one heavy pack, she'll be glad to lighten her load.

| | |
|---|---|
| diamond-shaped | 2 pairs of socks |
|   backpack | sneakers |
| sleeping bag | toothbrush |
| raincoat | cup/spoon/plate/ |
| 1 change of clothes |   canteen |

bread. The bandannas will be your pot-holders, scarves, dishtowels and wash-cloths, for they are much lighter than ter-rycloth, and the plastic jars will hold food from home like honey or jam.

Backpackers follow the same proce-dures for setting up as campers do, but since they have no ice chest, all food is hung in the big plastic bag on the nylon line (too high for raccoons to reach). Also, if there's no portable toilet nearby—and there usually isn't on these rugged trails—you'll need to dig a small hole with a stick for potting, at a respectable distance from camp.

### Cooking

All the food you carry should be put in plastic self-sealing bags with the finer ones in double bags. Carry powdered milk, dried vegetables, potato flakes or lentils, dried soups, fruits, some onion and garlic flakes and spices, as well as packages of powdered drinks like lemonade and mar-garine in plastic tubs, since they don't leak.

For protein, carry canned fish or sau-sage that needs no refrigeration. Good cooks find these foods have enough variety to let them be imaginative.

### The Trail

When you hike with a full pack, you'll want to teach your child to distribute the weight evenly on her back, to hunker down a little when she goes up a hill and to list slightly backward when she comes down, planting her feet sideways, rather than forward, with each step, as she would on a snowy hill.

You should walk at a steady pace and rest when anyone is tired, for you're not in a race to see how far you can travel or how fast. Drink a little water from the canteen, have a bit of Hiker's Snack for energy and take the time to rub elbows with nature. That's what backpacking is all about.

---

## HIKER'S SNACK

Before leaving home, have your Four

**COMBINE**
1 c. raisins
1 c. Spanish peanuts OR walnuts
1 c. semisweet chocolate morsels OR candy-coated chocolate bits
1 c. chopped dried apples

Put them in a plastic bag.

---

# CELEBRATIONS

◇                                                                    ◇

The first holiday may have been invented to celebrate fertility or planting or harvest, but we're sure a mother was behind it. Even then she must have known that nothing could cure her day-to-day drudgery or brighten the eye of a small child so quickly.

We have touched on the main holidays in this section but have skipped Mother's Day and Father's Day since they are capers a child should initiate and also in deference to first-time parents who no doubt are as appalled by their commercialism as we once were. As our children grew older we learned to take anything we could get and found ourselves happy to exchange our principles for the guarantee of a late sleep and breakfast in bed once a year. There were also the rewards of ill-made treasures and, one joyful year, a two-wheel bike all our own: not bad for a nonbeliever.

Whether you encourage these holidays or not, we don't think a month should go by without a celebration of some sort, even if you have to invent it. However, the only thing worse than having a month without a holiday is having a holiday without your child's help. She has every right to be a part of the preparation of each festivity, as she is a part of everything else that happens in a family.

When she polishes the silver bowl, roasts pecans or draws the place cards, she'll anticipate the party that much more—and that's where most of the fun comes from. The celebration itself will be over in hours, but the memory of those giddy days of preparation will last for years.

## BIRTHDAY

When your child has her first birthday party, she needs only her doting family and perhaps one young guest, the "happy birthday song," a little help blowing out the candle and then the cake itself, placed right on her high chair tray. You can expect her to burrow into the icing with two hands and a face: a spectacular snapshot.

By Five, the happiness of a party is in the weeks of anticipation, the hours of planning, with lists and invitations, the surprise of the cake cut into the shape of a sewing box or a train (with candy for the trim and boiled icing to cement the pieces together).

Some mothers dread these parties, but we think they're great if you plot them well in advance. We finally learned that everyone has a better time if the party is limited to two hours (most of which will be spent eating and opening presents), if you invite no more guests than the birthday child has years and if you drive the children home. We never met a mother who fetched her child on time, including us.

### THE BIRTHDAY ALBUM

One splendid mother makes a birthday album for—and about—each child each year, full of the lesser family photographs that feature him as well as a record of his accomplishments that year. Not surprisingly, it is always the birthday child's favorite book.

However you handle the invitations, you should put a limit on the gifts your child can accept. Tell each mother not to spend more than a dollar or two on a present, or to let her child make it, for you want your own child to realize that the present from a guest is not as important as the presence of that guest. The limit should be kept when you give too. For peace of mind, keep a few gifts in reserve, for a pre-Six is invited to more parties than a New Orleans debutante.

The joy a birthday party brings a child

beforehand and the sweet memories afterward completely erase the anxiety she may feel during the party itself. Be prepared for a deathly quiet for the first half-hour, punctuated by the guest who weeps when she surrenders her gift—typical of a Two—and the host who says "yuk" when she opens it—typical of a Six.

Turn the music high before they arrive and have a favor for every child—wrapped like a present—to give in return for the one she gives. We don't recommend competitive games often, particularly in this situation, for a child may be ready to win publicly but not even a Six is ready to lose. If you do give prizes, however, every person should get one for whatever reason you can concoct.

If you have one balloon per child, she will cry when it breaks, but if you have several she should have one left to bring to her little sister (who will cry when it breaks). For extras, rub inflated balloons on your hair to generate static electricity and stick them to the wall to be plucked down as needed.

## ICE CREAM POTS

The chocolate "dirt" on top of these pots is much too realistic for a very young child to eat, but a silly Four will think it's so funny she'll want to make these pots for her equally silly friends. First she should wash small

clay flower pots—one for each child—plug the holes with aluminum foil and into them

**PACK**          **ice cream**

Over it

**GRATE**          **chocolate candy bar**

Freeze until the party begins. Poke a hot skewer into the center of each ice cream pot, so you can stick the stem of a fresh flower into it—both your jobs, for your child has better things to do.

For the first few years one mother is necessary to help, but if all the mothers stay, they may deaden the party since they are sure to spend some of the time correcting the children's behavior. By Six your child will want to invite a few of her grown-up friends—both men and women—and this is a grand idea. A mixture of ages and sexes miraculously turns a party into a celebration.

### Penny Pitch

To pass time simply at a birthday party, have the children stand behind a starting line and, one at a time, have them toss pennies into a wastebasket. This is much harder than you might think. A Two may be successful at a distance of 2′ and a Six may manage at 6′, but if it's too hard, make the distance less and give them all another turn. As at all parties, each child must be a winner—either for accuracy or distance, noisiness or style, and they'll want the pennies as well. To the victors belong these spoils.

Your child also may like to play this game on an ordinary day, using a deck of cards, and either playing alone or with company.

### Copycat

Giggling little girls of Five like to stand in a circle while one of them shakes her arm for all the others to imitate. The next child adds another motion, for both to be copied, and so it goes, around and around, until you have a roomful of St. Vitus dancers. Anyone who forgets a motion is out of the game.

### Dining Room Ping-Pong

This game requires one Ping-Pong ball in the middle of the table and two Sixes facing each other, hands behind their backs. One child tries to blow the ball over the opposite edge of the table to score a point while the other child blows against it. It takes five points to win, or less, if one of the children can't stand this much competition. If balls dent, they usually reinflate when dropped in boiling water.

## PASSOVER

The Seder, to open the eight days of Passover, has to be one of the most inspiring—and dramatic—of all religious feasts, especially for children, for the significance and the history of each step are explained in this dinner table ritual.

In the Seder, everyone takes part, from the young child who asks the four questions of faith to the patriarch who answers them, helping each person relive the saga of the Jews' flight from Egypt. In many homes, it's a child's job to open the door for the prophet Elijah—the sign that any stranger away from home is welcome—and to end the festivity, there is the wild search for the afikomen—the broken matzoh. This is what the father hides at dinner for all the children to seek later and then gives a prize to the winner (and often to the losers).

A child can help prepare for the Seder, as sacred as it is, by setting the traditional fine glass on the table for her father to pour the wine for Elijah and by helping to make the individual Seder plates.

A Two can roast the dry shank bone of lamb—a recollection of the ancient Passover sacrifice of the Paschal Lamb—baking it in a 325° oven for several hours. She also can prepare another symbolic offering—the roasted egg—by baking a boiled one (wrapped in foil, in case it explodes), leaving it in the same oven with the bone for about an hour until its shell is streaked with brown. A Three can mix the salt and water in little bowls for every plate, to represent the tears shed, and cut the top of the horseradish root to dip in this water: bitter herbs to represent the bitter lot of

the Israelites. She also can give each plate its sprig of parsley—the green vegetable usually chosen to mark the festivity of the day—and at Four is trustworthy enough to make the charoses, to signify the mortar that Jews had to make to build the pyramids for the pharaohs. Finally, in the most symbolic of all foods, there is the matzoh, the big square cracker made without leavening so everyone will remember the haste of the flight, when there wasn't even time to get the yeast. Three matzohs are placed on the table under a folded linen napkin—the middle one to be broken and the afikomen taken from it.

Like Christmas, we think any child should celebrate at least one Seder, even if it's not part of her faith. It's unforgettable.

## CHAROSES

This doesn't look much like any mortar we've ever seen, but the story of the Jews and their enslavement by the Egyptians is so dramatic your child will think this simple recipe is the most significant part of the Seder if only because she can mix it. In a bowl

| GRATE | ½ lemon |
|-------|---------|
| ADD   | 1 c. chopped apple |
|       | ¼ c. chopped walnuts |
|       | 1 tsp. honey |
|       | 1 tsp. cinnamon |
|       | 1–2 tbsp. Passover or sweet wine |

You'll need enough wine to bind the mixture together.

## EASTER

Rituals are built into all cultures—some sacred, some silly—and every child should have a chance to sample them, especially Easter. It comes just when nature erupts with such a miracle of life that there should be a way for your child to celebrate it. What could be better than to wake up once a year to find dyed eggs, chocolate eggs and jelly eggs hidden everywhere?

You either can dye the Easter eggs yourself the night before (which can be a bother) or let your child help you the day before (which will be a mess). Even when she leaves them openly in the basket, she'll understand it's only a favor for such a busy bunny.

Buy much less candy than you're tempted to, particularly chocolate, since pre-Sixes don't digest it too well, and forget about serving Easter breakfast. Even one hard-boiled egg with some milk or juice will be a fine meal, if strange.

Hide the candy and eggs, either indoors or out, choosing obvious places in a confined area for a pre-Three—and have a camera ready. An older child likes to look a little harder, will stay cleaner and be less picture worthy.

Watch carefully that your child collects all the dyed eggs and stores them in the refrigerator. We once smelled the results when our flock left an egg between the cushions of their dear Aunt Mary's fancy sofa. Unfortunately, it took three weeks to find it.

## BAKED AND STUFFED CHICKEN

SERVES 4–6

It's hard to match the pride a little girl feels when she presents the whole chicken she has roasted for Easter dinner. It is much, much easier than it looks and combines interesting jobs, like cutting the bacon strips with scissors, tearing the bread and poking the dressing inside—all work a Five can do.

| SAUTÉ | 2 bacon strips, cut up |
|---|---|
|  | 2 tbsp. chopped onion |

Remove from the heat when the onions are clear.

| ADD | 4 slices bread, torn |
|---|---|
|  | 1 stalk celery, chopped |
|  | 1 egg |

|  | ½ tsp. salt |
|---|---|
|  | ¼ tsp. sage |
|  | ¼ tsp. pepper |

Stir. If the mixture is too dry

| ADD | ¼ c. hot water OR chicken broth |
|---|---|

Let cool.

Preheat Oven 400°

Wash and dry 3–4 lb. fryer, inside and out. Inside the bird

| RUB | ½ lemon |
|---|---|

Poke stuffing into the cavity, a handful at a time, and leave open. It will puff out, but little will be lost. Into your child's hands

| POUR | 1 tsp. oil |
|---|---|

Have her rub the chicken and over it

| SPRINKLE | ½ tsp. salt |
|---|---|
| BAKE | 1¼–1½ hours |

When it's ready, the meat should pull away from the bones, the joints should wiggle when touched and the juice should run clear, not pink, when the breast is poked with a fork.

## EASTER EGG TREE

Before Easter, when your Six is intrigued with colored eggs, teach her how to blow raw eggs right through the shells and into the skillet, saving the shells for this egg tree—a fine holiday decoration. Have her poke each end of the shell with an embroidery needle or an ice pick, deep enough to break the yolk. She'll blow the small end like a whistle and the egg will slide out of the bigger one. About half the eggs will break, for children are not too adept, but save the rest until you have a collection. You can paint these for her with clear shellac, which toughens the shells enough for handling, then let her color them with felt-tipped pens or paste gold stars or sequins on them. To hang these eggs

**CUT**　　　　**6″ lengths of thread**

You need one length for each egg. Fold the thread in half, knot the ends to make a loop—your job—and lay the knot over the fat end of the shell for her to seal in place with dripping candle wax. You'll hang the eggs gently from a branch, tied from some high place like a stairwell, or from the Hair Ribbon Tree (see page 208).

---

## THE NEW BABY

Every newborn deserves a party, whether it's to celebrate a baptism, a bris or simply the birth itself. It's especially important if you have an older child, for with forethought you can give her a role to play. She's really the one who needs to grab a little glory.

　For Christians, the christening is generally in the first six weeks, while Jews have a bris on the eighth day (but only for a baby boy, since it's the rite of circumcision). In either case, it involves a weepy baby, a weary mother, a few old friends, a little wine and whatever goodies the grandmother and aunts are willing to make, with perhaps rugelach—the rolled pastry—at a bris and chicken salad or a ham at a christening. Whatever the occasion, there's sure to be a fine dessert, like a cheesecake, which a child can make—with guidance.

---

## CHEESECAKE

A Five can make this magnificent cake because you'll prepare the crust the night before.

*The Crust*
In a food processor or blender

**PULVERIZE**　　　**1 box of Zwieback**

**ADD**　　　　　　½ c. sugar
　　　　　　　　　⅓ c. sweet butter
　　　　　　　　　¼ tsp. nutmeg

When well mixed, press this mixture into a 9″ springform pan and refrigerate, so the crust gets firm and crumbs won't fall into the cake.

*The Cake*
SERVES 16　　　　　　　　　　　Preheat Oven 350°

Have her make this cake a day in advance, because chilling makes it firmer, and have her make it before her nap, because it rises best in a quiet kitchen.

**SEPARATE**　　　**6 eggs**

This is a job for you. Your child then beats the egg yolks with a portable, twin-beater mixer, so they will get thick quite quickly. In a large bowl, have your child

**CREAM**　　　　　**1 c. sugar**
　　　　　　　　　**1 tbsp. flour**
　　　　　　　　　**3 8 oz. pkgs. cream cheese**

**ADD**　　　　　　**well-beaten egg yolks**
　　　　　　　　　**1 tbsp. lemon juice**
　　　　　　　　　**1 tbsp. vanilla**
　　　　　　　　　**zest of ½ lemon, grated**

When well beaten

**ADD**　　　　　　**1 c. heavy cream**

Set this aside and wash and dry the beaters well—another job for you—so both the mixer and the child are ready for the next important step.

**BEAT**　　　　　　**egg whites**

They're ready when she can draw them into stiff points with the beaters, but have her turn the mixer off first, or the egg whites will splatter everywhere. Both of you should then use rubber spatulas to fold the whites into the batter—under and over, again and again—but do it quickly, so she won't have time to help you too much: this is a delicate job. Pour the batter into the cold Zwieback crust, a mother's work, but let her scrape the bowl with a rubber spatula and add the rest.

**BAKE**　　　　　　**1 hour**

Let the cake cool in the oven for another hour, with the door propped open slightly. Refrigerate or freeze. Because a cheesecake cracks easily, cover it with Currant Glaze to hide the crevices.

*Currant Glaze*
In a skillet, have your child

**MELT**　　　　　　¾ c. currant jelly
　　　　　　　　　2 tbsp. water

**ADD**　　　　　　1 c. fresh berries or sliced peaches

Pour over the top of the cake. The glaze will jell again in about 10 minutes. If you whip some cream and put it into a small plastic bag with a hole cut in the corner, your child can pipe a design, of sorts, to cover any cracks that still show. Remove the springform and present the cake on your very best plate.

*Christening Hat*

Your Four will need 6 straight pins, a threaded needle, some ribbon, a beautiful lace and linen handkerchief and a lot of help from you to make a christening hat for the new baby—a nice thing to do in that tiresome ninth month of pregnancy.

A 12″ square, when pleated and folded, will fit a newborn.

Have your child first lay the handkerchief on a table, then fold each corner to the center and pin it into place. The four points should meet.

You now have a smaller square. Pleat it into 4–5 parallel rows, which makes accordion-like folds that will cover the head, from ear to ear.

Pin the ends while your child holds these pleats in place. She has now fashioned the hat—narrow over the ears (where it's pinned), and expanded in the middle (where it isn't).

Your child can sew the corners in place and tack the four corners too, but you must tie the knots. Pin, and then sew, a ribbon over the pleats on each side, so the hat can be tied under the chin, and a bow to cover the top where the four points meet.

At the risk of sounding sentimental, the hat can become a handkerchief again, to be used by your daughter on her wedding day or for your son to give to his bride.

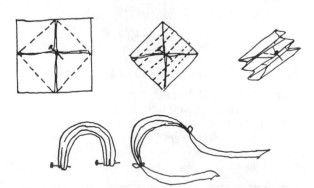

# HALLOWEEN

Some mothers can handle Halloween efficiently—and then there are people like us. We're the ones whose jack-o-lanterns draw fruit flies on October 28 and whose children, year after year, were either ghosts or tramps—the two easiest costumes these mothers could make.

Still Halloween is a marvelous event, if only for the amazement it will bring your toddler when she opens the grumpy neighbor's gate and for once you don't say, "Come back." She marches up the front steps and suddenly the lady who frowns so much is giving her candy by the handful. It's like winning the lottery.

By now we've learned a thing or two, mostly from all those mothers who've done Halloween right. Following their example, we think you should go on a pumpkin hunt a week ahead of time, with your child making the choice. Once home, have her draw a face on the pumpkin with a felt-tip marker, but do wait to cut it until two days before Halloween, so it won't rot. After it's carved she can clean the inside, refrigerating the seeds until she's ready to roast them, and put a candle inside. Any jack-o-lantern looks all right with a candle shining inside and it's safe enough if you do the lighting.

You'll want to prepare the costume in advance and together, either buying one of those dreadful ones from the dime store, which so many pre-Fours prefer, or making it at home. It should be funny or beautiful, but never truly scary, for the only person who'll be afraid will be your child and she'll be terrified. Let her wear her mask for days ahead of time, because it's so exciting and because she'll need practice to become accustomed to it. Claustrophobia, we've found, is automatic with a store-bought mask, unless you enlarge the holes for the eyes.

By Halloween itself, excitement is so high you may want to contain it better by having a few children over in the morning, either for them to dunk for apples in a

roasting pan of water—a nice, wet thing to do—or to bite into ones you've hung by strings from a doorway. In either case, their hands must be clasped behind their backs.

A nap is impossible on Halloween, even for the children of mothers like us, for the anticipation is overpowering. Put her down to rest at least, so you can do the same, then dress her in costume and take her door to door to the homes of people you know, and preferably with one of her friends, who will be sure to giggle better than you do. We've found if a child goes trick-or-treating before she gives candy away at her door, she'll be in a more giving frame of mind.

Some of our children hoarded their Halloween candy for months, others would eat it in a remarkable forty-eight hours, but we never knew a child who wasn't eager for a taste of salt instead of sugar the day after Halloween. For this we recommend roasting the pumpkin seeds.

## ROASTED PUMPKIN SEEDS

*Preheat Oven 250°*

Help your Four wash the seeds in a colander—a tedious job. Drain them and pat dry with a paper towel. In a large skillet

**SAUTÉ**          2 c. pumpkin seeds
              1½ tbsp. peanut oil
              1 tsp. salt

Stir 3 minutes, until all seeds are coated with butter, and pour them on a cookie sheet.

**BAKE**          30 minutes

If not roasted enough, bake 15 minutes longer, or until brown. Crisp on a paper towel and eat them, shells and all.

## THANKSGIVING

This poor holiday, so arduously arts and crafted in school, is scarcely mentioned at home except in terms of cooking, cleaning and company. When the day does arrive, most little children are cross to find it's just one big dinner. It's sure to last too long, because any meal longer than twenty minutes is too long for a child, and have too many vegetables, for one vegetable is often too many.

Some of the disappointment is lessened simply by talking about the holiday in advance. It may seem like an old story to you, but the classic tale of the pilgrims will be a wonder to your child. We've found a museum visit is helpful too, but nothing makes a modern Thanksgiving better for your child than to feel a part of it. We assign the flashiest, fanciest little jobs we can find, like the relish tray, for it's praise that keeps pre-Sixes good. One of the simplest and most praiseworthy of all recipes is Curry Dip.

## CURRY DIP FOR RAW VEGETABLES

YIELD: 1½ cups

A Four can make this sauce very easily, although she may like the compliments better than the taste. In the blender

**COMBINE**          1 c. mayonnaise
                2 tbsp. green onions, chopped
                2 sprigs parsley
                1 tbsp. green pepper, chopped
                2 anchovies
                3 tbsp. ketchup
                1 tbsp. curry
                dash cayenne

Make a day ahead to ripen in the refrigerator. Serve with peeled and quartered carrots, cucumbers and celery sticks and cauliflower broken into flowerets all of which you'll prepare yourself. Crisp them in cold water and dry before serving.

## PECAN PIE

SERVES 6                 Preheat Oven 425°

Southern cooking became famous with recipes like this. And so will your Five. In a bowl let her

**BEAT**
- 1 c. light corn syrup
- 1 c. sugar
- 3 eggs
- 1 tsp. vanilla
- ¼ tsp. salt

Pour into unbaked pie shell

**ADD**       1 c. pecan halves

**BAKE**      10 minutes

This high heat seals the top and crisps the pecans. Lower the heat to 325° and bake another 40 minutes. Serve cold.

## CHRISTMAS

The commercialization of Christmas may offend many of us, but a young child never sees it. To her, each decorated store window, each advertisement, makes expectation all the sweeter. For once the world is turned upside down and it's decidedly a better place.

Slowly, you'll help your child realize that Christmas is a celebration of charity, when the joy of giving is at least as fine as the joy of getting. A Two, however, can't hear enough about such dazzling ideas as a tree in the living room and elves who know how to make wagons. But you also should explain the religious history of Christmas, for a child deserves to know what any hullabaloo is about. If you are a church-goer, carry the magic one step further, by letting her discover little baby Jesus tucked in the cradle of your crèche on Christmas morning—the cradle that had been empty the night before. To young Dennis, it was just one more miracle.

Whether Christmas is a spiritual holiday for you or not, to a child it's the ultimate in family unity, like a vacation at the beach or a trip to Grandma's. She feels wrapped in a cocoon of closeness that comes from sharing so many good times and special traditions. These traditions will be your own blend of the customs you and your husband have inherited and others you've evolved together. This is what makes Christmas a unique experience for each child.

There will be cookies to bake and presents to make, carols to sing and popcorn to string, until, on the night before Christmas, when stockings are hung and the poem is read for the last time, the electricity of your child's excitement almost shocks you. You may be exhausted on Christmas morning—for what mother is not?—but her poignant expectancy on Christmas Eve will catch your heart: one of the more obvious blessings of motherhood.

### GIVING

It will be your job to emphasize the charity of Christmas by asking your Three what she's going to give for Christmas, before you ask her what she would like to get. Help her make her list and count her money and then take her on at least three trips to the museum shop and the dime store for the presents she can afford—the sea shells, the pen, the address book. Most of the gifts, however, should be home-made, for it only takes money to buy presents while the drawings and book-marks and sculptures of wood are presents that come from the heart. When a child sees how much they mean to you, she'll want to give presents all year long.

We reactivated the custom of candy-making, as we did in our childhood when there was little for gifts but a sack of sugar and pecans from the trees. It was, we found, as horrendous and hilarious as we remembered. We organized our children by having one child in charge of her own recipe for the evening, and the rest of us working as assistants. Although the parents read the instructions and checked the measurements, it was the chef for a night

who would assign the jobs, giving orders with all the frantic pomposity of a bad French general just before his next defeat. The mess was major and the voices shrill, but somehow the candy was great, the memories better. Each child would put a few pieces of her candy in the small baskets to give to their grown-up friends, and, alas, to eat sometimes, as we discovered at the end of the long ride to see Uncle Jim, when Mike sat absolutely still in the back seat, aghast to find himself holding an empty basket. This was the candy that lured him on.

## BUTTERSCOTCH CRUNCH

When we were retesting this recipe we offered some to a pretty Three and asked for her opinion. She put the candy in her mouth, solemnly pronounced, "Yumm," and picked up two more pieces to take home to her daddy.

The ingredients are so pure no child can fail—as long as you use butter instead of oleo. Since the sugar mixture gets so hot when it cooks, however, only a Six should stir it, with you standing by. Line a jelly roll pan or a 15″ × 10″ baking dish with foil, and crack and chop the nuts in the blender in advance, because this recipe allows no time for these steps after the ingredients are combined. In a microwave

| MELT | ½ lb. butter |
| ADD | 1 c. sugar |
| COOK | 8 minutes |

Do this over medium heat, stirring with a wooden spoon. It will look like bubbling bread dough after 3 minutes and be pale caramel when it has cooked the full time. Remove from the heat and spoon evenly into the pan—definitely a job for you.

| COOL | 2 minutes |

Over it

| SCATTER | 6 oz. butterscotch morsels |

The hot butter and sugar layer will melt the morsels in about 4 minutes. When they are shiny and soft to the touch, spread them with a rubber spatula, covering the first layer completely—definitely a job for your child.

| SPRINKLE | ¾ c. Brazil nuts, finely chopped |

Chill until firm, about ½ hour. Break into tiny pieces, for it's very rich.

## GETTING

Before Christmas, retire a few more toys than usual to the closet shelf and repair all the broken toys and torn books. Give away the ones she's outgrown and discard the irreparable. This will give you a clearer idea of your child's needs, which are never quite as extensive as you think. In fact, we recommend you cut your shopping list in half at least once, for too many toys baffle a child of any age, especially when she gets them all at once.

Your Five will need some help for that letter to the North Pole (the one you'll keep in the Bible for years) with cutout pictures of the things she'd like and not too many of them. You must tell your child to expect only some of the things on her wish list, and then stick to that, for a parent shouldn't be in the spoiling business.

Anything you give should be sturdy and of good quality, so your child won't feel she's a destructive person. The promotion of ill-made toys, particularly on television, has devastated many a Christmas morning, including one of ours, when we bought Mike a flashy, short-lived mechanical monster, his heart's desire. The next October we mentioned, casually of course, how sad it was that TV toys never worked and we certainly were glad to hear that Santa wouldn't give them any more. By November, he began to believe us and by December, as much as he may have hankered after the red, white and blue robot, he had the good sense not to ask for it. We found this technique so infallible our children would turn off the set if they thought their special toy might be advertised.

### SANTA

You can give the Santa Claus legend as much or as little emphasis as you want—one of us thinks it should be a lot, to stimulate the imagination; the other, very little, to keep it in perspective. We do know, however, that if you deny the fancy of the elves completely, your child will not.

We remember a Six, reared with unbending realism, whose parents told the sitter to forget about reading "The Night Before Christmas" on Christmas Eve. "David," they announced, "has never believed in Santa Claus," and yet, the minute they left, David chortled and said his parents pretended every year that they bought all the presents but, of course, he knew better. Santa Claus had. He had no doubts at all.

A child will believe in elves (and bunny rabbits and the tooth fairy) if she needs to believe and as long as it makes her happy to believe. No matter when a child accepts the truth, she always is wise enough to recognize the Santa Claus story for what it is—another way to show your love.

The only bad effects seem to be caused by some department store ringers who misinterpret their job. Although your Six will rationalize—without any help from you—that this man isn't the *real* Santa Claus, it's better to tell her beforehand that all the Santas she'll see in the stores and on the sidewalks will be only "helpers."

We've found the best helpers work in the swankiest stores, where they don't dare push or promise certain toys. The richer the customers, apparently, the softer the sell. To have this visit run even smoother, call the store first to check Santa's schedule and avoid a wait.

We almost can guarantee that your child will be stricken with a chill of conscience late in the day on Christmas Eve, even though you've never mentioned charcoal and switches. Suddenly she wonders if she and Santa Claus really have the same standards for goodness after all. We find it helps to tell a child she's wonderful—about fourteen times—and then let her prepare the cookies and sugar cubes for Santa Claus and the reindeer. A little giving can assuage a lot of last-minute doubts.

### THE TREE

In some families, the parents put up the tree on Christmas Eve, after the child goes to bed, so that Christmas will be one big ball of magic the next morning. We think that's a terrible idea. It isn't just because the buying and decorating of a tree is a family project that thrills a child, but because you'll be starting a tradition.

The most docile child will expect you to repeat everything you do, Christmas after Christmas, and this can turn the holiday into chaos.

In a few years you and your husband not only have the breakfast cart to prepare, the stockings to fill and the presents to arrange, but you'll have the tricycle, the twenty-four cardboard blocks and the doll's crib to assemble, and as years and babies progress, at least one frantic trip to the all-night drugstore when you realize that one child has fewer presents than another. To decorate a tree between bedtime and dawn would be just too much. There's such a thing as too many traditions.

If you plan to keep the tree in the house more than ten days, you may want to fireproof it. Do this before you bring the tree inside, by spraying the needles with the Fireproofing Solution (see page 51).

For safety, cut off the bottom inch of the trunk and put the tree in a bucket, but do this within thirty minutes of making the cut, so the sap won't seal and the tree can continue to draw water. The tree will drink its fill in about six hours, and then you can put it in a tree stand with a basin. If you fill this basin every day, the tree won't get dangerously dry.

Where and how you place the tree may decide on how smoothly Christmas will go. For stability, keep the tree and the stand either on a sturdy table or in a playpen, and tie it in place to a window catch or a nail driven into the bookcase, so it won't fall down and lose its ornaments. It's trouble enough just to decorate it once.

When you do decorate, at least one parent is sure to scream at the other—the way it happens before a dinner party—and the Four will take an age to string popcorn and cranberries. It will be the blowing of the tinsel, strand by strand, that makes adults pleasant if breathless again, but you'll find your child ignores all dissension. She'll let nothing spoil this good time.

We allowed our children, beginning at late Two, to help hang the unbreakable ornaments around the bottom of the tree and we put the breakables near the top, but after all these children, only the unbreakables are left, top or bottom. These scruffy family favorites still look beautiful to us, but the ones our children like best are the ones that belong to them.

### THE DOWRY

Every year we give each child one decoration, all her own and unlike any other we have. She hangs it where she pleases and wraps it in her own box to put in the trunk after Christmas. We figure a good education and a box of memories are as much a dowry as any child needs. We also make other ornaments of bread.

## ECUADORIAN BREAD DOUGH

YIELD: 10–15 decorations        Preheat Oven 250°

These are charming, seldom break, last for years and make good holiday presents for your Five to give. For reasons unknown to us, this recipe can't be doubled or halved and must be mixed, shaped and put in the oven within 2 hours. In a bowl

| MIX | 2 c. flour |
| | 1 c. salt |
| | ¾–1 c. water |

If the dough still doesn't hold together, add a tablespoon of water.

| KNEAD | 7 minutes |

Shape, according to suggestions in Hand-building (see page 302), and use a pencil to poke a small hole in the top for the hanger. To make a bas-relief to hang on the wall all year, open a paper clip partially and press half of it into the back of the decoration, before baking. Lay all decorations on a lightly greased cookie sheet. They may look rough when cooked if you don't smooth any edges with a wet knife before baking.

| BAKE | 2 hours |

They will be light brown and maybe a little puffy. Paint with acrylics when cool and then with clear shellac.

## CANDY ORNAMENTS

Preheat Oven 300°

These are the prettiest, easiest, tastiest decorations a mid-One can make—and not bad for a Thirty either. Lay any hard candies on a cookie sheet, but the delicate ones with flowers in their centers will look best, for the flowers will bloom as they expand.

| BAKE | 10 minutes |

Let cool a few minutes, but before they harden, poke a nutpick or the point of a pencil near the edge of each candy to make a hole for the ornament hanger. These decorations can be stored from year to year—if they're not eaten first.

*CHRISTMAS DINNER*

Christmas Eve is the best time for a child to prepare her treat for the Christmas dinner. We think this one is best and even a Two can make it.

## ROASTED PECANS

YIELD: 1 cup                Preheat Oven 300°

This is likely to earn more compliments at Christmas dinner than the turkey. The nuts can be reheated 10 minutes before eating, while the meat rests to draw back its juices. In a baking pan

| COMBINE | 1 c. pecan halves |
| | 4 tbsp. butter |
| | ½ tsp. salt |
| | |
| BAKE | 15 minutes |

Take the pan from the oven midway so your child can stir the pecans with a long wooden spoon. When roasted, let them crisp on a paper towel. Serve in small dishes at the dinner table, as you do the green onions and celery sticks.

*THE SLUMP*

Even if your child didn't get enough candy in her stocking to get a sugar shock, the post-Christmas slump can be pretty bad. To make it a little less slumpy, we think you should plan two to three low-key activities for the week after Christmas, so your child can simmer down slowly. We've found it pleasant to go to a movie matinée, see the animated displays in the store windows, drive through town to look at the decorations on other people's houses—in short, those adventures we never found the time for before Christmas.

## COMPANY DINNER

The pleasure in giving a dinner is mostly the pleasure of giving yourself. The effort you take is your way of showing your company that you care about them enough to give them a good time. Your Three wants to be a part of this too, even if she's never met the guests or if she must go to

bed after passing the hors d'oeuvres only once. When you let her help with some of the preparations, you're letting her share your gaiety.

## COLD ARTICHOKE

SERVES 4

No one keeps as busy as a child, which might be why even a Two will plow through a whole artichoke. Even though it is a lot of work to pluck each leaf, dip the base in sauce and scrape it between her teeth for just a little pulp, she is sure that everyone else will want to do it too. And they will.

Cut the stem yourself with a knife and use scissors to nip the pointed tips, but let your child stand the artichoke in the pot.

| ADD | 1″ water |

Simmer covered for twenty minutes. When cool, you—not your child—should pull out the inner leaves in a bunch, scoop out the thistle with a teaspoon and put the leaves back in place. Let your helper serve the artichoke with Lemon Sauce, or with Hollandaise (see page 344). When the company has finished with the leaves, she can cut the heart into pieces and offer it with toothpicks. A child can get a lot of mileage out of that.

*Lemon Sauce*
It takes a Four to make this sauce.

| MELT | 6 tbsp. butter |
| | |
| ADD | juice of 1 lemon |
| | 1 tsp. salt |
| | ½ tsp. dried dill OR tarragon |

Serve at room temperature.

## EGGPLANT CAVIAR

Once we knew a fellow who, when our Nell offered him this fine hors d'oeuvre, heartlessly said, "My Gawd, she's serving rat." We've camouflaged the eggplant's distressing gray color with chopped parsley ever since, which simply makes it better.

You could have the eggplant turn out pale and pretty green, however, if you let your Six bake it for 8–10

minutes in the microwave on high. Just have her cut a large eggplant in half, lengthwise, cover loosely with plastic film, turn it once if the oven doesn't have a carousel and then complete the recipe.

To make the traditional gray—and equally good—hors d'oeuvre

Preheat oven 425°

Let your Six put a large eggplant in a pan and prick it with a fork before cooking so it won't explode.

**BAKE          1 hour**

The rest of the recipe is the same, whether you microwave the eggplant or bake it. When it is cool enough to touch, slash it lengthwise, scoop it out of its skin—a mother's job—and put the pulp in a bowl. Have your child

**ADD**
- 2 tbsp. olive oil
- 2 tbsp. green onions, chopped
- 1 tbsp. parsley, chopped
- 2 tsp. lemon juice
- 1 garlic clove, pressed
- 1 tsp. salt
- ¼ tsp. pepper

The eggplant will absorb flavors better if it's still slightly warm when these ingredients are added. Your child should squeeze the pulp through her fingers until well mixed, and over it

**SPRINKLE          2 tbsp. parsley, chopped**

Serve at room temperature with chunks of French bread.

---

## LUMINARIOS

Spanish lanterns turn a neighborhood barbecue into a fiesta—and a Two can make them out of brown paper lunch bags.

Sit your child in the sandbox with as many bags as you'll need to light the table, the garden and the edge of the driveway. Have her fill each bag halfway with dry sand, poke a candle stub into it and leave it open, so the flame can breathe. The luminarios will look magical by night but a little scruffy until the sun goes down. If that bothers you, use fancier bags, which your child will like, or bring them out after dark, which she will not.

---

### *ARRANGING FLOWERS*

Flowers are sure to win praise at a party—which is reason enough for a Five to ar-

range them. The job is done best in the afternoon, before you feel pressured. With your guidance, she can do almost every step herself.

If the stems are tough, like those of daisies, have her smash 2″ of the base of the stem with a hammer. Cut any other stems diagonally—your job—and have your child put them in a bucket of very warm water for 1–2 hours to harden the stems so they last longer.

Spread newspaper on the table (a child makes this messy work much messier) and have her remove all the lower leaves and at least half of the others, since they foul the water and rob the flower of energy. She can pour sand in a vase to hold the flowers or mash her oil-based clay into the bottom of it and press either a styrofoam block or a frog in it. Before arranging the flowers, have her add water and one squirt of detergent or soap, which extends the life of the flowers.

You need to teach your child the rudiments of flower arranging, and the reasons. First, have her count the number of blooms—since the best bouquets have an odd number of flowers—and then have her stuff only one flower into the frog at a time, so the arrangement looks natural, with the bigger blooms at the bottom and the tallest one in the center. You also want to tell her to keep the setting of the vase in mind. It matters whether the flowers will be seen up on the mantelpiece or down on the dinner table, so she may have to stretch and crouch as she works. When done, give her some filler of ivy or hedge cuttings to poke into the inevitable gaps, just like a florist.

Flowers, like parties, don't last forever, more's the pity. Have your child change the water every 3–4 days, adding new soap. The flowers can be rejuvenated if you trim the stems, mashing again any tough, woody ones. Dip them in very hot water for 1–2 minutes to shock them into new life, then return them to cold, soapy water.

## THE NONHOLIDAY

When the weather turns foul or friends are away, melancholy may strike your child too. These days are no fun at all, and when you have a string of them you have to manufacture a good time. Use any small milestone—your son's new molar or your daughter's first go on the potty. Life is meant to be celebrated and here are three fine ways.

## SIDEWALK SUNDAES

This is called a sidewalk sundae because you'll be sorry if your child eats it inside the house. In an ice cream cone

| PACK | ice cream |
| --- | --- |
| ADD | chocolate syrup |
| | coconut |
| | nuts |
| | cherry |

Wrap a napkin around the cone and send her running.

## ICE CREAM SODAS

SERVES 1

This home treat shouldn't have gone out of style. In a tall glass

| MIX | ¼ c. milk |
| --- | --- |
| | 3 tbsp. chocolate syrup OR |
| | 3 tbsp. strawberry jam OR |
| | 5 tbsp. frozen fruit |

| ADD | 1 scoop ice cream |
| --- | --- |
| | 2 ice cubes |
| | club soda to fill |

Stir quickly.

## CREAM PUFFS AND ÉCLAIRS

YIELD: 12                           Preheat Oven 375°

This will seem almost too simple to a Five. It's easier to make than a cake from a box and requires only six utensils. Cream puffs can be used in a main dish—as in the Chipped Beef—(see page 347) but add no sugar. In a heavy saucepan

| COMBINE | 1 c. water |
| --- | --- |
| | ½ c. butter |
| | 1 tsp. sugar |
| | ½ tsp. salt |

Bring to a boil. Remove from the heat.

| ADD | 1 c. flour |
| --- | --- |

Stir with a wooden spoon for several minutes until smooth and return to a low fire. Stir constantly until the dough leaves the sides of the pan and rolls into a ball, then remove from the fire again.

| ADD | 5 eggs |
| --- | --- |

Drop in one egg at a time, but show your child how to beat the batter firmly with the spoon, so the egg disappears. She should mix the batter well after each egg, but she may need some help from you. Drop 12 round spoonfuls on a greased cookie sheet for cream puffs and trail long spoonfuls for éclairs.

| BAKE | 45 minutes |
| --- | --- |

The puffs are ready if the first one doesn't fall immediately when you take it from the oven. Split them and pull out any gooey dough—both jobs for you—and return them to the oven to crisp, leaving the heat off and the door open about an inch.

| WAIT | 10 minutes |
| --- | --- |

Cool on a rack and let your child fill them with whipped cream or ice cream. Cover éclairs with Chocolate Icing I (see page 362).

# EXPRESSIONS

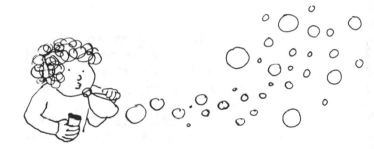

A baby is curious about everything, creative about some things and capable of almost nothing. His curiosity and his creativity will grow or shrink, depending on the limits he meets, and his capabilities will never develop well unless they are nurtured.

The more your child is allowed to expand, in every direction, the better he can express himself. These expressions take many forms. While one child might speak best with words, another uses his easel or his carpenter's kit, and still another prefers clay or needle and thread or a suitcase full of dress-ups. This doesn't mean he'll automatically be a writer, a builder or an actor when he grows up, but his preferences often point out his talents. Unless he has the chance to sample a little bit of everything, he may never find out where these talents lie.

A child clearly has likes and dislikes from the day he is born. Simply the way he snuggles in the bassinet, tummy up or down, is a matter of choice. You'll want to accept as many of his preferences as you can, for this is how you show respect for him as a person, just as you do later when you let him choose which flavor he gets in an ice cream cone or whether he'll wear the red sweater or the blue one. The more a child realizes that he can be different from other people—including you—the more original he can be.

Any expression your child attempts will need some help from you—sometimes just a little, as in drawing, sometimes very much as in carpentry. You're the one who'll show the world to him, pointing out the ants on a stick and the moon in the daylight sky. Later it will be the fractions he makes when he cuts his apple and the letters he finds in the headlines. It isn't that you're trying to nurture the superchild (a scary idea), but there are degrees of ability, in originality and in intelligence, and any help he gets will make him just a little bit better—and, therefore, a little bit happier too.

You'll gasp at his curiosity when he probes the first mysteries of science just as you will at his lip-biting concentration when he cooks and at his imagination when he plays store. All of his activities, as well as his adventures, his friendships and his toys, give his intelligence a tug every day. The mind is not taut like the skin of a drum, but rather like taffy. The more it's stretched, the farther it can reach. Each time you help him look for the nest when he sees a tree and look for the eggs when he finds the nest, he'll be more likely to grow up with a zesty "What's next?" view of life. He'll not only see beauty in the world and try to create more, but see problems and try to solve them.

# CURIOSITY

Curiosity is the basis of creativity. A baby's fresh mind strives to make sense of the world from the day he is born, gulping every sensation. He begins life as hungry to know as he is to eat.

From the first he pieces his ideas together into a patchwork of knowledge—however erroneous—which he reorganizes each time he gets a new piece of information. Every mind-stirring thing he meets will add to his wonder, which is as it should be. The more a child wonders, the more inventive and resilient his mind will be. Each new idea will make him more capable of thinking for himself, of exploring his own head for answers. At this age, he'll look at life from the underside, not only finding the unusual but expecting it: a viewpoint to be encouraged for the rest of his life.

We try not to be sentimental, but the flowering of a child is a triumph of nature. When you feed his senses and his mind, you feed your own soul. This is the flowering of a mother too.

## THE SENSES

In his early years a child learns only by specific example, never by concepts, and this is most obvious when you help him stretch his sensitivity.

You begin the day he's born, with the teasing of his senses, for even a day-old child can follow moving objects, feel temperature changes and turn his head to sound.

Soon his fingers want to reach whatever he sees and then he wants to smell it, taste it and squeeze it too. He'll make every possible noise, screeching his voice up the wall and dropping it down to the floor simply for the pleasure of hearing such sounds. The joy of each new dawn brings exquisite knowledge to a child. He'll be amazed the first time he rubs satin on his cheek, smells cloves, listens to raindrops or licks a few grains of sugar. Every new sensation, every new idea, gives him something else to wonder about.

## SIGHT

Visual stimulation is easy to give, for all things are new to a baby's eyes. Although his sight in the early weeks is blurred, a baby can see well and focus on anything that is eight to ten inches from his face and can recognize his mother's face in the first twenty-four hours. Your newborn baby sees so well he may even, very briefly, move his arm when you move yours, and ooh at you when you ooh at him.

Even in the quiet alert state—that hour or so immediately after a fairly quiet, drug-free birth—a baby can get so fascinated he won't suck, he won't move. He just stares, wide-eyed. During this period some babies may look at something for a few minutes, others for as long as ten, but all show certain preferences. Studies show that even in the first hour they like human faces better than abstract designs; abstract designs better than plain surfaces; complicated abstract designs better than simple ones; bright colors better than pale ones; objects that move better than those that stay still, and in a few days they show another startling preference: they like new objects better than familiar ones.

In the hospital your child is enchanted by the glow of a lamp, and the faces of those who hold him, and will try to follow the light if you strike a match a few feet away and pass it back and forth across his vision. This makes the eye muscles work and there isn't part of the body that doesn't profit by exercise.

A young child will revel in the pictures and mobiles in his room, but he'll be just as intrigued by the picture of the baby on the box of disposable diapers, the foil gum wrappers in the park, the stoplight on the corner. He is so visually oriented he needs picture books before six months are past and at One a full-length mirror, because it always has a picture of his best friend in it: his mirror image will be his favorite conversationalist for the next year.

A child will see the world in Technicolor but it's for you to point out the hidden surprises—the pigeon's nest (and the fact that it's almost impossible to catch sight of a baby pigeon), the weathervane on a barn, the "eyebrows" on old brownstones. He needs you to show him that each kind of flower has its own kind of petal, every type of spider its own type of web and every animal a different gait. Once you help a child see the unseen, he'll always see it again.

### "I SPY"

You can teach concepts and colors and still prevent trouble with this game. When mischief looks imminent, shout, "I spy something blue," picking the obvious blue chair. Your child will touch everything, while you say no, that's red or brown or whatever, but eventually he gets to the chair and learns the color of blue—indelibly.

You also can spy something square or metal or soft or something that starts with a "t" but use its sound, rather than the letter itself, so he can guess better.

Even a brand-new talker can play if you choose a new word, like "I spy a ruler"—or a rug or a candle. This is a painless way to expand a child's vocabulary and is ideal in a doctor's office or a traffic jam. A Three will want you to guess too.

## TOUCH

Touch is better developed in a newborn than any other sense and is the one most responsive to your attention. Your baby grasps your finger automatically when you put it in his palm and within a few weeks he'll poke his thumb in his mouth, try to squeeze his toes and soon may treasure a terry-cloth toy or a magic blanket to tickle his lips.

As he gets older, you'll watch his delight when he rubs his finger along a rubber tire, tries to pinch running water, scrambles his hand through garden soil. A Two can be irritating when he stops to touch the bark of every tree on a walk, but he does it because each texture is different and he wants to touch them all.

A Two sees with his fingertips when he glides them over the contours of a banister, a bench or the edge of a kitchen table. He'll enjoy going with you on a nature trail for the blind and touching the trees with his eyes shut (at least most of the time). The sense of touch is always arrested to some extent, first when you (quite rightfully) stop your baby from yanking your glasses or from bumping a playmate and later when you stop him from picking zinnias in the park.

To touch in freedom, however, helps a child develop the gentleness he needs to cup a flower in his hands or pat a baby's head, so we think you should curb him by rules rather than warnings. If you insist that snacks be eaten at the table and hands be washed as soon as he leaves it, there will be fewer fingerprints to wash from the walls and less need to fuss, and if you keep breakables out of reach, you seldom have to say, "Don't touch."

Some cities have barnyard zoos where animals can be petted, and museum exhibits where children can feel the sculptures and touch the dinosaur bones: all lovely places to go.

Since touch is the sense that makes sex so sexy, we think it's unwise to start limiting it now.

### GRAB BAG

A grab bag heightens the sense of touch in a child's fingertips and makes a good guessing game too, with no more reward than the promise of being right.

A Two can feel inside a paper bag, naming easy objects first, like a ball and a nail, and then more difficult ones, like a grape, a square of sandpaper, a napkin ring, a hard-boiled egg, a piece of elbow macaroni (yes, uncooked). As he gets older, he can learn to discriminate among six objects, all about the same size, or only among those that are round or those that are square.

## SOUND

You automatically introduce sound to your baby when he's in the womb, as he listens to your heartbeat—like no other heartbeat in the world—and to your body's noisy symphony.

When he's born, he has the shock of hearing his own cries and begins to adjust to a whole new set of noises. The best will be the music of your own words and your lullabies as soon as you feel less self-conscious about being a mother.

When you get home from the hospital, give your baby more music, through the radio, tapes, wind chimes, soft bells. Let him have a long, skinny rattle to clutch in his fist, which he can soon shake for several minutes. The tinkling of a music box or a soft musical toy is excellent and the one toy a newborn should have. If you have an older child let him turn the key: a small task to diffuse some of the jealousy.

Your baby's need for new sounds increases rapidly as he gets older, but he needs to hear these sounds singly and not in unison. Studies show that the child who hears a conversation, a song on the CD player, a radio and a game on television simultaneously hears only noise, but if he hears sound from only one source, he absorbs it and can develop into a quality listener. A child can't learn in cacophony and, in fact, he savors individuality in all the senses.

## SOUND SETS

One of the best ways to teach a Four to listen closely is with a game from Montessori, the school system that stresses the senses so much.

This game is played with a handkerchief and sixteen pairs of small containers, each pair filled with something different. You can make this game yourself by buying clear one-ounce plastic medicine containers with childproof caps from your druggist and filling the pairs halfway with rice, water, syrup, gravel, peppercorns, orange pips, 4-penny nails, birdseed, peanuts, lentils, spaghetti sticks, dimes, chips of glass, buttons, bells and bolts—whatever pleases you. Offer only three sets at first, letting your child look at them and shake them, then cover his eyes with the handkerchief so he can shake each container blindfolded, pairing them by their sound alone. Add new pairs as his ears become more attuned to the old ones.

## SMELL

The stimulation of the sense of smell is often ignored, but it shouldn't be. A child is never too young to learn about lilacs.

Your child will like the smell of his baby lotion and the breath of perfume you wear every morning (and therefore both should be used). Wave a blossom under his nose when you take your carriage walks and in the kitchen let him smell the ingredients you use—the onions and the garlic, the apples and oranges, the cinnamon and celery salt.

A mortar and pestle do more to enhance smell than almost anything else. Let your Three pulverize a cinnamon stick or some allspice; a tomato, a strip of green pepper or a handful of rose petals. Other spices, like ginger, are too hard for a child to crush but heat can release the smell too.

Odors have a vocabulary of their own and a child wants to learn all the words. In forty years he'll be bathed with warm memories of his father's face when he smells eucalyptus in the shaving cream or of a childhood summer when he smells grapes on the vine.

## GINGER TEA

We've found this especially good for a cross child with a stuffy nose. In a teacup, have him

| MEASURE | ⅛ tsp. powdered ginger |
|---|---|
| ADD | boiling hot water |

Pour the water yourself.

| STEEP | 5 minutes |
|---|---|

Let him add a spoon of sugar—or honey, if he's a year or more—and a squirt of lemon juice. They're the basis of so many good, safe cough medicines.

## TASTE

This is one sense that's sharper in a baby than in his mother. Salt is saltier, sugar is sweeter, for his taste buds are unsullied.

For the first year a baby uses his mouth as he uses his fingertips, trying to touch his tongue to everything he sees, tasting every surface, every texture. He often will spit out food, not always because the taste is unpleasant, but because his tongue is savoring the touch, rolling it around his mouth as if he were using it to explore a cave.

Because of possible allergies and because you want eating to be a happy, nutritious experience, you should stimulate the sense of taste quite slowly. A child usually prefers a sweet taste from the first day of his life, perhaps because he is often given dextrose shortly after birth—or perhaps because sugar tastes so good.

As tempting as it is, beware of giving even a "taste of a cookie" or "just one lollipop" to a six-month-old, for your child is smart. He'll never see another

cookie or another lollipop again without screaming for it. We think it's no use asking for a tantrum any sooner than you must.

Alcohol seems to cause the same reaction. If you casually offer a sip of beer to your mid-One, you can expect him to reach for any drink he sees—no matter who's drinking it—for years. We don't think you should share even your cranberry juice, because he'll badger you for that too, which will be a pain. It's easier to give your child his own juice in his own cup when you have a drink of any kind.

All children develop some eccentricities in their diet, but the pattern of a truly poor eater is set early, when he's given too many candies or cookies or repeatedly given food he doesn't like, with gritty textures, like fish roe, or dishes with more than one flavor at a time, like stew. This is the way a child learns to say no to other foods too.

By the time he's mid-Two, he's old enough to be tested on difficult foods like melon and peanuts; in fact, at this point, there's nothing your child can't taste. This is when you begin to stretch his sense of taste, letting him lick not only the bowl of frosting, but also the bowl of chili. Let him eat bagels and lox, some gumbo, a raw clam. He'll never know what he likes until he tries it.

Your child's taste—adventurous or cautious or finicky—will depend on the way you cater to it.

One of our favorite Twos, whose mother buys pomegranates by the case and whose sister gives kosher pickles for birthday presents, was enchanted to find a jar of stuffed olives in her stocking at Christmas. Since they had to be shared (for this was as expected in Suzannah's house as good eating), she couldn't bear to open them until March. This treat, she felt, was just too tasty to give away at first.

### TASTE TEST

If someone could freeze liver in an ice cube, we think a child might like it, for taste is affected by touch as well as smell. He rolls his tongue around anything he puts in his mouth, examining every surface with it, and generally the slicker and smoother it is, the better he seems to like it. After the first year, when most food has been tested, you can let him lick the spoon of anything you cook, shutting his eyes and guessing what it is. Later, have him hold his nose too and see how hard it is to tell what it is without any smell. He'll like this game if you offer only the tastes you think he'll like, for, after all, this is a game to help him discriminate, not to trick him into eating new foods—although he will be a more experimental eater because of it.

## EMPATHY

When a child is born, his senses fairly vibrate with response. There isn't a sensation he doesn't savor, and yet, for all these inborn reactions, he still needs you to arouse his empathy—that sixth and most important sense, which will bloom only if you nurture it.

*"WHAT IF?"*

*"WHAT IF?"*

This is a game that brings empathy home to a Four. Ask him what would happen IF
People had wings?
The car was never invented?
You knew what dolphins were talking about?

There was no gravity?
You lived on a bay
or in a castle
or on a farm
Or in a tarpaper shack without plumbing or heat or much to eat?

---

◇ # MIND ◇

The better a child uses his body, the better he can use his mind, because all basic mental skills are built on physical accomplishments. When he transfers his rattle from one hand to the other, reaches for his ball, rolls over, crawls, stands, falls, climbs and walks, he's programming the circuits in his brain in the same patterns he'll need one day to read a story, add numbers or draw abstract conclusions.

Your child registers these patterns when he fights against the obstacles you forgot were there. The battle is repeated intensely each time he grasps a wooden spoon in his fist or coordinates his thumb and forefinger well enough to pick up a scrap of paper, and it continues when he climbs a step over and over or teeters on a little stone wall—both stunts that help his sense of balance and perception. His coordination becomes significantly better as soon as he decides whether he's right-handed or left-handed, for this lets one side of the brain dominate. Until this is set, any learning will be harder.

Slowly your child will begin to master his equilibrium, first by crawling, then by walking on the balancing board (not just forward but backward), riding a scooter, walking on a twisted rope and imitating the gaits of different animals—all of which are preludes to reading.

A child must be given the chance to practice each skill again and again, from learning to stand to tying his shoes. This stretches his attention span and the longer it is, the better he can observe and concentrate. It's this concentration on a task—and the repetition of it—that makes a child so articulate with his body that his mind is freed to think. You can expect your Two to focus intensely on an activity for as long as ten minutes; your Six, as long as thirty.

This concentration is part of his drive for independence, which is why you let him do things for himself. Since anything he does requires a fusion of mental, physical and emotional readiness, he'll need a lot of practice before he can use the potty, clean his closet or learn to read.

Your child gathers the concepts of math when he sorts blocks by sizes or aligns row after row of beans, and he'll get a feeling for science, not just through simple preschool experiments, but through the notice you call to small details—in pictures, in buildings, in people. This gives your child a good eye for observation—the heart of scientific study.

Every young child is logical, not because he knows so much, but because he knows so little. Each day more information will clutter his mind, but if he can pigeonhole his knowledge he can digest it and keep his mind logical and precise all his life.

Some children, of course, are clearly more logical and more precise than others, but any child thinks better if he grows up with both physical and mental order. The first he gets from clearly drawn bounda-

## IMAGINATION

Imagination brings glory to some—to architects like Eiffel, to statesmen like Lincoln—and it brings satisfaction to all, from shoemakers and plumbers to very young children. It's imagination that turns the mundane into the marvelous. With it, a smart child conceives with brilliance, a normal child displays extra perception and a slower child delights you with a special, original turn of mind.

Everyone is born with imagination, but no flower in the soul of man is more easily crushed—or more easily nourished. You nurture this imagination when you let your child explore, when you trust in his ability—to climb a tree, to create a song, to dress up like a king and simply to sit and dream. In these ways, you're giving him the right to think for himself.

Your own inventiveness can stretch his imagination. The questions you ask, the fancies you suggest, the problems you pose, all put visions in his head. When you encourage your child to substitute the unusual for the obvious—a rock for a hammer, a can of beans for a rolling pin, a different mug instead of his favorite—you're stirring his imagination too.

Every time you offer him a choice between a trip to the park or a trip to the zoo, or even between an apple and an orange, you're asking him to exercise his imagination, for he must use it to recall the adventures he's had and the fruits he's tasted before he can reach a decision. The child who is asked to shut his eyes and listen hard enough to describe every sound he hears—the blue jay and the diesel brakes; the dryer tumbling clothes; scissors clicking—will not only have a better awareness of sounds but a richer reservoir of words, for he becomes more conscious of them. Each time he's pushed to be clever with words, he can express himself better and he can think better too.

The music he hears and the stories you tell also broaden his ideas, but he'll get even more from an activity if he takes part in it—singing, dancing, painting and especially in playing games of make-believe. For the same reasons, the best toys are also the ones that invite participation, like blocks, a tricycle or a ball.

While the potential of each child is different, his need for ingenuity is the same. Imagination gives wings to the intellect.

---

ries, limited choices, the encouragement to finish what he starts, and such specifics as a place to put his toys. Mental order comes from logical questions, which help him use his memory and his imagination to arrive at logical answers. When a child finds his own answers he remembers them better.

He will put himself through many physical exercises, big and little. The more complicated they are the more circuits he'll energize and the easier it will be for him to think. When he connects plumbing pipes and strings beads he's helping his eyes and his hands work together; when he plays Follow the Leader or Simon Says he's coordinating his whole body with his mind; and when he moves his eyes from left to right, rather than up and down, he's preparing them unknowingly for the printed page.

It's tempting to play the schoolmarm at home, teaching your child reading and math as if they were separate entities rather than knowledge woven through life, but he learns from his own actions rather than your lectures and he learns only when his body says it's ready. It is, after all, as hard for a child to identify numbers and letters as it is for you to decipher a code. If he isn't interested in these symbols, fine. That's the way he says that his body and his mind aren't in tune yet for this kind of learning. He'll get there in his own dear time, after he's perfected the physical skills he needs to do it.

Despite our fascination with computers today, it's important for a child to feel comfortable with letters and numbers, for these symbols are the cybernetics of the mind. A child usually can translate numbers into tangibles and tangibles into concepts long before he can identify letters, but he'll be more interested in the alphabet when you draw the "S" that looks like a snake that goes "hiss" and the "M" that looks like a river, humming along. It's all part of a child's insatiable need to know the reason why.

The body and the mind are one package. A child can't rush to skip the physical—or the mental—stages any more than he can skip the psychological ones.

## MATHEMATICS

One child can be as nimble with numbers as another is with paints, but this doesn't happen as often as it should.

An agility for math would be more common, we think, if arithmetic were woven into a child's world before first grade and if so many parents didn't pass on their prejudice against it as if their dislike was genetic. If this has happened to you, we think you should look at math in a fresh way. It's like scanning a column of figures in your checkbook to see if the answer is sensible, rather than adding one digit to the next and perhaps repeating the mistakes. By looking at arithmetic as a mosaic, not a series of unrelated bits, your child can use it as an exciting pastime, whether he has a flair for it or not.

As in anything else, if you do a job with zest, so will your child—a truism demonstrated to us well by one scientist we know who weaved numbers through the minds of her boy and girl until Ben and Missy, at Nine and Eleven, think math is as fascinating as a Nancy Drew mystery.

And she started when they were One.

### ONE

To do this, train yourself to be specific. Instead of promising a walk "in a few minutes," or "after a while," be exact. Say fourteen minutes. It doesn't matter if the time isn't quite accurate, since we have never met a One (or a Six) who could tell time anyway.

Be equally specific about the plane and solid geometry in your life. Give every shape a name—a triangle, a cylinder, a cube or a sphere. Show the logic of math by cutting a cake and pointing out that the wider the angle of the knife, the bigger the slice will be. The more a child can see the rationale of math, the more sense he can make of it later.

### MID-ONE

This child enjoys counting if you teach him how. Name each object as you count it—one apple, two apples and, of course, only count those objects that are the same, so he won't add apples and oranges when he can count by himself. He'll need this reminder for years.

Most children like to count food best, but our Kate, the chatterbox, regularly counted the steps in her row house: one step, two steps, right up to seventeen, not because she knew what the numbers meant, but because the words amused her.

### TWO

A Two recognizes that a part is smaller than the whole, as every mother knows who has tried to give her child a cookie that's been broken in half. Even if you fit the parts together, it won't taste as good.

Now your Two begins to fathom concepts. He speaks in numbers, not parroting them like a mid-One but thinking like a primitive tribesman who understands one, two and many. For this you help him by counting together: "one blue car, two blue cars, three blue cars." The concept of zero is clear now too. When he finishes a banana, for instance, he has none left and the example is graphic. This idea is the basis of negative numbers, which is why we think you should say "zero" quite as often as you say "all gone."

### THREE

Fractions come alive to a Three, for now he can see that a fraction is a number too, coming between whole numbers like the colors in a spectrum. He can see that an apple cut into fourths is ⁴⁄₄ of an apple and can be put together and that a pear sliced into fifths is ⁵⁄₅, which makes a whole pear. Amazingly, he can grasp that ⁷⁄₆ of a pecan pie is one pecan pie and an extra sixth of another, but they should be pies he can see and touch and eat and, even better, pies he has made.

He won't be able to read fractions of course, but he can recognize a few written numbers, like the ones on his house or the "3" on his cake. He also can count up to ten, but doesn't understand the meaning of a number bigger than his own age.

We have watched mid-Threes in a Montessori school juggle binomial and trinomial cubes, not as a geometric exercise to decipher the formulas of cube and square roots, but as amusing three-dimensional puzzles. However, a child will benefit from these cubes or an abacus only if you know how they work and will explain them as games and not as lessons.

### FOUR

Inexplicably, children love to learn numbers in another language. Our Mali, no genius in math but comical as a clown, learned to count in Spanish. We remember watching her stand on a farmyard fence counting *uno, dos, tres* cows until, instead of eight or *"ocho,"* she shouted *"fuchi"*— a rather scatological bit of Mexican—to

make her family laugh. Mildly dirty words are every child's inspiration—and for her they made math nice and naughty.

A Four adores to play store and can add and subtract with beans, marbles, apples, pencils, pennies, fingers and toes. This isn't because he has memorized 3 + 2 = 5 but because he can align the beans, for instance, adding 2 beans to 3 beans to get 5 beans. Slowly he begins to see that each time he adds 1 bean to the total he is counting one number higher, and if he removes a bean he has one number less. This is the basic concept he will need for arithmetic.

A mid-Four starts to appreciate a little algebra, for he can grasp the concept of variables (a word that still terrifies us), realizing that two oaks can be the same size but each has a different number of leaves.

A child keeps his fresh awareness of mathematics as long as it is applicable and practical. This is why you let him pour water by the tablespoon into a graduated cup, make a game of finding parallels in a room and help him measure his shadow with a yardstick.

At this age he and his buddies will play store for hours with his cash register and your canned goods, which they'll leave strewn about as if you're the worst housekeeper since the Collier brothers' mother.

### FIVE

A Five can learn to find the area of a room not because he can multiply but because he can count. If a room is 8 × 10 he can lay out 8 beans in a row and make 10 rows of tens. He will count every one of them for he has great patience now.

Your Five will like to shop for you, and should, buying bread and counting the change. He'll be much more impressed, however, with the number and weight of a handful of coins than he will be with paper money.

### SIX

A Six should feel so comfortable with arithmetic when he starts school that he'll savor the concepts and appreciate the rote as a way to get his answers in a hurry. Since every mother likes to look ahead, remember that a child who is articulate with numbers develops a sense of logic and a respect for precision—the backbone of dozens of careers, from music to architecture.

### MONEY

The concept of money teaches arithmetic better than anything else. It's tangible, it has a purpose—and adults respect it. As long as you treat it as a commodity, and not the most important thing in your life, a child will use it for the tool that it is.

### The Penny Candy Store

When we had three children under Five, such a sense of what-the-hell inevitability overcame us that for a year we invited two more pre-Fives from an orphanage to join us each Sunday. Although they endured the museums and were amused by the zoo, it was the weekly trip to an old-fashioned penny candy store that delighted them.

The five walked, stiff and tense, palms sweaty from squeezing their pennies. Each got an equal number but never nickels or dimes, for the concept of change is impossible now. Once in the little store, they pressed their noses to the glass like Norman Rockwell figures, choosing candies and then exchanging them, almost as fast. At home they opened their small paper sacks, smelled the candies, licked an occasional one and traded some more: five children who learned what pennies meant.

Although these stores and their patient owners are vanishing—small wonder—the dimestores and supermarkets have these loose candy selections. They cost much more than a penny, but self-service works almost as well.

### Playing Store

By now your Four may start saying, "Buy me" to everything he sees, which you won't do, of course, but playing store will satisfy him a little bit.

The props need be no more elaborate than a card table and some canned goods, but you'll want a sturdy cash register, for it will get hard use. It should jingle, its numbers should jump and its door should pop open as sharply as a jack-in-the-box. The earlier you let your child use real coins, the quicker he can understand how to make change.

### The One-Dollar Game

On one long, long car ride, we instituted the One-Dollar Game—100 pennies if our Five could count to one hundred without falter or flaw. This wasn't given, we tell ourselves still, as a bribe for good behavior or a payment for work, but because money translates one hundred more graphically than anything else. For Mike, we gave a 50-cent piece, a quarter, a dime, two nick-

els and five pennies, which explained it even better. Anyone would rather count money than beans.

## CARDS

A deck of cards, with its symbols, colors, pictures and numbers, teaches a child to classify—an essential part of learning. First he separates cards into reds and blacks, then into suits, but even before he's old enough to put them in numerical order he's ready for some card games.

### Battle

A Four is ready to play a simple game like Battle—some call it War—where winning and losing are obfuscated by all the action and the hours it takes to play. Two players split a deck, each playing one card at a time with the higher card taking the match, and a rematch in case of a tie. Since the winner must take all the cards, the game is seldom finished.

### Concentration

This game reinforces a child's memory skills at the same time it teaches numbers. A Four can play Concentration with you if you use only five pairs from a deck, but a Six can use them all.

Lay the cards singly and face down, in orderly rows. Each player has a chance to turn over two cards at a time and at random, and if he finds a pair he gets another turn. If the cards don't match—which they seldom do at first—they're turned down again in the same place. When the next player chooses his first card he tries to remember where to find its mate. The player with the most pairs wins, but it better not be you. A Six isn't ready to lose to anybody.

## READING

When a child can read even a few simple words, he experiences the same glorious boost to his ego that he did when he learned to talk.

There's nothing in the chemical or biological makeup of people that prevents reading before Six. Some children—the ordinary variety, mind you—can translate speech into sight reading if taught in simple, relaxed games. Later when a child recognizes the letters in a word and can connect their sounds, he is reading. He may learn sight reading as early as Two (a rare occurrence) and phonetic reading as late as Seven, which happens more often. By the start of second grade, a child should be able to read simple books with some ease and if he can't he should be tested to find out why. When the reading problem is defined, it's easier for a teacher to choose the right approach to help that particular child.

A child's ability to read depends on his control over his muscles—the coordination of his hands with his eyes—but he must be interested too. This depends not only on how he's taught, but how important books are to you, how many he has and how often you read them to him.

However, never teach a child to read—or to do anything else—for your own pleasure or to satisfy your pride. This not only would be damaging, but it wouldn't give him a head start in school either. Just as an early walker doesn't predict an athlete, neither does an early reader reveal a genius.

You just want to give your child the chance to read, if he wants, by letting him become familiar with letters and sounds, as well as books. Tantalize him with bits of information. Draw out the Ssss when you show him a picture of a snake, and then draw a snake, so he can see the S. Let him watch "Sesame Street" and "Reading Rainbow," and encourage him to type, particularly if you have a computer. It's easier for a preschooler to touch a key than to make his pencil go in the shape of a letter. New studies find that a child learns to read—and spell—best, if he learns to write first, guessing at the letters by the sounds they make.

## PRE-READING

We never figured how to teach our children to read before they went to school, but the alphabet was a cinch. The daily newspaper was the best tool, as it allowed us to point out letters by sight, by order and especially by sound—the basis of phonetics.

Pick out a capital *A* in a headline, say it by name and by its short sound, for a child can't learn more than one sound and the short one is the simplest. Let him draw over the letter, then circle all the *A*'s in other headlines on that page. In a day or two, when he has a fair grasp of the letter *A*, go on to *B* and have him circle both *A*'s and *B*'s in the headlines. Continue this routine at his pace until he learns the whole alphabet. Unless he is pushed, he'll be very pleased with himself for he'll see letters everywhere, pointing them out for you on signs, in books and by singing about them with his alphabet tape.

Another mother had great luck with stiff letters she made of corrugated cardboard so big her child could almost climb through them as well as with them. It's a particularly good method for the child who learns best when he's moving at the same time.

It helps any child to involve his whole body in the learning of letters, however, even if he only imagines them. To do this, let him use his arms to draw them in the air, as children with dyslexia are taught to do.

We recommend the consistent use of capital letters in all these techniques, simply because most schools do the same. If he's learned all the uppercase letters before first grade, you then can introduce lower-case.

As your child learns his alphabet, he will want to stick magnetic letters to the refrigerator or felt letters on a flannel board. This keeps him familiar with letters, although he may not try to combine sounds until first grade.

## SIGHT READING

We once knew a mother who taught her Two to read many simple words within a year. She created a book for her daughter, drawing and coloring pictures of simple nouns like MAMA, DADDY and BALL, printing the words beside them in capital letters and binding the pages in ribbon. Annie carried her book everywhere, for anything a mother makes for her child has enormous impact. She would ask her mother to write down a word or two wherever they were, just for the joy of reading them again. Her interest flourished with these relaxed, one-minute lessons and as the book got fatter, she was able to read many simple words. Because it was treated so casually, Annie never realized how extraordinary that was.

Even without making a book, any child will like to see you write simple words when he says them—especially if you put them on a postcard, for him to get in the mail the next day. These first lessons in sight reading will trigger his interest in all reading, but you shouldn't expect him to get beyond this point until he starts first grade.

## PHONETIC READING

If you were to teach reading phonovisually—so the child learns the sounds that turn letters into words—you would use phonovisual charts, tapes and about six months of lessons. That's more pressure than we think a kindergartner should feel, however. Just knowing letters, sounds and a few sight words is enough to enchant most children.

### READING CLOCKS

You can't expect a preschool child to tell time on a mechanical clock—or to care about time on a digital clock—but you can help him grasp its concept better if you use precision when you talk, like "fifteen minutes after twelve," rather than "around noon," and if you let him set the timer for the rice and put the money in the parking meter. When your child knows his numbers by sight, he may understand that the little hand points only to the hour, but the big hand will baffle him. You only can hope that he'll remember which is the before side and which the after. It helps if you give him a cardboard clock from the stationer's—the kind with a face that says "Be Back at——," so he can spin the cardboard hands the way he's told and hang it on his bedroom door when you take a walk.

### READING MAPS

So your Six can learn to use streets and numbers too, draw a big freehand map of the few blocks around your house. Name the streets and let him color the stores and churches and the places where friends live. Naturally, his house will be in the center.

## SCIENCE

Once a bright, bright child named Eliza, a mid-One, amazed her parents when she pointed to the first real horse she had ever seen and said, "Horsey!" Clearly, the picture books her mother had shown her, and the prancing and neighing like a horse had been a success. And then the next day Eliza, sprawled on the kitchen floor, pointed to a train of ants and said, "Horsey, horsey, horsey."

The conclusion was as logical as it was erroneous. Until a child knows that horses, ants and dogs are called animals, he has to find a word that fits; no puzzles are permitted in a small child's head. Instead, his conclusions are based on the little he knows and the many things he sees.

A child needs to examine all things closely and find their points of similarity and their points of difference so his knowl-

edge can rest on firm foundations. This testing, either by experience or by observation, is the heart of science and he must do it as much as he can. He'll feel tall next to a seedling, almost equal to a sapling, small near an oak, but dwarfed beside a television tower. Every new fact, every new experience, makes him sort and reclassify his information, so that each fact is relative to the next.

When your child organizes his collection of cars, beads or shells, he's sorting them by size, by color or by favorites, as carefully as he sorts the ideas in his head. You'll find him classifying the intangibles too, curious about the dandelion that's alive but doesn't move and the wind that moves though it isn't alive. He'll wonder what happens to the sugar in the lemonade, to the milk when the batter is baked and to the moon when he goes to bed. The answers, so obvious to you, are a discovery to a child.

You'll not only want to answer his own lively questions but also the ones he hasn't thought to ask. This is when you teach him about concepts like gravity, explaining how the spinning earth keeps his feet on the ground, that all the world is made of matter and all matter is made of molecules; that energy comes from a hundred sources and that gasoline is an unimportant source compared with the sun. When your child jumps, runs, scrubs a table, kicks a ball, kneads dough or picks up his toys, he's using energy, but energy is also used when the rays of the sun make the plants grow, the current in a stream carries a log and the campfire roasts the marshmallows. A child needs to know these things.

If his experiences are broad he'll have a smattering of every science. He'll learn some botany when he gardens and some biology through the care of his pets, while the blocks he stacks teach him about physics, and cooking introduces him to chemistry. It will be the basic experiments of science, however, that help your child understand and value the laws of nature. When he can examine air, heat, light and water as separate entities and use the same sort of wheels, ramps and pulleys that built the Roman roads, he'll recognize one day that concrete examples are the basis of abstract concepts.

You'll want to use scientific terms when he does the experiments in this section because symbols, either in words or on paper, help you be precise and they help him express himself accurately. You also should have him use small containers to hold the ingredients he adds, since any child becomes so interested in the pouring that he can forget the point of the experiment.

Some of these experiments require many steps, like lifting a weight with a pulley or making a volcano erupt, while others, like tracing shadows or making a water lens, are very simple. The best experiments are the ones your child can do almost entirely alone. This is how he makes sense out of science.

## WATER

Water is sure to make a baby laugh more than anything else, but as much as he enjoys splashing in it, nothing will baffle him quite so much. He can sit in it, pour

it and shake it, yet he can't pick it up in his hands. It's in the faucets, the ocean and the skies, sometimes fresh or salty; sometimes clear, green or brown—an astonishing creation.

A Two can spend many, many minutes pouring water back and forth from one cup to another, letting it trickle through his fingers. When a Three tries to float dishes and toys in the kitchen sink, he'll discover that glass and crockery fall to the bottom; that a sponge will float and so will crayons and blocks (because wax and wood can float), but only some metals, and only in some shapes, can ride the water. Later he can check this if you help him roll, bend, fold, wad and flatten foil, finding, like every sailor before him, that the shape of a boat floats best. A Four wants to understand how the water can only be horizontal and how it seeks its own level. By now he's most curious to find why sugar and salt and baking soda dissolve in water but pepper, sand and cinnamon don't, and why some liquids, like milk and chocolate syrup, will unite and others, like oil and vinegar, are as unfriendly as some people and avoid each other as much as possible.

### Evaporation and Condensation

When a Five starts to wonder what happens to the mud puddles or where the dew comes from, he's ready for experiments on evaporation and condensation.

### Humidity

The air in an average-sized room usually has eight cups of water suspended in it. Although no one can see the water floating about—since it's been broken into molecules—a child can believe it when he makes his own humidity. In a pot

**MEASURE**        **8 c. water**

Let him place it near a radiator or a sunny window and measure it daily for the next few weeks until there isn't any left at all.

*Dew*

Your child can bring some of the evaporated water back by filling a metal pitcher or a glass with ice and leaving it untouched for a few minutes, until the container is covered with dew. This begins to teach him that the cold air around the pitcher has cooled the wayward molecules of moisture and turned them back to water again. The chill from the ice turns mist to moisture, just as it does outdoors when the cool night squeezes the air dry and leaves dew on the grass. Your child may be surprised to learn that the grass really has nothing to do with the dew. It will settle on anything that's handy—the house, the car in the driveway or himself if he is out in the cold night air.

*Rain*

Any child who has seen steam rising from a boiling kettle has seen heat change liquid into a gas. If he pretends that the steam is a cloud in the sky your Six can see how the cloud carries water and with your help, he even can make it fall from the steam again like rain.

Boil a kettle of water and fill a saucepan with ice, choosing a long-handled one so you won't burn yourself. Hold the pan about 4″ from the spout. Almost immediately the chilled pot will change the steam back into drops of water—the way cold air changes a cloud of humidity into raindrops. If your child puts a cup under the saucepan, he can measure how much rain he's made.

*Water Levels*

The report of a study of college students found that most boys pass this test and most girls don't. We don't believe that for a minute—even if it did work that way for us.

Have your Four partly fill a clear glass with water, showing him how the level of water is parallel with the table. Tip the glass for him and then ask if the water is still horizontal. If your child thinks the water tips as well as the glass, do the experiment again, holding a pencil even with the surface so he can see that the glass tips, but the water always remains level.

*Skin Test*

In science a child learns, but only if you tell him, that all fluids—liquids or gases— have an invisible skin, which is called surface tension. Nothing proves it quite so well as water. This skin, as delicate as it is, stretches over water like a rubber sheet. Show him how insects can skate across the surface of a pond, how a superthin razor blade can be dropped flatly and lightly to rest on top of a bowl of water and how the water in a full teacup curves ever so slightly above the rim without spilling.

Your Five can use any kitchen spice and a bar of wet soap to prove that water does indeed have a skin. When he sprinkles the spice into a bowl of water, the tiny grains will rest on this skin. If he pokes his fist or a spoon into the water the spice hardly budges, but when he dunks the soap into it, the spice skitters away because the soap molecules break the surface tension that supports the tiny grains and chases them away—the same way they chase dirt from the clothes in the washing machine.

## LIGHT

A child's eyes track light from the day he's born and they'll keep doing it for the rest of his life. He'll follow the glow that filters from the moon, a street lamp, the night light, the luminous hands on a clock or a firefly. As he gets older you can help him experiment with light.

A Two will like to work in a dim room with a flashlight of his own (taped shut so he won't dismantle it). Just by shining it about he'll discover that light travels almost forever in a straight line, cutting through glass or paper, but not around corners or through wood or foil. He'll find it magnified when he flashes it in a mirror and that it turns his face into a horror show when he stuffs the lighted end in his mouth—a trick he'll enjoy again at Six, and by then he'll be brave enough to do it alone in the dark.

Brilliant sunshine can give color its full depth as he'll find when he looks at multicolored fabrics under the noon sun. Some, like tan, hardly change. Some, like blue, soothe the eyes. And others, like yellow and orange, are dazzling. But when night falls, colors fade into a common drabness—which is why all cats are gray in the dark.

Your child also can learn how to splinter white light into a spectrum, using a prism or a spray of hose water against the sun to bend the rays until they open like a fan, separating into a rainbow of purple, violet, red, orange, yellow, green and blue.

### Shadows

When a child plays with shadows, he's really playing with light. A Two will enjoy reflecting his fingers on the walls to make pictures in a lamplit room, and a Four will find his shadow is a friend on a lonely day outdoors: someone to chase when he's silly and hit when he's mad. With company, a shadow becomes a foil in tag, as children catch each other by stepping on their shadows—a particularly good game for the late afternoon, when shadows are longest and tempers are shortest.

By Six, your child will be skilled enough to chalk the shadow of some immovable object, like a fence post, on the sidewalk. This lets him see how big it is at the start and the end of the day and how small it is at noon—changes that are apparent even in fifteen minutes. In this way a child gathers his first concept of the movement of the earth around the sun—but only if you explain it.

### Lenses

Lenses come in six basic shapes and every one of them bends light, not enough to make a rainbow, but enough to make the eye see better. They may be made of glass or plastic or even water, but at least one side of the lens must be curved.

A Six may be able to understand that one lens can make an eyeglass and sometimes more must be fused together to get the right correction, but even a Two can see that a convex lens will enlarge a picture, whether with a magnifying glass, the side of a jar, a silver spoon or a drop of water.

At first he'll be less interested in the lens than in his own reflection. When he looks into the concave bowl of the spoon, he'll be upside down and when he turns it over to the convex side he'll look broad, chubby and silly enough to make him feel the curve of each surface and peer into the shiny sugar bowl, the toaster and the refrigerator handle as if they were fun-house mirrors.

---

## WATER LENS

Your Five can make a lens out of a drop of water and because the surface is convex, this lens becomes a magnifier. Since the water wobbles if he moves it, this isn't too practical, but it does teach the principle of a convex lens very well. To make it

**ASSEMBLE**  a piece of window glass (any size)
1 dark crayon
eyedropper

Lay the clean, dry glass over a newspaper. Have him use the crayon to draw a freehand circle on the glass, about the size of a penny, pressing hard to make the wax stick to it. He should fill the eyedropper with water and release a drop of it at a time until the circle is filled and the letters in the paper beneath it look bigger. If he adds too much water it will spill over the boundary and there will be no curve—and therefore no magnification. Dry the glass so he can make many more lenses and discover that they come in all sizes. The fun of this experiment is more in the making than the looking.

*Magnifying Glass*

Giving a child a magnifying glass is like giving him an extra eye; there seems to be no limit to what he can see.

A mid-Two puts it up to his thumb and yours, his father's big nose and the baby's little toes. The glass is taken on more outings than anything else, for it gives him the chance to examine leaves, grains, rocks and wood. For this you'll want to buy the inexpensive magnifier with a handle, which is easier for him to focus. The better the lens, the more carefully he'll have to hold it, since it must be held at exactly the right distance above the specimen for him to see clearly. One of the best magnifiers, begin-

ning at Three, is a large one set in the center of a child-sized stool, so the legs regulate the distance.

*Magnified Matter*

A child has a hard time believing in molecules, but the idea seems more sensible to a Four when he can examine a sugar cube, charcoal, chalk or a clay shard by breaking any of them into pieces to study under a magnifying glass. First, have him crack a cube of sugar, then break it into small chunks, then crumble it into grains and finally pulverize it with a hammer until he can see that even powder is made up of particles. Like most of his laboratory work, this is best done outside.

*Sponge Sprouts*

You almost can see some seeds sprout, particularly if you use a magnifying glass to watch them grow on a sponge. Set the

sponge in a cake pan with 1″ of water and on it have your Three

**SPRINKLE**          **1 tsp. grass/radish/birdseed**

Set the pan in a warm place and have your child add enough water to keep the sponge wet. This garden will sprout in about 48 hours.

*AIR*

Since air is invisible, a child never stops to think about it unless you mention it first— and even then he may think you're fooling. Somehow he's supposed to believe that he can't see it and yet it's there and that it's terribly strong and yet—as little as he is— he can push right through it.

If he believes all that, he's a trusting child—and you're a powerfully fine teacher.

While your child has seen the wind bend treetops and bang the back door shut, he'll need some experiments before he can understand that the air that surrounds him on a still summer day is the same as the wind that whips his hat away. It just isn't going anywhere.

He begins to believe it's a substance if he can lock it inside a bubble, and for this he can blow through a straw into water. He also can water the soil of an extremely dry flower pot and watch bubbles collect on top. If you blow up a balloon for him, he can see that air takes up space, and when you tie it and put a lightweight toy or a couple of socks on top of it, he can see that the balloon is strong enough to support it. This is the way a child learns that there is no such thing as nothing. Air fills the empty wastebasket just as it fills his shoe when his foot isn't in it and his cup until the milk is poured, with more air returning every time he takes a swallow.

When he realizes that air is all around him, he can accept the idea that it's pushing against his head, his fanny and his ribs, with a pressure that would be strong enough to crush him if he didn't have enough air inside him to balance the force—the same principle that keeps all things from exploding or collapsing, from the box turtle to the boxwood.

If you start early enough and simply enough a child can understand almost anything.

### Experiments with Air

When these tests are done, your child still may wonder if air is really everywhere but he can't have any doubts about water and neither will you. After he finishes playing with a dishpan full of it, water will be everywhere. Work outdoors.

### Experiment I

To make this experiment work, let your Four use a dishpan and a slightly shorter glass to put in it. Have him fill the pan with water, turn the glass upside down and plunge it straight to the bottom of the pan. The water will try to rush in but the air pressure in the glass will fight to keep it out. The air wins and only a very little bit of water will enter the glass. If he tips the glass as he plunges it into the water he'll see air bubbles escape from the jar and rise to the surface.

### Experiment II

Instead of a glass, give your Four an empty plastic carton with a small hole punched in the bottom and have him plunge the carton upside down into the pan with his finger a half-inch above the hole, so he can feel the air coming out of the container as the water rises in it. If you dry the carton he can try the experiment again, plugging the hole with his finger. This time the carton will stay as dry as the glass, because he's plugged the hole.

### Parachutes

A Five knows that all things fall down eventually, but he doesn't know that the

same things fall at different rates of speed if they are in different shapes—all because of the air's resistance. To show him this principle, give him two sheets of typing paper and have him crumble one into a wad. He can let them go at the same time to discover that the flat sheet takes longer to fall than the crumbled one because the flat sheet has a bigger surface and the air resists it more, slowing down the fall. He'll understand this better if he makes a parachute out of cloth and string, with a small block of wood or a key for the weight.

**CUT**          **15" square of fabric**
                **four 16" lengths of string**

Help him tie each string to a corner of the cloth and tie the four loose ends around the block like a package. Your child will toss parachutes into the air and watch them fall again and again for the next five years. So far Nell has made 127.

### SOUND

After a child learns that light can travel in a straight line, he's ready to learn that sound does not.

A pebble tossed in a pond explains it best, for the shaky rings of water radiate from the splash like sound waves, engulfing twigs and rocks but getting less and less distinct the farther they travel. The bigger the stone, the bigger the splash and the more distinct the vibrating waves. A shout is like a big stone; a whisper like a pebble.

Your Two will be pleased to find that some sound vibrations—like those of a

guitar string—can be felt as well as heard. When he sings he can hear the sound with his ears and feel the vibrations if he stretches his fingers to touch the side of his throat, his nose and his jawbone. He also can hear the difference between a noise and a note of music and, even though he can't count the number of vibrations in a note, he'll be curious to know that each one must have a set number of them in a second to ring true.

Unlike light, which can travel through a vacuum, sound waves must flow through a medium. Some media, like air and water, are very good conductors of sound, and others, like cotton batting, foam rubber or feathers, muffle it.

A Four finds that metal, glass and wood conduct sound too, if he puts his ear against a door, a metal cabinet or a glass pane while you rap on the other side. To test air as a conductor, let him collect sound waves from it by putting a cone of cardboard to his ear; he also can put the cone up to his mouth to amplify the waves of his own voice.

Water, however, makes the best test of all, if only because it's a child's favorite toy. Have him sit in a full bathtub and rest his ear on the water while you splash a few pennies into the tub. When they strike the bottom it will prove that water not only carries sound but amplifies it, which is why whales can hear each other talking three hundred miles away, even though they have no ears poking out of their big, sleek heads.

### Tuning Fork

Your Five can make a classic telephone by connecting two cans with a long piece of string. Unfortunately, children have been disappointed by such toy phones for decades, since the voice is barely carried and a child usually can hear his colleague as easily without this phone as with it. To make the principle clearer, cut one yard of string and tie a fork in the center. Have him hold one end of the string in each ear while the fork hangs down, keeping the string taut. He then walks around, striking the fork against a desk, a stove, a table leg—whatever's around. He'll be amazed how loud and clear each bump sounds and how well a simple length of string can carry vibrations directly to his ear.

### Thunder

A storm is the finest show that nature can produce, releasing vast quantities of energy as it scrubs the air as clean as an hour in the tub cleans him. To many children, however, it's about as scary as a spook show.

We've found science takes some of the mystery—and therefore the fear—out of thunder and at the same time teaches a child that light does indeed travel faster than sound.

Use a globe and a watch with a second-hand to show your Four that light is so fast it could go around the earth seven times in just one second. And then take a four-block walk and tell him that sound is so slow it takes a second to go just that far. Once he accepts the idea that the sound of a thunderclap comes long after the sight of the lightning, he's ready to measure the distance to the point where the lightning struck. He can do it if he counts slowly from the time he sees the flash until he hears the thunder, measuring a mile for every five seconds, so that fifteen seconds are three miles, ten seconds are two miles, five seconds are one mile—and one second is unfortunate.

### HEAT

Heat is as ubiquitous as air, but unless it's uncomfortable, it almost goes unnoticed.

Quite properly you've warned your

baby against "hot" before he can talk, but by Three he can begin to treat heat more as a friend than an enemy. Without it, his food couldn't cook, his plants couldn't grow and his body couldn't burn the germs when he gets a fever.

The more your child understands about heat the more curious he'll be to do experiments and learn to read the thermometer outside his window. It will be years, however, before your child truly realizes that everything in the world has a temperature—not just the fire in the barbecue and the ice in the freezer, but the heat in his kitchen, in his pencil and certainly in himself. He'll be surprised to find out that the 98.6° temperature that registers on the thermometer outside his window in July is the same as the temperature inside of him, all year long.

### Heat Energy

The energy of heat will stir water, as your Five will find when he dyes water near a sunny window. Have him fill one glass with cold water, the other with hot. Into each

**ADD**          **2 drops food coloring**

The color acts as a tracer so he can see that hot water is a swirling force, for it mixes the dye evenly, while most of it sinks in cold water.

### Conductors

Everything has heat, but it has it in different degrees, and everything conducts heat, but some things, like metal, conduct it better than others. Even the metals themselves differ, as your Five can find with a quarter, a nickel, a dime, a penny and four ice cubes.

Have him lay a coin on each cube, leaving them alone for a few minutes—until the heat of the room can transfer through the metal and into the ice. Help your child lift each coin with a knife blade (a trickier feat than you might think). He'll find the nickel is the worst conductor, because it makes the least imprint of all, and the penny is the best, for the copper etches deepest.

### Insulation

Unless there's some insulation to block it, heat flows like water to make all temperatures equal. A child can understand this flow when he watches his ice cream melt in a warm room and learns that as the ice cream gets warmer, the air above it gets colder.

The observation becomes more graphic when you have him put an ice cube on a plate and one inside a mitten. He'll find the one on the plate melts quicker, because the mitten keeps the warm air in the room from entering just the way it keeps the cold air out of his mittened hands in wintertime.

When your Four wraps his hands around a cup of hot chocolate he's learning that his hands take heat away from the cup and into themselves, but when he puts them around a glass of iced water, they'll raise the water's temperature enough to melt the ice.

### Hot Air

At one time or another, your child is sure to ask why campfire smoke goes up; why those wavy lines squiggle over a hot pavement and what good are chimneys anyway.

A Five can feel for himself that heat rises, by putting his hands first above and then below both a light bulb and a radiator. There is always more warm air above.

The proof is more memorable with a plastic sandwich bag, a jar, a rubber band, a saucepan and the stove. Fit the bag over the neck of a jar, wrapping the rubber band around it to make it fit tightly. Have him fill the pan with 1″ of water, set the jar in the pan and put it over low heat for five minutes. Indeed it is true. As the air in the bottle gets warm, it will rise and inflate the sandwich bag. It won't puff completely but it will puff enough for him to feel the pressure. Hot air rises and—the experiment has a double lesson—it also expands.

### Friction

A little bit of friction holds a family together and too much will tear it apart, just as it does to anything else.

If you have the sort of Four who wears down the heels of his shoes before they ever need a shine he has had a clear lesson in friction. On the one hand it's a culprit—always rubbing away at a surface—and on the other hand it's like glue. If the nails that hold the heel in place were as slick as icicles they would fall from the shoe, for there would be little friction, and without friction there would be no bond.

Your child either can erase some of the friction around him—by making a surface more slippery—or he can create more. To prove it, have him examine the ridges and whorls on his hands that give him the friction to open a jar, then have him erase the friction by rubbing them with wet soap, so they are too smooth to turn the lid.

He also can sharpen a stick by scratching it to a point on the sidewalk until it's warm to the touch, an experiment which helps him understand that friction can create so much heat it even may send sparks.

And then on the day he falls and

scrapes his knee, you can tell him that the friction between the knee and the sidewalk wore away the skin. And he'll cry, just the same.

### TOOLS

Like you, a child can multiply his strength with tools and do work he couldn't possibly do alone. Some tools are big, powerful and complicated like a concrete mixer, others are fragile like a straw or pretty like a teaspoon. Most tools were designed for just one purpose—a hammer, a garlic press or a needle—but if your child understands tools well enough he can be inventive with them.

All hand tools combine the principles of the five basic ones: the lever, the inclined plane, the wheel and axle, the wedge and the pulley. Every child is interested in tools, but he'll like them even more if you identify them by their technical names and give him the chance to use each one.

### Lever

A pair of shears, a shovel, a nail clipper, a spoon, a seesaw, a car jack and even your child's lower jaw are levers, for a lever is any tool that moves to lift or pry. A child knows that his scissors won't cut if the blades are apart, and the seesaw is no fun unless it rests on a stand—or, as it's called in the tool game, a fulcrum.

Your child can dig with a shovel, eat his ice cream with a spoon and even borrow his father's jack to raise the coffee table, but he won't understand how much work a lever and its fulcrum do until at Five he makes his own. For this he'll need a wooden plank about four feet long to serve as the lever, a large rock, a sturdy box or a concrete block to be the fulcrum and a bag of something heavy from the garden shed or the kitchen as the weight he will lift.

Have your child rest the lever on the fulcrum with the weight on one end, but for safety you'll have to steady it. Like a seesaw, the plank can hit him when he lets the other end go. After a few tries he can slide the plank up and down the fulcrum to understand that the longer the lever extends, the more force it has.

### Inclined Plane

An inclined plane, as stuffy as this name sounds, will intrigue a Four by its very simplicity. It's the bedway of his slide and the gangplank to a boat as well as the ramp that carries furniture into a moving van, wheel chairs into the museum and toy cars down the box he tilts. As your child will learn from the hills on a hike, the longer the incline, the gentler the slope and the easier it is to climb it.

### Wedge

A wedge is a little inclined plane, like the ones your child has in his box of blocks, but a wedge can be as skinny as a blade or as fat as a doorstop. The chisel that cracks a brick, like the hatchet that splits a log, are wedges too, but so is a dull knife slicing through cheese—and that's a wedge that is safe enough to use.

### Wheel and Axle

While a child tries to push every chair, every toy, every shoe box around the house from the time he can toddle, he'll automatically invent the wheel and axle when he gets his first wooden construction set—a glorious day. You'll watch him painstakingly fit a rod through a disc (which you'll call a wheel and axle), but it will be months before even the most mechanically minded Two will put a disc at each end of a rod to make a set of wheels (which you'll also call a wheel and axle). By Five, when your child is a champion truck pusher, you can show him how the axle turns the small hub of the wheel to make the big rim turn. Although they both will turn the same amount of times, the

rim will go much further. The moral of this story: the bigger the rim, the faster the wheel will go, although it does take more energy to push it.

### Pulley

The principle of the pulley—the oddest of all the tools—is the most complicated for a child (or a mother) to understand. The fact is, a pulley enables your child (or you) to lift a weight with half the effort it would otherwise require.

Start by letting your Two lift an encyclopedia in his hands to see how heavy it is and then tie some twine around it, leaving a long tail for you to drape over the pole in the closet. When he pulls on this string he can feel how much easier it is for him to lift the book, although it will be years before he can understand the neat relationship between the distance an object is moved by the pulley and the effort it takes to move it.

A Five is ready for a backyard experiment with real pulleys and a rope from the hardware store, so he can try to lift something too heavy for him to move alone. When you add another pulley, he'll find he can lift twenty pounds and it will feel like five, because every time one more pulley is added, his effort is halved—comforting information for the child who spends hours figuring how to move mountains and monuments. Now he knows.

### MAGNETS

A magnet is one of the best friends a curious Two can have. At first the Chinese used lodestones for magnets, but the ones today are made of hard iron or steel that has been permanently magnetized. Their strength will vary from the industrial magnet, so powerful it can lift huge girders, to a horseshoe magnet, just strong enough to gather slag in the street. It's one tool of learning that seems to have a touch of mystery, and the more a child learns about a magnet, the more mysterious it becomes.

While you know that only iron and steel are attracted irresistibly to magnets, your child does not. Let him try the refrigerator door, the tacks on the carpet, the scissors, needles, pins, pliers, hammer and nails. He can be certain that a piece of metal contains iron only if he touches it with his magnet and feels a pull.

Even though a magnet isn't attracted to cloth, glass, paper, plastic, pottery or wood, its magnetic force passes through them. To test this, have your Five lay a paper clip on a stiff sheet of bond paper, moving the magnet beneath the paper to pull the clip. He also can repeat the experiment by putting the clip in an aluminum pan and running the magnet beneath it or by putting it in a jar. Even if it contains water, the clip will skate around the glass.

### Magnet Making

A Six can make a magnet himself, although it will be temporary. Teach him to rub a nail against the end of a permanent magnet about twenty times—always in the same direction—until the nail can attract a paper clip. When the nail loses its magnetism, he can recharge it by rubbing it on the mother magnet.

He also can make magnets with only a momentary life span by using his permanent magnet to attract pins, paper clips or any lightweight iron that is easy to bend. It will lift them up like a row of elephants, with each paper clip hanging onto the other one's tail, because each clip becomes a magnet and draws the one next to it. The clips lose their attraction as soon as the magnet is removed.

### Magnetic Poles

A Six can understand that a magnet has magnetic poles and a magnetic field—if you tell him.

All magnets, no matter what their size or shape, have more force at their ends than at their centers. To test this, have your child lay a piece of brown paper over a magnet and sprinkle the paper with as many as a hundred pins, which will skitter to either end of the magnet.

If you lay a paper plate over a magnet and crumble steel wool all over its surface your child can see the radius of its energy—the magnetic field.

### Bar Magnet

If your Six has two bar magnets he can discover not only that a magnet is strongest at its poles but that one pole is different from the other. Have him place the two magnets end to end, almost touching each other, so he can see if the magnets pull together. If they do he's put the opposite poles next to each other and learned that great truth of love and science: opposites attract.

To show your child how each magnet has a north pole and a south pole, help him tie a string around the center of each bar magnet and hang one string from one end of a clothes hanger and one from the other, far enough apart for the magnets to swing freely without interacting. When they've stopped twirling and hang parallel, show him that one end points north and the other points south (which you can figure by the rising of the sun). Let him mark the poles "N" and "S" and, facing north like the magnet itself, he can learn that west is to his left and east to his right.

### ENERGY

Energy comes in many forms, but the experiments your Five likes best are either dramatic or goofy.

## VOLCANO

Air has energy and a child can see it if he makes a fuel of carbon dioxide by combining baking soda and vinegar.

This homemade gas, if mixed with powder paint, will look a little like an erupting volcano—especially since your Six has never seen one.

Cover the table with about 8 layers of newspapers, put a small, inverted flower pot on them—to serve as a pedestal—and set a coffee mug on it. Staple a piece of construction paper into a cone: the volcano. Trim the bottom of it so it will be level and adjust the top of the cone to fit tightly over the mug. To make the lava, use a 6-oz. paper cup for each color. Into each one

**BLEND**          4 tbsp. baking soda
                   1 tsp. powder paint

Drop one cup through the cone and into the mug (which keeps it steady), and into it

**POUR**           ¼ c. vinegar

When its overflow stops, add another quarter cup of vinegar to prolong the eruption. After this display, remove the paper cup and drop the next one into place and add the vinegar, continuing until all the colors are used. You may be ready to quit, but your child wants to use every color—and still will be ready for more.

## DANCING GARDEN

This same carbon dioxide form of energy can provoke a lot of laughs. Make the garden in a goldfish bowl of stones/buttons/beads. In a jar, let your Five

**MIX**            3 c. water
                   2 tsp. baking soda
                   1 c. vinegar

Pour it slowly into the bowl to make the gas.

**ADD**            20 mothballs

Do this yourself, for mothballs are poisonous. The balls will bounce up and down, fizzing as they go. When the bubbling stops, reactivate the garden with an occasional sprinkle of club soda.

## CRYSTAL GARDEN

These snowy salt crystals grow for three days, clustering together like little cauliflowers. Have your Six prepare the bed first and then in a pie pan let him

**COMBINE**        6 charcoal brickettes
                   6 clay shards

In a glass

**MIX**            4 tbsp. noniodized salt
                   4 tbsp. liquid bluing
                   4 tbsp. water

He should mix the ingredients in this order, stirring with a wooden spoon until the salt is partially dissolved. You must use regular salt, since any trace element inhibits the growth of crystals.

**ADD**            1 tbsp. ammonia

This is needed because crystals grow best in an alkaline solution. There will be a dramatic change in color—from blue to a muddy brown. Have him stir it some more, then drizzle it into the pan, making certain that the sediment of salt falls over both the coals and the shards. The crystals begin to grow immediately and last about three days, but the strong odor of ammonia disappears in about an hour. For bright (but tacky) colors, your child can add a few drops of Mercurochrome or food coloring on each lump of coal, right after he's poured the solution.

### Rubber Egg

This experiment in quiet energy produces a fascinating, if short-lived toy. It doesn't even smell bad when it breaks. Have your Six slip an uncooked egg, still in its shell, into a clear glass jar with a mouth wider than the egg since it will expand. Fill the jar with white vinegar, cover and let it rest for two weeks.

As the shell and the vinegar combine, your child will see tiny bubbles form on the shell—a sign that the acid is acting on the alkaline shell and slowly dissolving it.

Your child may open the jar regularly to test very gently how it feels; if he's rough at first he may crack the shell. The egg will grow slightly in size and in time the vinegar will dissolve the shell and cook the membrane so that it's as firm as a little balloon full of water.

Let him empty the jar in the sink, rinse it, rub away the residue of grit and hold the egg to the light to see the yolk floating in the white. He can then roll it gently and bounce it a little too. Our friend Kathy even bounced it on the ceiling (once).

# CREATIVITY

Every child must express herself every day, with words and music, with dance and make-believe, with the pictures she paints and the dolls she makes. Somehow she has to tell what's on her mind and she doesn't care if she has talent or not; it's what she says that counts. Her work may not be beautiful, but it will be creative, for it is her own.

Since no two children follow exactly the same interests or the same timetable, you'll want to offer your child a little bit of everything. The help she needs will depend on her age and your suggestions.

In the beginning most of her self-expression will be simple and as brief as it is giddy. She'll draw for a few minutes, run around in her fireman's hat or plink her xylophone, but by mid-One, she also needs you to plan at least three to four special creative activities a week. Naturally, these aren't the only moments that let her imagination soar. Some of the best times will be the ones you have together as a family: the "What Am I?" guessing games of charades, the dancing and even the writing, when you encourage your child to singsong the poems and stories she invents while you or your husband take down those brilliant words.

Other expressions of creativity take more guidance. The supervision of art projects will vary from a lot, with plaster casting, to very little, with pasting. Sewing and other complicated crafts, like dyeing cloth or pressing flowers, require a calm morning and much of your attention. The more time you must give the more likely you are to get cross about it. Unless you have the nerves of a sphinx, your dear little child and a mound of papier-mâché may be your undoing. Paradoxically, we've found company helps. A young guest more than doubles the chaos but she also can inspire you with a what-the-hell spirit. The project will be noisy, confused and memorable even with firm rules, so at first only ask one extra child at a time. You eventually can invite as many as five, but don't expect the children—or you—to last more than a half-hour and still enjoy it.

You'll be more apt to promote creativity (with or without company) if you have good work space and handy supplies; if you make the cleanup a part of the project and if you explain the techniques. As a child gets more adept with a paintbrush and play dough, she can concentrate more on the results. She'll paint the same picture a dozen times in a week and roll out snake after snake of clay—practicing until she's figured out how to paint the best tree and make the finest cigar. In the process of repetition she learns to accept small setbacks—the only way she can sample the pleasures of success. If a child could paint her best picture and dance her best dance the first time she would never be challenged to grow.

While creativity is a vital release to a child, it's also an absolute lark. Little else gives her more day-in, day-out good times and therefore more good times to you too. A happy child is mighty nice to have around the house.

# ⬦ ART ⬦

**A**rt is not only the food of the soul but the one form of self-expression that bewitches every child. A One, young and inept as she is, wants to fiddle with it as soon as she's coordinated enough to squiggle a crayon across a page.

Drawing precedes all other art forms by at least a year and probably is enjoyed longer than all of them too, as a worldful of doodlers knows well. No other art causes so little trouble, because it can be done almost anywhere and anytime.

To many mothers, creativity not only is limited to art, but art is limited to painting. It's easy to see why, for almost any broad, swooping strokes with a paintbrush will be beautiful to you and a great physical and even spiritual release to your child. But other art does this too. Although pancakes of clay and blobs of paste may not appeal much to you, the tactile pleasure they give a child is just as important to her as the pleasure she gets from a colorful picture.

Sculpting—in clay, mâché or plaster—gives a child the chance to create everything from a medallion to a horse and even a preschool child can hand-build well enough to make thumb pots (see Handbuilding, page 302).

Pasting may not seem like an art form to you, but to a child, it's a brilliant accomplishment and the basis for many

crafts and most collages. Here she learns how to give a picture an extra dimension, combining different materials into a single composition—considered one of the most sophisticated talents any artist can master.

Whatever medium you offer, you'll have to teach your child the techniques, so she can feel comfortable enough to express herself well, and you'll have to teach her to wash her tools and herself when she's done. If you don't, you'll resent her dependence so much that the art supplies will become a treat instead of a routine. It's easier if you're near her when she works, both because most art is messy enough to require supervision and because your conversation will pique her fancy.

Even though her talent and her originality come from within, you refine it every time you help her notice a ladybug on the lily or the cumulus clouds in the sky, for then you can ask if the flower she's drawing has a bug on it or if her sky has clouds. While your questions will be casual (for anxiety has no place in art either), they can inspire her work and make it livelier.

By Five, your child still will be proud of all her art, but you can tell that she leans either toward sculpting or painting by the way she handles these media. The painting style of one child may stay the same while her clay figures suddenly become wonderful creatures, but another child—even in the same family—is content to roll simple snakes of clay and yet paint complicated murals on the freezer wrap. This is classic. Almost no one is equally adept in both two-dimensional and three-dimensional art because the painter and the potter have a different set of abilities.

Although your child may have more of a bent for drama or music, any child who has wrestled with clay and swirled color on paper not only knows its joy but she'll appreciate Rodin and Van Gogh a little more too. Every effort of her own trains her eye to see more clearly, and all the museums in the world can't stretch a child's love of art any better than this.

## DRAWING

Drawing isn't just an easy expression of creativity, but an exercise as necessary to the development of a child's small muscles as running is to her big ones.

A One falls in love with paper and pencil—a romance that lasts about five years. She begins with dull pencils, in either graphite or color, and crayons and then prefers felt-tipped pens. These are the most satisfying of all drawing tools for their colors are so vibrant and their lines so crisp. Still, every child has a special loyalty to that green-and-gold box of crayons—a love that will last as long as childhood.

The first drawings at mid-One will be formless but by late Two your child will graduate to stick men to whom she'll give pants and shirts and curly hair at Three— if you suggest them and are willing to recognize them, no matter how hazy the

resemblance. Generally, however, she'll draw a sun, because it's a sign of happiness, and a tree, because it's a phallic symbol and that's a sign of happiness too.

A Three also can make three letters— O, X and T—which you should call by name and with enthusiasm, even if they were accidental. You won't expect much at the start, for a young child will only "scribble-scrabble," as our Six haughtily said, but she likes to savor the experience quietly, imitating you at your desk.

A Four can make most of her letters and print her first word—her name.

By Five, her name is such a mania she writes it everywhere, as you'll see even ten years later, when you find it etched into the bedpost.

A Five, bless her heart, culminates her love for writing by treating her tablet and pencil box—with its five pencils, its sharpener and its eraser—as if they were her best friends. They often are.

The older your child gets, the more she'll restrict her pictures, in both size and fluidity. You can prevent this somewhat by spending a few minutes outdoors encouraging her to draw great, sweeping pictures in the air with her arms—both of the things she sees and the things she would like to see. This helps a child draw with new scope, so her trees, while they still will look like phallic symbols, will look like BIG phallic symbols.

### PENS AND PENCILS

By the time a child is fifteen months she'll try to use ballpoint pens and pencils, both because they're handy and because they help her imitate you and other important people. While it's restrictive to draw with them, you always will want to keep one or two in your purse; they've carried many a child through the doldrums of a waiting room.

### Rubbings

A hundred years ago members of the English gentry laid parchment over brasses and tombstones and rubbed the paper with lampblack and beeswax to transfer the silhouettes.

Your Four can make rubbings too, with no more than a pencil, a penny and the back of an old envelope. Have her put the coin on anything flat, like a tabletop, cover it with a single thickness of paper and scratch it lightly back and forth with the side of the pencil until the picture emerges. This is an especially good trick if you're stuck somewhere you don't want to be, like an airport. However, if your child is getting fussy, don't try to show her the trick—just do it. The crossest child will want to try it.

### CRAYONS

Your child is ready for crayons as early as mid-One or as soon as she's stopped putting everything in her mouth; even if she eats one, she won't get sick. You'll want to begin with the flat-sided jumbo crayons for your pre-Three, working up to magnificently elaborate boxes with built-in sharpeners for the kindergartner. All should be of such high quality that your child can get good results.

We've found the so-called erasable,

washable ones make waxy, muddy colors on paper, and they're hard to remove from the walls too, since they leave a film of wax. Besides, if you give your child washable crayons, you imply that drawing on the walls is in the same category as leaving fingerprints on them. Instead, expect the best from your child, use regular crayons and when she has an occasional accident, have her help you remove the marks with Basic Cleaner (see page 226) or a little scouring powder.

A beginning artist will draw for only a few minutes at a time, using several sheets of paper and a choice of several colors. She must work under very close supervision and in a confined space, like a high chair, so she won't slip away and draw elsewhere. Of course, put the crayons away in some clever spot when she's done, because it's cruel to tempt such a young child.

A Three can take care of her own crayons fairly well, but she still should work at a specific place, like a work table. Even then some crayons will drop so you'll have to walk more carefully. You also must check your child's overall pockets, for only one crayon melted in the dryer can stain a whole load of clothes.

A Four is ready for you to teach her to cover paper with quick little dots, to rub crayons sideways and to lay one color over another gently to create a third color. Like any other techniques, these aren't automatic.

Contrary to all nursery school precepts, a Five is happiest when she colors between the lines of a dimestore coloring book, for she likes to impose limits on herself now. This is part of her new conformity, and no, it won't stifle creativity if you have other art forms available. Also, it's the same exercise for hand control that prepares her to write in school.

Your child can stay within the lines

easier if you teach her to make the long strokes within the picture just a little shorter and to use a series of tiny circles close to the edges, so she won't slop across the lines.

A Six creates her own pictures again, although they're seldom as original as they were at Four, and she often fills them in heavily and completely. Now she can etch designs on these pictures by drawing on them with an empty ballpoint pen, which shaves away some of the wax. To a child, that's magic.

---

## CRAYONED BATIK

Preheat iron: Warm

Your Four can do this if you supervise the ironing. Have her draw a picture or a design on a white handkerchief or a piece of a plain sheet, pushing the crayons down hard to sink the wax into the cloth.

**DAMPEN**          **2 paper towels**

Lay the fabric between them and iron until the paper is dry and the melted wax has set.

---

## PICTURE WINDOW PICTURES

Preheat iron: Warm

The sun will filter through these pictures as if they were stained glass. Use any broken crayons, in any colors. On a newspaper have your Five

**GRATE**          **Crayons**

**CUT**          **2 squares of wax paper**

Cover the ironing board with newspapers to keep it clean and lay one square over the other with the crayon shavings sprinkled in between like a sandwich. Cover with more newspaper and have your child press the paper with the warm iron until the wax is melted. Trim the edges for her and hang by a cord in the window.

---

### Transfers

A Six can transfer pictures without carbon paper. Have her fold a small sheet of your notepaper like a book, filling the inside left page completely with crayon, shutting the book and then drawing a picture with a pencil on the front page. The drawing is duplicated, in color, on the inside right page when she opens the book.

### CHALK

Chalk is one of the most imaginative, if impermanent, of all art forms.

A Two will be fascinated with it. At last she has something she can make appear and disappear, over and over—something she can control. For your sake, the chalkboard should be near your work space.

The best we ever saw belonged to our friend Guy, whose mother covered every low cabinet door in her kitchen with blackboard paint and hung a rag for an eraser.

However, you may want to keep at least the colored chalk under your care, because chalk is so fragile that one mashed red stick can cause a remarkable amount of mess and tears.

A Three will like to use white chalk on dark construction paper and learn to make swirling patterns by rubbing a stick on its side. A Four certainly can handle her own supply, in any color, with no more than the usual problems, and she'll be happy to draw pictures with her friends on the garage floor for a half-hour at a time, although the sidewalk is preferable, for everyone can admire it there. Little old ladies may object, but that will just delight the children more.

A Five, with her great admiration of school, likes her chalkboard on an easel, so she can play teacher, and a Six is quite ready for her own box of pastels to use on brown wrapping paper. Cover any work she wants to keep with a fixative like hair spray, or it won't last. We wish Picasso's mother could have done the same.

### FELT MARKERS

These pens must be one of our finest inventions, for they flow so easily and respond so well that a child as young as Two feels like a winner when she uses them. For best results, buy pens with broad tips and fat cases, and for your sanity, buy only water-based ones. You also must supply plenty of newsprint and much supervision, because it's hard for a child to contain herself to the paper. If she goes too far, remove the ink from the walls with strong detergent.

Keep these pens capped when not in use, but if they're not too dry they may be rejuvenated with a ten-minute soak in a cup of warm water. Waterproof pens need denatured alcohol or acetone to bring them alive again, which also removes most of the traces when they're left where they shouldn't be left.

## PAINTING

No one is as logical as a child—even a Two—which may be why she likes painting so much. This medium, more than any other art form, forces a child to look for logical answers to problems—in composition, in color, in perspective.

You'll see her paint her version of a tree, day after day, with little variation, until she feels she's mastered it, much as she climbs a stone animal in the park over and over until she thinks she can do it blindfolded.

The trees she paints between June and September may look the same to you, but she'll want you to notice the differences and comment on some aspect of each painting, as thoughtfully (and as kindly) as you would to an artist at his show of twenty landscapes. A child adores to be taken seriously.

You also show your respect when you tell her how to hold the brush, how to catch the drips and later how to mix the colors. This doesn't hurt her creativity, it simply makes her more adept. The better a child can handle her tools, the more she'll enjoy working with them—just like you.

There are five kinds of paint available, but we think a child should skip oils and watercolors entirely, even though they're cunningly boxed. Oils are not only indelible and messy, but they take weeks to dry,

and watercolors are so subtle they must be laid on with a small, delicate brush, each color blending into the next. A child, accustomed to vivid poster paints, can't resist rubbing the brush into the paper to enliven these pale colors—one of the hardest habits to unlearn if she ever should become a serious artist.

You'll find acrylics have spectacular colors (and prices), which a Five or a Six can use on her sculptures or crafts, but she might think the paint is too thick to glide easily on paper.

This leaves the two paints made from powdered tempera: finger paints, which most young children unaccountably like, and poster paints, the classic choice, since the brush fairly flies across the paper.

Whether your child uses poster paints or acrylics, she never needs more than red, blue and yellow—the source of every color in the prism—and white to make the shadings. It's particularly good for a child to make her own dark shades, because they'll be more interesting than any you can buy (see Poster Painting, page 297). You'll notice she instinctively avoids black—a good idea. It's the most dominating and therefore the most difficult color for anyone to use.

You can keep a painting session simple if the supplies are always ready. You'll need slick paper you can dampen, like freezer wrap, for finger paints; simple newsprint for poster paints; and good brushes with long handles and bristles of various thicknesses—one for each basic color. Buy fat, pointed camel's hair brushes for poster paints, which have a plastic base, but acrylics will ruin these natural bristles. You child will need special blunt brushes with synthetic bristles that can feed these paints more smoothly.

She'll poster-paint best at an easel and needs a table for either finger paints or acrylics, but you always should use newspapers or an Art Mat on the floor and her father's T-shirt on her; paint is a pain to scrub.

While these measures help your child to be a somewhat independent painter, she'll have some work to do when she's done—capping her own paints, folding her Art Mat and washing, drying and standing her brushes upside down in a tin can—and if she's not ready to do these things for herself she's not ready to paint the next time she asks.

### ART MAT

This mat will depress you less than a littering of newspaper on the kitchen floor. To make it

**CUT**        **4' × 4' vinyl-coated cloth**

Lay on the floor under her work space when she's painting, fold in a cupboard between use and hose clean when it looks too grungy.

### FINGER PAINTING

Finger painting is a delight of the very young, the bold and the messy, but it also is grand for loosening the shy and proper child. Where else can she smear paint with anything from her elbow to her fanny and be applauded for her creativity? Unfortunately, we ourselves never felt comfortable with finger painting but then we began late in life.

### The Techniques

Sit your well-smocked Two at a well-protected table and give her thick, slick paper, like shelf paper, the matte side of freezer wrap or, as a last resort, wax paper. Wet it first, either with a sponge or by skimming it under the tap, for this makes the paint slide better.

Drop a blob of the special paint onto the paper, and with some initial encouragement from you she'll make swirls and splats, dot and squiggles, using her elbows, her fingertips, her nails, her palms or if she wants to be less physical, a cork, a piece of a sponge, a comb.

## FINGER PAINT I

Liquid starch makes a fast and adequate finger paint and your Two can make it herself. In a cup

**MIX**            **¼ c. liquid laundry starch**
                   **2 drops food coloring OR**
                   **1 tsp. powder paint**

## FINGER PAINT II

Let your Three help you stir this to see the starch go through its magical change when mixed with boiling water. You can find the starch at the supermarket; the gylcerin at the drugstore. In a 2-quart saucepan

**COMBINE**        **½ c. dry laundry starch**
                   **½ c. cold water**

The mixture will be sticky and hard to stir.

**ADD**            **4 c. boiling water**

Add this yourself, a half cup at a time, but your child can stir it with a long wooden spoon. To keep it soft

**ADD**            **1 tbsp. glycerin**

When blended, separate into small baby food jars and into each one

**ADD**            **3 drops of food coloring**

You can make it as intense as she likes. Liquid or powder paints may be substituted, but they will leave color on her hands. Cap tightly and refrigerate between use.

### POSTER PAINTING

Poster painting encourages more freedom of movement—and therefore more originality—than other painting, partly because the exquisite tip of the brush makes the paper almost reach out to greet it. Newsprint is the paper you'll usually use, but a roll of brown wrapping paper is a good investment. It invites a big picture and forces a child to use vivid colors for contrast.

While a Two may like to lie on her Art Mat to paint, any child will do better at an easel. We found we could make a simple one by tacking a sheet of newsprint onto pressed wood, leaning it against the back of a kitchen chair and putting the paint pots over newspaper laid on the seat. If you can afford to buy an easel, however, it should be the best: sturdy, so it doesn't bring grief and make your child feel awkward; double, so a friend can paint too, and with a rack on each side to hold the paint without tipping.

The best paint pots are plastic jars with screw tops, baby food jars or even small juice cans, but if she's painting on a kitchen chair, use tuna fish cans. They're harder to tip, although you must cover any open can with foil between use or the paint will harden.

Because the mechanics of poster painting are hard to coordinate, a Two does better with only one color at a time at her easel, but an early Three can handle two colors at once, and a late Three can use all the primary colors at the same session.

To keep any color true, show her how to clean her brush between colors, dipping

### PAINTING TO MUSIC

We once endured a duty day at the cooperative nursery school by experimenting with music and art at the same time—a dandy way to stimulate a bored child and a bored mother too.

Without any direction, each child painted blue skies and sunshine as she listened to some soupy Hawaiian love songs and added darker colors and more detail with *American in Paris,* but when we switched to *Slaughter on Tenth Avenue,* they slowly covered their pictures completely with browns and blacks. While we don't recommend such drastic mood changes regularly, we did find that any child likes to translate sound into sight.

it first into a water pot and then wiping it on an old rag—a custom she'll learn to follow when she sees it makes sense.

Your Four is ready to mix her own colors. To do this give her small amounts of red, blue, yellow and white paints and a few extra cans so she can pour the colors back and forth like a mad scientist. At first all her colors will turn mauve, but by Five she'll be a fairly competent mixer and soon will like to fiddle with a color wheel from the art store. It teaches her that some colors are warm, others are cold and the combinations that look best to her are usually the ones that look best to all the other artists too.

The easiest kinds of poster paints your child can use are already mixed and pretty costly, but you can make excellent, and much cheaper, paints at home with paint powder if you add flour or a detergent to give them body and make the colors bright.

These powders are sold with art supplies in hobby shops and in some toy stores. We recommend the brands that come in pint-size cans—a mighty supply of creativity. You need only four colors—the three primary colors and the white to tone them.

## FLOUR-BASED POSTER PAINTS

Your Three can mix her paints herself if you have the stamina to stay with her and explain each step. To store them, have small wide-mouth plastic jars ready, one for each color. Measure all ingredients over the sink. In a saucepan

**STIR**          ¼ c. flour
                  1 c. water

Add the water slowly to make the paste smooth.

**HEAT**          3 minutes

Stir constantly, removing the pan from the fire when it begins to thicken. Cool. Into each jar

**MIX**           ¼ c. flour paste
                  3 tbsp. powder paint
                  2 tbsp. water

If the mixture is too dry add more water, a teaspoon at a time. Store in the covered jars and stir each time your child uses them. For a more opaque finish

**ADD**           ½ tsp. liquid starch

Or for a glossier finish

**ADD**           ½ tsp. liquid detergent

## DETERGENT POSTER PAINTS

This velvety mix makes each color as vivid as an acrylic, a dramatic paint for a Five. These proportions make enough for one color and one painting session. In a paper cup

**COMBINE**       1 tbsp. clear liquid detergent
                  2 tsp. powder paint

### THE WASH

A Six can draw a picture with a fine-lined felt-tipped pen, a pencil or a ballpoint pen and make it look almost professional by giving it a wash with poster paint. To do this, have her dip a wet cotton ball into any

pastel shade, press it lightly against the side of the cup to remove most of the paint, and pat or wipe it over or around the picture. The touch must be gentle and the drawing must be waterproof so it can't smear.

### DESIGNS

Your child can get a wholly new effect with paint if you introduce other materials to use with it.

### Texture

Texture comes through if you have your Three lay net, burlap or any other loosely woven material on a piece of paper and brush paint over it. Lift it carefully for her.

### String

To make this abstract design, let your Four dip a length of string in poster paint, then hold one end taut in the center of a sheet of paper and sweep the other end around the paper like a hand on a very fast clock.

### Stencil

Have your Five make a stencil in reverse by cutting a piece of construction paper into any shape and laying it on drawing paper. Have her paint its edges with short, feathery strokes that leave a design when she lifts the shape.

### BLOCK PRINTING

This art form brings instant success and requires little but an interesting stamp, a pad, some paper and a steady bang-stamp rhythm, which a Two can master. For paper, use newsprint, shelf paper, brown

bags or wrapping paper, freezer wrap or a piece of an old sheet, but by the time your child is Six, she may want to use manila paper and make her own stationery.

To block print, she can use a cork stopper, a piece of sponge, a scrap of smooth wood, the base of a bunch of celery or a head of lettuce or any firm fruit or vegetable, like a potato, which you first slice in half. A Five is ready to scoop a design ¼″ deep from the heart of the potato or trim the edges to make a shape, but at any age the child simply bangs the block she's made on the Stamp Pad and then on the paper.

## STAMP PAD

Wet one section of a paper towel, fold it and place it on a flat dish. On it

**SPRINKLE**      **1 tsp. powder paint OR**
                         **1 tbsp. liquid tempera paint**

Use the back of a spoon to blend the powder or paint into the pad, adding more water and more paint if it dries before she's done.

### ACRYLICS

Acrylics are the most beautiful paints of all—shiny, vivid and true—perfect for decorating crafts.

Like oils, they're not diluted but squirted directly from the tube to the palette. Unlike oils, however, a coat of acrylics will dry fairly well in just twenty minutes and the paint is water soluble. However, it must be rinsed out of the brushes and clothes with soapy water—or plain water—within thirty minutes, or they can't be rinsed at all.

To use, your child should have brushes with synthetic bristles and the easiest palette of all: a paper plate with dabs of white, blue, red and yellow on it. She can mix more colors by using the brush to lift some of the paint to other parts of the plate, stirring each new color with it. Teach her to rinse the bristles before touching the next dab to keep the colors pure.

You can make the paint go further if you add a gel medium to each color. This also retards the drying time but it doesn't change the color.

Even with gel, these acrylics are thick, so your child should dip the brush into water and then into the paint to make the strokes smoother. She can skip this step if she wants to drop the paint in blobs—a technique that takes longer to dry but gives a three-dimensional look.

## PASTING

Pasting is integral to a child's creativity, for it gives her another way to build. Besides, paste actually feels good to a child, which is one more way you can tell the difference between her and a grown-up.

The younger your child, the less she minds the smears of paste left on every picture. Thinned White Glue leaves the least trace, but the flour pastes are cheaper and easy to make. All must be stored in airtight containers, and the flour pastes must be refrigerated.

A child applies paste better with a 1″ brush than anything else, although a pre-Four may like to dip her collage materials into a saucer of paste instead. Have her work on newspapers and in her father's T-shirt, for a child and her paste are soon parted.

When she uses the Thinned White Glue recipe, she'll find it easier to glue two sides together if they're covered first with the glue and then she waits 10 minutes before pressing them together.

## UNCOOKED PASTE

This paste is good for an emergency and not much else. Into a cup

| MIX | ½ c. flour |
|     | ½ c. water |

Always add the water to the flour slowly so it won't lump.

## COOKED PASTE

The heat blends this paste well. In a 2-quart saucepan

| MIX | 1 c. flour |
|     | 1 tsp. salt |
|     | 2 c. water |

Add the water slowly, stirring until cooked.

| SIMMER | 5 minutes |

Cool and refrigerate in an airtight container.

## THINNED WHITE GLUE

This cold-water glue lasts longer than the cooked paste, is just as safe and doesn't look crusty when dry. Be sure to keep in an air-tight container.

| MIX | ½ c. white glue |
|     | ½ c. water |

# CUTTING

A child judges herself, in part, by the way she handles her tools, particularly a pair of scissors. Nothing else brings such pride if she's successful or such despair if she's not—which she surely will be if their quality is poor or if she's offered them too soon. It takes the skill of a Four to manipulate scissors perpendicular to paper, but not even a couturier could cut a pattern with clean edges if she used a pair of child's scissors from the dimestore. It's much more sensible to buy decent, blunt-tipped scissors from an art, surgical or school supply house—two pairs, in fact, in case of company or loss—and if your child is

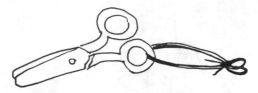

left-handed, the scissors must be too. For some reason, you usually can find good southpaw scissors at a toy store.

Your Four's frustration will be even less if you teach her to sharpen the blades by cutting sandpaper or trying to cut the neck of a soda bottle, which hones the edges too.

Still, the best scissors will bring despair unless you hang a long, bright ribbon on the handle so they won't get lost so easily, and unless you hide your scissors, in case they do. As we remember too well, once a child learns to cut, she doesn't quit easily.

Since every child will use pointed scissors sometimes, the safety rules apply to all. Explain carefully that she mustn't run with them or wave them and she must carry them with the blades wrapped in her fist and the tips extending just below the palm, and pointing backward, so she won't hurt herself if she falls.

When your Four begins to cut, she'll make endless chains of construction paper stapled or pasted together, and can cut simple swatches of crisp cloth for collages and for sewing. Scissors become the biggest mainstay of the school-happy Five and she practices with them almost continuously. A Six becomes adept enough to cut out paper snowflakes and the simplest paper dolls—not well, but well enough for the costume to hang on the figure.

# COLLAGES

A collage is a three-dimensional picture made from any combination of textures, weights and shapes, pasted into an abstract design at first and perhaps a realistic mural later.

Although early collages may not win a wholehearted "Wow" from you, your Two is learning to judge the feel and dimension of different objects and slowly she can harmonize a paper doily, a piece of fur, some ticket stubs and a pussywillow into an interesting, balanced composition.

The material will come from your kitchen cabinets, your sewing box and those slow walks to the park. Help her collect anything that's vivid, shiny, soft, brittle, geometric, common, rare—anything as long as it's reasonably clean and can't choke her. Give her a few empty oatmeal boxes to hold her collections, but don't let her keep buttons, stones or beans if she's a pre-Three and don't save paper or cloth that will need cutting until your child is Four and old enough to handle scissors.

A young child pastes collage material on anything stiff, like construction paper or paper bags, and by Five, uses glass jars and wood as well, with more expensive felt or burlap for a special tapestry.

As in any artwork, your child should wear her father's T-shirt and work over newspaper. Work alongside her at first, to explain the technique—particularly of pasting. She can take it from there. A Two will dip the scraps into Cooked Paste, but a Three will want to use Thinned White Glue to hold the heavier mosaics of beans, stones or pasta.

## FIRST COLLAGE

Choose anything that's easy and safe for a Two to pick up and paste.

**COLLECT**         cottonballs/leaves/feathers
                    eggshell bits/fabric and ribbon

Pour Uncooked Paste in a saucer and teach her to dip scraps into it and press them onto paper.

## GEOMETRIC COLLAGE

On that rare day when you have extra time, cut a dozen sheets of construction paper into rectangles, circles, triangles and squares, ranging from 1″ to 4″ in size. Your Three will need only one lesson to see that two circles and a rectangle make a car, but if she adds another, skinnier rectangle, it's a handle and the car becomes a wagon. She can glue the shapes onto a piece of paper with Cooked Paste and a 1″ brush and save the rest in an envelope for that ordinary day when she has extra time.

## GRAVEL MOSAIC

Let your Four dye gravel with various colors of poster paint, by dropping the stones into shallow tin cans of paint and then scooping them onto newspaper with a slotted spoon, where they can dry. While she waits, have her draw a picture or a design on a stiff paper and cover one section of it at a time with Thinned White Glue, then cover each section with stones of a different color.

## TISSUE COLLAGE

This collage looks best with paper scraps about the size of a Five's hand.

**TEAR**            3–6 colors of tissue

Using Thinned White Glue

**PAINT**           a wine bottle OR a block of wood

When it's completely covered, have her wash the glue from her hands, then paste overlapping scraps of paper on it. Wait about 10 minutes and wipe with a damp cloth to remove the extra glue and to stick the edges firmly in place—a delicate job you may have to do yourself.

## GLASS COLLAGE

A crafty Five we know invented collages made from the broken bits of colored glass she collected on her walks. Some were lovely, some ghastly, but she never cut herself, and she always had presents to give. A plastic lid made both the backing and the frame. On the inside of it, have your child

**SMEAR**           Thinned White Glue

Let it rest until tacky—about 10 minutes—then she can arrange the glass bits in the lid.

## FABRIC COLLAGE

This only looks handsome if your Six uses your good sewing scissors, for all edges must be clean.

**COLLECT**          yarn/string/twine
                     fabric scraps
                     trimmings/ribbons

Staple burlap or felt to a thick section of the daily paper to keep the surface firm—a job for you. Your child can paint the back of a scrap with Thinned White Glue and press it into place, adding pieces from day to day until she's made a picture. Unstaple the paper for her when the glue is dry.

# SCULPTING

Sculpting takes many forms, and if the medium is soft enough a young child can handle it. You'll want to offer the clays as early as Two, the plasters at Three and, finally, at Four, the papier-mâché.

## *CLAY*

The tactile joys of pounding, rolling and flattening clay strengthen a child's sense of touch as much as painting at the easel expands her sense of sight.

There is the Flour Clay and the Cornstarch Clay in this section, as well as the Play Clay (see page 207) and the Ecuadorian Bread Dough (see page 259), all of which are homemade, and the splendidly messy oil-based clay from the dimestore, which you'll want to buy only once a year—but no more, since it sticks so well to the floor. Finally, there is natural clay, that blessedly tough earth in the backyard where you thought the topsoil would be.

All of these are pliable enough to be shaped again and again and all, except the oil-based clay, can be baked and painted with powder paints or acrylics, which you can spray with a fixative later.

Your child can help you make the recipes but she needs you to give offhand suggestions and many compliments to learn the techniques.

## *Hand-building*

A Two automatically shapes clay into a ball, which you'll call an orange, and flattens it with her fist, which she'll call a cookie, imprinting the circle of clay with a fork, a key or a piece of your jewelry.

At Three she'll make paperweights, pressing clay over and around a rock and sticking a collage of shells, stones and dried flowers on it. She also can make snakes—if you teach her to lighten her touch enough to roll a ball of clay into a skinny rope. From there she learns the coil construction of a potter, circling the rope around and around from the center to make a basket.

A Four can make a gingerbread man— fixing the eyes and a mouth onto a ball, adding hair that's been squeezed through a garlic press (the one trick that won't work with natural clay) and twisting a body out of snaky clay, pressing it with a rolling pin. Almost any figure can be hung on the wall or on a Christmas tree if you embed a paper clip in its back before baking. At this age, your child can make and bake ropy rings and threaded beads of Cornstarch Clay—fragile gifts indeed, but the love they carry will outlast them by years.

The Five achieves real sophistication in her figures, dressing them in skirts and pants and hats. They can perch upright (if they're squat enough) and they like to be painted. She can lay snakes of clay on the table too, in the outline of the pussycat and the neighbor lady, glasses and all. The more classic hand-building starts with natural clay when, with much help, your Six can dig it herself and make her own thumb pots. Teach her to do this by shaping the clay into a ball the size of her fist, pressing her thumb in the center and then pressing it against the sides, all the way around, until it turns into a pot.

## FLOUR CLAY

This is easy for your Two to make, but you still must help her measure and knead as directed in the bread-making instructions (see page 355). In a bowl

| COMBINE | 4 c. flour |
|---|---|
| | 1½ c. salt |
| | 2 c. water |

Add the water slowly, stopping when the dough is still a little dry, and begin to work by hand. While the salt keeps this recipe pliable, it dries the skin, so you and your child should rub a little salad oil on your hands first.

| KNEAD | 10 minutes |
|---|---|

When it's soft and smooth, divide the dough into batches and add food coloring to each one. Refrigerate leftover clay in self-sealing plastic bags, between use, but have your child oil her hands whenever she sculpts with this clay.

## CORNSTARCH CLAY

Your Four will appreciate the smooth texture of this clay, for it's a pleasure to touch and it can be worked into delicate shapes. It also absorbs colors better than any other clay. In a 2-quart saucepan over a low fire

| STIR | 2 c. baking soda |
|---|---|
| | 1 c. cornstarch |
| | 1¼ c. cold water |

Add the water slowly to prevent lumps and help your child stir, because the job is hard until half the water is mixed.

| COOK | 6 minutes |
|---|---|

Stop when it looks like mashed potatoes and spread the dough on a cookie sheet to cool—your job. Cover with a damp cloth to keep it moist.

| KNEAD | 10 minutes |
|---|---|

Divide the clay into batches when it's pliable and add food coloring unless your child plans to paint it later. Refrigerate in self-sealing plastic bags, one for every color, or let your child shape it as soon as it's cool.

These works of art will harden in 24 hours if exposed to the air at room temperature or if they're left overnight in an oven that was first preheated to 275° and turned off, but most children would rather see the results a little quicker. To bake the clay

Preheat Oven 200°

Place the decorations on a lightly greased cookie sheet.

| BAKE | 2 hours |
|---|---|

Cool in the oven for 2 hours longer, removing when the decorations are hard underneath.

### *Natural Clay*

Probably the nicest reason for having your child work with natural clay is that you get a chance to do the same. Like making bread, anything that's been done for thousands of years is irresistible. You also don't need a potter's wheel, tricky tools, glazes or a kiln to know its joy. A young child is much too inept and impatient to throw clay on a wheel, but she can hand-build with a few kitchen utensils and her own little fingers. As for glazes, we think natural clay is meant to look natural, for it lets a child concentrate on the texture and the shape and this is where the pleasure lies. Finally, an oven is much handier than a kiln and although success is less certain, you can salvage enough to be proud. At this age, her cups are meant to be admired, not used.

There are many clays available, including the plasticized (and comparatively expensive) clay at the art supply stores, which can be air-dried without crumbling, or the ready-to-use and much cheaper clay sold in five-pound boxes, but your child probably would like to dig it for herself, at least once. It's a nice thing to do on a country vacation.

Clay is found everywhere—in tan, gray, white or red—depending on its minerals. Dig near a construction site—wherever the topsoil has been cut away—but avoid sandy areas for sand weakens its

strength, and be careful of broken glass. Before taking some clay, add a little water to it, twisting and squeezing the clay to see if it's pliable enough to hold a shape. Good clay is almost as springy as half-kneaded dough. Plan to take no more than half a bucket of clay, because the preparation is hard work.

You'll have to help with both the digging and, when you get home, the spreading, for it must dry in thin layers and then be crumbled into tiny pieces. Put them in a big bowl with enough water to turn the clay into "slip." This stage, about the consistency of pea soup, is so gloriously messy your child will want to do the next job herself: pouring the slip first through a colander and then through a window screen several times, which is necessary to filter the debris. Let the slip settle, drain the excess water and store in sealed plastic bags, where it will mature and perhaps smell sour as the organisms decompose. This adds some plasticity to the clay but it still can't be used until it's wedged—a nice potter's term that means to pound it and slam it down hard, again and again, both to make it pliable and to knock out the bubbles that can splinter clay as it dries. Your child will help with this hard work (but not much), but she will like to wrap a piece of heavy thread around both hands, pull it taut and slice the clay in half in several places. If no bubbles show, it's been wedged enough.

Generally a potter wedges and handbuilds on a "bat"—a slick, 2"-thick plaster of Paris slab that absorbs extra moisture—but the wrong side of oilcloth works just as well and the clay won't stick to that either. The clay stays moist if she covers it with the cloth or a damp towel between uses.

If the clay should get a little dry before you use it, add only a sprinkling of water to make it elastic. No matter how old or hard it gets, it will come to life if you soak it in water and roll it with a rolling pin, putting each layer between thicknesses of newspaper to get that plastic consistency.

However, any clay that has been wedged—either by the factory or by you—should be kneaded a little before using it, which your child can do for herself.

Any of the hand-building techniques can be used to make figures, boxes, animals or thumb pots, but if you and your child stop between shaping, cover your works with the oilcloth or the damp towel so you can work with them the next day. A fairly thin piece—less than an inch thick—can be baked in a 550° oven for six hours or more but clay shouldn't be too thick, even in a kiln, for it fractures easily under heat. That's why a potter leaves his finished sculpture uncovered overnight to dry a little and then scoops away some of the innards before he bakes it. Even then it must be treated gently afterward, for the pieces will always be fragile.

### PAPIER-MÂCHÉ

No art requires as much imagination as papier-mâché—or as much faith. It's hard for a Four to believe that water, paste and the classifieds ever could look like a cat. While a Five can't make the classic mâché of absorbent paper that's been torn, soaked, boiled, drained, squished and perhaps mixed with sawdust or plaster of Paris, she can dip strips of paper into wheat paste or starch. This sculpts quite as well, as long as she learns some techniques from you.

### The Armature

Since a good sculptor makes an armature first, your child should do the same—a subtle way to compliment her, for any child likes to feel she's doing adult work. This mâché armature is simply a few sheets of newspaper rolled into a primitive shape (her job) and bound with string or masking tape (your job). It won't look like much until she's molded the wet strips of paper around it.

### The Snake
Roll 4 sheets of newspaper into a tube and tie. Voilá—a snake!

### The Horse

Roll 5 double sheets of paper into a tube, tying to make the head, neck and body. Make two more tubes for the legs, using 2 sheets for each one and sealing the paper shut with masking tape. Leave room at one end for the head and neck and bend the legs across the top of the body so they go down straight. Tie with string in a secure X, under and over the body. The same armature makes a dog, a cat or a pig, but you must make shorter tubes, for the neck and legs must be much shorter.

### The Puppet

Have your child wad newspaper into a ball for the head, doing it around a toilet paper tube (so half of the tube extends to become the neck), while you wrap the head with string to keep it round. After the puppet's head has been sculpted and painted, cover the neck with a skirt of material, held in place by a rubber band.

### The Mâché

A mâché sculpture should please most children and mothers too, for the work not only can be stretched over several days—it must be. Your child has to tear the paper, make the armature, make the paste, wet the paper with it, press it on the frame, dry it and finally paint it. To begin,

**TEAR**      **8 sheets of newspaper, 3″ wide**

The paper rips straighter if several sheets are torn at once. To stick it on the armature, your child should drop each strip, as needed, into a bowl filled either with an inch of undiluted liquid starch, which is handy, or with Wallpaper Paste, which bonds better and can be sanded when done—a step some purists follow.

---

### WALLPAPER PASTE

Your Four can make this recipe easily.

**MIX**      **2 c. wheat paste**
                  **2½ c. water**

You'll find wheat paste at a paint store and can keep this mixture in the refrigerator for a few days in a covered container.

---

### The Sculpture

Have your child cover any armature by dipping one strip of paper at a time into the solution and pressing it over the frame, repeating the process again and again until the body, legs and head are covered. As layers accumulate, the figure will be wet enough for your child to pinch and poke the nose, the ears and the eyes into shape—or to transform a two-legged animal into a fat duck, for instance, by puffing its chest, pulling out its beak and flattening the ends of its legs, covering them until they turn into web feet.

If your child is making an animal with a tail, have her cut paper ¼″ wide and poke the lengths into its behind with a pencil, which will cause wicked laughter from scatologically minded children (and all children are). Broom straws, yarn or serpentine confetti will give as many yocks. Keep adding more strips until the animal has the right shape, then add a layer of paper towel for final smoothness.

**HARDEN**      **2 days**

This may take more time, or less, depending on the humidity of the room and the size of the sculpture. When completely dry—it will feel very light—the sculpture is ready for her to sand any rough edges and to paint with acrylics or poster paints. She can decorate if she wants, using Thinned White Glue (see page 300) to stick buttons for eyes, glitter for grandeur and elbow macaroni (or feathers) for feathers.

## MÂCHÉ MASKS

Our younger children hit an artistic peak in Kate's art class, making masks embedded with mirrors, fur, feathers and fancies and then painting them in brilliant colors—too fragile to wear but each a knockout on the wall. Your Five can make a mask, but your Six can make it better.

| ASSEMBLE | 8 sheets of newspaper |
| | 1 c. Wallpaper Paste |
| | 1 balloon |

Tear most of the paper into pieces the size of playing cards and the rest into strips, 5″ long. Drop these pieces into the paste, inflate the balloon and cover half of it with the wet paper. Add fangs, beaks, noses and ears by holding balls of paper in the proper places while your child covers them with wet strips.

| DRY | 2 days |

He can pop the balloon—an exhilarating step—then trim the edges with scissors, but you'll have to cut holes for the mouth and eyes. Have your child sand the rough edges and paint the mask with poster paints. When dry, paste on the decorations with Thinned White Glue (see page 300).

## LAMINATED SHIELD

A knight, if she's Five, can make this shield and she can laminate a crown too, in case she gets promoted. Mix half the recipe for Wallpaper Paste in a bowl. Dipping a 2″ brush into it,

| PAINT | 6 sheets newspaper |

Press one sheet on top of the other and cover with a layer of paper towels. She'll need your help to trim and bend it in the shape of a shield, rolling the edges under. Dry before painting.

## PLASTER

Since plaster is about the messiest art form of all, you'll want to use it on your more tolerant days.

Unless you're mixing your own exotic blend of lime and gauging plaster (a bother), you can choose between plaster of Paris, patching plaster and spackling compound. They differ in color and in drying time, but any can be used to cast a handprint or repair a wall, and all may be found in the hardware store.

Plaster of Paris (which naturally was invented in Paris) is a crisp, snowy mixture made mostly of gypsum. Because it's slick and white, it's still the favorite of some old-time plasterers and because it's so quick to dry, it's also preferred by impatient Twos. As your child becomes more adept, she probably would rather work with patch plaster, which takes twice as long to set. It's much cheaper too, since only 3⅓ cups of plaster equal a pound, and you can buy it in 25-pound sacks. The spackling compound is the slowest to dry and to a child it seems to take forever, which makes it best to fill nail holes. It's a little gray in color and has more lime, sand and hair than the others and very little gypsum.

The drying time of any plaster can be retarded by adding some extra water or sand. Use a tin can to mix it and never, never dump the leftover plaster down the drain unless you want to cast your pipes.

## PLASTER MIX

You can use these proportions to make any casting plaster, but don't mix more patch plaster than you can use in an hour or more plaster of Paris than you can use in several minutes. In a big tin can have your child

| STIR | 2 c. patch plaster OR |
| | plaster of Paris |
| | 1¼ c. water |

It should be as thick as pea soup so it can cast without air bubbles. Plaster of Paris goes to the consistency of thick stew in 3–4 minutes and dries in 10–20. Patch plaster takes 20–40 minutes to dry, but all drying time depends on the humidity, the size of the mold and how much the plaster was stirred. The more air you whip into it, the quicker it sets.

## THE MOLD

Plaster casting enchants the Three who first uses her hands as a mold. Make a small batch of plaster of Paris, wait about 2 minutes and then pour it into her cupped hands. Help her hold them together for several minutes more until the plaster feels quite warm and the shape is set. She'll think it beautiful.

## HANDPRINTS

A new handprint (or footprint) every six months makes a nice frieze around a child's wall, as fascinating to her as her growth chart on the wall. It's all part of the No-Belly-Button-Is-As-Interesting-As-One's-Own syndrome. Start at any age, but it seems to have a special appeal to a Three. Into a paper plate

**POUR**      **1″ Plaster Mix**

Wait 2 minutes for plaster of Paris; 6 minutes for patch plaster.

**IMPRINT**      **1–2 minutes**

Have her press her hand gently into the plaster so it doesn't go right to the bottom. Let the handprint set overnight, peel the plate from the print and paste a picture hook on the back for hanging.

## PLASTER MEDALLION

A Five can make a free-form medallion pretty enough to be proud of.

**CUT**      **27″ thong OR yarn OR string**

Spoon thickened Plaster Mix onto a piece of wax paper or a plastic lid. Let her use an opened paper clip to make a hole for the thong. When plaster has set, she can paint the medallion with a felt-tipped pen or poster paint and scratch a design on the medallion with a nail when the paint is dry.

## BIRDCAGE BALLOONS

This is a recipe that needs plenty of time, help and compliments, but your Five will be rewarded by airy make-believe birdcages to hang from her ceiling or small Christmas ornaments for the tree, both made of plastered yarn that's been dried around balloons. Have your child make enough to ensure some success and, if possible, make them outdoors, because the yarn is so drippy.

**ASSEMBLE**      **6 round balloons, large and small**
                       **3 c. Plaster Mix**
                       **six 12′ lengths of vivid yarn**
                       **six 2′ lengths of string**

You'll need less yarn and less string for the small ornaments. Have your child inflate the balloons, securing each with a 2′ string, so she can hang it later to dry. She can cut the yarn into lengths equal to the diameter of its inflated balloon and then dip them into the plaster. The thinner the yarn and the less plaster it attracts, the more delicate the cages will look. The yarn should be wrapped lengthwise, but the pieces must cross securely at the top and bottom, even if you have to reinforce them with a teaspoon of wet plaster. Tie the balloons by their strings to a hanger, suspending it from a door frame indoors or from a tree branch outside.

**DRY**      **30 minutes**

Your child should clean the mess while waiting, which she'll scarcely mind in her excitement to pop the balloons. When the scraps are pulled out of the cage, the rigid yarn should keep its shape.

## ◇ CRAFTS ◇

Since crafts are once again a part of our culture, every child deserves the chance to become adept at them. While a young child can't have the ability of an artisan, each of her attempts makes her appreciate the value of handwork.

Her best work will spring from ideas of her own, which will be prolific if she has scissors, paste, tissue, yarn, paper doilies, straws, pipe cleaners and those blessed scraps of telephone wire sometimes given away by the repairmen. The tiny, brightly colored wires, which you'll pull from the casing for her, can make everything from sculpture to jewelry (of a sort).

Your child will need your guidance to follow most of these craft recipes—at least until she understands the techniques—but the time is well spent. It's important for a child to know that she can capture the beauty of the flowers in a meadow with more than a memory; that she can gather berries and roots to dye cloth in rich, if muted, colors; that the doll she makes herself is quite as good a friend as the one you buy and that, with needle, thread and a little skill, she can make simple clothes for it or make a beanbag to toss. A child is never too young to learn that everything in life doesn't come from the store.

## DOLLS

Since dolls are among the few toys that are cheaper than they used to be, children are likely to have many more than they need—and yet, they'll all look alike. Tell your child how it used to be, long before you were born, when rich children had china

dolls from the store and the rest had dolls they made with their parents from a hundred odd things. Some they stuffed with rags, some they whittled of wood, some they made of cornhusks and some they carved from apples into wonderful, awful old crones. With help, your twentieth-century child can also make dolls. Although some may not last long, like the foil doll, others—like the yarn doll—will hang on the wall for years. The joy, we find, isn't just in the making but in the chance it gives a child to breathe some life into a creation all her own.

## LIFE MASK

Aluminum foil holds a shape, bends easily and can be decorated with poster paints. A Three can use it to make her own life mask and, in fact, wants to make so many you'll think she found her face in an assembly line.

**CUT**     **18″ length of foil**

Double to make it stiffer. Help her press it evenly over her face, molding it against her eyes, nose and mouth. Lift the fragile mask gently for her, poke holes at the temples with a knife and run string through them to hang it.

## ALUMINUM FOIL DOLL

By Four, a boy sometimes won't play with dolls but he likes to make one out of foil—especially if he can make a bosomy girl.

**CUT**     **9″ length of foil**

Help him roll it into a cylinder and pinch twice: once in the center for the waist and then higher for the neck. Press the foil into a ball for the head and wrap a pipe cleaner once around the neck with ends extending for arms. Probably without any prompting he'll strategically plump out the cylinder above the waist and flatten it below. If his girl wears pants he can rip the lower half in two, but for a dress, he must press an extra piece of foil around the middle for a skirt. So much for the life of a couturier.

## NUTSHELL CREATURES

A hundred years ago, when children were more prevalent than toys, the walnuts they ate became fine and fanciful creations. With clay, your Four can transform a shell into a basket for tiny dough fruit, a turtle shell with clay feet, head and tail or into a sailboat. To make this one, he should cut a triangle from the corner of an index card, thread it with a toothpick and anchor it in the shell with clay. The boat will float, because the shell is waterproof.

## ORANGE DOLL

One orange and a piece of material about 24″ × 36″ make a doll, would you believe, as cuddly and floppy as any little girl could want. We saw a Five named Molly, lonesome for her doll back home, ask for an orange, cover it with a dish towel, tie it with her hair ribbon and draw a face on it. The day wasn't done before she had embroidered the eyes and mouth, not too well, but well enough for the doll to be her constant companion for the rest of the week.

## YARN DOLL

A Five can wrap yarn around the width and length of a book to make a fat, old-fashioned yarn doll, but you'll have to count as she winds and tie the ends for her too. The width becomes the arms; the length becomes the head, the body and the legs.

Choose a thick book that is roughly 5″ × 8″, and wrap the long side of the book 80–100 times. Slip a 5″ piece of yarn underneath one end of the book to tie the loops so they stay together when she slips them from the book. Make the head by tying a knot 4″ from the top.

To make the arms, wrap more yarn 40–50 times around the width of the book, slipping it from the book carefully for your child and tying a short piece of yarn near the ends to form the hands. Have her slip the arms under the head—through the strands—and use a short piece of yarn to tie under the arms to bind the waist. If your child wants the doll in a dress, it's finished when she cuts all the loops; if the doll wears pants, she'll

have to divide the yarn into legs for you to tie at the feet.

## OCTOPUS

Braiding is an important and tricky skill for a Five to learn, and this Octopus teaches it well. This stuffed animal is made with the fattest yarn you can find and in three colors, so a child can see what she's doing.

ASSEMBLE      twenty-four 30″ lengths of yarn
one 3″ styrofoam ball
10 rubber bands
ten 3″ lengths of ribbon
white glue
2 felt discs

Have your Five band all the yarn an inch from one end and smoothe the strings evenly over the ball, if possible keeping the colors in sequence for easier braiding. Tie them just below the ball with another band to make the head of the octopus and hang this head on a hook or a nail so your child can have both hands free. She'll plait three strings, each a different color, stopping near the end while you band it, for she mustn't let the braid go. Do this 7 more times—and by then they may look right. Tie a bow ribbon on each octopus arm, around the neck and at the topknot to cover the bands—another job for you. Your child can paste the felt in place for eyes.

## CORNHUSK DOLL

Any cornhusk doll charms an adult, but your Six will be more enchanted by the one she makes herself. Creating the doll is a project that thrives best in a gentle atmosphere, when both of you feel like being together, for she'll need your help to bind the husks with heavy-duty thread and glue the corn silk hair.

Dry the inner husks and the silk in a brown paper bag months ahead of time and take them out on a quiet winter's day. Have your child soak the husks in warm water for 5 minutes to make them pliable again.

To form the head and body, have her choose the biggest husk and fold it in half over a small wad of thin husks to round out the head. Tie at the neck with thread. To make the arms, fold a long husk lengthwise 4 times and slip it through the body just below the neck. Tie the thread under the arms to make the waist. The doll can stand by itself if you cut the husks straight across the bottom when dry. Your child can cut another husk and tie it around for a skirt.

When the doll is dry, have your child draw the face

with a felt-tipped pen and cover the back of the head with white glue, pressing corn silk onto it.

## APPLE DOLL

An apple doll needs to cure in a dry, warm house as we discovered one September when it grew a beard of mold after three weeks of rainy weather. So the head won't mildew, make it in late winter when the fruit is dry and rather cottony.

Peel a whole apple—one without bruises—and help your Six use a corer to dig out two small holes for eyes and a crescent for the mouth. Shape the nose into a bump by whittling bits of apple from each side—a job that may be too tricky for a child. If your child wants the doll to have a rather fair skin, she should paint the apple with lemon juice. To dry the fruit, poke a popsicle stick into the base, drop the stick in a soda bottle and place it in a well-ventilated place, but not near a window or you may get fruit flies. If you put it near a radiator in the winter it will dry a little quicker.

### DRY            55–60 days

When the apple begins to pucker and form a skin, it's time for your child to pinch and poke the features to exaggerate a smile or to make the cheeks sag.

### CURE            2–3 weeks

After the face has set, help your child gather a ruffle of material around the stick with a rubber band to make the dress. Tie a bow ribbon around the neck. Raisins are glued in place for eyes and cotton turns into the snowy hair.

Now she won't think Great-Grandma looks so old anymore.

## DYES

Over three thousand years ago some clever Phoenicians built their fortunes on snails, taking a tiny gland from each one and baking it in sunshine before making the best, most expensive and one of the most complicated dyes in the world. Your child can make dye too, although it won't make her rich, it won't be kingly purple and unless you set it first with a mordant, it won't be colorfast either. Nevertheless, she can make a dye with almost anything—except perhaps snails.

Dyes come from chemicals, minerals, fruits, vegetables, roots, barks and, although you won't want to use them, insects.

Whatever you use must be boiled long enough to reach a deep color, then strained, measured, salted and cooled enough for your child to soak the cloth in it—a dripping job best done outside. It's the experiment that pleases your child and in the process she realizes that every color has a different source. At least she'll never wonder if sheep come in pink, blue and plaid.

Since synthetic fibers take natural dyes so poorly, your child should use natural cloth: linen, wool or cotton. Cotton is the cheapest and a good first choice and old cotton is the best, because you must remove the sizing in new cloth by washing it several times in hot water before the dye can be absorbed.

We've found an old cotton sheet from a yard sale is ideal, since it can be ripped into small squares and dyed in many colors. These can either turn into rather wretched, ragged but much treasured handkerchiefs or they can be pieced together into a drape for the playhouse, which is much prettier. A patchwork cover like that, machine-stitched by their mother, delighted Sarah and her sister Rachel.

## MORDANT

If your child dyes fabric in cooled water—the safest way for her to do it—the color will bleed unless you treat it first with a mordant to bind the dye to the fiber. Boil the material in an enamel pot with a metallic salt, like chrome or potassium or the much more common aluminum potassium sulfate, known as alum at the drugstore. The salt you use will affect the color of the dye, which makes the results even more interesting. A Four can do this measuring and return to help you when the water has cooled.

*Cotton and Linen*
To prepare these fabrics

**COMBINE**   1 gal. water
1 oz. alum
¼ oz. washing soda

**ADD**   material

**BOIL**   1 hour

Cool, rinse and dry before dyeing.

*Wool*
To prepare this fabric, substitute ¼ oz. cream of tartar for the soda.

## NATURAL DYES

Your Three can dye cloth simply by wetting it with vinegar and laying it on damp clay so it can draw the stain, but she's ready for more sophisticated techniques at Four.

All dyes must be made in an enamel pot, 2 quarts or bigger, with enough water to cover the leaves, flowers, berries or roots. Each takes a different length of time to release all its color and all must be stirred with a wooden spoon, cooled, strained and measured. If the cloth hasn't been treated with a mordant you'll need to add table salt, but even then it won't be very fast. To each cooled pint of dye

**ADD**   1 tsp. salt

Now your child can drop the cloth in the pot.

**SOAK**   10–15 minutes

Rinse the excess color in clear water and lay the material in the shade to dry.

*Onionskin*
For a dark honey color, have your child peel the brown shells from 5 pounds of onions.

**BOIL**   30 minutes

*Goldenrod*
When the goldenrod has just begun to bloom, pick about 3 dozen flowers. Chop both stems and flowers into small pieces.

**BOIL**   15 minutes

*Cranberry*
A half pound of cranberries bleeds a lovely magenta.

**BOIL**   30 minutes

*Beets, Dandelions and Sassafras*
The beets make a red-violet color; the dandelion roots are magenta; and the sassafras roots and bark are pink.

**BOIL**   45 minutes

This is one dye that requires salt, with or without a mordant. To each cooled pint

**ADD**   1 tsp. salt

## STRING

There's something about string that elicits inventiveness in a child. Since primitive times, people have used leather strips and grasses to bind tools and thread ornaments, and we still follow the same techniques today.

Your Two will begin by stringing a thick cord through her big wooden beads, gradually learning by Four to move the string to the bead and never the bead to the string: a basic exercise of coordination she'll need when she wants to thread a needle or read. Such ability seems to come naturally to a child if she's given a ball of twine and a few casual lessons in the simplest knot tying. She also can use long leather shoelaces, a packet of pipe cleaners, some delicate telephone wires—or, of course, long grasses.

## STRING DESIGNS

Three-dimensional geometric pictures can be very pleasing. Into a block of pine, let your Four

**HAMMER**   twenty 8-penny finishing nails

They should be driven 2″ deep, at random, although you may have to give the final rap to keep them steady. To any nail she chooses

**TIE**   5′ colored twine

Your child takes the string from nail to nail, twisting it once under the head to hold it in place. Tie the tail to the last nail when she's done. A Six can do it all, using a variety of lengths, colors and textures of string to create complicated geometric patterns—and also to look pretty.

## YARN PICTURES

If your Five soaks yarn or string in glue and pastes it on tissue paper, it can become a mobile, a sculpture or a window decoration. Cover the table with newspaper and have a washrag handy, because this is messy.

| CUT | 4–6 lengths of yarn |
|-----|---------------------|

They should be about as long as her arm. Cover another part of the table with newspaper and over it

| LAY | 1 sheet tissue paper |
|-----|----------------------|

In a bowl

| MIX | 2 tbsp. white glue |
|-----|--------------------|
|     | 2 tbsp. water      |

Have your child soak the yarn in the glue, squeezing each piece through her fingers to get rid of the excess, and then pressing in on the tissue and snaking each piece of yarn across another so the picture will hold together. To make a mobile or a sculpture, use plain tissue, tearing it away when the glue dries, but for a window decoration, use vivid tissue and trim the edges. It will catch the sunshine rather like stained glass.

## FLOWER KEEPING

The child who can dry flowers will never be insensitive to beauty. This is the art that makes her notice each petal, each leaf, until every flower in the field becomes unique in her sight.

Although flowers and foliage need water to keep them fresh, it must be removed as quickly as possible to dry them. Some hardy flowers can dry upside down in the closet—simple enough work for a Two—but others can be pressed in a thick book, which requires a Four. Drying them in a medium, like sand or silica gel or dipping them in wax, is the work of a Six (and a most patient mother).

Unless you're buying the flowers or cutting them from the yard, it takes some foresight to keep them fresh until you can get home from an outing in the country. If you want to press flowers you should take a thick phone book with you, so you can slip a few between the pages wherever you stop, but if you want to dry them you'll need to put them in a well-sealed plastic bag, a canister with a tight lid or a bucket of wet sand, so they won't wilt. If they do, they'll dry badly. Finally, you'll have to get the owner's permission to take any flowers from his field, but wherever you are, cut only one wildflower from each plant, so it can reproduce itself.

When you get home, remove the leaves and either hang the flowers immediately, or, if you're drying them in a medium like sand, put the stems in very warm water for 1–2 hours to harden them. If you're still not ready to work with them, poke the stems into a damp sponge, so they won't get any wetter than necessary, but for best results, try to dry them before the day is done. Most weeds and many flowers will cure well in air, but the finer flowers—pansies, roses and daisies—need a medium to keep their shape and color. Even so, only half of these flowers will be usable. If you collect them often enough, the losses won't matter so much.

### AIR-CURED FLOWERS

This is an easy method for a late Two, but it only works for hardy, fresh field flowers with long stems and small flowers, like goldenrod, and never with petal flowers, like ox-eyed daisies.

Have your child remove all leaves and help her tie the stems into loose bunches. Hang upside down from clothes hangers in a warm, dry place, like an attic or a utility room, so they won't mildew.

| CURE | 10–14 days |
|------|------------|

They can, of course, stay longer.

### TREATED FOLIAGE

There is as much subtle beauty in a finely veined leaf as there is in a flamboyant flower. Your Three will see it well when she soaks branches in glycerin, for this drugstore chemical makes the leaves turn color dramatically. Some become deep brown, some mahoghany, some bronze, depending on the species and the season, but the dogwood, that maverick, turns a bright green.

Not all foliage works and not every time but the experiment will fascinate a child. She'll have best luck with deciduous hardwoods like beech, birch, crabapple, maple and oak, but holly usually works too and so does bayberry, blueberry, forsythia, privet, rhododendron and rose. Once treated, the foliage keeps indefinitely in a vase without water, without shriveling and without losing its color. Our record is three years for ligustrum—a little dusty but still a rich chocolate brown.

Cut foliage when the leaves are green— a sign that the sap is running and the solution can run with it. Your child should crush the bottom 2″ of each stem with a hammer, which is a job she'll do enthusiastically. In a jar

| COMBINE | 1 c. glycerin |
|---------|---------------|
|         | 3 c. hot water |
| ADD     | foliage       |
| SOAK    | 1–3 days      |

They're done when the top leaves feel oily to the touch and all the leaves have a startlingly different color. The hotter the water, the quicker this change will be. You can use the solution over and over if it's reheated each time.

## PRESSED FLOWERS

Some pretty—and pretty expensive—pictures today are made with pressed flowers. A Four can press them with a fifty-fifty measure of success, if the flowers have only one or two layers of petals, like pansies or vinca minor. Fat flowers, like roses, carnations, hydrangeas or geraniums, should be pulled apart and pressed as petals.

Flowers press best in a thick telephone book, since its paper is so absorbent, or within a 3″ stack of newspapers. Don't use the Sunday comics, because they may stain, and don't use paper towels or napkins, because the embossed design may transfer.

**COLLECT          Flowers/ferns/leaves**

The flora mustn't be damp or cold—which means a sunny day, perhaps as late as noon—and the book shouldn't be cold either, or the flowers will be brown when they dry. Remove stems and leaves and lay the flowers in the book carefully, smoothing the petals so they don't crease and adding an entry every 4–6 pages.

Weight the book with a six pack of beer or the family Bible (whichever is handiest and heaviest) so light won't enter, and keep in a dry place.

**PRESS          7–10 days**

It's best for your child to keep the flowers in the book until she's ready to use them. If she removes them too soon they'll wilt and the leaves and fronds will curl, although these can be rescued by ironing them between two sheets of wax paper.

### Pressed Flower Pictures

Your Six can make a picture of her pressed flowers if she dots the center area of construction paper with Thinned White Glue (see page 300) and waits 10 minutes, until it's quite tacky. With tweezers, have her lift a few leaves and fronds gently, one at a time, dropping them on the glue as a background. The flowers go on top of them, each slightly overlapping the next like a bouquet with petals scattered among them for balance. This is a case where too many are better than too few.

These flowers will fade unless you frame them under glass so air can't reach them. However, if you're going to that much trouble, glue the flowers to a ground of velvet or taffeta, which looks much better. Seal the back of the frame with tape.

### PARAFFIN FLOWERS

It takes only seconds to wax fresh flowers and success is instant though not everlasting. Fresh flowers contain so much water they'll only look beautiful for a week or two, then they'll wither and brown like a pansy in Dorian Gray's lapel. Truth to tell, most fresh flowers last just as long, but this is such a wacky thing to do you'll be glad you did it—once. Since paraffin melts at a low temperature, it's safe enough for your Five to work with you, but you need many papers on the counter to catch the drips.

Choose fresh flowers that have only a single layer of petals—like daisies—so that every surface can be covered, and have your child cut off the bottom part of each stem that's been under water so the wax will stick. Set a 16-ounce tin can in 2″ of gently boiling water. Into the can

**ADD        1 lb. paraffin**

Melt the wax slowly and turn off the flame when it's clear. Use an imperfect flower to check the temperature of the wax. Too cool, it will show on the petals; too hot, the flower will shrivel. When the temperature is in between—about 130°—let your child dip a stem quickly into the wax, let it dry, then hold the stem to twirl the flower in the wax, coating it well. She should shake it slightly to lose any extra wax and then drop each stem into its own soda bottle to cool, so they don't bump each other and damage their waxy coats.

Remove any wax on clothes or counter by rubbing it with ice and peeling it free, and never, never pour leftover paraffin down the drain.

### DRIED FLOWERS

Almost all flowers can be dried in sand, silica gel or in a mixture of cornmeal with borax, using the same technique with each, but petunias are too sticky for success,

violets too fragile and bulb flowers too wet. Other flowers will be a little smaller and paler when they're dried, although just as beautiful as before.

Some flowers take as long as two weeks to dry; but most take 2–4 days, depending on their delicacy, the size of their seed pods (which store water) and the humidity and the temperature in the room.

Dried flowers either can be used to make a picture, as with pressed flowers, or arranged in a bouquet, although wire stems must sometimes be used.

Most of these flowers will last at least a year, and some, like pear blossoms, will last two, because the woodier the stems the longer the blossoms keep. Seal all dried flowers in plastic in summer for the humidity will ruin them unless you have an air-conditioned house.

### Drying Media

Sand is the oldest method and the favorite of purists. You'll need sterilized sandbox sand, builder's sand or sharp quarry sand, which are sold in toy stores or garden centers. Sea sand is a bad substitute; it's not only salty but dirty and the bacteria in the dirt will spot the flowers.

Silica gel, sold in garden centers and through seed catalogues, is the quickest drying method, as well as the easiest and most expensive. The deep blue gelatin bits scattered in this fine sand will turn pale lavender as they absorb the moisture.

Although the cornmeal medium fades flowers more than the other two media, the ingredients are at the grocery store, and it's quick to prepare. To make,

| MIX | 5 lbs. cornmeal |
| | 2 lbs. borax |

The sand, the silica gel or this cornmeal mixture can all be reused if baked to get rid of the water they've drawn from the flowers. Bake the sand for 1 hour at 200°, the gel for 30 minutes at 350°—until the beads are dark blue again—and the cornmeal mix for 1 hour at 150°. Stir the sand and the gel several times while they're baking, and stir the cornmeal mixture twice as much and then pour it through a colander, since the borax may harden and get lumpy. Whatever the medium, it should be poured into airtight containers while it's still hot.

### Technique

You can use flowers from the yard or from the market, or you can pick them from a meadow if you have permission, if you pick only the most common ones, and if you take a bucket of wet sand with you. The flowers must keep drinking to stay fresh until they're put in the medium.

| ASSEMBLE | drying medium |
| | #20 OR #24 florist wire |
| | florist tape |
| | large lidded canister or suit box |

Before drying the flowers, your child may need to make new stems out of wire. The real ones usually can't support the blossoms when they're dried, and even if they could, the foliage takes much longer to dry than the flowers, and this would burn the petals. To make new stems, help your child bend one end of each piece of wire to look like Bo-peep's crook. Cup the blossoms in your fingers while your child pushes the length of the wire through the flower so the crook is embedded in the center.

Your child will need the canister for smaller flowers, burying them vertically and upside down on a layer of mix and adding another layer for each layer of flowers, bending the wires down if they're taller than the container. When you near the top of the container, poke the wires into the mix so the last layer of blooms is upright. Cover with 1″ of medium.

Use a large suit box for tall, spiky flowers or for branches of fruit trees or dogwood (your own, since most states conserve theirs). Pour some mix in the box, make trenches in which to lay the flowers and then cover the flowers with another inch of mix.

Seal any containers with tape, to keep out damp air, and keep them in a warm place. Help your child check the flowers after two days, for they can disintegrate if left too long in a medium. Flowers with a single layer of petals should dry in 2–3 days and multilayered ones in 4–5 days. If they take much longer, you may have packed too many in the box.

When petals are crisp, lift the top layer of flowers for your child and gently empty the container into a colander, so she can collect the rest. She can blow the dust from the blooms, while you gently brush any residue with a poster paint brush.

Twirl the wire so the florist tape will wrap around it—a task we found too tricky for our children and almost for us, but, fortunately, it isn't essential.

### Arranging

Your Six should arrange these dried flowers as she would fresh ones, choosing a container a third as high as the tallest flower. Fill it halfway with sand, pebbles or sea shells, instead of water, for a tall arrangement but a short one requires a frog, florist's clay or a styrofoam ball, held in place with clay or tape. Use a variety of shapes in flowers and a good frog for a small arrangement, so that flowers can be poked from any angle, but these flowers must be handled gently for they are quite brittle. Use cured flowers or dried grasses as filler.

## SEWING

In other countries, a child is taught to tat, embroider, knit or crochet as early as Four and yet in our culture the simplest sewing is often considered too hard for a child under Eight.

There are, of course, exceptions. When our good friend Leah was Four, she asked her mother to thread a needle for her and she's been sewing ever since, learning almost every step on her own. Today at Eleven, Leah makes skirts and shirts and weaves cloth on a loom, and if they're not perfect yet, they show as much creativity as any picture or any pottery her friends have made.

Your child's first attempts at sewing should begin at late Three, we think, with yarn, sewing cards and a crewel needle, which is blunt and has a big eye. First use blank index cards, in which you've punched some holes for her to make her own designs, and later use the follow-the-picture cards from the dimestore, which are harder.

A Four is ready to work with cloth if it's a small piece and if the material is crisp. She also needs a table, a good pair of scissors—and a mother nearby. At this age your child can learn the basic Running Stitch—the key to all hand sewing—and will like to sew scraps of cloth together for no reason at all (except perhaps to her). As in all her hand sewing, have her use a doubled thread, which you'll have to knot

at each end, a job too complicated even for most Sixes.

A Five begins simple embroidery and uses the stitches to make toys, like a beanbag, but a Six is ready to handle a sewing machine if you keep it threaded.

The mechanics of either hand or machine sewing aren't easy to master, but if you have patience, if you stop the lesson before one of you cries and if your child believes that everyone else has trouble at first (and they do), she'll feel confident enough to pursue this avenue of expression too.

### UNWEAVING

Some children enjoy precise work and this is one of the precisest. To make these fringed cocktail napkins, use any loosely woven fabric, like burlap. The smaller the child, the looser the weave should be, for it's the removal of various threads that makes the design.

**CUT**          **3″ × 6″ pieces**

Have your child wrap two threads around her forefinger and pull them at the same time, so they won't break so easily. The unweaving of one napkin needn't, and probably couldn't, match another. We call that creativity.

### RUNNING STITCH

This simple stitch is as essential to hand sewing as it is to embroidery and is no more than the weaving of a needle in and out, in and out, as evenly as possible, so the thread is tight enough to lie flat on the cloth but not tight enough to pucker it. To help your child keep it like that, have her smooth the material across her bent knee every time she's taken a few stitches.

## THE APRON

An apron is an admirable thing to sew; it brings out the virtue in us all. To make,

ASSEMBLE      1 yd. ribbon, 1″ wide
1 terrycloth tea towel

The ribbon covers one end of the towel to make the sash and the other end is folded to make pockets—all steps that use the Running Stitch. Have your child sew across the top of the towel and then pull the thread a little to gather it, but you'll have to knot it in place. Lay the towel on the table and help her pin the sash over these gathers. To make pockets, fold the bottom third of the towel over on itself and pin in place. Have her sew the sides together with No. 50 thread and sew the pocket down the center so it won't flop open. The ribbon should be sewed in place twice, to withstand washing.

## THE PILLOW

Every dolly needs a place to rest her empty head. To make a pillow, have your Four

ASSEMBLE      two 9″ squares of cloth
many old, clean pantyhose

Any elastic on the hose should be cut away and the stockings heaped between the squares. Help your child pin the squares together and, using embroidery thread and a needle, sew them together with a Running Stitch 1″ from the edge. Knot the thread yourself and pink the material to prevent raveling.

## THE BEANBAG

The beanbag is almost as necessary in childhood as the storybook and a child can make it herself. With a funnel, have her pour any small beans, like lentils, into an odd mitten or sock until it's about two-thirds full—still heavy enough to carry through the air but not so packed it could hurt anyone if it hit her. Have your Four sew the bag together with embroidery thread and a crewel needle, using a small Running Stitch.

## DOLL'S SERAPE

The moment your child can cut with scissors, she can make this serape, which boy dolls and girl dolls wear with aplomb.

ASSEMBLE      1 strip of cloth
10″ length of ribbon

The material should be slightly wider than the doll's shoulders and twice the distance between the shoulders and the knees, for that's how long this costume reaches. The serape slides over the doll's head, through a cross cut in the exact center of the strip. Your child can do this by folding the material in half horizontally and then vertically, cutting perpendicular to each fold, as deeply as necessary. The ribbon becomes the sash.

## HEADDRESS

Your Four will take longer to collect exactly the right feathers on her walks than she will to make this head-dress. Help her measure the cloth but she can cut it herself.

ASSEMBLE      one 6″ × 12″ strip of cloth
9 feathers

Help her fold the cloth in half, then fold again, until the strip is only 1½″ wide. Your child should slide the feathers between the folds, with the biggest in the center, and pin them in place. Because the quills are tough, push the needle once or twice through each one yourself, to secure them, then have your child sew tightly around each quill to finish the job. Tie around her head.

## EMBROIDERY

All hand sewing is improved by the skill of embroidery, which your Five can learn if you teach her the stitches and let her sew her own design as she goes. Keep the supplies tidy, as the skeins are a mess to untangle, and have your child cut three very long strands of embroidery thread, for you to separate from the rest and then double and thread for her. A hoop is essential to embroider the Running Stitch and the Cross-Stitch but not the Blanket Stitch.

### Cross-Stitch

To begin, let your Five draw a line of X's on the top of the cloth, then follow this pattern by crisscrossing two Running Stitches over each X and moving on to the next from the underside. The only thread that shows should make an X.

### Blanket Stitch

This is much harder and is used only on a border, forming a series of square U's. To make each U, have your child poke the needle from the underside of the material, about ⅛″ from the edge, then stick the needle under the stitch before the thread is tightened so the thread will run along the edge. She'll make three stitches before she sees the pattern.

### MACHINE SEWING

The sewing machine is such a clever invention that it won't break if your Six uses it—so she should.

It will be a while before she cares how it's threaded or how the tensions make the threads knot in the cloth every time the needle meets the feeder. These are incidentals; right now she wants to run it.

When your child presses the starter foot it will be quite as exciting for her as the first time you pressed the accelerator of a car and, like you, your child will want to know how to stop it. Let her sew on scraps of cloth to practice starting and stopping the motor, both to give her the feel of the machine and to help her realize that it doesn't have a will of its own.

She can slip the material beneath the presser foot and lower it, pull the balance wheel to bring the needle down into the fabric to keep it still, then hold her left hand behind the needle to hold and guide the material as it moves. Her right hand must be far in front of the needle, so it won't hit her finger.

After this practice, she's ready to learn the gentle one, two, three, four process that finishes a seam: lifting the presser foot, lifting the needle, pulling away the fabric and cutting the thread.

To begin real sewing, choose a simple idea, like a bag to hold her jacks, using a pretty, crisp material that has obvious right and wrong sides to make the pieces easier to match. Draw a pattern first on smooth brown paper and have your child cut and pin it to the material and then cut the material itself. Help her pin the pieces together (there should be no more than three) and baste the seams with a Running Stitch to make the machine stitching smoother and easier. It also lets her remove the pins before she starts to sew—a good idea for they can cause a novice a lot of trouble.

You can expect to tie all threads yourself, although a late Six is ready to secure the seam by reversing several stitches at the beginning and end of it—if reminded. When she's done, have her pull the basting threads from the seams and sew any hems by hand, using any of the basic stitches. This not only looks prettier, it's also the way for your first-class child to do a first-class job.

## DOLL'S COAT

A very adept Six can make a simple three-piece coat for a doll, varying it in size according to the size of the doll. Cut one thickness for the back and cut the front twice—once with the sleeve facing right, once with it facing left. Have her sew the sleeve seams, top and bottom, then the side seams. The rest is done by hand. Your child should fold and pin the raw edges at the neck, the sleeves and the hem, sewing them with embroidery thread in the Blanket Stitch.

# DRAMA

◇ ◇

The child with a dramatic imagination has a hundred playmates and a thousand games. Like many other creative expressions, it all begins in infancy. A baby is a consummate actor; she knows exactly how to make her audience laugh and how to wring their hearts. She'll flirt and sigh, giggle and coo, scowl and shriek, experimenting with every emotion and technique. She'll improvise, pretend and invent, but how far she goes depends on the sights, sounds and ideas in her memory bank and how rich those images are.

A child can't hop like a bunny if she's never seen a rabbit or at least seen its picture, and she surely can't imagine what it's like to row a boat if she's never heard of a boat. Her frame of reference is stretched with each new experience you offer and when you heighten the experience it's stretched even more. You do this with dress-ups and props and with your questions and suggestions. To tie a helium balloon to your child's wrist and ask if she thinks she can float to the stars will focus her imagination on that slight tug so sharply she can dream of a dozen balloons sailing her anywhere.

It isn't that you'll make-believe all day long, but if her imagination is jostled enough, she'll seldom be bored—or boring.

Her first planned brush with make-believe is around three months when you play peekaboo, covering your face and quickly appearing again, first behind a handkerchief, then as she understands the game, behind the sofa, the chair, the curtain.

To let your child act her dramatic best, she'll need props. By six months, she'll start to play with a latch-free pocketbook, a set of old keys and a comb to rub over her head (whether she has any hair or not). In a few months she can respond to peekaboo, crawling behind the skinny avocado

plant or under the receiving blanket, and then inventing a whole new game, she pretends the blanket is first a hat, then a handkerchief in which she blows her nose.

By One, she improvises in earnest and everything in the house is likely to become something else. Ramon would push a carrot stick around his high chair tray, humming as if it were a car, and Nadia used the cotton balls to dust—a chore she must have learned in heaven for she couldn't have learned it at home.

Since "moo-moo" and "arf-arf" are among a child's first words, it will be no surprise when she imitates the way animals walk, run and eat, and you can expect her to imitate "Mama" too—scrubbing when you scrub, talking on a toy telephone when you answer the real one. A mid-One will copy the way you stand, the way you take off your glasses or raise your eyebrows. At times she'll want to wear your gloves and shoes and want to carry your briefcase too. Different children have different fixations. We had one child so addicted to hats that she even wore one in the bathtub and Kate would have walked naked past the White House as long as she had her rubber beads around her neck. It's fine, we think, to let these eccentricities flourish, as long as they don't hurt anyone, for the drama your child puts in her life helps shape a distinct personality.

A pair of tall boots, you'll find, will make a performer of the most timid child, and high heels turn a tree-climbing tomboy into a mincing, prancing lady—briefly. Day-to-day clothes, in fact, affect a child so much that we relied on party clothes and patent slippers to make little Meg behave and found our quiet Nell became twice as outgoing when she wore her tough-guy jeans.

A Two spends hours pretending to be all the grown-up people she's ever seen—another reason for her to see many people. For this she needs one flexible costume, like a shawl, which she can drape forty-two ways, or perhaps a piece of fake fur with its silky, sexy texture. Whether she's wearing a costume or not, she'll still spend many minutes a day before her beloved mirror and this is dandy. A mirror not only encourages a child to make bizarre faces but it makes her be good too. No child can cry or even stay angry in front of one, proving once more that children are no different from adults.

A Three needs props, as she begins to play mother and father with a doll and a carriage or a tricycle. She wants to sit in a large cardboard box—a train—or under a card table covered with a sheet—a playhouse—and she's ready for her first charades, pretending to be a stop sign, a car and a chair, as well as a tree, a gust of wind, a flower or the seed itself. All she needs is an occasional suggestion and an audience who may laugh at her antics, but never at her.

A Four needs costumes too. One day she's an Indian, the next a cowboy, the third a sailor and, while she'll be expected to improvise most of her outfits, she'll be very happy to have one that's beautiful,

complete and by all means of good quality. A cheesecloth Halloween costume will fall apart quickly, no matter how well your child takes care of it, and then she'll be sure to think it's her fault—a lesson that makes her wonder why she should take care of anything.

Between now and Five, your collection of dress-ups will get so big you'll need a suitcase to hold it, and then the case becomes a prop itself. Your child will want to enact her fantasies with her friends. Together they'll develop elaborate stories and they're sure to dragoon a smaller child to play the baby because every children's play has a baby just as surely as it has tears, misery and at least one fight. Pathos is the trademark of all young actors.

A Five will translate her dramatics into puppet theater, making figures out of anything from peanut shells to paper bags, and for this she'll like the Puppet Theater (see page 323) our friend Priscilla used so much. It's the easiest design we've ever seen.

By Six, charades can become a family ritual (we hope it does) with everyone enacting the simplest titles from your child's library. Now she becomes so self-confident about her abilities that she and her friends will produce a show, anytime, with many props, a curtain, a great opening line and then a collapse into an unintelligible script, giggles and then recriminations, all of which are forgotten before the next production—seldom more than a week later.

For our children, this love of drama made them beg for old-fashioned home theatricals. This has led to an annual production for neighborhood children, wittily written and improbably plotted by one of the fathers, stage-managed and costumed by two of the mothers and fantastically acted by children from Five to Twelve who don't mind the hours of rehearsals so long as they're treated like professionals—and so long as they all have the same number of lines.

## DRESS-UPS

While a child doesn't need a set of props for every role, she does need a selection from many—enough to tickle her fancy.

A secondhand shop is a fine source for pocketbooks, jewelry and especially canes, which teach children to strut, but of all the imaginative dress-ups, we've found hats are best. A hard hat, a plastic fireman's hat from the toy store, a baseball cap, a football helmet and a cowboy hat all will spark hundreds of Walter Mitty games. You'll find a big selection of authentic hats for soldiers and sailors, workmen and trainmen at a surplus store, which apparently acquires leftover sizes, for many are very small. You can find a magnifying glass here too—for your detective—and a real stethoscope, which encourages the more positive side of that great favorite—playing doctor. This is a game where children are wont to strip and take temperatures, bottoms up; a game, therefore, that you'll want to supervise more carefully than almost any other since their thermometers are likely to range from pencils to popsicle sticks.

You also will want to consider not only how a prop will be used, but how safe it is and the younger the child, the more careful you'll have to be. She can't wear neckties or necklaces to bed, nor have props that contain harmful dyes, sharp edges or pins, or shoes that have straps or high heels and, of course, she can't stomp the stairs in any dress-up shoes.

The props she likes best will be the ones that make her feel heroic, for no young child is ready to pretend to be a villain. To make fairy tales come alive, children enjoy a sword, made of one long piece of lathe with a shorter piece nailed across it for the guard; a baton, which is both a scepter and a magic wand; a bridal veil of net, and a royal train: three feet of fabric with a grommet at one end to fasten the cloak under the chin and a mantle made by doubling the materials back over the shoulder and pasting cotton to it. She

doesn't know what ermine looks like anyway.

Sarah, ordinarily one of our most magnanimous friends, could let another child wear her gauzy fairy princess gown from Grandma only for ten minutes without agony, so we suggest you might make two of any simple but glamorous costume. Harmony is its own reward.

All of these dress-ups should be kept together in a trunk or that big suitcase, where you'll also want a false beard (hard to find, but a dramatic delight); a wig; a chapstick (but not a lipstick, since that's asking for trouble); powder and rouge puffs; aprons that can turn into Superman capes; one of your husband's old hats, a vest and a pair of his pants; several pairs of discarded slippers, tennis shoes and boots—yours and his; an old dress that reaches to the floor like an evening gown and gloves—the longer the better, but they don't have to match.

These all help a child play the role she thinks is the most heroic of all: the role of parent.

### PLAYING HOUSE

When a child can play-act the everyday role, she feels more in charge of her destiny—and certainly nothing is as everyday as housework. While she'll do most of her cooking at your stove, it's nice to have this one just for make-believe. Choose a box that's as high as her elbow, remove the flaps and turn it upside down. Paint the box the color of your own stove, with four black circles on top, four knobs on the front for decoration. Cut out an oven door and screw a knob to the front for a handle. Keep the flap shut by poking a cotter pin just above the door, from inside to the outside, so she can slide the prongs horizontally to open the oven and vertically to keep it shut. Later you may want to get a colorful, sturdy plastic stool, when you know how much your child likes to play house.

### BROADCAST GAME

It's a little ridiculous to describe this game, but if you give a Four a hairbrush and call it a microphone, she'll sing, broadcast, tell a story or just gab—a particularly good game of drama when you're on a long car trip. Even the quietest child becomes garrulous in front of a mike.

### FORTUNE-TELLING

Once you've tied a scarf on your head and read your child's palm, she'll reenact this scene a dozen times with her friends. To get her started, explain

the head line
the heart line
the life line

Predict anything as long as the forecast is happy and she lives one hundred years. Let any little wrinkles represent the children and promise as many as she has in her nursery school, which will please her. She won't care a whit about marriage, however, since every little girl knows she'll marry her dad and every little boy will marry his mom. Instead, concentrate on her heroic future. If you're like other mothers, you'll just be dreaming out loud.

## CHARADES

Props, let us emphasize, needn't and shouldn't be part of all drama, because you want your child to know the joy of creating through action alone—the essence of all good stagework.

It won't take long before your Three can be an animal, a vegetable or a mineral at the merest hint. She is at once a stationary, solitary rock; a pinwheel flailing its arms; a bud opening its petals.

As we learned from Jennifer, a fascinating Four whose mother schools her in sensitivity the way another mother might teach reading—a child can pretend to be any animal from a ferocious lion to a sweet mouse, stalking first through a shag rug whose pile feels taller than bamboo, then nibbling real cheese held tightly in tiny front paws.

You help your child learn to feel from within herself each time she can pretend to be something else—even a lima bean. After she's seen one sprout in a clear plastic pot, clinging its tendrils around a popsicle stick, she can imagine she's been planted in some nice, rich earth where it's cozy and warm, growing plump in her shell beneath the earth. Suddenly she can burst out of it pushing through the soil with a well-bent head and wrapping her arms around a sturdy broomstick. She begins to flower and then to fruit, every step of which she can enact as you talk about the story of a seedling and imagine what it's like to grow up green.

We've found it takes little practice before a Five can perfect her improvisational techniques well enough to take part in a simple family game of charades. For this game, use book titles she knows, limited to three words, and place little emphasis on winning. No Six is ready for competition like that.

## PUPPETS

A child can create drama in many ways, but as she gets older she often feels more freedom if she can have puppets do the talking instead of herself. For the classic puppet of papier mâché, see page 305.

### PAPER BAG PUPPETS

A Two can bring two small paper bags to life, one on each hand. Draw a face for her on each bag and fasten them on her wrists with a string, some tape or a rubber band. She can make them herself by Three.

### ANIMAL PUPPETS

Your old glove can become a rabbit for your Four if you sew the thumb to the palm and make ears out of the fingers by sewing or stapling the index and middle finger together and the ring finger to the middle finger. Sew buttons on the other side for the eyes and the mouth and then have your child wear it backward, with her fingers wriggling in the ears and her hand twitching the face: a rabbit.

### FINGER PUPPETS

Although these sound simple, it takes the steady hand of a Six to put a face on a peanut shell. To make, have your child break five peanut shells in half and draw the eyes and mouth with a fine, felt-tipped pen. She then covers her fingers and thumbs with these puppets, like 10 little thimbles, so they can bow and talk to each other—the only players in a single-member cast and good company on a nothing day.

### PUPPET THEATER

This theater has a double dividend. It's so inviting it encourages frequent use and the rest of the time it stands flat against the wall, looking pretty.

**ASSEMBLE**

one 2′ × 3′ piece of interior plywood, ½″ thick
one sheet 0 sandpaper
two small cabinet hinges
eight 1″ No. 8 roundhead wood screws
one 4″ length of 2″ × 4″
paneling adhesive
one 24″ length of 2″ molding
one 16″ length of 2″ molding
enamel paint
two 12″ × 15″ panels of fabric
30″ length of string
two cup hooks

The theater will stand 3′ high with a window across the top of the stage with simple braces in both front and back, so it won't topple.

Measure and draw a 6″ × 16″ rectangle on the sheet of plywood, leaving 1″ of wood along the top and 4″ on either side. Cut out the rectangle cleanly with a jigsaw to create the stage, and smoothe all the rough edges with sandpaper.

Cut the rectangle into 2 triangles, 6″ × 16″ × 17″, to make the side braces. Use the cabinet hinges and wood screws to hinge the short side of each brace to the front of the theater—one alongside the lower right corner and one alongside the

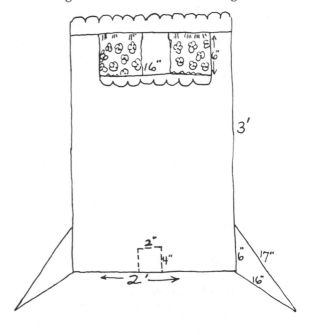

lower left. This lets the 16″ side of each triangle swing forward and distribute the weight of the plywood.

The theater still needs another brace in the back, and for this you'll use the length of 2′ × 4′. Set the wood on its side, perpendicular to the center of the base, to give it a 4′ support on the floor so it can't fall backward. Glue it in place with the adhesive and for extra strength, screw the block in place from the front with the other 4 screws. To trim the stage, glue the 24″ length of molding across the top to cover the narrow strip of plywood and use the 16″ piece to finish the bottom of the window. Sand any other rough edges and paint the theater.

Make the curtains by hemming the top of the material and running the string through it. The string is held from cup hooks, which should be screwed into the upper corners of the stage, but from the back, so they won't show. Your child can slide the curtain open for her productions.

---

◇                         # DANCE                         ◇

---

To a child, dancing is as natural as laughter. She bounces to the beat of music from the time she can stand, for dancing is bred in her bones. It's been part of every civilization, every culture, for all ages.

You encourage this love of rhythm when you bounce her on your knee and twirl her about the room in your arms, and when she's a toddler you and your husband will dance with her while she sways and spins to music without any self-consciousness at all. She learns to move her whole body in any way the music affects her: hopping, tiptoeing, jumping, crawling or rolling into a ball. Only dance releases so much energy so creatively and spontaneously.

If dancing has been a natural outlet for your child, by Three she'll like to dance regularly with other children, not as a show-off, but as if she were painting a picture with her body. All you'll need is a cleared room, a smooth floor, bare feet and music with many moods and beats. Leotards, perhaps a flashy scarf, a peasant shirt for a boy, a full skirt for a girl, all make it much more exciting.

If your child pines for a pair of dancing shoes, the best you can give her are rhythmic shoes, those ugly suede sandals, because they do give good leverage and they last much longer than the snug-fitting ballet shoes. Tights are good too, because they're safe, if you rip the seams in the soles so she can dance barefoot. They not only keep her legs warm, they help her pretend she's a real dancer.

Dancing can take care of a rainy day and Arsenic Hour too. Just put on some Motown and hunker down with your child for some serious rock and roll. It will chase those blues away.

## DANCING SCHOOL

You may want to advance to lessons at Four, for they can counteract the bad posture and clumsiness that sometimes begin at this age. Classes in tumbling, gymnastics, modern dance, rock and roll and especially eurhythmics help a child feel more in command of her body, but the contortions of acrobatics are too strenuous for her and ballet requires too much concentration. Even a Six can't swivel the whole leg from the hip joint and will use her foot to direct her leg, which will cause bulging muscles and poor posture later.

Toe shoes, as fetching as they are, cause trouble too, since young bones aren't developed well enough to take the strain. The most gifted ballerina must wait until she's at least Ten, has had several years of ballet—and the teacher says she's ready.

And then there's tap. Agile Sixes love to go to tap class because it's fun, it's tricky, and it makes so much nice noise.

If your child does take lessons, the time she spends on them should be just a fraction of the time she spends dancing, for dancing is meant to be as much a part of life as art or sunshine.

If you plan to send your child to dancing school, you'll want to visit it first, as you would any school.

Beware of high-pressure salesmanship that indicates that the business of the school comes before the pleasure of the children, and avoid schools that insist on fancy recitals. They may make a mother happy, but we never saw a young child who enjoyed them.

The building should have well-lighted rooms, big enough for easy movement, but not a ballroom. This is unnecessary since the classes should be limited to twenty.

The best dancing schools have a good pianist to accompany the children, but the teacher may make or buy her own special tapes which substitute well. She also needs a bongo drum or some percussion instrument to emphasize the beat.

In a good class, a teacher extracts each child's individual expression, giving only enough direction to create the order the children need to respond to the music as well as to each other. You can judge the teacher's ability by the grace and ease of her own body, the warmth and encouragement she shows the children and how well she understands how they're built, so that none of the movements she suggests will strain their young muscles—the most critical knowledge she can have.

# ◇ MUSIC ◇

Long before your child ever begins to play a musical instrument or even to sing, her ear will record a dictionary of sounds, categorizing noises, imitating them and creating new ones.

If songs and music are part of your baby's life she'll perform before she can talk, ahhhhing strings of sounds, and even at six months, shaking a tambourine and blowing into a wooden horn. She only needs you to blow the horn in front of her first, with great, obvious breaths, then hold it in her mouth for her to copy. Sooner or later she'll produce a magical toot. Once she can do this she's ready for

a huge and, therefore, quite safe policeman's whistle, although you may not be. It's much too loud for frequent use, but an occasional blast certainly delights a child.

You'll want these and the tambourine

to be your baby's first musical instruments. After that we think she'll profit by simple, one-note percussion instruments because they let her concentrate on pitch. A primitive bongo drum is a good starter, followed by small cymbals, bells and a triangle (any of which cost less than a child's hardcover book), and by Three, Sandpaper Blocks, one of the first musical instruments she'll make.

A Four is ready for something more complicated, like a wooden xylophone or a marimba, and if her interest in music is strong enough you might consider tone bars too. Again, make sure the pitch is true. Your child will like to play any of these instruments with her friends, but she needs to practice alone too, discovering, experimenting and repeating the different sequences she invents. A children's synthesizer is great for this.

When you encourage music you also must set limits. A fine musical instrument needs a loving touch, just like a little baby. Although you'll let her sound the notes occasionally, she must be expected to do it gently.

We don't think these limits will curb her creativity any more than it will curb a future writer who's expected to scribble on paper and not on the walls. A child has to learn to express herself and still be able to respect all things, from pianos to people.

You probably will be able to notice a musical bent in your child by the time she's Three or Four, just by the way she behaves. This child will talk about music

more, move her body in time with the songs in her head, ask for tapes at least as often as books and perhaps beg to learn to play a particular instrument. Do what you can, but you should realize that standard lessons are not ideal for a young child. Not only are they expensive, but a child usually isn't ready for them until she's old enough to read well.

There are, however, some very successful methods that teach a child to play before she can read notes, the way she learns to talk before she can read letters. Both the Carl Orff and the Suzuki systems use group lessons, believing that children find the same pleasure in making music together in a class as adults do in a symphony orchestra.

In the Orff approach, a group of children learn to play the simplest songs in unison. In Suzuki—the widely taught Japanese method for violin—a child as young as Three is given a tiny fiddle and plunged into sophisticated musical scores, concentrating first on making music and then refining it later. Here a child studies both in individual and group lessons, with the mother not only supervising the practice and attending the classes, but often becoming so involved that she studies the violin with her.

When your child is ready for traditional training she'll need a teacher so good she can stretch her potential to its limits and still make the half-hour happy.

## HOMEMADE MUSICAL INSTRUMENTS

A baby absorbs some sense of sound when you give her a wooden spoon and a metal one so she can hear the different tones they make when they're banged first on a metal pot and then on a wooden salad bowl.

A mid-Two will like a primitive maraca you make by filling half of a small tin can with dried beans, covering it with a plastic lid and taping it shut. A tambourine is made by safety-pinning small bells around a sturdy paper plate, which any young child will shake (and shake and shake).

With some help an older child can make other instruments herself, and she should, for it's the making of them that helps her learn how sound is made and pitch is changed.

### WATER PIPES

A Three can fill six heavy glasses with water, each at a different level, and tap tunes against them with either a metal or a wooden spoon for a drumstick. Different amounts of water make different tones. When she's Six she can align the glasses so the levels are graduated to make the scale.

### SANDPAPER BLOCKS

These wooden blocks, which sound rather dreadful to us, are rubbed together to the beat of the music and are popular with children and nursery schools. For your

Four to make a pair

| | |
|---|---|
| SAW | two 5″ lengths of 2″ × 4″ |
| CUT | two 4″ × 5″ pieces 00 sandpaper |

You'll do the sawing but your Four will do the cutting and can paint one wide side of each piece of wood with Thinned White Glue and paste the paper to it (see page 300).

| | |
|---|---|
| DRY | 1 hour |

The noise these blocks make will be music to her ears, if not to yours.

### HARP

A Five can combine eight large rubber bands and a little shoe box to make a harp. Have your child wrap the empty, topless box with bands, roughly equidistant and, if possible, using both thick and thin ones to produce different tones. For a Six to make a more elaborate harp

| | |
|---|---|
| SAW | one 10″ square of wood shelving |

Cut it diagonally; you will only need one of the pieces. Along one 10″ side have your Six

| | |
|---|---|
| HAMMER | eight 8-penny nails |

You'll have to pound 8 more nails into the other 10″ side so the nails will be in line with his row. To string it

| | |
|---|---|
| CUT | two 4″ lengths of nylon fish line |
| | three 10″ lengths of nylon fish line |
| | three 14″ lengths of nylon fish line |

If your child can tie a knot, let her tie a length to every nail she's hammered, with the short ones near the right angle, the long ones at the far end. So the harp strings will be tense enough for twanging, you'll have to tie them to the other side yourself, giving any string a few extra loops around its nail head if the line slackens. She can cut the tails when the strings are secure.

## MAKING BOOKS

Your Three can make her own book if you collect a few pictures she draws and write the captions, helping her tie them together into the simplest story by the discreet questions you ask. Later you can turn the tables on her "Tell me a story," by asking her to tell you a story of her own. It may be her own version of "The Three Bears" or her trip to the zoo, or it may be a dream or a nice bit of fantasy, but if you take it as dictation and type it onto several sheets of paper, she can draw the pictures to illustrate her text. Give any of these books a title page and either staple the sheets together or bind them with yarn. She'll be so impressed she'll memorize the words and read them back again and again.

## POETRY

At Four, when every child rolls words on her tongue as if they were lollipops, you'll find that many of them are as sweet as poetry. At this lyrical age, her conversation often has an instinctive beat, her ideas are as free as space and her words are so simple and direct that they can be as precise as a poet's. Since this almost excessive pleasure with words doesn't last, you'll want to keep a record of it, just as you would a photograph. We found long family car trips could become quite passable when we'd scribble Kate's prattle into the format of verse. If poems didn't have to rhyme for T. S. Eliot they didn't have to rhyme for her either.

## ROUND-ROBIN STORY

To tell a story in the round is almost as exciting to a Five as going to a movie—and possibly a lot more memorable. You'll need several children sitting in a circle while you invent maybe the first two paragraphs of a story and then, in mid-sentence, point to a child to continue it, letting her talk for two to three minutes before you point to the next child, again at random, again mid-sentence, so the plot takes wacky turns. By Six, the children need no more than "A boy named Ramon went to the circus and . . ." to follow with an idea. If you take notes and type the story for them the treat is compounded. The charm of a byline begins very young.

## SYNONYMS AND OTHER NYMS

Every time a mid-One masters a word, teach her another in its place. Use only that one for a while, then switch back and forth. Our Kate and Mike, at Five and Four, used to race each other to find synonyms for the easy words we'd suggest, like happy and sad, which occupied them on long, crosstown bus rides. Antonyms and homonyms work just as well.

## CLICHÉ GAME

In our writing family, each child knew what synonyms and antonyms were by the time she was Four (but nothing, alas, about fishing or baseball).

It was the Cliché Game, however, that pleased our Nell best, for it bailed her out of any argument. When the insufferable little boy said, "Naah, naaaah, you're a . . ." she could counter with exquisite sophistication, "That's a cliché." This was such a surprise it let her leave the scene in dignity.

Your late Three can understand clichés when you tell her that some phrases, like "black as night," are used again and again because they mean the same to everyone. Together you can pick out old ones and invent new ones, for if there's another way to describe the blackness of night, you can expect your original Four to find it. A nice game for a wet day.

## TYPING

It's as hard for a child to write before she can form letters well as it is for her to run with a weight on her back. We found the faster our children learned to put words on paper, the more creative they could be. Cursive letters are quicker than printed ones for a Six and calligraphy makes them more fun to learn, but since we weren't patient enough to teach either one, we taught typing instead. It was a small miracle; the touch system turned out to be a cinch.

A child masters typing the same way she masters printing, which is not very well. Still, it makes her more eager to learn the other forms of writing and that's what it's all about.

Unlike the sewing machine, a typewriter does get out of kilter easily, but you can fix it easily too, unless you're using a toy, which is an impossible contraption. Instead, use either an electric typewriter or if you're lucky, a computer, which has such a lovely light touch and is almost impossible to break.

To teach typing, color your child's fingernails with waterproof, felt-tipped pens in five colors—the same on each hand— and then paint the keys, including the space bar, to match the pattern his fingers will follow: left forefinger in orange and the letter F too. The code lets a child use the proper finger to hit the proper key.

Set the left hand on ASDF and the right hand on JKL; and remind your child to return to them every time she hits a letter, so she won't jam the keys. Although she'll look at them before she strikes the letters, she'll almost always use the correct fingers and after two or three lessons, she can remember the system for months. As for spelling, we don't worry much about that. A child is mainly interested in typing her name and some basic words, which you'll be able to decipher if she knows about half of the letters—and the sounds—of the alphabet. While your child will never be a speed typist until she takes one of those dreary courses in school, she probably will do better than you expect. As our friend Andy announced after his first lesson, "I really typed fast when *she* left the room."

# CAPABILITIES

Any capability a child acquires—even in the smallest degree—will help him feel more comfortable to develop it as he grows older. Although your child still will learn to carpenter or cook as an adult, he'll be much less clumsy if he's had a chance to practice as a child.

To help your child be as self-confident in his skills as he is in everything else, he needs a chance to garden, to cook and to handle tools. When a child can know the pride of painting a baseboard or transforming a packet of seeds into a row of lettuce—or a head of lettuce into a salad for supper—he'll find that there is a joy in production just as there is joy in creation.

To be sure, it's a bother to begin to teach a Two these skills, but this is another way you show respect to a child—an unspoken compliment that tells him he's smart enough and adept enough to be a part of the work in the household, as well as the play. While his efforts won't be perfect even at Six, they'll be a real help at Twelve, and there are psychic rewards at any age. A family is strong not for what the parents give to it, but for what every member gives.

## ◇ WORKSHOP ◇

Whenever you accomplish something permanent, you feel better about yourself. Your child is just the same, which explains the joy that manual labor brings him. Refinishing, plumbing, carpentry, bricklaying and plastering all develop a child's dexterity and self-assurance and satisfy his drive to feel part of the real world, which is particularly important for girls, for they need extra help to break outdated social conventions.

We give more advice on the restoration of furniture than anything else, both because we know a lot about it and because tangible accomplishments win compliments—the bread and wine of life.

You'll need to take more safety precautions in these activities than in any others we suggest, and to keep yourself and the rest of the house safe, you'll need to work alongside your child except when he uses the Plumber's Box or, when he gets more adept, the carpentry tools. At the same time, you must let him do as much of the work as he can, for the more you intrude, the more you chip away his ego—exactly the opposite of your goal.

Beginning at Two, your child can guide the electric sander, oil the squeaks out of hinges, help you revive dirty furniture and, before the year is done, can use his Plumber's Box—an assortment of pipes and joints he likes to fit together. Most of this is about as productive as painting the pave-

ment with water and a 2″ brush and he should do this too. It's one more workshop triumph.

A Three is ready for a Carpenter's Box, for he can handle many workshop tools and he can help you with more of the odd jobs: scrubbing carved wood with hot red wine and a toothbrush, feeding furniture with oil and soaping the runners of bureau drawers.

The masterful Four, always his own favorite hero, can lay bricks if you mix the concrete and sink the first course with him. He also can help you strip some furniture with denatured alcohol (and a lot of fresh air), wipe a stain—a pleasantly messy job—and paint the first wash coats of shellac, but he won't do any of these for more than twenty minutes and, of course, he won't do them very well.

A Five and a friend can saw three-inch logs with a bucksaw, but he should work with you and no one else when he cuts with pruning shears, because in his enthusiasm he may move too fast and hurt a little child. He also might hurt the bush, unless you keep a sharp eye, for pruning is a hard job to quit, but don't withhold the shears, for nothing inflates his ego so much. One day he'll discover that the length of the levers governs the power of the tool, but now it teaches him that he's the smartest, biggest, strongest person around.

A Six can give a prime coat of latex to a radiator or a fence, patch small nail holes in plaster and hold the wood you saw—all with enough skill to be rather helpful.

## PLUMBING

A late Two can assemble and reassemble pipes into a dozen designs with little help, and by Four can work for thirty unsupervised minutes—a joy for both of you. A little boy especially enjoys the role of a master mechanic and is often about as successful as his father. His interest is stimulated by one of the big events of his life— the Great John Overflow, which usually leads to the Coming of the Plumber. Later you can commemorate the occasion by giving him some pipes and fittings.

### PLUMBER'S BOX

In a carton or a wooden box

**ASSEMBLE**  **6–12 lengths of pipe, 6–24″ long**
**12–24 fittings**
**petroleum jelly**
**striped cap**
**plunger**

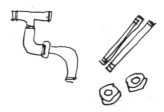

Have the pipes cut at the hardware store and rub all threads with the jelly, so your child can screw the pipes to the fittings more easily. The fittings, you'll find, have lovely names— crosses, bends and elbows—and nipples, unions, eccentric couplings and female adapters. This should appeal to his sense of silliness and yours. The box itself appeals to your worker's sense of order (which he does have) and to you because it encourages your young worker to put away his tools. If he doesn't, put them away yourself and keep them away for a time. A plumber can't leave his tools about and still go to the next job.

Some may argue that the striped hat— available at surplus stores—is not essential, but it does give that element of staging your child likes. The same thing is probably true for plumbers.

## CARPENTRY

To pretend that a young child could make a bookcase would be fatuous, but the simplest carpentry gives him both pleasure and a sense of dignity. It also gives a child enough coordination in the handling of tools to feel familiar with them for the rest of his life.

## CARPENTER'S BOX

As your child knows, building is a serious business and for this he needs real tools and a box in which to keep them. You'll feel more comfortable (and so will he) if he uses his tools

when he has no company. We don't include pliers, because they're too complicated, or a screwdriver, which can be lethal in a fall, but other tools are dandy. In a wooden box, gradually

| ASSEMBLE | simple block plane |
| --- | --- |
| | 10 oz. claw hammer |
| | 10-point crosscut saw |
| | brace and bit |
| | small monkey wrench |
| | wood chisel |
| | hinged rule |
| | yardstick |
| | assortment of nuts and bolts |
| | 8-penny nails |
| | lightweight aluminum discs |
| | 2 doz. scraps of pine |

In the beginning, your Three will make designs with wood, nailing discs and nuts and wood scraps together as if they were trucks and boats and other curiosities. Although the wrench is of no use to a Three (nor a Six), it causes no harm, it weighs enough to make him feel important, it can't come apart and the bolt is big enough for the most awkward fingers to manipulate. Hammering, however, is the big entertainment. The hammer should have a flat face, a claw to pull out nails and a tight-fitting shank of wood, for an all-steel hammer is very tiring. Above all, the hammer must be heavy or it will bounce back as if the nail is being sunk into ironwood. Nails should be big, so his fingers can grasp them, and they should have heads so they can be hit more easily. You may have to make a hole first to rest the nail while he drives it, but a Six should be able to hammer one without bending it and to pull it out with the claw. A Three can begin to cut wood with your help, if the saw has a good set, and by Six he can saw with the whole length of the blade. A Four can use the hammer to split a length of wood at intervals with the chisel, can shave the edges smoothly with a plane and wants to measure everything with his hinged rule and his yardstick. Your Five can operate the brace and bit, just to drill holes. Of course, you should be in the same room with a Three or a Four while he works, but a Five or Six who's familiar with tools can be left alone safely—which is more than you can say for some carpenters.

## PLASTERING

A mother we know, whose home had been full of plumbers, carpenters and plasterers for months, was startled to see her mid-One begin some renovation of his own. This child examined a small hole in the wall in silence, then toddled up and down stairs three times: first for his brother's chalk, then for his wooden hammer to beat it to bits and finally for a cup of water to pour on the chalk. Still flabbergasted, she watched him stir it to mush with his fingers and poke it into the hole.

Padraic had made plaster.

## PATCHING

Like Padraic, we think nail holes are meant to be filled by young children, although a Six does it much better than a mid-One and spackling compound does it much better than chalk. Cover the floor with newspaper and in a tin can

| POUR | 1 c. spackling compound |
| --- | --- |
| ADD | ½ c. water |

Let him stir until the paste is smooth and stiff. You'll find it's thinner and easier to handle than prepared spackling and it takes longer to dry than patch plaster, which is good too; a young plasterer needs all the time he can get. He should press the plaster into the hole or into a small crack with his fingertip, until it won't hold any more, then dip a sponge or a paintbrush into a cup of water, wiping it back and forth over the new plaster until the patch is exactly even with the wall—a professional trick. If the plaster pulls out of the hole while it's being patched, add 1–2 tablespoons of water to the plaster mix and fill the hole again. The next day—when the spackling is completely dry—he should wipe the excess dust from the wall with a wet cloth. Later you can sand it if it's necessary.

## PAINTING

You may say that giving a child real paint is silly and it probably is, but it will make him feel twelve feet tall—a noble height for a Five. Although your child surely will make a mess, some things are worth it. Besides, the child who has the chance to help you when you paint either will get

bored in ten minutes, leaving you to work alone for an hour, or he'll like it enough to be quite helpful, painting as long as thirty minutes.

Latex paint, because it's water soluble, is best, but it won't hurt him to try acrylics and oil-based paint too. We've found a Five can cover a small area like a door panel or a simple piece of furniture with a thin prime coat of enamel and can help paint closets with latex, but by Six he can paint a two-inch latex border on the walls above the baseboards, in the corners where the walls meet and around any window and door frame he can reach while standing on the floor. This border makes it much easier when you use a roller, for there's no temptation to go too close to the edges and your own job will be neater and faster.

To be a successful painter, your child will need the floor covered with newspaper, his father's T-shirt covering him, a foam brush and a few holes punched in the lip of the can, so the drips fall into the bucket rather than down the label. You also will have to remind him, rather regularly, that each side of the brush must be wiped against the lip of the can each time he gets more paint, that two thin coats are better than one thick one and that if he steps in a blob of paint it will track him around the house like a shadow, so he must clean the soles of his feet each time he starts to walk away from the dropcloth.

When he quits painting with latex, have him wash his own brush in soapy water and himself in a tub of warm water with a squirt of detergent to soften the paint on his skin. If he used enamel, remove the paint from both his brush and his skin with petroleum solvent before putting him in the tub, but never bathe him in very warm water or it will sting wherever you have rubbed the solvent. Whatever paint he used, coat his skin with mineral oil after his bath to keep it soft.

Even though your child has left most of the painting for you, he still should help you clean the room when you quit, for a good worker must finish his job. The more mess he has to clean, the more careful he'll be the next time; he sees the reason why.

## BRICKLAYING

As you've discovered on many walks, construction fascinates a child—boy or girl. The roaring of trucks, the scooping of earth, the hoisting of beams all mesmerize him, but simple bricklaying has a special appeal. It's so much like blockbuilding that he thinks he can do it—and he can.

At Two, he watches with fascination as

the hod carrier balances a load of bricks across his back and a mason lays them in a rapid, one-two-three motion.

If you buy twenty to thirty bricks from a demolition or construction site and then leave them in the backyard, your mid-Three will lug them, stack them and lay them without being told. He also will drop them, and since each brick weighs four pounds, he'd better wear shoes.

He'll soon be ready to lay a flat square of bricks in sand and by Four can set them in mortar. He can build a little wall, al-though it will take days. When he gets to the wall-building stage, you'll want to ex-plain the reason for each step and the correct technical terms; he'll savor every bit of this exotic information. He may want to know what mortar is made of (sand, cement, lime and water) and that the end of the brick is called the header, the flat side the stretcher—names that also make it easier for you to give clear instruc-tions. You can tell him that bricks are laid in different patterns, called bonds, not just to be pretty but to reinforce each other.

## THE WALL

A low brick wall in the corner of the yard offends no one and it's one of the biggest ego builders your child will ever know. We recommend a wall that's three bricks long, with five courses of brick—two below ground for the foundation and three above—and laid in the most basic pattern: Simple Running Bond.

**ASSEMBLE**

15 common bricks
hammer
chisel
bucket
20 lbs. prepared
    mortar mix
paper bucket
broomstick
small pointing
    trowel

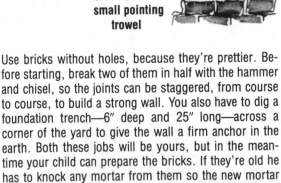

Use bricks without holes, because they're prettier. Be-fore starting, break two of them in half with the hammer and chisel, so the joints can be staggered, from course to course, to build a strong wall. You also have to dig a foundation trench—6″ deep and 25″ long—across a corner of the yard to give the wall a firm anchor in the earth. Both these jobs will be yours, but in the mean-time your child can prepare the bricks. If they're old he has to knock any mortar from them so the new mortar can stick and soak either old or new bricks in water so they won't draw moisture from the mortar and crumble it. To do this, have him drop 3–6 bricks in the bucket of water—as many as he probably can lay in a day—and leave them there for about 15 minutes.

The joints also will crumble if the mortar sets too soon, which is why it's mixed in small batches. Make no more than he can use in a half-hour. In the paper bucket.

**STIR**       5 lbs. mortar mix
              1¼ c. water

Use the broomstick to stir it well. This consistency is fairly stiff, although you may add more powder if it seems too runny or more water if it's too thick. Much depends on the dampness of both the bricks and the weather.

Without using any mortar in the trench, have your child lay a brick flush against one end of it. Before laying the second brick, he should butter the header with mortar, ½″ thick, and then zigzag the tip of the trowel across it for a better grip. Help him press the buttered end of this brick against the first one, tamping it hard with the butt of the trowel, and then lay the third (and last) brick in the row the same way. He'll use two half-bricks at each end of the second course (as well as the fourth), so each brick in the wall can overlap half of the one beneath it. To lay this second course, have him smear and score mortar on the first brick he's laid and press a half-brick on it. From then on, the bricks should be laid as before, with mortar splatted on the ends and on the course below and each brick tamped into place. Because mortar drips everywhere, your child should clean the bricks that are above the ground as he goes, wiping the excess with his trowel. The wall is finished when he has pounded the earth close to the foundation, rubbed oil on his hands (for mortar will dry them) and been given many, many compliments.

From then on, your child will scrutinize every brick building he sees, noticing the fancy Victorian fret, the arched doorways and the different bonds. He'll trace the patterns with his forefinger as if it were obligatory and seriously tell you how the shade or the pointing in the mortar of one house is quite different from the one down the street. Professionals have to start sometime.

## PATIO SQUARE

This square of bricks looks good under a big potted plant or a portable barbecue grill, where the grass won't grow. You'll do the digging, but your child will do the rest.

| ASSEMBLE | 30 lbs. building sand |
|----------|----------------------|
|          | 8 common bricks      |
| DIG      | 17″ square, 4½″ deep  |
| FILL     | 2″ sand               |

He can lay the bricks flat in the sand in two parallel rows, although a true construction buff may work out more complex patterns. Over them

**POUR**        **sand**

Have him sweep the square clean when the cracks are filled completely—and then quickly cover it with the plant or the grill before he takes the bricks out again.

## REFINISHING FURNITURE

A child finds that cooking and gardening have their place, but working with wood brings a pleasure all its own. It's such a grown-up thing to do.

Like many women, we were as inept as Twos with hammers and nails and instead found that refinishing furniture suited us exactly. With our children trailing behind we would look for pieces from one seedy junk store to the next, plunking Meg for safety in the great toy box at our favorite, the Alley Store, until at eight months she

said her first words—not "Mama" or "Dada," but "Alley Store."

We think you'll find, as we did, that the revitalization of the treasures is easier than you'd think. Most furniture needs only revival, not refinishing, which is fortunate, since stripping is hard to do around a child and, while he enjoys helping you sand and add the many coats of finish, the job can outlast the enthusiasm.

While your child will need more precautions and more supervision in this work than in any other we recommend, we found it safe for a child to strip and paint shellac. In fact, there never was a time when any of them were tempted to drink the solutions we used or to splash them around—perhaps because we warned them of their dangers and kept them out of reach or perhaps because they didn't smell like cherries or lemons and they weren't kept in bottles that looked like soda pops.

The restoration of furniture fascinated the children and it was a blessing to us too, psychologically and financially. It not only fitted into those fragments of time we called a schedule, but it was a cheap way to furnish a home. More than that, it made the children so aware of the beauty of wood they've never been blind to it since.

You'll find it's like magic to see the lines of a tree reappear as you strip a piece of furniture, watching it glow stronger and stronger with every coat of finish and wax you add.

This is the kind of magic a child can understand.

### REVIVAL

Five-year-old furniture, like any Five, is bound to be dirty even if it hasn't been playing in mud—and you can expect fifty-year-old furniture to be very dirty. Your child can help you rejuvenate wood by cleaning white stains with the Ring Remover (see page 226) or rubbing a piece of furniture with either American Polish (see page 228) or Mediterranean Polish (see page 207) to give it a fresh matte finish.

The scruffiest table may just need a good cleaning instead of a new finish. Either of these revivers will remove most of the checks in an old finish and make the grain of the wood come alive again.

## REVIVER I

A Three can help you restore the warm color of dark wood while cleaning it. In a saucepan

**HEAT**          **1 c. red wine**

Dip a soft cloth into it and squeeze it, so the wine will be cool enough for your child's touch and warm enough to melt the wax. Have him rub the wood with the cloth and use a toothbrush, dipped in wine, to scrub any carvings. Apply paste wax and buff—a job for you or a Five.

## REVIVER II

A fine Swiss cabinetmaker we knew claimed that all furniture, whether varnished, shellacked or oiled, should be washed twice a year, then oiled to feed the wood and waxed to protect it.

For a time estimate, it took us three hours to revive a large antique grandfather's clock, from the bath to the final shine, but we worked alone. If your child helps double the time (as always) and stretch the job over several days, to suit his attention span.

### Washing Wood

You'll need to dip a well-squeezed cloth diaper or a terry-cloth towel into this solution to clean the wood. In a bowl

**COMBINE**      **1 qt. warm water**
                    **2 tbsp. detergent**

Let your Five start in the most conspicuous place you can find—just to make him feel proud—rubbing a small patch with this solution until a clean cloth shows no trace of dirt. Rinse with clear, warm water and dry thoroughly. Wash the rest of the wood to match the color of the cleaned area, rinsing and drying each part before starting the next, or the water will swell the grain of the wood.

### Feeding Wood

This treatment completes the cleaning, lightens the wood a little more and smooths away light crazing. We find paraffin oil—available in a big, or an old-fashioned hardware store—is the best, because it's thin enough for a Five to help you wipe away the excess easily and it doesn't show our housekeeping like boiled linseed oil, which can attract dust. Rub it on the furniture with 0000 steel wool, working in tiny circles with the grain of the wood. Rub one patch down to the finish—but not hard enough to remove it—and match the next patch to it. Let the oil soak into the wood for two hours or more, then rub dry with a clean cloth. Apply paste wax thinly and buff.

## *STRIPPING*

Your Four can help you remove shellac—the protection on almost all furniture built before 1910 and much of it built afterward—but paint and varnish is too dangerous for a child to strip.

Some furniture, in fact, shouldn't be stripped at all, like an antique with its original painted or shellacked finish (for that hurts its value and its charm), or one with an unappealing wood, but most pieces look best when you can see the grain. To tell the difference between varnish and shellac, touch some nail polish remover to the finish. Shellac softens immediately.

Strip the wood outdoors or in a well-ventilated room, working for no longer than a half-hour at a time, and don't worry if the wood has some painted or stenciled designs. It won't budge them. Paint, as well as varnish, requires removers usually based on lye. If you do use them, work alone and, to get the job done quicker, use a marine grade. Like marine paint, it's much stronger.

## SHELLAC STRIP

Fast work, an old rag and denatured alcohol melt shellac as an oven melts ice. This solvent won't hurt the skin but it will dry it, for which you and your child will need hand cream afterward, and you also should wear simple gauze masks to avoid the fumes. Cover the floor with newspaper, open all windows for ventilation and into a bowl

**POUR          Denatured alcohol**

Give your child a piece of a diaper in each hand, one to dip in the alcohol, the other left dry to wipe away the softened shellac. Have him work with the grain of the wood, dipping and wiping in a quick 1-2 motion that takes less than a minute—not easy for a pre-Six to coordinate. Help by wiping after him before the shellac hardens again, wherever it's been smeared. Repeat many times, adding more alcohol to the bowl occasionally. Sand the wood when a cloth still looks clean after the wood is wiped with fresh alcohol.

---

## SANDING

While your child can sand by hand, he'll like a machine better. The most timid Two unfolds at the chance to run an electric sander, for it's such a heavy, noisy, masterful tool and it's the only power-driven workshop tool that's safe for a child to handle. Use an oblong sander (a circular one is too difficult) and let him turn it off and on, over and over, as you help guide it with the grain.

**USE          0000 aluminum oxide sandpaper**

This production paper is best, because it lasts longer. Also this grit is so fine and his pressure so light that you can erase any cross-grain scratches he makes by a little more sanding with the grain. How long it takes depends on how hard the wood is and how bad the damage. The wood is ready for a finish when it's as smooth as a baby's bottom. Onto a clean cloth

**POUR          petroleum solvent**

Wipe the wood lightly with it to remove any dust and let it dry before applying the stain, if necessary, and the finish.

## FINISHING

Any wood that has been stripped must be protected again, either by paint, varnish, shellac or oil. Wax alone can't give enough protection or a lasting sheen.

We've let our Twos—and our visiting Twos—apply both oil and shellac finishes

with us and never had a problem. Their help also has never lasted more than ten minutes nor amounted to more than 2 percent of the work. In the next four years, your child can learn to apply the first coat of paint, to wipe a stain, to rub oil into wood and brush on thin wash coats of shellac—all with your constant help—but no young child can apply varnish well, for it must be laid on rather than brushed into the pores.

By Six he can steel wool and paint the shellac finish for 20–30 minutes at a time—the longest this job takes unless the furniture is very big—and will do maybe 20 percent of the work. Still you can expect him to grow up and remind you of the time he refinished that picture frame in the hall "all my myself."

Finishing furniture is a great image builder for him too.

### The Stain

Let your Four spit (once) on bare wood to see the color it will be when it's shellacked. If this color isn't dark or warm or soft enough to suit you he can help you brush one of the many oil-based stains on the wood and wipe it away again with cheesecloth, before you apply the finish.

You also can make a stain in any color by cutting oil-based enamel paint in half with petroleum solvent. Brush this solution on the wood, rest it a few minutes and wipe with cheesecloth. All paint and most of the stain can be removed with pure solvent if you think the tone is too blatant. Always work with the grain.

Cover with either an oil or a shellac finish.

### Oil Finish

This is durable and subdued, well suited to modern furniture and painstaking mothers. A good oil finish is impervious to heat, alcohol, water and stains. Give your Four a wad of cheesecloth, saturated with boiled linseed oil, and have him rub it into the stripped wood, going with the grain, catching all the places he has missed yourself. Wait 20 minutes and, with dry cloths, rub and rub the wood—again with the grain and especially in corners—until it isn't sticky anymore.

Apply a new coat every few days for weeks, but never give another treatment until the first one is absolutely dry or the furniture will draw dust. Quit when the wood has a warm matte glow and it can't absorb any more oil.

### Shellac Finish

A Two can rub this shellac finish with steel wool and a Four can brush on the shellac itself. Altogether, stripped wood needs five of these wash coats to be well protected, but don't use shellac straight from the can; it's too thick. In a paper cup

**MIX**  1 part orange shellac
1 part white shellac
3 parts denatured alcohol

The orange brings out the richness in the wood and the alcohol makes the layers thinner and easier to apply and makes the finish look much deeper. Stir gently to avoid air bubbles, then have your Four paint a light coat with a 2″ brush, going back and forth but with the grain—a reminder to be given often. Wait 24 hours—so the shellac is dry beneath the surface too—then, still going with the grain of the wood

**RUB**  0000 steel wool

This slices the tops of the tiny bubbles in the finish to make it smooth. If you don't do this each succeeding coat will make the bumps look bigger. Your child should know the reason for each instruction before he asks, for anyone feels silly when he has to follow rules and he doesn't know why.

After rubbing the shellac with the steel

wool—very quick work—have your child blow at the dust and then wipe the wood with an old diaper dipped in petroleum solvent, to catch the rest of it. Let the solvent dry and repeat all of these steps with each succeeding coat. When complete, add two very thin coats of paste wax to protect the finish, for shellac can be damaged by alcohol, by vinegar and by water.

### French Finish

For a special treasure, our Fives have helped us paint as many as twelve coats of this special finish—invented, it's said, by a craftsman in Marseilles. This recipe, applied daily, gives a depth and a sheen to wood that's only improved by applying it with the French Polish, but it will still look grand if you use the conventional 2″ brush instead of a wad of cheesecloth.

Start using this recipe after you've applied three coats of the Shellac Finish. To make it,

**COMBINE**  1 drop olive oil
1 c. Shellac Finish

Add 2 drops of oil to his mixture for the second coat, 3 for the third, increasing a drop a day until you add a dozen drops to the cup on the last day.

### French Polish

In our collection of little European cabinetmakers, we found one from Spain who insisted that this technique—the prince of them all—was simple enough for a child to do. Consequently, he was able to teach it to our Six, who found it easy, and to us, who did not. It takes a wad of cheesecloth, instead of a brush. Dip the cloth in the Shellac Finish or the French Finish and press it against the side of the cup to get rid of the excess, then have your child rub it on the wood in tiny circles, going with the grain. Dip and press each time the cloth dries, which happens very quickly. We recommend polishing something quite small, like a picture frame. You'll find it very messy, very successful and worth trying—once.

# ◇ COOKING ◇

The same mother who can find words in the babble of an eight-month-old will take a cake to the table and say her Two made it. And we think she should.

Even though you'll read the instructions, gather the ingredients, explain each step and check each measurement, the person who measures the flour and beats the batter is the cook. If your attitude to his accomplishments is positive he not only will grow up thinking he can do anything, he'll think he's already done it.

We believe a child can gain more self-esteem in a kitchen than anywhere else, for to him, cooking probably is the most important job in the world. Although you may have an office job eight hours a day, he still sees you spend most of your time in the kitchen—so it must be important. Every moment you allow him to cook with you is one more sign of his own worth.

A child also is learning a lot about creativity, about cause and effect, about arithmetic—even about sex. To us, a child whose sensitivity is encouraged in any way, including the cooking and savoring of many foods, will be an adult alive and sensitive in all ways—including sex. Which is as it should be. When he splashes the walls with his Hollandaise, be cheered. The cause is good.

We can't pretend that cooking with a child is always jolly and if you truly don't like to cook, you should do little of it together. Conversely, if it's a skill you enjoy it's much easier to work intensively with him for ten to thirty minutes in a day than to work by yourself for an hour while he whines and plucks at your skirt. There's another advantage. Although it will take twice as long to cook with your child (as it does to do anything else with him), the joy of a shared experience will be the joy you remember twenty years from now.

We think you should start cooking with a child when he's very young. Many mothers think a hot stove and a rowdy Two are

a dangerous combination, but we never found a child who behaved foolishly when he was given a small but grown-up job to do and we never saw an accident when the Safety Rules were followed. Besides, most of the kitchen work is in the preparation and not at the stove at all.

We've directed all instructions to you (since you're the one who reads), but unless we've specified otherwise, a child will be able to do each step himself with some assistance and advice—and as little of both as you can manage. The recipes offer a variety of tastes and textures, all chosen because they're easy to make, nutritious to eat and most people like them. Some are adult favorites—good to make and serve to company since a child is enriched quite as much by compliments as by vitamins.

You may notice that few of our recipes have chocolate, for this, like cola, has such a high caffeine content it can kill B vitamins and make some children jumpy, but don't deny your child the joy of the Ultimate Chocolate Cake (see page 360). That would be going too far.

Because a child needs a purity of tastes, we recommend natural cheese, pure vanilla and top grade soy sauce and instead find our economy in less expensive meats and vegetarian dishes. The optional ingredients we suggest are listed parenthetically, but even these trimmings aren't for looks alone. A child needs his parsley and almonds for magnesium, walnuts and cashews for protein, wheat germ for vitamin E.

We do, however, sometimes call for the great no-no's of the nineties—eggs, butter and cream. The pediatrician will almost surely tell you that the eggs are all right for your child, unless he has an allergy, and the butter and cream are all right for special occasions. You can substitute margarine and milk the rest of the time, but let your child taste the best.

Other ingredients—and recipes—should bring cheers from the nutritionists, who are used to children's cookbooks full of sweets and rather silly foods. Less than a fourth of the recipes in this book are sweet, none of them are fried, and only cholesterol-free peanut and olive oils are used.

We use no mixes in our recipes, because the directions are on the boxes anyway, because it's much more fun for a child to cook from scratch and because, like potato chips and candy, they fill the stomach only briefly and whet the taste buds for more of the same.

We particularly object to toy store "mixes," for their flavors are so synthetic and stale that no child could be proud of the results. Also, we don't like to see everyday foods dressed up to look like animals or faces or to have a child cook with miniature pans in a toy oven. No person wants to think his cooking is a joke—especially a small person.

When your child is between Two and Six, you'll demonstrate, casually and often, that two tablespoons make an ounce and that a pint and two cups are just the same. You'll show him the degrees on the oven knob and the way the broiler flame is high for the ten minutes it takes to reach the right temperature. Children are very logical people, and they need to understand that cooking is logical too—that meat must be dried before it can brown, and eggs help a cake to rise. You should give a child the reason for each instruction and identify each ingredient, encouraging him to taste as he goes (unless it contains raw eggs), and to smell everything, re-minding him that he's expected to eat a little of everything he makes—and also everything you make.

### TWO

At this age he can hold the portable electric mixer with both hands if you're ready to push it deep into the bowl every time he forgets. He can roast bacon, snap the ends of the beans and wash the salad greens—but not very well—and decorate a cookie with a nut but not with icing. He can take out utensils now and knead hamburgers, but be cautioned: his attention span will last about ten minutes in a job, whether it's cooking or cleaning.

### THREE

He'll gather most of the ingredients and drop very few and you'll spend a lot of time explaining kitchen safety. He can make applesauce—with skins to keep the food value—and crack eggs, squeeze lemons (if he has no cuts) and shake stew beef in a paper bag with flour. Now he'll be fascinated with the properties of yeast and make his own Lost Bread, left over from the bread he's baked.

### FOUR

This child makes granola for the family and because he's such a show-off now, he may eat it. He'll cut parsley and green onions with scissors—the best way to cut them—make salad dressings, bake a cake and be very daring if you don't watch out. This is a good time to let the Great Experimenter bake just one loaf of bread without yeast—the biblical way—although no one may want to eat it.

### FIVE

This child makes fried bologna sandwiches, a daube, a pound cake, and uses a blender to make a fine Hollandaise Sauce. By now he should be cleaning as he goes and not even minding it too much.

## SIX

Now he can make any of the recipes we've included, but even if he can read and is a genius at organization, you still must check his accuracy, do the steps he doesn't like to do and, generally, be around for safety and to keep him from feeling like a slave. Of course, you can't expect him to gauge his time or prepare dishes for simultaneous serving.

Any child who contributes a little to the meal, even the salad dressing, will feel more responsible for the conviviality of the dinner itself, for he's part of the work as well as the play. Every time you help your child achieve an ability of his own, you have put a stone beneath his feet where only sand has been.

## KITCHEN CODE

A child has the right to learn each skill with as much simplicity and safety as you can give him. He learns best when the instructions are simple and the action verb is the same every time. Here are the Rules and Techniques your child needs to follow.

## RULES

☐ Wash hands before starting, so they can be used to mix anything.
☐ Wear an adult T-shirt to keep clothes clean.
☐ Assemble all ingredients on one side of the working area, all utensils on the other—before you start.
☐ Use only one bowl, if possible, rinsing and reusing, to prevent a huge cleanup—a practice you may one day learn yourself.

## TECHNIQUES

*Measure*—Spoon dry ingredients lightly into a measuring cup and level with

### Safety Rules

You should

☐ Avoid all recipes involving hot grease or boiling syrups, which cause the worst kitchen burns.
☐ Stand your child on a kitchen chair, with its back to the counter or stove, so he can hang on while he works.
☐ Turn on the stove yourself and always stand next to him if he's cooking on the burners.
☐ Give him a long wooden spoon for stirring, so heat can't transmit.
☐ Have him hold the pot handle with one hand, with a pot holder if necessary, while he stirs with the other, which gives the extra balance a small child needs.
☐ Aim all pot handles to the back of the stove when he isn't stirring, so he can't knock over the pots—a rule for all the family to follow, for a child's height is handle high.

a knife. To avoid a mess, work over wax paper, and measure wet ingredients in the sink.

*Sift*—Omit this standard step; it isn't necessary in any of our recipes.

*Chop*—Work on a cutting board, slicing as much as possible with kitchen shears, which takes the coordination of a Four. A younger child uses a knife, holding each end of the blade with his fingertips and walking it away from him, working it up and down like a seesaw.

*Pare*—Peel as few fruits and vegetables as possible, since most of the nutrition is just below the skin. Scrape away the thinner skins with a pot scrubber and use a peeler on the thicker ones, working away from the body, but it's healthier and easier to cook the foods in their skins, then let

your child peel them with his fingers when they're cool.

*Grate*—Hold any object with the fingertips to avoid the curse of the kitchen: grated knuckles. Grate only the colorful zest of citrus, not the bitter white beneath it.

*Stir*—Use a wooden spoon and stir gently, so the bowl can contain the ingredients.

*Beat*—Use a mixer on medium speed with the blades deep in the bowl to avoid spatter and place the bowl on a wet dishcloth so it won't spin while mixing.

*Blend*—Use a blender as directed, holding the base of the blender for your child.

*Process*—Use the food processor as directed, but with very great care, while you hold the base firmly.

## BREAKFAST

Children eat their meals much better when they help to make them—especially breakfast.

## SPANISH GRANOLA

One afternoon Nell brought dismay to her mother (the sort who says, "So eat," so often) when she announced, "Guess what! Today I wasn't hungry until lunch."

That was the morning we served not fish or eggs and certainly not cold cereal, but our own homemade Spanish granola. It's as filling as it is nutritious and, ounce for ounce, it's cheaper than any puffy, commercial cereal. It also makes a good cookie base instead of oatmeal, it's a fine snack and a Four likes to make it.

YIELD: 7 cups                    Preheat Oven 250°

In a saucepan

| HEAT | ½ c. peanut oil |
|------|----------------|
|      | ½ c. honey     |

| ADD | 1 tsp. vanilla |
|-----|----------------|

In a roasting pan

**MIX**

4 c. rolled oats
1 c. raw wheat germ
4 oz. chopped almonds OR pecans
1 c. unsweetened coconut
3 tbsp. soy flour

Add the honey mixture and stir until all ingredients are sticky.

**BAKE**            **30 minutes**

Stir every 10 minutes. When cool, store in airtight plastic bags. Serve less than usual since it's so filling. Like any cereal, it should be served with milk to make a whole protein.

## ROASTED BACON

SERVES 4                              Preheat Oven 350°

Even an early Two can handle this if the bacon is room temperature.

**SEPARATE**        ¼ lb. bacon

Lay strips on a cake rack placed over a baking dish.

**BAKE**            **20 minutes**

Dry on paper towel.

## LOST BREAD

SERVES 1

The frugal French have turned stale bread into a toast treat and so can your Three. In a bowl

| BEAT | 1 egg |
|------|-------|
|      | ¼ c. milk |
|      | 1 tsp. sugar |
|      | ½ tsp. orange flavoring |

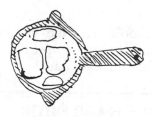

**ADD**   3 slices stale bread

The more stale it is, the more egg mixture the bread will absorb and the better it will cook. In a skillet

**MELT**   2 tbsp. butter

Help your child lift the slices with a slotted spoon, frying them first on one side, then on the other. Butter and serve with honey.

## CINNAMON TOAST

SERVES 1                                    Preheat Broiler

We hate to admit it, but only the Health Bread (see page 356) or one made of a whole grain makes this recipe nutritious. Still the taste and the smell are worth a great deal. Your Five can

**MIX**   ¾ tsp. cinnamon
          3 tbsp. sugar

In the broiler

**TOAST**   4 slices bread

Toast on one side only. Spread the other with butter and sprinkle with the cinnamon sugar. Broil until bubbly, lifting it with a spatula yourself and serve when cooler, because caramelized sugar can cause a bad burn.

## SOFT AND HARD COOKED EGGS

The most inept toddler can make these eggs, and they are more digestible than boiled ones. In a saucepan

**COMBINE**   2 cups cold water
              unshelled eggs

The rest of the job is yours. Bring to a boil. To cook a soft egg, reduce boil to a simmer and remove in four minutes. Drop the fat end of the egg into an egg cup; its gentility will delight him.

To cook a hard egg, turn off the heat when the water boils, cover and wait 20 minutes. Your child can peel a cool egg under running water, for slick removal, but we think unshelled ones are meant to be colored by a small

child, so you can identify them in the refrigerator. Let him use crayons, paints or felt-tipped markers.

### EGGS

We once knew a college professor who, despairing of modern youth, applied for a job as a houseman on an estate. He listed such a grand spread of skills that he was hired, even though he said he "would have nothing to do with eggs."

This is understandable. A person can become quite uncomfortable with an egg, particularly a very small person. The best way to overcome this reaction is to teach your child to cook his own.

## SCRAMBLED EGGS

SERVES 4

If scrambled eggs are beaten first they lose the stringiness a good chef insists upon, and besides—there's another bowl to wash. A Three will enjoy cracking the eggs directly into a skillet, but a Six likes to blow them into a bowl first and save the shells for an Easter Egg Tree (see page 252). In an iron skillet

**SAUTE**   1 tbsp. butter
            ¼ c. green onions, chopped

**ADD**   5 unbeaten eggs
          1 tbsp. water

The water slows down the cooking process. Have your child stir the eggs with a wooden spoon until they're almost set. They'll finish cooking by the time he spoons them into the serving dish.

For variety, he can add parsley, chipped beef or crumbled cheddar cheese with the eggs instead of the green onion—or none of them, depending on the whim of your child.

## POACHED EGGS

SERVES 4

Surprisingly, a Four can poach the breakfast eggs. In a skillet

**SIMMER**   2 c. water
             1 tsp. vinegar (optional)

The vinegar helps older eggs hold their shape. In a bowl, have your child

**BREAK**          **4 eggs**

Help him slide the contents into the skillet—an extra step that usually keeps the yolks from breaking—and cook 3–4 minutes, until the whites have set. Remove the eggs yourself with a slotted spoon. Serve on buttered toast or on English muffins as in Eggs Benedict.

## EGGS BENEDICT

SERVES 4

Every Six should have the chance to eat this dish at least once—and even to make it.

**TOAST**          **2 split English muffins**

**SAUTÉ**          **4 slices Canadian bacon**

**POACH**          **4 eggs**

In a double boiler to prevent curdling

**HEAT**          **Hollandaise Sauce**

Even a tablespoon of leftover Hollandaise per egg is enough, but more is better. Butter the muffins, lay a slice of bacon on each one and then an egg. Cover with the sauce.

*Hollandaise Sauce*
YIELD: 1 cup

Nothing is sacred anymore. Even a child can make Hollandaise if he has two helpers—you and the blender—and with this recipe, he can make it in advance. Serve over meat, fish or vegetables, hot or cold. Separate the eggs yourself. In a small pan

**MELT**          **½ c. butter**

**BLEND**          **3 egg yolks**
**2 tbsp. lemon juice**
**¼ tsp. salt**
**⅛ tsp. pepper**

Blend at high speed. A child then can add the butter very slowly through the hole in the top or by stopping the blender repeatedly to add a few drops each time. It will begin to thicken after two-thirds of the butter is added. If this Hollandaise should curdle

**ADD**          **1 tbsp. hot water**

Blend again for a second. Reheat slowly in a double boiler.

## LUNCH
A preschooler still has enough energy to make one of these simple recipes before he takes his afternoon nap.

## HOMEMADE PEANUT BUTTER

YIELD: 1 cup

Old-fashioned, unhydrogenated peanut butter is a cinch for a new-fashioned Three to make. The hulling should be done outside, away from the wind and over a large bag.

**BLEND**          **1 c. hulled, roasted peanuts**
**1½ tbsp. peanut oil**
**⅛ tsp. salt**

Have him start the blender on a low-speed, while you hold the lid down, then switch to high, stopping it once or twice for you to scrape the jar with a rubber spatula. Stop when it's as smooth as he likes. Make 1 cup at a time but never more than 2, or it might jam the blender. Refrigerate. It will keep indefinitely.

## BANANA AND PEANUT BUTTER SANDWICH

This sandwich will surprise you. It tastes good. It also combines two of the most nutritious foods available. On one slice of bread, let your Two

**SPREAD**          **2 tbsp. peanut butter**

**ADD**          **½ banana, sliced lengthwise**

Fold the bread over itself, like a hot dog roll.

## EGG SALAD SANDWICHES

SERVES 4

A Four's favorite because all the ingredients can be mixed by squeezing them through his clean fingers until the whites are broken into small pieces.

**COMBINE**          **4 hard-cooked eggs**
**3 tbsp. mayonnaise**
**1 tsp. Dijon mustard**
**½ tsp. Worcestershire sauce**
**dash pepper**

Have him spoon the egg salad on a slice of bread and cover it with another. Be sure to wash your child's hands again when he's finished making the sandwiches, or he'll leave a trail of egg prints.

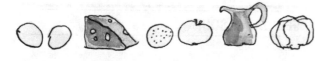 

## GRILLED BOLOGNA SANDWICH

For some inexplicable reason, children adore this sandwich—possibly because it was invented by a child. A Five makes it well. Use a nonstick skillet but no grease.

**FRY**              **1 slice bologna**

Remove when the bologna puffs in the center. Lay it on a slice of buttered bread and roll it like a taco.

## GRILLED CHEESE SANDWICH

This makes a Six feel skillful. Have him

**BUTTER**              **2 slices bread**

Put the slices together, with the butter on the outside.

**INSERT**              **1 slice cheddar cheese**

Fry the sandwich in a hot skillet, about 4 minutes on one side, two on the other, to melt the cheese and toast the bread. For a change, you also can insert sliced cold cuts, tomatoes, chopped olives or apple slices before cooking.

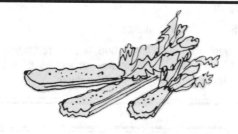

## CELERY BOATS

This recipe gives your child almost every vitamin he needs as a lunch supplement, and a Two can do it all.

**CLEAN**              **celery stalks**

Into their scoops

**SPOON**              **peanut butter OR**
                       **cream cheese**

Skim a knife across the top to level the boats.

**ADD**               **raisins OR**
                      **nuts**

## APPLESAUCE

Suzannah, a neighborhood favorite, could make this recipe at Four, since the apples were neither peeled nor cored, but she needed her big brother to help her stir and strain. Into a heavy soup pot

**ADD**              **12 uncored apples, quartered**

Since apples contain so much water you don't need to add any if you cook them covered over the lowest fire. Stir every 5 minutes with a wooden spoon—a job that needs your help—for about 20 minutes, or until the apples are soft. Squeeze through a food mill or use a colander, pressing the pulp through with a small wooden bowl or a tin can. Most children like this without any sugar or spices.

# DINNER

*SOUPS*

French cookbooks have introduced more mystery to the soup pot than Sherlock Holmes did to Baker Street. We can't imagine why. Although we've never known a parent who could spare a burner to simmer a stockpot around the clock (and, consequently, a stockpot that didn't turn sour in a week), we've found it very easy to turn out a good soup. The smell alone is reason enough to make it.

Soups require two or three hours to cook—not necessarily consecutively—including short spurts of time when your child lobs something into the pot. A Three only needs to know what to add and when.

Children generally like to eat thick soups better than thin ones and soups that keep them curious, with bits of meat and fresh vegetables and certainly a pasta like alphabet noodles floating in them. There

are so many soups and so many flavors of each one that anything your child makes will be right. If it has a pallid flavor, add more salt and pepper or a few bouillon cubes and boil to reduce the liquid. If it's too strong add water, and if it's too salty add a few extra potatoes to absorb the salt.

Any canned vegetables (except tomatoes) should be drained if the soup is to keep its homemade flavor and they should be added during the last few minutes of cooking.

## SOUP BASE

YIELD: 6–8 cups

This base can be used for either beef or chicken, depending on the protein you add. The turnip is essential for the sweet taste it gives, whether it's eaten or not. The carrots are added for their nutty flavor and the pasta, potatoes or rice for their thickening powers. This is a base to make yourself, and later let your child make the soup, which, as you both will discover, is much less formidable than it seems. In a heavy soup pot

| COMBINE | 2 qts. water |
| | 1 large onion, peeled and quartered |
| | 1 turnip, quartered |
| | 3 whole unpeeled carrots |
| | 2 stalks celery |
| | 1 bayleaf |
| | 1 bunch parsley, tied |
| | 1–2 tsps. salt |
| | 6 peppercorns |

Bring to a boil.

| ADD | 1 lb. stew beef OR |
| | 2 lbs. beef bones OR |
| | 1 cut-up chicken |

Simmer covered for two hours. Strain and chill in the refrigerator until fat solidifies. Then your child can lift the fat and dramatically throw it away.

Either chicken or beef base is good for most soups, but only use the chicken base for a fancy cream soup. Any meat in this recipe can be used for salads, sandwiches or for baby food when blended with a little broth.

## VEGETABLE SOUP

YIELD: 16 cups

This is a nutritious, quick soup—using the stock and stew beef from the Soup Base. The ingredients are listed in order of the time it takes to cook and the flavors to marry—a 30-minute job. In a heavy pot

| COMBINE | 6–8 c. beef Soup Base |
| | 1 c. boiled beef |

Bring to a simmer. Now's the time to tell your Three what to toss in the pot and when.

| ADD | 3 potatoes, peeled and quartered, OR |
| | ⅓ c. barley OR |
| | ⅓ c. uncooked brown rice |
| | 1 28-oz. can plum tomatoes with liquid |
| | 2 tsp. dried basil |
| | 1 tsp. dried oregano |
| | 2 celery stalks, chopped |
| | 2 carrots, sliced |
| | 1 turnip, peeled and quartered |

Simmer covered for 15–20 minutes, until the potatoes, barley or rice are almost tender.

| ADD | ¼ lb. snapped beans |
| | 1 10-oz. pkg. frozen limas |
| | 1 8½-oz can white corn, drained |
| | salt and pepper to taste |

Cover again.

| SIMMER | 10 minutes |

If you want to freeze this soup, either remove the potatoes—they lose their texture—or use ⅓ c. pasta instead, adding it in the last 10–12 minutes.

## CHICKEN SOUP

YIELD: 8–10 cups

After making a soup base with chicken, cool the bird enough for your child to pull away the skin and bones, a gruesome, 20-minute task every Four strangely enjoys. Tear into bite-sized pieces. In a heavy soup pot

| SIMMER | 6–8 c. chicken soup base |

In a skillet

| SAUTÉ | 1 T. olive oil |
| | 1 carrot, chopped |
| | 1 celery stalk, chopped |
| | 2 green onions, chopped |

He'll need your help to do the chopping, because the vegetables should be fine—and because it's boring to work alone. When the onions are translucent

**ADD**              2 tbsp. flour

Ladle a little hot soup base into the skillet and stir to dissolve the flour, so it won't lump. Empty the skillet into the soup pot (a job for you) and bring to a full boil.

**ADD**              ⅓ c. pasta OR
                     ⅓ c. uncooked rice
                     ½ c. cooked chicken

Simmer covered 15 minutes before serving. You can add dumplings of Homemade Biscuit Mix (see page 356).

## PISTOU

YIELD: 12 cups

If you managed to plant an herb garden, try this "pea stew." And if you didn't, use dried herbs and still feel blessed. This has the triple virtue of tasting good, requiring short segments of working time—about as long as a small child's interest can stretch—and sounding obscene enough to delight a Five. In a soup pot have him

**COMBINE**          1½ qts. water
                     1 c. dried white beans

Boil two minutes, then simmer covered for 1½ hours. In a skillet

**SAUTÉ**            ¼ c. olive oil
                     2 medium onions, peeled and
                        chopped

When onions are soft, add them to the soup pot and boil 5 minutes.

**ADD**              16-oz can tomatoes with liquid
                     2 potatoes, peeled and chopped
                     ½ lb. snapped green beans
                     2 zucchinis, chopped
                     ½ c. fresh basil OR
                     2 tbsp. dried basil
                     5 whole garlic cloves, peeled
                     2 tbsp. tomato paste
                     2 tbsp. salt
                     ½ tsp. pepper

Simmer covered for 15–20 minutes, until potatoes are done and colors are still vibrant. Over it

**SPRINKLE**         ¼ c. chopped parsley

---

*MAIN DISHES*

These entrées are great for either lunch or dinner.

## TUNA MELTS

SERVES 4                                         Preheat Broiler

This is a fine, fast supper for a mother and a Six to make together, and it's extranutritious if it's made with natural, rather than processed, cheese.

**MASH**             one 7-oz can drained tuna
                     2 tbsp. mayonnaise
                     1 hard-cooked egg, chopped
                     1 green onion, chopped
                     1 celery stalk, chopped
                     ½ c. diced natural cheese

Spread on 4 slices of bread. Broil until bubbly—about five minutes.

## CHIPPED BEEF ON TOAST

SERVES 4

The best thing about this recipe (besides its good taste) is its speed. It requires about 10 minutes of stirring, which a Four thinks is dandy. Serve hot on toast or a baked potato.

**SAUTÉ**            2 tbsp. butter
                     ½ medium onion, peeled and
                        chopped
                     ½ green pepper, sliced

Stir until the onions are clear. Turn off the heat.

**ADD**              2 tbsp. flour

Stir over a low fire for 2 minutes, until there are no lumps. If they develop, beat them with a whisk.

**ADD**              1½–2 c. milk.

Do this slowly, stirring until thick.

**ADD**              4 hard-cooked eggs, quartered
                     4 oz. chipped beef, shredded
                     ½ tsp. salt
                     ¼ tsp. pepper

## CHEESE SOUFFLÉ

SERVES 4                                    Preheat Oven 425°

This recipe should be tried once, because it's very easy, it doesn't fall if dinner is late and because most children love it. The rest of them hate it. There is no in-between. Have your Four start this recipe in a bowl.

| MIX | 3 eggs |
|-----|--------|
|     | 1 c. milk |
|     | 1 tsp. dry mustard |
|     | ½ tsp. salt |
|     | ⅛ tsp. pepper |

Butter a 1-quart baking dish, and into small bits

| TEAR | 4 slices bread |
|------|----------------|

Lay the bread in the bottom of the dish.

| SLICE | ⅓ lb. cheddar cheese |
|-------|----------------------|

A child does this best with a vegetable peeler. Lay the cheese on top of the bread. Pour the egg mixture over the bread and cheese and bake 20 minutes, or until lightly browned on top.

## SPICED CHICKEN

SERVES 4

There is a large if dreary school of people who thinks food shouldn't be touched. Children know better. This is the touchiest recipe we know. In a large bowl have your Three

| COMBINE | 1 cut-up fryer |
|---------|----------------|
|         | ⅓ c. soy sauce |
|         | 3 tbsp. peanut oil |
|         | 1 garlic clove, pressed |
|         | 1 tsp. ground ginger |
|         | ¼ tsp. pepper |

Rub the chicken completely with this marinade and let it soak in it for a half hour to overnight in the refrigerator.

Preheat Oven 350°

Arrange chicken in a baking dish, with no overlapping so it will cook crisply. Cover with the marinade and baste three times while it is baking—a mother's job.

| BAKE | 50 minutes |
|------|------------|

## CHICKEN WITH FRUIT

SERVES 4

If children get enough natural sugar they won't crave sweets so much, but don't skimp on the onions here. They balance the flavors. A Five is quite old enough to make this recipe. In a Dutch oven

| SAUTÉ | 1 medium onion, peeled and sliced |
|-------|-----------------------------------|
|       | 2 apples, unpeeled, quartered and cored |
|       | 2 tbsp. butter |

Cook until onions are clear. Remove onions and apples with a slotted spoon, a step for you. In the same pan

| BROWN | 1 cut-up fryer |
|-------|----------------|

This is another job you do yourself.

| ADD | ¼ c. raisins |
|-----|--------------|
|     | ⅔ c. mixed dried fruits |
|     | 1 c. apple juice |
|     | 1 tsp. salt |
|     | ¼ tsp. pepper |
|     | sautéed onions and apples |

If you're using a very large pot you may need to add more apple juice, for it should be about an inch deep when all the ingredients are added.

| SIMMER | 1 hour, covered |
|--------|-----------------|

Serve with Baked Rice.

## GRILLED HAMBURGERS

SERVES 6                                    Preheat Broiler

A Two likes to smash these into shape.

| KNEAD | 1½ lbs. ground beef |
|-------|---------------------|
|       | ⅓ c. water |

The water prevents dryness. Make 6 patties 1½" thick for rare hamburgers, less thick if you want them well done.

| BROIL | 5 minutes |
|-------|-----------|

Turn and repeat—a job for you. Season with salt and pepper.

## CHILI

SERVES 6

We never knew a Six who didn't like to make chili, perhaps because it dresses up so easily. In a heavy iron skillet

| BROWN | 1 lb. ground beef |
|---|---|
| ADD | 1 18-oz can tomatoes with liquid |
| | 1 18-oz can red beans with liquid |
| | 2 tbsp. tomato paste |
| | 1 tsp. cumin |
| | ¼ tsp. chili powder |
| | ¼ tsp. garlic powder |
| | ½ tsp. celery salt |
| | ½ tsp. salt |

For lower cholesterol use ground turkey and double the amount of spices. Simmer uncovered for a half hour. Serve with Baked Rice (see page 351) or in a bowl with saltines or in hot tortillas to make tacos, every child's delight. To make them, spoon the chili inside and

| ADD | chopped Muenster cheese OR |
|---|---|
| | Monterey Jack |
| | sour cream/chopped parsley/ |
| | chopped green onions/shredded |
| | lettuce/diced tomatoes |

You can use any or all of these ingredients.

## DAUBE

SERVES 6                                   Preheat Oven 350°

The layering involved in this beef dish intrigues a Five, who is as orderly as he is inept. The gin tenderizes the meat and then evaporates, as all alcohol does under heat. Into a large bowl

| COMBINE | 2 c. sliced carrots |
|---|---|
| | 2 c. sliced onions |

This is your job—the only one—for the slices must be thin.

| ADD | one 28-oz. can tomatoes, mashed |
|---|---|
| | ¼ c. gin OR vodka |
| | 1 beef bouillon cube |
| | 2 tbsp. olive oil |
| | 2 garlic cloves, pressed |
| | 1 bay leaf |
| | ½ tsp. dried thyme |
| | 1 tsp. salt |
| | ¼ tsp. pepper |

In a paper bag

| COMBINE | 2 lbs. cubed stewing beef |
|---|---|
| | ¾ c. flour |

Shake the bag to coat the cubes.

| SEPARATE | ½ lb. bacon |
|---|---|

Line a Dutch oven with bacon strips. With a slotted spoon, scatter a layer of the vegetables and then of the beef. Repeat these three layers and end with the rest of the bacon. Add the vegetable and gin marinade and, if necessary, enough water to reach the top layer. Cover.

| BAKE | 1 hour |
|---|---|

Lower heat to 300° and cook two hours longer. Remove the bay leaf and serve with Baked Rice (see page 351) or buttered noodles.

## PIZZA

SERVES 4                                   Preheat Oven 450°

In an Italian household, this is known as "Mama's pizza"—good, plain pizza with no frills, the way a Four usually likes it best. The mix is found on page 356.

| MIX | 2 c. Homemade Biscuit Mix |
|---|---|
| | ⅔ c. milk |

Knead gently for 30 seconds. Grease a cookie sheet and roll the dough on it with a glass or simply pull it to the edges as thin as possible. A child gets less sticky if his hands are oiled first. To prevent a soggy crust

| BAKE | 10 minutes |
|---|---|
| COOL | 10 minutes |
| DRAIN | one 16-oz. can tomatoes |

With a vegetable peeler

| SLICE | 1 c. mozzarella OR cheddar cheese |
|---|---|

Let your child break the tomatoes between his fingers and scatter them on the pizza crust. Cover with the cheese.

| ADD | 1 tsp. olive oil |
|---|---|
| | ½ tsp. salt |
| | dash pepper |
| BAKE | 10 minutes |

## BOILED SHRIMP

SERVES 4–6

In New Orleans, mothers cover the supper table with newspaper and pile spiced shrimp on it, for everyone to peel his own—even a Three. A Four can put everything in the pot but the shrimp, and a Five can make the sauce. In a large soup pot

| COMBINE | 3 qts. water |
|---|---|
| | 1 bunch leafy celery, broken |
| | 2 large onions, peeled and quartered |
| | 2 lemons, quartered |
| | 2 bay leaves |
| | 4 cloves garlic, peeled |
| | 4 whole allspice |
| | 5 tbsp. salt |
| | 1 tbsp. cayenne pepper |
| | ½ tsp. dried thyme |
| BOIL | 10 minutes |
| ADD | 2 lbs. shrimp |

Do this yourself, for the water may splash.

| BOIL | 5 minutes |
|---|---|

Cool in the broth to absorb more flavors. Drain in a colander, and serve shrimp warm or cold with Mayonnaise Sauce.

*Mayonnaise Sauce*
YIELD: 1½ cups

| MIX | 1 c. mayonnaise |
|---|---|
| | 4 green onions, chopped |
| | 3 tbsp. chopped parsley |
| | 1 tsp. lemon juice |
| | ¼ tsp. hot sauce |
| | salt and pepper |

## LENTILS AND SAUSAGE

SERVES 8

This is the sort of hearty meal so popular with a father, whose appreciation will encourage a Three to eat some of the beans and all of the sausage, just as a way of saying, "You're welcome."

Lentils, a staple in Europe, are found in the supermarket with other dried beans. This dish needs no rice or potatoes to complement it.

| COMBINE | 6 c. water |
|---|---|
| | 1 lb. lentils |
| | ¼ lb. salt pork |
| | 4 stalks leafy celery, broken |

| | 4 onions, peeled and quartered |
|---|---|
| | 2 whole carrots, unpeeled |
| | 1 bunch parsley, tied |
| | 2 bay leaves |
| | ½ tsp dried basil |
| | 1–2 tsp. salt |
| | ½ tsp. pepper |

Simmer covered for 1½ hours.

| ADD | 2 lbs. smoked sausage |
|---|---|

Simmer covered a half-hour longer—until the water is absorbed—and remove the limp celery, parsley and bay leaves before serving. Use leftover lentils as a salad, served in equal parts with chopped tomato and green onion. Mix with a vinegar and oil dressing.

## BEEF STEW

SERVES 6                          Preheat Oven 250°

This is the perfect stew for children who don't like their flavors mixed. The heat is kept so low each vegetable remains whole, crisp and colorful and each taste is pure. The gravy is dark brown. A Three can make this stew right after nap and not look at it again until dinner. In a Dutch oven

| COMBINE | 1½ lbs. stew beef |
|---|---|
| | 1 medium onion, peeled and quartered |
| | 2 whole carrots, unpeeled |
| | 2 sprigs parsley |
| | 2 c. hot water |
| | 1 16-oz. can tomatoes, drained |
| | 1 tsp. salt |
| | ½ tsp. peppercorns |
| Cover. | |
| BAKE | 2½ hours |

In a small saucepan, have your child

**MELT**          **3 tbsp. butter**

**ADD**           **3 tbsp. flour**

Stir and let bubble for 2 minutes. To prevent lumps, add a tablespoon of hot broth to the flour—a job for you—blend well and return all to the casserole. Stir over a low fire on top of the stove for about 5 minutes, until thickened. If you use a 2-lb. frozen chuck instead

**BAKE**          **3½ hours**

Now you have a pot roast and with a lot less trouble.

## RED BEANS (AND RICE)

SERVES 6

In almost every culture, a native dish has evolved with such balance that it makes a whole protein, whether it has meat in it or not. Red beans and rice are like that. This dish is such a staple in Louisiana that Louis Armstrong signed letters "Red Beans and Ricedly Yours."

The food value will be less if you use white rice but still much higher than it would be if either the beans or the rice were served alone. A Four can boil the beans and a Five can bake the rice.

**WASH**          **1 lb. red kidney beans**

In a soup pot

**MEASURE**       **8 c. water**

Add beans. Soak overnight or boil for 2 minutes, turn off the heat, cover, and soak 1 hour. A child feels a sense of accomplishment just watching his beans soak. Pour out the water and replace it with fresh water, so it won't cause gassiness.

**ADD**           **ham bone OR**
                  **½ lb. salt pork**
                  **1 large onion, peeled and quartered**
                  **1 green pepper, seeded and**
                  **quartered**
                  **2 garlic cloves, peeled**
                  **1 bay leaf**
                  **½ tsp. dried thyme**
                  **1 tsp. salt**
                  **½ tsp. pepper**

Stir and cover.

**SIMMER**        **2 hours**

Stir occasionally. The water must cover the beans at all times, to soften them. Remove the bay leaf and serve with Baked Rice.

## BAKED RICE

SERVES 6                          Preheat Oven 350°

Few dishes are as easy to ruin as rice—unless you bake it. In a heavy iron casserole have your Five

**SAUTÉ**         **2 tbsp. butter OR oil**
                  **2 tbsp. chopped onion**
                  **1 c. long grain rice**

Stir until the grains are clear—about 5 minutes.

**ADD**           **2 c. boiling water**
                  **2 bouillon cubes**
                  **½ tsp. salt**

Stir and cover.

**BAKE**          **20 minutes**

All water should be absorbed. For some reason if you double the recipe you should cook it 10 minutes longer. With brown rice

**ADD**           **3½ c. boiling water**

**BAKE**          **1 hour**

For a Mideastern flavor

**SAUTÉ**         **¼ c. raisins**
                  **¼ c. blanched almonds**
                  **2 tbsp. butter**

Add just before serving.

*VEGETABLES*

If you want your child to like vegetables you should use fresh ones and he should help you fix them. The tastiest vegetables—and the most nutritious—are the most colorful and the easiest to prepare. A Two can wash and snap green beans (catching about half of them), a Three can shell peas, and a Four can scrub carrots. No vegetables should be peeled before cooking, because most of the vitamins are just below the skin, and green and yellow vegetables should usually be steamed, because water dissolves some vitamins.

## STEAMED VEGETABLES

You'll need a steamer or a pot big enough to hold a colander. In it have your child

**BOIL**              **1″ water**

Add the colander of vegetables—green beans, beets, carrots, summer squash, spinach or whatever. Cover.

**STEAM**             **10–20 minutes**

Remove as soon as they're cooked, when the color is still bright; the texture, crisp; the flavor, fresh.

## CRISP BAKED POTATOES

SERVES 4                                    Preheat Oven 350°

Some baked potatoes are more equal than others. Like these. A late Two can make them.

**HALVE**             **4 medium potatoes**

Lay flat side down, on a well-buttered cookie sheet.

**BAKE**              **30 minutes**

Small potatoes take 20.

## ZUCCHINI AND TOMATO CASSEROLE

SERVES 4                                    Preheat Oven 350°

This recipe requires very fresh vegetables to bring out the purity of flavor. An old zucchini tastes bitter and a hothouse tomato doesn't taste at all. A Six can make this handily over 1″ boiling water.

**STEAM**             **1 large zucchini, thickly sliced**

Cover and cook for 10 minutes only. Grease a 2″-deep casserole with olive oil and layer the following ingredients, in this order, saving some of the cheese for an extra layer on top. You'll have to add the zucchini yourself with a slotted spoon if it's still hot.

**LAYER**            **steamed zucchini**
                     **2 large tomatoes, sliced**
                     **¼ lb. Swiss cheese, sliced**
                     **¼ tsp. dried basil**
                     **salt and pepper**

**POUR**             **1 tbsp. olive oil**

**BAKE**             **10 minutes**

It's ready when the cheese on top is melted.

*SALADS*

There's nothing quite so rewarding for a child to make as a salad. He plays in water, stirs the ingredients with his hands, tears the lettuce to pieces—and everyone congratulates him for being so good. Even if he eats earlier than his parents he'll enjoy joining them for his specialty, and he may eat it too, just to play grown-up.

All raw fruits and vegetables are more nutritious than they are when they're cooked, but leafy greens—the darker the better—have vitamins and minerals that are hard to find anywhere else.

A Two can wash and dry the greens reasonably well, but a Four can do the whole job himself, which he should start after a nap and return to at dinnertime. First the leaves are floated in a pot of cool water about 10 minutes, so dirt sinks to the bottom, and then they're shaken in a colander and dried or whirled in a salad spinner so the oil coating will stick when it's added later.

Your child should remove spinach stems and for better flavor, have him tear, but not cut, the lettuce leaves. Refrigerate in a plastic bag with more paper towels inside to absorb any moisture that remains and to crisp the greens again.

## BASIC DRESSING

Any vegetable oil can be used. The French use peanut oil, the Italians use olive. In a large measuring cup, have your Four

**POUR**             **1 c. oil**
                     **⅓ c. balsalmic vinegar OR lemon**
                         **juice**
                     **½ tsp. salt**
                     **½ tsp. pepper**

Let him transfer the dressing to the cruet with a funnel, or he'll surely lose some of it.

He also can use four 3-ounce baby food jars instead

of a single bottle and put a different flavor in each one. In the jars

**ADD**  1 oz. crumbled blue cheese OR
1 garlic clove OR
¼ tsp. curry OR
1 tbsp. fresh OR 1 tsp. dried herbs

These dressings keep indefinitely if refrigerated. Shake well before using.

## GREEN SALAD

SERVES 4–6

Aplomb is a Four mixing salad at dinner, but don't use the word "toss," or no bowl will be big enough.

**PEEL**  1 garlic clove

Cut and rub the inside of a wooden bowl.

**COMBINE**  1 head romaine lettuce OR spinach,
torn in pieces
1 tsp. peanut oil

The leaves are coated first with oil so the acid in the dressing won't wilt them. Any or all of these additions may be used in the salad.

**ADD**  ½ c. croutons
2 crisp bacon strips, crumbled
3 raw mushrooms, sliced
2 tomatoes, quartered
½ c. leftover vegetables
1 hard-boiled egg, grated

Just before serving

**ADD**  2 tbsp. Basic Dressing

After dinner your child should wipe the bowl clean with a paper towel so the residue of oil continues to season the wood.

## TOMATO SALAD

SERVES 4

Fresh basil is to tomatoes what ham is to eggs. A third as much of the dried herb will always do, but in this case it doesn't do so well. To make this salad, have your Five

**COMBINE**  2 tomatoes, sliced
2 tbsp. chopped fresh basil
2 tbsp. Basic Dressing

## DESSERTS

If most children had their way, every meal would end with a dessert. These are some of the best.

## RASPBERRY PEACHES

SERVES 6

We've probably never seen a dessert so pretty or so simple, and though we first found it in our fanciest French cookbook, we discovered a Four could make it.

Into a deep saucepan

**STIR**  6 c. water
2¼ c. sugar
1 vanilla bean OR
2 tbsp. vanilla

Bring to a simmer.

**ADD**  6 whole peaches

Cook, just below the simmering point, for 8 minutes. Lift the peaches with a slotted spoon—your job—and let them drip onto a cake rack over a plate for 30 minutes. Have your child slip the skins from the peaches when they're still warm—a very easy act which transforms them from sodden, tan blobs into fruit that looks more luscious than they did when they were picked. Refrigerate until dinner. For the sauce

**BLEND**  one 8-oz. pkg. frozen raspberries,
unsweetened
¼ c. sugar
½ lime, squeezed

It works just as well to beat this sauce for 2 minutes or even stir it, if the berries are thawed. Just before serving, in the place of the peach stem.

**ADD**  1 pair mint leaves

Pour the sauce over part of each peach so the blush of the fruit can show.

## CHOCOLATE MOUSSE I

SERVES 6

If you like chocolate, this dessert has no rivals. Its elegance is almost overwhelming; its simplicity, disarming, and if you do a few of the steps yourself even your

Three can make it. There's just one drawback: you have to know your poultry farmer or raise the chickens yourself, to make sure the raw eggs will be free of salmonella. The recipe is worth it. In a heavy saucepan let your child

**COMBINE**      6 oz. semisweet chocolate bits
                 2 tsp. hot water

Cook over a low fire, for chocolate burns easily, and use a rubber spatula to scrape the melted bits into the blender—your job. Let him

**ADD**          ½ c. whipping cream
                 2 tbsp. confectioners sugar
                 4 egg yolks

Separate the eggs yourself, but your child can operate the blender.

**BLEND**        3 minutes

**ADD**          4 egg whites
                 2 tsp. vanilla

Blend 3 minutes longer. Chill in demitasse cups for 2 hours to set the cream. If your child is cooking for adults, you can use 2 teaspoonfuls of strong coffee for the water and a tablespoon of brandy for the vanilla.

## CHOCOLATE MOUSSE II

SERVES 6

For those of us who don't have our own chickens, try this delectable number. In a clean dry bowl, let your Five

**ADD**          6 oz. sweet Lindt chocolate

Put in the microwave, uncovered. At medium power,

**COOK**         2½–3½ minutes

Let your child stir the chocolate at the halfway mark, but you should take it out of the oven for him since it is hot. When cool

**ADD**          1 tsp. vanilla
                 2 cups whipping cream

Refrigerate 4 hours.
Have your child whip the mixture until it peaks, then help him fill the dessert dishes and refrigerate.

*BREADS*

Bread became the staff of life because even a Cro-Magnon bride couldn't ruin it. Any miscalculation simply became a new kind of bread. Since measurements don't have to be too exact, a modern Three can make it too—with your help.

The process is both a scientific and a physical exercise as well as a civilized way for a child to work out his aggressions. As you have learned by now, if one person in the house is tense at breakfast you can expect chaos by noon. Fortunately, 10 A.M. is a good time to start making bread. It takes five hours, with hardly more than an hour's help altogether from the baker, and you can control the rising time to fit your schedule.

Bread-making does require a real understanding of the process before you start the recipe itself. You should know—and tell your child—that the whiter the flour the finer the texture, but darker flours have more nutrition and, we think, more flavor. It's the yeast that makes the bread rise and sweetening that makes it rise higher, but the salt you need for flavoring does hinder this a little. Shortening tenderizes bread and keeps it fresh, and milk adds nutrition and freshness and helps it brown better.

Your child will be fascinated with the science of bread-making from the moment he learns that the yeast in the package is alive but asleep and only warm water will make it wake up and grow (and hot water will kill it).

He watches the fungus bubble and grow, kneads the dough until it builds

## BAKER'S BOX

By the time your child is nine months, he'll lose more and more interest in his toys—in favor of yours. Since each room should have its collection of playthings, we recommend for the kitchen a Baker's Box of unbreakable tools, duplicating many of your own. He still will play with yours, but when he starts cooking at Two, he can assemble most of the equipment he needs from his own assortment. We've found a Baker's Box is one of the cheapest—and to be candid, the noisiest—toy investments you can make. In the box, put

- plastic measuring pitcher
- measuring spoons
- wooden spoon
- rubber spatula
- large metal bowl
- cookie sheet
- cake pan
- pie tin
- cake rack

enough gas to be pliable, hears the "whoof" it makes when he punches down the first rising, watches it double its height again and then discovers the odd smell of fresh yeast that has baked itself into an ovenful of glory. He'll admire his bread hugely—almost as much as himself. Following these principles, you and your child can make any yeast bread—including the Swedish Rye (see page 209).

### Preparations

You'll have much less mess if you cover the part of the floor where you work with newspaper and even the space where you measure the dry ingredients, or they will turn pasty when you wash the counter. Measure wet ingredients in the sink and mix everything together with a long wooden spoon in a 4-quart bowl or a refrigerator crisper to contain them best, because a child is a messy mixer. If you use a pair of 5-cup meat loaf pans to bake

the bread, it will rise as high as the bakery's best.

### Techniques

*Mix*—Stir all ingredients with the spoon, adding as much of the extra flour as needed and stopping when the dough sticks to itself and not much else—about 15 minutes.

*Rest*—Cover the dough with a cloth and let it sit for 10 minutes before kneading or shaping so the gluten relaxes and the dough won't fight back.

*Knead*—Divide the dough for easier handling, keeping half on a floured table top for you and the rest in a floured bowl for your child, which is less messy. Put the bowl on the seat of a kitchen chair, so he can have more leverage. Push your batch forward with the heel of the hand and fold it back on itself—the classic kneading style—but let your child pull, twist and slam it down, then punch it like a boxer. Swap batches to give them an equal workout and add more flour as needed until the dough loses its stickiness and is smooth and springy—about 10 minutes although his help may make it take a little longer.

*Rise*—Let the dough grow in a greased bowl so it can climb up the sides as high as it would like but first roll the dough in the bowl so it won't form a crust, for this also inhibits rising. Cover with a dry dishtowel to prevent evaporation and place it in a warm spot in the kitchen (about 72°) or in an oven which was preheated to 200°, then turned off and left open. In about an hour your child can start poking the dough with his finger to see if it has doubled in bulk. The dough will spring back if it's too soon (which does no harm) but will stay indented when finished—usually no more than 2 hours. Refrigerate the dough whenever you want to double the rising time.

*Shape*—Divide dough and stretch each batch into a rectangle, 14″ × 7″ and ½″ thick. Roll the short side and pinch the long seam and the ends, tucking the ends underneath as you put the loaves in their pans to rise again—about 1 hour.

*Bake*—Center pans in a preheated oven and remove when the loaves shrink from the sides, sound hollow when thumped with the wooden spoon, are light brown on the top and smell great—about 45 minutes. After baking, rub the top of each hot loaf with a stick of butter if you want soft crusts. The bread is then removed from the pans and cooled on a rack to prevent sogginess.

## HEALTH MIX

YIELD: 3 cups

For a better nutrition and texture, your Two can make a batch of this mix for you to add to bread and cookie recipes.

**MIX**
1 c. soy flour
1 c. powdered milk
1 c. raw wheat germ

Store in a small canister or a jar with a lid. Use in breads, biscuits, muffins or cookies by removing 2 tablespoons of flour from each cup and replacing it with this mix.

## HEALTH BREAD

YIELD: 2 loaves

This is an easy recipe to double, but don't attempt it the first time. You may be overwhelmed. If you don't read the preceding Bread rules first you surely will be and so will your Three. He can add everything except the boiling water. In a teacup

**DISSOLVE**
1 pkg. yeast
¼ c. warm water

Into a very large bowl

**ADD**
1 c. water, boiling
1 c. cold milk
1 c. Health Mix
1 c. unbleached flour
2 tbsp. sugar OR honey
2 tbsp. vegetable oil
1 tbsp. salt

Stir this mixture with a wooden spoon and add the dissolved yeast. Since the milk cools the water there's not enough heat to kill the yeast.

**ADD**
4 c. unbleached flour

Mix and add as much as 2 more cups of flour until the dough loses most of its stickiness. Rest, covered with a cloth, for 10 minutes. Knead until springy, adding a little more flour to prevent stickiness if necessary, and scatter more on the counter. Roll the dough around in a greased bowl to coat the surface and cover with the cloth.

**FIRST RISING** 1½–2 hours

Punch down, divide, cover and let it rest for 10 minutes before shaping the dough into loaves. Put in greased loaf pans and cover with the towel.

Preheat Oven 350°

**SECOND RISING** 1 hour

**BAKE** 45 minutes

Butter tops, remove loaves from pans and cool on racks. You can make standard white bread by using unbleached flour in place of the Health Mix.

## HOMEMADE BISCUIT MIX

YIELD: 9 cups

This is the basis for biscuits, muffins, dumplings and pizzas.

**STIR**
8 c. flour
¼ c. baking powder
1 tsp. salt

**ADD**
1 c. vegetable shortening

The shortening should be beaten in one small lump at a time, at very low speed for 4 minutes, until dough looks like coarse bread crumbs. Store in a 3-quart canister with a tight lid. It will stay fresh for many weeks in the cupboard or for 4–6 months in the refrigerator.

## BISCUITS

YIELD: 1 dozen                                              Preheat Oven 450°

Would you believe, a Two can make these biscuits. Let him

**STIR**           **2 c. Homemade Biscuit Mix**
                   **⅔ c. milk**

Knead 10 times to give the biscuits a smoother shape. Spoon onto greased cookie sheet.

**BAKE**           **10 minutes**

They are done when they are light brown and smell delicious.

## MUFFINS

YIELD: 1 dozen                                              Preheat Oven 400°

Have your Three butter the muffin tins before he combines these ingredients. Then in a bowl he can

**STIR**           **2 c. Homemade Biscuit Mix**
                   **3 tbsp. sugar**
                   **2 eggs**
                   **⅔ c. milk**
                   **2 tbsp. oil OR melted vegetable**
                   **shortening**

Fill each cup halfway with the lumpy mixture or, for variety, spoon ½ teaspoon of preserves, raisins or chopped dates between 2 tablespoons of the batter. Stir only until dry ingredients are moist.

**BAKE**           **15–18 minutes**

They are ready when the tops have turned light brown.

## DUMPLINGS

YIELD: 1 dozen

A Two can make these dumplings, but you'll have to drop them into the hot pot. In a bowl

**MIX**            **2 c. Homemade Biscuit Mix**
                   **¾ c. milk**

Knead dough a few times and drop by spoonfuls into a bubbly stew pot, after the gravy has been made, or into soup. Cover and simmer 10 minutes. Remove lid, turn them and cook 10 minutes more.

## *COOKIES*

A cookie is to a child what a cigarette might once have been to you: tasty, soothing—and mighty addictive. It will be easier to limit cookies to morning and afternoon snacks if you bake just a dozen at a time and use a recipe so nourishing that two cookies will satisfy.

Cookie baking should be a pleasant, half-hour interlude, with little mess, one bowl and no tears. Gathering the utensils from the Baker's Box—a spoon, a spatula, the bowl, a cookie sheet, and a cake rack—have your child dump in the ingredients and beat with the portable mixer. Unless the recipe calls for a great deal of butter, the cookie sheet must be greased.

A child can drop the balls of dough onto the sheet and decorate them with nuts, raisins or the tines of a fork, pressed flat to make a checker board. We don't recommend a cookie press even for a Six and, in fact, except for special occasions, it takes much too long to ice cookies or cut them into shapes. Cookies should be baked in a preheated oven until the edges brown—usually no more than 10 minutes—then removed with a spatula (your job) and left to crisp on the rack.

You can substitute up to ½ cup of sugar with honey in any recipe, but you'll need to use ¼ cup more flour and bake them

25° lower than the required temperature. Refrigerate or freeze leftover dough in cylinders of wax paper ready to use later.

## AGGRESSION COOKIES

YIELD: 15 dozen                          Preheat Oven 350°

We don't know where this recipe came from, but we don't know a better one for That Kind of Day. In a huge bowl, let your Two

| COMBINE | 6 c. oatmeal |
| | 3 c. brown sugar |
| | 3 c. butter OR |
| | 3 c. half butter/half margarine |
| | 3 c. flour |
| | 1 tbsp. baking soda |

Mash, knead and squeeze, it says, "until you feel better"—and until there aren't any lumps of butter. Your child will need some help, but he can form the dough into small balls himself, not as big as a walnut, and put them on an ungreased cookie sheet. Butter the bottom of a small glass and have him dip it into granulated sugar. This is what he uses to flatten each ball of dough, dipping it into sugar each time.

| BAKE | 10–12 minutes |

Remove when lightly brown, cool a few minutes and crisp on a rack. Store in a tight container. The dough keeps well in the refrigerator.

## SUGAR COOKIES

YIELD: 4 dozen                           Preheat Oven 350°

The nutmeg makes these so special, they'll win many compliments for your Two.

| BEAT | 1 c. sugar |
| | ½ c. soft butter |
| | ½ tsp. nutmeg |
| | ½ tsp. vanilla |
| | 1 egg |
| | 1 tbsp. milk |
| ADD | 2 c. flour |
| | 1 tsp. baking powder |
| | 1 tsp. baking soda |
| | ⅛ tsp. salt |

Help him hold the beaters deep into the bowl until mixed and then drop by spoonfuls onto greased cookie sheets. He can decorate each cookie with a nut if he likes.

| BAKE | 10 minutes |

Crisp on a rack.

## BANANA COOKIES

YIELD: 4 dozen                           Preheat Oven 375°

Two of these cookies with juice after a nap can carry most energetic children through the 5 o'clock miseries. A Two likes to mash the bananas best of all (and through his fingers, of course) but it takes a Four to add the rest of the ingredients. In this order

| BEAT | ¾ c. honey |
| | ¾ c. soft butter |
| | 1 egg |
| | 1 tsp. vanilla |
| | 1 c. (2–3) very ripe, mashed bananas |
| | 1½ c. flour |
| | ¼ c. soy flour |
| | 1½ c. rolled oats |
| | ¼ c. wheat germ |
| | ½ tsp. baking soda |
| | 1 tsp. salt |
| | ½ tsp. nutmeg |
| | ¾ tsp. cinnamon |
| STIR | ½ c. chopped nuts |
| | ½ c. raisins |

You can substitute a third of the butter with soft peanut butter, but the dough will be sticky either way. Chill for 30 minutes. Drop by teaspoons onto greased cookie sheets.

| BAKE | 12 minutes |

Crisp on a rack. Your child can coat them with confectioners sugar on high feast days.

### PIES

There are many complicated skills a pre-Six can master—stitching on a sewing machine, catching crabs, skiing—that have one common point. The child is regularly with an adult to whom that particular task is very easy.

Pie dough is like that. If you can handle dough deftly a Six or even a well-coordinated Five will be able to handle it too,

although not so well. However, until you learn to be an adequate pastry chef, don't let him help you or at least one of you may cry.

We recommend our fast, simple method to learn and then to teach, but no matter what kind of pie shell you use—homemade, frozen or lady fingers end to end—it will delight your child. A pie guarantees so much praise that your baker will glow with success, and it is the success of a job, and not the doing of it, that grows a child.

## PASTRY

YIELD: Two 8–9″ pie crusts

Before we knew any better, we beat our pie dough with an electric mixer—and it worked. It's heat that toughens pastry, but this method is so quick the dough stays cold if the butter is very cold before you start. Add as little of the water as possible, so the crust will flake, and use the extract for fruit pies only. A Six can do everything but lift the dough. In this order

| BEAT | 2 c. flour |
|---|---|
| | ¼ lb. cold butter |
| | 3 tbsp. cold lard OR oil |
| | 3–5 tbsp. ice water |
| | ¼ tsp. salt |
| | ⅛ tsp. sugar |
| | 1 tsp. almond extract |

Use a low speed for 1 minute, quitting when the shortening is cut to the size of peas and the dough sticks together when squeezed. Slap it around several times with the heels of your hands (the palms are too warm) to break down the fat further.

Divide the dough in half and roll each ball between sheets of wax paper for easier, cooler handling. Your child should roll the dough in quick, short strokes with a rolling pin or a smooth water glass, making each circle slightly bigger than the pie pan. For the first crust, peel away the top piece of paper in strips—often the only way it can be done—and lay the pie pan over the dough. Invert the pan for him. The dough will sink to the bottom and the second sheet of paper can be pulled away. He then presses the torn dough together like modeling clay and fills the pie, slowly but well.

Have your child pull away the top sheet of paper from the second crust, turn it over gently—a job for you—and drop it on the top of the filling. He again tears away the last sheet, cuts his initial on top for steam to escape and presses the flat tines of a fork around the rim, which mashes the crusts together to contain the juice. Bake as each individual recipe requires.

*Baked pieshell*—Prick the bottom of a single crust to prevent puffing and bake at 400° for 15–20 minutes.

*Cinnamon Strips*—Dip leftover dough in cinnamon sugar (see Cinnamon Toast, page 343) and bake at 400° for 15 minutes.

*Jam Tarts*—Fill scraps with a spoonful of jam and fold the dough over itself, sealing them shut with a fork. Bake at 400° for 15 minutes.

## UNBAKED BLUEBERRY PIE

SERVES 6

This is a summer wonder, with or without a baked pie shell. A Three can make the filling.

| CLEAN | 1 qt. blueberries |
|---|---|

You'll do most of this tedious job yourself. In a saucepan

| COMBINE | 1 c. sugar |
|---|---|
| | 1 c. blueberries |
| | 1 c. water |
| | 3 tbsp. cornstarch |
| | ⅛ tsp. salt |

Stir over low heat about 10 minutes, until thick. Turn off heat.

| ADD | 3 c. blueberries |
|---|---|
| | 1 tbsp. butter |

Stir and mix well. Cool.

| WHIP | ½ pt. heavy cream |
|---|---|
| | 1 tbsp. sugar |

Pour berry mixture into a baked pie shell, or simply into a bowl, just before serving. Cover with the cream.

## CHERRY PIE

SERVES 6                                              Preheat Oven 425°

Fresh cherries are hard to find but canned ones aren't

worth your time. A Five is not too young to learn that sometimes you go first class or not at all.

**PIT**         **1 qt. sour cherries**

A dreary job, much of which you'll do yourself. Pour them in a pie shell, heaping most in the center. In a bowl, have your child

**MIX**         **1 c. sugar**
                   **1 tbsp. flour**
                   **⅛ tsp. salt**

Sprinkle over the cherries, then cover with a crust, seal edges and slit dough.

**BAKE**         **40 minutes**

Take the pie out of the oven for your child when the cherry juices bubble through the crust.

---

## CAKES

Once upon an unbelievable time, the cook just added water to a cake mix, but it wasn't very good. Then fresh eggs were required, sometimes milk or juice instead of water, then oil and, finally, pudding or gelatin mixes. We think if you look at the list of ingredients you have to add to a prepackaged mix and the chemicals the company already has added, you'll find a homemade cake is easier, healthier, cheaper and certainly better.

Cakes call for a light touch, which is why old recipes have the butter and sugar whipped to a pale froth, the eggs separated and beaten, the flour sifted and the dry and wet ingredients added alternately. Despite what the cookbooks say, today's flour has been milled so much it only needs sifting for the most elegant recipes and the electric mixer whips such a fast, airy batter, you needn't separate the eggs. You only need to add dry and wet ingredients alternately to avoid spatter.

When mixing, a child must keep the beaters deep in the bowl and scrape the sides often with a rubber spatula. We suggest the pans you'll need for baking, but you don't have to be too precise. The batter will rise just as well in a couple of tin cans. All containers should be buttered

and floured, filled no more than halfway and positioned slightly off center in the oven, each on a different shelf, so the air can circulate around them.

When the cake has smelled good for at least five minutes, it's probably done. Let your child see if it has pulled away a little from the sides of the pan, if a broom straw comes clean when he pokes it in the middle and if the center springs back when he touches it—all true signs of readiness.

Any cake must be cooled on a rack for 10 minutes after taking it from the oven, so the air can circulate around the layers, or it may break when you take it out of the pan. When cool, invert it on a flat plate—a job for you—run a knife blade around the sides and rap the bottom of the pan with your knuckles if the cake sticks.

---

### ULTIMATE CHOCOLATE CAKE

YIELD: 12 servings         Preheat Oven 375°

This is the chocolate layer cake that stops you and your Four from trying any other chocolate cake. There's no need to keep looking. In a cup

**COMBINE**       **½ c. milk**
                       **1 tsp. vinegar**

Canned milk is better; cream is best. The vinegar sours it, to act upon the soda. In a saucepan

**COMBINE**       **1 c. boiling water**
                       **4 sqs. unsweetened chocolate**
                       **½ c. chopped butter**

Stir until melted, heating if necessary, and add the soured milk. To the saucepan

**ADD**            **2 c. flour**
                       **2 c. sugar**
                       **1½ tsp. baking soda**
                       **2 eggs**
                       **½ tsp. vanilla**

Beat well with a wooden spoon. Pour into two greased and floured 9″ cake pans.

**BAKE**            **40 minutes**

Cover with Chocolate Icing II.

## POUND CAKE

YIELD: 16 servings                    Preheat Oven 350°

This is a good traveling cake—sturdy enough to carry, rich enough to be proud of and big enough for a little girl of Five to give her big brother's Scout troop. Use buttermilk or let her curdle sweet milk so it can combine with the soda for the batter to rise. To do this

**COMBINE**         **1 c. tepid milk**
                    **2 tsp. vinegar**

Let it curdle—about 10 minutes. Meanwhile, in a large bowl

**BEAT**            **2 c. sugar**
                    **1 c. vegetable shortening**
                    **4 eggs**
                    **1 tsp. vanilla**
                    **1 tsp. almond extract**

Beat at high speed for 3 minutes. In a separate bowl

**COMBINE**         **3 c. flour**
                    **½ tsp. baking soda**
                    **½ tsp. baking powder**
                    **¾ tsp. salt**

Add half the flour mix to the sugar mixture, then add half the milk, beating thoroughly each time. Repeat and beat 2 minutes at medium speed. Pour into an un-greased 9″ tube pan.

**BAKE**            **60–70 minutes**

## LEMON TEA CAKE

YIELD: 1 loaf                         Preheat Oven 325°

If you decide to have a tea party with your daughter, this is the cake to make. It deserves a party. Since it's more delicate than our other cakes, all ingredients must be well beaten, which is why it takes a Five to make it. Grease and flour an 8″ × 4″ loaf pan. In a bowl, let her

**BEAT**            **½ c. butter**
                    **1 c. sugar**

**GRATE**           **zest of 1 lemon**

Add the zest to the sugar.

**ADD**             **2 eggs**
                    **1½ c. flour**
                    **1 tsp. baking powder**
                    **⅛ tsp. salt**
                    **½ c. milk**

Beat each ingredient into the batter well, before adding the next. Once all ingredients are in the bowl, beat 2 minutes, using the medium speed.

**BAKE**            **1 hour**

Remove the cake from the oven when the sides leave the pan and immediately pour over it:

*Lemon Sugar*

**MIX**             **juice of 1 lemon**
                    **¼ c. sugar**

Remove from the pan, right side up and serve cold.

### Icings

Icing cakes, like gilding lilies, isn't necessary, but even a Two wants to do it and he can, if you help him follow some basic principles.

☐ Lay a square border of 4 wax paper strips on the cake plate, to catch the drips of icing, then lay the bottom layer on them.

☐ Cool any cake before covering it, or the icing will melt and the cake will shed crumbs.

☐ Mix any additions, like raisins or nuts, at the last minute or the icing might not harden.

☐ Ice between layers, then the top of the cake and ice the sides last.

☐ Spread the icing with a knife, dipping it regularly into a glass of warm water for smooth results.

☐ Beat a teaspoon of hot water into the bowl of icing if it hardens before you finish.

☐ Put extra icing in a small plastic bag, cut a tiny corner and let you child squiggle a picture on top.

☐ Pull away the paper strips before serv-ing.

## CONFECTIONERS DUST

This is the easiest icing of all. Simply let your child—a pre-Two will do—sift confectioner's sugar over a single-layer cake or one baked in a bundt pan. It gussies up a cake nicely.

## CHOCOLATE ICING I

This icing is rich, dark, drippy and shiny enough to justify an éclair and it can be mixed, beaten or blended. In a pan let your Three

**MELT**          4 sqs. unsweetened chocolate
                  2 tbsp. hot water

Cook over low heat, stirring and watching carefully so it doesn't burn. Remove from the stove for him.

**ADD**           1 c. confectioners sugar
                  2 eggs
                  6 tbsp. chopped butter

When smooth, your child can use it to ice a 9″ cake, spoon it over a dozen éclairs or dip the tops of cupcakes into it.

## CHOCOLATE ICING II

This recipe is so simple it can destroy a child's belief in the mumbo-jumbo of the kitchen. We hope it does. In a double boiler have your Five

**HEAT**          one 14-oz. can condensed milk
                  2 sqs. unsweetened chocolate

Stir until the chocolate has melted and then spread on the cake.

◇ # GARDENING ◇

There's no magic in making plants grow. Any plant hardy enough to survive in a dime store is magic in itself. If you take it home and give it its quota of light and soil and water, it will love you. Your child will find that a few house plants can satisfy his parental instincts almost as much as a puppy and, besides, they don't throw up on the rug. In fact, there will come a time, we guarantee, when you'll decide a Bird of Paradise looks better than a bassinet.

A child's efforts at gardening will be very clumsy, but this is part of his learning process. These early years should be his time of slow appreciation when he learns from you to draw as much pleasure from the first shoot as he will from the full flower. Gradually he'll learn the principles of botany—probably just a step behind you.

You will teach him that every seed develops into four basic parts—the roots, the stems, the leaves and the flower, which in turn fruits with new seed. He learns that plants eat minerals through their roots, that earthworms fertilize the soil and aerate it so the roots can breathe better and that the leaves inhale carbon dioxide and exhale oxygen, which is why nature needs a balance between its animals and its plants. You'll need to explain that plants are the only living things that make their own food and that this chlorophyll is like blood to them.

Your child will learn that indoor plants enjoy each other's company, growing best when the pots are grouped together, and that cross-pollination is to petunias what making love is to people—productive, if not as jolly.

Whether you live on an Iowa farm or

in a New York City apartment, there always should be room in your life to bring the outdoors inside. The smallest infant deserves to smell fresh earth in his room and watch a young plant inch higher, just like himself. When a child feels he is a part of nature he is better able to sort out his place in it.

When you begin your walks—in the first few weeks of life—you stimulate his awareness. There is always something new every season, whether you're brushing his cheeks with mimosa puffs or letting him smell the differences between geraniums, roses and violets. His sense of observation is sharpened every time you show him a new plant or an autumn leaf.

Between six months and a year, a baby is thrilled to crawl through grass and blow away enough dandelion puffs to seed a city block. In the next eight months, he'll start to dig in the dirt while you weed the flower bed and if you aren't watching, he may help you by flowering the weed bed.

Gardening and a Two go best together we think, not because a child does it well (which he doesn't), but because by then a mother's ego is so low she needs to nurture something that won't have a tantrum when watered, fed or taken inside.

Now you'll have him soaking the clay pots (especially the gurgling new ones), finding pebbles for drainage and cracking charcoal in a paper bag for the potting soil. He'll stick his orange seeds in sphagnum moss, plant carrot tops and a whole sweet potato in water and feel as clever as Mendel when anything sprouts. In fact, we suspect a Two can find more beauty in a morning glory than an adult finds in a whole art gallery. This sensitivity either will grow or diminish, depending on the encouragement you give it.

A Three can root his own cuttings, tend his first cactus and help water the plants, which takes a deft touch. This is the time to tell him that some gardeners think plants grow best when people sing to them. This may or may not be true, but the sound of a small child's tune will put

equanimity in your day. This also is the time to emphasize the names of different plants, particularly the fifty or more that are named for animals, like the orange tiger lily with its black stripes, the ever-multiplying hens and chickens and the flappy green elephant ears. We've even seen a Three run off the Latin names of every plant in her garden, simply because it was the normal way to learn about them in her family. As always, whatever comes easily and customarily to parents will be simple for their child to master: a good reason for parents to develop more skills. This is the time to plant bulbs outdoors—the easiest of all flowers to grow—but it takes a patient Six to make tulips bloom in the house.

A Four should grow some of the food he eats, starting with the sprouts of beans and seeds that he mixes with soups and sandwich spreads. He can grow an herb garden in the kitchen, lettuce in the garden and cast birdseed into a flower bed to see what corn and wheat and sunflowers look like. Since a Four likes to show off so much, let him help you lug the house plants outside in summer. He'll learn for himself how direct sunshine gives a plant enough energy to thrive the rest of the year indoors with filtered light.

The curious Five likes to grow exotic fruit seeds—dates, pomegranates and mangoes—and he wants to hear about the lands they come from and why they need the care they do. You'll need to explain that most house plants are tropical and need warmth and moisture and rich soil, but cacti need extra sand and sunshine to make them feel at home. Help your Five compare the woody-stemmed plants to the succulents, which store water in their fat stems so they don't need it so often, and let him find the spores on the fern and grow pineapples, the best known of all the peculiar bromeliads.

With your guidance, a Six can plant a 3′ × 3′ outdoor garden or a smaller rock garden—in his own haphazard way—but he needs help to transplant delicate seedlings and make a terrarium. Let him sow a few melon seeds in a tub outdoors, which will come to fruition with its vine creeping along the patio floor. You can move it out of the way when necessary, the way watermelon farmers do in Indiana, before the cultivator goes through.

We've found if you have enough plants growing all the time, your child won't be disappointed at the ratio of success to failure—about 50-50. In fact, we've found the most successful gardeners are the ones who plant so much no one notices their mistakes—especially themselves. That's the attitude your child should have about gardening and everything else.

## HOUSE PLANTS

It took a lot of house plants—and a lot of children—for us to learn that a preschool child can't care for a plant all alone any more than he can care for a kitty—or for himself. As always, he needs experience, he needs competence and, above all, he needs to know exactly why he's doing what. The more he knows, the better gardener he'll be. Unless you're quite knowledgeable yourself, you'll probably want to start your indoor garden with plants from the dime store.

This is where you first begin to see that a green thumb is no more than a sharp eye for the right plants. The inexpensive ones, like the spider plant or the philodendron, are usually the easiest to care for, but all plants should be chosen from a fresh shipment and all should have a few light green leaves—the sign of new growth—and no brown or yellow ones—the sign of disease or poor care. You'll have better luck with a flowering plant if you buy it during the blooming season, and not before—or its adjustment will be difficult—and if you can baby it with winter sunlight, a cool house by day and a colder one by night—all necessary to force most blooms although African violets will take a warmer room.

As you learn to gauge the water and light your plants need, you and your child will want to start others from seeds or cuttings. Finally you succumb to those luscious beauties at the nursery. They can be as disastrous to the budget as a day at the races, but when you can keep them alive they're a lot better for the morale.

### LIGHT

All house plants need light to photosynthesize water and carbon dioxide into food, but the more direct the rays, the less they need. If you're lucky enough to have the triple exposure of a bay window with three hours of sun a day, you have almost as much intense light as a greenhouse. If not, you must gauge the intensity of indoor sunlight by the size and location of the window and how brightly the sun can shine through it. For us, this was enough to make us wash the windows.

Most plants should live no farther than three feet from a window since the sunlight diffuses quickly. The time we give for indoor sunlight is based on this distance, and it's always one to two hours more than a plant needs when placed outdoors.

A bushy plant from a nursery, acclimated as it is to special lights, can't feed so much foliage at home and it rapidly drops all the leaves it can't support. If the bushy plant means so much to you, you might consider a light unit, but every room can have greenery if you rotate the plants and if you choose them carefully.

Any strong plant can live in a dark corner for a few weeks and some, like the Chinese evergreen and the spider plant, need no sunlight, thriving in bright, well-lighted areas, although they grow more slowly. A rubber tree needs only an hour of sun, a flowering plant needs three to five hours, and a citrus tree needs four to five.

All plants are heliotropic and must be turned around a little every few weeks or they will grow crooked: an important assignment for a Two.

### Wintering

Group potted plants together, since they are as convivial as children. They enjoy sitting on a radiator, either in a planter on a bed of dampened peat moss or sand or simply with their pots resting on saucers full of stones and water. The heat raises the moisture and envelops their leaves in humidity, which gives them, like English maidens, nifty complexions. However, if you place them near hot or cold air vents, the intermittent blasts will choke the plants.

### Summering

If possible, bury pots in the ground outdoors in summer but bring them inside several weeks before you turn on the heat in the fall, so they may adjust. If you forget them outdoors, you may have to treat them for frostbite by showering the pots and then by soaking them in a bucket. Place the pots in a room below 70° until they begin to gain consciousness.

### WATER

One of the best parts of gardening is the side interests it develops—in food, in beauty, in all the wonders of science. One

of the most wonderful must be the story of evaporation, which every child should

know. Explain that the soil dries when some of the invisible water molecules become restless (not unlike children) and rush to the top and out into the air. More of them slip out of the leaves. The most obvious facts to you are revelations to a child.

Although water is essential to plants, the soil needs to dry out between waterings so it can fill with oxygen and the tiny root hairs can breathe. It is these root hairs that also draw food and water into the roots themselves.

Some plants need more water than others, depending on their origins, and the smaller the pot the more frequent the watering. All plants need more water when they're flowering, so the blossoms don't fall, and less when they're dormant. Plants, like people, can't eat and sleep at the same time.

A plant needs water when it droops or when the soil feels as dusty as it looks, which a Three can discover if he carefully pokes his finger down near the side of the pot, as deep as it can go. If the soil is loose, you can pour water until it runs out through the bottom. However, the water will race through old, hard soil, without absorption, or puddle on the top, which means the pot needs cultivation, a long soak or new soil.

There are four ways to water plants, but it is best to do it very slowly with lukewarm water (for better absorption) and only as the plants need it. This is seldom a daily need—a hard lesson for an enthusiastic child to learn.

### Method I

Soak the pots—especially new transplants or large plants—in a basin of water, letting them drink as long as they wish. Unlike people, they know when to quit. Remove the pots when the soil is damp on top—an hour to overnight.

### Method II

Poke a fork deep into the soil around the sides of the pot, 4–6 times, and drizzle water around and around the plant with the spout of the can close to the earth. The drier the earth, the more it will gurgle.

### Method III

Use 6 ice cubes in a hanging pot, instead of water. They melt so slowly, they cause no drips and a child can carry them without dribbling water from the kitchen.

### Method IV

Water the pineapple and other bromeliads from above, filling the leaves.

### Misting

Although the fuzz on some leaves, like the African violets, protects them from dust, the slicker the leaves the more they need to be bathed. Dust blocks sunlight and without that, the leaves can't photosynthesize. In a job your child will chortle over, let him spray them with a mister filled with lukewarm water. Some overzealous housekeepers wipe the leaves with oil to make them shine, but this just clogs the pores, attracting more dust. It's a great bother, besides.

## SOIL

We once knew a proper headmistress of a proper school for young ladies whose gardenias were the most splendid in town, but no one knew she got them that way by sending her distinguished husband outdoors every night for a "turn in the garden." However, you don't have to ask your husband to pee in the pots if you use the right soil mixture.

Although it's hard to believe, plants don't grow very well in dirt. They need a combination of sterilized potting soil for food; a humus such as peat moss to hold water and anchor the tiny root hairs; sand, vermiculite or perlite for drainage and grit, as well as charcoal to keep the soil sweet.

Although most house plants will thrive in the balanced Basic Soil some, like delicate woodland plants and the exotic gardenia, need extra peat moss for more acidity, and others, like succulents and cacti, need extra sand for quicker drainage.

We recommend making a big batch of fertilized Basic Soil with your child and using it as needed, adding the extra sand or peat moss if necessary for some plants. As you make it, rub the soil between your fingers so you and your child can learn to judge textures. The quality of soil isn't constant and it's time to change it when the consistency changes—probably about once a year.

### Definitions

In this gardening section we use the same technical names you and your child will hear at the garden center. This is what they're talking about:

*Potting soil*—a prepackaged mix of soil, sterilized to kill bacteria, mold and weed seeds. It's blended with some sand and humus, but not enough to hold water and anchor roots well. We use it in our Basic Soil recipe.

*Humus*—anything that was once alive and has decomposed, such as rotted sawdust, leaf mold from the woods, compost and any of the peat mosses. All humus anchors roots, distributes fertilizer and helps the soil hold water, but it contains no nutrition. Humus is used in Basic Soil.

*Peat moss*—an assortment of plants that has decayed in water. It's commercially packaged, the easiest humus to find and comes from many parts of the world. Sphagnum and Michigan peat are the most common.

> *Sphagnum*—an especially good medium for sprouting seeds, because it prevents mildew. It must be scalded to make it absorbent—a bother, but it's worth it.
>
> *Michigan peat*—the most acidic peat moss. It's packaged wet, which accounts for its rich, dark color and its higher cost.

*Drainage*—an important ingredient of Basic Soil, needed to aerate the roots and anchor them. Sand, vermiculite and perlite are used interchangeably, but none have any nutrients.

> *Sand*—the grittiest of all. The more you add to the soil, the faster the water will drain. Use builder's sand sold in garden centers, but never use sea sand, which packs too hard and is salty.
>
> *Vermiculite*—refined mica, mined in flat brittle sheets and expanded by extreme heat into spongelike bits that absorb water more than the other drainage. It's excellent for cuttings and for germinating seeds.
>
> *Perlite*—a volcanic mineral also treated under heat to expand, but it absorbs no water.

*Charcoal*—a freshener used in either soil or water to keep it sweet and sold commercially in chips.

*Fertilizer*—either organic or chemical. All fertilizers contain nitrogen, phosphorus and potash in varying proportions, all of which are needed by plants.

> *Nitrogen*—causes leafier plants and is found in cow manure, blood meal and any organic fertilizer.
>
> *Phosphorus*—makes strong roots and promotes development of flowers and seeds. It's found in bonemeal, rock phosphate and manure.
>
> *Potash*—helps improve the quality and size of fruits and vegetables and is found in the ashes of wood, cigars and cigarettes.

*Cow manure*—contains nitrogen and some phosphorus and is dehydrated, pre-packaged, nearly odor-free, socially acceptable and can be added to Basic Soil.

*Bonemeal*—acts slowly but very well. This fertilizer, ground from animal bones, is safe enough for young roots. It's used instead of manure and is excellent for bulbs, but since it takes as much as two years to be absorbed, most gardeners use it outdoors. For pots they prefer steamed bonemeal, which is fat-free, enabling root hairs to absorb it quicker. Too much of either kind will mildew the top of the soil but this is harmless.

*Chelated iron*—corrects the yellow leaves caused by anemia—a special problem for citrus.

---

## BASIC SOIL

YIELD: three 4″ pots

Your Three will want to help you mix this batch. In a big roasting pan

| COMBINE | 2 c. sphagnum OR peat moss |
|---------|----------------------------|
|         | 2 c. potting soil |
|         | 2 c. sand OR vermiculite OR perlite |
|         | ⅓ c. cracked charcoal |
|         | 1 tbsp. steamed bone meal OR |
|         | 2 tbsp. dried cow manure |

All three drainage materials work well but perlite is the least messy when a child is helping you. If you use peat moss as the humus, we recommend the sphagnum—the least acidic, most available, most compact to store. It's highly absorbent if scalded first, for its fibers remain expanded. This definitely is a job for you. Put it in a colander and over it

| POUR | boiling water |
|------|---------------|
| COOL | 3 hours |

Don't touch any sooner for it stays hot much longer

than you'd think. Extra sphagnum can be stored in a plastic bag after treatment.

### Sandy Soil

Your child can transform Basic Soil to suit cacti by doubling the amount of sand.

### Spongy Soil

To make the spongy soil that ferns need, have your child add twice as much humus as he did in the Basic Soil mix.

---

## TECHNIQUES

It's no use pretending. Your child needs to use some tricks to grow happy house plants, but they're not nearly as esoteric as the experts say they are.

### Potting

There are three types of containers—the clay pot, which allows plants to breathe better but requires more watering; the plastic pot, which is especially good for the forgetful (but holds water so well the roots sometimes rot), and the nonpot, which is any container, like an enamel bowl, that has no drainage holes. Any but the nonpot needs a saucer to catch the water.

### Preparing the pot

Have your Two soak a clay pot in water before using it, for a soaked pot won't draw moisture from the soil just as a soaked brick won't dry out its mortar. In a bucket.

**SOAK**   small pot—1 hour
           big pot—overnight

Stop when the pot quits gurgling. Over the drainage holes of a plastic or a clay pot.

**PROP**   large clay shard

**ADD**    1″ pebbles OR shards

**FILL**   Basic Soil, dampened

Line the pot with this soil, pressing it down and against the sides, to prevent mold and to snuggle the roots. Leave a hole as deep and wide as the plant you'll press into place. In a nonpot use 2″ of pebbles and the special commercial soil mixture found at the dime store, which is much airier than other packaged potting soil or our own mix.

### Transplanting

Seedlings should be transplanted when they have four leaves, but most house plants should be transplanted every year. The old soil is worn out and often the pot should be bigger. If the pot is too small the roots become bound and push through the drainage hole—a clear sign that the plant needs more room. Plants with thick leaves and stems—succulents, bromeliads and cacti—need larger pots only every two or three years, because they like to feel snug. No plant should be transplanted into a pot that's more than two inches bigger in diameter than the old one. If the pot is too big the soil can sour, like a child whose boundaries are so wide his roots have no stability.

Although moving is traumatic for any plant, the crisis will be less severe if the job is done in the more temperate times of the year. First have your Four water it well and then slide a knife around the sides of the old pot while you hold the stem of the plant between your thumb and index finger as he thumps out the plant. He can knock away the old soil and sink the plant into a prepared pot, tamping the earth firmly around the plant and adding more soil if needed. The soil level on the stem must stay the same: if it's higher it may rot the stem; if lower, it may expose the roots. This is the only trick of transplanting. Water once more and keep it out of direct sunlight for two days.

### Fertilizing

Any plant in a pot needs extra vitamins. We find fish emulsion, that smelly stuff, is best. As with any fertilizer, be sure to use only half as much as it says on the label, because the roots are burned so easily. Mix it with lukewarm water—so the root hairs can absorb it in only hours instead of days—and feed the plants in spring and summer. Plants also should be fertilized when you see new buds or shoots, but in any case only once a month.

### Cultivation

Watering packs the soil if there are no bugs or worms to aerate it as there are in the garden. If it doesn't crumble when you press it have your Four ruffle the earth by poking it with a fork to a depth of 2–3". This is necessary every 4–6 weeks—a good job for a so-so child on a bad day.

### Pinching

Good-looking plants, unlike good-looking bottoms, need to be pinched. To have a bush plant, instead of a stick, have your Four press off the top pair of leaves. This frustrates the plant into sending side shoots.

### Cross-Pollination

Without the help of bees, butterflies and south winds, a flowering tree, like the miniature orange, may need sex on a toothpick to bear fruit indoors. Let your Six use a cotton swab or his soft poster paint brush to dip inside each bloom, which shakes the pollen from the pistils down into the stamen. This fertilizes the seeds in the ovule, which expands to become the fruit—something for your Six to remember the next time he sinks his teeth into an apple.

### THE HOTHOUSE

A homemade hothouse makes rooting and germination much faster and even waters plants when you're on vacation since the water in the soil evaporates and rains down again and again. To make, have your Four water the pot well, then enclose it in a self-sealing plastic bag, and place it near an east or west window but not in direct sunlight or the plastic will intensify the heat and damage the leaves. The bag should look dewy in the morning and dry in the afternoon. If it doesn't dry, open the bag temporarily so the extra water can evaporate.

### PROBLEMS

The leaves of your plant will show the first symptom of trouble, whether it's caused by bugs, disease or the wrong sort of care. Help your child look under the leaves for insects, and if they're there, protect the top of the soil with foil, then hold the plant upside down to dunk the leaves into hot soapy water. Rinse in cold water and isolate it until you're sure all the bugs are gone.

If there were no bugs but the leaves are brown, then the plant is burned, either by too much sunlight or too much fertilizer. If the leaves are yellow, the plant needs more light, better drainage or a fertilizer with iron to correct its anemia. If many leaves fall without replacement, most plants need more light or water—and then there are the aralia and the zebra plant, which drop their leaves every time their feet get too wet.

For final proof of a problem, run a knife around the sides of the pot and tip out the plant. You can see any damage from disease, because it strikes the roots first, or from too much water, because they will smell bad. There's no hope for such a plant; weep and throw it away. If no trouble is obvious your plant needs about the same thing you should give a peaked child—better food, more sunshine, new friends, much love.

## THE BEGINNINGS

There are three ways to start a plant. The easiest are from seeds and bulbs, but plants can be started from cuttings too. It's especially good for that most particular child, the pre-Three, to understand that there are a lot of ways to do anything.

### SOWING SEEDS

A child's sense of drama swings to the miracle of life as he watches a simple bean unfold almost overnight. Most seeds will sprout in a warm place eventually, planted in either soil, water or wet cotton. The seed contains all the nutrition a plant needs until its second, or true, set of leaves appears. The first set is merely the seed's division of itself.

The seeds in a child's food can be divided into two categories: the ones he eats and the ones he spits. Even to show a child these seeds encourages his curiosity, but a fussy eater often improves enormously when he tries to grow his own food right from the meals he is served.

Let your child study the eating seeds in a tomato, an eggplant, a cucumber, a squash, a strawberry or a lima—a seed that sprouts best if it has another lima for company. Every one of these can be planted even by a Two and some of them will grow, although the smaller the seed, the harder it is to keep it alive after it germinates, for these seedlings are very fragile.

The bigger, spitting seeds have longer pregnancies (like elephants to ants). Their shells are tougher, such as peaches and pecans, but their sprouts have much more endurance. Citrus seeds and pips from grapes and apples and pears are in this category and so is an avocado, a fine handling size for a child.

Some kitchen gardeners dry the seeds first to imitate the life cycle, but this doesn't seem necessary to us. For faster germination, however, you can soak any seed overnight in a cup of water. This softens the shell.

## KITCHEN TABLE POT

The French have their *pot au feu* simmering on the back of the stove, but we prefer our pot germinating on the kitchen table. This is the place to plant the seeds of the day. They need no window light to sprout, but the soil must stay moist. Use a clear plastic pot so your child can see what's going on below. In a 6″ pot

**LAYER**
  1″ pebbles
  3″ Basic Soil
  1″ scalded sphagnum moss

The layer of moss keeps the seeds from mildewing. Press the tiny seeds into the moss, cover bigger ones with a dusting of it and bury any large seed just below the surface. Transplant when 4 leaves have appeared.

**WATER**      **2 times weekly**

Kitchen pots prefer to sit in a saucer of water to drink through their drainage holes, so the small seeds don't float.

## CITRUS TREE

We know a little girl named Alix whose mother planted a grapefruit seed in a pot when she was born. Both now are Twelve and beautiful, but the tree is much taller and, unlike Alix, very thorny, vibrant green and bushy. Use a Kitchen Table Pot. A Two can start this tree but it takes a Five to care for it.

**GERMINATION**      **15–30 days**

When it has 4 leaves, transplant into a small, individual pot.

**SOIL**                **Basic**

**INDOOR SUNLIGHT**   **4–5 hours**

**OUTDOOR LIGHT**     **partial sun**

**WATER**               **3 times weekly**

This frequent watering is essential in the first six months, when citrus trees often die from dehydration, and in spring and summer, when they bloom. The trees may fruit in seven years if you crosspollinate them, which your child will do, but if the trees live outdoors year round, the bees will do it for you.

## DATE TREE

Date pits from the dates you put in your Christmas fruitcakes will sprout into palm trees for your Five, but they need good aeration—helped by bits of leaves and twigs—and a tall pot, because their roots have learned to travel deeply for water. A plastic pot is best, for the roots should never dry completely. Dig up one seed in about three weeks to show your child how the silvery eye in the center begins to form a pearl, the first sign of growth.

| | |
|---|---|
| **SOIL** | Sandy |
| | **1 tbsp. dried manure (cow or camel)** |
| **GERMINATION** | **8–10 weeks** |
| **INDOOR SUNLIGHT** | **3 hours** |
| **OUTDOOR LIGHT** | **partial sun** |
| **WATER** | **2 times weekly, in the saucer** |

Keep young palms away from drafts. Your child won't have to transplant for a year if there are no more than three pits in a 5″ pot.

## MANGO

Every seed deserves to be tried at least once, especially when it's four inches long, heavy, flat, hairy and has a big eye at one end. Have your Five scrub the seed first. In a bowl

| | |
|---|---|
| **COMBINE** | **1 pt. water** |
| | **⅓ c. cracked charcoal** |
| | **seed** |

Soak for a week to soften the tough shell. In a tall 5″ pot

| | |
|---|---|
| **PLANT** | **vertically, eye pointed down** |
| **SOIL** | **Basic** |
| **WATER** | **heavily** |

Let the pot dry out completely once a month to develop good breathing space for the root hairs.

| | |
|---|---|
| **GERMINATION** | **4 months** |
| **INDOOR SUNLIGHT** | **4–5 hours** |
| **OUTDOOR LIGHT** | **partial sun** |

A mango chills easily. Keep it away from cold windows inside, beware of frosts outside, and use only tepid water. It needn't be transplanted for a year.

## AVOCADO

This seed grows into a lush, bushy tree if your Four pinches it. Otherwise, it will be straight as a flagpole and about as handsome. We've found the California fruit you buy in January often has roots when you open them, which makes it easy. If not, have your child dry the seed for a couple of days, peel the papery brown skin and warn him that the seed may take up to three months to sprout. Some people start these seeds in a cup of water but we find Basic Soil in a 5″ pot is better. Plant base down ⅔ into the soil leaving the pointed tip exposed. For a stronger root system, keep well watered in a dark cupboard until the seed germinates.

| | |
|---|---|
| **GERMINATION** | **30–90 days** |
| **SOIL** | **Basic** |
| **INDOOR SUNLIGHT** | **3–5 hours** |
| **OUTDOOR LIGHT** | **light shade** |
| **WATER** | **weekly** |

Remind your child to pinch off the top leaves every few inches.

## POMEGRANATE

A Five finds a pomegranate such an adventure to eat he'll want to grow his own.

This fruit develops into a bushy shrub if pinched and finds the dry heat of a city apartment rather like its native Persia. The flowers are brilliant orange and they can fruit outdoors as far north as Baltimore, but if yours fruits inside, write "Believe It or Not" and make your own grenadine.

To begin, have your child suck the seeds clean before he plants them in the Kitchen Table Pot.

**GERMINATION       6–8 weeks**

Transplant several seedlings into a 5" pot and keep them away from the humidity of other plants.

| | |
|---|---|
| **SOIL** | Sandy |
| **INDOOR SUNLIGHT** | 2–3 hours |
| **OUTDOOR LIGHT** | partial sun |
| **WATER** | weekly |

### CUTTINGS

It's easier to meet a neighbor over a rose-bush than a coffee party and a lot more interesting to a child. The old-fashioned custom of swapping the cuttings of favorite plants is a good way to multiply your friendships and your house plants too.

Swap anything—chrysanthemums, impatiens, begonias—and expect best results in spring to midsummer, when plants are most energetic. Make many cuttings; they like to root around with friends.

**CUT          2–4" stems**

Slice just below the node, a growth point that looks like a bump. The lower leaves should be removed. Keep the stems turgid in water or refrigerated in a plastic bag with a little water in it, or the cuttings may wilt and lose their rooting power. Otherwise, almost anything seems to root if you wait long enough—but some people help luck along by dipping the cut ends in a commercial root booster before planting in a rooting medium, whether they use water or the sand mixture given below.

## WATER METHOD

In a glass have your Two

**ADD          1 tbsp. cracked charcoal
6 oz. water
cuttings**

The first root hairs will sprout within a week or so, whether the glass is on a windowsill or not.

## SAND METHOD

In a pot or a plastic tray, have your Three

| | |
|---|---|
| **LAYER** | 1" pebbles |
| **ADD** | 1 c. vermiculite OR perlite OR sand
1 c. scalded sphagnum moss
⅓ c. water |
| **PLANT** | cuttings or leaves |

Embed them at a slant, so water can't collect at their bases, and about 2" apart, so the roots don't tangle. Press drainage material around cuttings and add a little more water so these particles can fill the air pockets. If you put the entire pot in The Hothouse (see page 369), the cuttings will root faster.

**INDOOR SUNLIGHT 1 hour**

**ROOTING        3–6 weeks**

Transplant when the roots are 2–3" long and keep out of sunlight for the next two days.

## ROOT CUTTINGS

Plants store all extra food in their roots, which is why carrots and other tap roots are so good for your child and why they have the energy to send up new stalks when only the tops of the roots are planted. No new roots will grow, but you'll have a few weeks of pretty foliage. Use a cake pan, either nestling the carrot, beet or radish tops in drainage or in a little water with charcoal to keep it smelling fresh. Keep in a well-lighted area.

## PINEAPPLE

This air plant only uses its roots to keep it from flying away. Cut the top ½″ of the pineapple and let it dry for a day or two. Remove 1″ of leaves from the base and you can see the tiny roots; they look like worms. In a pot

| | |
|---|---|
| **FILL** | **sand OR vermiculite OR perlite** |
| **EMBED** | **pineapple top** |

Water from above to fill the cupped leaves. It will send out new leaves within 10 days. The old ones will die at about the same rate this new core grows and they should be clipped with scissors as they brown, for good looks. Transplant when the new leaves are 1–2″ long and treat like any bromeliad.

If you wait a few years, you may be able to make the pineapple fruit by putting an apple in the pot and putting the entire pot in a sealed plastic bag for 5 days. The apple releases ethylene, a gas that inspires the pineapple to flower in 2–3 months. If cross-pollinated it eventually will bear a baby pineapple, growing at the end of a tall spike in the center of the foliage.

## INDOOR BULBS

There is magic abroad in the land (as every child knows), but a bulb in bloom is the best example we know of nature at its most miraculous. Before you start a bulb garden, let your child slice down through the center of a bulb—any one from the lowly onion to the exotic amaryllis—to see its tiny woody core. This is the embryo of the plant itself, with the stem, the flower and the leaves in miniature. It will draw all the nutrition it needs to bloom from the layers of skin around it. This is why many bulbs are so easy to grow.

It's easy to make hyacinths, paperwhite narcissus, crocuses, daffodils and tulips bloom indoors if you buy the bulbs in early fall, when they're plentiful—and if you remember to move them from place to place for the next four months. This schedule lets them think they're following the seasons, since bulbs, like bears, need to hibernate. This just proves that bulbs have many positive qualities, but they are not very smart.

Have your Three put them in a brown paper bag to winter in the refrigerator for at least one month—the longer they "winter," the better their blooms will be—and then help him plant the bulbs in water, sand or soil. Move them next to a cold, dark place to root—as if it were early spring—and when the first green shoots appear, move them to a bright sunny window and tell them it's spring.

If you add a few more bulbs every week or two, the blooms will be staggered, but date the bags, so you can take them out in sequence.

*Planting*—Because even indoor bulbs root best in cool weather, your child should plant them when the air is nippy (not freezing) on the back porch or in the garage or wherever he'll keep them. He can put them in water, sand, rocks, or, for tulips, in Basic Soil. All bulbs should be planted point up. If your child uses water the bulb should fit snugly in its own container or the flower will topple, but if he uses sand or soil he can crowd many together in a bowl, which makes a better effect. Use a pretty container, since the bulb won't be transplanted, and fence the edge of it with 3–4 popsicle sticks and a length of yarn to keep the plants from flopping. Start a new pot every two weeks if you want continual flowering.

*Water*—Suspend the bulb over its jar with just enough water to tickle its base. Since bulbs rot easily, they mustn't be deep enough to soak. You can buy special glass jars designed for bulb forcing, if you prefer, but they are expensive.

*Soil*—Put 1″ of pebbles into the bottom of a pot, for drainage, fill with Basic Soil, water thoroughly and imbed the bulbs up to their waists. You can also put the bulbs in a bowl, skip the drainage and use sand, peat moss or pebbles instead of the soil.

*Rooting*

No matter what medium you've chosen, the bulbs, once potted, must start to grow in a cold, dark place. Some gardeners who force bulbs in soil like to bury their pots outdoors in the earth and under glass, because here they need no watering. Your child will have the same effect with sand, which is cleaner than dirt and never freezes. Have him sit the pots in a wooden liquor box filled with 4″ of sand and then fill the top of the box with more sand to insulate the bulbs. Unless the pots are buried in soil or sand, they should be checked every two weeks to make sure the medium is moist, but be careful not to soak them.

| | |
|---|---|
| **TEMPERATURE** | **40–55°** |
| **LIGHT** | **none** |

The longer the bulbs are in darkness, the better they will root.

| | |
|---|---|
| **GERMINATION** | **6–8 weeks** |

When the shoots are 2–3″ tall they can be moved indoors. To check the buried pots you must lift them out of the sand. Even if the shoots aren't tall enough, they can live without another burial until they're ready.

*Blooming*

Move the plants to the coolest room in the house where the leaves and stalks get their color and grow tall enough to bloom.

| | |
|---|---|
| **TEMPERATURE** | **65°** |
| **WATER** | **constant moisture** |
| **INDOOR SUNLIGHT** | **indirect** |
| **BUDDING** | **2–3 weeks** |

When the bud is full, have your child move the pot to its place of honor, away from any source of heat, for any flower lasts longer if it isn't too warm.

| | |
|---|---|
| **TEMPERATURE** | **68–72°** |
| **WATER** | **twice weekly** |
| **FRUITION** | **1 week** |

The blooms will last two weeks. After they have bloomed, have your child save the bulbs to plant outdoors when the weather permits. Forced bulbs can't get enough sunlight or nutrition in their pot to form a new embryo even if the soil has been fertilized, but they can flower again if planted in the garden.

## THE VARIETIES

There are hundreds of kinds of plants and you'll want your child to have as many as possible—a fern and a bromeliad, because they have a story to tell; a vine, because it's the mainstay of the dimestore; a succulent, because it's the most varied of all, and a flowering plant, because it will bring such happiness.

*FLOWERING PLANTS*

Like a lady in a corset, pot-bound plants have bigger blooms.

| | |
|---|---|
| **SOIL** | **Basic** |

Use Sandy Soil for flowering cactus.

| | |
|---|---|
| **INDOOR SUNLIGHT** | **3–5 hours** |
| **OUTDOOR LIGHT** | **partial sun** |
| **FERTILIZE** | **weekly in budding season** |
| **WATER** | **2–3 times weekly** |
| **MIST** | **weekly** |

Sunlight triggers the blooms and cool temperatures keep them fresh. If you limit the water and sunlight in summer, you'll enforce dormancy and have winter flowers instead.

## VINES AND FOLIAGE PLANTS

A vine like pothos is the easiest for a child to grow, since it even thrives in water. Other foliage plants such as schefflera, ficus or a palm tree are almost as easy if you keep them indoors in winter, for most are tropical.

| | |
|---|---|
| **SOIL** | Basic |
| **INDOOR SUNLIGHT** | 1 hour or less |
| **OUTDOOR LIGHT** | shade |
| **FERTILIZE** | monthly in spring and summer |

Water when the soil feels dry when you poke into it. Keep the leaves dusted so they can photosynthesize.

## FERNS

Ferns, once as tall as dinosaurs (before there were any dinosaurs), are the most primitive plants of all. They reproduce not by seeds in fruit but by a two-step operation of spores and eggs. Let your Five see the rows of black spores that dot the back of each frond or hide in their own stalk case—and which people once thought could make them invisible. The fern skips a generation when their spores drop to the ground and sprout a scarcely noticeable little plant that hatches eggs and dies within a few hours. These eggs send up new stems several inches from the fern, which sends up new shoots too. Old stems continually wither and need to be clipped every week so the pot looks pretty. If a child keeps his potted fern on a bed of stones it can have the same humid atmosphere it knew in the forest to produce more spores.

| | |
|---|---|
| **SOIL** | Spongy |
| **INDOOR SUNLIGHT** | 2 hours |
| **OUTDOOR LIGHT** | shade |
| **WATER** | 3 times weekly |

## SUCCULENTS

Any plant that stores water in its thick stems and leaves, such as a jade tree or a cactus, is a succulent. It usually hates to be pinched, likes to be potbound and, because of its shallow roots, wants only 2–3″ of soil, which may mean a few extra inches of gravel in the pot. Flowering succulents, like geraniums, impatiens and begonias, need more earth, two more hours of sunshine a day and the casual care of a Three.

| | |
|---|---|
| **SOIL** | Sandy |

Water lightly at transplanting, drench it several days after settling and allow the soil to get dry as dust before each watering.

| | |
|---|---|
| **INDOOR SUNLIGHT** | 2 hours |
| **OUTDOOR LIGHT** | partial sun |
| **WATER** | heavy and infrequently |

After eons in the desert the cactus developed prickles to protect itself against punctures and the loss of water from its leaves. It only needs water every 2 weeks—less often if it is bigger, more often when it's blooming—and enjoys as much as 5 hours of indoor sunlight a day, anytime.

## BROMELIADS

These Latin American plants come in an astonishing variety and often have exotic flowers that take weeks to unfold and last just as long. At home their shallow roots are attached to tall trees so their feet can stay dry and so they can get near some sunlight. Bromeliad leaves are cupped to catch and ration rainfall and also to trap dead leaves and insects, which feed the plant as they decompose. One gardener we know claims a few dead flies dropped in the cups during budding season improve the blooms as well as delight the children in her kindergarten class. Bromeliads make interesting indoor plants and need little soil and small pots.

| SOIL | Spongy |
|---|---|
| INDOOR SUNLIGHT | 3 hours |
| OUTDOOR LIGHT | partial sun |
| WATER | twice weekly, from above |
| MIST | weekly |

A new plant will grow from the side. Transplant it when the big mother dies.

### TERRARIUM

A terrarium is an excellent present to get and to give and is also a good way to teach a child about the environment, for he sees the terrarium create its own life cycle, turning its little bit of sunshine into food and its dew into rainfall. Growth here is so slow the scene is almost static, so you'll need very small plants and much variety. You can use ones from a dimestore, if they're divided to fit the small space, and rooted cuttings, but there are tiny plants in every backyard if your child looks closely enough. You need at least six plants—tall and short, fat and skinny, and even one with berries—and then you need some ground covering and moss. No clumb of earth you collect should be bigger than 2″ square. In a glass canister, a goblet, a little jar or a big fish tank

| LAYER | ½″ stones |
|---|---|
| | gravel |
| | cracked charcoal |
| | 2–3″ Basic Soil |

The stones are for drainage and the bigger the terrarium, the thicker this layer should be. The gravel fills in the bigger spaces between them and the charcoal keeps the soil sweet. Have your child make a hilly terrain of the soil, to make the garden more interesting. He should poke holes in the earth with a pencil and press the plants into them, firming the soil around the roots with his fingertips. Each plant must include roots, a stem and a leaf. Cover the earth with the moss and add a few stones, sea shells, bits of bark or tiny pine cones for contrast.

| ADD | water |
|---|---|

It should partly cover the bottom layer of stones. Clean the plants and the inside of the bowl by spraying with a mister. Cover with clear plastic or glass.

| INDOOR SUNLIGHT | 1 hour OR |
|---|---|
| | 3 hours lamplight |

The terrarium should look dewy in the morning and be clear by evening. Add more water if it doesn't cloud, but if it doesn't clear all day, remove the cover so some of the extra moisture can evaporate. If your child has added a flowering plant like a begonia, the terrarium needs 2–3 hours of sunlight a day or 6–8 hours of lamplight. A desert terrarium requires Sandy Soil, a top layer of pure sand instead of moss and no cover at all.

If the terrarium is big enough your child can add a chameleon, a small box turtle or even a frog, but you must include a bowl of water. Cover this terrarium with a screen and water it more often.

## OUTDOOR GARDEN

Perhaps babies recognize beauty because they're so beautiful themselves, but we've never known a child who didn't smile at the sight of a flower or call each one "pretty" almost from the time that he could talk. These are the moments that make your soul sing.

You cultivate your child's love of

beauty in many ways, but a little garden patch of his own, no bigger than a window box, does it very well. Your Two likes his own trowel—the only tool he'll need for years—and then he's ready to begin.

We found bedding plants are better than seeds because he'll step on them less than on young sprouts, and flowers are better than vegetables because blooms come long before fruition, and this satisfies his eagerness. We don't recommend insecticides at all, not only because ladybugs and praying mantises are superior, but because every child eats a certain number of flowers in his time and eating a peck of dirt is a lot healthier than eating a pinch of insecticide.

A Three can plant his first bulbs, and a Four plants both flower and vegetable seeds. The patch he had at Two can grow bigger every year until a Six can handle a rock garden too. No matter what kind of garden he has, this child can care for his land if the area is small, if the plants are easy to tend—and if you're taking care of your own plot nearby.

## BASIC GARDEN

An outdoor garden, either for flowers or vegetables, needs a half day of sunshine and dark, rich, well-drained soil. If the soil is reddish—a sign of clay—buy some topsoil and pile your old dirt in a corner of the yard, the foundation for a rock garden. If the drainage is bad there will be moss on the ground, puddles after a rain and plants that rot at the roots. In that case, dig up a 6–7′ patch of earth—a job for grown-ups to do and for your child to pretend to do.

In a 3′ × 3′ plot

| LAYER | 1″ gravel |
|---|---|
|  | 2 bushels topsoil |
| ADD | 2 c. dried cow manure |
|  | 1 c. bone meal |

Crumble the soil and water thoroughly.

| ADD | 100 earthworms |
|---|---|

Unless you saw many worms when you dug, this addition is necessary to keep the soil friable. Buy them at a garden center or a bait store, releasing them at sundown so they have time to get into the ground before the birds eat them. The worms will thrive if you don't use a heavy dose of chemical fertilizer.

## VEGETABLE GARDEN

Help your Four plan an interesting garden, but he should choose which vegetables to plant. He might like squash, with their blossoms that could have come from Mars, and a tomato plant—a delight, for he'll never forget the taste of the warm, red tomatoes eaten right in the garden—and green peas, which are lovely to shell. Add onions and marigolds to keep away the bugs and lettuce to edge the plot. Plant seeds as directed on the package, but for planned gardenhood, don't plant many more than the soil can support. Thin the extra seedlings after the second set of leaves appears and you can tell which plants are the strongest.

## BULB GARDEN

Bulbs send up shoots in spring, an anticipation almost as joyful to a child as Christmas.

Choose the driest spot in the yard, for bulbs rot easily if drainage is bad. To look their best, bulbs should be planted in clumps about 6″ apart. Dig a trench or individual holes, with your child measuring the depth with his ruler, for arithmetic makes more sense when it can be applied. The bigger the bulbs the deeper they're planted. The lowest depth for tulips will let them bloom as long as five years. Into each hole

**SPRINKLE**          1 tbsp. bone meal

**PLANT**               crocus, 4″ deep
                        hyacinths, 6″ deep
                        daffodils and tulips, 8–10″ deep

Cover and tamp, a job every child enjoys. If the soil is clay, you'll have to dig 6″ deeper to line the bed with stones for drainage and add a layer of top soil—the nutrition for next year's flowers—before the bulbs are planted. This is hard enough work to make it a family production.

### ROCK GARDEN

This is especially good because it calls for as much creativity as it does energy. A rock garden should look like a rough hillside, with flowers and mosses growing between the rocks. Either arrange it against a corner of the fence or dig out a small slope in the yard to embed it. It can be any size or height, depending on the strength of your small child's arms. It's his garden, from the collection of rocks to the compliments, although he'll need your help to make it and to keep it going. For a low garden

**COLLECT**           small, angular rocks

**LAY**               1″ gravel OR cinder drainage bed

**COVER**             8″ Basic Soil

**ARRANGE**           rocks

The rocks should be planted rather irregularly but close together, jammed two thirds of the way into the earth and, for harmony, with the grain of the rocks going in the same direction, like wood. Press more soil between the rocks.

**PLANT**             sweet alyssum/bulbs/phlox/
                      candytuft/forget-me-nots/moss

Nestle these or other plants among the rocks and embed smaller rocks beneath the plants to hold them and to help with drainage. A child will enjoy this garden best if he gradually adds other rocks and plants, rather than planting all at once. Cacti may be substituted if Sandy Soil is used.

## CANDY TREE

There are some days so full of sameness the mind seems stultified. For this you need a different sort of gardening. Our Kate and Mike, at Seven and Eight, invented the Candy Tree.

They took their pennies to the corner store, selected a crop of candies, ran home, balanced the candy in a camellia bush and called their little sister quickly.

The Candy Tree had bloomed.

The bush gained enormously in prestige and became the wonder of the block, watered by young gardeners when all other plants were ignored. Now the little sister has a little sister who occasionally gets bored and for whom, very occasionally, the Candy Tree blooms again.

Naturally it's never asked for, because no one knows how it happens, and it's never expected, because no one knows when it will happen, but there are always enough blooms to give each child an equal amount.

This is a simple diversion, costing little in time or money, and it will boggle a child's imagination nicely.

# EPILOGUE

Each of us weeps—at least inside—when a child begins first grade, not because of the child we are losing, but because of the chances we've lost. So much is left undone.

Certainly it was that way for us. We hadn't the time, the knowledge or the sense of duty to use every recipe and suggestion in this book for each of our seven children, and we were still learning what to do for the youngest when the oldest were practically grown.

When we disciplined one child with kindness and firmness, it was only because we had learned at the expense of those who had gone before, and if we helped all to know the joys of play we did have some trouble when it came to teaching them the rewards of work.

In the years between first and sixth grades, you may be surprised to find your child change gears so slowly you can't believe he's going through stages anymore. His accomplishments are harder to notice; his moods, though not so merry, last much longer. A boy particularly seems to go through agony, for he needs to prove himself—to himself—day after day.

We'll leave it to *The Mother's Almanac II* to tell you the full saga of children from Six to Twelve—the still years that prepare them for their yeasty teens. It is the continuum that makes parenthood so rich and rewarding.

We think you'll find, as we did, that a child's ups and downs during his first six years are repeated during the next twelve, when his disposition falls apart and comes together, again and again. Still you'll want to give as much of yourself as you ever did before, keeping the channels open by talking and especially by listening, but now it's not so easy. This is his period of absorption, when his social and physical and mental development all must learn to mesh again.

You start to notice the change at Seven when you watch him twist his way through the first bout of puberty (now he knows for sure that the world is against him), and by Eight, you see him try harder every day to act like all the other Eights. This fledgling is alert to every sight and sound, but seldom makes a move that's different from the flock: the opinions of his friends are paramount. This has mixed effects. For the first time, your extraordinary child may be just a little bit boring. Where once he was full of bright sayings, now he only repeats those same silly riddles you knew as a child, and when he goes to a movie he has to tell you the whole plot, which takes almost as long as the movie itself. Even his teeth look too big for his face, and besides, he whistles a lot.

At Nine, he may limit himself to one super best friend, each reinforcing the other to be as much alike as possible until you almost think your child has lost his originality. By Ten he will surprise you one more time. Slowly all the ideas he's absorbed in the last few years begin to surface. Now he amazes you with his fresh insights, his new competence and even his wit, a rebirth that continues for the next two years. At the same time he rebels in a dozen small ways to break those molds he made. Feel blessed. Each stage is as right for him as all the ones that have gone before.

Between Thirteen and Sixteen your child will go through the same outrageous rule breaking as he did at Two and Four, and although it may wrench your heart, these should be good years too. If your teenager still can count on you for as much time and praise and affection and respect and trust as he's had at every age, he can grow up to be a strong, happy, self-confident adult—and a good friend for life. You can't ask for anything more.

# RECOMMENDED READING

## MOTHER

### PREGNANCY
American College of Nurse-Midwives, *Your Pregnancy Calendar*. A.C.N.M., 1522 K St., N.W., Suite 1000, Washington, D.C. 20005. A good, simple wheel to show you what happens when, in English or Spanish, for $2.50.

Carter, Lanie, with Ostrow, Lauren Simon, *The Miracle Year*. New York: Pocket Books, 1990. A fine account of the six months before and after the baby's birth.

Eisenberg, Arlene; Murkoff, Heidi E.; and Hathaway, Sandee E., B.S.N., *What to Expect When You're Expecting*. New York: Workman, 1988. A general, month-by-month guide on What to Do When There's Nothing to Do.

Hotchner, Tracy, *Pregnancy & Childbirth*, revised. New York: Avon, 1990. A classic book that covers all fronts.

Jones, Sandy, with Freitag, Werner, *Guide to Baby Products*. Yonkers: Consumer Report Books, 1991. The best for your baby, but not the most expensive.

McCartney, Marion, C.N.M., and van der Meer, Antonia, *The Midwife's Pregnancy & Childbirth Book*. New York: Harper/Perennial, 1991. A truly excellent account, not just of midwifery but obstetrics too.

Morales, Karla, and Inlander, Charles B., *Take This Book to the Obstetrician with You*. Boston: Addison-Wesley, 1991. A consumer's guide to pregnancy and childbirth.

Nilsson, Lennart, *A Child Is Born*, revised. New York: Dell, 1989. No one has ever matched these photographs of fetal development.

### PREGNANCY PROBLEMS
Hales, Dianne, and Johnson, Timothy R. B., M.D., *Intensive Caring*. New York: Crown, 1990. The latest medical information for high-risk pregnancy, in a low-key style.

Manning, Barbara Eck, *Infertility*. New York: Prentice-Hall, 1988. A guide for the childless couple.

Rich, Laurie A., *When Pregnancy Isn't Perfect*. New York: Dutton, 1991. Sensible, nonhysteric guidance for those who need it.

Stangel, John J., M.D., *The New Fertility and Conception*. New York: Plume, 1989. A book to give hope and chances.

### CHILDBIRTH
Bean, Constance A., *Methods of Childbirth*. New York: Morrow, 1990. A straightforward book to help the mother decide which delivery is best for her.

Fenlon, Arlene; Oakes, Ellen; and Dorchak, Lovell, *Getting Ready for Childbirth*. Boston: Little, Brown, 1986. A good guide, full of hows and whys.

Lieberman, Adrienne B., *Giving Birth*. New York: St. Martin's, 1987. A blow-by-blow and pant-by-pant description of birth—warm, reassuring and accurate.

### CHILDBIRTH PROBLEMS
Hausknecht, Richard, M.D., and Heilman, Joan Rattner, *Having a Cesarean Baby*. New York: Plume, 1991. Complete guide for a happy and safe Cesarean childbirth experience.

Henig, Robin Marantz, with Fletcher, Dr. Anne B., *Your Premature Baby*. New York: Ballantine, 1983. A clear, positive explanation of the care and feeding of a preemie.

Rosen, Mortimer, M.D., and Thomas, Lillian, *The Cesarian Myth*. New York: Penguin, 1989. The pros—and cons—of a C-section.

### BREASTFEEDING
Huggins, Kathleen, R.N., M.S., *The Nursing Mother's Companion*. Boston: Harvard Common Press, 1990. Comprehensive, nonjudgmental advice on everything from milk production and breast pumps to the kind of medicine you can take when you nurse.

La Leche League, *The Womanly Art of Breastfeeding*, 5th edition. New York: Plume, 1991. The group—and the book—that led mothers back to the basics.

Pryor, Karen, and Pryor, Gale, *Nursing Your Baby*. New York: Pocket Books, 1991. First-rate advice, especially for the working mother.

### POSTPARTUM DEPRESSION
Ciaramitaro, Barbara, *Help for Depressed Mothers*. Edmonds, Wash.: Charles Franklin Press, 1982. A

clear explanation of postpartum depression and how to treat it.

Dix, Carol, *The New Mother Syndrome*. New York: Pocket Books, 1985. A total picture of this unsettling problem, and what to do about it.

## WORKING MOTHER

Lew, Irvina Siegel, *You Can't Do It All*. New York: Berkeley, 1987. The book that puts work, and family, into perspective, and tells you how to do it a little easier.

# CHILD

## CARE AND FEEDING

Boston Children's Hospital with Baker, Susan, M.D., Ph.D., and Henry, Roberta R., R.D., *Parents' Guide to Nutrition*. Boston: Addison-Wesley, 1987. A thorough book for thorough parents.

Satter, Ellen, R.D., *Child of Mine*, expanded edition. Palo Alto: Bull, 1986. Feeding with love and good sense.

Schneider, Vimala, *Infant Massage*. New York: Bantam, 1989. A short book about one of the most soothing techniques you can use on a baby.

Wilson, Miriam, *Help for Children*, 5th edition. Shepherdstown, W. Va.: Rocky River, 1987. A national—and invaluable—directory of hotlines to help children from infancy to adulthood.

## DAY CARE

Miller, Jo Ann, and Weissman, Susan, M.S.W., *The Parents' Guide to Daycare*. New York: Bantam, 1986. Just what you need to make the best decision.

Muscari, Ann, and Morrone, Wenda Wardell, *Child Care That Works*. New York: Doubleday, 1989. A positive look at child care, and how it works best.

Squibb, Betsy, *Family Day Care*. Boston: Harvard Common Press, 1986. How to be a day care provider yourself.

## DEVELOPMENT

Ames, Louise Bates, and Ilg, Frances L., *Your One (or Two, Three, Four, Five or Six)-Year-Old*. New York: Dell, 1982. An excellent series, with a book for every year.

Biracree, Tom and Nancy, *The Parents' Book of Facts*. New York: Ballantine/Ivy, 1989. A concise report on the mental, physical, emotional and moral growth of a child.

Brazelton, T. Berry, *Toddlers and Parents*, revised. New York: Dell, 1989. It delivers what it promises.

Fraiberg, Selma H., *The Magic Years*. New York: Macmillan, 1984. One of the best books you can find on the behavior of the child, but with a strong Freudian bent.

Galinsky, Ellen, and David, Judy, *The Preschool Years*. New York: Ballantine, 1988. A thorough account of the young child and how he grows best.

Gesell, Arnold, M.D., *The First Five Years of Life*. New York: Harper & Row, 1940. This book is the basis for all other books on early childhood, but it may only be available at your library.

Gilligan, Carol, *In a Different Voice*. Boston: Harvard University Press, 1982. A book to remind you that boys and girls really are different, no matter what we do.

Ilg, Frances L., M.D., Ames, Louise Bates, Ph.D., and Baker, Sidney M., M.D., *Child Behavior*, revised. New York: Harper/Collins, 1982. You need hardly go further.

Kiersey, David, and Bates, Marilyn, *Please Understand Me*. Del Mar, Calif.: Prometheus Nemesis Books, 1978. A key to decode your child's temperament.

Klaus, Marshall H., M.D., and Klaus, Phyllis H., M.Ed., C.S.W., *The Amazing Newborn*. Boston: Addison-Wesley, 1985. The very best book on the marvelous first ten days of life, by the doctor who taught us about bonding.

Leach, Penelope, *Your Baby & Child*. New York: Knopf, 1981. Beautifully done book on the total child.

Stone, L. Joseph, and Church, Joseph, *Childhood and Adolescence*, 1984. New York: Random House. Probably the most thorough, succinct overview on the child from birth to college.

White, Burton L., M.D., *The First Three Years of Life*, revised. New York: Prentice-Hall, 1987. A classic, brought up to date.

## HEALTH

Pantell, Robert H., M.D.; Fries, James F., M.D.; and Vickery, Donald M., M.D., *Taking Care of Your Child*, 3d edition. Boston: Addison-Wesley, 1990. A clear, concise medical reference.

Prudden, Bonnie, *How to Keep Your Child Fit from Birth to Six*. New York: Ballantine, 1986. Body development, exercises, play equipment and some psychology, in a book that excels in both text and photographs.

Shelov, Steven P., M.D., and Hannemann, Robert E., M.D. *Caring for Your Baby and Child*. New York: Bantam, 1991. The definitive medical reference about children from birth to five, under the auspices of the American Academy of Pediatrics.

Spock, Benjamin, M.D., *Baby and Child Care*. New York: Pocket Books, 1981. An old and trusted medical guide for mothers and an excellent one, if not relied upon more than the baby's own pediatrician.

## HEALTH PROBLEMS

Crook, William, M.D., *Help for the Hyperactive Child*. Jackson, Tenn.: Professional Books, 1991.

An allergist writes this easy-to-follow book that makes diet management easy to follow too.

Rapp, Doris, M.D., *Is This Your Child?* New York: Morrow, 1991. A book on allergies and how they can affect a child, physically and emotionally.

Thompson, Charlotte E., M.D., *Raising a Handicapped Child.* New York: Ballantine, 1991. Just what you need if you have a physically disabled child.

## MIND

Copeland, Richard W., *How Children Learn Mathematics.* New York: Macmillan, 1984. A book to show how Piaget methods are applied to math.

Gardner, Howard, *Frames of Mind.* New York: Basic Books, 1983. A full, intelligent account of intelligence, at any age.

Healy, Jane M., Ph.D., *Your Child's Growing Mind.* New York: Doubleday, 1987. An informative, easy-to-read book that describes the way your child thinks.

Pulaski, Mary Ann Spencer, *Understanding Piaget.* New York: Harper & Row, 1980. Paiget deciphers the way children learn; this book deciphers Piaget.

Smutny, Joan F.; Veenker, Kathleen; and Veenker, Stephen, *Your Gifted Child.* New York: Facts on File, 1989. This book can help you through some thickets.

Webb, James T.; Meckstroth, E.; and Tolan, S., *Guiding the Gifted Child.* Columbus: Ohio Psychology Publishing Co., 1982. A classic introduction to this special child.

## GOOD TIMES

### ACTIVITIES

Katz, Adrienne, *What to Do with the Kids on a Rainy Day.* New York: St. Martin's, 1989. A little book that may save your sanity.

Rich, Dorothy, *Mega Skills.* Boston: Houghton Mifflin, 1988. Inexpensive, interesting things to do with a child—and why.

### ART

Brittain, W. Lambert, and Lowenfeld, Viktor, *Creative and Mental Growth,* 8th edition. New York: Macmillan, 1987. This definitive book explains why every child needs art in his life.

### BOOKS

Lipson, Eden Ross, *The New York Times Parents' Guide to the Best Books for Children.* New York: Times Books, 1988. The last word on the best words for children.

Trelease, Jim, *The New Read-Aloud Handbook,* revised. New York: Penguin, 1989. To remind you that all children need their parents to read books to them and how to do it best.

### CRAFTS

Croft, Doreen, and Hess, Robert, *Activities Handbook for Teachers of Young Children.* Boston: Houghton Mifflin, 1984. Just what you need to know.

### DANCE

Findlay, Elsa, *Rhythm and Movement.* Evanston, Ill.: Sengstack, 1971. Uses principles of eurhythmics to help a child get the most out of music and dance.

Laban, Rudolf, *Modern Educational Dance.* Princeton, N.J.: Princeton Book Company. Laban is to movement what Piaget is to the mind.

### MUSIC

Jarnow, Jill, *All Ears.* New York: Penguin, 1991. How to choose and use recorded music for children.

Judy, Stephanie, *Making Music for the Joy of It.* Los Angeles: Tarcher, 1990. Enhancing creativity and musical skills.

Suzuki, Shinichi, *Nurtured by Love.* New York: Accura, 1987. An explanation of the worldwide Suzuki violin method for preschool children.

### SCIENCE

Katz, Adrienne, *Naturewatch.* Boston: Addison-Wesley, 1986. A book to help you enchant your child.

Ontario Science Centre, *Scienceworks.* Boston: Addison-Wesley, 1986. A fine introduction to the wonders that grown-ups take for granted.

### TRAVEL

Lansky, Vicki, *Trouble-Free Travel with Children.* Deephaven, Minn.: Book Peddlers, 1991. Traveling with children is never perfect, but this book will make it better.

### VIDEOTAPES

Green, Diana Huss, and the editors of Consumer Reports Books, *Parents' Choice Guide to Videocassettes for Children.* Mt. Vernon, N.Y.: Consumer Reports Books, 1989. An indispensable collection of reviews to help you rent and buy videotapes for your child.

## PRESCHOOL

Ames, Louise Bates, Ph.D., and Chase, Joan Ames, Ph.D., *Don't Push Your Preschooler.* New York: Harper & Row, 1985. Shows the dangers of expecting too much of a child.

Brenner, Barbara, *The Pre School Handbook.* New York: Pantheon, 1990. A thorough explanation of all the preschool options.

Hainstock, Elizabeth, *The Essential Montessori,* 2d edition. New York: Plume, 1986. A book to explain this special teaching style.

Paley, Vivian Gussin, *Mollie Is Three.* Chicago: University of Chicago Press, 1986. The perfect account of a year in what appears to be a perfect preschool.

Robinson, Jacqueline, *Is Your Child Ready for School?* New York: Arco, 1990. Straightforward explanation to find out what both public and private schools expect.

Steiner, Rudolf F., *A Modern Art of Education.* London: Anthroposophic, 1981. Explains the Waldorf brand of education.

Wade, Theodore E., Jr., et al., *The Home School Manual*, 3d edition. Auburn, Calif.: Gazelle, 1984. For those who want to teach their children at home.

# PARENTS

## PARENTING

Bell, Roselyn, ed., *The Hadassah Magazine Jewish Parenting Book.* New York: Avon, 1989. To help you rear your child within your own culture.

Briggs, Dorothy Corkille, *Your Child's Self-Esteem.* New York: Doubleday, 1975. How to give your child self-esteem—the key to good parenting.

Budd, Linda S., Ph.D., *Living with the Active Alert Child.* New York: Prentice-Hall, 1990. A splendid, practical book to deal with the child on the go-go-go.

Cohen, Miriam Galper, *Long Distance Parenting.* New York: Signet, 1989. How to manage one of the toughest jobs any parent could have.

Elkind, David, *The Hurried Child*, revised. Boston: Addison-Wesley, 1985. A four-star book to slow you down, when you're tempted to push your child too fast.

Friedrich, Elizabeth, and Rowland, Cherry, *The Parents' Guide to Raising Twins.* New York: St. Martin's, 1984. To help you give your best to your multiples and still have some left for yourself.

Ginott, Hiam G., *Between Parent and Child.* New York: Avon, 1976. Basic techniques to encourage good behavior.

Greywolf, Elizabeth S., *The Single Mother's Handbook.* New York: Morrow, 1984. The problems of a single parent and many of the solutions.

Hopson, Dr. Darlene Powell, and Hopson, Dr. Derek S., *Different and Wonderful.* New York: Prentice-Hall, 1990. To guide black parents down their own special path.

Hymes, James, *Teaching the Child under Six*, 3d edition. St. Paul, Minn.: Consortium, 1990. Straightforward and informative.

Kelly, Marguerite, *The Mother's Almanac II.* New York: Doubleday, 1989. To help you enjoy the Middle Years from six to twelve, and make the teenage years much smoother.

Kersey, Katharine C., Ed.D., *The Art of Sensitive Parenting.* Washington: Acropolis, 1983. The ten keys to guide your child with greater grace.

Krueger, Caryl W., *Six Weeks to Better Parenting.* Gretna, La.: Pelican, 1981. One of the great unsung books on parenting.

Kutner, Lawrence, Ph.D., *Parent & Child.* New York: Morrow, 1991. The psychologist uses communication to strengthen this essential connection.

Newman, Susan, *Parenting an Only Child.* New York: Doubleday, 1990. A popular book on an increasingly popular choice.

Novotny, Pamela Patrick, *The Joy of Twins.* New York: Crown, 1988. The title speaks for itself.

Schulman, Michael, and Meker, Eva, *Bringing Up a Moral Child.* Boston: Addison-Wesley, 1985. A well-documented book with many clear how-to examples to guide your child well.

Sullivan, S. Adams, *The Father's Almanac*, revised. New York: Doubleday, 1991. The riches of parenthood, from a father's point of view.

Weiss, Joan Solomon, *Your Second Child.* New York: Summit, 1981. It may not be the best book on the second child, but it's one of the few.

## PARENTING PROBLEMS

Faber, Adele, and Mazlish, Elaine, *How to Talk So Kids Will Listen and Listen So Kids Will Talk.* New York: Avon, 1982. These Ginott disciples teach parents to get respect, by giving it.

Ingersoll, Barbara, Ph.D., *Your Hyperactive Child.* New York: Doubleday, 1988. Traditional views on this puzzling problem.

Lansky, Vicki, *Getting Your Child to Sleep . . . and Back to Sleep.* Deephaven, Minn.: Book Peddlers, 1991. A truly practical book on the many strategies that work, for some child, somewhere, so you can find out which one works for you.

Turecki, Stanley, M.D., and Tonner, Leslie, *The Difficult Child.* New York: Bantam, 1985. A psychiatrist lays out helpful methods to help a problem child.

## DISCIPLINE

Ames, Louise Bates, Ph.D., with Haber, Carol Chase, and the Gesell Institute of Human Development, *He Hit Me First.* New York: Warner, 1985. A book on sibling rivalry—the bane of any household with two or more children.

Faber, Adele, and Mazlish, Elaine, *Siblings Without Rivalry.* New York: Norton, 1987. The masters of the field.

Martin, Judith, *Miss Manners' Guide to the Turn of the Millennium.* New York: Pharos, 1989. Hundreds of clever, insightful ways to use etiquette to keep children (and grown-ups) in line—and why.

Mitchell, Grace, *A Very Practical Guide to Discipline with Young Children.* Marshfield, Mass.: Telshare, 1987. How to discipline children well.

Reit, Seymour V., *Sibling Rivalry*. New York: Ballantine, 1985. A book to help you handle a big problem.

Samalin, Nancy, with Jablow, Martha Moraghan, *Loving Your Child Is Not Enough*. New York: Penguin, 1987. You'll see that positive discipline brings positive results.

Shaefer, Charles E., Ph.D., and DiGeronimo, Theresa Foy, *Teach Your Child to Behave*. New York: Plume, 1990. Dozens of time-tested, child-tested ways to help a child be good.

## FAMILY

### ADOPTION

Gilman, Lois, *The Adoption Resource Book*. New York: Harper & Row, 1984. It delivers just what it promises.

Koh, Frances M., *Oriental Children in American Homes*. Minneapolis: East-West Press, 1981. A must-have book for parents who adopt Asian children.

Michelman, Stanley B., and Schneider, Meg, with van der Meer, Antonia, *The Private Adoption Handbook*. New York: Dell, 1988. Here is the key to this complicated pursuit.

Siegel, Stephanie E., Ph.D., *Parenting Your Adopted Child*. New York: Prentice-Hall, 1990. A book to guide you through these somewhat different waters.

### FAMILY RELATIONSHIPS

Bradshaw, John, *Bradshaw On: The Family*. Deerfield Beach, Fla.: Health Communications, 1988. This book will reach into your past so you can figure out your present.

Curran, Delores, *Traits of a Healthy Family*. New York: Ballantine, 1983. An unpretentious book that will make you think for weeks.

Gottlieb, Daniel, Ph.D., with Claflin, Edward, *Family Matters*. New York: Dutton, 1991. One of the most helpful books you can find.

### GRANDPARENTS

Levy, Michael T., M.D., *Parenting Mom & Dad*. New York: Prentice-Hall, 1991. For those who take care of their parents as well as their children.

Wassermann, Selma, *The Long Distance Grandmother*. St. Paul, Minn.: Hartley and Marks, 1990. How to keep the connection strong.

### DEATH

Friedman, Rochelle, *Surviving a Pregnancy Loss*. Boston: Little, Brown, 1982. A book to guide you and ground you through these dark days.

Ginsburg, Genevieve Davis, M.S., *When You've Become a Widow*. Los Angeles: Tarcher, 1987. A guide to get you through it at least a little more easily.

Ilse, Sherokee, *Empty Arms*. Maple Plain, Minn.: Wintergreen Press, 1982. A poignant book for those who have lost a baby through miscarriage and infant death.

Kübler-Ross, Elisabeth, *On Children and Death*. New York: Macmillan, 1985. A classic in this field.

———, *On Death and Dying*. New York: Macmillan, 1970. Another classic.

### DIVORCE

Clair, Bernard, and Daniele, Anthony, *The Ex-Factor*. New York: Donald Fine, 1986. A do-it-yourself guide to get you through it, once the divorce is done.

Jewett, Claudia, *Helping Children Cope with Separation and Loss*. Boston: Harvard Common Press, 1982. This book will help you help children who lose grown-ups, through absence, divorce or death.

Lansky, Vicki, *Vicki Lansky's Divorce Book for Parents*. New York: NAL, 1989. To help children heal.

Shapiro, Robert, Ph.D., *Separate Houses*. New York: Prentice-Hall, 1989. Covers all those sticky problems that come with divorce.

Trafford, Abigail, *Crazy Times*, revised. New York: Harper/Collins, 1992. Such an honest description on the death of a marriage that you may decide to work it out instead.

Walther, Anne N., M.S., *Divorce Hangover*. New York: Pocket Books, 1991. A book to help you get on with your life.

### FAMILY PROBLEMS

Andreasen, Nancy C., M.D., Ph.D., *The Broken Brain*. New York: Harper/Collins, 1985. One of the first, and best, books on biopsychiatry.

Beattie, Melody, *Codependent No More*. New York: Walker, 1989. A thoughtful book to help you deal with an addicted personality in your family.

Rubin, Dr. Jeffrey, and Rubin, Dr. Carol, *When Families Fight*. New York: Morrow. When we know the real reasons for the fights, the fighting often goes away.

Stearns, Ann Kaiser, *Living Through Personal Crisis*. New York: Ballantine, 1985. An extremely helpful book for any adult.

Viorst, Judith, *Necessary Losses*. New York: Fawcett, 1985. To explain the lessons we learn from our losses.

### MARRIAGE AND REMARRIAGE

Coleman, Dr. Paul, *The Forgiving Marriage*. Chicago: Contemporary Books, 1989. A good guide.

Klagsbrun, Francine, *Married People*. New York: Bantam, 1986. A book to help you stay together in an age of divorce.

Lorimer, Anne, with Feldman, Philip M., M.D., *ReMarriage*. Philadelphia: Running Press, 1980. So this marriage can be stronger.

## STEPPARENTS

Burns, Cherie, *Stepmotherhood*. New York: Times Books, 1985. To help you have reasonable expectations, and enjoy your role more.

Savage, Karen, and Adams, Patricia, *The Good Stepmother*. New York: Avon, 1988. Warm, reassuring advice to deal with a difficult, but rewarding, job.

# RESOURCES

## BEHAVIOR

Gesell Institute of Human Development, 310 Prospect St., New Haven, CT 06511; (203) 777-3481.

## CHILD ABUSE

National Center for Missing and Exploited Children, 2101 Wilson Blvd., Suite 550, Arlington, VA 22201; (703) 235-3900.

National Committee for Prevention of Child Abuse, 332 S. Michigan Ave., Suite 1600, Chicago, IL 60604; (312) 663-3520.

Parents Anonymous, 520 S. Lafayette Park Pl., Suite 316, Los Angeles, CA 90057; (213) 388-6685.

## CHILD CARE

Experiment in International Living, Au pair/Homestay USA, 1015 Fifteenth St., N.W., Suite 750, Washington, D.C. 20005; (202) 408-5380.

## DEATH

Children's Hospice International, 901 N. Washington St., Suite 700, Alexandria, VA 22314; (800) 24-CHILD or (800) 242-4453.

The Compassionate Friends (for parents whose child has died), P.O. Box 3696, Oak Brook, IL 50422-3696; (708) 990-0010.

National Hospice Organization, 1901 N. Moore St., Suite 910, Arlington, VA 22209; (800) 658-8898.

National SIDS Alliance, 10500 Little Patuxent Pkwy., Suite 420, Columbia, MD 21044; (800) 221-SIDS or (800) 221-7437.

## DISABILITIES

The Arc (the Association for Retarded Citizens), P.O. Box 1047, Arlington, TX 76004; (817) 261-6003.

Federation for Children with Special Needs (mental and physical disabilities), 95 Berkeley St., Suite 104, Boston, MA 02116; (617) 482-2915.

National Information Center for Children and Youth with Disabilities, Box 1492, Washington, D.C. 20013; (800) 999-5599.

Sibling Information Network, 991 Main St., Suite 3A, East Hartford, CT 06108; (203) 282-7050.

## DRUGS

Alcoholics Anonymous, Adult Children of Alcoholics, Al-Anon and Narcotics Anonymous: see your local directory.

American Council for Drug Education, 204 Monroe St., Suite 110, Rockville, MD 20850; (301) 294-0600.

National Clearinghouse for Alcohol and Drug Information, Box 2345, Rockville, MD 20852; (301) 443-6500.

## ENRICHMENT

American Library Association, 50 E. Huron St., Chicago, IL 60611; (800) 545-2433.

Chinaberry Book Service (children's books by mail), Suite B, 2780 Via Orange Way, Spring Valley, CA, 91978; (800) 776-2242.

Listening Library, 1 Park Ave., Old Greenwich, CT 06870; (800) 2243-4505, to buy videos, books and recordings.

Parents' Choice, Box 185, Waban, MA 02168; (617) 965-5913.

Secret Garden (children's books by mail), 5309 Oakland Rd., Chevy Chase, MD 20815; (301) 654-1365.

## FAMILY

Catholic Charities USA, 1731 King St., Suite 200, Alexandria, VA 22314; (703) 549-1390, or see your local directory.

Children's Defense Fund, 122 C St., N.W., Suite 400, Washington, D.C. 20001; (202) 628-8787.

Family Service America, 11700 W. Lake Park Dr., Milwaukee, WI 53224; (414) 359-1040, or see your local directory.

National Military Family Association, 6000 Stevenson Ave., Suite 304, Alexandria, VA 22304; (703) 823-6632.

## GIFTED

Council for Exceptional Children (for gifted and disabled children), 1929 Association Dr., Reston, VA 22091-1589; (800) 845-6232.

National Association for Gifted Children, 1155 Fifteenth St., N.W., Suite 1002, Washington, D.C. 20005; (202) 785-4268.

## HEARING AND SPEECH

American Speech-Language-Hearing Association, 10801 Rockville Pike, Rockville, MD 20852; (800) 638-8255.

Gallaudet University, 800 Florida Ave., N.E., Washington, D.C. 20002; (202) 651-5000.

National Association of the Deaf, 814 Thayer Ave., Silver Spring, MD 20910; (301) 587-1788, TDY (301) 587-1789.

Self Help for Hard of Hearing People, Inc. (SHHH), 7800 Wisconsin Ave., Bethesda, MD 20814-3524; (301) 657-2248, TDY (301) 657-2249.

## HYPERACTIVITY

Feingold Association, Box 6550, Alexandria, VA 22306; (703) 768-3287.

## ILLNESS

Association for the Care of Children's Health, 7910 Woodmont Ave., Suite 300, Bethesda, MD 20814; (301) 654-6549.

Candlelighters Childhood Cancer Foundation, 1312 18th St., N.W., Suite 200, Washington, D.C. 20036; (800) 366-2223.

Juvenile Diabetes Foundation International, 432 Park Ave. South, 16th Floor, New York, NY 10016-8013; (800) 223-1138.

## LEARNING DISABILITIES

Learning Disabilities Association of America, 4156 Library Rd., Pittsburgh, PA 15234; (412) 341-1515.

Orton Dyslexia Society, Chester Bldg., 8600 LaSalle Rd., Suite 382, Baltimore, MD 21204-6020; (800) 222-3123.

## MENTAL ILLNESS

National Alliance for the Mentally Ill, 2101 Wilson Blvd., Suite 302, Arlington, VA 22201; (703) 524-7600.

## MARRIAGE/REMARRIAGE

Clergy Services, Inc., 706 W. Forty-second St., Kansas City, MO 64111; (800) 237-1922, for the service and the Family Medallion to include the child in the vows.

## NUTRITION

Center for Science In the Public Interest, 1875 Connecticut Ave., N.W., Suite 300, Washington, DC 20009-5728; (202) 332-9110.

## PRESCHOOL

Home and School Institute, 1201 Sixteenth St., N.W., Washington, DC 20036; (202) 466-3633.

National Association for the Education of Young Children, 1834 Connecticut Ave., N.W., Washington, DC 20009; (202) 232-8777.

## SEX

Alan Guttmacher Institute, 2010 Massachusetts Ave., N.W., Washington, DC 20036; (202) 296-4012.

Planned Parenthood Federation of America, 810 Seventh Ave., New York, NY 10019; (800) 829-7732.

## TWINS AND MORE

Mothers of Twins Clubs, Inc., 12404 Princess Jeanne NE, Albuquerque, NM 87112.

The Triplet Connection, P.O. Box 99571, Stockton, CA 95209; (209) 474-0885.

*Twins*, a magazine about multiples, Box 12045, Overland Park, KS 66212; (800) 821-5533.

# ACKNOWLEDGMENTS

The knowledge and wisdom of professionals and friends, parents and children, helped to send the first edition of *The Mother's Almanac* into thirty-six printings and have given a good start to the second. Our warmest thanks to them all, and a little daisy for those who helped out with both.

## THE FIRST EDITION

Audubon Naturalist Society
Helen Baldwin
Lillian Barrett
Jeanette and Robert Bernstein
Sophy Burnham
Constance Burr
Mary Cassidy, Ph.D.
Doris Celarier
Beverly Baumgart Chalker
Susan Chalker
Shirley Cochrane
Margaret Coughlan
Sheila Cowen, Ph.D.
Kay Crane
❀Clare Crawford-Mason
Sally Crowell
❀Edward F. Dillon, R.Ph.
Tom Donnelly
Patricia Driscoll
Asher Etkes
Eve Eggers
Minor Elson
Lydia Finkelstein
J. Morton Franklin
Amy Gardner
Sue Gartner
❀Mariana Gasteyer
Jean Getlein
Judy Gleason
Bette Glickert
Judith Goldinger
Bea Hackett
Ann Hanks
Sharon Hanley
Marifrances Hardison
Sallie Ann Robbins Hart
Virginia Haviland
Robin Hirsh
Ann Hochstein
Carl I. Hoffmann
Jane Horton
Margaret and Susan Howard
Clara Davidson Huus
Faith Jackson
❀C. Tim Jensen
Helmut Jaehnigen
Joan Keenan
Leonard Kirsten
Adelaide Krizek
Barbara Kubeck
❀Louise and Marion Lelong
Gail McCarthy Lunenfeld
Nancy McCrae
Judy McKnight
Virginia Mahoney
Thomas Mann
Amelia Manning
Mary Markley
Rita and Kathy Markley
Rita Mendez
Beverly Mischer
Patricia Molumby
Roberta Mora
Betty Moskowitz
Barney Nehring
Dorothy Newman
Nutrition Department, Cornell University
Gloria Panton
Edith Parsons
Ida Prosky
Audrey Pugh

Pat Rafuse
Susan Reid
Enid Requé
Judith Reynolds
Arlene Roback
Julia D. Robertson
Lisa Romberg
Miris and Richard Sanchez
Mary Scheltema
Kathryn Shollenberger
Helen Skinner
Mildred Skinner
Myra Sklarew
Charlotte Smutko
Janet Stratton
❀ Martha Swaim
Stephen Swaim
Kathryn Smith, Ph.D.
Nancy Stewart
Robert Thurston
Cora Toliver
James True
Elizabeth Van Kluyve
Kenneth Watkins, Jr., D.V.M.
Kitty Weaver
Kathryn Williams
Lorna Williams
Miriam Wolf, M.D.
Elizabeth Young
Katharine Zadravec
Joanne Zich

*Children*
Priscilla Burr
Sara Burr
Eben Burr
Andrew Hackett
Alan Keenan
Leah Swaim
❀ Michael Swaim
Suzannah Swaim

**THE SECOND EDITION**
Rabbi Nathan Abramowitz
Heidi Almy

Claudette Best
John Milton Best
Kara Blanchard
Roberta Blanchard
Maria J. Burrington
Keith Cheely
Stephanie Deutsch
Carol Fitzsimmons
Julie Giles, D.V.M.
Diana Huss Green
Barbara Geyger
Vicki Hall
Elizabeth Harper, M.S.W.
Kate Holwill
Doremus Jenkins
Stephen Johnson
Beverly Lemmon
Michael Levy
Heather Linnell
Katie Linnell
Froma Lippmann
Marion McCartney, C.N.M.
Judith Martin
Martha Mechelis
Alfonsa Micutuan
Fiona Morris
Prudence Nelson
Greenie Neuberg
Joanne Omang
Virginia L. Penn
Sharon Raimo
Sara Rimensnyder
Pam Sacks
Maria Salvadore
Robbi Scharfe
Shari Ostrow Scher
Charlotte Smutko
Jewell Stoddard
Franklin Stroud, M.D.
Danielle Tarantolo
Anne and Fred Vinson
Hilary Winkler
Tom Winkler
*and to the ladies of the Reading Circle*